In Memory Of

The
Wiman
Family

NEONATAL NUTRITION AND METABOLISM

Neonatal Nutrition and Metabolism

WILLIAM W. HAY, JR., M.D.
Professor of Pediatrics
Section of Neonatology and Division of Perinatal Research
University of Colorado School of Medicine
Denver, Colorado

Mosby
Year Book

St. Louis   Baltimore   Boston   Chicago   London   Philadelphia   Sydney   Toronto

ᴍ Mosby
Year Book

Dedicated to Publishing Excellence

Sponsoring Editor: James F. Shanahan
Assistant Editor: Joyce-Rachel John
Assistant Director, Manuscript Services: Frances M. Perveiler
Production Coordinator: Nancy C. Baker
Proofroom Manager: Barbara Kelly

Library of Congress Cataloging-in-Publication Data
Neonatal nutrition and metabolism / [edited by] William W. Hay, Jr.
        p.   cm.
    Includes bibliographical references.
    Includes index.
    ISBN 0-8151-4215-3
    1. Infants (Newborn)—Nutrition.   2. Infants (Newborn)—
  -Metabolism.   3. Infants (Newborn)—Growth.   4. Infants (Newborn)—
  -Diseases.   I. Hay, William W.
    [DNLM: 1. Infant, (Newborn)—metabolism.   2. Infant Nutrition.
  WS 120 N438]
  RJ216.N45   1991   91-13225
  618.92′639—dc20   CIP
  DNLM/DLC
  for Library of Congress

To Judy, and her love for me and our children, Emily and Andrew ———————

CONTRIBUTORS

WILLIAM F. BALISTRERI, M.D.
Dorothy M.M. Kersten Professor of
  Pediatrics
University of Cincinnati Medical Center
Director, Division of Pediatric
  Gastroenterology and Nutrition
Children's Hospital Medical Center
Cincinnati, Ohio

MICHELE N. BRONSTEIN, PH.D.
Assistant Professor of Pediatrics
University of Colorado School of Medicine
Denver, Colorado

IRENE CETIN, M.D.
Assistant Professor of Obstetrics and
  Gynecology
Universitá Degli Studi di Milano
Milano, Italy

SHYH-FANG CHENG, M.D.
Neonatology Fellow
Baylor College of Medicine
Texas Children's Hospital
Houston, Texas

RICHARD M. COWETT, M.D.
Professor of Pediatrics
Department of Pediatrics
Brown University
Women and Infants Hospital of Rhode Island
Providence, Rhode Island

JANE E. DiGIACOMO, M.D.
Research Fellow
Department of Physiology
University of Pennsylvania School of
  Medicine
Philadelphia, Pennsylvania

CAROL L. GREENE, M.D.
Assistant Professor
Director, Inherited Metabolic Diseases
  Clinic
University of Colorado Health Sciences
  Center
Denver, Colorado

HARRY L. GREENE, M.D.
Professor of Pediatrics
Associate Professor of Biochemistry
Vanderbilt University School of Medicine
Head, Division of Nutrition
Vanderbilt University Medical Center
Nashville, Tennessee

K. MICHAEL HAMBIDGE, M.D., SC.D.
Professor of Pediatrics
Department of Pediatrics
University of Colorado School of Medicine
Denver, Colorado

MARGIT HAMOSH, M.D., PH.D.
Professor of Pediatrics
Department of Pediatrics
Chief, Division of Developmental Biology
  and Nutrition
Georgetown University Medical Center
Washington, D.C.

WILLIAM W. HAY, JR., M.D.
Professor of Pediatrics
Section of Neonatology and Division of
  Perinatal Research
University of Colorado School of Medicine
Denver, Colorado

WILLIAM C. HEIRD, M.D.
Associate Professor of Pediatrics
Department of Pediatrics
Columbia University College of Physicians
  and Surgeons
New York, New York

OUSSAMA ITANI, M.D.
Fellow in Neonatology
University of Cincinnati
Cincinnati, Ohio

VICKI JOHNSTON, M.D.
Neonatology Fellow
Case Western Reserve University
Rainbow Babies and Childrens Hospital
Cleveland, Ohio

JOSEPH KAEMPF, M.D.
*Neonatologist, Director of Pediatric
    Intensive Care
Bess Kaiser Hospital
Portland, Oregon*

SUDHA KASHYAP, M.D.
*Associate Professor of Clinical Pediatrics
Columbia University College of Physicians
    and Surgeons
Assistant Attending Pediatrician
Babies Hospital
New York, New York*

ROBERT M. KLIEGMAN, M.D.
*Professor of Pediatrics
Case Western Reserve University
Vice Chairperson
Department of Pediatrics
Rainbow Babies and Childrens Hospital
Cleveland, Ohio*

JAMES A. LEMONS, M.D.
*Professor of Pediatrics
Director, Section of Neonatal-Perinatal
    Medicine
Indiana University School of Medicine
Director, Section of Neonatal-Perinatal
    Medicine
James Whitcomb Riley Hospital for Children
Indianapolis, Indiana*

PAMELA K. LEMONS, M.S., N.N.P.
*Assistant Professor of Nursing
Indiana University
James Whitcomb Riley Hospital for Children
Indianapolis, Indiana*

ALAN LUCAS, M.A., M.R.C.P.
*Member of Scientific Staff of Medical
    Research Council
Dunn Nutrition Unit
Cambridge, England*

MARTHA J. MILLER, M.D., PH.D.
*Assistant Professor of Pediatrics
Case Western Reserve University
Assistant Professor of Pediatrics
Rainbow Babies and Childrens Hospital
Cleveland, Ohio*

MARGARET C. NEVILLE, PH.D.
*Professor of Physiology
University of Colorado School of Medicine
Denver, Colorado*

DAVID K. RASSIN, PH.D.
*Professor, Department of Pediatrics
The University of Texas Medical Branch at
    Galveston
Director, Pediatric Developmental Nutrition
    and Metabolism Laboratory
The University of Texas Medical Branch
    Hospital at Galveston
Galveston, Texas*

BRIAN D. RIEDEL, M.D.
*Assistant Clinical Professor of Pediatrics
Wright State University School of Medicine
    and Uniformed Services University of the
    Health Sciences
Chief of Pediatric Gastroenterology and
    Nutrition
USAF Medical Center
Wright-Patterson Air Force Base
Dayton, Ohio*

RICHARD J. SCHANLER, M.D.
*Associate Professor of Pediatrics
Children's Nutrition Research Center
Baylor College of Medicine
Attending Neonatologist
Texas Children's Hospital
Houston, Texas*

JOAN K. SHARDA, M.D.
*Fellow, Neonatal-Perinatal Medicine
Indiana University
James Whitcomb Riley Hospital for Children
Indianapolis, Indiana*

C. JEFFREY SIPPEL, M.D., PH.D.
*Fellow, Children's Hospital Medical Center
Cincinnati, Ohio*

RONALD J. SOKOL, M.D.
*Associate Professor
University of Colorado Health Sciences
    Center
Pediatric Gastroenterologist
The Children's Hospital
Denver, Colorado*

JOHN W. SPARKS, M.D.
*Associate Professor of Pediatrics
University of Colorado School of Medicine
Denver, Colorado*

SHARON F. TAYLOR, M.D.
*Assistant Professor
University of Colorado Health Sciences
    Center
Pediatric Gastroenterologist
The Children's Hospital
Denver, Colorado*

REGINALD C. TSANG, M.D.
*Professor of Pediatrics and Obstetrics and
    Gynecology
Director, Division of Neonatology
Director, The Perinatal Research Institute
Children's Hospital Medical Center
University of Cincinnati Medical Center
Cincinnati, Ohio*

JOHN E. E. VAN AERDE, M.D.
*Associate Professor of Pediatrics
University of Alberta
Staff Neonatologist
University of Alberta Hospitals
Edmonton, Alberta, Canada*

Lawrence T. Weaver, M.D.,
M.R.C.P., D.C.H.
*Member of Scientific Staff of Medical
Research Council
Dunn Nutrition Unit
Cambridge, England*

Steven Yannicelli, M.M.Sc., R.D.
*Metabolic Nutritionist
Professional Research Assistant
University of Colorado Health Sciences
Center
Denver, Colorado*

FOREWORD

Neonatal nutrition has been a major concern of pediatricians as growth is the province of pediatrics. Indeed, the beginnings of pediatrics as a specialty occurred with the development of foods to supplement or replace breast milk in the late 19th century. The host of formulas and books that were published competes in number and effectiveness with the number of articles and books published now on weight-reducing regimens.

For the next 100 years, pediatricians made numerous trials and experiments first to lower mortality, then to lower morbidity, then to improve long-term effects. With the development of hi-tech devices within the past third of a century nutrition as an area of study of the newborn was displaced as an area of research and practical interest. Pediatricians became more involved not only with mechanical devices but also with sophisticated metabolic studies and outcome studies of low-birth-weight and full-term infants.

As survival of infants improved in the past two decades infant nutrition has again become an added concern to both neonatologists and all those caring for children. As a result, major advances have occurred in the understanding of metabolic processes—an understanding that is applied not only to infants, but to children and adults as well. As a result, a host of informative articles and a number of books on infant nutrition have been published.

A need was recognized to collate knowledge in the diverse areas of nutrition and metabolism of the neonate. The result is the current volume, which summarizes in a delightfully readable form the bases for present clinical management. The road from basic science to applicability proceeds without detours. The considerations of practical methods of feeding and the avoidance of feeding problems and their treatment when they occur are detailed in a lucid manner. Complicated nutritional problems are not bypassed. Even some of the social problems are handled with finesse.

Feeding prematurely born and low-birth-weight infants properly requires familiarity with embryology and knowledge of physiological and biochemical development, as well as dietary requirements and limitations of the present information. All of these are addressed. A chapter on methods of feeding provides advice and empathy. The impact, limitations, and complications of tests and procedures are compared and contrasted with nutritional needs.

The interweaving of metabolic processes, nutritional demands, and social developments are presented, just as they occur in the growing and thriving neonate.

LEWIS A. BARNESS, M.D.
Visiting Professor
Department of Pediatrics
University of Wisconsin Medical School
Madison, Wisconsin

PREFACE

Somewhere between what we feed to babies and the molecular biology of cellular biochemistry lies the interaction of nutrient substrate supply and the metabolism, for energy and for growth, of these substrates. This is the subject of this book. It is intended to provide a detailed examination of the general phenomena of neonatal growth and energy balance, and specific aspects of how different supplies of selected nutrients and various developmental and clinically significant conditions in the newborn infant (particularly those born prematurely and with altered fetal growth patterns) interact to produce special requirements for the use of nutrients for growth and for energy balance in these infants. All of this has grown out of my concern that at bedside teaching rounds in the newborn and intensive care nurseries, it has made much more sense (to me) to encourage students (of all kinds) to think of why different nutrient supplies might be important because of how they are used rather than according to a more traditional "intake and output" balance. This approach has proven useful for medical students, nursing students, nurse "specialist" trainees, residents in pediatrics and neonatology, and colleagues in basic science and clinical disciplines. This joint interest of clinicians and scientists also has shaped this book to include an important mixture of practical clinical material and more detailed accounts of metabolic phenomena. Central to all of these issues is my major concern that babies and their nutrition, growth, and health will benefit from clinicians and scientists thinking and working together, just as nutrient substrates and their metabolic interactions combine to successfully produce normal growth and the energy to thrive.

WILLIAM W. HAY, JR., M.D.

ACKNOWLEDGMENTS ───────────

I should like to acknowledge first Dr. William Ballard of Dartmouth College and Dr. Donald Barron, formerly of Yale University and now of the University of Florida, both of whom encouraged me to take up a career in science and to look for how things are put together and how they work. Second, I thank Dr. Giacomo Meschia and Dr. Frederick C. Battaglia who gave me the opportunity and the education to pursue my interests in fetal and neonatal nutrition and metabolism. Finally, I appreciate greatly the patience and support provided by Jim Shanahan and his colleagues at Mosby–Year Book who made this book possible and got it finished; and Jeanette Vafai, Kathy Wallace, and Casey Johnson who did all those things that secretaries do that make an enterprise of this sort successful.

WILLIAM W. HAY, JR., M.D.

CONTENTS

Growth and Energy

Chapter 1

Intrauterine Growth

John W. Sparks, M.D.

Irene Cetin, M.D.

INTRAUTERINE GROWTH

Human intrauterine growth has received considerable attention in recent years. In obstetrics, intrauterine growth remains a most important sign of fetal well-being; in neonatal care, many therapeutic strategies are directed at matching rates of intrauterine growth.[1] Moreover, treatment of infants whose growth has been restricted by a process of intrauterine growth retardation presents clinical challenges in both acute management and long-term follow-up. Expanded clinical capabilities in both obstetrics and neonatology, better understanding of the physiology and pathophysiology of the fetus and premature infant, and changing attitudes, among other factors, have led to dramatic reductions in morbidity and mortality rates in small premature infants.[2, 3]

It is almost paradoxical, then, in an era of rapidly expanding clinical technology as well as rapid scientific advances at the molecular level, that clinicians and scientists alike are increasingly interested in reexamining a relatively old literature employing classic technologies to describe human intrauterine growth and nutrient accretion. Many cited observations of physical and chemical growth considerably predate modern analytic techniques, accurate assessment of gestational age, or modern statistical analysis.

While perinatologists have developed enormously their abilities to evaluate and treat neonates—and to an increasing extent, the fetus—this technology does not intrinsically supply "yardsticks" for understanding the newer technologies. Reassessment of older approaches may be increasingly important in providing a foundation for integration of concepts relating to intrauterine growth.

Definitions

Several important concepts and definitions underlie considerations of intrauterine growth. First, one should note the many terms in common usage to describe variations in fetal growth (Table 1–1). *Low-birth-weight (LBW)* and *very low birth weight (VLBW)* describe infants with birth weights less than 2,500 g and 1,500 g, respectively. These terms do not incorporate a concept of gestational age. In contrast, *small-for-gestational age (SGA)* or *small-for-dates* refers to those infants below the 10th percentile in growth,

TABLE 1–1.

Terminology Basic to Intrauterine Growth Studies

Term	Definition
Low birth weight (LBW)	Birth weight < 2,500 g
Very low birth weight (VLBW)	Birth weight < 1,500 g
Macrosomic	Birth weight > 4,000 g
Premature	Gestational age < 38 wk
Postmature	Gestational age > 42 wk
Large-for-gestational age (LGA)	Percentile > 90%
Appropriate-for-gestational age (AGA)	Percentile between 10% and 90%
Small-for-Gestational age (SGA)	Percentile < 10%
Intrauterine growth retarded (IUGR)	Process of growth restriction

adjusted for gestational age; *large-for-gestational age (LGA)* or *large-for-dates* refers to infants above the 90th percentile, adjusted for gestational age. Those between 10th and 90th percentile in growth are termed *appropriate-for-gestational age (AGA)*.

Second, in common usage, *intrauterine growth retarded (IUGR)* is often used synonymously with SGA. However, within this chapter, IUGR will be used to denote a pathophysiologic process resulting in restriction of fetal growth, whereas SGA will refer to a statistical grouping of infants below the 10th percentile. From a practical standpoint, there may be considerable overlap of the two groups; however, at a conceptual level, the distinction may be important. Statistically, 10% of infants should be below the 10th percentile regardless of medical intervention, and this group may reflect biologic diversity as well as restriction of growth. In contrast, a fetus who by clinical or ultrasound criteria has stopped growing, but is delivered before the 10th percentile crosses the estimated weight, may be considered as subject to a process that restricts growth, even if AGA. If the processes restricting growth result in other long-term consequences, then it would be reasonable to regard such infants as at risk, even if above an arbitrary percentile.

Third, estimations of the duration of pregnancy present recurrent problems. The importance of dating gestation is a historically modern concept, and many earlier studies relate development to weight, length, foot length, or other indices of fetal size. Gestational duration may be dated from the last menstrual period, conception, or implantation. Alternatively, gestation may be staged by the developmental stage of the fetus, as is commonly referenced in early embryology.

Clinically, events are generally dated in terms of *gestational age,* which estimates age from the first day of the last normal menstrual period (LMP). The *estimated date of confinement* (EDC) is the projected date of delivery, measured from the LMP. Näegele's rule calculates the EDC as the date of the first day of the last menstrual period, less 3 months, plus 1 week. Dated from the time of the LMP, the average duration of pregnancy is 279 ± 17 days.[4] Embryologic *postconceptional age* is measured from the time of conception. Since the time of conception is generally not known accurately, the clinical use of LMP dating is reasonable. However, gestational age differs from postconceptional age by the time from LMP to conception, typically about 2 weeks. Estimation of gestational age becomes difficult in the presence of irregular or abnormal menstruation.

Other terms have also been used, including *fetal age* or *developmental age,* measuring from the time of implantation. Additionally, in literature on the newborn, *corrected age,* dating actual postnatal age from the EDC, is frequently used in newborn follow-up to adjust for differences in prematurity. Thus, an infant 6 months post delivery at 32 weeks might be considered as 4 months corrected age.

The accuracy of gestational dating poses some serious conceptual problems. In clinical practice, LMP data is not infrequently unavailable or unreliable, and estimations must be made from other clinical criteria of actual gestational age. In obstetric practice, physical examination and ultrasound assessment of growth and development provide assessment of gestation. Similarly, in the neonatal period, assessments proposed by Dubowitz et al.,[5] Ballard et al.,[6] and Lubchenco,[7, 8] which are based on both neurologic and physical findings, are used to estimate gestational age in neonates. Each of these examinations ultimately calibrated its estimate of gestational age on maternal dates, and each has an error of about ± 1 to 2 weeks. Both the obstetric and neonatal examinations provide useful estimates of gestational age where LMP data are unavailable or obviously incorrect. However, "correction" of gestational age by these examinations invites circularity in reasoning and complexity in interpretation of abnormal growth patterns. Infants may not infrequently be categorized differently, depending on which gestational age (e.g., LMP, neonatal examination, fetal ultrasound) is used.

Finally, it is important to recognize that measurements of fetal growth depend both on the timing of the measurements and the techniques used to make such measurements. Each neonatal gestational age assessment has an optimal time of performance to achieve accuracy and precision. With increasingly short neonatal hospital stays, the examinations may be performed outside this optimal period.

Widely used curves of "intrauterine growth" typically span the last trimester with either serial or cross-sectional measurements. Many standard "growth curves," including those of Lubchenco et al.,[9] Usher and McLean,[10] and Gruenwald[11] are in fact cross-sectional measurements collected near the time of birth, and do not represent serial measurements in the same subject over time. While limitations of this approach will be discussed in detail later, it is important to note that these types of somatic measurements are subject to both measurement errors and conceptual concerns.

Ultrasound has more recently provided serial estimates of fetal growth in individual subjects during pregnancy. This technology has advanced rapidly, with greatly increased precision and accuracy of fetal measurement. Nonetheless, in many studies, the measurement error is large relative to fetal size, complicating interpretation of such curves.

Stages of Intrauterine Growth

From a conceptual point of view, three periods appear important for intrauterine growth. The *preconceptional period* includes the time leading up to conception. The *embryonic period* includes time from conception through embryogenesis and the development of all major organ systems. For the human, this includes the first 8 weeks of development. The *fetal period* spans from the end of the embryonic period through delivery. Each of these intervals may impact on development and growth; however, the issues are somewhat different for each period.

Periconceptional Issues

There is evidence that alterations in the maternal milieu may impact subsequent development of the conceptus. The mechanisms of such effects are generally poorly understood, but may include genetic, nutritional, biologic, and environmental factors.

Biologically, maternal weight and nutritional status may affect the environment in which conception is to occur. Body fat appears to be related to normal reproductive function. Loss of body fat through undernutrition or intensive exercise may lead to loss of reproductive function; refeeding may restore it. Early in human pregnancy, women ordinarily begin to store fat; they continue to do so through the second trimester. A rapid rate of maternal fat deposition is shared by many species.[15]

An interesting epidemiologic literature also describes the impact of maternal events on fetal growth. For example, early menarche,[16] low prepregnancy weight [17, 18] and low prepregnancy height,[19] and short interpregnancy interval[20, 21] have each been associated with shifts in growth curves or increased risk of delivering a small baby. Of perhaps more concern are epidemiologic data suggesting that a history of delivery of a prior growth-retarded infant predisposes to an increased risk of growth retardation in subsequent pregnancies.[17, 22] Indeed, there is evidence that growth retardation may span generations. Careful review of maternal birth weight and infant birth weight suggests that mothers who were themselves of low birthweight are more likely to produce LBW infants.[23]

It is also likely that maternal genetic variations affect fetal growth. There are differences in growth curves in different geographic regions and among different racial and ethnic groups within the United States. For example, evidence has been presented that blacks have several-fold higher rates of fetal death or delivering premature and SGA infants, after statistical correction for social and demographic factors.[24, 25] However, it is extremely difficult to factor environmental factors from true genetic differences, and such data should be interpreted cautiously.

Embryogenesis and Differentiation

During early growth and differentiation, teratogenesis is a major consideration, and there is also evidence that maternal periconceptional status may impact on embryogenesis and development. Major concerns have been expressed regarding teratogenicity of uncontrolled maternal diabetes, with the recommendation that good control be established before conception.[26, 27] More recently, evidence is accumulating that suggests a relationship between maternal vitamin status, particularly with regard to folic acid, and the frequency of neural tube defects.[28, 29] Similarly, there is evidence that some forms of vitamin A may be associated with a teratogenic syndrome.[30, 31] While mechanisms may be poorly understood, a variety of teratogenic factors may impact on differentiation, with an effect on fetal growth.

Fetal Growth

Many factors may impact on the rate of growth during fetal life. Such effects may be mediated by many mechanisms, including nutrition, hypoxia, environment, and genetic factors.[16–18] These will be discussed in detail later in the chapter.

Standards of Intrauterine Growth

Graphical standards for percentiles of birth weight, length, and head circumference of infants at increasing gestational age have become traditional tools in perinatal medicine. The curves of Lubchenco and associates (Fig 1–1),[7, 9] among others, are widely disseminated on clinical perinatal services, and the assessment of appropriateness for gestational age based on such standards has proved usefulness in projecting neonatal risks for mortality[2, 3, 9] as well as many morbidities, such as hypoglycemia.[32]

Colorado Intrauterine Growth Charts

Name

Birth date

Hospital number

Date

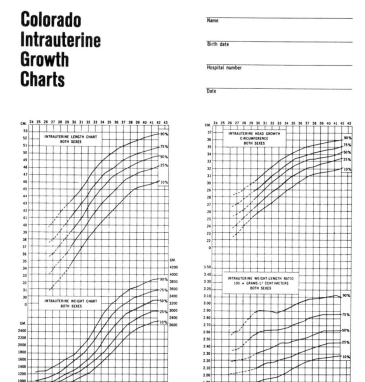

FIG 1–1.
Colorado Intrauterine Growth Charts. (Courtesy of Ross Laboratories, Columbus, Ohio.)

Growth in Fetal Size

Measurements of weight and length at birth provide the largest published body of information describing intrauterine growth of the human fetus. Several studies have addressed the cross-sectional distribution of birth weights at gestations from 24 to 42 weeks in populations differing in geographic location, altitude, ethnic composition, and socioeconomic status. Babson et al.[33] published birth weight standards for approximately 40,000 Caucasian infants born at sea level receiving private medical care. Gruenwald[11, 34] published data describing birth weight in approximately 15,000 infants of mixed socioeconomic status born in Baltimore. Lubchenco et al.[9] recorded the weights, lengths, and head circumferences of 5,635 infants of a medically indigent, mixed Caucasian and Spanish American non-black population born at 5,000-ft altitude. This study population included only infants whose stated gestational ages based on maternal dates were consistent with size and who did not have gross pathologic defects. More recently, Miller[18, 35] has presented anthropometric data on carefully selected infants in Kansas City, excluding infants with an obstetric history or neonatal physical findings that might inhibit fetal growth. Infants were excluded for factors such as maternal smoking, obstetric course, maternal medical conditions, or neonatal anomalies, among other factors, in order to generate a hypothetically optimal curve. While the data of Usher and McLean[10] include only 300 infants, these data describe measurements of a single observer using consistent techniques in an inborn Caucasian population of mixed socioeconomic status. The data excluded infants who had congenital anomalies or whose clinical gestational age was not consistent with the gestation calculated from the date of the LMP. Similarly, Wong and Scott[36] used clinical assessment of gestational age in verifying the calculated gestation in approximately 5,000 infants, excluding infants with poor dates or known conditions affecting intrauterine growth. In addition, standards for birth weight are also available for populations in other countries.[19, 37-41]

Interpretation of Intrauterine Growth Curves

The published data demonstrate several common features. First, these human weight curves can be approximated as roughly sigmoidal in shape, curvilinearly increasing with gestational age. Second, the curves show a steady rate of increase from approximately 24 weeks to approximately 37 to 39 weeks, depending on the series. Third, there is a flattening of the curve in most of the reported series, occurring at 37 to 39 weeks, followed by a period of a diminished rate of increase in wet weight. Finally, there may be an actual decrease in average birth weight after about 44 weeks gestation.

Measurements of length and head circumference follow similar steady rate of growth until weeks 35 to 38, with growth slowing toward term; and indices such as the weight/(length)^3 ratio or ponderal index have proved useful in differentiating the premature from the growth retarded infant.

While the differences among series are frequently emphasized in comparison of effects of altitude, socioeconomic status, or other factors, the reported series typically differ by less than 10% for a given percentile at a given gestational age. These interstudy differences at the same percentile may have epidemiologic and public health significance, but such differences are much smaller than the intrastudy cross-percentiles differences (500 g at term between 10th and 50th percentile), so that percentiles are generally not very different between series. As an example, the 5th percentile of Babson et al.,[33] which is representative of the studies with larger weights at percentile and gestational age, corresponds approximately to the 10th percentile of Lubchenco et al.,[9] which is frequently cited as one of the series with smaller weights at percentile and gestational age.[7, 42, 43]

Many factors are known to affect the birth weight of a population. The classic studies of McKeown and Record[44] have documented differing growth curves of human multiple-gestation infants, compared to singleton gestation. The curves for multiple gestations are similar through the first and second trimesters, and diverge from those of singleton gestation at 26 to 30 weeks. Pregnancies with more fetuses diverge earlier and by greater magnitude from the singleton curve.

Similarly, smoking appears to decrease birth weight; the curve for infants of smoking mothers parallels that for nonsmoking mothers with a decrement of weight without shortening of gestation.[45] Altitude has also been implicated in reducing birth weight among singletons at given gestational ages.[46] Maternal starvation appears to reduce birth weight, typically by a few hundred grams.[47-49]

Mathematical Description of Intrauterine Growth

The abundance of birth weight data corresponds to an equal abundance of mathematical techniques for analysis and modeling of birth weight in relation to gestational age. Such analyses have proved of theoretical interest in comparing large populations of birth weights and have utilized a variety of sophisticated mathematical approaches, including series expansions and multiple regressions. As pointed out by Hoffman and associates[50] and by Wilcox,[45] there is considerable opportunity for systematic statistical bias in constructing such curves. In comparisons of populations, or determinations of the effects of maternal smoking, nutrition, or other factors, these statistical problems may seriously complicate analysis.

However, functions describing the relationships of weight and length to gestational can be modeled by much simpler mathematical functions if one imposes limits in the range of gestational age to be approximated. As an example, for the gestational age range of 24 to 39 weeks, the data of Usher and McLean[10] can be approximated within approximately 50 g as a simple exponential function, of the form:

$$\text{Birth weight} = K1 \times e^{(K2 \times GA)},$$

where $K1$ and $K2$ are constants and GA is the gestational age in days. In this analysis, the constant K2 represents the growth rate, in units of percent per day, while K1 represents a scaling factor. Of particular interest, the value K2 is 0.0145 ± 0.0001 for the reported 5th, 50th, and 95th percentiles, yielding a similar rate of growth of about 1.45%/day, or about 14.5 g/kg/day for all three groups. The values of K1 of 50, 65, and 80 establish an approximate proportionality for the SGA, AGA, and LGA infant, respectively. In simple terms, the curves for the 10th and 90th percentile are proportional to the 50th percentile curve, and are scaled at about $\pm$ 25% from the 50th percentile curve. The classic Dancis curves demonstrate a family of curves for extrauterine growth, with more rapid growth (g/day) of larger infants, consistent with this approach.[51]

Thus, from 24 to 39 weeks, the curves of Usher and McLean[10] may be approximated within 50 g by this simplified model, with SGAs and LGAs approximately 77% (50/65) and 123% (80/65) of the 50th percentile value at each gestational age. The curves of Lubchenco and associates[9] can be similarly well approximated by a simple exponential function increasing at approximately 15g/kg/day over a slightly narrower range, from 24 to 37 weeks.

Similar simplifications of the intrauterine growth curve can be made for the other reported series. While such simplifications are inadequate for precise characterization of population data, the slight loss of accuracy is small compared with the differences between percentiles and is offset by considerably increased practical ease of calculation. Of particular note is the expression of intrauterine growth rate in units of g/kg/day rather than g/day. Intuitively, however, if caloric intake postnatally is customarily expressed per kilogram body weight, it is not surprising that resultant growth should be better expressible per kilogram body weight.

Theoretical Concerns With Growth Curves

Regardless of the technique for mathematical modeling of intrauterine growth, these models produce curves that are generically known as "intrauterine growth curves," suggesting that dynamic rate of change can be inferred from them. In fact, these curves represent percentiles of static perinatal measurements, and the growth of individual fetuses need not follow such curves. Measurements at birth represent a static, cross-sectional measurement in an individual neonate following delivery.

While such measurements can properly be used to establish percentiles for the measured static parameter at a given gestational age, it may not be legitimate to estimate a dynamic measurement of rate of change for the longitudinal growth of a hypothetical fetus based on differences among static measurements of different fetuses. Restated, such a "growth curve" represents a statistical statement of mean percentile values in a population at the fixed time of delivery, and an individual fetus need not follow such percentiles during growth. Indeed, Wilcox[45] has argued that unthinking acceptance of the "intrauterine growth curve hypothesis" may be an impediment to understanding intrauterine growth.

Contributing to this conceptual problem is an underlying assumption that gestational age is a true independent variable, against which somatic measurements can be plotted. In an experiment, an investigator might time gestation accurately, and electively deliver infants or animals over a range of gestations, plotting data against gestational age as a true independent variable. However, in clinical practice, we rarely know why a given baby delivers at a given time, and it is therefore reasonable to ask whether the group of babies delivering at one period in gestation differ biologically from those delivering spontaneously at another. Restated, is it reasonable to assume that a premature baby would have grown to the same size as a postmature baby had gestation continued, or alternatively, would the process leading to prematurity also lead to altered growth? It has been argued, for example, that the apparent slowing of the weight curve near term and post-term gestation results not from a true biologic slowing, but from an artifact of the way in which data are collected (Naeye).[51a]

Another theoretical problem in the cited studies is that the statistical methods for establishing percentiles for intrauterine growth are generally poorly described, and generally cite without reference the curve smoothing techniques used to beautify the data. Application of such methods may be complicated by the non-normality of the distributions of measurements at a given gestational age. Some observers have commented on a non-normal distribution of birth weight at gestational ages less than 32 weeks. Furthermore, usual least squares regressions minimize deviations of observed data from the calculated function along the y-axis only; Brace[52] has demonstrated that such methods may systematically underestimate true slopes when there is significant error along the x-axis, in this case gestational age.

It should also be recognized that the use of percentile data at gestational age to construct an intrauterine growth curve for an idealized fetus presupposes that a single growth curve in fact exists. The classic observations of Walton and Hammond[53] demonstrate interactions of genetic and environmental factors in determining birth weight and postnatal growth. The original data of Lubchenco et al.[9] document population differences in neonatal anthropometric measurements based on sex, and the observations of Tanner and Thomson[19] suggest differing growth curves based on maternal height and weight. It seems more likely that the "intrauterine growth curve" may be better described as a family of growth curves. The selection of the best growth curve would then be based on knowledge of the individual fetus, as well as on sophistication of analyses of the family of curves. On a practical basis, comparison of percentile curves between white and non-white populations in the United States presents special problems.[45, 50]

Finally, the use of any of these individual series to extrapolate to the more general population is subject to question. In analyzing U.S. birth weight data, Hoffman and associates[50] identified several important biases that might be present in data any hypothetical individual series. This report details extensive statistical analyses on the combined U.S. data, and generate sophisticated mathematical functions describing the percentiles for the combined population data at varying gestational age.

Practical Problems With "Intrauterine Growth Curves"

While the data on birth weight are many, they clearly show some major types of practical problems in the analysis of intrauterine growth. Parturition can be characterized as a short and unusual event in a long gestation characterized by the lack of labor and delivery. Measurements during or after delivery (e.g., cord blood lactate concentrations; head circumference following vaginal delivery) may be significantly distorted by intrapartum events, and may not be representative of the same measurement in utero prior to delivery. In addition, there is a significant problem with error in measurements. Plotting of percentile curves based on measurements postnatally assumes accuracy in both gestational age assessment and in physical measurement.

The errors implicit in gestational age assessment based on maternal dates are well known, and may yield gestational age assessment within a range of 4 weeks (± 2 weeks), potentially contributing considerable variance to mathematical modeling. In cases where maternal dates appear close to clinical estimates, maternal dates may be used. However, inaccurate maternal dates based on postimplantation bleeding or irregular menses are not infrequent, and assessments of gestational age based on physical or neurologic examination has proved very helpful.[7]

Moreover, weight can be easily measured with good precision, and length and head circumference to a lesser extent. One is confronted with an unusual situation in statistics in which variation along the x-axis may be considerably greater than variation along the y-axis.

Gestational age assessments based on clinical criteria may "correct" or exclude obviously erroneous gestational ages based on dates, but theoretically can introduce systematic errors if such clinical criteria systematically exclude the extreme variance that is biologic in nature. Moreover, the standardization of such assessments must rest ultimately on an external standard of gestational age such as maternal dates, permitting the possibility of circular reasoning and systematic bias.

Measurement of weight, length, and head circumference are also subject to technical problems.[7] For weight, almost 500 g separates the 50th and 5th percentiles at term, and scales are readily available with relatively negligible error. However, measurements of length and head circumference are considerably less precise, and are dependent on skill of the examiner and perinatal factors such as molding. Thus, weight may be optimally assessed at birth in order to minimize postnatal weight loss, while head circumference may be more reflective of intrauterine growth after resolution of molding. Thus, the choice of time and method of postnatal anthropometric measurement may materially affect "intrauterine" growth assessment.

Fetal Deposition of Fat, Carbohydrate, and Protein

From a nutritional point of view, body weight is an important but relatively crude measurement. Thus, the rapid weight gain of an infant with heart failure need not imply good nutrition. While this may be an obvious exception, convenient clinical tools are limited that accurately assess the nutritional value of increasing weight in ostensibly normally growing infants, and such assessment is extremely limited for the fetus. Chemical analyses of macronutrient contents of human fetuses may provide important insights into the nutritional consequences of intrauterine growth.

As noted earlier, the growth in wet weight can be approximated with reasonable accuracy as increasing at approximately 15 g/kg/day. However, it is well known that the human fetus changes dramatically in composition as well as weight during the last half of gestation. Thus, assessment of nutrient needs of the fetus requires some estimate of the rate of change in chemical composition as well as the rate of increase in weight.

Analysis of the data on intrauterine nutrient accretion has proved useful. Ziegler et al.[54] carefully selected among the aggregate data in the available series to generate typical accretion curves for a "reference fetus." Sparks et al.[55] partitioned the chemical components of growth in order to estimate the caloric value of daily tissue growth. In late gestation, the caloric value of new tissue accretion was approximately 40 kcal $\cdot$ kg^{-1} $\cdot$ day^{-1}, of which approximately 80% is required for deposition of fat in the human.

More recently, the data have been reexamined[56] to generate typical curves for SGA, AGA, and LGA infants within the aggregate data reported. Such analyses show substantial differences in total body fat among the three groups, with approximately 250, 500, and 1,000 grams body fat for the SGA, AGA, and LGA groups, respectively, at term. Similar analyses for non-fat dry weight or nitrogen content show much greater overlap for the three groups, suggesting that the fat component is disproportionately affected by variations in growth.

Figure 1–2,A demonstrates the dry weight of fetuses plotted against reported gestational age. The three lines given are the exponential regressions for the LGA, AGA, and SGA groups, respectively. Note that there is little overlap between groups, with a consistent order of lower dry weight content at gestational age in SGAs than AGAs, and in AGAs than LGAs. Figure 1–2,B demonstrates similar curves for the fat contents of the reported fetuses, and again demonstrates a consistent order at gestational age, with larger differences and little overlap between groups. Figure 1–3,A shows the non-fat dry weight of the same groups, plotted against gestational age. While the same order exists, there is more overlap between groups at the same gestational age. Figure 1–3,B demonstrates the nitrogen content of the same group of fetues.

Several conclusions are evident from this type of analysis. First, the data in the aggregate are considerably biased toward the SGA fetus. Thus, usage of combined data in estimating intrauterine accretion rates of chemical components of growth might give in-

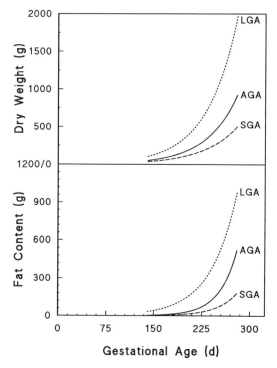

FIG 1–2.
Dry weight (**A**) and fat content (**B**) of fetus vs. reported gestational age.

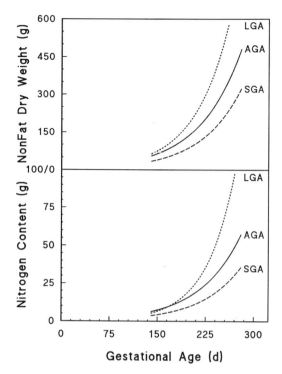

FIG 1–3.
Non-fat dry weight (**A**) and nitrogen content (**B**) of fetus vs. reported gestational age.

correctly low values.[54] Second, the reported data support the concept that in ostensibly normal fetuses, LGAs, AGAs, and SGAs show considerable differences in fat content at a given gestational age. The curves for the three groups intercept 280 day's gestation at approximately 1,000, 500, and 250 g fat, respectively. Thus, a LGA fetus demands of the mother considerably more calories for fat deposition than does an AGA or SGA. Third, the three groups also differ in content of non-fat dry weight and nitrogen. However, for these components, the differences are of lower magnitude and there is more overlap between groups, raising the hypothesis that differences in intrauterine growth may predominantly affect the fat component of growth.

It should be noted that the published data report nitrogen content rather than protein content. Based on observations in the sheep[57] and guinea pig,[58] it appears that only about 80% of the nitrogen content of the fetus of these species is found in protein. Thus, if the human fetus is similar in proportion of nitrogen in protein, the protein content can be estimated from the nitrogen content, with the protein content approximately

$$0.8 \times 6.25 \times \text{nitrogen content}$$

The rate of increase of protein content may be estimated in a similar fashion from the rate of nitrogen accretion.

Characteristics of Infants With Measured Chemical Composition

In using the published data to establish norms of intrauterine growth, ideal data could be considered as points on the growth curve of a hypothetical normally growing fetus without defect. Among the tests that could be applied for compliance of actual data with this ideal standard are (1) that fetal gestational age is accurately known, (2) that the fetuses came to autopsy for reasons not expected to alter growth or nutrient accretion, (3) that the analyzed fetuses conform to norms for growth of fetuses in the general population, (4) that fetuses analyzed are selected randomly from the general population, (5) that the fetuses are analyzed rapidly after death, with accurate, precise and modern methods used.

Features of the studies reporting chemical analyses of human fetuses have been extensively summarized.[54] Approximately 169 ostensibly normal fetuses have been described chemically in some detail, while another 38 have been described preliminarily.[59-61] In addition, Fee and Weil[62] have described the chemical composition of 11 infants of diabetic mothers. As noted by Ziegler et al.[54] and Sparks,[56] the published data fall considerably short of the ideal data noted earlier. First, the information describing the fetuses analyzed is limited. Fetal sex is described in only half the fetuses, and fetal length in only two-thirds. Reason for fetal demise leading to availability for analysis is infrequently given, and when given, may be insufficient to preclude significant fetal abnormality. Thus, when considered as aggregate data, male fetuses predominate over females 2.5:1, and approximately 45% of analyzed fetuses are SGA by modern standards, some severely SGA. Thus, use of the published data to develop intrauterine accretion curves potentially skews such curves considerably. Of particular interest, however, the data of Widdowson[12, 63] appear more appropriately distributed.

It should be further noted that there is considerable variation in the reported methods of chemical analyses in the reported fetuses. First, Widdowson et al.[12, 63, 64] and Apte and Iyengar[65] analyzed unpreserved fetuses, while many of the fetuses in the series reviewed by Kelly et al.[66] were preserved before analysis. Moreover, series differed in analyzing the fetus as a whole, or as aliquots of body organs, with mathematical reconstitution based on organ weight. Finally, a variety of chemical methods for constituent analysis have been applied over the years in the reported fetuses. The least variation probably applies to the measurement of body water, which is determined by drying to constant weight, although some variation is reported in the temperature at which the tissues are dried. Considerably more variation is reported in methods of fat analysis.

Several other problems are evident in describing the published human fetal accretion data. First, gestational age is rarely accurately known, and is frequently estimated from length. This factor led Ziegler et al.[54] to exclude the data of Widdowson from their construction of an idealized growing fetus. Secondly, the methods of chemical analyses differ considerably over the 100 year span of published data. Such error would be expected to be less for dry weight measurement and greater for troublesome measurements such as fat content. Finally, conceptual problems, including choice of normalizing factors in expressing the data, have complicated data analysis.

Alternative Expressions of Human Fetal Accretion Data

While it is traditional to regress statistically or to plot against gestational age in generating intrauterine curves, different information becomes available if one plots against body weight. Surprisingly, when the latter is done, single curves appear to estimate body water, non-fat dry weight, nitrogen content, body fat, and total body caloric value for SGA, AGA, and LGA infants. In these data, dry weight increases steadily from approximately 10% at 24 weeks' gestation to approximately 30% at term, an approximate tripling in this calorically important component. The differences for SGA, AGA, and LGA infants result from different rates of progress along the same curve in this analysis: that is, growth at 15g/kg/day is slower in grams per day for smaller SGA infants and faster for larger LGA infants. The plots of fat contents and of caloric value against wet weight is shown in Figures 1–4,A and 1–4,B. Fat content and estimated caloric equivalent of dry weights follow single curves for SGA, AGA, and LGA infants when plotted against weight.

The issue of fat accretion presents some unresolved problems. Given the concern occasionally expressed regarding adult obesity with the possibility of a relationship to infant growth, the desirability of matching these rates of fat accretion could be questioned. However, by adult standards, all infants are fat, peaking at approximately 25% body fat by 2 months postnatal age, and declining toward adult values of 8% to 12% throughout infancy and childhood. This enormously rapid fat deposition beginning in the last trimester is a consistent finding in human biology, and is unusual in other species. Our understanding of the implication and consequences of this phenomenon is limited at present.

In these analyses, several general points should be emphasized. First, there appear to be considerable differences in intrauterine growth depending on the appropriateness for gestational age. Second, such differences appear to resolve when plotted against weight rather than gestational age. One must caution that these could result from statistical artifact: such measurements are considerably more precise than assessment of gestational age, and the reduction in variance by using such measurements may thus be a technical rather than biologic statement. Thirdly, it is important to recognize that such allometric relationships need imply nothing about mechanism. For example, there is some reason to believe that the increased fat content in older or LGA infants, as compared with SGA infants, may result from entirely different mechanisms, which may include altered endocrine milieu. However, it remains an interesting philosophical ques-

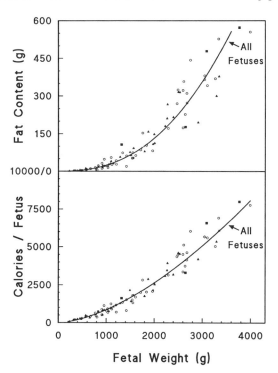

FIG 1–4.
Fetal fat content (**A**) and total calories (**B**) of fetuses vs. fetal weight.

tion whether the biologic clock of development ticks in minutes or some other biologic unit, such as size.

Caloric Implications of Fetal Growth

The analyses thus far permit estimation of the caloric demands placed on the mother for accretion of fetal tissues. In these estimates, the caloric values of fat and non-fat dry weight were taken as 9.5 and 4.5 kcal/g. Based on these analyses, the growth in non-fat dry weight in each group requires approximately 10 to 12 kcal/kg/day. However, the requirement for fat deposition varies considerably, requiring approximately 15, 28, and 40 kcal/kg/day, respectively. Thus, the total value of new tissue accreted at term is about 25, 38, and 52 kcal/kg/day. Using the approach based on weight, one can estimate that approximately 3 kcal are required per gram of new tissue growth at term; this appears in reasonable agreement with the slope of caloric requirement for growth reported in the careful studies of Reichman et al.[67]

These estimates for the intrauterine accretion rate of calories can be compared against two types of standards. First, caloric accretion rates can be approached from previous estimates of intrauterine growth.[54, 68–70] Previous estimates have suggested somewhat lower rates of fat accretion, with concomitant lower caloric accretion. These studies have estimated the intrauterine accretion of fat at term to be approximately 1.75 g · $kg^{-1} \cdot d^{-1}$, while these data estimate fat accretion to be approximately 2.6 to 3.6 g · $kg^{-1} \cdot d^{-1}$ for the AGA subgroup. The mathematical models used in previous series are not completely described, and the reasons for the lower estimates than in the present series are not certain. The fetuses used for the "reference fetus" of Ziegler's group appear to have been skewed toward the SGA, as all but two of the 22 fetuses used were less than the 50th percentile.

These estimates for intrauterine accretion can also be compared against recent rates of fat accretion estimated in the balance studies in rapidly growing premature infants.[67, 71] In each of these studies, the measured accretion rate of calories was somewhat higher than estimated here or in previous estimates of intrauterine caloric accretion. The increased caloric accretion appears primarily a result of a more rapid rate of fat accretion, and the caloric value of non-fat dry weight accretion appears in the range estimated for the intrauterine rate of 8 to 12 kcal · $kg^{-1} \cdot day^{-1}$. The rapid rate of fat accretion in each study is interesting, and may reflect high net caloric intakes or possibly catch-up growth in a rapid growth phase after resumption of steady growth. In each study, the caloric value per accreted gram new body weight was 3 to 5 kcal/g new weight; similar values for 1-, 2-, and 3.5-kg infants using the intratuterine data are approximately 1.4, 2.2, and 3.1 kcal/g new tissue. Whether a better reference standard is the term infant growing postnatally[72, 73] remains unclear.

In estimating the total caloric demand of pregnancy on the mother, two additional factors need to be considered. First, the oxidative metabolic rate of the fetus must be added to the caloric rate of accretion to give the total demands of the fetus. The fetal oxidative rate has been estimated at approximately 50 kcal/kg/day for the human.[73, 74] The biosynthesis of tissue components appears generally efficient, particularly the synthesis of fat from triglyceride;[75] the energy required for biosynthetic processes is derived oxidatively and is therefore included in the caloric requirement for oxidation (indirect calorimetry). There is little information in humans permitting separate figures for fetal oxidative rate in LGA, AGA, or SGA infants; thus the total rate of caloric utilization for an AGA fetus is approximately 90 to 100 kcal/kg/day, of similar magnitude to the AGA neonate. Second, the support of pregnancy requires the support of the placenta as well.

While infrequently considered as a metabolic organ, data from the chronically catheterized sheep suggest that as much as half the oxygen and three-quarters the glucose provided from the mother is consumed within the placenta and does not reach the fetus.[74, 76] Thus, the above estimates based on fetal measurements alone may considerably underestimate the caloric demands placed on the mother by the continuation of gestation.

Mineral Accretion in the Fetus

Calcium accretion has attracted considerable attention in recent years, with the increasing recognition that many premature infants appear unable to take in adequate calcium for growth, resulting in demineralization of bone during rapid growth. Tsang et al.[77] has estimated the intrauterine accretion rate at approximately 140 to 150 mg Ca · kg^{-1} · min^{-1}. Shaw[78, 79] has approximated the calcium accretion data of Widdowson as an exponentially increasing function of gestational age. Comparing reports, Sparks has noted that plotting calcium accretion as a function of weight systematically underestimated the calcium content of SGA infants, while overestimating that of LGAs. In contrast, plotting calcium content against reported fetal length in 65 fetuses (Fig 1–5) provides an alternative relationship that appears similar in both SGA and AGA infants. The choice of normalizing denominators thus seems to affect or reduce systematic deviations, reemphasizing the theoretical problems of choosing an appropriate normalizing factor. When length is used instead of gestational age as the independent variable, it appears that the intrauterine rate of calcium accretion is about 85 mg/kg/day, significantly lower than estimates based on weight. It is not unreasonable by biologic standards, however, for calcium to relate to length better than to weight, as bone represents the major structure determining length. The calcium:phosphorous ratio does not change with gestational age after 16 weeks at approximately 1.8:1, consistent with the major locus of calcium in bone.

By any standard of analysis, the requirement of calcium in late gestation is large. Thus, whether expressed as 300 mg/day, 150 mg/kg/day (weight calculation) or 85 to 90

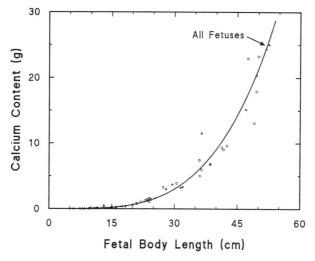

FIG 1–5.
Calcium content of human fetuses against fetal body length.

mg/kg/day (length calculation), it appears important for rapidly growing premature infants to receive large net intakes of calcium. Given the solubility of calcium, the net retention of calcium, and other nutritional goals, the provision of these large amounts of calcium has presented considerable clinical problems.

Use of Intrauterine Growth as a Neonatal Nutritional Standard

It is important to emphasize that the goal of achievement of intrauterine growth rate provides only one among many nutritional yardsticks in common clinical nursery use. Several of these standards may be in use simultaneously in the same patient. In general, achievement of intrauterine growth rate is a nonspecific and, in many cases, untestable goal. This goal is frequently superseded as more specific information is known. Thus, one might order a humanized milk formula for infants in general, order a calcium supplemented premature formula for the subgroup of newborns who are premature, and provide additional calcium and/or vitamin D for the subgroup of prematures with specific evidence of rachitic disease. Similarly, the dosage of iron may differ when providing at the Recommended Daily Allowances to prevent iron deficiency in the general population, compared with therapeutic regimens for individual iron-deficient infants.

Intrauterine Growth in Animal Fetuses

The intrauterine growth of other species may provide some insight into understanding the human data. Curiously, however, there are more data carefully describing chemical growth of humans than of experimental animals. Widdowson[80] has described the chemical composition of a number of mammals at term, and has noted that while most mammals are relatively constant at 12% to 14% protein at term, the fat content of almost all land mammals at term is about 1% to 2%. Among commonly studied laboratory animals, only the guinea pig (12%) approaches the fat content of human term infants (16%). Besides composition differences, the rate of growth varies widely among mammals. Human fetuses grow quite slowly when compared with common laboratory animals such as the sheep (6%/day), rabbit (30%/day), and rat (35%/day). Thus, the demands placed on a pregnant rat growing 11 low-fat fetuses at 35%/day may be very different from the demands placed on a pregnant human mother, growing a single, fatty fetus at 1.5%/day. Measurements of growth in length are also available in many species.[81]

Recently, fetal growth in the guinea pig has been extensively examined.[58] Measuring weight, dry weight, fat, total calories, amino acids, nitrogen, and carbon, we have constructed accretion curves for this species. This species is of considerable interest in view of its slower growth rate (7%/day), higher fat concentration at term (12%), and more recently, the ability to study gestation in this species in unstressed animals. These data have demonstrated several features supporting the analyses of human data presented earlier. First, these data provide direct experimental support for the values of 4.5 and 9.5 kcal/g non-fat and fat dry weight, respectively, which have been used in the earlier calculations of human caloric content. Second, these data demonstrate analogous increases in percent dry weight, fat content, and nitrogen to the human data. Of particular interest, these data provide direct evidence that approximately 80% of the nitrogen in fetal animals is in protein. Finally, these data suggest a very high rate of caloric deposition, totaling approximately 220 kcal/kg/day. The higher than human value results from the more rapid growth in wet weight (7%/day). As with the human, however, more than half the calories are required for fat deposition.

Static measurements at term of the chemical composition of animal fetuses are available for several species.[80, 82-88] Widdowson's[80, 82, 83] analyses of chemical composition at birth in several species are of particular interest in demonstrating biologic consistency in the contents of the protein portion of dry weight. Each of the species described has a protein concentration of about 12% at term. Furthermore, non-protein non-fat dry weight appears as a relatively small fraction of dry weight. In contrast, the fat component of dry weight exhibits considerable variation among fetuses at term. Fetuses of commonly studied laboratory animals, including the rat, rabbit, and sheep, are relatively low in fat, in contrast to the very high fat content of the human. The rhesus monkey appears also to produce a low-fat fetus.[85] Among laboratory animals, the guinea pig comes closest to the human in fetal fat concentration at term.[58, 80]

Measurements of fetal body composition throughout gestation are curiously limited. Increases in dry weight concentration appear well approximated as linear in the human, monkey, sheep, and guinea pig.[57, 58, 84, 88] Accretion rates of amino acids and protein have also been estimated in the sheep[57, 88] and guinea pig.[58] Fat concentration in most experimental animals is about 1% to 2% at term.[80] For these species, changes in fat concentration probably provide a small contribution to the total fat accretion rate, and it is probably reasonable to estimate accretion rate of fat in these species from growth in wet weight. More recently, fat accretion in the guinea pig has been measured,[58] and it appears that fat predominantly accumulates in the last third of gestation, similar to its development in the human. For the guinea pig, the more rapid rate of growth leads to a caloric accretion rate at term of approximately 220 kcal $\cdot$ kg^{-1} $\cdot$ d^{-1}, of which approximately 60% is required for fat accretion.

In interpreting these data, the considerable variation among species in fetal growth and composition demands considerable care when one attempts direct extrapolation to the human. As an example, if a low-fat rat fetus increases in weight at 35%/day, the implications for the high-fat human fetus growing at 1.5%/day remain to be demonstrated.

While such interspecies differences may make direct extrapolation problematic, such differences may be exploited in a comparative physiologic approach, and such data may therefore be of considerable interest in framing hypotheses regarding comparative intrauterine growth. In particular, it seems a reasonable hypothesis that measurements of non-fat dry weight accretion in a number of species may provide insight into human fetal non-fat accretion. Second, just as the fat component may be the most greatly affected by variations in human fetal growth, the accretion of fat in animal species may be comparatively more species-specific. Third, the large variation in fetal number, fetal percentage growth rate, and length of gestation may impose considerable interspecies differences in the nutritional and metabolic demands placed on the mother by gestation. Thus, effects too small to measure in one species may be readily observed in another. For example, the large fetal mass and rapid growth of the guinea pig in late gestation are associated with a 50% increase in maternal food intake,[89] and increases in maternal glucose turnover correlated directly with increasing fetal mass and number.[90] Finally, the comparative study of several species with regard to fetal growth and composition may help resolve such questions raised in individual species.

Intrauterine Growth Retardation in Experimental Animals.—Experimental fetal growth retardation has been induced in a variety of experimental animals. Reduction of uterine blood flow by uterine or umbilical artery ligation[86-88] produces small fetal weights and altered composition; differing effects result from microsphere ablation of the placenta.[91] A reduction in placental blood flow has also been observed in guinea pig spontaneously growth retarded fetuses and increased flow in spontaneously macrosomic fetuses.[92] This same phenomenon was confirmed in chronically catheterized guinea pigs[93]; a strong correlation was found between placental blood flow and spontaneous fetal weight. Myers et al.[93] have demonstrated in the guinea pig that spontaneously small guinea pig fetuses receive spontaneously lower uterine blood flow, and that spontaneous birth weight appears related as a power function of spontaneous placental blood flow. Growth retardation can be induced in the sheep by several methods, including nutritional restriction,[94-97] placental infarction with microspheres,[98, 99] or limitation of placental implantation,[100] umbilical artery ligation,[101-103] and maternal heating.[104] Growth-retarded fetal lambs show a reduction in the concentration of most metabolites. Average blood glucose levels are lower in the growth-retarded fetuses, although this difference has been found to be significant only in the carunclectomized animals.[100] Lactate and pyruvate concentrations were also diminished; however, lactate concentrations were significantly increased when growth retardation was induced by embolization.[98] Total α-amino nitrogen was reduced in all experimentally induced growth retardation.

Umbilical blood flow was also significantly reduced in growth-retarded fetal sheep. When total uptake was calculated, glucose uptake was reduced in both spontaneous and experimentally induced growth retardation. Total uptake of α-amino nitrogen was reduced in one study where growth retardation was induced by dietary deprivation.

Asymmetric growth retardation has been induced in rhesus monkeys by experimental placental insufficiency.[105] The newborn monkeys showed reduced muscle mass and less fat in the carcass than healthy control newborns. Moreoever, the pattern of organ involvement demonstrated that reduction in weight was small in brain and large in liver and spleen. These results closely parallel findings in human newborns.[106, 107]

In severe fetal growth retardation, brain growth is no longer maintained, and fetal head size as well as length and weight are decreased.[108] Those areas of the brain that grow more rapidly during late gestation are the most affected. In the monkey, greater changes were found in the cerebellum than in the cerebrum, as the cerebellum has a later growth spurt.[105] Total deoxyribonucleic acid (DNA) (as an index of cellularity) in the cerebellum was significantly reduced in growth-retarded animals when compared with normal control animals, but the concentrations of DNA, ribonucleic acid, and proteins were unchanged. These changes appear similar in different mammalian species. A similar reduction in brain weight and cellularity has been found in growth-retarded infants who die during the neonatal period.[109, 110]

Static cross-sectional measurements of chemical composition during spontaneous and experimentally induced growth variation are also available in several experimental animal species.[91, 111-117] The guinea pig is of particular interest, in light of the fat content of the fetal guinea pig. Widdowson has measured fat content of spontaneously small guinea pig fetuses at term and reports increased fat contents of spontaneously small guinea pig fetuses. In contrast, measurement of fat content in fetuses of nutritionally restricted mothers demonstrates significant reductions in body weight and in fat content. Interestingly, the fat content per body weight does not appear to be reduced. The data of Saintonge et al.[114] support reduced uptake of carbohydrate and amino acid analogues in growth-retarded fetal guinea pigs studied in the acute phase.

In summary, there are many models of spontaneously occurring and experimentally induced growth retardation in several animal species. These biologic experiments exploit natural interspecies diversity and illustrate the impact of different processes on fetal growth. However, given substantial biologic diversity in fetal size, fetal number, growth rates, body compositions, placentation, and maternal diet, direct extrapolation to human IUGR is potentially misleading. Nonetheless, these data are of great importance in illustrating general principles of normal and abnormal fetal growth, and in providing foundations for asking precise questions of human biology.

CLINICAL ISSUES IN FETAL GROWTH AND INTRAUTERINE GROWTH RETARDATION

Intrauterine Growth Retardation and Growth Excess

Intrauterine growth is one of the most important clinical signs of fetal well being. Normal intrauterine growth depends on the genetic potential of an individual, modulated by environmental factors including maternal health and nutrition. Normal growth of the fetus reassures the clinician that fetal development is proceeding well, while abnormal fetal growth should alert the clinician to evaluate the fetus in more detail. Excessive fetal growth may lead to the diagnosis of unsuspected complications of pregnancy, including multiple gestation and maternal glucose intolerance. Similarly, slow fetal growth should alert the clinician to further evaluation for diseases that result in the final common pathway of intrauterine growth retardation. A classification of causes for IUGR is presented in Table 1–2.

Classically, diminished fetal growth has been divided into two major patterns. In the first pattern, "symmetrical" IUGR, the fetus grows at a constant, but slower, rate than normal. Head circumference and length are reduced proportionately to weight. In

TABLE 1–2.

Factors Associated With Reduced Fetal Growth

I. Epidemiologic factors
  A. Female
  B. Racial/ethnic
II. Fetal factors
  A. Fetal infections
    1. Rubella
    2. Cytomegalovirus
    3. Toxoplasmosis
  B. Fetal anomalies
    1. Potters sequence
    2. Cardiac
    3. Anencephaly
    4. Pancreatic agenesis
    5. Gastrointestinal anomalies
    6. Discordant twins
  C. Fetal genetic/chromosomal disorders
    1. Syndromes
      a. Cornelia De Lange
      b. Genetic dwarfs
    2. Chromosomal syndromes
    3. Inborn errors of metabolism
      a. Galactosemia
      b. PKU
    4. Osteogenesis imperfecta
    5. Transient neonatal diabetes

Continued.

TABLE 1-2 (cont.).

III. Placental factors
    A. Microscopic
        1. Thrombosis
        2. Avascular villus
        3. Diffuse fibrinosis
    B. Macroscopic
        1. Infarction
        2. Separation
        3. Single umbilical artery
        4. Abnormal cord insertions
IV. Maternal factors
    A. Epidemiologic factors
        1. Small maternal size
        2. Previous SGA infant
        3. Mother herself SGA
        4. Reduced interpregnancy interval
        5. Poor maternal weight gain
    B. Multiple gestation
    C. Altitude
    D. Parity
        1. Primipara
        2. Grand multipara
    E. Smoking
    F. Drugs
        1. Narcotics
        2. Cocaine
        3. Alcohol
        4. Teratogens
    G. Maternal Diseases
        1. Chronic renal disease
        2. PIH
        3. Anemia
        4. Gastrointestinal, e.g., ulcerative colitis
        5. Hemoglobinopathies
    H. Extrauterine pregnancy
    I. Postmaturity
    J. Maternal floor infarction

the second pattern, "asymmetrical" IUGR, the rate of fetal growth slows and may even stop. Brain growth is relatively preserved, while growth of liver, spleen, and somatic body are more affected, resulting clinically in disproportionate body measurements. Head circumference is less affected than length, while weight is most affected. While clinically useful in conceptualizing processes that cause IUGR, Kramer et al.[118] have recently examined the distribution of growth parameters in IUGR and questioned whether there is a clear division between symmetrical and asymmetrical growth retardation.

The symmetrical pattern of IUGR is typical of a limited growth potential, which may be either hereditary or congenital. Because head circumference and length are reduced in proportion to weight, this pattern is referred to as "symmetrical." For some babies this is completely normal; they are small but otherwise healthy. In other cases, growth retardation is only a sign of a more complex pathologic process. Chromosomal abnormalities, severe congenital anomalies, and some inborn errors of metabolism are associated with growth retardation. The growth arrest in congenital viral infection may result from several factors, including altered fetal growth potential due to viral growth inhibiting factors[13] and altered substrate delivery caused by placental villous inflammation.[117]

The asymmetrical pattern of growth retardation has been intensively studied, in part because it leads to interesting physiologic questions and therapeutic possibilities. In this pattern, the brain and the heart are preserved while the liver, spleen, and somatic tissues are affected sooner. This phenomenon has been described as "brain sparing."

Growth retardation has been associated with many clinical conditions (see Table 1–2). Usually, however, no etiologic factor can be identified and the condition is commonly defined as idiopathic.

From a physiologic point of view, asymmetrical growth retardation may imply a decrease in oxygen or nutrient supply to the fetus. Conceptually, this decrease could be due to a decrease in maternal supply to the placenta or to a reduction in placental substrate transfer to the fetus. A reduction in oxygen and nutrient concentration has been found in both animal and human growth retardation.[108] Human studies have also measured nutrient concentrations in umbilical venous and arterial blood of growth-retarded fetuses at the time of spontaneous vaginal delivery or cesarean section. Total α-amino nitrogen concentrations were found to be significantly reduced in SGA as compared with AGA fetuses.[119] Moreover, the branched chain amino acids valine, leucine, and isoleucine, all essential for the growing fetus, accounted for most of the difference. In growth-retarded fetuses the mean umbilical arteriovenous difference for total α-amino nitrogen was not significantly positive and was much lower than for AGA fetuses. Since Doppler studies have suggested a significant reduction in umbilical blood flow in growth-retarded fetuses, the α-amino nitrogen umbilical uptake would appear to be significantly reduced.

These results have been recently confirmed in growth-retarded fetuses sampled in utero by cordocentesis.[119] Umbilical venous concentrations are significantly related to maternal arterial concentrations in both AGA and SGA fetuses. However, in SGA fetuses, at any given maternal concentration, umbilical venous concentrations of the branched chain amino acids are significantly lower than in healthy fetuses. The branched chain amino acids share a common transport system, the "L" or leucine-preferring, transport system.[120] These findings are consistent with recent findings in isolated placental membrane vesicles,[121] in which placental uptake of methylaminoisobutyric acid by vesicles isolated from the villous membrane of the syncytiotrophoblast was found to be significantly reduced in SGA as compared with AGA pregnancies.

Glucose concentrations were not found to be reduced in SGA fetuses when compared with normal fetuses at term.[122] The glucose/oxygen (G/O_2) quotient in SGA fetuses was similar to that in AGA fetuses and was significantly related to maternal arterial concentrations. Because umbilical blood flow is likely reduced in pregnancies complicated by IUGR, the maintenance of a normal umbilical G/O_2 quotient suggests that there may be a proportionate reduction in glucose and oxygen delivery.

At birth, growth-retarded neonates present reduced umbilical venous concentrations of glucose and have a steeper postnatal drop in blood glucose.[123, 124] These findings were concomitant with higher concentrations for lactate and alanine in SGA neonates, supporting a functional delay in the development of hepatic gluconeogenic enzymes.

Maternal nutrient concentrations have also been studied in pregnancies carrying an SGA fetus. Maternal amino acid concentration has been found to be related to birth weight.[125] Mothers with amino acid levels below 4 mg/100 mL had lighter babies with smaller cranial volumes than those whose amino acid levels exceeded 4 mg/100 mL.

However, mothers of SGA infants do not present mean total α-amino nitrogen concentrations different from mothers of AGA infants. Alanine is the only amino acid found to be significantly increased in mothers of SGA children consistently,[119, 126, 127] but fetal umbilical concentrations do not vary from those of healthy fetuses, leading to a lower fetal:maternal alanine ratio.[118] Total maternal amino acid concentrations have also been shown to be significantly increased in mothers of LGA infants.[127a] Total plasma amino acid concentrations and six individual amino acids correlated significantly with birth weight, whereas late pregnancy profiles of glycosylated hemoglobin A and plasma glucose did not. The amino acid serine correlated best with birth weight. Fetal pancreatic islet insulin secretion can be stimulated in early to mid gestation by certain amino acids long before glucose stimulation occurs in the last trimester.[128] This early effect might be partially responsible for the fetal hyperinsulinemia seen in these pregnancies.

A strong correlation has been described between uteroplacental blood flow, placental size, and fetal size. Doppler studies have estimated increased resistance in the uterine vessels of mothers of SGA fetuses as early as the second trimester.[129]

Another factor affecting substrate flow to the fetus is placental size and functional capacity. Placental transport of nutrients to the fetus is a function of placental surface area. A linear relationship between fetal and placental weights has been documented in several mammalian species, including the human, where SGA infants have small placentas and LGAs large placentas.[130] The incidence of perinatal problems is also increased in infants with high fetal/placental weight ratios.[131]

Maternal malnutrition in humans interferes with normal placental growth, reducing placental weight, size, and DNA content.[132, 133] In various studies, the decrease in mean placental weight has ranged between 14% and 50%, with placental weight being more affected than fetal weight. One hypothesis is that maternal malnutrition causes a reduction in the normal expansion of blood volume in pregnancy. This is associated with an inadequate increase in cardiac output and leads to decreased placental blood flow and therefore to reduced placental size. This has been reported in acutely catheterized fetal rats; food restriction was associated with decreased fetal and placental size.[133]

Various histologic conditions may result in defective placental substrate transfer. Several types of histologic change have been described in placentas of SGA fetuses, including umbilical vascular thrombosis, diffuse deposition of fibrinoid, edema, and thickening of the basement membrane and vascular terminal villi.[108, 134]

More recently, morphological changes in the microvillous membrane have been described in cases of severe fetal growth retardation associated with a marked reduction in the surface area of exchange at the peripheral villous level.[135] These changes were characterized by an increase in the microvillous surface density and surface enlargement factor, associated with a reduction of the intermicrovillous space. Such changes could represent an adaptation to the reduction in the placental surface area of exchange.

Intrauterine growth is also regulated by hormonal and growth factors. However, the humoral regulation of fetal growth differs significantly from postnatal growth regulation. Neither growth hormone nor thyroid hormone is an important regulator of fetal size.[136] Instead, insulin appears to play a significant role in fetal growth. The macrosomia of infants of diabetic mothers has been related to hyperinsulinemia. Pedersen et al.[137] suggested that the somatic changes seen in these infants resulted from maternal hyperglycemia, leading to fetal hyperglycemia followed by increased fetal insulin secretion. Similar somatic changes have been observed in infants with nesidioblastosis or the Beckwith-Wiedemann syndrome, which are also associated to increased insulin secretion.[138, 139] Insulin can act as a fetal growth factor first by increasing nutrient uptake and utilization and second by exerting a direct anabolic effect. Moreover, insulin can modulate the release of growth factors from the fetal tissues.[140] The growth-promoting effect of insulin seems to vary throughout gestation: cell proliferation and protein synthesis appear to be induced in early gestation, changing to energy storage in late gestation.[141] Insulin release is inhibited by adrenergic stimulation in fetal sheep.[142] Therefore, the release of catecolamines that occurs during fetal hypoxia could result in the inhibition of insulin release and consequently of fetal growth.

Other growth factors have also been found to influence fetal growth. Somatomedin concentrations in human fetal cord blood correlate with size at birth.[143, 144] Numerous fetal tissues contain specific somatomedin binding or receptor sites, including placenta, brain and monocytes.[144] Growth factors can interact with each other. Mitogenesis of limb bud cultures is stimulated by several factors such as epidermal growth factor, fibroblast growth factor, insulin, and somatomedin C. However, maximal growth is achieved where different factors are present simultaneously: conditioned medium from liver explants, epidermal growth factor, fibroblast growth factor, and either insulin or somatomedin C.[145]

Clinical Assessment of Intrauterine Growth

Growth is the process of increasing size (body dimensions) over a period of time. The clinical objective of assessing fetal growth is the identification of those fetuses with decreased or excessive fetal growth. Postnatal growth can be easily and directly estimated from serial measurements of the neonate. Unfortunately, the estimation of fetal growth is complicated by the difficulty of extrauterine observers measuring an intrauterine fetus. Therefore, clinicians must either rely on indirect measurements of fetal growth or apply imaging techniques to visualize and measure the fetus.

Clinical Assessment of Gestational Age

Traditionally gestational age has been defined according to reliable clinical dates by applying Näegele's rule, dating pregnancy from the first date of the last menstrual period. However, an optimal menstrual history is not always available, and between 6% and 45% of pregnant women have been reported to be unable to give such a history.[146]

Intrauterine growth is reflected very obviously in maternal abdomen expansion. Experienced obstetricians recognize the importance of determining fundal height in defining fetal growth during a normal pregnancy. This measure has been standardized into the symphysis-fundus distance, with several charts of normal growth. However, fundal height has not proved very accurate in detecting growth retardation: in a recent study one measurement below the 10th percentile identified 64% of IUGR but the positive predictive value was only 29%.[147] However, the sensitivity of fundal height has been reported as high as 85% in detecting IUGR when gestational age had been assessed sonographically early in pregnancy.[148, 149]

Ultrasound Assessment of Gestational Age

Gestational age can also be assessed with ultrasound examination. Ultrasound measurements performed between 12 and 18 weeks of gestation have been shown to be significantly better at predicting the date of delivery than Näegeles rule, even in mothers with optimal clinical dates.[146] Different parameters are used at different gestational ages: fetal crown-rump length (CRL) is used during the 1st trimester,[150] whereas the biparietal diameter (BPD) is utilized at later gestational ages.[151]

The CRL is defined as the distance from the top of the head to the outer part of the rump, and represents the longest length of the embryo. The mean error in predicting the day of delivery by CRL varies from 5 to 8 days.[150, 152] This measurement is not recommended after 12 weeks because of loss of accuracy due to flexion of the fetal spine. After the first trimester the BPD becomes the parameter of choice to assess gestational age; the BPD is measured from the outer to the inner edge of the proximal skull (outer-inner measurement), perpendicularly to the midline echo. Equal accuracy in predicting gestational age has been shown with CRL measured in the first trimester and BPD measured between 20 and 24 weeks of gestation.[152] The femur length, measured from the greater trochanter to the lateral condyle, has been shown to be as reliable as the BPD in assessing gestational age.

Alternative methods of establishing gestational age include clinical examination and recording the first recognizable fetal movements; however, both have been shown to be imprecise.[153, 154] If ultrasound measurements are used, it is recommended that the actual measurement be reported on the defined curves for normality at the gestational age calculated from the last menstrual period. Maternal dates should be used, unless estimated dates by ultrasound are considerably discrepant from maternal dates.

The best timing for a screening ultrasound examination in pregnancy has been estimated to be between 16 and 20 (or 24) weeks of pregnancy, when assessment of gestational age has been shown to be as accurate as during the first trimester,[152] and when it is also possible to screen for structural malformations of the central nervous, cardiovascular, musculoskeletal, gastrointestinal, and genitourinary systems.[155, 156]

Ultrasound has proved to be an invaluable tool to study both fetal morphology and fetal growth, and the application of ultrasound has become progressively more widespread.

Ultrasound Assessment of Intrauterine Growth

Two different patterns of growth can be found with ultrasound in IUGR. In the first, growth is decreased from early in pregnancy, with a sustained, low rate of growth. In the second, growth may be normal through early in the third trimester, but then flattens. These patterns are thought to reflect two different pathophysiologic mechanisms. In the first, the fetus is persistently small, probably reflecting a reduced growth potential. In the second, a fetus that had been growing well reduces its growth rate, and may come eventually to a complete growth arrest. "Uteroplacental insufficiency," an imprecise term suggesting that failure of the placenta to continue to provide adequately for the fetus, is thought to be responsible for this latter case.

In this late growth slowing, fetal organs are affected differently, with the greatest effect on weight, and to a lesser extent, length. There is often relative preservation of head growth, or "brain sparing." For this reason, head measurements may be a poor predictor of IUGR, and the sensitivity of the BPD in predicting growth retardation is only 50% to 60%.[157]

The femur length is affected late in most cases of IUGR[158] and may therefore not be a good indicator of severe IUGR. The liver is affected the most in states of IUGR.[159] The measurement of the abdominal circumference at the level of the umbilical vein was first described in 1975.[160] Since then, this has been widely accepted as the best single predictor of fetal growth[149, 157] with a sensitivity of 95%, a specificity of 60%, and a negative predictive value of 99%.[161] However, the positive predictive value varies from 21%[161] to 50%.[149] The ratio between the head and abdominal size has also been evaluated,[162] showing a decline during gestation due to increases in fetal fat and subcutaneous tissues. This ratio can be increased in many cases of asymmetric IUGR, but it is not involved in those cases when there is a symmetric involvement of the fetal organs. Oligohydramnios is also frequently found in association with IUGR.[163] The absence of a pocket of amniotic fluid greater than 1 cm had a sensitivity of 93% and a specificity of 89% in detection of IUGR.

Fetal weight can be estimated from measurements of the fetus, based on the assumption that volume is related to weight. Multiple parameters have been used to derive equations for the prediction of fetal weight; one of the most widely used, described by Shepard et al.,[164] derives the estimated fetal weight from the BPD and the abdominal circumference. This measurement has been used in the detection of fetal macrosomia, with a sensitivity of 73%, a specificity of 95%, but a positive predictive value of only 63%.[165] Head measurements are not necessarily affected in excessive fetal growth, since the fetal brain does not appear to be sensitive to the growth-promoting effect of insulin,[166] while the liver and the abdominal organs are likely to be enlarged. Therefore, abdominal measurement is probably the most reliable parameter for the detection of fetal macrosomia in utero. In diabetic pregnancies, an abdominal circumference exceeding the 90th percentile has a positive predictive value of 78%.[167] This value increases slightly when both abdominal circumference and estimated fetal weight are considered.[168]

In conclusion, no single ultrasonically measured parameter can be performed alone to detect with confidence intrauterine growth retardation or growth excess. Therefore, multiple parameters should be monitored, and followed longitudinally when an abnormality is suspected. A recent study analyzes by multiple regression analysis the value of different clinical and ultrasound parameters in predicting IUGR and develops an IUGR scoring system based on sonographically estimated fetal weight, amniotic fluid volume, and maternal blood pressure.[168] This scoring system introduces a functional evaluation of the uteroplacental vascularization through the measurement of maternal blood pressure.

Doppler Flow Velocimetry

Recently, new ultrasonic Doppler techniques have made possible the estimation of maternal uterine blood flow and fetal umbilical blood flow. A significant advantage of Doppler studies over more invasive procedures (i.e., cordocentesis) is that they can be repeated in problem pregnancies with minimal risk. In the last few years, several studies have focused on the prediction of perinatal distress by Doppler ultrasound.

In Doppler studies, sound of a known frequency is transmitted, and the change in the frequency of reflected sound reflected is proportional to the velocity of the blood moving through vessels. A flow velocity waveform (FVW) is recorded that describes flow. Absolute quantitation of blood flow requires knowledge of the diameter of the vessel and the angle the ultrasound beam makes with that vessel. Because these values are difficult to measure simultaneously with the waveform, quantitation of absolute flow presents a technical challenge. Simpler ratios between systolic and diastolic values have been developed that are independent of angle.[169] Based on flow velocity, it is also possible to estimate vascular resistance.

Both uteroplacental and fetoplacental blood flows have been studied with this method and normal standard curves have been developed. On the maternal side, a significant fall in maternal blood pressure and systemic vascular resistance occurs at mid pregnancy, and this is reflected in a fall between 16 to 20 weeks in the resistance indexes measured on the arcuate arteries on the placental side with no change thereafter.[170] Indexes from FVW measured from the fetal arteries demonstrate a continuing decrease throughout gestation, from an increase in diastolic velocities with increasing gestation.[170, 171]

Changes in perfusion indexes have been shown to occur very early in pathologic pregnancies. Blood flow velocity profiles in the uterine vessels (arcuate arteries) can be altered as early as the second trimester in pregnancies associated with hypertension, proteinuria, or suspected fetal growth retardation.[129] The failure to observe a fall in uterine resistance indexes has been ascribed to a failure of trophoblast cells to invade the intima and media of uterine spiral arteries in complicated pregnancies.[171] This invasion occurs normally by the 20th week and is thought responsible for the fall observed in resistance indexes between 16 and 20 weeks.

On the fetal side, many studies have reported an increase in resistance indexes in the umbilical arteries and in the descending aorta of growth-retarded fetuses. Moreover, in intrauterine growth retardation, raised pulsatility indexes (PI) in the umbilical arteries have been found together with reduced PI in the internal carotid arteries, confirming the presence of a "brain sparing" effect in these fetuses.[172]

Doppler study is particularly powerful in identifying those cases of IUGR that will develop perinatal distress. In a recent study, all growth-retarded fetuses that had fetal distress requiring obstetric intervention in the perinatal period presented extremely raised PI, in most cases with absence of end diastolic flow.[173] The absence of end diastolic frequencies in the fetal aorta has been associated with poor perinatal outcome (i.e., perinatal death, necrotizing enterocolitis, and hemorrhage).[174] Doppler measurements have also been compared to fetal heart rate monitoring in identifying fetal distress. Doppler presented a higher sensitivity than FHR and was especially powerful in detecting newborns who required an admission to the intensive care unit.[175]

The PI of the fetal umbilical arteries has been correlated to biochemical monitoring in growth-retarded fetuses both at the time of cesarean section and in utero by cordocentesis.[176] Cordocentesis is a technique that allows transabdominal cord blood sampling under ultrasonic guidance and provides a direct insight into fetal status.[177] The evaluation of oxygenation and acid–base balance by cordocentesis in growth retardation has shown that lactate concentrations are the earliest indicator of fetal distress and that high lactate concentrations can be present in fetuses with normal fetal heart rate tracings.[178] The PI of the fetal umbilical arteries presents a significant relationship with pH and lactate concentrations measured on umbilical venous blood by cordocentesis,[176] supporting PI as a valid method to follow high-risk pregnancies noninvasively.

Biochemical Endocrine Assessment

Biochemical endocrine assessment has been advocated for many years in the management of high-risk pregnancies. The rationale to study hormones that are produced by the placenta or by both fetus and placenta in order to evaluate fetal growth is that an impairment of fetal growth would lead also to a decrease of hormone production. Abnormal estriol excretion patterns have been found in pregnancies complicated by diabetes, hypertension, and fetal distress or fetal death.[179] However, estriols are subject to great variations, with large diurnal and day-to-day variations. Each patient has to serve as her own control, and longitudinal determinations are necessary.[180]

Human placental lactogen (HPL) has also been correlated with functional placental mass. High HPL levels have been reported in multiple gestation, Rh isoimmunization, and diabetes, conditions associated with a large placental mass, whereas a chronic reduction in placental size has been associated with a decrease in HPL levels. However, the accuracy of low HPL levels in predicting IUGR has been reported to vary from 32% to 100%.[181] Moreover, the cost and sophistication of assays limit their use. Therefore, despite their interest in physiologic terms, measurement of hormone levels are not currently used to evaluate fetal growth and fetal well-being.

Management of Intrauterine Growth Retardation

Early Diagnosis, Counseling, and Timing In Pregnancy

The major focus of the management of the IUGR pregnancy is the early identification of growth retardation, followed by careful attention to the needs of the identified pregnancy. Specific interventions may be indicated in some cases, such as smoking, substance abuse, poor nutrition, or maternal illness. In other cases, careful attention to the diagnosis of congenital anomalies, chromosomal disorders, or congenital infections may warrant more invasive diagnostic studies such as amniocentesis or cordacentesis. In these cases, specific diagnoses may guide subsequent family counseling as well as obstetric management. In most cases, however, the specific cause for the growth restriction is unknown. Consequently, specific therapeutic interventions may not be available. In such cases, the major goals are to provide meticulous obstetric care and to assure proper timing and preparation for delivery.

Experimental Treatments During Pregnancy

There has been considerable interest in the obstetric literature examining nonspecific maneuvers for treatment of IUGR fetuses. Bedrest has been widely proposed, but its efficacy has been the subject of only limited actual study.[217, 218] In one recent study, bedrest was shown not to be efficacious for fetal growth or pregnancy outcome. Use of betamimetics[182] and prostacyclin[183] has been reported, with both mixed effectiveness and serious complication. Oxygen has been shown to improve fetal gases by cordacentesis,[184] and its usage has been reviewed in detail.[185]

Aggressive nutritional intervention has also been tried in experimental animals. Charlton and Johengen have shown that intravenous, intraamniotic, and maternal nutritional supplementation is at least partially efficacious in restoring fetal weight in sheep fetuses experimentally made growth retarded.[187, 187a] Similarly, transamniotic feeding has been shown to improve growth and outcome in experimental IUGR rabbits.[188, 189] However, maternal hyperalimentation did not improve fetal growth in IUGR rats.[190]

Human studies have shown mixed results in aggressive nutritional management of suspected IUGR pregnancies. A recent analysis of the Women Infants Children (WIC) program demonstrated no increase in mean birth weight in supplemented women.[190] Maternal dietary supplementation has resulted in minimal alteration of mean birth weights.[191] Of more concern, Rush and associates have shown an increased rate of prematurity, higher mortality, and lower birth weight when women were given a high-protein supplement,[192] and birth weight correlated negatively with the protein content of supplements.[191]

A few case reports have demonstrated that it is possible to provide intravenous nutrition in pregnancy. However, the limited data in humans have not shown aggressive intravenous nutrition to be effective in augmenting growth in IUGR pregnancies.[192, 193]

Obstetric Complications

If carriage of pregnancy represents a chronic stress to the growth-retarded baby, it is not surprising that the growth-retarded fetus may not tolerate the additional stress of delivery. Failure to tolerate labor may be manifested in many clinically evident ways, including decreased fetal activity, poor fetal heart tones, abnormal fetal monitoring, abnormal scalp and cord pH, and abnormal cord gases. Increased risk of fetal distress and even fetal death may be associated with IUGR. Poor tolerance of labor, with increased cesarian section rate and increased perinatal asphyxia, has been noted.[194] Accordingly, it is essential that pregnancies with suspected IUGR be carefully evaluated and monitored. Associated findings of fetal distress, particularly including passage of meconium and asphyxial organ damage, may significantly complicate neonatal management, and a clinician skilled in newborn resuscitation should be available at deliveries of infants suspected of growth retardation.

Neonatal Consequences

It is well known that SGA infants are subject to increased risks of metabolic problems in the nursery. Hypoglycemia and hypocalcemia are common in all neonates, but the risk of these derangements is significantly greater in SGA infants. Several factors may contribute to the observed hypoglycemia. First, SGA infants do not appear to accumulate liver glycogen late in gestation, as do healthy infants. Shelley and Neligan[195] presented evidence showing a dramatic increase in liver glycogen in healthy human fetuses beginning at 32 to 34 weeks, reaching very high glycogen concentrations and contents by term. The SGA infants in the same study did not accumulate liver glycogen normally. Secondly, perinatal stress may cause a transient early mobilization of glycogen postnatally in stressed infants, followed by hypoglycemia as stores are consumed. Finally, there is evidence in humans and experimental animals that IUGR infants may regulate glucose poorly, with altered postnatal gluconeogenic substrate and gluconeogenesis.[196, 197] Direct measurement of conversion of alanine to glucose in human IUGR infants, however, has not confirmed abnormal maturation of gluconeogenic pathways.[197a]

Amino acid and fat metabolism are probably affected by growth retardation as well. An SGA infant may be more sensitive to excess protein in the diet than AGA controls, possibly on the basis of hepatocellular consequences of IUGR.[196, 198] Direct measurement of rates of protein synthesis using stable, isotopically labeled glycine has not yielded consistent results.[195, 199–201] More recent measurements of protein turnover with stable, isotopically labeled leucine[201a] have suggested a positive relationship between body weight and protein synthetic rate.

Composition studies cited earlier demonstrate that SGA fetuses have considerably less fat than AGA or LGA fetuses, and there is limited evidence that fat metabolism may be abnormal in IUGR infants as well. The IUGR infants have decreased fat detectable by several methods,[202] and there is evidence in IUGR animals of abnormal fat oxidation and triglyceride synthesis.[197]

Long-Term Consequences of Fetal Growth Restriction

There is considerable evidence that the process of growth retardation is associated with significant consequences in the infant. Some IUGR infants have obvious anomalies, and some of the long-term effects result from the associated anomalies in these infants. However, even after exclusion of infants with obvious anomalies, there remains significant residual concern regarding the consequences of IUGR. Some of these effects are immediate and are subject to evaluation and treatment in the newborn period. Of significant concern, however, is the repeated observation that restriction of fetal growth may have effects on growth and development that persist long after birth.

Neurologic Development

The long-term neurologic and developmental outcome of IUGR infants has been of major concern. Clearly, many individual causes of IUGR, particularly including congenital infections and obvious anomalies, may be associated with poor neurologic outcome, and proper diagnosis of cause of IUGR is important for outcome prognostication.

However, there remains considerable concern regarding outcome even after exclusion of infants with known diagnoses. Several studies suggest minimal change in intelligence (IQ) after exclusion of infants with infections and anomalies.[203–205] Taken as a group, however, it would appear that a significant body of recent evidence supports concern regarding developmental outcome and school performance in IUGR infants.[204, 206–209] Normally, growth monozygous twins appear to have better developmental outcome than their IUGR twin.[210] Moreover, IUGR infants appear abnormally represented in the population of developmentally disabled children. It should be noted that, excluding infants with anomalies and congenital infections, major neurologic findings are infrequent in this population. Generally, sequelae associated with IUGR are the more subtle changes in activity, attention and behavior, and tone. These types of "soft" findings are poorly understood and are likely to be multifactorial, but likely contribute to a perception of poorer outcome and school performance.

Several factors significantly complicate the interpretation of these data. First, gestational age assessment postnatally, as prenatally, is susceptible to error, with resultant misclassification of infants. In particular, postnatal assessment of gestational age relies in large part on neurologic tone and motor activity, which may be affected by stress and asphyxia. Moreover, the postnatal timing of the examinations is important in view of the normal postnatal changes in tone and activity. With the tendency for early discharge from nurseries, many infants are examined before these examinations are most valid. Second, even if there is increased risk in the IUGR population, that risk appears to be heterogeneous, and may relate as much to other consequences of IUGR than to IUGR itself. A recent reevaluation of the National Collaborative Perinatal Project data suggests that perinatal stress is a major determinant of neurologic outcome in IUGR infants.[207] Finally, socioeconomic factors may confound interpretation of the data.

Postnatal Growth

There is general agreement that IUGR infants are at increased risk for reduced rates of postnatal growth. Infant growth appears to correlate with infant birth weight and length,[211] and many studies document that IUGR infants tend to be shorter and slimmer than other infants.[211–215] Of importance, however, is the observation of heterogeneity in the postnatal growth of IUGR infants: a large proportion of this population will evidence "catch-up" growth in the first 2 years of life, achieving weight and length typical of healthy infants.[212] Both insulin and growth hormone have been proposed to have a role in this catch-up growth.[216]

REFERENCES

1. American Academy of Pediatrics Committee on Nutrition: Nutritional needs of low-birth-weight infants. *Pediatrics* 1977; 60:519–530.

2. Koops BL, Morgan LJ, Battaglia FC: Neonatal mortality risk in relation to birth weight and gestational age: Update. *J Pediatr* 1982; 101:969–977.

3. Lubchenco LO, Searls DT, Brazie JV: Neonatal mortality rate: Relationship to birth weight and gestational age. *J Pediatr* 1972; 81:814–822.

4. Nakano R: Post-term pregnancy. *Acta Obstet Gynecol Scand* 1972; 51:217.

5. Dubowitz LMS, Dubowitz V, Goldberg C: Clinical assessment of gestational age in the newborn infant. *J Pediatr* 1970; 77:1.

6. Ballard JL, Novak KK, Driver M: A simplified score for assessment of fetal maturation of newly born infants. *J Pediatr* 1979; 95:769.

7. Lubchenco LO: *The High Risk Infant.* Philadelphia, WB Saunders Co, 1976, pp 65–98.

8. Lubchenco LO: Clinical estimation of gestational age, in Kempe CH, Silver HK, O'Brien D (eds): *Current Pediatric Diagnosis and Treatment,* ed 3. Los Altos, Calif, Lange, 1974.

9. Lubchenco LO, Hansman C, Dressler M, et al: Intrauterine growth as estimated from live-born birth-weight data at 24 to 42 weeks of gestation. *Pediatrics* 1963; 32:793–800.

10. Usher R, McLean F: Intrauterine growth of live-born Caucasian infants at sea level: Standards obtained from measurements in 7 dimensions of infants born between 25 and 44 weeks of gestation. *J Pediatr* 1969; 74:901–910.

11. Gruenwald P: Growth of the human fetus: II. Abnormal growth in twins and infants of mothers with diabetes, hypertension or iso-immunization. *Am J Obstet Gynecol* 1966; 94:1120–1132.

12. Widdowson EM, Spray CM: Chemical development in utero. *Arch Dis Child* 1951; 26:205–214.

13. Plotkin SA, Vaheri A: *Science* 1967; 156:659–661.

14. Lederman SA, Rosso P: Effects of food restriction on fetal and placental growth and maternal body composition. *Growth* 1980; 44:77–88.

15. Elphick MC, Hull D: Transfer of fatty acid across the cat placenta. *J Dev Physiol* 1984; 6:517–25.

16. Schell LM, Hodges DC: Longitudinal study of growth status and airport noise exposure. *J Phys Anthropol* 1985; 66:383–389.

17. Cnattingius S, Axelsson O, Eklund G, et al: Factors influencing birthweight for gestational age, with special respect to risk factors for intrauterine growth retardation. *Early Hum Dev* 1984; 10:45–55.

18. Miller HC, Merritt TA: *Fetal Growth in Humans.* Chicago, Year Book Medical Publishers, 1979.

19. Tanner JM, Thomson AM: Standards for birthweight at gestation periods from 32 to 42 weeks, allowing for maternal height and weight. *Arch Dis Child* 1970; 45:566–569.

20. Ferraz EM, Gray RH, Fleming PL, et al: Interpregnancy interval and low birth weight: Findings from a case-control study. *Am J Epidemiol* 1988; 128:1111–1116.

21. Miller JE: Determinants of intrauterine growth retardation: Evidence against maternal depletion. *J Biosoc Sci* 1989; 21:235–243.

22. Yang P, Beaty TH, Khoury MJ, et al: Predicting intrauterine growth retardation in sibships while considering maternal and infant covariates. *Genet Epidemiol* 1989; 6:525–535.

23. Klebanoff MA, Meirik O, Berendes HW. Second-generation consequences of small-for-dates birth. Pediatr 1989; 84:343–347.

24. Kessel SS, Kleinman JC, Koontz AM, et al: Racial differences in pregnancy outcomes. *Clin Perinatol* 1988; 15:745–754.

25. Myers SA, Ferguson R: A population study of the relationship between fetal death and altered fetal growth. *Obstet Gynecol* 1989; 74:325–331.

26. Hollingsworth DR, Jones OW, Resnik R: Expanded care in obstetrics for the 1980s: Preconception and early postconception counseling. *Am J Obstet Gynecol* 1984; 149:811–814.

27. Berne C, Wibell L, Lindmark G: Ten-year experience of insulin treatment in gestational diabetes. *Acta Paediatr Scand [Suppl]* 1985; 320:85–93.

28. Holmes LB: Does taking vitamins at the time of conception prevent neural tube defects? *JAMA* 1985; 260:3181.

29. Milunsky A, Jick H, Bruell CL, et al: Multivitamin/folic acid supplementation in early pregnancy reduces the prevalence of neural tube defects. *JAMA* 1989; 262:2847–2852.

30. Rosa FW, Wilk AL, Kelsey FO: Teratogen update: Vitamin A congeners. *Teratology* 1986; 33:355–364.

31. Lungarotti MS, Marinelli D, Mariani T, et al: Multiple congenital anomalies associated with apparently normal maternal intake of vitamin A: A phenocopy of the isotretinoin syndrome? *Am J Med Genet* 1987; 27:245–248.

32. Lubchenco LO, Bard H: Incidence of hypoglycemia in newborn infants classified by birth weight and gestational age. *Pediatrics* 1971; 47:831–838.

33. Babson SG, Behrman RE, Lessel R: Fetal growth. Liveborn birth weights for gestational age of white middle class infants. Pediatrics 1970; 45:937–944.

34. Gruenwald P: Growth of the human fetus: I. Normal growth and its variation. *Am J Obstet Gynecol* 1966; 94:1112–1119.

35. Miller HC: Intrauterine growth retardation—an unmet challenge. *Am J Dis Child* 1981; 135:944–948.

36. Wong KS, Scott KE: Fetal growth at sea level. *Biol Neonate* 1972; 20:175–188.

37. Lindell A: Prolonged pregnancy. *Acta Obstet Gynecol Scand* 1956; 35:136–163.

38. Sterky G: Swedish standard curves for intrauterine growth. *Pediatrics* 1970; 46:7–8.

39. Kloosterman GJ: The obstetrician and dysmaturity, in; Jonxis JHP, Visser HK, Troelstra JA (eds): *Aspects of Prematurity and Dysmaturity*. Nutricia Symposium. Springfield, Ill, Charles C Thomas, 1968; pp 263–284.

40. Kloosterman GJ: On intrauterine growth: The significance of prenatal care. *Int J Gynaecol Obstet* 1970; 8:895–912.

41. Arbuckle TE, Sherman GJ: An analysis of birth weight by gestational age in Canada. *Can Med Assoc J* 1989; 140:157–160.

42. Brandt I: Growth dynamics of low-birth-weight infants with emphasis on the perinatal period, in Falkner F, Tanner JM (eds): *Human Growth,* vol 2. *Postnatal Growth.* New York, Plenum Publishing Corp, 1978; pp 557–617.

43. Introduction to comparative growth studies: Methods and standards, in Eveleth PB, Tanner JM (eds): *Worldwide Variation in Human Growth*. London, Cambridge University Press, 1976, pp 1–14.

44. McKeown T, Record RG: Observations on fetal growth in multiple pregnancy in man. *J Endocrinol* 1952; 8:386–401.

45. Wilcox AJ: Birth weight, gestation, and the fetal growth curve. *Am J Obstet Gynecol* 1981; 139:863–867.

46. Lichty JA, Ting RY, Bruns PD, et al: Studies of babies born at high altitude. *Am J Dis Child* 1957; 93:666–678.

47. Stein Z, Susser M, Rush D: Prenatal nutrition and birth weight: Experiments and quasi-experiments in the past decade. *J Reprod Med* 1978; 21:287–297.

48. Stein ZA, Susser MW: The Dutch Famine, 1944/45, and the reproductive process: I. Effects on six indices at birth. *Pediatr Res* 1975; 9:70–76.

49. Stein ZA, Susser MW: The Dutch Famine, 1944/45, and the reproductive process: II. Interrelations of caloric rations and six indices at birth. *Pediatr Res* 1975; 9:76.

50. Hoffman HJ, Stark CR, Lundine FE, Jr, et al: Analysis of birth weight, gestational age and fetal viability, U.S. Births, 1968. *Obstet Gynecol Surv* 1974; 29:651–681.

51. Dancis J, O'Connell JR, Holt LE: A grid for recording the weight of premature infants. *J Pediatr* 1948; 33:570–571.

51a. Naeye RL, Dixon JB: Distortions in fetal growth standards. *Pediatr Res* 1978; 12:987–991.

52. Brace RA: Fitting straight lines to experimental data. *Am J Physiol* 1977; 233:R94–R99.

53. Walton A, Hammond J: The maternal effects on growth and conformation in the Shire-Shetland pony crosses. *Proc R Soc Lond [Biol]* 1938; 125:311–335.

54. Ziegler EE, O'Donnell AM, Nelson SE, et al: Body composition of the reference fetus. *Growth* 1976; 40:329–341.

55. Sparks JW, Girard JR, Battaglia FC: An estimate of the caloric requirements of the human fetus. *Biol Neonate* 1980; 38:113–119.

56. Sparks JW: Intrauterine growth. *Semin Pertinatol* 1984; 8:74–93.

57. Meier P, Teng C, Battaglia FC, et al: The rate of amino acid nitrogen and total nitrogen accumulation in the fetal lamb. *Proc Soc Exp Biol Med* 1981; 167:463–468.

58. Sparks JW, Girard JR, Callikan S, et al: Growth of the fetal guinea pig: Physical and chemical characteristics. *Am J Physiol* 1985; 248:132–139.

59. Southgate DAT, Hey EN: Chemical and biochemical development of the human fetus, in Roberts DF, Thomson AM (eds): *The Biology of Human Fetal Growth.* London, Taylor and Francis, 1976, pp 195–214.

60. Southgate DAT: Fetal measurements, in: Falkner F, Tanner JM (eds): *Human Growth,* vol 1, *Principles and Prenatal Growth.* New York, Plenum Publishing Corp, 1978, pp 379–395.

61. Widdowson EM, Southgate DAT, Hey EN: Body composition of the fetus and infant, in Visser HKA (ed): *Nutrition and Metabolism of the Fetus and Infant.* Fifth Nutricia Symposium. The Hague, Martinus Nijhoff, 1979, pp 169–177.

62. Fee BA, Weil WB, Jr: Body composition of infants of diabetic mothers by direct analysis. *Ann NY Acad Sci* 1963; 110:869–897.

63. Widdowson EM, Dickerson JWT: Chemical composition of the body, in: Comar CL, Bronner F (eds): *Mineral Metabolism,* vol 2, part A, New York, Academic Press. 1964, pp 1–247.

64. Widdowson EM, McCance RA: Some effects of accelerating growth: I. General somatic development. *Proc R Soc London [Biol]* 1960; 152:188–206.

65. Apte SV, Iyengar L: Composition of the human foetus. *Br J Nutr* 1972; 27:305–317.

66. Kelly HJ, Sloan RE, Hoffman W, et al: Accumulation of nitrogen and six minerals in the human fetus during gestation. *Hum Biol* 1951; 23:61–74.

67. Reichman B, Chessex P, Putet G, et al: Diet, fat accretion, and growth in premature infants. *N Engl J Med* 1981; 305:1495–1500.

68. Shaw JCL: Parenteral nutrition in the Management of sick low birthweight infants. *Pediatr Clin North Am* 1973; 20:333–358.

69. Widdowson EM: Importance of nutrition in development, with special reference to feeding the low birthweight infant. In: Meeting Nutritional Goals for Low Birthweight Infants: Proceedings of the Second Ross Clinical Conference 4-11, 1982 (Ross Laboratories, Columbus OH)

70. Adam PAJ, Felig P: Carbohydrate, fat, and amino acid metabolism in the pregnant woman and fetus, in Falkner F, Tanner JM (eds): *Human Growth,* vol 1, *Principles and Prenatal Growth.* New York, Plenum Publishing Corp, 1978; pp 461–547.

71. Whyte RK, Haslam R, Vlanic C, et al: Energy balance and nitrogen balance in growing low birthweight infants fed human milk or formula. *Pediatr Res* 1983; 17:891–898.

72. Fomon SJ: Body composition of the male reference infant during the first year of life. *Pediatrics* 1967; 40:863–870.

73. Meschia G, Battaglia FC: Principal substrates of fetal metabolism. *Physiol Rev* 1988; 58:499–527.

74. Meschia G, Battaglia FC, Hay WW Jr, et al: Utilization of substrates by the ovine placenta in vivo. *Fed Proc* 1980; 39:245–249.

75. Millward DJ, Garlick PJ. The energy cost of growth. Proc Nutr Soc 35:339–349, 1976

76. Sparks JW, Hay WW Jr, Wilkening RB, et al: Partition of maternal nutrients to the placenta and fetus in the sheep. *Eur J Obstet Gynecol Reprod Biol* 1983; 14:331–340.

77. Tsang RC, Steichen JJ, Brown DR: Perinatal calcium homeostasis: Neonatal hypocalcemia and bone demineralization. *Clin Perinatol* 1977; 4:385–409.

78. Shaw JC: Trace metal requirements of preterm infants. *Acta Paediatr Scand [Suppl]* 1982; 296:93–100.

79. Shaw JC: Evidence for defective skeletal mineralization in low-birthweight infants: The absorption of calcium and fat. *Pediatrics* 1976; 57:16–25.
80. Widdowson EM: Chemical composition of newly born mammals. *Nature* 1950; 166:626–627.
81. Evans HE, Sack WO: Prenatal development of domestic and laboratory mammals: Growth curves, external features and selected references. *Anat Histol Embryol* 1973; 2:11–45.
82. Widdowson EM: Immediate and long-term consequences of being large or small at birth: A comparative approach, in Elliott K, Knight J (eds): *Size at Birth*. New York, American Elsevier, 1974, pp 65–82.
83. McCance RA, Widdowson EM: Glimpses of comparative growth and development, in Falkner F, Tanner JM (eds): *Human Growth,* vol 1, *Principles and Prenatal Growth*. New York, Plenum Publishing Corp, 1978.
84. Behrman RE, Seeds AE, Battaglia FC, et al: The normal changes in mass and water content in fetal rhesus monkey and placenta throughout gestation. *J Pediatr* 1964; 65:38–44.
85. Hill DE: Experimental growth retardation in rhesus monkeys, in Elliott K, Knight J (eds): *Size at Birth*. New York, American Elsevier, 1974, pp 99–125.
86. Renfree MB, Meier P, Teng C, et al: Relationship between amino acid intake and accretion in a marsupial, *Macropus eugenii. Biol Neonate* 1981; 40:29–37.
87. Alexander G: Birth weight of lambs: Influences and consequences, in Falkner F, Tanner JM (eds): *Human Growth,* vol 1, *Principles and Prenatal Growth*. New York, Plenum Publishing Corp 1978, pp 215–245.
88. Meier PR, Peterson RG, Bonds DR, et al: Rates of protein synthesis and turnover in fetal life. *Am J Physiol* 1981; 240:E320–E324.
89. Sparks JW, Pegorier JP, Girard JR, et al: Substrate concentration changes during pregnancy in the guinea pig studied under unstressed steady state conditions. *Pediatr Res* 1981; 15:1340–1344.
90. Gilbert M, Sparks JW, Girard JR, et al: Changes in glucose metabolism during pregnancy induced by fasting in chronically catheterized guinea pigs. *Fed Proc* 1981; 40:469E.
91. Clapp JF, Szeto HH, Larrow R, et al: Umbilical blood flow response to embolization of the uterine circulation. *Am J Obstet Gynecol* 1980; 138:60–67.
92. Saintonge J, Rosso P: Placental blood flow and transfer of nutrients analogs in large, average and small guinea pig littermates. *Ped Res* 1981; 15:152–156.
93. Myers SA, Sparks JW, Makowski EL, et al: The relationship between placental blood flow and placental and fetal size in the guinea pig. *Am J Physiol* 1982; 243:H404–H409.
94. Wallace L: The growth of lambs before and after birth in relation to the level of nutrition: I and II. *J Agric Sci* 1948; 38:243.
95. Wallace L: The growth of lambs before and after birth in relation to the level of nutrition: III. *J Agric Sci* 1948; 38:367
96. Koritnik D, Humphrey W, Kaltenbach E, et al: Effects of maternal undernutrition on the development of the ovine fetus and the associated changes in growth hormone and prolactin. *Biol Reprod* 1981; 24:125–137.
97. Charlton V, Johengen M: Metabolism of the fetal lamb growth retarded by maternal malnutrition (abstract), *Pediatr Res* 1982; 6:109A.
98. Clapp J, Szeto H, Larrow R, et al: Fetal metabolic response to experimental placental vascular damage. *Am J Obstet Gynecol* 1981; 140:446–451.
99. Creasy R, Barrett C, Deswiet M, et al: Experimental intrauterine growth retardation in the sheep. *Am J Obstet Gynecol* 1972; 112:566–573.
100. Robinson J, Kingston E, Jones C, et al: Studies on experimental growth retardation in sheep. The effect of removal of endometrial caruncles on fetal size and metabolism. *J Dev Physiol* 1979; 379–398.
101. Emmanouilides G, Townsend D, Bauer R: Effects of simple umbilical artery ligation in the lamb fetus. *Pediatrics* 1968; 42:919–927.
102. Hobel C, Emmanouilides G, Townsend D, et al: Ligation of one umbilical artery in the fetal lamb. *Obstet Gynecol* 1970; 6:582–588.

103. Oh W, Omori K, Hobel C et al: Umbilical blood flow and glucose uptake in the lamb fetus following simple umbilical artery ligation. *Biol Neonate* 1975; 25:291.

104. Alexander G: Birth weight of lambs: influences and consequences, in Dawes G (ed): *Size at birth*. Ciba Symposium 27. Amsterdam, Elsevier, 1974, pp 215–245.

105. Hill DE: Experimental growth retardation in rhesus monkeys, in Dawes G (ed): *Size at birth*. Ciba Symposium 27. Amsterdam, Elsevier, 1974, pp 101–125.

106. Gruenwald P: Chronic fetal distress and placental insufficiency. *Biol Neonatorum* 1963; 5:215–265.

107. Naeye RL: Malnutrition. Probable cause of fetal growth retardation. *Arch Pathol* 1965; 9:284–291.

108. Charlton V: Nutritional supplementation of the growth retarded fetus: Rationale, theoretical considerations and in vivo studies, in Milunsky A, Friedman E, Gluck L (eds): *Advances in Perinatal Medicine,* vol 5. New York, Plenum Publishing Corp, 1986, pp 1–42.

109. Chase P, Welsh N, Dabiere C, et al: Alterations in human brain biochemistry following IUGR. *Pediatr* 50:403–411, 1972.

110. Gonzales-Sastre F, Rodes M, Sabater J, et al: Intrauterine growth retardation: Biochemical changes in human central nervous system. *An Esp Pediatr* 1978; 11:13.

111. Wigglesworth JS: Experimental growth retardation in the foetal rat. *J Pathol Bacteriol* 1964; 88:1–13.

112. Oh W, D'Amodio MD, Yap LL, et al: Carbohydrate metabolism in experimental intrauterine growth retardation in rats. *Am J Obstet Gynecol* 1970; 108:415–421.

113. Oh W, Omori K, Hobel CJ, et al: Umbilical blood flow and glucose uptake in lamb fetus following single umbilical artery ligation. *Biol Neonate* 1975; 26:291–299.

114. Saintonge J, Rosso P: Placental blood flow and transfer of nutrient analogs in large, average, and small guinea pig littermates. *Pediatr Res* 1981; 15:152–156.

115. Greizerstein HB: Placental and fetal composition during the last trimester of gestation in the rat. *Biol Reprod* 1982; 26:847–853.

116. Lederman SA, Rosso P: Effects of fasting during pregnancy on maternal and fetal weight and body composition in well-nourished and undernourished rats. *J Nutr* 1981; 111:1823–1832.

117. Driscoll SG: in Gruenwald P (ed): *The Placenta and Its Maternal Supply Line*. Baltimore, University Park Press, 1985; pp 80–97.

118. Kramer MS, McLean FH, Olivier M, et al: Body proportionality and head and length 'sparing' in growth-retarded neonates: A critical reappraisal. *Pediatrics* 1989; 84:717–723.

119. Cetin I, Marconi AM, Bozzetti P, et al: Umbilical amino acid concentrations in appropriate and small for gestational age infants: A biochemical difference present in utero. *Am J Obstet Gynecol* 1988; 158:120–126.

120. Enders RH, Judd RM, Donohue TM, et al: Placental amino acid uptake: III. Transport systems for neutral amino acids. *Am J Physiol* 1976; 230:706–710.

121. Dicke JM, Henderson GI: Placental amino acid uptake in normal and complicated pregnancies. *Am J Med Sci* 1988; 295:223–227.

122. Bozzetti P, Ferrari MM, Marconi AM, et al: The relationship of maternal and fetal glucose concentrations in the human from midgestation until term. *Metabolism* 1988; 37:358–363.

123. Haymond MW, Karl IE, Pagliera AS: Increased gluconeogenic substrates in the small-for-gestational-age infant. *N Engl J Med* 1974; 291:322–328.

124. Mestyan J, Soltesz G, Schultz K, et al: Hyperaminoacidemia due to the accumulation of gluconeogenic amino acid precursors in hypoglycemic small-for-gestational age infants. *J Pediatr* 1975; 87:409–414.

125. Churchill JA, Moghissi KS, Evans TN, et al: Relationships of maternal amino acid blood levels to fetal development. *Obstet Gynecol* 1969; 33:492–495.

126. Young M, Prenton MA: Maternal and fetal plasma amino acid concentrations during gestation in retarded fetal growth. *J Obstet Gynaecol Br Commonw* 1969; 76:333–344.

127. Metcoff J, Costiloe JP, Crosby W, et al: Maternal nutrition and fetal outcome. *Am J Clin Nutr* 1981; 34:708–721.

127a. Kalkoff RK, Kandaraki E, Morrow PG, et al: Relationship between neonatal birth weight and maternal plasma amino acid profiles in lean and obese nondiabetic women and in type I diabetic pregnant women. *Metabolism* 1988; 37(3):234–239.

128. Milner RDG, Ashworth MA, Barson AJ: Insulin release from human foetal pancreas in response to glucose, leucine and arginine. *J Endocrinol* 1972; 52:497–505.

129. Campbell S, Diaz-Recasens J, Griffin DR, et al: New Doppler technique for assessing uteroplacental blood flow. *Lancet* 1983; 1:675–677

130. Molteni RA, Stys S, Battaglia FC: Relationship of fetal and placental weight in human beings: Fetal/placental weight ratios at various gestational ages and birth weight distributions. *J Reprod Med* 1978; 21:327–334.

131. Bonds DR, Gabbe SG, Kumar S, et al: Fetal weight/placental weight ratio and perinatal outcome. *Am J Obstet Gynecol* 1984; 149:195–200.

132. Rosso P: Placental growth, development and function in relation to maternal nutrition. *Fed Proc* 1980; 9:250–254.

133. Rosso P, Kava R: Effects of food restriction on cardiac output and blood flow to the uterus and placenta in the pregnant rat. *J Nutr* 1980; 2350–2354.

134. Shanklin DR: The influence of placental lesions on the newborn infants. *Pediatr Clin North Am* 1970; 17:25–42.

135. Teasdale F, Jean-Jacques G: Intrauterine growth retardation: morphometry of the microvillous membrane of the human placenta. *Placenta* 1988; 9:47–55.

136. Johnson JD: Regulation of fetal growth. *Pediatr Res* 1975; 19:738–741.

137. Pederson J, Bojsen-Moller B, Poulsen H: Blood sugar in newborn infants of diabetic mothers. *Acta Endocrinol* 1954; 15:33–52.

138. Heitz PV, Kloppel G, Hacki WH: Nesidioblastosis: The pathologic basis of persistant hyperinsulinaemic hypoglicaemia in infants. *Diabetes* 1977; 26:632–642.

139. Filippi G, McKusick VA: The Beckwith-Wiedemann syndrome. *Medicine* 1970; 49:279–298.

140. Hill DJ, Milner RDG: Insulin as a growth factor. *Pediatr Res* 1985; 9:879–886.

141. Sipha MD, Miller JD, Ganguli S, et al: Differential maturation of insulin sensitivity for glucose and amino acid metabolism in rat hepatocytes (abstract). *Pediatr Res* 1983; 17:142A.

142. Bassett JM: Glucagon insulin and glucose homeostasis in the fetal lamb. *Ann Rech Vet* 1977; 8:362–373.

143. D'Ercole AJ, Foushee DB, Underwood LE: Somatomedin-C receptor ontogeny and level in porcine fetal and human cord serum. *J Clin Endocrinol Metab* 1976; 43:1069–1077.

144. D'Ercole AJ, Applewhite GT, Underwood LE: Evidence that somatomedin is synthesized by multiple tissues in the fetus. *Dev Biol* 1980; 75:315–328.

145. Kaplowitz PB, D'Ercole AJ, Underwood LE: Stimulation of embrionic limb bud mesenchymal cell growth by peptide growth factors. *J Cell Physiol* 1982; 112:353–359.

146. Warsof SL, Pearce JM, Campbell S: The present place of routine ultrasound screening. *Clin Obstet Gynecol* 1983; 10:445–457.

147. Calvert JP, Crean EE, Newcombe RG, et al: Antenatal screening by measurement of symphysis-fundus height. *Br Med J* 1982; 205:846–849.

148. Warsof S, Pearce JM, Campbell S: The present place of routine ultrasound screening. *Clin Obstet Gynecol* 1983; 10:446–457.

149. Warsof SL, Cooper DJ, Little D, et al: Routine ultrasound screening for antenatal detection of intrauterine growth retardation. *Obstet Gynecol* 1986; 67:33.

150. Robinson HP, Fleming JEE: A critical evaluation of sonar "crown-rump length" measurements. *Br J Obstet Gynecol* 1975; 82:702–710.

151. Kurtz AB, Wapner RJ, Kurtz RJ, et al: Analysis of biparietal diameter as an accurate indicator of gestational age. *J Clin Ultrasound* 1980; 8:319–326.

152. Kopta MM, May RR, Crane JP: A comparison of the reliability of the estimated date of confinement predicted by crown-rump length and biparietal diameter. *Am J Obstet Gynecol* 1983; 145:562.

153. Beazley JM, Underhill RA: The fallacy of fundal height. *Br Med J* 1970; 4:404–406.

154. Campbell S: The assessment of fetal development by diagnostic ultrasound. *Clin Perinatol* 1974; 1:507–519.

155. Devore GR, Hobbins JC: The use of ultrasound in the diagnosis and management of fetal congenital anomalies: The challenge of the 1980's, in Warshaw JB (ed): *The Biological Basis of Reproductive and Developmental Medicine*. New York, Elsevier, 1983, p 391.

156. Campbell S, Pearce JM: The prenatal diagnosis of fetal structural anomalies by ultrasound. *Clin Obstet Gynecol* 1983; 10:475–506.

157. Kurjak A, Kirkinen P, Latin V: Biometric and dynamic ultrasound assessment of small-for-dates infants: Report of 260 cases. *Obstet Gynecol* 1980; 56:281.

158. Woo J, Wan CW, Fang A, et al: Is fetal femur length a better indicator of gestational age in the growth retarded fetus as compared with biparietal diameter? *J Ultrasound Med* 1985; 4:132.

159. Evans MI, Muhkerjee AB, Schulman JD: Animal models of intrauterine growth retardation. *Obstet Gynecol Surv* 1983; 38:183.

160. Campbell S, Wilkin D: Ultrasonic measurement of fetal abdominal circumference in the estimation of fetal weight. *Br J Obstet Gynecol* 1975; 82:689.

161. Brown HL, Miller JM, Gabert HA, et al: Ultrasonic recognition of the small-for-gestational age fetus. *Obstet Gynecol* 1987; 69:631.

162. Campbell S, Thomas A: Ultrasound measurement of the fetal head to abdomen circumference ratio in the assessment of growth retardation. *Br J Obstet Gynecol* 1977; 84:165.

163. Manning FA, Hill LM, Platt LD: Qualitative amniotic fluid volume determination by ultrasound: Antepartum detection of intrauterine growth retardation. *Am J Obstet Gynecol* 1981; 139:154.

164. Shepard MJ, Richards VA, Berkowitz RL, et al: An evaluation of two equations for predicting fetal weight by ultrasound. *Am J Obstet Gynecol* 1982; 142:47–54.

165. Ott WJ, Doyle S: Ultrasonic diagnosis of altered fetal growth by use of a normal ultrasonic fetal weight curve. *Obstet Gynecol* 1984; 63:201.

166. Ogata ES, Sabbagha R, Metzger BE, et al: Serial ultrasonography to assess evolving fetal macrosomia: studies in 23 pregnant diabetic women. *JAMA* 1980; 243:2405.

167. Tamura RK, Sabbagha RE, Dooley SL, et al: Realtime ultrasound examinations of weight in fetuses of diabetic gravid women. *Am J Obstet Gynecol* 1985; 153:57.

168. Benson CB, Boswell SB, Brown DL, et al: Improved prediction of intrauterine growth retardation with use of multiple parameters. *Radiology* 1988; 168:7–12.

169. Rightmire DA: Clinical Doppler ultrasonography: Uterine and umbilical blood flow. *Clin Obstet Gynecol* 1988; 31:27–43.

170. Pearce JM, Campbell S, Cohen-Overbeek T, et al: References ranges and sources of variation for indices of pulsed Doppler flow velocity waveforms from the uteroplacental and fetal circulation. *Br J Obstet Gynecol* 1988; 95:248–256.

171. Cohen-Overbeek T, Pearce JM, Campbell S: The antenatal assessment of uteroplacenta and fetoplacental blood flow using Doppler ultrasound. *Ultrasound Med Biol* 1985; 11:329.

172. Wladimiroff JW, Wijngaard JAGW, Degani S, et al: Cerebral and umbilical arterial blood flow velocity waveforms in normal and growth retarded pregnancies. *Obstet Gynecol* 1987; 69:705–709.

173. Reuwer PJHM, Sijmons EA, Rietman GW, et al: Intrauterine growth retardation: Prediction of perinatal distress by Doppler ultrasound. *Lancet* 1987; 2:415–418.

174. Hackett GA, Campbell S, Gamsu H, et al: Doppler studies in the growth retarded fetus

and prediction of neonatal necrotising enterocolitis, haemorrhage, and neonatal morbidity. *Br Med J* 1987; 294:13–16.

175. Trudinger BJ, Cook CM, Jones L, et al: A comparison of fetal heart rate monitoring and umbilical artery waveforms in the recognition of fetal compromise. *Br J Obstet Gynecol* 1986; 93:171.

176. Ferrazzi E, Pardi G, Buscaglia M, et al: The correlation of biochemical monitoring versus umbilical flow velocity measurements of the human fetus. *Am J Obstet Gynecol* 1988; 159:1081–1087.

177. Daffos F, Capella-Pavlovsky M, Forestier F: Fetal blood sampling during pregnancy with use of a needle guided by ultrasound: A study of 606 consecutive cases. *Am J Obstet Gynecol* 1985; 153:655–660.

178. Pardi G, Buscaglia M, Ferrazzi E, et al: Cord sampling for the evaluation of oxygenation and acid-base balance in growth retarded human fetuses. *Am J Obstet Gynecol* 1987; 157:1221–1228.

179. Greene JW, Touchstone JC: Urinary estriol as an index of placental function. *Am J Obstet Gynecol* 1963; 85:1.

180. Ray DA: Biochemical fetal assessment. *Clin Obstet Gynecol* 1987; 30:887–898.

181. Spellacy WN: The use of human placental lactogen in the antepartum monitoring of pregnancy. *Clin Obstet Gynecol* 1979; 6:245.

182. Cabero L, Cerqueira MJ, del Solar J, et al: Long-term hospitalization and beta-mimetic therapy in the treatment of intrauterine growth retardation of unknown etiology. *J Perinatol Med* 1988; 16:453–458.

183. Steel SA, Pearce JM: Specific therapy in severe fetal intrauterine growth retardation: Failure of prostacyclin. *J R Soc Med* 1988; 81:214–216.

184. Villar J, Khoury MJ, Finucane FF, et al: Differences in the epidemiology of prematurity and intrauterine growth retardation. *Early Hum Dev* 1986; 14:307–320.

185. Metcalfe J: Oxygen supply and fetal growth. *J Reprod Med* 1985; 30:302–307.

186. Charlton V, Johengen M: Fetal intravenous nutritional supplementation ameliorates the development of embolization-induced growth retardation in sheep. *Pediatr Res* 1987; 22:55–61.

187. Charlton V, Johengen M: Effects of intrauterine nutritional supplementation on fetal growth retardation. *Biol Neonate* 1985; 48:125–142.

187a. Mulvihill SJ, Albert A, Synn A, et al: In utero supplemental fetal feeding in an animal model: Effects on fetal growth and development. *Surgery* 1985; 98:500–505.

188. Flake AW, Villa RL, Adzick NS, et al: Transamniotic fetal feeding: II. A model of intrauterine growth retardation using the relationship of "natural runting" to utering position. *J Pediatr Surg* 1987; 22:816–819.

189. De Prins F, Hill DJ, Milner RD, et al: Effect of maternal hyperalimentation on intrauterine growth retardation. *Arch Dis Child* 1988; 63:733–736.

190. Rush D, Alvir, JM, Kenny DA, et al: The National WIC Evaluation: Evaluation of the Special Supplemental Food Program. *Am J Clin Nutr* 1988; 48:412–428.

191. Rush D, Kristal A, Navarro C, et al: The effects of dietary supplementation during pregnancy on placental morphology, pathology, and histomorphometry. *Am J Clin Nutr* 1984; 39:863–871.

192. Rush D, Stein Z, Susser M: A randomized controlled trial of prenatal nutritional supplementation in New York City. *Pediatrics* 1980; 65:683–697.

193. Mughal MM, Shaffer JL, Turner M, et al: Nutritional management of pregnancy in patients on home parenteral nutrition. *Br J Obstet Gynaecol* 1987; 94:44–49.

194. Wennergren M, Wennergren G, Vilbergsson G: Obstetric characteristics and neonatal performance in a four-year small for gestational age population. *Obstet Gynecol* 1988; 72:615–620.

195. Shelley HJ, Neligan GA: Neonatal hypoglycemia. *Br Med Bull* 1966; 22:34–39.

196. Smart JL, Massey RF, Nash SC, et al: Effects of early-life undernutrition in artifically reared rats: Subsequent body and organ growth. *Br J Nutr* 1987; 58:245–255.

197. Kliegman RM: Alterations of fasting glucose and fat metabolism in intrauterine growth-retarded newborn dogs. *Am J Physiol* 1989; 256:E380–E385.

197a. Brar HS, Platt LD: Antepartum improvement of abnormal umbilical artery velocimetry: Does it occur? *Am J Obstet Gynecol* 1989; 160:36–39.

198. Boehm G, Senger H, Muller D, et al: Metabolic differences between AGA- and SGA-infants of very low birthweight: II. Relationship to protein intake. *Acta Paediatr Scand* 1988; 77:642–646.

199. Pencharz, PB: The 1987 Borden Award Lecture: Protein metabolism in premature human infants. *Can J Physiol Pharmacol* 1988; 66:1247–1252.

200. Cauderay M, Schutz Y, Micheli JL, et al: Energy-nitrogen balances and protein turnover in small and appropriate for gestational age low birthweight infants. *Eur J Clin Nutr* 1988; 42:125–136.

201. Duffy B, Pencharz P: The effect of feeding route (i.v. or oral) on the protein metabolism of the neonate. *Am J Clin Nutr* 1986; 43:108–111.

201a. Denne SC, Kalhan SC: Leucine metabolism in human newborns. *Am J Physiol* 1987; 253:E608–615.

202. Peterson S, Gotfredsen A, Knudsen FU: Lean body mass in small for gestational age and appropriate for gestational age infants. *J Pediatr* 1988; 113:886–889.

203. Berg AT: Childhood neurological morbidity and its association with gestational age, intrauterine growth retardation and perinatal stress. *Paediatr Perinatol Epidemiol* 1988; 2:229–238.

204. Matilainen R, Heinonen K, Siren-Tiusanen H: Effect of intrauterine growth retardation (IUGR) on the phychological performance of preterm children at preschool age. *J Child Psychol Psychiatry* 1988; 29:601–609.

205. Pena IC, Teberg AJ, Finello KM: The premature small-for-gestational-age infant during the first year of life: Comparison by birth weight and gestational age. *J Pediatr* 1988; 113:1066–1073.

206. Holst, K, Andersen E, Philip J, et al: Antenatal and perinatal conditions correlated to handicap among 4-year-old children. *Am J Perinatol* 1989; 6:258–267.

207. Schauseil-Zipf U, Hamm W, Stenzel B, et al: Severe intra-uterine growth retardation: Obstetrical management and follow up studies in children born between 1970 and 1985. *J Obstet Gynecol Reprod Biol* 1989; 30:1–9.

208. Touwen BC, Hadders-Algra M, Huisjes HJ: Hypotonia at six years in prematurely-born or small-for-gestational-age children. *Early Hum Dev* 1988; 17:79–88.

209. Matilainen R, Heinonen K, Siren-Tiusanen H, et al: Neurodevelopmental screening of in utero growth-retarded prematurely born children before school age. *Eur J Pediatr* 1987; 146:453–457.

210. Henrichsen L, Skinhoj K, Andersen GE: Delayed growth and reduced intelligence in 9–17 year old intrauterine growth retarded children compared with their monozygous co-twins. *Acta Paediatr Scand* 1986; 75:31–35.

211. Binkin NJ, Yip R, Fleshood L, et al: Birth weight and childhood growth. *Pediatrics* 1988; 82:828–834.

212. Fitzhardinge PM, Inwood S: Long-term growth in small-for-date children (discussion). *Acta Paediatr Scand [Suppl]* 1989; 349:27–33.

213. Walther FJ: Growth and development of term disproportionate small-for gestational age infants at the age of 7 years. *Early Hum Dev* 1988; 18:1–11.

214. Tenovuo A, Kero P, Piekkala P, et al: Growth of 519 small for gestational age infants during the first two years of life. *Acta Paediatr Scand* 1987; 76:636–646.

215. Piekkala P, Kero P, Sillanpaa M, et al: The somatic growth of a regional birth cohort of 351 preterm infants during the first two years of life. *J Perinatol Med* 1989; 17:41–49.

216. Rochiccioli P, Tauber M, Noisan V, et al: Investigation of growth hormone secretion in

patients with intrauterine growth retardation. *Acta Paediatr Scand [Suppl]* 1989; 349:42–46, 53–54.

217. Viehweg B, Ruckhaberle KE, Zimmermann G, et al: Zur Therapie bei Verdacht auf intrauterine fetale Retardierung. *Zentralbl Gynaekol* 109:818–829.

218. Brar HS, Platt LD: Anterpartum improvement of abnormal umbilical artery velocimetry: Does it occur? *Am J Obstet Gynecol* 1989; 160:36–39.

Chapter 2

Energy Requirements and Protein Energy Balance in Preterm and Term Infants

Michele N. Bronstein, Ph.D.

In the term infant there is a paucity of data with regard to total energy expenditure and balance. As a result, energy requirements for the healthy term infant have been defined from measurements of intake rather than factorial determinations of energy need. While this approach is not optimal, it is generally believed that there have been no serious ramifications on the nutritional care of these infants, as appetite mechanisms are adequately developed and breast milk is an appropriate nutrient mixture.[74] It is inappropriate, however, to define the dietary requirements of the preterm or low-birth-weight infant (LBW) from observed intakes, as appetite mechanisms are not adequately developed and it is uncertain what fuel mixture is optimal. Furthermore, growth is much more rapid in these infants and energy stores limited. Therefore, it is imperative to ensure that energy and other nutrient needs are met.

In response to the need for a scientific foundation from which to prescribe a dietary energy recommendation for the premature infant, numerous studies of energy expenditure and protein energy balance have been performed in recent years. The goal of this chapter is to summarize this research. Although the primary focus of this discussion will be upon the appropriate-for-gestational age (AGA) LBW infant, special reference will be made to how the small-for-gestational age (SGA) infant may differ. Mention will also be made of recent efforts to assess the requirements of the term infant from measurements of energy expenditure.

COMPONENTS OF THE ENERGY REQUIREMENT (FIG 2–1)

The infant requires dietary energy for expenditure and growth. Energy intake must be somewhat in excess of that need to provide for energy that is not absorbed or utilized. The latter can be quite significant and variable in early infancy when immaturities exist that impair digestion.

Under conditions of thermoneutrality, energy is expended for basal or resting metabolism, postprandial metabolism, activity, and tissue synthetic processes. Additional

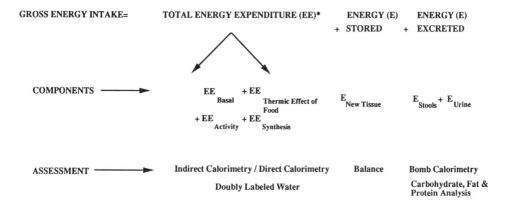

GROSS ENERGY INTAKE=   TOTAL ENERGY EXPENDITURE (EE)*   ENERGY (E)   ENERGY (E)
                                                          + STORED   + EXCRETED

COMPONENTS ⟶ EE_{Basal} + $EE_{Thermic\ Effect\ of\ Food}$ $E_{New\ Tissue}$ E_{Stools} + E_{Urine}
                    + $EE_{Activity}$ + $EE_{Synthesis}$

ASSESSMENT ⟶   Indirect Calorimetry / Direct Calorimetry   Balance   Bomb Calorimetry
                         Doubly Labeled Water   Carbohydrate, Fat & Protein Analysis

*
Under non-thermoneutral conditions energy is also expended for thermoregulation.

FIG 2–1.
Components of energy balance and techniques utilized for assessing these components.

energy is expended if thermoneutral conditions are not maintained. Determination of infant energy expenditure has been performed most often by indirect calorimetry, which measures energy production through the assessment of oxygen consumption and carbon dioxide production. Direct calorimetry, which directly measures heat loss from the organism, has also been used to assess infant expenditure but with far less frequency as isolation of the infant is required. Both indirect and direct calorimetry are cumbersome techniques that are technically difficult to perform with the infant. A newer approach for assessing total energy expenditure (TEE) that is generating much excitement is the doubly labeled water ($^2H_2{}^{18}O$) stable isotope technique[61] (discussed later). With this technique an assessment of "free-living" energy expenditure is obtained, enabling measurements to be made in previously inaccessible infant populations.

The energy cost of new tissue has been evaluated through determination of energy balance, which involves the assessment of gross energy intake, energy losses in excreta, and energy expenditure. Retained energy intake or metabolizable energy intake is determined from the difference between gross energy intake and the energy content of excreta, and the difference between retained energy intake and TEE is attributed to energy stored. Nutrient balance techniques are also utilized to ascertain the composition of tissue growth.

Basal Metabolism

Basal energy expenditure is defined as the minimal amount of energy required to maintain life in the resting state. Inclusive in the cost of basal expenditure is energy expended for respiration, cardiac function, maintenance of body temperature, and other essential tissue functions. Measurement of basal metabolism is of particular interest as it is the largest component of total expenditure and is thus a useful starting point for estimating individual energy requirements. In order to validly assess the basal metabolic rate (BMR) the subject should be awake, resting quietly in a thermoneutral environment, and fasting for 12 to 18 hours. As these experimental conditions are both impractical and unethical for use in the infant, BMR is instead typically assessed while the infant is asleep and 2 to 3 hours following a meal. These conditions are not ideal, as sleep is known to depress metabolism and the effect of food on metabolism is stimulatory. In addition, inclusive in the measurement of resting metabolism in the "growing infant" is expenditure for tissue synthesis. While some researchers have attempted through theoretical calculations to separate synthetic costs from basal metabolism, most reported measures of BMR do not make this distinction.[13, 26]

In the adult human BMR is found to be highly correlated with fat-free mass (FFM).[33] This relationship is most likely observed as FFM better represents the metabolically active portion of the body. When expressed on the basis of FFM, interindividual differences in BMR among adults are frequently indistinguishable. During infancy, however, the relationship between lean body mass and metabolism is not as evident.[19] This may be due in part to the significant compositional changes that occur in the FFM compartment during infant life. As the infant matures, the expansion of metabolically less active muscle tissue is proportionally greater than that of extremely active organ tissues (brain, liver, lungs, heart, and kidney).[31, 68]

Following birth there is a rise in the BMR over the first week or so of life.[13, 26, 30, 41] This rise in BMR has been found to coincide with increased food intake and weight gain, leading to speculation that the increment in basal expenditure is due to the residual thermic effect of food and/or growth related metabolic activity.[13] During the first few days of life there are also numerous physiologic adaptations that the newborn must undergo in making the transition to extrauterine life and an independent existence. An increased cost for thermoregulation, respiratory function, and cerebral metabolism may also contribute to the postnatal rise in BMR.[63]

The pattern of postnatal change in basal expenditure differs in premature and term infants.[64, 72] The BMR (kcal/kg/day) is initially lower in the preterm infant and rises much more gradually over the first few weeks of life; but with increasing age, the BMR of the premature infant eventually surpasses that of the term infant. The greater immaturities (e.g., feeding difficulties) of the preterm infant may retard the transition to extrauterine life, and consequently delay the rise in basal expenditure.[64, 72] The later greater increase in the preterm infant's BMR could possibly reflect differences in body composition, greater food intake, or a faster rate of growth.

The BMR is also dependent on prenatal nutritional status. Growth-retarded or SGA infants demonstrate a relative hypermetabolism when compared with similarly sized AGA preterm infants (Table 2–1).[12, 15, 64, 67] Sinclair and Silverman, among others, have proposed that the hypermetabolism of the SGA infant may be the product of a

TABLE 2–1.

Comparisons of Basal Metabolism Between Appropriate-for-Gestational Age (AGA) and Small-for-Gestational Age (SGA) Infants

Reference	Group	No.	Gestational Age (wk)	Age at Study (day)	Birth Weight (g)	Basal Metabolism (kcal/kg/day)
Sinclair and Silverman[67]*	AGA	34	32	. . .	1,335	42.6
	SGA	4	38	. . .	1,638	61.3
Scopes and Ahmed[64]*	AGA	9	<36	8–11	1,972	44.9
	SGA	7	>36	8–11	2,088	52.2
Chessex et al.[15]	AGA	13	29	21	1,155	54.2
	SGA	6	33	26	1,120	57.6
Cauderay et al.[12]	AGA	11	32	21	1,563	57
	SGA	8	35	21	1,519	64

*Basal metabolic rate (kcal/kg/day) is estimated from oxygen consumption by assuming 4.83 kcal per liter oxygen.

larger ratio of brain to body weight.[31, 68] As cerebral metabolism is the most significant component of basal metabolism in the neonatal period, it seems feasible that a proportionally greater brain mass might significantly impact minimal energy needs. It has also been speculated that the elevated BMR of the malnourished infant may reflect a faster rate of growth.[15]

Table 2–2 is a summary of some of the efforts to quantitate the contribution of basal metabolism to overall energy expenditure in the premature infant.[9, 23, 42, 49] Reported BMR levels in Table 2–2 range from 35.4 to 61.6 kcal/kg/day, and constitute from 66% to 90% of total daily expenditure. Part of this variability among studies may result from some of the factors discussed earlier—such as differences in subject prematurity, postnatal age, and rate of growth. Differences in study experimental conditions (e.g., size and timing of latest meal, length of measurement, temperature) and application of the indirect calorimetric technique may have also contributed to the large interstudy variability observed.

Thermic Effect of Food

The thermic effect of food (TEF), or "specific dynamic action," has been traditionally defined as energy expended for the digestion, absorption, processing, and disposal of nutrients. In recent years it has been hypothesized that in addition to these obligatory costs, the TEF also contains a "facultative" or adaptive expenditure component, which may play a role in adjusting individual energy expenditure in response to energy balance.[33] The presence of an adaptive component in dietary induced thermogenesis has been offered as one explanation for apparent differences in the efficiency of energy utilization.

To measure the thermic response to a meal in the newborn, investigators typically assess a "fasting baseline" and then follow the postprandial rise in expenditure until administration of the next meal (about 2 to 3 hours). The TEF is calculated from the dif-

TABLE 2–2.

Studies of Total Energy Expenditure and Its Components in the Premature Infant*

Factor	Reichman et al.[49] PF (SMA 20/24)	Mestyán et al.[42] HM	Mestyán et al.[42] F (Adapta)	Freymond et al.,[23] PF (Alprem)	Brooke et al.[9] PF
Number of subjects	13	9	4	9	15
Birth weight, g	1,155	1,600	1,615	1,740	1,581
Gestational age, wk	29.3	—	—	33	32
Age at study, days	21	10	12	21	(14, 27, 42)†
Basal (resting) energy Expenditure (kcal/kg/day)	47.0	35.4	39.7	61.6	58.6
(% of total)	(75.1)	(80.1)	(72.2)	(90.0)	(66.4)
Activity energy expenditure (kcal/kg/day)	4.3	3.0	6.0	3.6	23.2
(% of total)	(6.9)	(6.8)	(10.9)	(5.3)	(26.3)
Thermic effect of food (kcal/kg/day)	11.3	5.8	9.3	3.2	6.4
(% of total)	(18.0)	(13.1)	(16.9)	(4.7)	(7.3)
Total energy expenditure (kcal/kg/day)	62.6	44.2	55.0	68.4	88.2

* PF = preterm formula; HM = human milk; F = formula.
† Data presented represent the combined means of three study periods at days 14, 27, and 42.

ference between the premeal and postmeal energy expenditure measurements. As it is not feasible to obtain a true fasting state in the infant, measurements of postprandial expenditure made in the infant most likely underestimate the thermic response. It is also difficult to ensure that differences in premeal and postmeal activity are not attributed to part of the thermogenic response.

Another complication is that it is not possible to clearly separate the TEF from metabolic expenditure for growth. As digestion, absorption, and nutrient processing are all prerequisites to nutrient storage, it is understandable why the distinction between the TEF and tissue synthetic expenditure is not straightforward. In fact, based on a high linear correlation between postprandial thermogenesis and growth in the infant, several researchers have interpreted the thermic response to food as primarily representing the cost of tissue synthesis.[4]

Rubecz and Mestyán performed serial measurements of the TEF in breast-fed very low birth weight infants from birth to 5 to 6 weeks of age.[58] With increasing age, the mean thermogenic response increased. Furthermore, when the thermogenic response was grouped based on weight gain, it was found that while those infants with the greatest weight gain had the largest response, even those infants with no weight gain had a significant thermic response to food. These observations suggest that infant postprandial metabolism is due to both the energy cost of digesting food and the energy cost of growth.

Interstudy comparisons of dietary induced thermogenesis are difficult, as experimental conditions (e.g., meal size and type, length of fast, mode of feeding and duration of measurement) vary among the studies, in addition to differences in the postnatal age and maturity of study populations. Also, although it is unknown whether facultative thermogenesis plays a role in the infant's thermic response to food, if present this could contribute to interindividual differences in the efficiency of food utilization. Considering the multitude of factors that can affect the thermogenic response it is interesting to note that there is surprisingly little variation among studies. Reported estimates of the daily cost for the TEF in preterm infants vary from 3.2 to 11.3 kcal/kg/day, constituting 4.7% to 18% of total energy expenditure (see Table 2–2).[9, 23, 42, 49]

Activity

Based on short-term measurements of energy expenditure during muscular activity in healthy, term infants, Benedict and Talbot observed as much as a 60% to 70% increase in energy expenditure.[6] The daily cost of muscular activity was suggested to be as high as 40% of total expenditure. However, actual measures of 24-hour energy expenditure in two term infants indicated that the cost for activity was considerably lower and only about 25% of total energy expenditure. While it is difficult to estimate a mean cost for activity, the effect of activity on expenditure has been observed to be consistent. Murlin et al. found that for each 1% of the time spent crying, a 1% increase in metabolism resulted.[43] As the infant develops physically, activity expenditure increases. Waterlow has estimated that the cost of physical activity for the term infant increases from 0.1 × (the 12-hour BMR) at 1 month of age, to 0.2 × (the 12-hour BMR) at 3 months of age, to 0.4 × (the 12-hour BMR) at 6 months of age.[74]

The quantitative importance of activity energy expenditure in the preterm infant appears to be smaller than in the term infant. Using an arbitrary scoring system to quantitate visible physical activity, Mestyán estimated that in the first few weeks of life the premature infant spends greater than 80% of the time either asleep or making only slight movements.[41] By subtracting postprandial and resting energy expenditure from total expenditure, several investigators have assessed the daily cost of activity expenditure to be only 3 to 6 kcal/kg/day (see Table 2–2),[23, 41–42, 49] indicating that activity probably accounts for less than 10% of total expenditure. It should be noted that the much higher estimate of activity expenditure of 23 kcal/kg/day reported in Table 2–2 was obtained using a different method of calculation.[9] Brooke et al. estimated activity expenditure by combining measurements of the metabolic cost of different activities with estimates of the proportion of each day spent at these different activity states.[9] The authors noted that the difficulties associated with this methodologic approach were considerable, and from their observations it appeared that the energy cost of activity was very small for the immature infant.

As the premature infant ages, the energy cost for activity increases,[41] similar to the term infant. This increase in expenditure has been shown to result from an increase in both the occurrence and intensity of activity. Mestyán reported that the percentage of time spent in very quiet activity dropped from 84% to 66% from age 2 days to age 16 to 39 days.[41] Maximum oxygen consumption in this same group of infants increased from 12.6 to 22.3 mL/kg/min. The increased cost for muscular activity with age may arise from the greater muscular strength of the older infant.

Energy Cost of Tissue Synthesis

There is both a storage component and an expenditure component to the energy requirement for growth (see Fig 2–1). While the storage component represents the energy deposited in newly acquired tissue, the expenditure component encompasses energy spent in the formation of this new tissue. With knowledge of energy balance, the cost of energy storage can be readily determined. However, measurement of the cost of tissue synthesis apart from the other components of energy expenditure represents a difficult challenge, and thus a separate estimation of this component is frequently not attempted.

In the term infant, the cost of growth has been calculated by applying values derived from animal studies for the separate costs of fat and protein deposition to estimates of the composition of infant tissue gain. Utilizing such an approach, Fomon and coworkers estimated the total energy cost of growth to be 5.6 kcal/g.[22] For this calculation the cost of laying down fat and protein was assumed to be 11.6 and 7.5 kcal/g, respectively, and the composition of tissue gain was assumed to be 40.8% fat and 11.6% protein. The 5.6 kcal/g value includes both the energy required to synthesize the tissue and the energy content of the tissue laid down. By deducting the caloric value of fat (9.25 kcal/g) and protein (5.65 kcal/g) from the 11.6 and 7.5 kcal/g values, the cost of tissue synthesis can be separately estimated to be 1.2 kcal/g, approximately 20% of the total cost.

Several strategies have been employed to approximate tissue synthetic costs experimentally in the preterm infant (Table 2–3).[9, 13, 26, 57, 59] Brooke et al. estimated the cost of tissue synthesis (1.72 kcal/g) by deducting the energy cost of storage from the total cost for growth (5.74 kcal/g).[9] The total cost for growth was calculated from the slope of the regression line relating weight gain to metabolizable energy intake. Others have estimated the cost of synthesis by taking advantage of the fact that synthesis expenditure is incorporated into the infant's metabolic rate.[13, 26] Thus if a positive linear relationship can be observed between metabolic rate and weight gain, the slope of the line can be interpreted to represent the cost of tissue synthesis. Employing this approach,

TABLE 2–3.
Estimates of the Cost of Tissue Synthesis in the Premature Infant

Reference	Gestational Age (wk)	Age at Study (days)	Energy Content of Tissue Gained (kcal/g)	Cost of Tissue Synthesis (kcal/g)	Mean Weight Gain (g/kg/d)	% of Total Energy Expenditure	Method Employed to Assess Tissue Synthetic Expenditure
Brooke et al.[9]	32	14, 17, 42	4.02	1.72	13.7	26.8	Total cost of growth minus cost of energy storage
Chessex et al.[13]	29	5–43	—	0.67	13.9	15.4	Regression of expenditure vs. weight gain
Gudinchet et al.[26]	31	7–42	—	0.54	15.9†	13.4†	Regression of Expenditure vs. weight gain
Sauer et al.[59]	32	8–14	6.09	0.76	10.5	12.6	Difference between energy expenditure determination by indirect and direct calorimetry
		29–35	2.94	0.26	18.0	7.1	
Roberts and Young[57]	29–31	12–38	2.9–6.0	1.3–1.4	14.0–20.9	—	Multiple regression analysis of published energy balance data

†Data presented represent mean measurements at day 21 rather than the mean for days 7 through 42.

Gudinchet et al.[26] and Chessex et al.[13] reported similar estimates for the cost of tissue synthesis: 0.54 kcal/g and 0.67 kcal/g, respectively.

A third, rather novel, experimental approach taken by Sauer et al. derives an estimate for the cost of tissue synthesis from the difference between indirect and direct calorimetric measures of energy expenditure.[59] The theoretical basis of this technique is that when energy is "stored" in the form of new chemical bonds during tissue synthesis, energy production (i.e., oxygen consumption) exceeds heat losses. Thus when growth occurs, indirect calorimetry (which measures energy production) diverges from direct calorimetry (which assesses heat losses), and the difference between the two measures represents tissue synthetic costs. Using this approach the cost of tissue synthesis was calculated to be only 0.26 kcal/g, a rather low estimate when compared with the other determinations noted in Table 2–3. An explanation for the relatively low cost determined by this approach is that while part of the energy used for tissue synthesis is stored, synthesis is not 100% efficient and thus part of the energy is also released as heat. As noted by these investigators, this approach solely estimates "net" tissue synthetic costs.

Using published energy balance data collected in preterm infants and a multiple regression approach, Roberts and Young derived values for the separate costs of fat and protein deposition in the premature infant.[57] The cost of depositing fat was calculated to be 10.8 kcal/g and that of protein was determined to be 13.4 kcal/g. After subtracting the energy content of fat (9.25 kcal/g) and protein (5.65 kcal/g) from these values, the costs of fat and protein synthesis were estimated to be 1.55 and 7.75 kcal/g, respectively. The high energy cost of protein synthesis was not unexpected, given that the preterm infant has been shown to have a low ratio of protein gain to protein turnover.[44, 57] It has been estimated that the preterm infant retains only 1 g of protein for each 5 g of protein synthesized. Employing their calculated values for fat and protein deposition (i.e., 10.8 and 13.4 kcal/g), Roberts and Young calculated the energy requirement for weight gain of a varying chemical composition (Fig 2–2). Based on reported values for the composition of weight gain in the term infant, these investigators estimated that the total cost of growth lies between 2.9 and 6.0 kcal/g, of which 1.3 to 1.4 kcal/g represents tissue synthetic costs (23% to 45% of total cost). If a mean growth rate of 15 g/kg/day is also assumed,[69] then daily synthetic expenditure ranges from 19.5 to 21.0 kcal/kg/day, a significant component of total expenditure.

Although the cost of tissue synthesis has not been directly assessed in the SGA infant, there are indications that synthetic expenditure may differ between growth-retarded and appropriately grown LBW infants. Postprandial expenditure, which is believed to represent synthetic expenditure, has been shown to be reduced in the SGA infant.[2] This has led to the suggestion that the SGA infant utilizes energy more efficiently for growth. In support of this hypothesis, in a recent study SGA infants were found to have a higher ratio of protein gain to protein synthesis than AGA infants of a similar postnatal age, suggesting that the acquisition of protein was a more efficient process in the SGA infant.[12] Alternatively, a reduction in synthetic expenditure could reflect differences in the composition of tissue gain. Chessex et al. found both the protein and fat content of tissue gain to be substantially reduced in the SGA infant compared with the AGA infant (Table 2–4).[15] Utilizing the factors developed by Roberts and Young for the preterm infant,[57] the cost of tissue synthesis can be estimated for the SGA and AGA infants studied by Chessex et al. This calculation suggests that the cost of tissue synthesis is substantially reduced in the SGA infant: 0.94 kcal/g for the SGA infant vs. 1.49 kcal/g for the AGA infant.

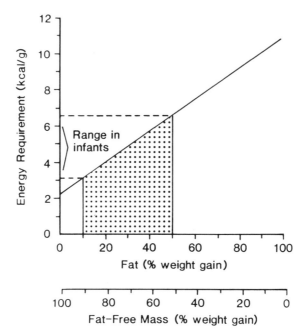

FIG 2–2.

Dietary energy requirement for weight gain as a function of the composition of tissue gain. A protein content of 16% was assumed for the fat-free mass. Shaded area (2.9 to 6.0 kcal/g) represents expected range for growth expenditure in first year of life based on literature values (Foman et al.; ref 22) for the composition of tissue growth during infancy. (From Roberts SB, Young, VR: Energy costs of fat and protein deposition in the human infant. *Am J Clin Nutr* 1988; 48:951–955. Used by permission.)

Thermoregulation

It is well known that the term newborn, who has a high ratio of surface area to body weight, is susceptible to thermal instability.[71] Thermoregulation poses an even greater challenge to the smaller and developmentally immature preterm infant.[71] To minimize the cost and stress of thermoregulation, the metabolic response to different ambient temperatures has been studied and thermoneutral temperature ranges identified.[28, 65] The lower end of the thermoneutral temperature range (i.e., critical temperature) varies considerably with postnatal age, infant size, and maturity.[65] Over the first few weeks of life the critical temperature needed to maintain minimal oxygen consumption drops. Both intrauterine growth retardation and prematurity are associated with a higher minimal temperature.[65] Thus, smaller infants are more susceptible to cold stress.

Metabolic expenditure in response to cold can be considerable in the preterm infant. Mestyán et al. reported a 100% increase in energy expenditure for the naked preterm infant exposed to temperatures of 28° C to 29° C.[42] The increase in expenditure was required for both increased activity expenditure (16.1 kcal/kg/day) and the thermic response to cold (15.3 kcal/kg/day). Swaddled infants were also found to increase energy expenditure in response to cold (20° to 22° C), but not to the same extent as naked infants (10 vs. 31 kcal/kg/day) and only by increasing heat production.

Although maintenance of thermoneutral conditions will minimize heat losses in the preterm infant, it is likely that activities such as handling, bathing, and nursing prohibit warmer temperatures from being continually maintained.[16] Dietary energy recommenda-

TABLE 2–4.

Comparisons of Energy Balance Between Small-for-Gestational Age (SGA) and Appropriate-for-Gestational Age (AGA) Infants

	Chessex et al.[15]		Cauderay et al.[12]	
Factor	SGA (no. = 13)	AGA (no. = 6)	SGA (no. = 8)	AGA (no. = 11)
Gestational age, wk	33	29	35	32
Birthweight, g	1,120	1,155	1,519	1,563
Postnatal age at study, days	26	21	18	20
Gross energy intake, kcal/kg/day	156	149	124	122
Metabolizable energy intake, kcal/kg/day	126	130	110	108
Retained energy, %	81	87	89	88
Total energy expenditure, kcal/kg/day	67	63	67	62
Energy stored, kcal/kg/day	58	68	44	42
Stored fat (g/kg/day)	4.3	5.4	3.5	3.3
Stored protein (g/kg/day)	1.6	1.9	2.0	2.1
Weight gain (g/kg/day)	19.4	16.8	17.6	18.3

tions for the preterm infant estimate the daily cost of thermoregulation to be 5 to 10 kcal/kg/day.[3, 16]

Total Energy Expenditure

Given the difficulty in separately measuring the components of infant daily expenditure, most investigative efforts have instead focused on the measurement of TEE. This value has been most frequently assessed by extrapolating to an entire day (24 hours) indirect calorimetric measurements performed for a period of several hours. For the premature infant, reported TEE values range from 44 to 88 kcal/kg/day (see Table 2–2; Fig 2–3).[9, 23, 42, 46, 49, 50, 54, 76] Limited data available suggest that TEE is slightly higher in SGA infants than comparably sized preterm infants (see Table 2–4).[12, 15] Large interstudy variability in TEE may reflect differences in the age and maturity of the subject population studied, environmental and study conditions, diet, and feeding regimens. As previously discussed, all these factors play a role in basal, postprandial, activity, and synthetic energy expenditure, and consequently influence total energy expenditure.

Interstudy differences in methodologic approach may also contribute to the wide variability seen in the literature for preterm TEE. Researchers have differed notably in their selection of the time interval from which TEE is estimated. While some have documented that TEE can be reliably estimated from measurements of 3 to 6 hours,[26, 63] there has been some evidence to suggest considerable improvement in measurement precision with longer time periods of assessment.[55] In a recent study, the 95% confidence limit of variation was found to drop from 18% for a 3-hour measurement to 9% for a 24-hour measurement.[55] In addition, measurements of TEE showed less interindividual variability than intraindividual variability (2.1% vs. 3.8%), implying that a pooled group estimate of TEE may be a more useful measure than individual values.

In recent years an alternative technique has become available which may circumvent some of the limitations of calorimetric procedures. This method, referred to as the doubly labeled water method ($^2H_2{}^{18}O$), permits TEE to be estimated from a several day

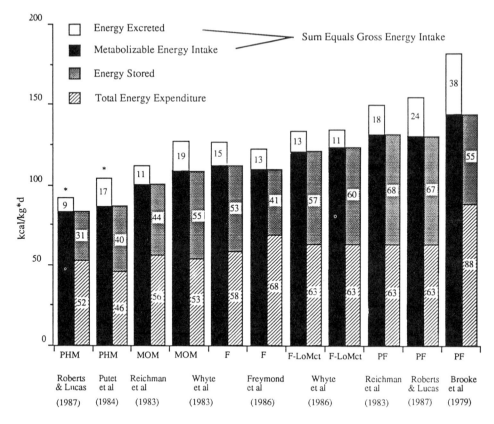

PHM (Pooled Human Milk); MOM (Mothers' Own Milk); F (Formula); PF (Preterm Formula)

*Weight gain < 15 g/kg*d

FIG 2–3.
Studies of energy balance in the preterm infant. (Numeric values represent kcal/kg/day) Metabolizable energy intake is equal to the sum of total energy expenditure and energy stored. Gross energy intake is equal to the sum of metabolizable energy and energy losses in excreta.

measurement period, as opposed to a several hour period.[61] An additional advantage is that no restriction or isolation of the subject is required. All that is required is consumption of a bolus of water labeled with deuterium and ^{18}O followed by spot urine collection to monitor the disappearance of the isotopes from the total body water pool. The basic theory underlying this technique is that the disappearance rate of deuterium reflects water turnover, while the more rapid clearance of ^{18}O represents water and carbon dioxide turnover combined. Thus, the difference in the disappearance rates of deuterium and ^{18}O should reflect carbon dioxide production. With knowledge of the metabolic fuel mixture (i.e., respiratory quotient), carbon dioxide production can then be utilized to estimate energy production.

Validation studies have shown good correlation between doubly labeled water and more conventional approaches to TEE assessment.[34, 52] When compared with indirect calorimetry, doubly labeled water has been shown to have an accuracy of 1% to 2% and a precision of 3% to 6% in infant populations. Subsequent to these promising results, a flurry of studies followed. The results of several investigations performed with infants are summarized in Table 2–5. For the term infant, 1.5 to 4 months of age, reported

TABLE 2–5.

Measurements of Total Energy Expenditure (TEE) by Doubly Labeled Water Technique During Infancy

Reference	No.	Age (mo)	TEE (kcal/kg/day)	Population Studied
Roberts et al.[52]	4	0.8	58	Preterm infants
Lucas et al.[39]	12	1.2	67	Breast-fed term infants
	12	2.8	72	
Butte et al.[11]	16	4	76	Breast- and bottle-fed term infants
Roberts et al.[56]	18	3	72	Breast- and bottle-fed term infants
Davies et al.[19]	39	1.2	64	Breast- and bottle-fed term infants
	40	2.6	67	

TEE ranges from 65 to 75 kcal/kg/day.[11, 19, 39, 56] The one study performed with young preterm infants indicated that expenditure was lower, at about 58 kcal/kg/day.[52]

A considerable benefit to doubly labeled water is that it enables measurement of "free-living" infant energy expenditure, thus making it feasible to assess how TEE is altered as the infant becomes progressively more mobile. Davies et al. longitudinally followed TEE in a cohort of about 40 healthy term infants at ages 6 weeks, 3 months, and 6 months.[19] From these measurements a graphic depiction of TEE over the first 6 months of life was generated that allowed for the variable effect of infant size (Fig 2–4). This information should prove particularly useful in establishing reference standards for daily expenditure in the term infant. Future research should be directed toward supplying similar longitudinal data for the preterm infant.

Although the doubly labeled water method shows tremendous promise, application of this technique is currently limited. Few research facilities have the equipment and

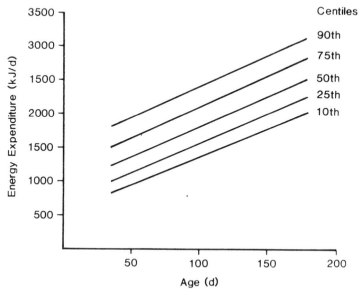

FIG 2–4.

Centiles for total energy expenditure (kJ/day) vs. infant age. Centiles were generated from the means and standard deviations of log transformed energy expenditure values determined for a cohort of about 40 term infants at 1.5, 3, and 6 months of age. (From Davies PSW, Ewing G, Lucas A: Energy expenditure in early infancy. *Br J Nutr* 1989; 62:621–629. Used by permission.)

personnel needed to perform these challenging stable isotope analyses. Experts have also cautioned against applying this technique in a casual fashion to infant populations, as the assumptions underlying doubly labeled water are quite complex and require careful consideration.[17, 18, 32, 61] Weaning, rapid growth, and alterations in body composition are all characteristics of infant life and are all factors that can potentially influence the interpretation of doubly labeled water data.[35, 51, 61] In addition, facile application of this technique necessitates the assumption of a mean respiratory quotient and a mean rate of evaporative water loss. The potential error introduced by making these assumptions can be substantial and is currently a topic of much debate.[17, 32, 61] Still, despite existing reservations, doubly labeled water has generated much enthusiasm for its potential to expand current knowledge of energy balance in infant populations for which conventional methodologies are impractical.

Energy Cost of Tissue Deposition

A prerequisite to assessing an energy requirement for tissue deposition is that one must first have defined standards for the optimal rate and composition of infant growth. Current definitions for "adequate" or "appropriate" growth during infancy are controversial, which has hindered the identification of dietary requirements.

For the term infant the National Center for Health Statistics (NCHS) data base has been most commonly used as a reference for appropriate infant growth.[27] A controversial aspect of the NCHS reference is that it is largely derived from anthropometric data collected for formula-fed infants. This has been problematic, as exclusively breast-fed infants demonstrate a different pattern of growth than the NCHS standard (50th centile); growth of breast-fed infants is more rapid during the first 3 months but then significantly drops off from the NCHS median at 3 to 4 months.[74, 75] As breast milk is supposed to define the optimal nutrient mixture, NCHS growth curves have come under criticism as being inappropriate reference standards.

Identification of growth standards for the preterm infant has proved equally challenging. The general premise most commonly accepted is that the most desirable growth pattern is one that mimics the pattern observed in utero. Researchers have attempted to define this pattern by utilizing data obtained from compositional analyses of infants who were stillborn or who died shortly (2 or less than days) after birth.[80] The composition of weight gain for the reference fetus is detailed in Figure 2–5. As estimated from infant weight curves, an appropriate mean daily weight gain for the premature infant from age 24 to 37 weeks is 15 g/kg/day, or 1.5% of body weight.[69]

In Table 2–6 the energy cost of storage has been calculated for the premature infant utilizing intrauterine growth data and by assuming a calorie value of 9.25 and 5.65 kcal/g for fat and protein tissue, respectively. For comparison, a similar calculation has been included for the term infant. It is interesting to note that despite a much more rapid growth rate in the premature infant, the calculated cost of tissue deposition is similar in both premature and term infants (1 to 2 months), reflecting the higher water and lower fat content of intrauterine tissue.

From a knowledge of retained food energy and energy expenditure, experimental determinations of the energy cost of storage have been made for the premature infant. The striking observation from these studies is that observed expenditure for tissue storage appears much greater than that predicted from intrauterine growth (see Fig 2–3).[9, 23, 46, 50, 54, 76] In only two studies has the energy cost for storage been found to be 40 kcal/kg/day or less, and in both, weight gain was less than the recommended level

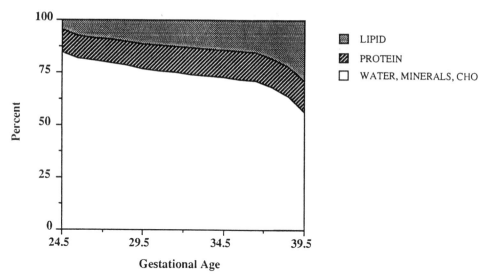

Gestational Age

FIG 2−5.
Profile of composition of tissue gain from weeks 24.5 to 39.5 of gestation (computed from estimates of the body composition of the reference fetus throughout the 3d trimester). The reference fetus was constructed from compositional analysis of fetuses and infants who were stillborn or who had died within 48 hours of birth. The data of Ziegler et al.[80] were utilized for this figure. (See Ziegler EE, O'Donnell AM, Nelson SE, et al: Body composition of the reference fetus. *Growth* 1976; 40:329−341.)

of 15 g/kg/day.[46, 54] For the remainder of the studies in Figure 2−3, weight gain ranged from 15 to 22 g/kg/day, and the energy cost of storage varied from 45 to 70 kcal/kg/day, about twofold to threefold greater than the predicted cost.

The reason for the high observed energy cost of storage can be visualized in Figure 2−6.[23, 46, 50, 54, 76] The calculated fat—and thus energy content of premature tissue-gain—appears to be much higher than the theoretically predicted amounts. While cal-

TABLE 2−6.
Estimates of Cost of Energy Storage in Premature and Term Infants

Factor	Premature		Term	
Age	28−30 wk	32−34 wk	0−1 mo	1−2 mo
Rate of weight gain, g/kg/day*	15	15	7.5	7.1
Mean body weight, kg†	1.318	2.020	3.998	4.980
Composition of tissue gain†				
% fat (g/kg/day)	10.6 (1.59)	13.25 (1.99)	20.4 (1.53)	40.2 (2.85)
% protein (g/kg/day)	11.75 (1.76)	13.15 (1.97)	12.5 (0.94)	10.0 (0.71)
% other (g/kg/day)	77.65 (11.65)	73.60 (11.04)	67.10 (5.03)	49.80 (3.54)
Energy cost of tissue deposition, kcal/kg/day‡	24.6	29.5	19.5	30.4
Energy content of tissue acquired, kcal/g‡	1.64	1.97	2.59	4.28

* Mean rate of growth obtained from Sparks[69] for the premature infant, and from Fomon et al.[21] for the term male infant.
† Mean body weight and composition of tissue gain taken from Ziegler et al.[80] for the premature infant, and from Fomon et al.[21] for the term male infant.
‡ To compute the energy cost of tissue deposition and the energy content of tissue acquired, the caloric content of fat and protein were assumed to be 9.25 and 5.65 kcal/g, respectively. The caloric content of the remaining tissue was assumed to be negligible.

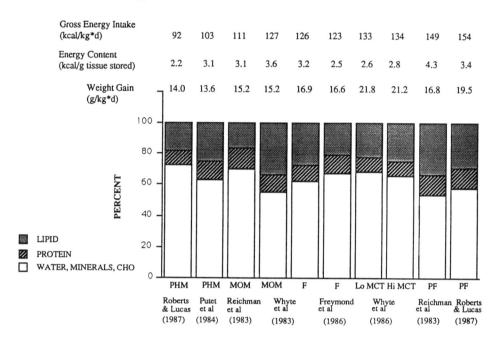

Gross Energy Intake (kcal/kg*d)	92	103	111	127	126	123	133	134	149	154
Energy Content (kcal/g tissue stored)	2.2	3.1	3.1	3.6	3.2	2.5	2.6	2.8	4.3	3.4
Weight Gain (g/kg*d)	14.0	13.6	15.2	15.2	16.9	16.6	21.8	21.2	16.8	19.5

LIPID
PROTEIN
WATER, MINERALS, CHO

PHM	PHM	MOM	MOM	F	F	Lo MCT	Hi MCT	PF	PF
Roberts & Lucas (1987)	Putet et al (1984)	Reichman et al (1983)	Whyte et al (1983)	Freymond et al (1986)	Whyte et al (1986)	Reichman et al (1983)		Roberts & Lucas (1987)

PHM (Pooled Human Milk); MOM (Mothers' Own Milk); F (Formula); PF (Preterm Formula)

FIG 2–6.
Gain in energy content and composition of new tissue in the premature infant. Except for the study of Reichman et al., the composition of tissue gain was computed by the "balance" approach; that is, protein gain was computed from nitrogen balance data and lipid gain was computed from the difference between total energy gain and energy deposited as protein (carbohydrate gain was assumed to be negligible). In the study of Reichman et al., macronutrient storage was estimated from the difference between metabolizable macronutrient intake and oxidation.

culations of intrauterine growth suggest that the fat component of weight gain should be in the range of 10.6% to 16.8% (weeks 29 through 37 of gestation) (see Fig 2–5),[80] the experimentally observed fat composition of weight gain for the preterm infant in Figure 2–6 ranges from 16.6% to 33.8% and is more similar to the growth of the term infant (see Table 2–6). The observation of a higher percent fat gain is consistent regardless of type of feed. Although a lower gross energy intake appears to produce a fat gain that is quantitatively (i.e., g fat gained/kg/day) more similar to that observed in utero, this reduction is typically accompanied by a substandard weight gain (<15 g/kg/day) (see Fig 2–6).[46, 54] In only one study was growth found to qualitatively and quantitatively mirror intrauterine growth (Reichman et al.; Fig 2–6).[50] In contrast to the observations for fat, the protein content of weight gain exhibits considerably less variability (range: 9.6% to 13.4%) and is more comparable to the theoretical estimate of 11.75% to 13.6% for the infant 29 to 37 weeks of age.[80] The influence of dietary protein content on lean tissue gain will be discussed later.

These observations have led many to question whether intrauterine growth is the most appropriate standard for extrauterine growth in the premature infant. Consequently, assessment of an energy allowance for tissue deposition has been controversial. Some have argued that a weight gain slightly below the recommended level of 15 g/kg/day is preferable, as excessive fat gain would be minimized.[47] Others have offered that the optimal pattern of growth for the premature infant might be one that is higher in fat and more similar to that exhibited by the term infant during the first 4 months of life.[48] Considering the increased challenges of thermoregulation and nutrition placed on the premature infant by an extrauterine existence, a higher fat content might be advantageous.[48]

Separate growth standards have not been identified for the growth-retarded LBW infant. Chessex et al. found significant differences in growth between SGA and AGA low-birth-weight infants fed similar diets (see Table 2–4).[15] The SGA infants grew at a faster rate, but the caloric content of tissue acquired by the SGA infant was significantly reduced. Thus, despite a greater rate of growth, the net cost of energy storage was lower for the SGA infants studied. Cauderay et al., however, observed no differences in growth quality or quantity between SGA and AGA low-birth-weight infants (see Table 2–4).[12] Future research should be directed at clarifying whether SGA infants utilize dietary nutrients differently for growth.

Energy Losses in Excreta

In estimating the metabolizable energy intake of the term infant, it is frequently assumed that digestibility in the infant is not appreciably different from that of the adult.[10] To convert from gross energy to metabolizable energy, it is commonly estimated that only about 5% of energy intake is lost in excreta. This assumption has been questioned, however, as macronutrient absorption has been shown to be quite variable in the neonatal period and not as efficient. Limited energy balance data available for the term infant suggest that about 88% to 92% of gross energy intake is retained.[10]

The even greater gastrointestinal immaturities of the preterm infant can lead to substantial excretion of dietary energy. The primary source of these greater energy losses is increased fecal excretion of fat.[10] As calculated from the energy balance studies shown in Figure 2–3, the mean coefficient of energy retention (metabolizable energy/gross energy) for the preterm infant ranges from 0.79 to 0.92.[9, 23, 46, 50, 54, 76] Factors contributing to the variability among studies include choice of diet, energy level fed, maturity, and postnatal age of population. In addition, intraindividual variability in energy digestibility appears to be considerable. Brooke et al. reported that energy retention ranged from 52% to 94% for a population of healthy preterm infants fed similar amounts of a formula diet.[9] This large variability emphasizes the inappropriateness of assuming uniform digestibility among preterm infants. It is unknown whether intrauterine growth retardation exerts a separate effect on nutrient digestibility. Chessex et al. found protein and fat digestibility to be 11% to 14% lower in SGA infants than in AGA infants, despite the greater maturity of the SGA infants studied (see Table 2–4).[15] In contrast, Cauderay et al. and Brooke reported no differences in digestibility between SGA and AGA infants.[8, 12]

Fat digestion has been speculated to be better in infants fed fresh human milk than in formula-fed infants because of the lipase present in human milk.[1] However, comparisons of human milk and formula have revealed inconclusive results. While some investigators have reported improved fat digestion,[1] others have found similar or lower fat digestibility for human milk–fed infants.[50, 77] Moreover, when human milk is pasteurized, nutrient digestibility appears to be considerably impaired.[46, 78] Putet et al. found preterm infants fed pasteurized human milk to have on average a 8% to 15% lower absorption of protein, fat, and energy than formula-fed infants.[46]

Two approaches that have been taken to increasing metabolizable energy intake in the preterm infant are (1) increasing the caloric density of the formula and (2) enhancing the fat digestibility of the formula. While high-energy formulas (84 to 90 kcal/100 mL) permit a higher metabolizable energy intake, the proportion of energy lost in excreta also increases. Roberts and Lucas found that with a 68% increase in gross energy intake, energy digestibility fell from 90% to 84%.[54] Similarly, Brooke found a 12% reduction in digestibility when the energy content of the formula was raised from 62 to 90 kcal/100 mL.[7]

To potentially enhance fat, and thus energy digestibility, infant formulas have been manufactured in which medium-chain triglyceride (MCT) oil has been used in place of the more customary long-chain triglyceride (LCT) fat sources. While some research has indicated that fat absorption is improved with the use of MCT, this improvement in fat digestibility does not necessarily translate into an improvement in energy digestibility as the energy content of MCT is also reduced (8.1 kcal/g in MCT vs. 9.3 kcal/g for LCT).[76] Whyte et al. calculated that a 7% enhancement in fat digestibility with MCT would only contribute to a 2% improvement in energy digestibility.[76] Furthermore, when these researchers actually compared the energy digestibility of a high-MCT formula to that of a low-MCT formula, no differences in energy digestibility were observed (see Fig 2–3). Brooke et al. similarly found no improvement in energy digestibility when MCT was used in place of LCT fat.[7]

Estimated Energy Requirement

Utilizing a factorial approach, estimates of the energy requirement for the preterm infant have been derived (Table 2–7).[3, 16] Although mean estimates generated by different expert committees show good agreement, it is striking to note the large range in energy requirements cited by the European Society of Paediatric Gastroenterology and Nutrition (ESPGAN) committee.[16] The large variability cited emphasizes the importance of carefully considering the "individual" when estimating energy requirements in the clinical setting. For example, if an infant is unusually active, is handled frequently, and shows poor nutrient retention, intake should be appropriately adjusted upward.[16]

While these requirements provide a reference point from which to prescribe dietary energy intake, several goals for refinement of current recommendations can be identified. First, estimated energy requirements for growth (20 to 30 kcal/kg/day) are incongruous with experimental determinations of energy used for growth. The merit of de-

TABLE 2–7.

Estimations of Energy Requirement (kcal/kg/day) for the Premature Infant

Factor	American Academy of Pediatrics[3]	European Society of Paediatric Gastroenterology and Nutrition[16]	
		Average	Range
Energy expenditure			
Resting metabolic rate	50	52.5	45–60
Activity	15	7.5	5–10
Cold stress	10	7.5	5–10
Synthesis/thermic effect of food	8	17.5	10–25
Energy stored	25	25.0	20–30
Energy excreted	12	20.0	10–30
Estimated energy requirement	120	130	95–165

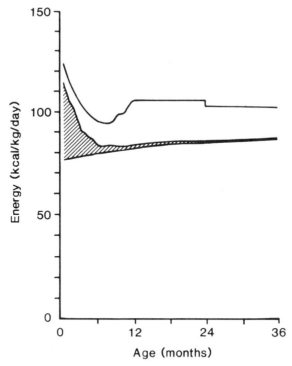

FIG 2–7.

Revised estimates of the metabolizable energy requirement for the term infant (data of Prentice and co-workers). The revised estimates *(middle line)* were generated by adding an energy requirement for growth *(hatched area)* to a mean curve for total energy expenditure derived from published and unpublished energy expenditure values determined by doubly labeled water. The *upper line* represents the current FAO/WHO/UNU recommendations (see reference 20) for comparison. (From Prentice AM, Lucas A, Vasquez-Velasquez L, et al: Are current dietary guidelines for young children a prescription for overfeeding? *Lancet* 1988; 2:1066–1069. Used by permission.)

fining premature infant growth requirements from the chemical composition of in utero growth needs to be evaluated in lieu of this consistent discrepancy. Second, guidelines are needed which take into account the variable influences of postnatal age, degree of prematurity, and infant growth on LBW infant energy needs. In addition, no separate guidelines have yet been established for the growth-retarded infant. Differences observed between growth-retarded and appropriately grown infants with respect to energy expenditure, digestibility, and storage suggest the need for a separate energy recommendation.

Metabolizable energy recommendations for the term infant put forth by the FAO/WHO/UNU* are shown in Figure 2–7.[20, 45] These recommendations are based on energy intake data collected for healthy term infants. With the advent of the doubly labeled water tool for assessing free-living infant TEE, research efforts have been directed at reevaluating these intake-based dietary guidelines. Prentice et al. recalculated metabolizable energy requirements for the term infant by employing pooled TEE data collected for term infants from 0 to 36 months and an energy allowance for growth.[45] As seen in Figure 2–7, their revised estimates fall below current recommendations. Pren-

---

*Food and Agriculture Organization of the United Nations, World Health Organization, and United Nations University.

tice and co-workers noted that the lower estimate is not surprising if one considers that the intake data utilized by the FAO/WHO/UNU in formulating recommendations includes data collected from infants fed older, high-energy formulas. More recent assessments of energy intake from infant populations receiving human milk suggest a lower caloric intake that parallels the revised estimates of energy need made by Prentice and co-workers.[45, 74]

PROTEIN ENERGY BALANCE

In assessing dietary requirements for infant growth it is critical to consider the dietary protein:energy ratio, in addition to overall energy needs. An important question that has arisen is how might manipulation of the protein concentration in the diet alter premature infant growth. In considering the ideal protein:energy mixture it should be recognized that protein and energy metabolism are interrelated.[20, 79] Protein synthesis for the maintenance of existing protein stores and the development of new lean tissue are energy-expensive processes that are significantly impacted by the organism's energy status. These costs are estimated to be considerable in the neonate, who has been calculated to have a protein synthetic rate approximately fivefold that of the young adult.[44, 79] If energy intake is limiting or inadequate, protein synthesis will be depressed and amino acid oxidation potentially increased. With provision of adequate dietary energy, protein retention becomes more a function of protein intake.[66] However, care must be taken in unnecessarily increasing the protein content of the preterm infant's diet, as excessive protein can potentially be harmful because of immaturities in the preterm infant's metabolic and excretory functions.[47]

Protein energy balance studies conducted over the past 15 years have been extremely helpful in clarifying how different mixtures of protein and energy affect postnatal growth and metabolic response, and this information has been utilized toward defining the optimal dietary regimen. However, certain limitations still remain in applying the knowledge obtained from these studies to the formulation of dietary goals. As discussed previously, physiologic ranges for growth have not yet been clearly defined in the premature infant. In order to define appropriate growth, longitudinal studies are needed that evaluate the potential effect of preterm infant growth on longer term growth. Controversy also exists regarding what should be viewed as a "normal" metabolic response.[38] Specifically, normal circulating amino acid and protein levels remain undefined. Some have argued that the lower levels of the breast-fed infant should be used as the standard,[47] while others have voiced the opinion that in the preterm infant the higher amino acid levels found in cord blood may be a more appropriate standard.[66] Prospective studies are needed to address whether different amino acid and protein profiles possibly influence later neurologic and clinical performance.[38] With these limitations in mind, protein energy balance studies performed in premature infants will be reviewed. Preliminary data from recent longitudinal studies will also be discussed.

Räihä and co-workers were among the first to examine the consequences of varying protein quantity and quality in a constant energy diet upon premature infant growth and metabolic status.[24, 47] Although protein balance was not assessed in this study, the striking findings and conclusions of these investigators deserve mention as they became the basis for a considerable number of balance studies that have followed. In this study, 106 preterm infants were evaluated and randomly assigned to either pooled human milk or one of four different preterm formulas that varied in protein quality (60:40 or 18:82

whey:casein) and quantity (1.9 or 3.8 g protein/100 kcal). Calorie intake was similar in all infant groups, with the mean intake ranging from 114 to 118 kcal/kg/day. With respect to growth, little difference was observed between the response of the different dietary groups. Formula-fed infants were found to gain weight at a faster rate than infants fed pooled human milk, but linear growth did not differ. More remarkable was the effect of the high-protein formula diets on metabolic response and status. Compared with infants fed pooled human milk, those fed the higher protein formulations developed elevations in blood urea nitrogen, blood ammonia, serum proteins, and urine osmolarity. Based on these findings, it was concluded that a protein:energy ratio higher than that found in pooled human milk should be carefully reconsidered, as (1) there was no linear growth advantage to further increasing the protein:energy ratio, and (2) the synthetic and degradative amino acid pathways of the premature infant did not appear adequately developed to support higher protein intakes; thus, higher protein formulations may be detrimental to the immature infant.

In response to this study the metabolic consequences of feeding protein at the comparatively enriched levels (2.2 to 3.2 g/100 kcal) found in preterm infant formulas have been more carefully examined. Kashyup and co-workers monitored the growth and metabolic response of premature infants fed a formula designed to mirror the protein content of typical preterm formulations (2.0 g protein/63 kcal), and compared the response of these infants to those fed a diet either lower in protein (1.3 g protein/63 kcal) or higher in energy (2.0 g protein/82 kcal) (Table 2–8).[36] Infants fed the higher protein intake demonstrated better growth than those fed the lower protein intake, as assessed by nitro-

TABLE 2–8.

Studies of the Effect of Varying Protein and Energy Intake on Protein Energy Balance in the Preterm Infant

Factor	Kashyap et al.[36] and Schulze et al.[62]			Kashyap et al.[37]		
Number of subject	9	9	9	14	15	15
Weight at birth, g	1,469	1,453	1,394	1,390	1,500	1,460
Protein content of formula, g/dL	1.3	2.0	2.0	1.6	2.1	2.2
Energy content of formula, kcal/dL	63	63	82	66	67	80
Gross energy intake, kcal/kg/day	115	114	149	118	120	142
Nitrogen intake, mg N/kg/day*	352	576	560	448	608	624
[g protein/kg/day]	[2.2]	[3.6]	[3.5]	[2.8]	[3.8]	[3.9]
Percent dietary energy intake as protein	11	18	13	14	18	15
Nitrogen retention, mg N/kg/day	268	422	425	346	420	473
Net protein utilization†	0.75	0.73	0.76	0.77	0.69	0.76
Protein:fat ratio of weight gain	0.40	0.79	0.46	0.53	0.70	0.52
Weight gain, g/kg/day	13.9	18.3	22	16	19.1	21.5
Change in length; mm/wk	9.4	12.1	12.4	10.4	12.1	12.8
Change in skinfolds, mm/wk‡	0.65	0.74	1.31	0.69	0.77	1.22

* Nitrogen intake computed from the following relationship: (g protein × 0.16) × 1,000.
† Net protein utilization = nitrogen retained/nitrogen intake.
‡ Sum of triceps and subscapular skinfolds.

gen retention, weight gain, linear growth, and head circumference. When compared to intrauterine estimates for growth (~320 mg N/kg/day; 15 g/kg/day),[80] only those groups with higher protein intake achieved adequate growth. Increasing energy intake had no further effect on net protein utilization, thus it appeared that an energy intake of 115 kcal/kg/day was sufficient to support a protein intake of 3.5 g/kg/day. In contrast to the observations of Räihä et al.,[47] these workers failed to detect azotemia or abnormalities in blood acid–base status in the infants fed higher protein levels, although blood amino acid profiles were elevated when contrasted with profiles generated by human milk–fed babies. Kashyup et al. postulated that the failure of Räihä et al. to observe a similar improvement in linear growth with increased protein intake may have been due to the low mineral content of the formulas used by these investigators.

As a follow-up to this first study, Kashyup et al. performed a second study in which both an intermediate protein level (2.4 g/100 kcal) and a more elevated protein level (3.1 g/100 kcal) were evaluated (see Table 2–8).[37] The 2.4 g protein/100 kcal level was chosen as it more closely imitates the protein content of preterm human milk, and 3.1 g protein/100 kcal was chosen to see if nitrogen retention could be further bolstered without promoting excessive fat storage. Although 2.4 g protein/100 kcal (2.8 g/kg/day) did not promote growth to the same extent as 3.1 g protein/100 kcal (3.8 g/kg/day), the lower protein formula was able to produce growth and nitrogen retention at the intrauterine level. Moreover, no evidence of metabolic intolerance could be found to 2.4 g protein/100 kcal, and the amino acid profile of this infant group was comparable to that of infants fed mothers' milk. Increasing the protein level of the diet 3.1 g/100 kcal did permit a further increase in nitrogen retention, but only when the energy intake of the diet was also enriched. Thus for a high-protein intake of 3.8 g/kg/day, an increased energy intake was necessary to enhance net protein utilization.

Based on the findings of these two studies Kashyup and colleagues suggested that the protein content of LBW feeds should not exceed 3 g/100 kcal.[37] Their data also demonstrated that the composition of newly acquired tissue in the LBW infant reflects the relative proportions of protein and energy in the diet (see Table 2–8).[37, 62] Thus, in instances of inadequate growth it is important to supplement with protein in addition to nonprotein calories, as long as the protein content of the diet does not exceed 3 g protein/100 kcal.

In recent years, the merit of pooled or banked human milk has been compared with both preterm human milk (i.e., mothers' own milk) and preterm infant formulas.[5, 25, 46, 73] Although pooled breast milk is considered appropriate for the term infant, the concern has been raised that the protein content is insufficient for the greater growth requirements of the preterm infant. Mothers' own milk, on the other hand, has been shown to be enriched in protein relative to term milk for the first few weeks of lactation,[25] and has subsequently been proposed to be a superior nutrient source for the preterm infant (Fig 2–8). It is interesting to note that with increasing postpartum age, the protein:energy ratio of preterm milk declines. Whitehead has proposed that as growth velocity declines during infancy the concentration of protein calories required for growth also decreases.[75] Perhaps the gradually declining protein:energy dietary ratio of preterm milk denotes an appropriate growth velocity curve for the immature infant.

Räihä et al. had concluded in their studies that there was no linear growth advantage to increasing the protein content of a feed beyond that provided by banked breast milk.[47] Subsequent studies have not repeated these findings, and have instead shown a distinct linear growth advantage to providing a higher enrichment of protein, such as is found in either preterm milk or preterm formula (Table 2–9).[5, 46, 53] Moreover, as seen in Table

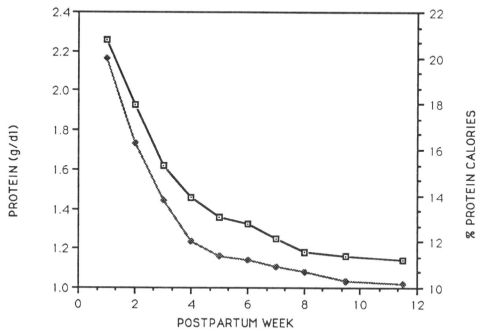

FIG 2–8.
Protein content (g/dL) of preterm human milk and percent dietary energy of this milk as protein calories are plotted against postpartum week, showing declines. Preterm human milk was obtained from mothers who had delivered infants at less than 35 weeks of gestation. The data of Gross were utilized for this figure. (See Gross SJ: Growth and biochemical response of preterm infants fed human milk or modified infant formula. *N Engl J Med* 1983; 308:237–241).

2–9, pooled human milk has consistently failed to produce intrauterine rates of nitrogen retention (~320 mg N/kg/day), whereas both mothers' own milk and preterm formulas have been more successful. In addition, other investigators have not necessarily found that this improvement in growth occurs at the expense of metabolic protein overload.[5, 73]

Most notable were the differences in nitrogen retention observed by Roberts and Lucas between LBW infants fed pooled human milk and those fed preterm formula.[53] Pooled human milk-fed infants received far less nitrogen, and in addition, the protein content of tissue gain also was reduced. Whereas infants fed pooled human milk gained 8.7 g protein/100 g tissue, infants fed preterm formula gained 12.8 g protein/100 g tissue. Given that the intrauterine recommended protein accretion rate for infants in the third trimester is 11% to 14% of weight gain,[80] the 8.7% value observed in the babies fed pooled human milk is strikingly low. The poor lean tissue growth exhibited by the infants fed pooled human milk mirrored the reduced amount and proportion of protein calories in their diet. Insufficient dietary energy may have also limited protein synthesis, as net protein utilization (nitrogen retained/nitrogen intake) was reduced in the infants fed pooled human milk compared with those fed formula (0.62 vs. 0.72).

There has been some hesitation to unequivocally recommend preterm human milk

TABLE 2–9.
Studies of Protein Balance in the Preterm Infant*

Factor	Atkinson et al.[5] Pooled HM	MOM	PF	Putet et al.[46] Pooled HM	PF	Roberts and Lucas[53] Pooled HM	PF	Schanler et al.[60] Fortified MOM	PF	Whyte et al.[77] MOM	F	Reichman et al.[50] MOM	PF
Subject number	8	8	8	6	6	8	8	17	14	9	19	11	13
Age at study, days	8	~14	8	21	29	35	37	17	16	12	16	21	21
Weight at birth, g	<1,300	<1,300	<1,300	1,318	1,302	1,096	1,054	1,180	1,195	1,320	1,250	1,160	1,155
Energy intake, kcal/kg/day	137	125	142	103	126	96	139	134	130	127	126	111	149
Nitrogen intake, mg N/kg/day‡	397	483	507	408	498	310	548	459	451	418	428	483	510
[g protein/kg/day]	[2.5]	[3.0]	[3.2]	[2.6]	[3.1]	[1.9]	[3.4]	[2.9]	[2.8]	[2.6]	[2.7]	[3.0]	[3.2]
Percent of dietary energy intake as protein§	10	14	13	14	14	11	14	12	12	12	12	15	12
Nitrogen retention, mg N/kg/day‡	233	324	305	264	373	194	397	303	311	258	272	315	307
Percent protein weight gain	...	...	...	12.1	10.5	8.7	12.8	11.8	11.4	10.7	10.1	13.4	12.5
Percent fat weight gain	...	...	...	25.1	23.2	...	...	...	...	33.8	27.7	16.6	33.8
Weight gain, g/kg/day	...	...	...	13.6	22.1	13.7	19.4	16	17	15.2	16.9	15.2	16.8
Change in length, mm/wk	...	...	...	10	14	7.5	9.7	10	9	8.6	9.4	9.8	10.2

* HM = human milk; MOM = mothers' own milk; PF = preterm formula; F = formula.
† Data presented represent the mean of two balance studies.
‡ Nitrogen and protein intake/retention computed from the following relationship: g N × 6.25 = g protein.
§ % Dietary energy intake as protein computed as follows: [(g protein intake × 5.65 kcal/g protein)/energy intake] × 100.

for the nutritional support of small infants.[16, 29] This hesitation stems from concern that mothers' own milk is too variable and borderline in nutritional content. Several research groups have evaluated protein energy balance for infants fed mothers' own milk (see Table 2–9).[14, 50, 60, 77] Reichman et al. found the protein and energy content of mothers' own milk able to support weight gain and nitrogen retention at the intrauterine rate (Table 2–9).[50] The composition of growth differed, however, from that demonstrated by formula-fed infants; infants fed mothers' own milk stored considerably less fat. The higher fat content of tissue acquired by the formula-fed infants was attributed to their greater fat intake. As for both the human milk and formula-fed infant groups, a similar strong association was observed between metabolizable macronutrient (fat, protein) intake and storage. Thus, the investigators concluded that diet-related differences in fat and protein accretion were apparently due to differences in metabolizable intake. It was also concluded that the macronutrient composition of mothers' own milk produces growth that mimics intrauterine growth more closely.

Other research groups have compared the growth-promoting abilities of mothers' own milk and infant formula when consumed at similar protein and energy intake levels (see Table 2–9).[60, 77] Under these circumstances, weight, protein, and fat gain appear similar for premature infants fed human milk and those fed formula. However, Whyte et al. found the energy content of tissue acquired by those fed human milk to be slightly higher than that of infants fed formula, reflecting a slightly higher percentage fat gain (34% vs. 28%).[77] This later result argues against the hypothesis that the growth of infants fed preterm human milk is lower in fat and consequently more like intrauterine growth than that of formula-fed infants.

Limited protein energy balance data are available for SGA infants. Studies of labeled amino acid turnover suggest however that significant differences in whole body protein metabolism exist between SGA and AGA low-birth-weight infants. Pencharz et al. found protein synthesis and breakdown to be 26% and 35% higher in SGA low-birth-weight infants compared to AGA low-birth-weight infants.[44] Studies of older malnourished children have similarly found the parameters of protein metabolism to be elevated during catch-up growth.[79] In contrast to these results, a recent study reported a 20% slower protein turnover rate in SGA low-birth-weight infants compared to AGA low-birth-weight infants.[12] Clearly, further studies are needed to define how protein metabolism differs in the SGA infant and the impact of potential differences in metabolism on the protein and energy requirements of the SGA infant for growth.

Protein energy balance studies have provided useful information on the immediate response of the premature infant to diet. Longitudinal studies are needed, however, to answer questions such as:

1. What are the long-term effects on the body composition of the infant who prematurely deviates from the intrauterine pattern of weight gain?
2. Is a premature high fat gain linked with later obesity?
3. Do infants fed pooled human milk demonstrate reduced stature later on and thus failure to achieve genetic growth potential?
4. Are the relatively elevated amino acid levels in premature infants fed high-protein formulations potentially detrimental to neurologic development?
5. Is there a relationship between different preterm dietary regimens and clinical outcome?

Given the difficulty and expense of carefully following the progress of a large cohort of premature infants, longitudinal data remain scarce. Svenningsen et al. longitudinally followed the growth performance and neurologic development of 48 LBW infants who were randomly assigned to one of three isocaloric diets varying in protein content during weeks 3 through 15 of postnatal life.[70] The diets evaluated were human milk (1.6 g protein/100 kcal), a moderate protein formula (2.3 g protein/100 kcal), and a high-protein formula (3 g protein/100 kcal). The majority (12 of 18) of the infants fed human milk were receiving their mothers' own milk. Mean protein intake was 1.9, 2.5, and 3.2 g protein/kg/day for the human milk, moderate protein formula, and high-protein formula, respectively. Early assessment of growth during weeks 15 through 20 indicated that infants fed human milk were gaining weight at a slower rate than infants fed the high-protein formula; however, subsequent assessment from 8 months to 2 years of age revealed no differences in the weight between infant groups. Length and head circumference gain were consistently similar among the breast-fed and formula-fed infant groups for the entire 2 years. These results suggest that early differences in protein intake (within the range of 1.9 to 3.2 g protein/kg/day) do not produce quantitative differences in "long-term" (i.e., 2 year) growth, although it is uncertain from this study whether qualitative growth differed. Neurodevelopmental examinations in these same infants similarly revealed no differences among the dietary groups. However, as a number of the infants fed the high-protein formula did develop metabolic acidosis, it was suggested that a protein:energy ratio of 3 g/100 kcal may be excessive.

In England a large multicenter study has been established to examine the effects of various preterm infant feeding regimens on short-term and long-term growth, neurologic development, and clinical performance.[38, 40] Initial findings from this study suggest that infants fed pooled human milk show reduced weight, length, and head circumference gain when compared with LBW infants fed preterm formula. Although detailed data have not yet been published, preliminary findings from this study indicate that these early differences in growth may still be visible at 2 years of age.[38] Longitudinal growth data that are anticipated from this study should provide much needed insight into the question of whether later growth reflects early differences in growth.

Summary and Current Guidelines

Protein energy balance studies have indicated that growth in the LBW infant is very much reflective of dietary composition and content. While preterm human milk, fortified human milk, and infant formulas appear capable of supporting nitrogen retention and weight gain resembling in utero conditions, pooled human milk does not appear to be an adequate nutrient source. Longitudinal studies are needed, though, to assess the impact of early diet-induced growth patterns on longer term quantitative and qualitative growth. Protein intakes in excess of those provided by human milk do result in increased circulating amino acid and protein levels and in some instances high-protein intakes have been associated with metabolic acidosis, azotemia, or hyperammonemia. These abnormal metabolic responses indicate that the biochemical and excretory immaturities of the preterm infant need to be carefully considered prior to enriching the protein content of the diet.

Based on a careful review of the literature, ESPGAN established guidelines for adequate, yet nonexcessive ratios of protein:energy in the diet.[16] The lower limit suggested was 2.25 g protein/100 kcal, which if fed at the recommended energy level of 130 kcal/kg/d would provide 2.9 g/kg/day. An upper limit of 3.1 g protein/100 kcal (4.0 g/kg/day) was suggested with the proviso that this high protein:energy ratio may exceed the metabolic tolerance of the preterm infant. Although the ESPGAN committee acknowledged the possible difficulty of achieving the lower limit of protein:energy with human milk, breast milk was recommended as providing a "safe" protein intake and also for its non-nutritional attributes (i.e., host defense). To optimize nutritional status, mothers' own milk is preferred, and an intake of 185 to 200 mL/kg is recommended. The committee noted that fortification of human milk is suggested if clinical signs of protein deficiency are evident.

REFERENCES

1. Alemi B, Hamosh M, Scanlon JW, et al: Fat digestion in very low-birth-weight infants: Effect of addition of human milk to low-birth-weight formula. *Pediatrics* 1981; 68:484– 489.
2. Alvear J, Brooke OG: Specific dynamic action in infants of low-birth-weight. *J Physiol* 1978; 275:54P.
3. American Academy of Pediatrics, Committee on Nutrition: Nutritional needs of low-birth-weight infants. *Pediatrics* 1985; 75:976–986.
4. Ashworth A: Metabolic rates during recovery from protein-calorie malnutrition: The need for a new concept of specific dynamic action. *Nature* 1969; 223:407–409.
5. Atkinson SA, Bryan MH, Anderson GH: Human milk feeding in premature infants: Protein, fat, and carbohydrate balances in the first two weeks of life. *J Pediatr* 1981; 99:617–624.
6. Benedict FG, Talbot FB: *Metabolism and Growth from Birth to Puberty.* Carnegie Institute, publication 302. Washington DC, 1921.
7. Brooke OG: Energy balance and metabolic rate in preterm infants fed with standard and high-energy formulas. *Br J Nutr* 1980; 44:13–23.
8. Brooke OG: Energy requirements and utilization of the low birthweight infant. *Acta Paediatr Scand [Suppl]* 1982; 296:67–70.
9. Brooke OG, Alvear J, Arnold M: Energy retention, energy expenditure, and growth in healthy immature infants. *Pediatr Res* 1979; 13:215–220.
10. Butte NF: Energy requirements during infancy, in Tsang RC, Nichols BL (eds): *Nutrition During Infancy.* Philadelphia, Hanley & Belfus, 1988, pp 86–99.
11. Butte NF, Wong WW, Lee LS, et al: Energy expenditure of 4-month-old breast-fed and formula-fed infants. *Proc Nutr Soc* 1988; 47:37A.
12. Cauderay M, Schutz Y, Micheli J-L, et al: Energy-nitrogen balances and protein turnover in small and appropriate for gestational age low birthweight infants. *Eur J Clin Nutr* 1988; 42:125–136.
13. Chessex P, Reichman BL, Verellen GJE, et al: Influence of postnatal age, energy intake, and weight gain on energy metabolism in the very low-birth-weight infant. *J Pediatr* 1981; 99:761–766.
14. Chessex P, Reichman B, Verellen G, et al: Quality of growth in premature infants fed their own mothers' milk. *J Pediatr* 1983; 102:107–112.
15. Chessex P, Reichman B, Verellen G, et al: Metabolic consequences of intrauterine growth retardation in very low birthweight infants. *Pediatr Res* 1984; 18:709–713.
16. Committee on Nutrition of the Preterm Infant, European Society of Paediatric Gastroenterology and Nutrition: *Nutrition and Feeding of Preterm Infants.* Oxford, UK, Blackwell Scientific Publications, 1987.
17. Coward WA: The doubly-labelled-water ($^2H_2^{18}O$) method: Principles and practice. *Proc Nutr Soc* 1988; 47:209–218.
18. Coward WA, Roberts SB, Cole TJ: Theoretical and practical considerations in the doubly-labelled water ($^2H_2^{18}O$) method for the measurement of carbon dioxide production rate in man. *Eur J Clin Nutr* 1988; 42:207–212.
19. Davies PSW, Ewing G, Lucas A: Energy expenditure in early infancy. *Br J Nutr* 1989; 62:621–629.

20. FAO/WHO/UNU: *Energy and Protein Requirements*. World Health Organization technical report series, 724. Geneva, World Health Organization, 1985.

21. Fomon SJ, Haschke F, Ziegler EE, et al: Body composition of reference children from birth to age 10 years. *Am J Clin Nutr* 1982; 35:1169–1175.

22. Fomon SJ, Thomas LN, Filer LJ, et al: Food consumption and growth of normal infants fed milk-based formulas. *Acta Paediatr Scand [Suppl]* 1971; 223:1–36.

23. Freymond D, Schutz Y, Decombaz J, et al: Energy balance, physical activity and thermogenic effect of feeding in premature infants. *Pediatr Res* 1986; 20:638–645.

24. Gaull GE, Rassin DK, Räihä NCR: Protein intake of premature infants: A reply. *J Pediatr* 1977; 90:507–510.

25. Gross SJ: Growth and biochemical response of preterm infants fed human milk or modified infant formula. *N Engl J Med* 1983; 308:237–241.

26. Gudinchet F, Schutz Y, Micheli J-L, et al: Metabolic cost of growth in very low-birth-weight infants. *Pediatr Res* 1982; 16:1025–1030.

27. Hamill PVV, Drizd TA, Johnson CL, et al: Physical growth: National Center for Health Statistics percentiles. *Am J Clin Nutr* 1979; 32:607–629.

28. Hey EN: The care of babies in incubators, in Gairdner D, Hull D (eds): *Recent Advance in Pediatrics,* ed 4. London, Churchill Livingstone, 1971, p 171.

29. Hibberd C, Brooke OG, Carter ND, et al: A comparison of protein concentrations and energy in breast milk from preterm and term mothers. *J Hum Nutr* 1981; 35:189–198.

30. Hill JR, Robinson DC: Oxygen consumption in normally grown, small-for-dates and large-for-dates new-born infants. *J Physiol* 1968; 199:685–703.

31. Holliday MA, Potter D, Jarrah A, et al: The relation of metabolic rate to body weight and organ size. *Pediatr Res* 1967: 1:185–195.

32. James WPT, Haggarty P, McGaw BA: Recent progress in studies on energy expenditure: Are the new methods providing answers to the old questions? *Proc Nutr Soc* 1988; 47:195–208.

33. Jequier E: Energy utilization in human obesity, in Wurtman RJ, Wurtman JJ (eds): *Human Obesity,* vol 499. New York, Annals of the New York Academy of Science, 1987, pp 73–83.

34. Jones PJH, Winthrop AL, Schoeller DA, et al: Validation of doubly labeled water for assessing energy expenditure in infants. *Pediatr Res* 1987; 21:242–246.

35. Jones PJH, Winthrop AL, Schoeller DA, et al: Evaluation of doubly labeled water for measuring energy expenditure during changing nutrition. *Am J Clin Nutr* 1988; 47:799–804.

36. Kashyap S, Forsyth M, Zucker C, et al: Effects of varying protein and energy intakes on growth and metabolic response in low birth weight infants. *J Pediatr* 1986; 108:955–963.

37. Kashyap S, Schulze KF, Forsyth M, et al: Growth, nutrient retention, and metabolic response in low birth weight infants fed varying intakes of protein and energy. *J Pediatr* 1988; 113:713–721.

38. Lucas A: Does diet in preterm infants influence clinical outcome? *Biol Neonate* 1987; 52(suppl 1):141–146.

39. Lucas A, Ewing G, Roberts SB, et al: How much energy does the breast fed infant consume and expend? *Br Med J* 1987; 295:75–77.

40. Lucas A, Gore SM, Cole TJ, et al: Multicentre trial on feeding low birthweight infants: Effects of diet on early growth. *Arch Dis Child* 1984; 59:722–730.

41. Mestyán J: Energy metabolism and substrate utilization in the newborn, in Sinclair JC (ed): *Temperature Regulation and Energy Metabolism in the Newborn*. New York, Grune & Stratton, 1978, pp 39–74.

42. Mestyán J, Jarai I, Fekete M: The total energy expenditure and its components in premature infants maintained under different nursing and environmental conditions. *Pediatr Res* 1968; 2:161–171.

43. Murlin JR, Conklin RE, Marsh ME: Energy metabolism of normal new-born babies, with special reference to the influence of food and of crying. *Am J Dis Child* 1925; 29:1–28.

44. Pencharz PB, Masson M, Desgranges F, et al: Total-body protein turnover in human premature neonates: Effects of birth weight, intra-uterine nutritional status and diet. *Clin Sci* 1981; 61:207–215.

45. Prentice AM, Lucas A, Vasquez-Velasquez L, et al: Are current dietary guidelines for young children a prescription for overfeeding? *Lancet* 1988; 2:1066–1069.

46. Putet G, Senterre J, Rigo J, et al: Nutrient balance, energy utilization, and composition of weight gain in very-low-birth-weight infants fed pooled human milk or a preterm formula. *J Pediatr* 1984; 105:79–85.

47. Räihä NCR, Heinonen K, Rassin DK, et al: Milk protein quantity and quality in low-birthweight infants: I. Metabolic responses and effects on growth. *Pediatrics* 1976; 57:659–674.

48. Reichman B, Chessex P, Putet G, et al: Diet, fat accretion, and growth in premature infants. *N Engl J Med* 1981; 305:1495–1500.

49. Reichman B, Chessex P, Putet G, et al: Partition of energy metabolism and energy cost of growth in the very low-birth-weight infant. *Pediatrics* 1982; 69:446–451.

50. Reichman B, Chessex P, Verellen G, et al: Dietary composition and macronutrient storage in preterm infants. *Pediatrics* 1983; 72:322–328.

51. Roberts SB, Coward WA, Ewing G, et al: Effect of weaning on accuracy of doubly labeled water method in infants. *Am J Physiol* 1988; 254:R622–R627.

52. Roberts SB, Coward WA, Schlingenseipen K-H, et al: Comparison of the doubly labeled water ($^2H_2{}^{18}O$) method with indirect calorimetry and a nutrient-balance study for simultaneous determination of energy expenditure, water intake, and metabolizable energy intake in preterm infants. *Am J Clin Nutr* 1986; 44:315–322.

53. Roberts SB, Lucas A: The effects of two extremes of dietary intake on protein accretion in preterm infants. *Early Hum Dev* 1985; 12:301–307.

54. Roberts SB, Lucas A: Energetic efficiency and nutrient accretion in preterm infants fed extremes of dietary intake. *Hum Nutr Clin Nutr* 1987; 41C:105–113.

55. Roberts SB, Murgatroyd PR, Crisp JA, et al: Long-term variation in oxygen consumption rate in preterm infants. *Biol Neonate* 1987; 52:1–8.

56. Roberts SB, Savage J, Coward WA, et al: Energy expenditure and intake in infants born to lean and overweight mothers. *N Engl J Med* 1988; 318:461–466.

57. Roberts SB, Young VR: Energy costs of fat and protein deposition in the human infant. *Am J Clin Nutr* 1988; 48:951–955.

58. Rubecz I, Mestyán J: Postprandial thermogenesis in human milk-fed very low birth weight infants. *Biol Neonate* 1986; 49:301–306.

59. Sauer PJJ, Dane HJ, Visser HKA: Longitudinal studies on metabolic rate, heat loss, and energy cost of growth in low birth weight infants. *Pediatr Res* 1984; 18:254–259.

60. Schanler RJ, Garza C, Nichols BL: Fortified mothers' milk for very low birth weight infants: Results of growth and nutrient balance studies. *J Pediatr* 1985; 107:437–445.

61. Schoeller DA: Measurement of energy expenditure in free-living humans by using doubly labeled water. *J Nutr* 1988; 118:1278–1289.

62. Schulze KF, Stefanski M, Masterson J, et al: Energy expenditure, energy balance, and composition of weight gain in low birth weight infants fed diets of different protein and energy content. *J Pediatr* 1987; 110:753–759.

63. Schulze K: A model of the variability in metabolic rate of neonates, in Fomon SJ, Heird WC (eds): *Energy and Protein Needs During Infancy*. Orlando, Fla, Academic Press, 1985, pp 19–38.

64. Scopes JW, Ahmed I: Minimal rates of oxygen consumption in sick and premature newborn infants. *Arch Dis Child* 1966; 41:407–416.

65. Scopes JW, Ahmed I: Range of critical temperatures in sick and premature newborn babies. *Arch Dis Child* 1966; 41:417–419.

66. Senterre J: Nitrogen balances and protein requirements of preterm infants, in Visser HKA (ed): *Nutrition and Metabolism of the Fetus and Infant*. Boston, Martinus Nijhoff, 1979, pp 195–212.

67. Sinclair JC, Silverman WA: Relative hypermetabolism in undergrown human neonates. *Lancet* 1964; 2:49.

68. Sinclair JC, Silverman WA: Intrauterine growth in active tissue mass of the human fetus, with particular reference to the undergrown baby. *Pediatrics* 1966; 38:48–61.

69. Sparks JW: Human intrauterine growth and nutrient accretion. *Semin Perinatol* 1984; 8:74–93.

70. Svenningsen NW, Lindroth M, Lindquist B: Growth in relation to protein intake of low birth weight infants. *Early Hum Dev* 1982; 6:47–58.

71. Swyer PR: Heat loss after birth, in Sinclair JC (ed): *Temperature Regulation and Energy Metabolism in the Newborn*. New York, Grune & Stratton, 1978, pp 91–128.

72. Talbot FB, Sisson WR, Moriarty ME, et al: The basal metabolism of prematurity: III. Metabolism findings in twenty-one premature infants. *Am J Dis Child* 1923; 26:29–55.

73. Tyson JE, Lasky RE, Mize CE, et al: Growth, metabolic response, and development in very-low-birth-weight infants fed banked human milk or enriched formula: I. Neonatal findings. *J Pediatr* 1983; 103:95–104.

74. Waterlow JC: Basic concepts in the determination of nutritional requirements of normal infants, in Tsang RC, Nichols BL (eds): *Nutrition During Infancy*. Philadelphia, Hanley & Belfus, 1988, pp 1–19.

75. Whitehead RG, Paul AA: Growth charts and the assessment of infant feeding practices in the Western world and in developing countries. *Early Hum Dev* 1984; 9:187–207.

76. Whyte RK, Campbell D, Stanhope R, et al: Energy balance in low birth weight infants fed formula of high or low medium-chain triglyceride content. *J Pediatr* 1986; 108:964–971.

77. Whyte RK, Haslam R, Vlainic C, et al: Energy balance and nitrogen balance in growing low birthweight infants fed human milk or formula. *Pediatr Res* 1983; 17:891–898.

78. Williamson S, Finucane E, Ellis H, et al: Effect of heat treatment of human milk on absorption of nitrogen, fat, sodium, calcium, and phosphorus by preterm infants. *Arch Dis Child* 1978; 53:555–563.

79. Young VR: Protein-energy interrelationships in the newborn: A brief consideration of some basic aspects, in Lebenthal E (ed): *Textbook of Gastroenterology and Nutrition in Infancy*. New York, Raven Press, 1981, pp 257–263.

80. Ziegler EE, O'Donnell AM, Nelson SE, et al: Body composition of the reference fetus. *Growth* 1976; 40:329–341.

Chapter 3

Development of Gastrointestinal Structure and Function

L. T. Weaver

A. Lucas

The gut is the interface between 'diet' and 'metabolism' across which all nutrients must pass. At no time is its efficient function more vital to the growing infant than during the initiation of enteral feeding. Our understanding of the neonatal gastrointestinal tract has grown over the past decade as a result of increasing interest in two major areas: clinical neonatology and developmental biology. For the neonatologist, the gut has emerged as an organ of importance as advances in respiratory support of the very low birth weight infant have led to the survival of ever more preterm babies. The problems posed by their nutrition have directed attention to the development of the alimentary system and those processes involved in adaptation from intrauterine to extrauterine life. For the developmental biologist the gut offers opportunities to study the factors that regulate differentiation of an organ that undergoes a series of changes in structure and function during transition from embryologic to adult life. Much work in this area has been done in laboratory animals, but the techniques of tissue culture and organ transplantation offer exciting new ways in which insights gained from the study of the young of other mammals can be explored in man.

The gut of the newborn is faced by a major challenge: following division of the umbilical cord it must bear full responsibility for the nutrition of the growing infant. Prepared in utero by the passage of amniotic fluid, the gut has to cope soon after birth with passage of intermittent large volumes of milk. An adult ingesting a comparable feed volume per body weight would require 15 to 20 L of milk per day.[1] Successful adaptation to extrauterine life requires the hitherto untested gut to undertake the full nutritional support of the neonate rapidly and efficiently.

Enteral feeding demands a concerted response by the gastrointestinal tract comprising coordinated sucking and swallowing; efficient gastric emptying and intestinal motility; regulated salivary, gastric, pancreatic, and hepatobiliary secretions; enterocyte function capable of synthesizing and delivering appropriate brush-border enzymes; and providing effective absorption, secretion and mucosal protection, economical utilization of the products of digestion and absorption, and expulsion of undigested and waste products.

Two factors are of particular importance to the process of perinatal adaptation to enteral nutrition: the relative maturity of the gastrointestinal tract, and the composition of milk feeds received at birth.

PHASES OF GUT DEVELOPMENT

The human gut develops largely prenatally; by 20 weeks its final anatomic position is achieved, and by 33 to 34 weeks gestation it has reached a functional maturity sufficient to independently support the nutrition of the preterm neonate. The development of the gastrointestinal tract may be divided into ten phases (Table 3–1).

Embryogenesis

During the 2d week after conception the inner cell mass of the implanted blastocyst differentiates into an embryonic disk, which divides the amniotic cavity from the primary yolk sac. In the 3d week three germ layers are identifiable: ectoderm, mesoderm, and endoderm. The gastrointestinal tract is formed from the endodermal layer of the embryo by the incorporation of the dorsal part of the yolk sac during infolding of the embryonic disc. The splanchnic mesoderm and endoderm form a primitive two-layered gut wall (Fig 3–1).

Organogenesis

The intestine is identifiable by the 4th week after conception as a tube extending from mouth to cloaca, divided according to its blood supply into fore-, mid-, and hindgut. A short esophagus, fusiform gastric and cecal swellings, pancreatic and hepatic buds, and a midgut loop in continuity with the yolk sac, are recognizable (see Fig 3–1). Continuity of the gut lumen with the amniotic cavity is achieved when the buccopharyngeal membrane ruptures during the 3d week, and the cloacal membrane by the 7th, es-

TABLE 3–1.

Major Phases in the Ontogeny of the Gastrointestinal (GI) Tract With Some of the Developmental Abnormalities Associated With Each Phase

Phase	Abnormality
Embryogenesis	Ventral wall defects
Organogenesis	Malrotation
Epithelium formation	Intestinal atresias
Mucosal differentiation	Congenital enteropathies
Growth and maturation	Immature motile and mucosal function in the preterm
Perinatal adaptation	Necrotizing enterocolitis
Neonatal period	Milk protein intolerance
Weaning period	Weanling diarrhea
Adult life	Acquired GI diseases
Senescence	Diseases of waning GI structure and function

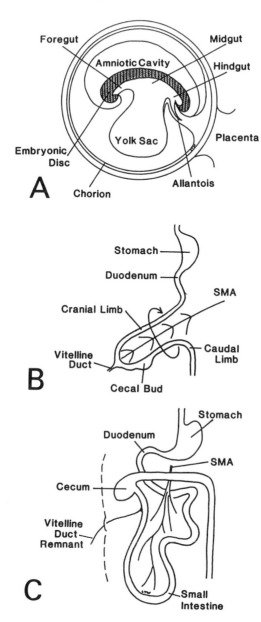

FIG 3–1.
Morphological development of the human gastrointestinal tract. **A,** median section of 3-week embryo showing primitive gut. **B,** intestinal loop before counter-clockwise rotation around superior mesenteric artery *(SMA)* at 6 to 7 weeks. **C,** position of gut in abdomen by 12 weeks, before descent of cecum to right lower quadrant.

tablishing free circulation of amniotic fluid through the gastrointestinal tract. The vitello-intestinal duct closes by the 5th week.

Epithelium Formation

Further differentiation of the mesoderm and endodermal tissue occurs during lengthening of the midgut, its herniation and rotation within the umbilical cord (extraembryonic celom), and its return to the abdominal cavity, completed by the 10th week (see Fig 3–1,B). Small intestinal villi and crypts are formed, the neuromusculature of the gut is identifiable, and a primitive multilayered epithelium is replaced by a monocolumnar epithelium. Ventral and dorsal pancreatic buds fuse, the liver and gall bladder are formed, and full patency of the gut is achieved.

Mucosal Differentiation

Differentiation of the gastrointestinal epithelium into absorptive, goblet, enteroendocrine, lymphoid, gastric parietal and chief cells, pancreatic zymogen, and other cells occurs between the 8th and 16th weeks. During the 2d trimester the columnar epithelial cells of the small intestine possess an apical tubular system capable of internalizing luminal material, which may play a part in the uptake of physiologically active macromolecules present in the amniotic fluid in utero.[2] Brunner's glands, Peyers's patches, and M cells make their first appearance around the 14th and 15th postconceptual weeks.

Growth and Maturation

During the 2d and 3d trimesters of pregnancy, growth and maturation of the gastrointestinal system occur in preparation for postnatal life. This is the period of maximal growth of the gut—which doubles in length between 25 and 40 weeks; at full term, gastric volume is about 30 mL, the length of the esophagus 10 cm, the small intestine is 250 to 300 cm, and the large intestine is around 40 cm. The cecum completes its descent to the right iliac fossa by 20 weeks when its mesenteric attachments are complete.

Perinatal Adaptation

The gastrointestinal tract appears anatomically prepared for oral feeding by the end of the 2d trimester: organogenesis is complete and the gut has assumed its final anatomic position in the abdomen. However, many of the physiological processes required for efficient enteral nutrition are not fully developed, and the resulting immaturity of gastrointestinal function may contribute to nutritional, metabolic, and clinical problems in the preterm neonate.

At birth the human neonate exchanges nutritional dependence upon two fluids of closely regulated composition (maternal blood and amniotic fluid) for a third (maternal breast milk). While varying greatly in its constituents from blood and amniotic fluid, human colostrum and milk contain all the nutrients required for the healthy growth and development of the newborn infant. In addition, human milk contains factors that may assist in digestion, the development of mucosal function and protection, and systemic metabolism. The non-nutrient components of colostrum and milk include viable white blood cells, enzymes, immunoglobulins, hormones, trophic factors, oligosaccharides, polypeptides and proteins which, secreted by the mammary gland, are active and/or absorbed at the intestinal mucosa (Table 3–2). Biologically the newborn remains an extragestate fetus until weaning when he or she achieves nutritional independence. Until that time the growing infant relies upon a diet of closely regulated composition for which the function of the gastrointestinal tract is well adapted.

There is an intimate interrelation between lactating mammary function and neonatal gastrointestinal function. During neonatal life the composition of colostrum and milk changes to meet the changing nutritional demands of the growing infant. Such changes

TABLE 3–2.

Macromolecules in Human Colostrum and Milk
Which May Play a Part in Neonatal Adaptation to
Enteral Nutrition and Extrauterine Life

Digestive enzymes
    Amylase, bile salt stimulated lipase, lipoprotein
        lipase
Hormones
    Thyroxine (T_3, T_4), thyroid stimulating hormone,
    thyrotrophin releasing hormone, corticosteroids,
    adrenocorticotrophic hormone, insulin, luteinizing
    hormone releasing factor, gonadotrophin releasing
    hormone, somatostatin, oxytocin, prolactin,
    erythropoietin, calcitonin
Growth factors
    Epidermal growth factor, nerve growth factor,
    somatomedin-C, transforming growth factor
Anti-inflammatory agents
    Prostaglandins E and F, alpha 1-antitrypsin, alpha
    1-chymotrypsin
Anti-infective factors
    Secretory IgA, IgM, IgG; secretory component;
    lactoferrin; lysozyme; complement; interferon;
    lactoperoxidase; antistaphylococcal factor; bifidus
    factor; vitamin B_{12}, folate binding proteins

are anticipated and reflected by the changing pattern of gastrointestinal function and metabolism in the postnatal period.

NEONATAL GASTROINTESTINAL FUNCTION

Motile Function

Amniotic fluid volume rises steadily during gestation to around 700 mL at term. Fetal swallowing and intestinal motility are detectable in the second trimester, and by term the fetus ingests around 300 mL of amniotic fluid per day. The fetal gastrointestinal tract is therefore exposed to the constant passage of a fluid that contains a range of physiologically active proteins and other macromolecules, including enzymes, immunoglobulins, trophic factors, and hormones. These may play a role in intrauterine gastrointestinal mucosal differentiation and fetal development.

A coordinated pattern of sucking and swallowing is absent in the neonate of less than 34 weeks gestation, and 75% of healthy preterm infants require tube feeding until this gestation. The mature suck–swallow pattern is characterized by prolonged bursts of 30 to 40 sucks at a rate of 2 per second, with swallowing occurring one to four times per burst. Bursts of non-nutritive sucking occur during rest and sleep. Gastroesophageal sphincter pressure is related directly to postconceptual age, ranging from a mean of 4 mm Hg before 29 weeks gestation to 18 mm Hg at full term. It rises during the 1st week in newborn infants. The rate and pattern of gastric emptying may be affected by composition and osmolality of feeds and by the infant's posture. The half-life of a feed in the stomach ranges from 30 to 90 minutes, and its emptying pattern follows a monoexponential curve. Gastric emptying rate may be delayed in prematurity and dysmaturity.

Infants of less than 30 weeks gestation exhibit disorganized random contractions of the small intestine, and those of 30 to 33 weeks have short bursts of motor activity (fetal complexes). Thereafter, organized migrating motor complexes are detectable, coincident with the development of coordinated sucking and swallowing. There is a direct relation between (1) increasing gestation and increasing gastroduodenal pressures, and (2) propagation and slow wave frequency.[3]

Passage of stool occurs within 24 hours of birth in 95% of healthy full-term infants. Meconium is passed for the first 2 or 3 days, followed by transitional and then fecal stools by the 7th day. During the 1st week of postnatal life the full-term neonate may pass up to 9 stools per day. Within 2 weeks this has declined to 3 or 4 per day. Breast-fed infants initially pass fewer stools, but by the mid neonatal period they pass more, softer, and bulkier stools than the formula-fed child.[4] Delay of passage of the first stool occurs in a significant number of preterm infants. In a recent survey by the authors of 844 preterm infants, delay was shown to be inversely related to gestational age: only 57% of infants less than 28 weeks at birth passed their first stool before the 3d postnatal day. Stool frequency is directly related to volume of milk ingested at all gestations. Like the full-term infant, the preterm infant fed human milk passes more and softer stools than the formula-fed infant.

Barrier Function

Mucosal protection is afforded by luminal, mucosal, and systemic mechanisms. Gastric acid, a first-line defense against the ingestion of potentially pathogenic bacteria, is present within hours of birth in both the full-term and preterm infant. Gastric pH rises gradually with age thereafter, and following feeds. The microvillus membrane and mucus of the intestinal epithelium may be immature in their barrier properties.

The neonatal gut is permeable to the passage of milk proteins and small water-soluble molecules, particularly in the preterm infant. However, the biologic and clinical significance of this is unclear. During intrauterine life the mucosa of the small intestine appears capable of taking up macromolecules, and the presence in amniotic fluid of physiologically active growth factors, and receptors on the microvillus membrane for them, suggests that intestinal uptake of macromolecules may be important in perinatal adaptation. Specialized 'M' cells overlying Peyer's patches are involved in recognition and processing of intestinal antigens. However, there is little evidence that there exists in the human neonate a period of enhanced macromolecular uptake, comparable to that operating in the intestinal mucosa of the suckling young of certain mammals, and essential to their adaptation to extrauterine life.[5]

The human infant derives its circulating immunoglobulins (largely IgG) prenatally by way of the placenta. Secretory IgA, with its capacity to agglutinate intraluminal antigens, is the first line of immunologic defense at the mucosal surface. Its high titers in human colostrum help to protect the mucosal surfaces of the breast-fed newborn (see Chapters 11 and 12), while circulating immunoglobulins (IgG and IgM) represent a further line of defense against absorbed antigens. A significant proportion of colostral IgA survives passage through the gastrointestinal tract of the infant. Secretory IgA has been detected in the gut wall and contents of fetuses of 11 to 32 weeks, and is detectable in the saliva of full-term infants by the end of the 1st week of life, reaching adult levels by 4 weeks. Exposure to food and microbial antigens probably induces IgA production from plasma cells in the lamina propria, where the immunoglobulin can be identified by immunofluorescence soon after birth. The time of onset of IgA synthesis appears to be similar in preterm infants as light as 1.5 kg, and in full-term infants.

Digestive and Absorptive Function

The newborn infant has an immediate requirement for carbohydrate and fat for energy, insulation, neural tissue synthesis, and membrane synthesis. Stores laid down during the last trimester of pregnancy meet these demands in the full-term child, but the preterm infant, with insufficient reserves, may be vulnerable. As well as satisfying these nutritional demands (see Chapters 11 and 12), breast milk contains enzymes (amylase and lipase) that assist intraluminal nutrient digestion and compensate for the relative deficiency of those secreted by the lingual, salivary, gastric, and pancreatic glands. Breast milk lipases are stable at low pH, active when bile salts are relatively deficient, and are present in preterm milk. Fat absorption is more efficient in the newborn infant fed breast milk rather than cow's milk formula, and in the full-term as opposed to the preterm infant. In the preterm infant of 32 weeks gestation the bile acid pool is only 50% of that of the full-term infant, in part due to poor ileal reabsorption of bile acids which, if levels in the gut fall below the critical micellar concentration, may lead to malabsorption of fat. Gastric lipolysis makes up for this deficiency and for that of the pancreas.[6]

Pancreatic function is relatively deficient at birth, and mature levels of pancreatic enzymes are not achieved until late infancy. Concentrations of pancreatic amylase, lipase, trypsin, and chymotrypsin are detected first in mid gestation at levels of about 10% of adult values. Infants of 32 to 34 weeks gestation at birth secrete lipase, alpha-amylase, and trypsin, at levels appreciably lower than those of mature infants. In the term infant trypsin is found at levels 50% of those in adults, while amylase and lipase remain at very low concentrations during neonatal life.

Glucose and amino acids are transported across the gut wall of the upper small intestine as early as 10 weeks after conception. Active D-glucose absorption is significantly lower in infants of less than 37 weeks gestation than those born at term, and a postnatal surge in D-glucose and D-xylose absorption occurs between the 1st and 3d weeks of life in the newborn. The use of nonmetabolizable sugars in infant feeds has provided a simple, noninvasive means of studying changes in the integrity of the gastrointestinal tract in the enterally fed newborn. Passive intestinal permeability to lactulose (an analogue of lactose) is elevated in the newborn—particularly in the preterm child and when the gut mucosa is damaged.[7] The initiation of enteral feeding is followed by a reduction in permeability during the 1st week of postnatal life in both the preterm and full-term neonate (Fig 3–2).

Intestinal mucosal disaccharidases are first detectable coincident with the appearance of villus ridges—around 8 weeks of gestation. Intestinal lactase activity of the human fetus of 26 to 34 weeks gestation is only 30% of that of the full-term baby, but from 35 weeks onwards there is a rapid rise to mature levels. By combining lactulose with lactose in milk feeds, the sequential changes in the intestinal lactase activity of 40 neonates ranging in gestation from 27 to 42 weeks was measured.[8] While lactose is hydrolyzed at the brush-border, lactulose resists lactase; both disaccharides may traverse the gut wall by passive permeation and are fully excreted in the urine, where their differential recovery may be used as a measure of intestinal lactase activity. Full-term infants displayed a fivefold greater increase in lactase activity than infants of 28 weeks' gestation during the first 10 days of milk feeding (Fig 3–3), but within 5 days intestinal lactase activity exceeded 98% efficiency even in the very preterm. Sucrase and maltase

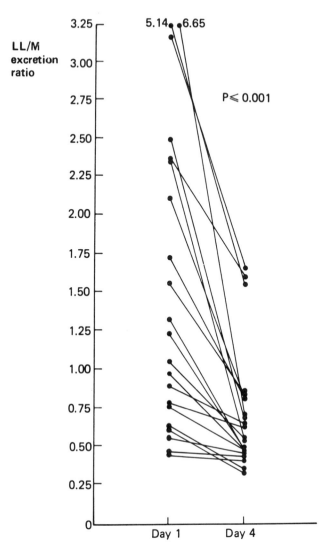

LL/M
excretion
ratio

5.14 6.65

P ≤ 0.001

Day 1   Day 4

LL/M urinary excretion ratios on days 1 & 4
Preterm babies ≤ 37 weeks gestation

FIG 3–2.
Urinary lactulose:mannitol *(LL/M)* excretion ratios of preterm infants fed milk feeds containing a fixed ration of markers (5:1). There is decline in intestinal permeability to lactulose with increasing age. (Modified from Weaver LT, Laker MF, Nelson R: Intestinal permeability in the newborn. *Arch Dis Child* 1984; 59:236–241.)

activities reach mature levels earlier in gestation even though these enzymes are not required in significant concentrations until weaning.

Intestinal Flora

The fetal gut is sterile. During vaginal delivery the newborn infant is exposed to microorganisms present in and around the birth canal. Bacteria may be detected in meconium within 4 hours of birth, and within 20 hours bacteria associated with the diet, and those colonizing the mother, are present in the child's large bowel. These may vary

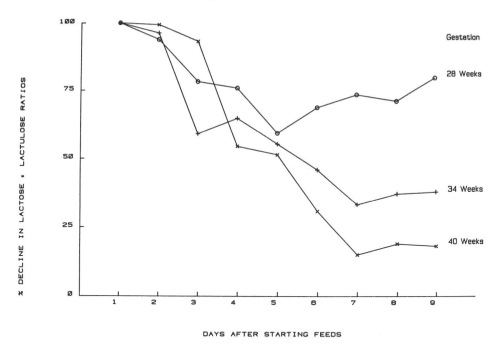

FIG 3-3.
Percentage decline in urinary lactose:lactulose excretion ratios after milk feeding in infants of 28, 34, and 40 week's gestation at birth. There was a significant trend in ratios with gestational age from day 7 onwards (P <.01). (From Weaver LT, Laker MF, Nelson R: Neonatal intestinal lactase activity. *Arch Dis Child* 1986; 61:896. Used by permission.)

according to the infant's age, gestation, place of birth, mode of delivery and nursing, type of feeding, and whether or not he or she receives antibiotics.

The full-term breast-fed infant is colonized first by a range of gram-positive and gram-negative organisms, mainly anaerobes, including *Escherichia coli, Bacteroides, Clostridia, Lactobacillus,* and *Bifidobacterium* species. Within a week of birth bifidobacteria predominate, accounting for 90% of the gram-positive saccharolytic bacteria present in the stools. Although preterm infants are also colonized by facultative anaerobes from the 1st day of life, bifidobacteria are not present in their stools in significant numbers until toward the end of the 1st week, even in those receiving breast milk. *Escherichia coli* is the dominant organism found in the stools of healthy preterm infants, and the ratio of gram-negative to gram-positive bacteria has been shown to increase steadily with age in this group.

Delivery by cesarian section is associated with a delay in colonization by anaerobes, and the gut may remain relatively sterile for some days, especially if the newborn infant receives antibiotics and is nursed in an incubator. Colonic flora may play an important role in the metabolism of undigested dietary components, releasing volatile fatty acids that are absorbed in sufficient quantities by salvage pathways to make a contribution to the nutrition of the preterm infant.[9]

REGULATION OF GASTROINTESTINAL DEVELOPMENT

The gastrointestinal tract develops under the influence of four major determinants: its genetic endowment, an intrinsic biologic clock, endogenous regulatory mechanisms, and environmental influences. At any time point in its development its capacity to respond to the demands of enteral nutrition depends on the interaction of these four (Fig 3–4).[10]

Early fetal life (phases 1 through 4) is a time of rapid growth and differentiation of the alimentary system. It is a critical period when the destiny of populations of cells is determined and when, if cellular differentiation unfolds incorrectly, developmental anomalies such as ventral wall defects and gastrointestinal atresias occur (see Fig 3 1, Table 3–1).

Mesoderm-endoderm interactions are central to tissue differentiation, and signals, which may be instructive or permissive, are probably transmitted in the form of peptide regulatory factors. Those best studied in the embryo are insulin growth factors, fibroblast growth factors, transforming growth factors and epidermal growth factor.[11] Systemic hormones, notably cortisone and thyroxine, have regulatory roles in mucosal development and enzyme expression during the perinatal period. Their influence has been especially studied in suckling rodents.[12]

During the phase of mucosal differentiation (6 to 16 weeks postconception) the human gut becomes diffusely populated with cell lines that secrete a range of gastrointestinal peptides. These "gut hormones," synthesized by this complex neuroendocrine organ, may act as true circulating hormones, locally acting hormones (paracrines or autocrines), and neurotransmitters. For most peptides examined, concentrations in gut tissue rise to values in the last 10 weeks of gestation that are at least as high as those seen in adults.[13] Aynsley-Green and co-workers[14] obtained samples of fetal umbilical arterial and venous blood and amniotic fluid by fetoscopy prior to therapeutic abortion at 18 to 21 weeks gestation in conscious, sedated mothers. Their studies demonstrated appreciable concentrations of gut hormones in the fetal circulation and amniotic fluid at this early stage. Enteroglucagon, for example, was higher in fetal than in maternal blood, of interest in view of the likely role of enteroglucagon as a trophic hormone for the gut. Gastric inhibitory polypeptide (GIP) was found in high concentrations in amniotic fluid. These findings raise the possibility that gut hormones might play a significant role in fetal gut development.

Gastrointestinal peptides are found in the venous cord blood at birth at concentrations similar to those found in fasting adults, though in the case of gastrin there is transient elevation, perhaps related to vagal stimuli. In fetal distress, however, a number of gut peptides are elevated, notably the gut motor hormone motilin, which might account for the passage of meconium in this condition.

Enteral feeding after birth induces major elevation of several circulating gut hor-

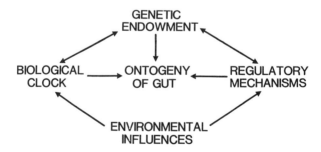

FIG 3–4.
Interaction of determinants of gastrointestinal development. (Modified from Lebenthal E, Lee PC: Interactions of determinants in the ontogeny of the gastrointestinal tract: A unified concept. *Pediatr Res* 1983; 17:19–24.)

mones (Fig 3–5) to values exceeding those found in adults.[15] Such changes are not seen in infants deprived of enteral feeding. These multiple gut hormone surges may induce adaptive changes in the gut and in intermediary metabolism that equip the infant for extrauterine nutrition. For example, motilin is thought to stimulate gastrointestinal motility and gastric emptying in adults, and it is possible that the postnatal elevation in plasma motilin (see Fig 3–5) could contribute to the increase in gut motility that occurs during

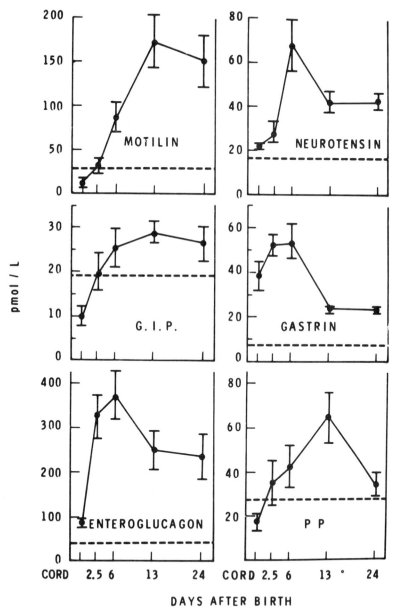

FIG 3–5.

Postnatal surges in basal (prefeed) plasma concentrations of gut hormones in preterm infants at birth and thereafter. *Dotted lines* show mean adult fasting values. *GIP* = gastric inhibitory peptide; *PP* = pancreatic polypeptide. (From Lucas A, Bloom SR, Aynsley-Green A: Gastrointestinal peptides and the adaptation to extrauterine nutrition. *Can J Physiol Pharmacol* 1985; 63:527. Used by permission.)

the neonatal period.[3] Enteroglucagon is thought to be trophic to the gut mucosa: evidence for this comes from the massive villus hypertrophy seen with enteroglucagon-secreting tumors, from the compensatory elevation in plasma enteroglucagon observed in association with gut hypertrophy following gut resection, and from experimental studies in animals. The rises in plasma enteroglucagon, gastrin, and pancreatic polypeptide (see Fig 3–5), may be an important factor in the intestinal mucosal and pancreatic growth that follows enteral feeding in neonates. Gastric inhibitory polypeptide is thought to be the principal stimulus to insulin release via the enteroinsular axis, a term coined to describe the transmission of signals from gut to pancreas. The presence of this axis explains the greater insulin response to oral as opposed to intravenous glucose. Thus the postnatal surge in the basal GIP concentration (see Fig 3–5), together with the development of a further GIP elevation following a feed, may result in the progressive enhancement of insulin release and glucose tolerance described in the neonatal period.[1]

The pattern of gut hormone release after birth is markedly influenced by the mode of feeding and by the nature of the diet.[15] Major differences in gut hormone release in 6-day-old breast-fed and formula-fed infants are shown in Figure 3–6. The long-term significance of these early differences is an important area for investigation.

Influence of Colostrum and Breast Milk on Adaptation

Human milk contains both nutrient and non-nutrient proteins. The former consist largely of alpha-lactalbumin and casein (see Chapter 11). Cow's milk casein is less well digested than that in human milk. The contributions of breast milk digestive enzymes were discussed previously. Immunoglobulin A is found in high concentrations in colostrum and, through the enteromammary circulation, may afford the newborn specific protection against exposure to microorganisms derived from the maternal gastrointestinal tract.[16]

There is evidence that breast-fed infants have a more rapid appearance and higher concentrations of IgA in mucosal secretions than those fed formula. We have been unable to detect differences in circulating levels of IgA in relation to either feed composition or postconceptual age in healthy neonates[17] (Fig 3–7), suggesting that, rather than

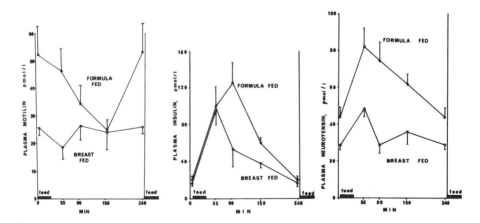

FIG 3–6.
Effects of breast feed and formula feed on plasma motilin, insulin, and neurotensin in 6-day-old infants [mean ± standard error of the mean (SEM)] (From Lucas A, Bloom SR, Aynsley-Green A: Gastrointestinal peptides and the adaptation to extrauterine nutrition. *Can J Physiol Pharmacol* 1985; 63:527. Used by permission.)

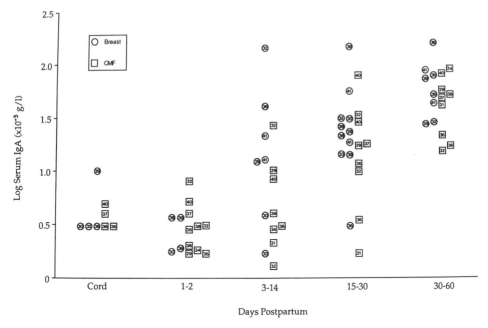

FIG 3–7.
Relation between gestational age at birth (numbers within symbols; weeks) postnatal age (days), compostion of feeds, and serum IgA concentrations in the newborn. (Unpublished data of Wadd N, Weaver LT, Taylor C, and Toms GL, 1989.)

representing uptake of colostral IgA, factors in breast milk stimulate local production of IgA or plasma cell proliferation in the intestinal mucosa, from which IgA or activated cells pass to other epithelial sites. Secretory IgA is active at mucosal surfaces and, with lactoferrin, lysozyme, complement, interferon, and protease inhibitors, may confer protection against microbial infection (see Table 3–2). Milk also contains viable white blood cells, including polymorphonuclear leucocytes, macrophages, and both T and B lymphocytes, which may contribute to induction of IgA activity.

There is a range of other physiologically active macromolecules in human milk which, secreted against a concentration gradient, may play a role in perinatal adaptation. These include hormones, trophic factors, prostaglandins, and other anti-inflammatory agents[18] (see Table 3–2). Of these, hydrocortisone and epidermal growth factor (EGF) present in amniotic fluid and milk, have been shown to modulate mucosal differentiation in the fetal small intestine and that of the suckling. The EGF, found in high concentrations in saliva, colostrum, and milk, as well as gastric and duodenal secretions, bile, amniotic fluid, and urine, has mitogenic, antisecretory, and protective effects. Together these properties suggest that EGF may be important in neonatal adaptation to enteral feeding.[19]

The recent development of methods of explant culture of fetal intestine, coupled with our growing understanding of the biologic effects of EGF in laboratory animals, has opened the way for examination of the regulatory mechanisms of this growth factor in human gut development. Cultures of human fetal jejunum of 11 to 14 days postconceptual age shows induction of lactase and suppression of sucrase, trehalase and glucoamylase activities, but depression of deoxyribonucleic acid (DNA) synthesis, in the presence of increasing concentrations of EGF. Simultaneous administration of hydrocortisone and EGF caused no synergistic action on expression of hydrolase activities, but hydrocortisone-stimulated DNA synthesis was inhibited by EGF.[20]

These studies are made all the more relevant by the detection of EGF in human fetal gut and amniotic fluid as early as 12 weeks of gestation, EGF receptors on fetal entero-cytes, and a recent report of a greater urinary excretion of EGF in the urine of infants fed breast milk containing the growth factor.[21] They suggest that physiologically active EGF, present in amniotic fluid, colostrum, and milk, may not only be active at the mu-cosal surface, but also be absorbed and contribute to systemic metabolism during the perinatal period.

CLINICAL IMPLICATIONS

Neonatal life is a critical period when the immature gut may be vulnerable to both luminal and extraintestinal insults leading to immediate and possibly long-term effects. It is also a period when the gut is sensitive to stimuli that may program later responses of the gastrointestinal mucosa and systemic metabolism.

Necrotizing Enterocolitis

Necrotising enterocolitis (NEC) is a severe failure of adaptation of the gastrointes-tinal tract to extrauterine life. It is primarily a disease of the preterm infant of very low birth weight and occurs most frequently within the 1st week of postnatal life. The inci-dence of NEC ranges from around 0.5 to 15 per 1,000 live births, and in infants weigh-ing less than 1.5 kg it may approach 8%. The disease appears to be a pathologic re-sponse of the immature intestine to injury by a variety of factors which have a complex interrelation (Fig 3–8). It has been suggested that damage to the mucosa, the presence of bacteria, and a metabolic substrate (feeds) in the intestine are all necessary for the development of the disease.

Mucosal Injury
The small intestine is served by the superior mesenteric artery, which divides into branches within the mesentery to form arcades of arterioles supplying the submucosa and mucosa. Vulnerable to underperfusion, reduced oxygenation of the mucosa may lead to ischemic damage. Aberrant patterns of blood flow in the fetal aorta suggestive of peripheral hypoxia may be associated with the development of neonatal NEC. Systemic hypotension may lead to diversion of cardiac output to organs apparently more precious than the gut, analogous to the diving reflex of aquatic mammals in which gut perfusion is reduced to maintain adequate cerebral blood flow in the face of hypoxia. Patent duc-tus arteriosus, with left-to-right shunting and retrograde flow in the aorta during diastole may diminish superior mesenteric artery blood flow, and umbilical artery and venous catheters may cause vascular insufficiency by either reducing mesenteric artery blood flow or generating emboli from thrombus in the aorta or its branches. The association between umbilical venous catheters and NEC may be related to the use of catheters for exchange transfusion, but with the disappearance of Rhesus factor disease this possible cause of NEC has diminished.

The microvillous membrane of the neonatal epithelium is immature in its barrier properties compared with that of the mature gut, and relative deficiency of mucus and secretory IgA may fail to protect the mucosal surface from damage by milk and bacterial

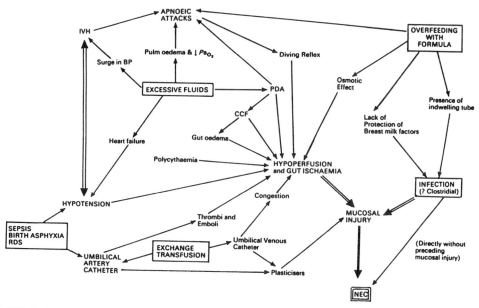

FIG 3–8.

Interrelation of etiologic factors associated with necrotizing enterocolitis. (From Lucas A, Roberton NRC: *Recent Advances in Obstetrics and Gynaecology, 14,* New York, Churchill Livingstone, 1982; pp 115–160. Used by permission.)

antigens.[22] Oral administration of IgA–IgG recently has been shown to lessen the incidence of NEC.[23] The neonatal gut, particularly that of the preterm infant, is more permeable to the passage of both small and large molecules. Mucosal damage may lead to further loss of integrity of the intestinal epithelium, and the resulting increased mucosal permeability may contribute to the uptake of microorganisms and toxins. Corticosteroids, which promote intestinal maturation in other species, given prenatally, may protect against the development of NEC.

Enteral Feeds

Enteral feeds may predispose to NEC by a number of mechanisms (see Fig 3–8), and nearly all infants who develop NEC have received oral feeds. Intraluminal milk may provide the substrate necessary for bacterial proliferation, and it has been shown that hydrogen (which accounts for 30% of both mural and intraluminal gas in infants with NEC) is produced in the gut only in the presence of milk or 50% glucose feeds. The incidence of NEC varies directly with the volume of enteral feeds; it is diminished when enteral feeding is delayed or replaced by total parenteral nutrition. Hyperosmolar feeding and a rapid rise in feed volumes (in an attempt to increase caloric intake) is associated with NEC. Cow's milk, soya proteins, and even nonhuman proteins in breast milk, may damage the immature gut, producing the syndrome, but there is no convincing evidence that the incidence of NEC is reduced when human milk is used in preference to nonhuman milk formulas.

Microbial Infection

Although there is little evidence that NEC is primarily and exclusively an infectious disease, microbial infection is clearly an important etiologic factor. Infants with NEC often have a septicemia, but no organism is consistently associated with the disease.

Blood cultures may be positive in many cases and often correlate closely with isolates from stool or peritoneal fluid. It seems likely that the damaged gut allows enteric organisms to traverse the mucosa to the circulation.[24]

The fecal flora of babies who suffer NEC may differ from those of the healthy preterm infant, and the relatively sterile environment of the hospitalized preterm infant may favor the unhindered proliferation of one or a few potentially pathogenic species. The *Clostridia* produce a potent toxin that may be isolated from the stools of infants during epidemics of NEC, though it is not usually found in sporadic cases of NEC, except in association with Hirschsprung's disease.

Prevention

Guidelines for the prevention of NEC are largely empirical because the precise etiology of the disease is unclear. Early removal of umbilical artery catheters—especially if there is evidence of thrombosis, such as difficulty withdrawing blood, or discoloration of the infant's toes or feet during infusion—should be undertaken. Because of the positive relation between fluid intake and incidence of NEC, maintenance of intravenous fluids to a minimum compatible with normal hydration is advised. In the low-birth-weight infant enteral feeding should be introduced slowly and a check made (by regular gastric aspiration) that milk is not pooling in the stomach. Evidence of normal gastrointestinal motility (meconium has been passed, the abdomen is not distended, and bowel sounds are audible) should be confirmed. Small, non-nutritional volumes of milk may contribute to the maturation of the gut of the preterm (discussed in the following section). The oral administration of milk or drugs of high osmolarity should be avoided and episodes of hypotension, hypoxia, and hypothermia minimized. Prophylactic antibiotics have not been shown to have a consistent benefit.

Minimal Enteral Feeding

As outlined earlier, trophic factors in the fetus, amniotic fluid, colostrum, and milk may all contribute to the regulation of gut development and perinatal adaptation. Those changes in circulating gut hormones that occur in the neonatal period in response to mode and composition of feeds, and to postconceptual age, probably play a part in the regulation of acid secretion, mucosal growth, gut motility, pancreatic secretion, gall bladder contraction, and epithelial differentiation and function. All these processes are involved in the adaptation of the neonatal gastrointestinal tract to enteral nutrition, and it has been shown that infants deprived of oral feeds exhibit no postnatal rise in gut hormones comparable to fed controls[15] (Fig 3–9). This observation has led to the speculation that "minimal enteral feeding" might have a valuable biologic role. Preliminary studies have indicated that very small quantities of intraluminal milk are required to induce postnatal gut hormone surges[25] (Fig 3–10). Such findings suggest that subnutritional quantities of food may have a maturational effect on the neonatal alimentary system and accelerate adaptation to oral feeding. In the preterm infant deprived of feeds for nongastroenterologic reasons, and in neonates who have undergone surgery for congenital gut anomalies, minimal enteral nutrition may be of clinical value. In one study of preterm infants, introduction of minimal enteral feeding (also described as hypocaloric feeding) was associated with improvments in weight gain, bone mineralization, and hepatobiliary function.[26]

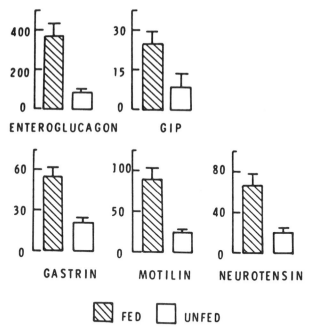

FIG 3–9.
Basal plasma concentrations of gut hormones (pmol/L ± SEM) on the 6th postnatal day in preterm infants enterally fed from birth compared with those deprived of oral nutrition and maintained on intravenous dextrose. (From Lucas A, Bloom SR, Aynsley-Green A: Gastrointestinal peptides and the adaptation to extrauterine nutrition. *Can J Physiol Pharmacol* 1985; 63:527. Used by permission.)

Programming by Early Diet

The possibility that the nutrient composition of diet in early life may have long-term effects on gastrointestinal function is an important area for future research. In animal studies phenotypic regulation of glucose and amino acid transport in the jejunum occur in response to changes in diet: prolonged lactose feeding in rats increases total intestinal lactase activity and diminishes the rate of enzyme decline at weaning. Adult mice switched from a high-protein, carbohydrate-free food to a low-protein, carbohydrate-rich diet exhibit a rise in glucose transporter activity and a decline in amino acid transporter activity. The reverse diet switch produces the opposite changes in transporter activity.[27] Early diet may also have long-term irreversible effects on nutrient transport, as well as gut and body size in rats. Animals weaned onto a high carbohydrate diet have higher rates of glucose absorption when full-grown than those weaned onto a carbohydrate-free, high-protein diet.[28] Such critical-period programming has potential implications for our nutritional management of the newborn. In humans, certain patterns of gut hormone release described in the neonatal period persist into infancy, raising the possibility that these hormones could act as intermediaries between early diet and later gastrointestinal function and metabolism.

From a deleterious point of view, antigenic components of milk and early diet may damage the intestinal mucosa and tolerize or sensitize the growing infant to food proteins encountered in later life. Milk protein intolerance, with small intestinal enteropathy and colitis, has been described in infants receiving cow's milk and soya formulas, and even breast milk.[29] Intrauterine growth retardation and postnatal malnutrition are associ-

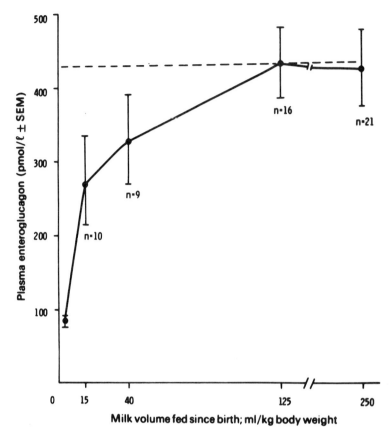

FIG 3–10.
Relation between plasma enteroglucagon concentrations (pmol/L ± SEM) and volume of milk consumed from birth (mL/kg body weight) in preterm infants. Rise after 15 mL/kg; $P < .001$. (From Lucas A, Bloom SR, Aynsley-Green A: Gastrointestinal peptides and the adaptation to extrauterine nutrition. *Can J Physiol Pharmacol* 1985; 63:527–537. Used by permission.)

ated with depression of mucosal and pancreatic enzyme activities. Neonatal life therefore appears to be a critical period when the immature gut is responsive to stimuli that facilitate neonatal adaptation and may program later nutritional and metabolic processes, but is also vulnerable to mucosal damage and stimuli that may mediate future disordered immunologic function.

FUTURE DIRECTIONS

The past decade has seen an enormous amount of illuminating work on the ontogeny of the mammalian gut, which has provided us with a growing understanding of the processes involved in gastrointestinal development. However, insights gained from the study of laboratory and farm animals should be generalized to humans with caution. While the overall development of the mammalian gut follows a common course, there are significant differences between species that are related to time of birth, neonatal nutrition (composition of colostrum and milk), and postnatal growth rates. Techniques of cell and tissue culture and organ transplantation now offer opportunities to transfer our studies of gut ontogeny to humans in order to test those hypotheses arising from animal models.

Transplantation of segments of gut to syngeneic or athymic hosts promises to extend the viability of explants and to permit studies of isolated gut segments over an extended period. Following its use in laboratory animals, where the influence of luminal and inherent ("hard-wired") triggers on mucosal enzyme expression have been elegantly distinguished,[30] the technique has now been extended to the study of the developing human gut.

Subcutaneous isografts of fetal human intestine in athymic mice regenerate, are revascularized, and become viable—affording an opportunity to study the late gestation phases of prenatal gut development. Through study of mouse and rat gut glucose and amino acid uptake, peristalsis and brush-border enzyme expression have been demonstrated.[31] Preliminary experiments on human gut of 20 week's gestation have been used to measure crypt cell production rate and enterocyte antigen expression, using monoclonal antibodies to disaccharidases and other microvillus membrane components.[32] This exciting new technique will shed light on the factors that govern the ontogeny of the human gut, in particular those of importance for our understanding of the gastrointestinal function and nutritional management of the newborn baby.

REFERENCES

1. Aynsley-Green A: The control of adaptation to postnatal nutrition. *Monogr Paediatr* 1982; 16:59–87.
2. Colony PC: Successive phases of human fetal intestinal development, in Kretchmer N, Minkowski A (eds): *Nutritional Adaptation of the Gastrointestinal Tract of the Newborn.* New York, Raven Press, 1983, pp 3–28.
3. Milla PJ (ed): *Disorders of Gastrointestinal Motility in Childhood.* New York, John Wiley & Sons, 1988, pp 17–50.
4. Weaver LT: Bowel habit from birth to old age. *J Pediatr Gastroenterol Nutr* 1988; 7:637–640.
5. Weaver LT, Walker WA: Uptake, sorting and transport of macromolecules in the neonate, and their relationship to the structure of the microvillus, in Lebenthal E (ed): *Textbook of Gastroenterology and Nutrition in Early Childhood,* ed 2. New York, Raven Press, 1989, pp 731–748.
6. Hamosh M: Lingual and breast milk lipases. *Adv Pediatr* 1982; 29:33–67.
7. Weaver LT, Laker MF, Nelson R: Intestinal permeability in the newborn. *Arch Dis Child* 1984; 59:236–241.
8. Weaver LT, Laker MF, Nelson R: Neonatal intestinal lactase activity. *Arch Dis Child* 1986; 61:896–899.
9. Potter GD, Lester R: The developing colon and nutrition. *J Pediatr Gastroenterol Nutr* 1984; 3:485–487.
10. Lebenthal E, Lee PC: Interactions of determinants in the ontogeny of the gastrointestinal tract: A unified concept. *Pediatr Res* 1983; 17:19–24.
11. Haffen K, Kedinger M, Simon-Assmann P: Mesenchyme-dependent differentiation of epithelial progenitor cells in the gut. *J Pediatr Gastroenterol Nutr* 1987; 6:14–23.
12. Henning SJ: Ontogeny of enzymes in the small intestine. *Ann Rev Physiol* 1985; 47:231–245.
13. Buchan AMJ, Bryant MG, Polak JM, et al: Development of regulatory peptides in the human fetal intestine, in Bloom SR, Polak JM (eds): *Gut Hormones.* London, Churchill Livingstone, 1981, pp 119–126.

14. Aynsley-Green A: Metabolic and endocrine interrelations in the human fetus and neonate. *Am J Clin Nutr* 1985; 41:339–417.

15. Lucas A, Bloom SR, Aynsley-Green A: Gastrointestinal peptides and the adaptation to extrauterine nutrition. *Can J Physiol Pharmacol* 1985; 63:527–537.

16. Kleinman RE, Walker WA: The enteromammary immune system. *Dig Dis Sci* 1979; 24:876–882.

17. Wadd N, Weaver LT, Taylor C, et al: Unpublished data, 1989.

18. Koldovsky O, Thornburg W: Hormones in milk. *J Pediatr Gastroenterol Nutr* 1987; 6:172–196.

19. Weaver LT, Walker WA: Epidermal growth factor and the developing human gut. *Gastroenterology* 1988; 94:845–847.

20. Menard D, Arsenault P, Pothier P: Biologic effects of epidermal growth factor in human fetal jejunum. *Gastroenterology* 1988; 94:656–663.

21. Gale SM, Read LC, Nascimento CG, et al: Is dietary epidermal growth factor absorbed by premature human infants? *Biol Neonate* 1989; 55:104–110.

22. Walker WA: Antigen penetration across the immature gut: Effect of immunologic and maturational factors in colostrum, in Ogra PL, Dayton D (eds): *Immunology of Breast Milk.* New York, Raven Press, 1979, pp 227–235.

23. Eibl MM, Wolf HM, Furnkranz H, et al: Prevention of necrotizing enterocolitis in low-birth-weight infants by IgA–IgG feeding. *N Engl J Med* 1988; 319:1–7.

24. Lake AM, Walker WA: Neonatal necrotizing enterocolitis: A disease of altered host defense. *Clin Gastroenterol* 1977; 6:463–480.

25. Lucas A, Bloom SR, Aynsley-Green A: Gut hormones and 'minimal enteral feeding.' *Acta Paediatr Scand* 1986; 75:719–723.

26. Dunn L, Hulman S, Weiner J, et al: Beneficial effects of early hypocaloric enteral feeding on neonatal gastrointestinal function: Preliminary report of a randomized trial. *J Pediatr* 1988; 112:622–629.

27. Karasov WH, Diamond JM: Adaptive regulation of sugar and amino acid transport by vertebrate intestine. *Am J Physiol* 1983; 245:G443–G462.

28. Karasov WH, Soldberg DH, Chang SD, et al: Is intestinal transport of sugars and amino-acids subject to critical-period programming? *Am J Physiol* 1985; 249:G770–G785.

29. Stern M, Walker WA: Milk allergy and intolerance. *Pediatr Clin North Am* 1985; 32:471–492.

30. Diamond JM: Hard-wired local triggering of intestinal enzyme expression. *Nature* 1986; 324:408.

31. Friedberg JS, Ryan DP, Driscoll SG, et al: Human small bowel transplants into athymic mice and rats. *Surg Forum* 1986; 375–378.

32. Weaver LT, Hendren RB, Quaroni A, et al: Crypt cell production rate and surface membrane characteristics of transplanted human fetal small intestine. *Gut* 1988; 29:A1493.

PART II

Specific Nutrients

Chapter 4

Carbohydrates: Metabolism and Disorders

Jane E. DiGiacomo

The importance of carbohydrates in the metabolism of the newborn has been recognized since the report of Cornblath in 1959 which associated the occurrence of neonatal hypoglycemia with increased neonatal morbidity and mortality. Carbohydrates provide substrates for fetal and neonatal metabolism, supplying both immediately usable and stored energy as well as carbon skeletons for macromolecule synthesis and tissue accretion.

FETAL CARBOHYDRATE METABOLISM

Glucose and lactate are the major carbohydrates which, along with amino acids, serve as substrates for fetal metabolism and growth. Glucose in the maternal circulation is transferred to the fetus by facilitated diffusion across the placenta and taken up by the umbilical circulation. At term, fetal plasma glucose concentration is approximately two thirds of the maternal plasma glucose concentration. Studics in animal models have established that in the unstressed physiologic state, umbilical uptake provides enough glucose to maintain the normal fetal glucose utilization rate. Thus when the normal maternal glucose supply is available, there is no significant fetal hepatic glucose production. However, gluconeogenic enzymes are present in the fetus as early as 10 weeks of gestation. Net fetal glucose production has been detected in fetal lambs during chronic stress (e.g., chronic maternal hypoglycemia),[11] although it is not known whether this glucose is produced by gluconeogenesis or glycogenolysis. A recent study[5] of the relationship between maternal and fetal glucose concentrations at mid gestation in humans also demonstrated that although fetal glucose concentration was usually less than the mother's, in several cases in which the maternal level was less than 80 mg/dL, fetal glucose concentration equalled or exceeded maternal concentration. This finding suggests that fetal glucose production was induced by the relative maternal hypoglycemia.

Glucose utilized by the fetus is available for both fetal oxidative metabolism and as a source of carbon for accretion of glycogen and synthesis of other organic compounds. Under normal conditions, 60% to 70% of glucose utilized by the fetus is oxidized to carbon dioxide, with the remainder available for synthetic processes. The glucose/oxygen quotient in most mammals is less than 1 (in the human fetus, for example, it is approximately 0.8), indicating that oxidation of glucose alone does not account for total fetal oxygen consumption and that other substrates must contribute to fetal oxidative metabolism. Estimates of the net fetal carbon accretion rate based on fetal body composition and rate of growth suggest that glucose also is not the sole source of carbon for tissue accretion.

Several factors regulate fetal glucose metabolism. Umbilical glucose uptake is affected by the maternal-fetal glucose concentration gradient, and may also be altered when uterine blood flow is severely reduced. Studies in fetal sheep have shown that both fetal insulin and glucose concentrations independently affect fetal glucose utilization rate.[16] Neither maternal nor fetal insulin concentration appears to regulate placental glucose consumption and placental-fetal glucose transfer; instead, studies have suggested that placental glucose metabolism is controlled by changes in fetal glucose concentration.

Insulin is present in the pancreas of the human fetus by 8 to 10 weeks gestation. Because insulin does not cross the placenta, the increasing levels noted during the last third of gestation must reflect increased fetal pancreatic release. Fetal insulin concentration affects fetal glucose metabolism but is probably more important as a growth factor. The fetal pancreas appears to be less sensitive to changes in glucose concentration than that of the adult. Nevertheless, insulin secretion is augmented by acute fetal hyperglycemia; this effect is intensified if amino acid uptake is increased concomitantly. Acute increases in insulin concentration enhance both fetal glucose utilization and glucose oxidation rates without increasing total fetal oxygen consumption. This implies that the oxidation rate of other substrates (e.g. amino acids) is reduced, making more substrate available for nonoxidative metabolism. Increased substrate availability may in turn promote tissue accretion and growth.

Glucagon is present by the beginning of the second trimester, but at normal fetal and maternal glucose concentrations does not appear to have a significant regulatory function. For example, Devaskar et al.[10] have reported that fetal glucose utilization is not altered by acute changes in fetal glucagon concentration. Acute hypoglycemia does not induce glucagon secretion, but increased fetal glucagon concentrations have been measured in response to chronic fetal hypoglycemia after maternal fasting. Because elevated glucagon concentrations induce synthesis of gluconeogenic enzymes, the glucagon response to chronic hypoglycemia may be one of the mechanisms responsible for the appearance of fetal glucose production under these conditions.

Glycogen is the major form of stored carbohydrate in the fetus. Although glycogen synthesis begins as early as the 9th week of gestation in the human embryo, most glycogen is accumulated during the last 30% of gestation; this pattern has been observed in several species.[30] Levels of glycogen in lung and cardiac muscle decline slightly as the fetus approaches term. The decrease in lung glycogen stores may reflect the energy requirement of ongoing developmental processes such as surfactant synthesis. Cardiac glycogen stores may serve as a significant energy source during periods of stress; for example, survival after asphyxia appears to be related to cardiac glycogen content.[26]

Both skeletal muscle and hepatic glycogen content reach 3 to 5 times adult levels by the end of gestation and form an important energy storage pool for the fetus and newborn. The relatively high insulin:glucagon ratio present in the fetus preferentially stimulates glycogen synthesis and suppresses glycogenolysis by means of a multi-enzyme regulatory system. Hepatic glycogen synthesis is controlled by the levels of the active forms of two enzymes: glycogen synthase and glycogen phosphorylase. Although insulin concentration does not alter the total concentration of these enzymes, the fetal insulin:glucagon ratio maintains glycogen synthase in the active form and glycogen phosphorylase in the inactive form, therefore favoring glycogen synthesis and inhibiting glycogenolysis.[4] (Fig 4–1) Cortisol and glucose also activate glycogen synthase and inactivate glycogen phosphorylase. An increase in fetal cortisol levels as well as insulin concentration appears to be necessary to induce the increased rate of glycogen synthesis during the last third of gestation. Although hypoglycemia alone does not change the amount of active synthase present, increased concentrations of glucagon or catecholamines stimulate phosphorylation of the enzymes, resulting in inactivation of synthase, activation of phosphorylase, and subsequent glycogenolysis. Thus when the fetus is stressed, for example, during hypoxia or chronic hypoglycemia, glycogenolysis may be stimulated and glycogenesis inhibited.

The role of lactate in fetal metabolism is less clear. The finding of significant lactate concentrations in fetal blood was originally interpreted as a metabolic response to the low fetal arterial oxygen content. However, recent studies have shown that lactate is synthesized in the placenta from other molecules—most likely glucose from the maternal or fetal circulation—and taken up by the umbilical circulation. It, too, can be oxidized or used to synthesize other compounds including glycogen and amino acids. Studies in animal models have shown both net hepatic uptake of lactate and incorporation of radioactive lactate into fetal hepatic glycogen, supporting its role as a fetal carbon source.

The importance of fructose and galactose in fetal carbohydrate metabolism has not been demonstrated in humans. Fructose is of interest to investigators because it is present in high concentrations in the ruminant fetus. Fructose turnover and oxidation rates are low, but a slow decline in fetal fructose concentration has been observed during prolonged maternal starvation, suggesting that it may serve as a metabolic substrate when glucose supply is reduced. Galactose also is not a usual substrate for fetal metabolism. However, the enzymes necessary for galactose metabolism are present in high concentrations during fetal life, and the fetus seems able to metabolize galactose when it is provided. Galactose activates glycogen synthase in the monkey, and a significant rate of galactose incorporation into hepatic glycogen has been measured following galactose administration to fetal rats. However, since virtually no galactose is transferred from the maternal to the fetal circulation, it is unlikely that galactose plays an important role in fetal metabolism. More likely the experimental observations reflect the preparation of the fetal metabolism for the transition to neonatal life.

CHANGES IN CARBOHYDRATE METABOLISM AFTER DELIVERY

At delivery, the glucose supply from the placenta is abruptly interrupted, and blood glucose concentration in the neonate falls. Several hormonal and metabolic changes occur at birth which facilitate the adaptation necessary to maintain glucose homeostasis. Both catecholamines and thyroxine levels increase shortly after birth, possibly in response to cold stress or cord cutting. Glucagon concentration also begins to increase, peaking during the first 2 hours of life and reversing the insulin:glucagon ratio. The increasing catecholamine and glucagon concentrations alter the ratio of the active forms of glycogen synthase and glycogen phosphorylase, stimulating hepatic glycogenolysis (see Fig 4–1) Simultaneously, the falling blood glucose concentration stimulates synthesis of glucose-6-phosphatase, which increases hepatic glucose output. During the first

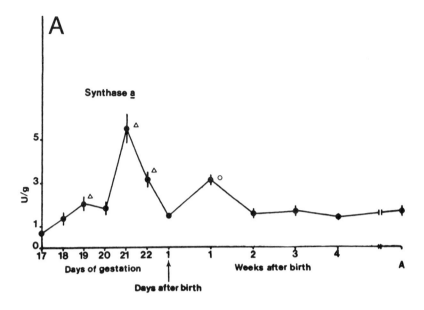

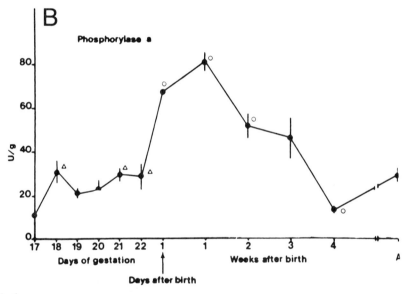

FIG 4–1.
Effect of gestational and postnatal age on **(A)** hepatic glycogen synthase content (active form); **(B)** hepatic glycogen phosphorylase content (active form); and **(C)** ratio of active glycogen synthase to active glycogen phosphorylase. Values shown are mean ± standard error of the mean (SEM) as determined in rat liver. (Adapted from Margolis RN: Regulation of hepatic glycogen metabolism in pre- and postnatal rats. *Endocrinology* 1983; 113:893–902. Used by permission.)   *(Continued)*

few hours of life, skeletal muscle glycogen is also rapidly consumed, producing lactate, which is used to meet local tissue energy requirements. Lactate may be oxidized directly through the tricarboxylic acid cycle, bypassing gluconeogenesis.

Gluconeogenesis is also promoted by the postpartum hormonal milieu. The reversal of the insulin:glucagon ratio after delivery induces synthesis of the gluconeogenic en-

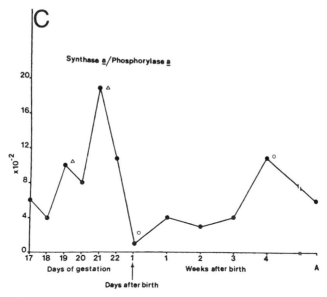

FIG 4-1   (cont.).

zymes, particularly phosphoenolpyruvate carboxykinase (PEPCK), which appears to be the rate-limiting enzyme in establishment of effective hepatic gluconeogenesis. Glucagon also stimulates an increase in the ratio of adenosine triphosphate to adenosine diphosphate in hepatic mitochondria and stimulates pyruvate carboxylase activity, two factors which may also contribute to the increasing rate of gluconeogenesis.[6] Because there is a time lag in synthesis of significant amounts of gluconeogenic enzymes, glycogenolysis remains the primary source of hepatic glucose production during the first few hours of life. By 4 to 6 hours, levels of PEPCK and other enzymes are high enough to promote glucose synthesis, although adult enzyme concentrations are not achieved for 1 to 2 weeks.

NEONATAL CARBOHYDRATE METABOLISM

Glucose metabolism in the neonate differs from adult metabolism in several ways. The normal glucose utilization rate in the term newborn is 3.5 to 5.5 mg/min/kg, approximately twice the weight-specific rate of the healthy adult. As in the fetus, approximately half of the glucose utilized is oxidized during normal metabolic processes, while the remainder is used in non-oxidative pathways, such as glycogen and fat synthesis.[9] The brain is the major consumer of glucose in the neonate, and under normal conditions relies almost exclusively on glucose for its metabolism. However, studies in rats suggest that the neonatal brain may be able to utilize lactate directly if glucose supply is reduced[25]; this metabolic adaptation has not been demonstrated in humans.

The regulatory system for maintaining glucose homeostasis is not fully mature in the newborn and is less sensitive to feedback control. Although glucose infusion suppresses hepatic glucose release in adults, some term and preterm infants maintain hepatic glucose production even when exogenous glucose is administered at a rate equal to utilization rate.[8] In contrast to the adult, hepatic glucose production in the neonate seems to be regulated not by a change in glucose concentration, but by the change in insulin concentration induced by variations in blood glucose.[34] At the same time, the neonatal liver is relatively insensitive to insulin effects. To produce similar changes in hepatic metabolism, a three times greater change in insulin concentration is needed in the infant than in the adult. The ratio of insulin to glucagon, rather than the absolute insulin concentration, may also be a factor in the control of hepatic glucose production.

If feeding with breast milk or a cow's milk–based formula is initiated, lactose becomes the major carbohydrate source for the neonate. To use lactose, the neonate must be able to convert it to the two monosaccharides, glucose and galactose, and then utilize these two components. The neonatal liver seems to metabolize galactose more readily than glucose. Thus galactose taken up by way of the portal circulation is rapidly cleared from the blood. Following a milk feeding, both galactose and glucose levels in the blood increase, but the change in glucose concentration is of greater magnitude, confirming the efficient clearance of galactose from the circulation[31] (Fig 4–2). While glucokinase levels are low at birth, galactokinase levels are at their peak, allowing phosphorylation of galactose and subsequent metabolism. Studies of glycogen synthesis from

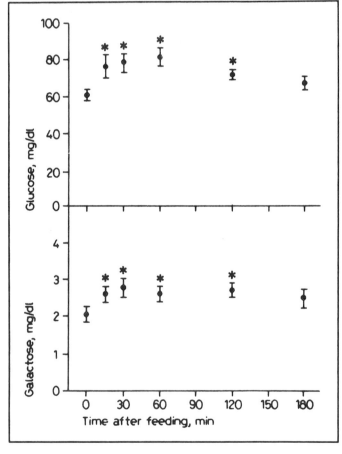

FIG 4–2.
Blood concentrations of galactose and glucose in milk-fed term infants after feeding (From Siegel CD, Sparks JW, Battaglia FC: Patterns of serum glucose and galactose concentrations in term newborn infants after milk feeding. *Biol Neonate* 1988; 54:301–306. Used by permission.)

glucose and galactose in newborn animals[20] have shown that galactose is incorporated more quickly, suggesting glycogen synthesis by a direct pathway, while incorporation of glucose into glycogen takes longer, suggesting that glucose may be incorporated indirectly by way of smaller intermediates that are recombined to form glucose-6-phosphate and then glycogen.

DISORDERS OF CARBOHYDRATE METABOLISM

Pathophysiology

Most disorders of neonatal carbohydrate metabolism result from disturbances of glucose homeostasis. Maintenance of normal glucose homeostasis depends on the balance between hepatic glucose output and peripheral glucose utilization. Hepatic glucose output, in turn, is a function of the rates of glycogenolysis and gluconeogenesis, while peripheral glucose utilization varies with the metabolic demands placed on the neonate. Some circumstances in which peripheral utilization are increased include (1) hypoxia, as anaerobic metabolism of glucose is less efficient than aerobic glycolysis; (2) hyperinsulinemia, which increases glucose uptake by the insulin-sensitive tissues; and (3) cold stress, which results in an increased metabolic rate. If rates of glycogenolysis and gluconeogenesis do not match the rate of glucose utilization because of failure of the hormonal control mechanisms or inadequacy of substrate supply, then disturbances of glucose homeostasis occur.

Hypoglycemia

Neonatal hypoglycemia has been defined as a whole blood glucose concentration in the first 72 hours of life of less than 35 mg/dL in the term infant and less than 25 mg/dL in the premature infant. These figures were obtained by determining the glucose concentration 2 standard deviations (SD) less than the mean of random glucose measurements obtained from a large population of infants. Although convenient as a guideline, these values may misdefine "physiologic" hypoglycemia for several reasons. First, as feeding practices have changed, the pattern of blood glucose concentrations measured in population studies has also changed. Srinivasan and associates[33] found that glucose concentrations were higher on the 2nd and 3rd days of life and suggested that the definition of hypoglycemia at 24 to 72 hours of age be revised upward accordingly (Fig 4–3). Second, brain glucose uptake is concentration dependent, and sensitive to changes in glucose levels. Thus for any given infant, hypoglycemia should be defined as the blood glucose concentration at which central nervous system (CNS) glucose delivery falls below the cerebral glucose requirement. By this definition, the presence of hypoglycemia may depend on factors other than the plasma glucose concentration. For example, infants with hyperviscosity syndrome may have normal plasma glucose concentrations but be symptomatic due to inadequate delivery of glucose to the CNS as a result of decreased cerebral plasma flow. A recent study[21] has also demonstrated that abnormal brain stem auditory evoked potentials may be detected in neonates at glucose concentrations ranging from 13 mg/dL to 45 mg/dL (Table 4–1). Thus the current definition of hypoglycemia must be considered a guideline to be combined with clinical observation to make an accurate diagnosis.

Many infants with hypoglycemia are asymptomatic when glucose concentration first declines. When present, signs of neonatal hypoglycemia are nonspecific and extremely

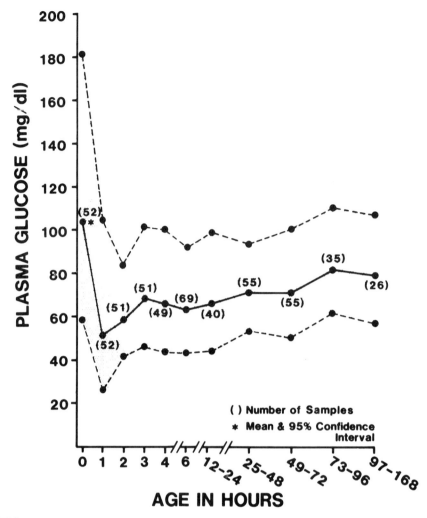

FIG 4–3.
Plasma glucose concentrations during the 1st week of life in healthy, appropriate-for-gestational age, term infants. (From Srinivasan G, Pildes RS, Cattamanchi G, et al: Plasma glucose values in normal neonates: A new look. *J Pediatr* 1986; 109:114–117. Used by permission.)

variable. They include general findings such as abnormal cry, poor feeding, hypothermia and diaphoresis; neurologic signs, including tremors and jitteriness, hypotonia, irritability, lethargy, and seizures; and cardiorespiratory disturbances, including cyanosis, pallor, tachypnea, periodic breathing, apnea, and cardiac arrest. These findings may also be seen in prematurity, sepsis, intraventricular hemorrhage, asphyxia, hypocalcemia, congenital heart disease, and structural CNS lesions, among other conditions. Resolution of symptoms following administration of glucose supports the diagnosis of hypoglycemia. Untreated hypoglycemic infants who are initially asymptomatic may develop symptoms if the low concentration of glucose persists.

Because hypoglycemia is often asymptomatic early in its course, most nurseries routinely screen infants considered to be at risk for this problem. Most screening methods used rely on the use of enzyme reagent test strips with or without a reflectance colorimeter to detect abnormal glucose concentrations. These methods must be used with

TABLE 4–1.

Effect of Glucose Concentration ([G]) on Neonatal Brain Stem Auditory Evoked Response (BAER)*

Patient	Age (days)	[G]normal† (mg/dL)	[G]abnormal‡ (mg/dL)	Symptoms	Time to Normal BAER§
1	1	43.2	25.2	None	1 hour
2	1	34.2	25.2	None	Immediate
3	2	37.8	34.2	None	Immediate
4	2	73.8	45.0	Drowsy	16 hours
5	3	75.6	12.6	None	2 days

* Adapted from Koh THHG, Aynsley-Green A, Tarbit M, et al: Neural dysfunction during hypoglycaemia. *Arch Dis Child* 1988; 63:1353–1358. Used by permission.
† Lowest glucose concentration at which normal BAER obtained.
‡ Glucose concentration when abnormal BAER obtained.
§ Time from administration of intravenous glucose until BAER returned to normal.

caution, since a detailed evaluation[7] has shown that the correlation between values obtained with these techniques and blood glucose values obtained from a blood sample using the glucose oxidase method is quite variable. Even when investigators were careful to use precise and proper techniques for specimen handling and reading results, these methods variably overestimated or underestimated glucose concentrations, and several cases of neonatal hypoglycemia would have been missed if test strips had been used as the sole diagnostic device. In the nursery setting, where technique is less likely to be consistent, more errors could be expected to occur.

Two groups of neonates are among those recognized to be at high risk of developing hypoglycemia. These are the infants of diabetic mothers (IDMs) and low-birth-weight (LBW) infants, whether premature or small for gestational age. Hyperinsulinemia is thought to be the cause of hypoglycemia in the IDM. In utero, maternal hyperglycemia directly causes fetal hyperglycemia, which stimulates the fetal beta-cells and produces fetal hyperinsulinemia as well as development of an abnormal pancreatic response to glucose. After delivery, the overabundant glucose supply ceases, but the abnormal pancreatic response is still present. Data suggest that the postpartum glucagon and catecholamine surge is also blunted in the IDM. These effects combine to maintain a high insulin:glucagon ratio, which inhibits glycogenolysis, lipolysis, and development of adequate gluconeogenesis. At the same time, the continued hyperinsulinemia increases peripheral glucose utilization by insulin-sensitive tissues such as skeletal muscle. As a result, the liver cannot produce enough glucose to meet the neonatal requirements, and hypoglycemia ensues. The incidence of hypoglycemia in IDMs ranges from 15% to 75% and is most often asymptomatic when initially diagnosed. Both the incidence and severity of the hypoglycemia may be related to the degree of maternal control during pregnancy, although this has not been adequately demonstrated experimentally.

Hyperinsulinemia causes neonatal hypoglycemia in a number of other clinical situations. Islet cell hyperplasia has been noted in infants with erythroblastosis fetalis. The proposed mechanism for this finding is that glutathiones released by hemolyzed red blood cells inactivate circulating insulin, leading to overproduction of insulin by the pancreas as it senses an apparent decrease in plasma insulin concentration. Exchange transfusion may further contribute to hypoglycemia in these infants, because the high dextrose content of banked blood further stimulates insulin release. Infants with Beckwith-Wiedemann syndrome have generalized organomegaly, including hyperplasia of the pancreas, and frequently have episodes of symptomatic hypoglycemia due to hyperinsulinemia. Idiopathic islet cell dysplasia such as nesidioblastosis and islet cell adenomas lead to persistent hyperinsulinemia, often with repeated episodes of severe, intractable hypoglycemia.

Drugs administered to pregnant women prior to delivery may also affect neonatal glucose homeostasis. The profound neonatal hypoglycemia noted after oral hypoglycemic agents were used to treat maternal diabetes mellitus led to discontinuation of their use in pregnancy. More recently, it has been suggested that use of beta-agonist tocolytic agents may stimulate pancreatic islet cell growth and cause fetal hyperinsulinemia. Elevated insulin concentrations have been measured in some infants following maternal tocolysis with such agents as fenoterol and terbutaline sulfate, but only one study noted any infants with hypoglycemia as a result.[29] Warburton and associates[35] have also reported stimulation of glycogenolysis in fetal lambs exposed to beta agonists in utero, which could compound the neonatal effects of hyperinsulinemia. Administration of intravenous fluids containing glucose to women in the 2 to 3 hours prior to delivery causes fetal hyperglycemia and hyperinsulinemia, and has been associated with neonatal hypoglycemia because of the persistent elevated insulin concentrations after delivery.[15]

The cause of hypoglycemia in LBW infants appears to be multifactorial. Glycogen stores are markedly reduced, but initial glycogenolysis proceeds at the same rate in infants with intrauterine growth retardation (IUGR) as in those with normal growth, resulting in rapid depletion of substrate.[19] Metabolic demands may also be increased for several reasons. All LBW infants, whether premature or growth retarded, have an increased ratio of surface area to body mass, which increases the amount of energy needed for thermoregulation. Glycogen and fat stores are also reduced, while metabolic demand may be increased by respiratory distress syndrome, infection, or asphyxia. In addition, infants with asymmetric growth retardation have an increased ratio of brain to body mass, which results in cerebral glucose requirements out of proportion to the liver's ability to respond. Some investigators have reported additional abnormalities of glucose kinetics in small-for-gestational age infants, including a higher than normal weight-specific glucose utilization rate, inappropriately high insulin levels, and a blunted metabolic response to hypoglycemia. In animal models for growth retardation that cause fetal hypoglycemia, induction of gluconeogenic enzymes is delayed despite increased glucagon levels.[17]

A number of other causes have been described in cases of neonatal hypoglycemia. These include sepsis, inborn errors of metabolism (such as glycogen storage disease type I), congenital heart disease, and malpositioning of umbilical artery catheters near the origin of the pancreatic artery. Endocrine disorders such as panhypopituitarism and hypothyroidism may also cause hypoglycemia, although other signs of endocrine dysfunction are usually present as well. Persistence of anaerobic metabolism following asphyxia may lead to rapid depletion of substrate and subsequent hypoglycemia, while hypothermia can also increase metabolic rate sufficiently to disturb glucose homeostasis.

Hyperglycemia

Criteria for the diagnosis of neonatal hyperglycemia vary from institution to institution, but blood glucose concentrations greater than 125 mg/dL in a term infant or greater than 150 mg/dL in a preterm infant are generally considered abnormally elevated. Many cases are iatrogenic and occur in infants receiving intravenous glucose solutions; incidence ranges from 5.5% overall to as high as 40% to 60% of infants weighing less than 1,000 g.[23] Hyperglycemia is usually asymptomatic and is diagnosed by screening for elevated blood glucose concentrations and the presence of glycosuria in infants at risk for this problem.

The physiologic consequences of hyperglycemia in the neonate are unclear. Glucose concentrations high enough to produce significant glycosuria and an osmotic diuresis may complicate fluid and electrolyte management. However, the development of this process in preterm infants with hyperglycemia has not been well documented; glycosuria is frequently noted in very low birth weight infants at normal glucose concentrations owing to renal immaturity, but rarely has a significant effect on urine output. There has been speculation that risk of intracranial hemorrhage is increased if serum osmolality is elevated due to high serum glucose concentrations; however, to produce a significant change in serum osmolality, glucose concentrations would have to be greater than 350 to 400 mg/dL, levels not often seen even in high-risk infants.

Several factors contribute to the development of glucose intolerance in the LBW infant. Pancreatic insulin secretion in response to a change in glucose concentration is blunted compared with secretion in term infants, as is the hepatic sensitivity to insulin.[18] Glucokinase levels are also reduced, limiting the ability to utilize glucose. Elevated catecholamine and glucocorticoid levels from the stress of pulmonary disease or infection may contribute to glucose intolerance in sick infants. Infants who are not receiving enteral feedings also have an increased incidence of hyperglycemia compared with those who are receiving some of their calories by the enteral route.

Although hyperglycemia is most often encountered in LBW infants, it has also been described in several other clinical settings. A number of cases of transient neonatal diabetes mellitus have been reported. This entity is characterized by insulin resistance present at birth but usually resolving over the first 1 to 2 weeks of life. Transient diabetes mellitus is often associated with IUGR but may also occur in appropriate-for-gestational age infants. Neonatal sepsis and treatment of apnea of prematurity with theophylline may cause hyperglycemia in some neonates. Elevated blood glucose concentrations have also been noted following surgery, probably due to stress-related hormones as well as the volumes of glucose-containing fluid sometimes administered during surgical procedures. This response may be reduced by the inclusion of opiates such as fentanyl citrate as part of the anesthesia regimen.[1]

Most disorders of metabolism of carbohydrates other than glucose are the result of inborn errors of metabolism, such as hereditary fructose intolerance and galactosemia, which are discussed elsewhere. However, disturbances of digestion and absorption of lactose are common in neonates, especially premature infants. Unlike the other disaccharidases (sucrase and maltase), lactase levels develop late in gestation. Small bowel lactase activity approaches term levels by 36 weeks gestation; at 28 to 30 weeks gestation lactase activity is only approximately 30% of activity at term. Infants less than 34 weeks gestation appear to digest most lactose in the large bowel, where colonic flora ferment lactose that has not been enzymatically digested in the small bowel. Thus these infants are especially susceptible to any disturbance in the normal colonic flora, such as occurs during treatment with broad spectrum antibiotics. Even in term neonates, use of antibiotics has been associated with lactose intolerance.[2]

Basic Requirements

Because the human brain uses glucose almost exclusively to meet its metabolic demands, there is an absolute glucose requirement equal to that necessary to provide an adequate glucose supply to the brain. Because glucose can be synthesized from a number of other molecules, including lactate, alanine, glycine, and free fatty acids, it is possible to meet this glucose requirement without direct administration of glucose. However, there are some advantages to the use of carbohydrates as a glucose source. While amino acids and fatty acids can be used, the metabolic processes used to convert these molecules to glucose are inefficient from a caloric standpoint, and may have other adverse metabolic effects. Metabolism of protein and amino acids may generate excessive amounts of nitrogenous waste and organic acids and contribute to metabolic acidosis, while metabolism of fats generates large quantities of ketone bodies as well as carbon dioxide, which the infant with lung disease may not be able to excrete. Provision of 40% to 60% of total caloric requirement as carbohydrate—corresponding to a carbohydrate intake of approximately 12 to 14 g/kg/day—will prevent these adverse effects. This is a minimum requirement and may need to be increased if metabolic demand is high (e.g., in tachypneic infants with increased muscle activity). In infants whose feedings consist of a lactose-based formula, half of administered carbohydrate will be glucose and half galactose. If lactose intolerance is present, however, substitution of sucrose or glucose polymers will adequately meet the recommended intake.

Treatment

Treatment of disturbances of carbohydrate metabolism are based for the most part on empirical regimens rather than careful clinical trials. In many institutions, mild asymptomatic hypoglycemia in otherwise stable infants may be treated with oral feeding of formula or glucose/water solutions. In prematures, infants with marked or symptomatic hypoglycemia, and those unresponsive to oral administration of glucose, intravenous glucose infusion is the treatment of choice. The "minibolus" regimen described by Lilien et al.[22] consists of a bolus of 200 mg/kg of glucose given as a 10% dextrose in water solution over 2 to 5 minutes followed by a continuous infusion of glucose at 4 to 6 mg/kg/min. Although this regimen has been shown to be superior to glucose infusion alone, no study has attempted to determine whether it is the optimum method for maintaining blood glucose concentrations.

The continuous infusion of glucose must be carefully titrated by following the infant's glucose concentration at frequent intervals, because some infants, especially those with hyperinsulinemia, may have much higher glucose utilization rates than anticipated. In such infants, there is a danger of overshooting the glucose requirement, causing increased insulin release and rebound hypoglycemia. Studies have shown that IDMs produce higher levels of insulin in response to a glucose infusion than normal infants[28] (Fig 4–4). In contrast, galactose infusion produced a smaller pancreatic response while resulting in similar blood glucose concentrations. Such data suggest that there may be an advantage to continuing feedings while administering intravenous glucose to treat hypoglycemia in such infants, or considering the possible use of a galactose infusion instead (discussed later). The glucose clamp technique, in which glucose infusion rate is adjusted according to an algorithm based on frequent (every 10 to 15 minute) monitoring of blood glucose concentrations has been used successfully in animals and humans to maintain blood glucose concentrations during studies of glucose metabolism. This technique has been used to establish glucose homeostasis in refractory neonatal hypoglycemia (W.W. Hay, Jr., unpublished data) and could prove useful in establishing normal glucose concentrations in infants with labile glucose metabolism, such as IDMs with severe hyperinsulinemia (Fig 4–5).

When intravenous glucose infusion rates of 12 to 15 mg/kg/min are required to

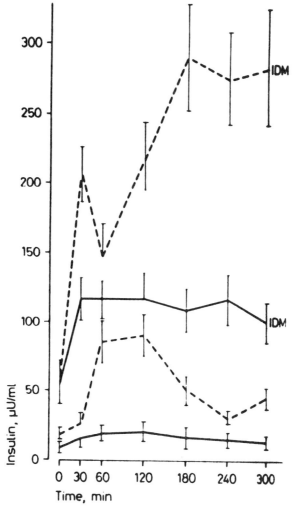

FIG 4–4.

Change in plasma insulin concentration (mean ± SEM) during infusion of glucose *(dashed line)* and galactose *(solid line)* in healthy infants and IDM's. (From Pribylova I, Kozlova J: Glucose and galactose infusions in newborns of diabetic and healthy mothers. *Biol Neonate* 1979; 36:193–197. Used by permission.)

maintain normal blood glucose concentrations, use of adjunct agents may be helpful. Drugs used include glucagon, diazoxide, steroids, and somatostatin. These have generally been used only in the rare cases of pancreatic islet cell dysplasias, as most other infants will respond to glucose infusion alone.

Hyperglycemia in LBW infants is usually treated by reduction of the amount of glucose administered until glucose tolerance improves. Several authors have reported use of continuous insulin infusions to improve glucose tolerance[3]; some infants demonstrated an apparent increase in carbohydrate tolerance while others developed resistance to insulin over the course of its use.[13] The secondary metabolic effects of insulin infusion in very premature infants have not been examined closely and must be considered before starting such treatment. Sparks and associates have suggested the use of galactose as an alternative carbohydrate source in glucose-intolerant infants.[32] Administration of an intravenous solution containing both glucose and galactose to six such infants resulted in a

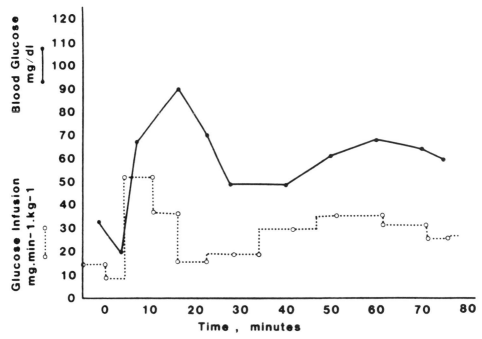

FIG 4-5.
Blood glucose concentration and intravenous glucose infusion rate in an IDM with severe hypoglycemia. Glucose infusion rate was titrated using the glucose "clamp" technique. (From Hay WW Jr: Fetal and neonatal glucose homeostasis and their relation to the small for gestational age infant. *Sem Perinatol* 1984; 8:101–116. Used by permission.)

65% higher carbohydrate intake than when glucose alone was infused. Normal blood glucose concentrations were maintained throughout. The advantage of this regimen is that the infant can maintain adequate caloric intake during the period of relative glucose intolerance. However, little is known about the effects of intravenous galactose administration, and further investigation is necessary before this treatment becomes part of the standard therapy.

Outcome

Long-term outcome in term infants with neonatal hypoglycemia appears to be related to the severity and duration of the hypoglycemia. Most follow-up studies have not shown any significant neurodevelopmental problems in term infants who had asymptomatic hypoglycemia. Those infants who were symptomatic, especially neonates with recurrent severe episodes of hypoglycemia (e.g., those with islet-cell dysplasias) were more likely to demonstrate CNS abnormalities at follow-up, including learning disability, cerebral palsy, seizure disorders, and developmental delay.[12] Prompt initiation of appropriate therapy is thought to improve outcome, although this has not been well documented.

In older studies, IDMs had a higher incidence of neurodevelopmental abnormalities than normal neonates, but this finding has not been supported by more recent surveys.[27] The discrepancy may be due to improvements in management of the diabetic pregnancy and the IDM. No studies have shown a correlation between the occurrence of neonatal hypoglycemia and neurologic disability in IDM's; outcome seems to be related to the presence of other significant morbidity, including prematurity and congenital anomalies.

The significance of episodes of hypoglycemia in the sick premature infant is not clear. Infants most likely to have hypoglycemia are the most severely ill infants, who are also those most likely to have long-term neurologic sequelae. However, Lucas et al.[24] recently performed neurodevelopmental testing in over 600 former premature infants and found significantly lower mental and motor scores in those who had five or more documented episodes of moderate hypoglycemia (defined as a blood glucose concentration less than 45 mg/dL) during the neonatal period. The correlation between incidence of hypoglycemia and decreased developmental scores remained significant when confounding factors (such as severity of respiratory disease and the presence of intracranial hemorrhage) were accounted for by multivariate analysis. If confirmed by additional long-term follow-up studies, such findings suggest that hypoglycemia in the premature infant must be prevented if possible and treated aggressively if it does develop.

Hyperglycemia per se has not been associated with adverse outcome in the neonate. One study did report an increased mortality in hyperglycemic premature infants compared with infants who maintained normoglycemia, but most surveys have not shown any difference in morbidity or mortality associated with the presence of hyperglycemia in infants when compared with controls matched for gestational age. No studies have been done to assess any long-term effects of hyperglycemia on neurologic outcome.

SUMMARY AND DIRECTIONS FOR FUTURE RESEARCH

In summary, the fetus relies on glucose supplied by the maternal circulation and lactate synthesized by the placenta to meet its metabolic requirements for carbohydrate. At birth, the neonate must provide carbohydrate to meet its glucose requirements by means of glycogenolysis and gluconeogenesis. In the newborn period, galactose joins glucose as an important carbohydrate for maintenance of glucose homeostasis. Conditions that interfere with the ability to maintain glucose homeostasis include maternal diabetes during pregnancy, prematurity, intrauterine growth retardation, sepsis, and respiratory distress syndrome as well as a number of other congenital disorders. Disturbances in glucose homeostasis may be manifested by either hypoglycemia or hyperglycemia. Treatment of these conditions is largely empirical and consists of altering the rate of carbohydrate administration to return glucose concentration to normal. The physiologic effects of these abnormalities of glucose metabolism are unclear, but recent evidence suggests there may be both short-term and long-term effects on CNS function.

Although neonatal energy metabolism is largely dependent on maintenance of normal glucose homeostasis, and disorders of carbohydrate metabolism are quite common, there has been little systematic investigation of these problems. Areas that require further study include the specific effects of variations in neonatal blood glucose concentration on CNS function, optimization of intravenous treatment regimens for hypoglycemia, evaluation of oral vs. intravenous treatment of hypoglycemia, use of preventive strategies in infants at risk of disturbances of glucose homeostasis, and proper use of insulin and other treatments (e.g., galactose) in the management of hyperglycemia. Such studies, as well as studies of the basic fetal and neonatal physiology of carbohydrate metabolism, will further our understanding of fetal and neonatal energy metabolism and growth.

Acknowledgment

Dr. DiGiacomo was supported by National Institutes of Health Training Grant HD07186.

REFERENCES

1. Anand KJS, Sippell WG, Aynsley-Green A: Randomised trial of fentanyl anesthesia in preterm babies undergoing surgery: Effects on the stress response. *Lancet* 1987; 1:243–248.
2. Bhatia J, Prihoda AR, Richardson CJ: Parenteral antibiotics and carbohydrate intolerance in term neonates. *Am J Dis Child* 1986; 140:111–113.
3. Binder ND, Raschko PK, Benda GI, et al: Insulin infusion with parenteral nutrition in extremely low birth weight infants with hyperglycemia. *J Pediatr* 1989; 114:273–280.
4. Bourbon J, Gilbert M: Role of fetal insulin in glycogen metabolism in the liver of the rat fetus. *Biol Neonate* 1981; 40:38–45.
5. Bozzetti P, Ferrari MM, Marconi AM, et al: The relationship of maternal and fetal glucose concentrations in the human from midgestation until term. *Metabolism* 1988; 37:358–363.
6. Brennan WA Jr, Aprille JR: Regulation of hepatic gluconeogenesis in newborn rabbit: Controlling factors in presuckling period. *Am J Physiol* 1985; 249:E498–E505.
7. Conrad PD, Sparks JW, Osberg I, et al: Clinical application of a new glucose analyzer in the neonatal intensive care unit: Comparison with other methods. *J Pediatr* 1989; 114:281–287.
8. Cowett RM, Oh W, Schwartz R: Persistent glucose production during glucose infusion in the neonate. *J Clin Invest* 1983; 71:467–475.
9. Denne SC, Kalhan SC: Glucose carbon recycling and oxidation in human newborns. *Am J Physiol* 1986; 251:E71–E77.
10. Devaskar SV, Ganguli S, Styer D, et al: Glucagon and glucose dynamics in sheep: Evidence for glucagon resistance in the fetus. *Am J Physiol* 1984; 246:E256–E265.
11. DiGiacomo JE, Hay WW Jr: Fetal glucose metabolism and oxygen consumption during sustained hypoglycemia. *Metabolism* 1990; 39:193–202.
12. Fluge G: Neurological findings at follow-up in neonatal hypoglycemia. *Acta Paediatr Scand* 1975; 64:629–634.
13. Goldman SL, Hirata T: Attenuated response to insulin in very low birthweight infants. *Pediatr Res* 1980; 14:50–53.
14. Gruppuso PA, Brautigan DL: Induction of hepatic glycogenesis in the fetal rat. *Am J Physiol* 1989; 256:E49–E54.
15. Grylack LJ, Chu SS, Scanlon JW: Use of intravenous fluids before cesarean section: Effects on perinatal glucose, insulin and sodium homeostasis. *Obstet Gynecol* 1984; 63:654–658.
16. Hay WW Jr, Meznarich HK, DiGiacomo JE, et al: Effects of insulin and glucose concentrations on glucose utilization in fetal sheep. *Pediatr Res* 1988; 23:381–387.
17. Jones CT: Reprogramming of metabolic development by restriction of fetal growth. *Biochem Soc Trans* 1985; 13:89–91.
18. King RA, Smith RM, Dahlenburg GW: Long term postnatal development of insulin secretion in early premature infants. *Early Hum Dev* 1986; 13:285–294.
19. Kliegman RM: Alterations of fasting glucose and fat metabolism in intrauterine growth-retarded newborn dogs. *Am J Physiol* 1989; 256:E380–E385.
20. Kliegman RM, Morton S: Sequential intrahepatic metabolic effects of enteric galactose alimentation in newborn rats. *Pediatr Res* 1988; 24:302–307.
21. Koh THHG, Aynsley-Green A, Tarbit M, et al: Neural dysfunction during hypoglycaemia. *Arch Dis Child* 1988; 63:1353–1358.
22. Lilien LD, Pildes RS, Srinivasan G, et al: Treatment of neonatal hypoglycemia with mini-bolus and intravenous glucose infusion. *J Pediatr* 1980; 97:295–298.

23. Louik C, Mitchell AA, Epstein MF, et al: Risk factors for neonatal hyperglycemia associated with 10% dextrose infusion. *Am J Dis Child* 1985; 139:783–786.

24. Lucas A, Morley R, Cole TJ: Adverse neurodevelopmental outcome of moderate neonatal hypoglycaemia. *Br Med J* 1988; 297:1304–1308.

25. Medina JM: The role of lactate as an energy substrate for the brain during the early neonatal period. *Biol Neonate* 1985; 48:237–244.

26. Mott JC: The ability of young mammals to withstand total oxygen lack. *Br Med Bull* 1961; 17:144–148.

27. Persson B, Gentz J: Follow-up of children of insulin-dependent and gestational diabetic mothers. *Acta Paediatr Scand* 1984; 73:349–358.

28. Pribylova I, Kozlova J: Glucose and galactose infusions in newborns of diabetic and healthy mothers. *Biol Neonate* 1979; 36:193–197.

29. Procianoy RS, Pinheiro CEA: Neonatal hyperinsulinemia after short-term maternal beta-sympathomimetic therapy. *J Pediatr* 1982; 101:612–614.

30. Shelley HJ: Glycogen reserves and their changes at birth and in anoxia. *Br Med Bull* 1961; 17:137–143.

31. Siegel CD, Sparks JW, Battaglia FC: Patterns of serum glucose and galactose concentrations in term newborn infants after milk feeding. *Biol Neonate* 1988; 54:301–306.

32. Sparks JW, Avery GB, Fletcher AB, et al: Parenteral galactose therapy in the glucose-intolerant infant. *J Pediatr* 1982; 100:255–259.

33. Srinivasan G, Pildes RS, Cattamanchi G, et al: Plasma glucose values in normal neonates: A new look. *J Pediatr* 1986; 109:114–117.

34. Susa JB, Cowett RM, Oh W, et al: Suppression of gluconeogenesis and endogenous glucose production by exogenous insulin administration in the newborn lamb. *Pediatr Res* 1979; 13:594–598.

35. Warburton D, Parton L, Buckley S, et al: Effects of beta-2 agonist on hepatic glycogen metabolism in the fetal lamb. *Pediatr Res* 1988; 24:330–332.

RECOMMENDED READING

Battaglia FC, Meschia G: Fetal and placental metabolism: Part 1. Oxygen and carbohydrates, in *An Introduction to Fetal Physiology.* Orlando; Fla, Academic Press, Inc, 1986.

Fisher DA: Endocrine physiology (I), in Smith CA, Nelson NM (eds): *The Physiology of the Newborn Infant,* ed 4. Springfield, Ill, Charles C Thomas, 1976.

Hay WW Jr: Fetal and neonatal glucose homeostasis and their relation to the small for gestational age infant. *Semin Perinatol* 1984; 8:101–116.

Hertel J, Kuhl C: Metabolic adaptations during the neonatal period in infants of diabetic mothers. *Acta Endocrinol* 1986; 277(suppl):136–140.

Ktorza A, Bihoreau M-T, Nurjhan N, et al: Insulin and glucagon during the perinatal period: Secretion and metabolic effects on the liver. *Biol Neonate* 1985; 48:204–220.

Margolis RN: Regulation of hepatic glycogen metabolism in pre- and postnatal rats. *Endocrinology* 1983; 113:893–902.

Marsac C, Saudubray JM, Moncion A, et al: Development of gluconeogenic enzymes in the liver of human newborns. *Biol Neonate* 1976; 28:317–325.

Mayor F, Cuezva JM: Hormonal and metabolic changes in the perinatal period. *Biol Neonate* 1985; 48:185–196.

Pildes RS, Pyati SP: Hypoglycemia and hyperglycemia in tiny infants. *Clin Perinatol* 1986; 13:351–375.

Chapter 5

Amino Acid and Protein Metabolism in the Premature and Term Infant

David K. Rassin

Investigations into the protein requirements of neonates have resulted in an evolution in the understanding of how to evaluate nutrient needs. Early studies delineated requirements for basic growth and development; more recent investigations have begun to concentrate on cognitive outcome. Optimal protein nutrition for the neonate should support appropriate growth, take into account health and genetic background, and result in fulfillment of the potential for maximal neurologic development. There has been a progression in the evaluation of protein nutrition in the neonate as growth and nitrogen balance studies have been supplemented by techniques that evaluate biochemical maturation, in vivo metabolism, and neurologic function.

Protein is a macromolecular carrier for approximately 20 amino acids. The quality of protein nutrition reflects the relative amounts of those amino acids contained within specific proteins or parenteral solutions used in the nutrition of neonates. Protein is not a generic nutrient requirement but is rather the vehicle by which amino acids—some of which are essential, some of which are not essential, and some of which are conditionally essential—are supplied to the neonate. Defining neonatal protein requirements necessitates an understanding of both the overall need of the neonate for growth and an appreciation for the roles that individual amino acids play in a variety of body functions. Thus, both requirements for protein quantity and for protein quality (amino acid composition) must be evaluated. In the following presentation the protein requirements of the neonate are discussed, followed by a review of amino acid metabolism during development and the effects of such biochemical development on the responses of neonates to various forms of protein intake.

PROTEIN REQUIREMENTS OF THE NEONATE

Requirements of the neonate for protein are divided into those for the preterm infant (a special situation with respect to body stores and biochemical maturation) and those for the term infant. In addition, it is important to define techniques by which protein requirements can be determined. These techniques have included studies of growth, nitrogen balance, enzymatic synthetic capacity, plasma amino acid patterns, stable isotope studies, and comparisons to human milk composition. Suggested protein requirements that were based on growth and nitrogen balance studies (reviewed by Irwin and Hegsted[32]) resulted in fairly large ranges of suggested intake: 2 to 7 g/kg/day for the preterm infant; 2 to 5 g/kg/day for the term infant (0 to 6 months); and less than 0.8 to 4 g/kg/day for the older (6 to 24 months) infant.

Various professional organizations have synthesized information in the literature, generally concentrating on growth and nitrogen balance data, and have made recommendations of their own. The Recommended Dietary Allowances (RDA)[62] suggest protein intakes of 2.2 g/kg/day for term infants (0 to 6 months) and 2.0 g/kg/day for older (6 to 12 months) infants. In addition, they state that preterm infants probably have a greater requirement for protein than term infants. The Food and Agriculture Organization of the World Health Organization (FAO/WHO) in 1973[70] divided the age categories into smaller blocks of time and recommended daily intakes of 2.4 g/kg (0 to 3 months), 1.85 g/kg (3 to 6 months), and 1.5 g/kg (6 to 12 months). These recommendations were reiterated in 1985[71] to further take into account available data on nitrogen retention and improved statistical techniques. One analysis of the FAO/WHO data has suggested that at least for 3- to 4-month old infants, the recommendations are too high.[3]

These latter investigators have suggested that 3- to 4-month old infants require 1.1 ± 0.1 to 0.2 g/kg/day of protein. They also point out the fact that current recommendations by this group are incompatible with the consensus that human milk is the most appropriate form of feeding for the healthy term infant.[3]

The European Society for Paediatric Gastroenterology and Nutrition[14] suggested that formulas for term infants contain 1.2 to 1.9 grams protein per deciliter (1.8 to 2.8 g/100 kcal assuming 68 kcal/dL), that follow-up formulas for infants 4 to 6 months of age contain 2.0 to 3.7 g/dL,[15] and that preterm infant formulas contain 2.25 to 3.1 g/100 kcal.[16] The Committee for the Revision of the Dietary Standard for Canada[8] recommended a progression from 2.4 g/kg (infants 0 to 2 months), to 2.0 g/kg (3 to 5 months), to 1.9 g/kg (6 to 11 months). The Committee on Nutrition of the American Academy of Pediatrics[9, 10] has recommended that formula protein intakes be within the ranges of 2.1 to 5.2 g/kg/day at birth and 1.9 to 4.7 g/kg/day by the end of infancy.

These various recommendations seem to be generally compatible with term infants receiving 2.0 to 2.2 grams protein per kilogram body weight during the first months of life, followed by a gradual decline to 1.8 to 2.0 g/kg from 4 to 12 months of age. It is usually recommended that preterm infants receive about 1 g/kg/day more protein than newborn term infants.

Interpretation of these recommendations in light of the emphasis on breast-feeding in the term infant is problematic. With the exception of the reexamination of the FAO/WHO data by Beaton and Chery,[3] these suggested intakes could only be met with great difficulty by feeding human milk. Human milk contains approximately 1 g/dL of protein compared with 1.5 g/dL for most term infant formulas. Human milk would have to be fed at rates of 200 mL/kg/day to meet basal recommendations of 2 g/kg/day of protein. However, breast-fed infants seem to stabilize at intakes of 720 to 750 grams of milk per day despite active growth, resulting in an apparent decline in intake from about 1.6 to 0.9 g/kg/day of protein.[7] These intakes are comparable to those reported elsewhere.[36, 69]

The use of human milk in preterm infants is also controversial, partly due to its relatively low protein content, even though the milk from mothers who deliver preterm infants appears to be somewhat enriched in protein compared with that from mothers of term infants.[2, 27, 41] Preterm infants have been observed to grow well on milk from mothers of preterm infants[26] and on pooled human milk fed in increased volumes.[35] However, the use of human milk in this population is still the subject of considerable difference of opinion.[12, 19, 21, 31]

The use of stable isotopes to measure protein synthesis and degradation in vivo has resulted in recommendations of protein intakes for premature infants in the range of 3.8 to 4.3 g/kg/day.[48-50] However, these and similar studies have been based on small groups of infants because of the technical difficulty in carrying them out. Use of this technique to evaluate protein requirements has also aroused some controversy.[45, 74] The major difficulty in evaluating protein needs of the preterm infant has been the lack of consensus on a control or goal for feeding such infants. The in utero fetus and the human milk–fed preterm infant have both been suggested to fill this role, but each has inherent biologic drawbacks. The fetus undergoes many different physiologic changes as it appears ex utero while the human milk–fed infant has not always gained weight at rates sufficient to avoid concern.

These recommendations have, in general, paid little attention to the components of the protein being fed: the amino acids. In fact, the variability among investigations may partly reflect the variability in the quality of protein being fed, especially the large differences in amino acid composition of human milk vs. cow milk proteins.

Milk proteins are vehicles for the supply of amino acids, so any evaluation of protein requirements must address amino acid requirements. On the basis of growth and nitrogen balance data, Irwin and Hegsted[33] divided the 20 amino acid components of protein into essential (indispensable), nonessential (dispensable), and conditionally essential (Table 5–1). Investigations into the growth of infants have led to particular attention to histidine,[66] cysteine,[51, 65] and tyrosine[65] as potentially essential for the neonate but not for the adult.

Improved understanding of the biochemistry of the amino acids, for example the ability of keto acid analogues to satisfy the requirement for some amino acids (such as leucine and isoleucine) in certain circumstances via transamination reactions, led to further modifications of the principal of essentiality and nonessentiality.[34] Amino acids could be classified as essential and nonessential depending on the body's ability to synthesize the carbon skeleton and/or to aminate the carbon skeleton. When the further in-

TABLE 5–1.

Classification of Amino Acids*

Essential	Nonessential	Conditionally Essential
Isoleucine	Alanine	Cysteine
Leucine	Arginine	Histidine
Lysine	Asparagine	Taurine†
Methionine	Aspartate	Tyrosine
Phenylalanine	Glutamate	
Threonine	Glutamine	
Tryptophan	Glycine	
Valine	Proline	
	Serine	

* Based on Irwin MI, Hegsted DM: A conspectus of research on amino acid requirements in man. *J Nutr* 1971; 101:539–566.
† Not a protein constituent.

fluences of health, developmental state, genetics, and other special nutritional circumstances are factored into the scheme,[40] eight different levels of amino acid essentiality could be defined (Table 5–2). Thus, for the neonate the assessment of the requirement for protein must not only factor in the amino acid composition of the protein being fed, but must also consider the biochemical maturity of the infant, the influence of underdevelopment and illness (in the preterm infant), and the influence of unusual nutritional circumstances, such as the use of total parenteral nutrition.

AMINO ACID METABOLISM IN THE NEONATE

Unusual biochemical responses of infants fed various protein/amino acid diets have resulted in particular interest in the development of the metabolic pathways that deal with sulfur amino acid metabolism, aromatic amino acid metabolism, and ammonia metabolism (the urea cycle). In general, the response of infants to various diets has resulted in unexpected changes in amino acids and metabolites. These changes have strengthened the suggestion that amino acids thought to be nonessential may be essential in the neonate. Investigation of associated enzymatic activities have, in most cases, implicated a biochemical explanation for these findings.

Methionine is the essential amino acid precursor of the sulfur amino acid metabolic pathway (Fig 5–1). Cysteine was suggested to have a methionine-sparing effect,[18] and, in addition, feeding studies[51, 65] and enzymatic studies[47, 67] indicated that cysteine itself may be essential for the neonate. Cystathionase, the enzyme responsible for catalyzing the synthesis of cysteine from cystathionine, was found to be immunologically absent from fetal liver[47] and to be present in less than adult activity in the livers of preterm and term infants.[67] Investigations of the activity of this enzyme in other tissues suggests that the neonate has some capacity to form cysteine in organs such as the kidney.[75] How-

TABLE 5–2.

Categorization of Amino Acids*

Classification	Definition (Example)
Nonessential	Amino acids whose carbon skeleton can be both synthesized and aminated (alanine, glutamate)
Essential carbon skeleton	Amino acids whose carbon skeleton cannot be synthesized but can be aminated (leucine, valine)
Semiessential	Amino acids whose carbon skeleton can be synthesized but not aminated (glycine, serine)
Essential	Amino acids whose carbon skeleton can be neither synthesized nor aminated (lysine)
Developmentally required	Amino acids that cannot be sufficiently synthesized due to biochemical immaturity (cysteine in premature infants)
Genetically required	Amino acids that cannot be sufficiently synthesized due to a genetic defect (tyrosine in phenylketonuria)
Disease-induced requirement	Amino acids that cannot be sufficiently synthesized due to a disease not specifically related to amino acids (branch-chain amino acids in liver dysfunction)
Nutritionally induced requirement	Amino acids needed due to special nutritional circumstances to correct imbalances of other metabolites (arginine in total parenteral nutrition)

*Compiled from references 33, 34, and 40.

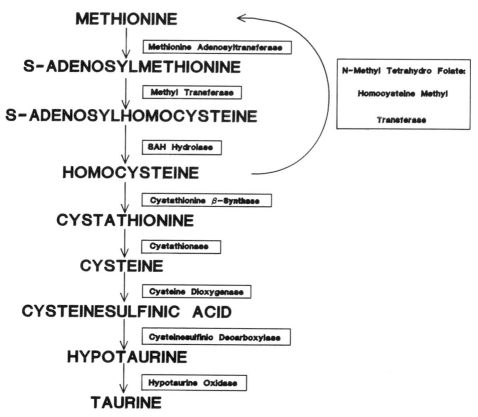

FIG 5–1.
Metabolic pathway of methionine metabolism.

ever, such activity does not always maintain cysteine concentrations in the face of nutritional regimens, such as total parenteral nutrition, in which cysteine is supplied in very low amounts or is absent.

Taurine is a second component of the sulfur amino acid pathway that has been suggested to be an essential nutrient for the neonate based on low plasma concentrations observed in feeding studies and relatively low activity of its synthetic enzyme, cysteine sulfinic acid decarboxylase.[22] Unlike cystathionase, the hepatic activity of which progresses from undetectable in fetal and premature infants to about 50% of adult in the term infant liver,[23] cysteine sulfinic acid decarboxylase, remains low in activity throughout life.[22] Cysteine sulfinic acid decarboxylase has an activity of 0.26 nmol per milligram protein per hour in human fetal liver and 0.32 in human adult liver; this activity is at least one order of magnitude lower than that observed in a number of other species. The cat, which is particularly susceptible to taurine deficiency,[30] has considerably more hepatic cysteine sulfinic acid decarboxylase activity[4, 46] than that measured in the fetal or adult human liver.[22] It is also interesting to note that, as for cystathionase, other organs contain greater activity of cysteine sulfinic acid decarboxylase, especially the brain.[56] However, this enzymatic capacity is insufficient to maintain taurine plasma concentrations in the face of nutrient deficiencies.

The aromatic amino acid pathway, that involving phenylalanine and tyrosine (Fig 5–2), has also been the subject of considerable scrutiny with respect to the interaction of development and nutrition. The catabolism of phenylalanine occurs primarily by

PHENYLALANINE

Phenylalanine Hydroxylase

TYROSINE

Tyrosine Transaminase

ρ–HYDROXYPHENYLPYRUVIC ACID

ρ–OH–Phenylpyruvic Acid
Oxidase

HOMOGENTISIC ACID

FIG 5–2.
Metabolic pathway of phenylalanine metabolism.

means of three enzymes: phenylalanine hydroxylase, which catalyzes the synthesis of tyrosine; tyrosine transaminase, which catalyzes the deamination of tyrosine to *p*-hydroxyphenylpyruvic acid; and *p*-hydroxyphenylpyruvic acid oxidase, which catalyzes the formation of homogentisic acid. Human fetal liver phenylalanine hydroxylase has an activity of about 60% of the adult[13] while tyrosine transaminase and *p*-hydroxyphenylpyruvic acid oxidase activities are about 8% and 18% of adult activities, respectively.[38, 39] The implication of these findings is that there is a functional block in the catabolism of tyrosine, resulting in large increases in tyrosine concentrations in plasma and urine when infants receive proteins enriched in the aromatic amino acids.[61]

A paradoxical response with respect to tyrosine is observed when nutrient regimens are fed that contain very low amounts of this amino acid in the presence of ample phenylalanine. Most total parenteral nutrition mixtures contain little tyrosine; yet despite supposedly adequate capacity to synthesize this amino acid from phenylalanine,[72] both adult rats[63] and human infants[4, 59] seem to lack the ability to maintain plasma tyrosine concentrations when fed these amino acid mixtures intravenously. Thus, the neonate seems to be at risk for both excess and deficient tyrosine nutrition, depending on the nutritional source of protein.

A major toxic metabolite that the body has to deal with is ammonia produced by the catabolism of protein. The primary route for detoxification is the urea cycle (Fig 5–3).

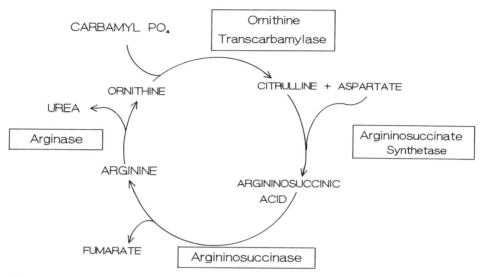

FIG 5–3.
The urea cycle.

The enzymes in the cycle are present fairly early during development as measured by hepatic activity.[54, 55] However, the activity of one enzyme in the cycle, argininosuccinate synthetase, is particularly low in fetal liver (2%) compared with adults. The other enzymes in the pathway have fetal hepatic activities ranging from 17% to 46% of adult. Argininosuccinate synthetase thus appears to be the rate limiting step in the cycle, apparently resulting in an increased requirement for arginine in the neonate. When arginine is fed it appears to exert a protective effect with respect to hyperammonemia during development.[11]

Other amino acids, such as threonine, glycine, and alanine, may also be subject to varying biochemical mechanisms during early development.[20, 25] However, the pathways described above involve amino acids and metabolites that appear to have a particular potential for toxicity[5]—methionine, tyrosine, and ammonia—as well as involvement in inherited metabolic diseases with serious consequences for the neurologic development of the infant (e.g., homocystinuria, phenylketonuria, ornithine transcarbamylase deficiency).

INFANT RESPONSES TO PROTEIN INTAKE

Neonates respond to various amounts and types of protein intake at the level of growth, at the level of their biochemical responses, and ultimately at the level of their neurologic outcome. Both breast-feeding and formula feeding, when used appropriately, support proper growth as defined by weight and length increases in the term infant. There have been some concerns that breast-fed infants do not grow as well as formula-fed infants over the first 6 months of life. In addition, some data indicate that breast-fed infants grow more rapidly than formula-fed infants during the early days of life.[53] The growth of preterm infants fed different forms of protein has been more controversial, and has been the basis for suggesting that these infants have a greater protein requirement.

However, growth lacks the specificity of response to the type of protein intake; of necessity, growth reflects the overall nutrient composition of the type of feeding used. In contrast, total serum protein, albumin, blood urea nitrogen, and individual amino acids are more specific reflections of the amount and type of protein in the diet. Total serum protein, serum albumin, and blood urea nitrogen all respond to the amount or quantity of protein fed in both term and preterm infants.[37, 52] The greater amount of protein in formulas, compared to human milk, is reflected by increases in the blood content of these general markers of protein intake.

On the other hand, the plasma amino acids provide markers for both the quantity of protein fed and the quality (amino acid composition) of protein fed. The major proteins used in enteral nutrition of preterm and term infants are obtained from human milk (70% human whey and 30% human casein) and bovine milk (either 18% or 60% bovine whey and 82% or 40% bovine casein).[29] These proteins differ in their supply of amino acids, with each having a typical individual pattern.

Bovine casein proteins are particularly rich in phenylalanine and tyrosine; so infants fed formulas in which bovine casein protein predominates typically have higher concentrations of plasma phenylalanine and tyrosine than do infants fed formulas in which bovine whey protein predominate or infants fed human milk.[37, 61] Bovine whey proteins are very rich in threonine, in contrast to bovine casein proteins or human milk whey proteins. Infants fed bovine whey protein–predominant formulas have increased plasma threonine concentrations than those fed either bovine casein protein–predominant formulas or human milk (which is also whey protein predominant, but different whey proteins).[37, 60]

Ammonia tends to increase in the blood of preterm infants fed various amounts of protein, reflecting the immature biochemical activity of the urea cycle.[52] The application of special nutrient regimens such as total parenteral nutrition have been of particular interest with respect to the urea cycle. Anderson et al.[1] found an increased requirement for arginine in infants fed total parenteral nutrition to prevent hyperammonemia and orotic aciduria. Other amino acids that appear to be particularly at risk for remarkable changes in infants fed total parenteral nutrition are tyrosine (reduced concentrations), cysteine (reduced concentrations), methionine (increased concentrations), and glycine (increased concentrations).[58]

These various amino acid modulations due to diet in the term and preterm neonate have the potential for affecting infant behavior.[57] Many of the amino acids are neuroactive themselves (glycine, glutamate, aspartate, taurine) or are precursors of neuroactive compounds (phenylalanine and tyrosine are metabolized to the catecholamines; tryptophan, to serotonin; glutamate, to gamma-aminobutyric acid). Behavioral changes have been documented related to excessive protein in the neonate,[24] and some of these changes may be specific to specific amino acids such as tyrosine.[43, 44] Low protein intake in the preterm neonate may also have short-term behavioral effects, as documented by the Neonatal Brazelton Assessment Scale.[6, 68] Long-term behavioral effects have been associated with formula feeding vs. breast-feeding,[64] and small improvements in intelligence and language development have been noted in 7-year-old children who were breast-fed compared to those who were formula fed.[17]

The amino acid responses noted earlier suggest a mechanism by which protein intake may influence long-term behavior. A sequence of events can take place that ultimately alters the nutrient milieu of the developing brain. First, protein intake alters plasma amino acid patterns. These plasma amino acid changes result in a competition for active transport sites at the blood-brain barrier for entry into the central nervous system.[46] Once inside the brain, amino acid pools are altered. The change in brain concentrations of neurotransmitter precursor amino acids results in changes in neurotransmitters because the enzymes responsible for catalyzing their synthesis are not saturated with respect to the amino acid precursors.[28, 42] Last, alterations in the biochemical environment of the brain result in behavioral changes. Support for this sequence of events exists, for example, in studies in which tryptophan (a precursor of serotonin, the neurotransmitter probably responsible for sleep regulation) and valine (an amino acid that competes with tryptophan for entry into the central nervous system) were fed to neonates.[73] These investigators found that tryptophan enhanced sleep behavior while valine had an opposite effect.

These findings illustrate the need to step beyond the classic approaches to determining protein requirements (growth and nitrogen balance studies) into investigations that better evaluate the functions of the amino acid components of protein and how variations in their nutritional availability interact with maturation of biochemical capacity for their metabolism, influencing brain development. The various nutritional regimens used in the neonate generally support the basic needs of these infants; what is still poorly understood is how these nutrients affect the long-term development of the brain.

Acknowledgments

The author appreciates the secretarial skills of Deborah LaVictoire and the graphic computer skills of Stacy Magliolo used in the preparation of this manuscript.

REFERENCES

1. Anderson TL, Heird WC, Winters RW: Clinical and physiological consequences of total parenteral nutrition in the pediatric patient, in Greep JM, Soeterz PB, Wesdorp RIC, et al: (eds): *Current Concepts in Parenteral Nutrition*. The Hague, Martinus Nijhoff, 1977, pp 111–127.
2. Atkinson SA, Bryan MH, Anderson GH: Human milk: Difference in nitrogen concentration in milk from mothers of term and premature infants. *J Pediatr* 1978; 93:67–69.
3. Beaton GH, Chery A: Protein requirements of infants: A reexamination of concepts and approaches. *Am J Clin Nutr* 1988; 48:1403–1412.
4. Bell EF, Filer LJ Jr, Wong AP, et al: Effects of a parenteral nutrition regimen containing dicaboxylic amino acids on plasma, erythrocyte and urinary amino acid concentrations of young infants. *Am J Clin Nutr* 1983; 37:99–107.
5. Benevenga NJ: Toxicities of methionine and other amino acids. *Agric Food Chem* 1974; 22:2–9.
6. Bhatia J, Cerreto MC, Rassin DK, et al: Behavioral differences in low-birth-weight infants fed formulas with differing protein concentrations. *Pediatr Res* 1986; 20:159A.
7. Butte NF, Garza C, Smith EO, et al: Human milk intake and growth performance of exclusively breastfed infants. *J Pediatr* 1983; 104:187–195.
8. Committee for the Revision of the Dietary Standards for Canada. *Recommended Nutrient Intakes for Canadians*. Ottowa, Canadian Government Publishing Center, 1983, pp 179–181.
9. Committee on Nutrition, American Academy of Pediatrics. Recommended ranges of nutrients in formulas. *Pediatric Nutrition Handbook*. Elk Grove Village, Ill, American Academy of Pediatrics, 1985, pp 356–357.
10. Committee on Nutrition, American Academy of Pediatrics. Commentary on breast-feeding

and infant formulas including proposed standards for formulas. *Pediatrics* 1976; 57:278–285.

11. Czarncki GL, Baker DJ: Urea cycle function in the dog with emphasis on the role of arginine. *J Nutr* 1984; 114:581–590.

12. Davies DP: Adequacy of expressed breast milk for early growth of preterm infants. *Arch Dis Child* 1977; 52:296–301.

13. DelValle JA, Greengard O: Phenylalanine hydroxylase and tyrosine aminotransferase in human fetal and adult liver. *Pediatr Res* 1976; 11:2–5.

14. ESPGAN Committee on Nutrition. Guidelines on infant nutrition: I. Recommendations for the composition of an adapted formula. *Acta Paediatr Scand [Suppl]* 1977; 262:1–20.

15. ESPGAN Committee on Nutrition. Guidelines on infant nutrition: II. Recommendations for the composition of a follow-up formula and beikost. *Acta Paediatr Scand [Suppl]* 1981; 287:1–25.

16. ESPGAN Committee on Nutrition. Nutrition and feeding of preterm infants. *Acta Paediatr Scand [Suppl]* 1987; 336:1–14.

17. Fergusson DM, Beautrais AL, Silva PA: Breast-feeding and cognitive development in the first seven years of life. *Soc Sci Med* 1982; 16:1705–1708.

18. Finkelstein JD, Mudd SH: Trans-sulfuration in mammals: The methionine sparing effect of cysteine. *J Biol Chem* 1967; 242:873–880.

19. Fomon SJ, Ziegler EE: Protein intake of premature infants: Interpretation of data. *J Pediatr* 1977; 90:504–506.

20. Gaull GE, Hommes F, Roux J: Human biochemical development, in Faulkner F, Tanner J (eds): *Human Development.* New York, Plenum Publishing Corp, 1978, pp 23–124.

21. Gaull GE, Rassin DK, Raiha NCR: Protein intake of premature infants: A reply. *J Pediatr* 1977; 90:507–510.

22. Gaull GE, Rassin DK, Raiha NCR, et al: Milk protein quantity and quality in low-birth-weight infants: III. Effects on sulfur-containing amino acids in plasma and urine. *J Pediatr* 1977; 90:348–355.

23. Gaull GE, Sturman JA, Raiha NCR: Development of mammalian sulfur metabolism: Absence of cystathionase in human fetal tissues. *Pediatr Res* 1972; 6:538–547.

24. Goldman HI, Freudenthal R, Holland B et al: Clinical effects of two different levels of protein intake on low birth weight infants. *J Pediatr* 1969; 74:881–889.

25. Greengard O: Enzymic differentiation of human liver. Comparison with the rat model. *Pediatr Res* 1977; 11:669–676.

26. Gross SJ: Growth and biochemical response of preterm infants fed human milk or modified infant formula. *N Engl J Med* 1983; 308:237–241.

27. Gross SJ, Geller J, Tomarelli RM: Composition of breast milk from mothers of preterm infants. *Pediatrics* 1981; 68:490–493.

28. Guroff G, Lovenberg W: Metabolism of aromatic amino acids, in Lajtha A (ed): *Handbook of Neurochemistry* New York, Plenum Publishing Corp, 1970, pp 209–223.

29. Hambraeus L: Proprietary milk versus human breast milk in infant feeding: A critical appraisal from the nutritional point of view. *Pediatr Clin North Am* 1977; 24:17–36.

30. Hayes KC, Carey RE, Schmidt SY: Retinal degeneration associated with taurine deficiency in the cat. *Science* 1975; 188:949–951.

31. Heird WC: Feeding the premature infant: Human milk or artificial formula. *Am J Dis Child* 1977; 131:468–469.

32. Irwin MI, Hegsted DM: A conspectus of research on protein requirements of man. *J Nutr* 1971; 101:539–566.

33. Irwin MI, Hegsted DM: A conspectus of research on amino acid requirements of man. *J Nutr* 1971; 101:539–566.

34. Jackson AA: Amino acids: Essential and non-essential? *Lancet* 1983; 1:1034–1036.

35. Jarvenpaa AL, Raiha AL, Rassin DK, et al: Preterm infants fed human milk attain intrauterine weight gain. *Acta Paediatr Scand* 1983; 72:239–243.

36. Jarvenpaa AL, Raiha NCR, Rassin DK, et al: Milk protein quantity and quality in the term infant: I. Metabolic responses and effects on growth. *Pediatrics* 1982; 70:221–230.
37. Jarvenpaa AL, Rassin DK, Raiha NCR, et al: Milk protein quantity and quality in the term infant: II. Effects on acidic and neutral amino acids. *Pediatrics* 1982; 70:214–220.
38. Kretchmer N, Levine SZ, McNamara H, et al: Certain aspects of tyrosine metabolism in the young: I. The development of the tyrosine oxidizing system in the human liver. *J Clin Invest* 1956; 35:236–244.
39. Kretchmer N, Levine SZ, McNamara H, et al: The 'in vitro' metabolism of tyrosine and its intermediates in the liver of the premature infant. *Am J Dis Child* 1957; 93:19–20.
40. Laidlaw SA, Kopple JD: Newer concepts of the indispensable amino acids. *Am J Clin Nutr* 1987; 46:593–605.
41. Lemons JA, Moye L, Hall D, et al: Differences in the composition of preterm and term human milk during early lactation. *Pediatr Res* 1982; 16:113–117.
42. Lovenberg W, Jequier E, Sjoerdsma A: A tryptophan hydroxylation in mammalian systems. *Adv Pharmacol* 1968; 6A:21–36.
43. Mamunes P, Prince PE, Thornton NH, et al: Intellectual deficits after transient tyrosinemia in the term neonate. *Pediatrics* 1976; 57:675–680.
44. Menkes JH, Welcher DW, Levi HS, et al: Relationship of elevated blood tyrosine to the ultimate intellectual performance of premature infants. *Pediatrics* 1972; 49:218–224.
45. Millward DJ, Rivers JPN: Protein and amino acid requirements in the adult human. *J Nutr* 1986; 116:2559–2561.
46. Pardridge WM: Regulation of amino acid availability to the brain, in Wurtman RJ, Wurtman JJ (eds): *Nutrition and the Brain,* vol 1. New York, Raven Press, 1977, pp 141–204.
47. Pascal TA, Gillman BM, Gaull GE: Cystathionase: Immunochemical evidence for absence from human fetal liver. *Pediatr Res* 1972; 6:773–778.
48. Pencharz PB, Farri L, Papageorgiou A: The effects of human milk and low-protein formula on the rates of total body protein turnover and urinary 3-methylhistidine excretion of preterm infants. *Clin Sci* 1983; 64:611–616.
49. Pencharz PB, Masson M, Desgranges F, et al: Total-body protein turnover in human premature neonates: Effects of birth weight, intrauterine nutritional status and diet. *Clin Sci* 1981; 61:207–215.
50. Pencharz PB, Stefee WP, Cochran W, et al: Protein metabolism in human neonates: Nitrogen-balance studies, estimated obligatory losses of nitrogen and whole-body turnover of nitrogen. *Clin Sci* 1977; 52:485–498.
51. Pohlandt F: Cysteine: A semi-essential amino acid in the newborn infant. *Acta Paediatr Scand* 1974; 63:801–804.
52. Raiha NCR, Heinonen K, Rassin DK, et al: Milk protein quantity and quality in low-birth-weight infants: I. Metabolic responses and effects on growth. *Pediatrics* 1976; 57:659–674.
53. Raiha NCR, Minoli I, Moro G: Milk protein intake in the term infant: I. Metabolic responses and effects on growth. *Acta Paediatr Scand* 1986; 75:881–886.
54. Raiha NCR, Siuhkonen J: Development of urea-synthesizing enzymes in human liver. *Acta Paediatr Scand* 1968; 57:121–124.
55. Raiha NCR, Suihkonen J: Factors influencing the development of urea synthesizing enzymes in rat liver. *Biochem J* 1968; 107:793–797.
56. Rassin DK: Taurine, cysteinesulfinic acid decarboxylase and glutamic acid in brain, in Huxtable RJ, Pasantes-Morales H (eds): *Taurine in Nutrition and Neurology.* New York, Plenum Publishing Corp, 1982, pp 257–268.
57. Rassin DK: Protein nutrition in the neonate: Assessment and implications for brain development, in Rassin DK, Haber B, Drujan B (eds): *Basic and Clinical Aspects of Nutrition and Brain Development.* New York, Alan R. Liss, 1987, pp 19–39.
58. Rassin DK: Amino acid requirements and profiles in total parenteral nutrition, in Lebenthal E (ed): *Total Parenteral Nutrition: Indications, Utilization Complications, and Pathophysiological Considerations.* New York, Raven Press, 1986, pp 5–15.

59. Rassin DK: Amino acid metabolism in total parenteral nutrition during development, in Friedman M (ed): *Absorption and Utilization of Amino Acids,* vol II. Boca Raton, Fla, CRC Press, 1989, pp 71–85.

60. Rassin DK, Gaull GE, Heinonen K, et al: Milk protein quantity and quality in low-birth-weight infants: II. Effects on selected essential and non-essential amino acids in plasma and urine. *Pediatrics* 1977; 59:41–50.

61. Rassin DK, Gaull GE, Raiha NCR, et al: Milk protein quantity and quality in low-birth-weight infants: 4. Effects on tyrosine and phenylalanine in plasma and urine. *J Pediatr* 1977; 90:356–360.

62. *Recommended Dietary Allowances,* ed 9. Washington, DC, Food and Nutrition Board, National Academy of Sciences–National Research Council, 1980.

63. Rivera A, Bhatia J, Rassin DK, et al: In vivo biliary function in the adult rat: The effect of parenteral glucose and amino acids. *JPEN* 1989; 13:240–245.

64. Rodgers B: Feeding in infancy and later ability and attainment: A longitudinal study. *Dev Med Child Neurol* 1978; 20:421–426.

65. Snyderman SE: The protein and amino acid requirements of the premature infant, in Jonxis JHP, Visser HKA, Troelstra JA (eds): *Metabolic Processes in the Foetus and Newborn Infant.* Leiden, Steinfert Kroese, 1971, pp 128–141.

66. Snyderman SE, Boyer A, Roitman E, et al: The histidine requirement of the infant. *Pediatrics* 1963; 31:786–801.

67. Sturman JA, Gaull GE, Raiha NCR: Absence of cystathionase in human fetal liver. Is cysteine essential? *Science* 1970; 169:74.

68. Tyson JE, Lasky RE, Mize CE, et al: Growth, metabolic responses and development in very low-birth-weight infants fed banked human milk or enriched formula: I. Neonatal findings. *J Pediatr* 1983; 103:95–104.

69. Wallgren A: Breast milk consumption of healthy, full-term infants. *Acta Paediatr Scand* 1945; 32:778–790.

70. WHO/FAO. Energy and Protein Requirements. WHO technical report series no. 522. Geneva, World Health Organization, 1973.

71. WHO/FAO. Energy and protein requirements. Technical report series no. 724. Geneva, World Health Organization, 1985.

72. Wurtman, RJ: Aspartame effect on brain serotonin. *Am J Clin Nutr* 1987; 45:799.

73. Yogman MW, Zeisel SH: Diet and sleep patterns in newborn infants. *N Engl J Med* 1983; 309:1147–1149.

74. Young VR: McCollum Award Lecture. Kinetics of human amino acid metabolism: Nutritional implications and some lessons. *Am J Clin Nutr* 1987; 46:709–725.

75. Zlotkin SH, Anderson GH: The development of cystathionase activity during the first year of life. *Pediatr Res* 1982; 16:65–68.

Chapter 6

Lipid Metabolism

Margit Hamosh, Ph.D.

Fats are vital for normal growth and development, and are the main energy source of the newborn infant. In addition to providing 40% to 50% of the total calories in human milk or formula, fats are an integral part of all cell membranes, provide fatty acids necessary for brain development, and are the sole vehicle for fat-soluble vitamins and hormones in milk.[1] Furthermore, these energy-rich lipids can be stored in the body in nearly unlimited amounts, in contrast to the limited storage capacity for carbohydrates and proteins. Before birth, glucose is the major energy source for the fetus, with the fetal requirement for fatty acids supplied mainly as free fatty acids from the maternal circulation. After birth, fat is supplied chiefly in the form of milk or formula triglycerides.[2]

Lipids are nonpolar or amphipathic substances that are insoluble in aqueous media (Fig 6–1). Absorption of fat permits the efficient assimilation of a great number of hydrophobic (fat-soluble) chemicals, some beneficial (such as the fat-soluble vitamins) and some detrimental (such as hydrophobic xenobiotics, drugs, and food additives).[3]

MAJOR LIPIDS IN INFANT NUTRITION

The major lipid classes are glycerides, phospholipids, sterols (cholesterol), and free fatty acids (see Fig 6–1).

Glycerides

Glycerides are non-phosphorus-containing lipids that result from the esterification of glycerol and fatty acids (see Fig 6–1). Triglycerides (neutral fat) are the most abundant lipids in animal tissue and serve as an important energy source. In triglycerides all three of the carbon molecules of glycerol are esterified with fatty acids. Monoglycerides and diglycerides are compounds resulting from ester links between glycerol and one or two fatty acids, respectively.

Phospholipids

Phospholipids, phosphorus-containing lipid compounds, may be subdivided into three classes: derivatives of glycerol-3-phosphate (phosphatidyl choline, phosphatidyl

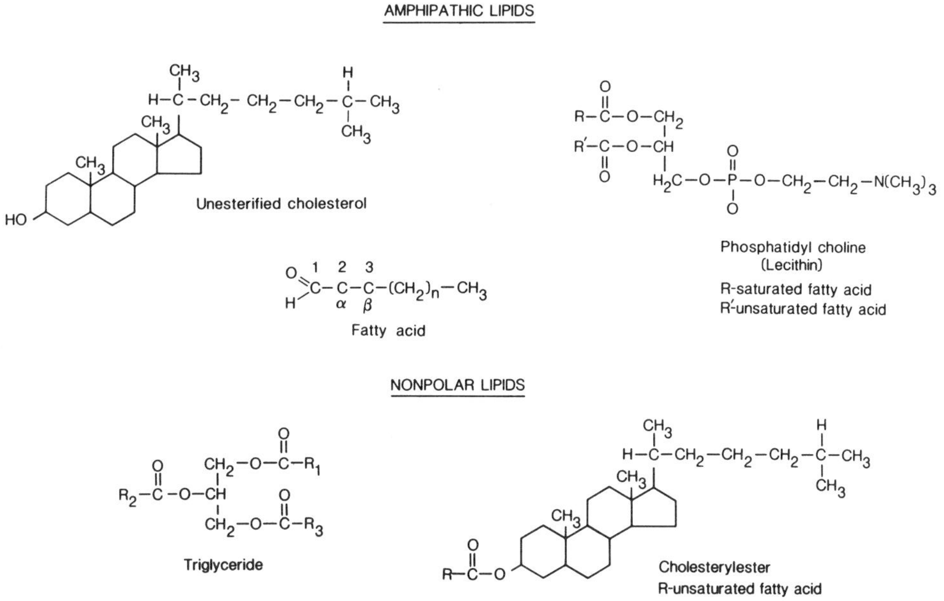

FIG 6–1.
Principal dietary lipid components. (From Hamosh M, Hamosh P: Lipoprotein lipase: Its physiological and clinical significance. *Mol Aspects Med* 1983; 6:199–289. Used by permission.)

ethanolamine, phosphatidyl serine, and phosphatidyl inositol), sphingosine, and the glycolipids. Phospholipids are found as structural components of all biologic membranes. They are important in oxidative phosphorylation, in transport across cell membranes, and in electron transport reactions. They are also the main components of pulmonary surfactant.

Sterols

Sterols are alcohols with the cyclopentanoperhydrophenanthrene skeletal structure. The principal sterol is cholesterol, the parent compound of the steroids, including the adrenocortical, ovarian, and testicular hormones. The bile acids, degradative products of cholesterol, are important in gastrointestinal absorptive processes.

Fatty Acids

Fatty acids of animal origin are usually unbranched, monocarboxylic acids containing an even number of carbon atoms, varying from 2 to 24 in chain length. The fatty acid chains may be either saturated or unsaturated (Table 6–1). Most biologically important fatty acids are esterified with glycerol; a small portion are linked with other compounds or are free.

The fat composition of commercially available infant formulas is listed in Table 6–2. The composition of lipids in human milk is discussed in detail in this chapter. The functions of the lipid classes discussed are summarized in Table 6–3. Storage lipid contains higher amounts of saturated fatty acids than structural lipids (Fig 6–2).

TABLE 6–1.

Structure of Fatty Acids*

Descriptive Name	Systematic Name	Carbon Atoms	Double Bonds	Position of Double Bonds†	Unsaturated Fatty Acid Class‡
Acetic	. . .	2	0	. . .	. . .
Butyric	. . .	4	0	. . .	. . .
Caproic	Hexanoic	6	0	. . .	. . .
Caprylic	Octanoic	8	0	. . .	. . .
Capric	Decanoic	10	0	. . .	. . .
Lauric	Dodecanoic	12	0	. . .	. . .
Myristic	Tetradecanoic	14	0	. . .	. . .
Palmitic	Hexadecaenoic	16	0	. . .	. . .
Palmitoleic	Hexadecaenoic	16	1	9	n-7
Stearic	Octadecaenoic	18	0	. . .	. . .
Oleic	Octadecaenoic	18	1	9	n-9
Linoleic	Octadecadienoic	18	2	9,12	n-6
Linolenic	Octadecatrienoic	18	3	9,12,15	n-3
Linolenic	Octadecatrienoic	18	3	6,9,12	n-6
Homolinolenic	Eicosatrienoic	20	3	8,11,14	n-6
Arachidonic	Eicosatetraenoic	20	4	5,8,11,14	n-6
§	Eicosapentaenoic	20	5	5,8,11,14,17	n-3
§	Docosahexaenoic	22	6	4,7,10,12,19,19	n-3

* Adapted from Montgomery R, Dryer RL, Conway TW, et al: *Biochemistry: A Case-oriented Approach,* ed 4. St Louis, CV Mosby Co, 1982.
† Position of the one or more double bonds listed according to the Δ numbering system. In this numbering system, only the first carbon of the pair is listed: that is, 9 means position 9, 10, starting from the carboxyl end.
¶ In the n numbering system, only the first double bond from the methyl end is listed and only the first carbon of the pair is written.
‡ Fatty acids are classified according to structure. In medium-chain fatty acids, chain length is <C12 carbon atoms. Long-chain fatty acids, >C12, are divided into saturated (no double bonds) and unsaturated (≤6 double bonds). Saturated fats are considered atherogenic, whereas unsaturated fats have the opposite effect.
§ No commonly used descriptive name.

TABLE 6–2.

Principal Fat Sources for Milk and Infant Formulas*

Milks and Formulas	Fat (%)	Source
Milks		
Human†	4.0*	. . .
Cow	3.7	Buttermilk
Formulas		
Enfamil 20	3.7	80% soy, 20% coconut oil
Similac 20	3.6	Coconut and soy oils
Similac PM 60/40	3.8	Coconut and corn oils
SMA	3.6	Oleo, coconut, safflower, and soy oils
Lonalac	3.5	Coconut oil
ProSobee	3.6	80% soy, 20% coconut oil
Soyalac	4.0	Soybean oil
Isomil	3.6	Coconut and soy oils
Nutramigen	2.6	Corn oil
Portagen	3.2	88% MCT oil, 12% corn oil‡
Pregestimil	2.7	60% corn oil, 40% MCT oil‡

* From Hamosh M: Fat needs for term and preterm infants, in Tsang RC, Nichols BL (eds): *Nutrition During Infancy.* Philadelphia, Hanley & Belfus, 1988, pp 133–159.
† The composition of human milk fat is given in Tables 6–4 and 6–5.
‡ MCT = medium-chain triglyceride.

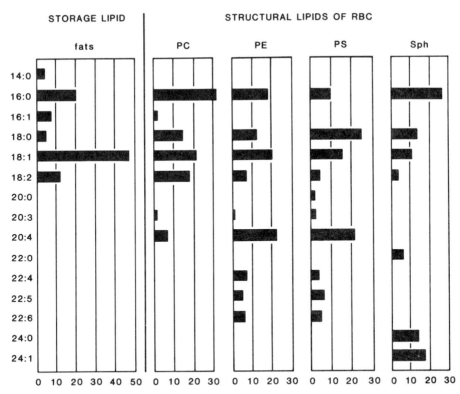

FIG 6–2.
Fatty acid composition of storage and structural lipids. Storage lipid is triglyceride, whereas structural red blood cell *(RBC)* lipids are phospholipids and sphingomyelin: *PC, PE,* and *PS* are phosphatidylcholine, phosphatidylethanolamine, and phosphatidylserine, respectively; *SPH* is sphingomyelin. (From McGilvery RW, Goldstein GW: *Biochemistry: A Functional Approach.* Philadelphia, WB Saunders, 1983, and Hamosh M: Fat needs for term and preterm infants, in Tsang RC, Nichols BL (eds): *Nutrition During Infancy.* Philadelphia, Hanley & Belfus, 1988, pp 133–159.)

DIFFERENCES BETWEEN THE FAT IN HUMAN MILK AND INFANT FORMULAS

Fat Composition of Human Milk

Mature human milk has a 3.5% to 4.5% fat content. The fat in milk is contained within membrane-enclosed milk fat globules.[4] The core of the globules consists of triglycerides (98% to 99% of total milk fat); the globule membrane is composed mainly of phospholipids, cholesterol, and proteins (Table 6–4). The packaging of triglyceride within the core of the globules permits the dispersion of these nonpolar lipids in the aqueous environment of milk and also protects them from hydrolysis by milk lipases.[5, 6]

Milk fat content and composition change during lactation. These changes are most pronounced during early lactation (colostrum, secreted 1 to 3 days postpartum), during the transition to mature milk (within the following 2 to 3 days), and again during weaning. Mature milk, however, maintains a constant fat composition.

Total fat content increases gradually from colostrum (2.0%) through transitional milk (2.5% to 3.0%) to mature milk (3.5% to 4.5%).[7] Cholesterol content is highest in colostrum and decreases to lower levels in transitional and mature milks; it is distributed as 87% free cholesterol and 13% cholesteryl ester (see Table 6–4). Phospholipids show

TABLE 6–3.

Function of Lipids in Mammals*

Lipid Class	Function
Glycerides	Fatty acid storage, metabolic intermediates
Phospholipids	Membrane structure, lung surfactant
Sterols	
Cholesterol	Membrane and lipoprotein structure, precursors of steroid hormones, degradation products are bile salts important in fat digestion and absorption
Cholesteryl ester	Storage and transport
Fatty acids	Major energy source, components of most lipids precursors of prostaglandins

* From Hamosh M: Fat needs for term and preterm infants, in Tsang RC, Nichols BL (eds): *Nutrition During Infancy*. Philadelphia, Hanley & Belfus, 1988, pp 133–159.

a similar decrease from high levels in colostrum to lower levels in mature milk. The decline in phospholipid and cholesterol levels agrees well with an increase in the fat globule size[8] and thus a decrease in the amount of membrane lipids (containing about 60% of milk phospholipid and 85% of milk cholesterol).

Over 98% of the fat in human milk is present in 11 major fatty acids from C10:0 to C20:4 (Table 6–5). Medium-chain fatty acids amount to 10% of total fatty acids in mature milk of mothers of term infants but contribute 17% of total fatty acids in milk produced by mothers of preterm infants.[7]

Saturated fatty acids constitute 42%, and unsaturated fatty acids 57%, of total lipid in human milk. Linoleic acid concentrations have been higher in recent studies[7] than in

TABLE 6–4.

Composition of Human Milk Fat*, †

Glycerides		3.0–4.5 gm/dL	
Triglycerides	98.7%‡	Major component of the core of milk fat globules	
Diglycerides	0.01%		
Monoglycerides	0		
Free fatty acids	0.08%		
Cholesterol		10–15 mg/dL	Major component of
Phospholipids		15–15 mg/dL	milk fat globule
Sphingomyelin	37%‡		
Phosphatidylcholine	28%		
Phosphatidylserine	9%		
Phosphatidylinositol	6%		
Phosphatidylethanolamine	19%		

* Data from Hamosh M, Bitman M, Wood DL, et al: Lipids in milk and the first steps in their digestion. *Pediatrics* 1985; 75(suppl):146–150.
† Mature milk from mothers of term infants.
‡ Percent in lipid class (glycerides and phospholipids, respectively).

TABLE 6–5.

Fatty Acid Composition (%) of Human Milk*†

Fatty Acid	Structure	VPT‡ 26–30 wk	PT 31–36 wk	T 37–40 wk
	10:0	1.37±0.17	1.27±0.18	0.97±0.28
Lauric	12:0	7.47±0.72	6.55±0.77	4.46±1.17
Myristic	14:0	8.41±0.83	7.55±0.89	5.68±1.36
	15:0	0.23±0.04	0.27±0.05	0.31±0.07
Palmitic	16:0	20.13±1.40	23.16±1.49	22.20±2.28
	16:1	2.56±1.40	2.92±0.26	3.83±0.39
	17:0	0.34±0.22	0.60±0.24	0.49±0.36
	18:0	7.24±1.13	7.25±1.21	7.68±1.85
Oleic	18:1	33.41±1.67	33.74±1.79	35.51±2.73
Linoleic	18:2	15.75±1.22	13.83±1.20	15.58±1.99
	18:3	0.76±0.13	0.76±0.14	1.03±0.21
	20:0	0.17±0.07	0.09±0.08	0.32±0.11
	20:2	0.35±0.13	0.33±0.13	0.18±0.20
	20:3	0.51±0.09	0.43±0.10	0.53±0.15
	20:4	0.55±0.18	0.58±0.19	0.60±0.29
	20:5	0.04±0.05	00	00
	21:0	0.05±0.07	0.07±0.08	0.17±0.12
	22:4	0.13±0.10	0.24±0.11	0.07±0.16
	22:5w6	0.11±0.05	0.04±0.05	0.03±0.08
	22:5w3	0.42±0.09	0.12±0.10	0.11±0.15
	22:6w3	0.24±0.09	0.21±0.09	0.23±0.14

* Comparison of milk* from mothers who delivered at 26 to 30 weeks (VPT), 31 to 36 weeks (PT), and 37 to 40 weeks (T) of pregnancy. Milk was collected at 6 weeks of lactation.

† Data from Bitman J, Wood DL, Hamosh M, et al: Comparison of the lipid composition of breast milk from mothers of term and preterm infants. *Am J Clin Nutr* 1983; 38:300–313. Used by permission.

‡ Means ± standard error of the mean.

earlier reports[9] and reflect the higher intake of polyunsaturated fats by the American population. Essential fatty acid contents are higher in colostrum and transitional milk than in mature milk.[10] Long-chain polyunsaturated fatty acids derived from linoleic acid (20:2n6, 20:3, 20:4, 22:5n6) and from linolenic acid (20:5, 22:5n3, 22:6) show a similar decrease throughout lactation. The level of these fatty acids is significantly higher in colostrum and milk of mothers of preterm infants than mothers of full-term infants.[7]

Differences Between Human Milk and Formula Fat

The major differences between the fat in human milk and in infant formulas are absence of long-chain polyenoic fatty acids greater than C18 in formulas and the presence of only traces of cholesterol as compared with an average amount of 10 to 15 mg/dL cholesterol in human milk. Furthermore, while formulas deliver a constant amount of fat to the infant during each feed, there are marked variations in fat content of human milk, fat concentration being lowest in fore milk and gradually increasing to highest levels in hind milk. In addition, fat content rises during the day, early morning milk having the lowest fat content.

Minerals, trace elements, and enzymes associated with the cream fraction of milk have similar diurnal variations. Nutrient content might also vary in the milk secreted from the right or left breast at the same feeding.

In contrast to the changes in fat concentration, the fat composition of mature human milk is remarkably constant. Only drastic changes in the diet, such as consumption of excessively large amounts of polyunsaturated fats, of carbohydrates, or severe limitations of total food intake, result in the increase of linoleic acid, medium-chain fatty acid levels, and palmatic acid, respectively. Recent studies show that the amount of eicosapentaenoic acid or of trans fatty acids (geometric isomers of cis fatty acids, formed during partial hydrogenation of fat) rises markedly in milk of women who consume large amounts of fish oil[11] or hydrogenated fats,[12, 13] respectively. The greatest increase in milk trans fatty acids occurred in women who were losing weight and consuming hydrogenated fat.[13] From these data it appears that trans fatty acids from the diet and from the mother's fat depots contribute to milk trans fatty acids.

Milk fat composition is markedly affected by maternal diseases such as cystic fibrosis,[10] diabetes,[14] and hyperlipemia.[15] Whether feeding human milk or formula in infancy might affect the health status of the adult is unknown at present. Careful studies are necessary in order to establish clearly whether early feeding of milk protects against obesity and atherosclerosis in later life. We have stressed, however,[16, 17] that metabolic changes associated with breast-feeding, such as rate of feeding when suckling as compared to being fed by bottle[18, 19]; differences in gastric emptying rates[20]; and different patterns of hormonal release in response to feeding human milk vs. formula[21] might affect weight and adiposity, with possible effects continuing into later life. Careful epidemiologic studies indicate a protective effect of human milk against obesity.[21] Breast-fed infants have a lower weight gain than formula-fed infants,[23] and recent studies show energy intake and growth velocity to be lower than National Center for Health Statistics standards, even in an affluent, well-educated population.[24]

The self-perpetuating nature of weight gain, associated with an increase in fasting levels of lipoprotein lipase activity[25] and in the responsiveness of this key enzyme in fat deposition[26] to feeding,[25] as well as the recent observation that fat calories may be preferentially stored in reduced-obese subjects,[27] suggests that great care has to be exercised in early life in order to avoid overweight at later ages.

It might be too early to assess the relationship of the presence or absence of cholesterol in the newborn diet to later atherosclerosis.[16, 17] The reason for this statement is the nature of the studies conducted (mainly in animals fed artificial diets as compared with suckled controls) and the fact that recent studies, with very sensitive techniques, show that the cholesterol content of human milk is only 15 mg/dL[7] (contrary to higher human milk cholesterol levels found in earlier studies). Whether this low cholesterol level in human milk—as compared with no cholesterol or only traces of cholesterol in formula—will affect cholesterol metabolism in later life is not known at present.

The role of polyenoic fatty acids (present in human milk, but absent from formulas) in brain development, especially in the preterm infant, will be discussed in a later section.

METABOLISM OF LIPIDS

Fat Digestion and Absorption

More than 95% of dietary fat (including that in human milk and infant formula) is triglyceride (see Fig 6–1; Table 6–4). Digestion and absorption of dietary fat can be divided into three steps. *The luminal phase* involves the solubilizing and hydrolysis of triglycerides to free fatty acids, monoglycerides, and glycerol, prior to their uptake by the intestinal mucosa. *The mucosal phase* involves the reesterification of free fatty acids to form triglycerides, which are assimilated into chylomicrons and very low density lipoproteins (VLDL) prior to their release from the mucosal cell into the blood via the lymphatics. In the *transport and delivery phase,* the fatty acids within chylomicrons and VLDL are taken up by the individual tissues for their metabolic needs.

Luminal Phase

Fat digestion requires adequate lipase activity and bile salt concentrations, the former for the breakdown of triglycerides and the latter for emulsification of fat prior to and during lipolysis.[3] The lipases, significant for fat digestion, are listed in Table 6–6. Fat digestion begins in the stomach with the action of lingual lipase, an enzyme secreted from lingual serous glands[28] and of gastric lipase secreted from glands within the gastric mucosa.[29] Further digestion takes place in the small intestine through the action of pancreatic lipase (Fig 6–3).

The Stomach

Initial hydrolysis of fat in the stomach leads to the formation of partial glycerides and free fatty acids.[30] This critical step is necessary for efficient fat absorption in the adult with adequate pancreatic function.[30] In the newborn and especially the preterm infant, pancreatic lipase and intraduodenal bile acid concentrations (the major components of intestinal fat digestion) are low.[31] Therefore, efficient fat absorption in the newborn depends on alternate mechanisms for the digestion of dietary fat.

Of special importance is intragastric lipolysis in which lingual and gastric lipases compensate for low pancreatic lipase (see Table 6–6).[29, 32] In addition, the products of intragastric lipolysis (fatty acids and monoglycerides) compensate for low bile salt con-

TABLE 6–6.
Compensatory Digestive Lipases in the Newborn*

Characteristic	Lipases in Gastric Aspirates†	Milk Bile Salt Stimulated Lipase
Origin	Lingual serous glands: gastric mucosa	Mammary gland (human, gorilla, and carnivores)
Ontogeny	Present from 24 weeks gestation	Present after term and preterm (26–36 weeks) delivery and in prepartum mammary secretions
Site of action		
Characteristics	Stomach (duodenum)	Intestine
pH optimum	3.0–6.5	7.0–9.0
pH stability	>2.2	>3.5
Rate	MCT > LCT	MCT = LCT
	FA unsaturated > saturated	Water-soluble esters
Reaction products	FFA, DG, MG	FFA, glycerol
Bile salts	20%–40% stimulation	Obligatory
Molecular weight	46,000–48,000	90,000–125,000
Function	Hydrolysis of 50%–70% ingested fat	Hydrolysis of 30%–40% of milk fat

* Data from Hamosh M, Bitman J, Wood D, et al: Lipids in milk and the first steps in their digestion. *Pediatrics* 1985; 75(suppl):146–150.
† MCT = medium-chain triglyceride; LCT = long chain triglyceride; FA = fatty acids, FFA = free fatty acids; DG = diglycerides; MG = monoglycerides.

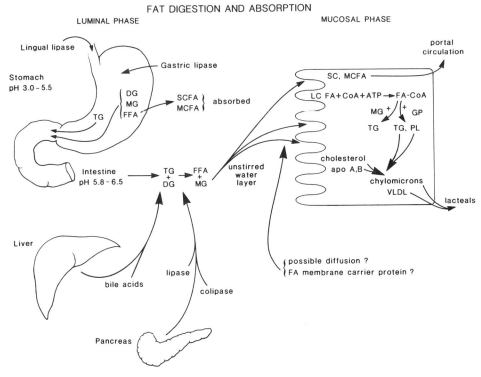

FIG 6–3.

Fat digestion and absorption. Abbreviated scheme of major steps in fat hydrolysis in the lumen of stomach and intestine and reesterification in the intestinal mucosa. *TG* = triglyceride, *DG* = diglyceride, *MG* = monoglyceride, *FFA* = free fatty acids, *GP* = glycerophosphate; α = glycerophosphate; *apo A, apo B* = apoproteins A and B, *PL* = phospholipid. (From Hamosh M: Fat needs for term and preterm infants, in Tsang RC, Nichols BL (eds): *Nutrition During Infancy*. Philadelphia, Hanley & Belfus, 1988, pp 133–159.)

centrations by emulsifying the lipid mixture.[30] As much as 10% to 30% of dietary fat is hydrolyzed in the stomach of the newborn.[32] Indeed, lingual and gastric lipases appear before 26 weeks gestation and have high activity levels at birth.[32] Furthermore, in pancreatic insufficiency, the lower pH in the duodenum enables these lipases (which have a pH optimum under 6.5) to continue the hydrolysis of fat in the upper small intestine.[33, 34]

Lingual and gastric lipase have a special function in the hydrolysis of milk fat. Milk fat globules are resistant to the action of pancreatic lipase but are readily hydrolyzed by lingual lipase, which penetrates into the core of the fat particles and hydrolyzes the triglyceride without disrupting the globule membrane.[35] Indeed, as much as 15% of core triglyceride is hydrolyzed without producing any change in the microscopic appearance of milk fat globules.[35] Lingual and gastric lipases hydrolyze medium-chain and short-chain triglycerides at higher rates than long-chain triglycerides. Short- and medium-chain fatty acids are absorbed directly through the gastric mucosa,[36] and these products of intragastric lipolysis appear rapidly in the circulation.

Intragastric hydrolysis of milk fat produces relatively large amounts of monolauryl glyceride, a substance with antibacterial, antiviral, and antifungal activity, indicating that anti-infective agents are formed in the infant's stomach during fat hydrolysis. Fat digestion in the stomach is probably quantitatively much more important for the newborn than for the healthy adult; the stomach is a large receptacle where food is mixed with enzyme through churning and squirting movements. Gastric pH is higher in the newborn and stomach emptying is slower, allowing for longer periods of food digestion than in adults. High fat concentration in gastric contents further delays gastric emptying.

Recent studies show that there are marked species differences in the origin of prepancreatic digestive lipases, in some species (such as rodents and ruminants) the enzyme being exclusively of oral origin, while in others (lagomorphs, primates) the lipase being predominantly of gastric origin.[37, 38]

The Duodenum

The hydrolysis of fat in the intestine is catalyzed primarily by pancreatic lipase in a complex interaction between the lipase, colipase, bile salts, and the triglyceride substrate (see Fig 6-3).[3, 39] The colipase is necessary to provide higher affinity for lipase attachment at the surface of a bile-salt-covered triglyceride–water interface. Bile salts enhance the hydrolysis by promoting the formation of a colipase-lipase complex, which then adheres to the triglyceride molecules at the region of the ester bonds.

Pancreatic phospholipase A_2 hydrolyzes phospholipids, including those in the surface layer of milk fat globules or formula fat emulsions.[34] The enzyme has an absolute requirement for calcium and bile salts for the hydrolysis of long-chain phospholipids. Pancreatic cholesterol ester hydrolase hydrolyzes cholesteryl esters, monoglycerides, and fat-soluble vitamins.[3, 39]

Little is known about these processes in the newborn except that, as mentioned, pancreatic lipase and bile salt levels are low (<critical micellar concentrations [CMC]) and the secretory response to exogenous and endogenous stimuli is diminished.[31] The newborn benefits, however, from the extensive intragastric lipolysis. The products of this process (protonated fatty acids and diglycerides) facilitate the action of pancreatic lipase; and fatty acids increase lipase–colipase binding and the binding of colipase to bile salts.

The breast-fed infant depends on an additional digestive enzyme, the bile salt–stimulated lipase of human milk.[40] (The characteristics of this lipase are described later in Table 6-6. Because of low substrate specificity, the enzyme hydrolyzes a large variety of triglycerides completely to free fatty acids and glycerol, thus continuing, in the intestine, the lipolytic process started in the stomach (see Fig 6-3).

Thus, even with very low levels of pancreatic lipase the newborn is able to absorb 90% to 95% of dietary fat through the combined action of gastric lipolysis and intestinal lipolysis by human milk lipase. Recent studies show that bile salt–stimulated lipase activity levels are similar in preterm and term milk and that the enzyme is stable at low temperature, indicating that preterm infants fed their own mother's milk receive adequate digestive lipase even when fed previously stored milk.[5, 41]

Absorption and Transport to Tissues

The products of luminal lipolysis pass into the enterocyte by passive diffusion. Recent studies suggest, however, that fatty acid transport across the enterocyte could be facilitated by a specific membrane fatty acid binding protein.[1] Once inside the enterocyte the fatty acids are transported to the reesterification site (the endoplasmic reticulum) by means of a soluble intracellular fatty acid–binding protein.[1]

After the fatty acids are activated to acyl-coenzyme A (CoA) (a step that is catalyzed by acyl-CoA ligase and occurs in the mitochondria), the reesterification to triglyceride occurs by two mechanisms, the monoglyceride and the phosphatidic acid pathways. In the first mechanism the acceptor of fatty acids is monoglyceride, whereas in the second pathway the acceptor is α-glycerophosphate produced from glucose metabolism. The monoglyceride pathway accounts for the reesterification of about 70% of absorbed fatty acids, whereas the phosphatidic acid pathway is the only mechanism for phospholipid synthesis in the intestinal mucosa (see Fig 6–3).

Studies in developing animals show that the mucosal phase of fat absorption is well developed and keeps pace with the higher fat intake of the neonatal period.[1]

Transport and Delivery Phase

The newly synthesized triglyceride, together with phospholipid, cholesterol, and protein, are assembled into lipoproteins, namely chylomicrons and VLDL. The large particles are released into the intercellular space by reverse pinocytosis and move across the basement membrane into the lymphatics.[42] Chylomicrons are released into the lacteals on the 1st day after birth, suggesting that this phase of fat assimilation is well developed in the newborn.

Lipids are nonpolar or polar amphipathic substances (see Fig 6–1) that are insoluble in aqueous media and can be transported in the circulation only in association with specific proteins. Polar lipids, such as free fatty acids and lysolecithin, bind to plasma albumin, whereas nonpolar lipids are transported within much larger particles—the lipoproteins. The nonpolar lipids (triglycerides and cholesteryl ester) from the hydrophobic core of the lipoproteins, while amphipathic lipids (phospholipids, cholesterol, small amounts of free fatty acids, and partial glycerides) combine with apoproteins to form the surface film.

The lipoproteins are generally divided into four categories: chylomicrons, VLDL, low-density lipoproteins (LDL), and high-density lipoproteins (HDL). The primary function of the lipoproteins is the transport of lipids, chiefly triglyceride (chylomicrons and VLDL) and cholesterol (LDL and HDL) (Table 6–7). In addition to their transport function—the solubilization of hydrophobic lipid in the aqueous environment of

TABLE 6–7.

Plasma Lipoproteins: Composition and Function*

| Lipoprotein | Protein[†] | Lipid[‡] | | | | Origin | Half-Life | Function |
		TG	CE	C	PL			
Chylomicrons	2.0	85	5.0	2.0	8.0	Intestine	5 min	TG transport
VLDL	8–10	56	13.0	8.0	20.0	Intestine§‖ Liver‖	Hours	TG transport
LDL	25	10	50.0	10.0	30.0	Circulation from VLDL	Hours	Cholesterol transport to tissues (anabolic)
HDL	41–55	1–8	28.0	6.5–9.0	50.0	Intestine Liver Circulation¶	Days	Cholesterol transport to liver (catabolic)

* Adapted from Hamosh M, Hamosh P: Lipoprotein lipase: Its physiological and clinical significance. *Molec Aspects Med* 1983; 6:199–289. TG = triglyceride, CE = cholesteryl ester, C = cholesterol, PL = phospholipid, VLDL = very low density lipoprotein, LDL = low density lipoprotein, HDL = high density lipoprotein.
  The lipoprotein profiles difer markedly between cord blood and postnatal blood specimens. Very little is known about the factors that modulate these rapid postnatal changes.
† Weight percent per particle.
‡ Weight percent of total lipid.
§ Dietary fat.
‖ Endogenous fat.
¶ Surface coat of chlomicrons and VLDL during lipolysis.

blood—the protein components of lipoproteins, the apolipoproteins, have important metabolic functions. Some apoproteins (apo B and apo AII) have a primary role in lipid transport, whereas others (apo CII and AI) are specific activators of enzymes involved in lipolysis (lipoprotein lipase) and the interconversion of lipoproteins [lecithin:cholesterol acyl transferase (LCAT)].

The catabolism of chylomicrons, VLDL, or Intralipid, occurs by a stepwise reduction of the triglyceride core through the action of lipoprotein lipase, an enzyme that hydrolyzes lipoprotein–triglyceride at the luminal surface of the capillary endothelium (Fig 6–4).[26] Concomitantly with triglyceride hydrolysis, surplus surface constituents (apoproteins and polar lipids, 60% of free cholesterol, 90% of phosphatidylcholine, and 100% of sphingomyelin) are removed from VLDL. These surface constituents are released in particulate form that associate into disk-shaped structures similar to HDL precursors (nascent HDL) isolated from intestinal lymph or from rat liver perfusate.

The hydrolysis of chylomicrons and VLDL by lipoprotein lipase reduces the core of the lipoprotein particles, producing chylomicron remnants and LDL from chylomicrons and VLDL, respectively. The surplus surface constituents are the precursors of HDL (nascent HDL) (see Fig 6–4).

A second lipase that hydrolyzes lipoprotein–triglyceride is hepatic lipase, located in the endothelium of liver capillaries. The enzyme acts on VLDL triglyceride as well as on HDL phospholipids. Another enzyme with a key role in lipoprotein metabolism is LCAT. This enzyme is released from the liver into the circulation, where it acts specifically on plasma HDL by converting the lecithin and unesterified cholesterol of HDL to lysolecithin and cholesteryl ester.[43] Once esterified, the cholesteryl ester leaves the sur-

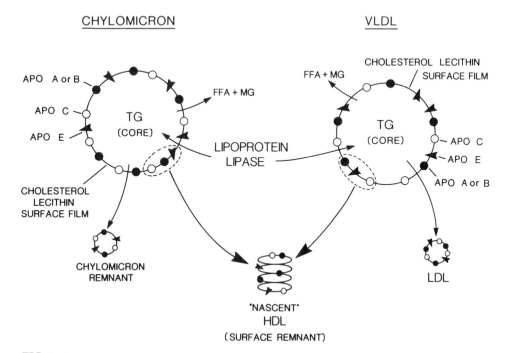

FIG 6–4.
Central role of lipoprotein lipase in the formation of low-density and high-density lipoproteins. (From Hamosh M: Fat needs for term and preterm infants, in Tsang RC, Nichols BL (eds): *Nutrition During Infancy.* Philadelphia, Hanley & Belfus, 1988, pp 133–159.)

face coat and moves into the nonpolar lipid core in the center of the particle, leading to the transformation of disk-shaped "nascent" HDL into spherical "mature" HDL.

Lipoprotein lipase, the key enzyme in removal of lipoprotein triglyceride, is thus important in the formation of both LDL and HDL lipoprotein. The enzyme LCAT catalyzes the synthesis of almost the entire cholesterol ester of circulating lipoproteins. These two key enzymes differ in one important respect: lipoprotein lipase is active at the capillary wall and under normal conditions is found only in trace amounts in the circulation. This specific location probably facilitates the uptake of lipolytic products (free fatty acids and monoglycerides) into tissues. On the other hand, LCAT acts exclusively in plasma, where it accomplishes its function of continuous modulation of the cholesteryl ester content of circulating lipoproteins.

Long-chain Polyunsaturated Fatty Acids and Brain Development

Lipids are major constituents of the brain, where they are essential for the structure and function of neuronal and glial membranes, and are the main components of the myelin sheath.[44] The biochemistry of brain development during the fetal and postnatal periods has been the subject of several reviews,[45, 46] while the specific subjects of lipid accretion in the fetus[47] and of very long chain fatty acids in the developing retina and brain[48] have received excellent reviews recently. Lipids constitute about 60% of fetal brain solids; in myelin, the weight of lipid amounts to 70% to 75% of dry weight.[49] The timing of growth and development of the human brain suggests that the brain might be more vulnerable to postnatal nutritional influence than previously assumed. The growth spurt is much more postnatal, ending only 3 to 4 years after birth. Thus, the statement of Kuhn and Crawford that, "human fetal development is a biological process in which both the blueprint (genetics) and building materials (nutrition) must be in good order for the construction of a healthy infant,"[50] is relevant not only to the fetal period, but also to infancy and childhood.[49] Because an increase in chain elongation–desaturation products does not occur for several weeks after birth in preterm infants,[51] placental transfer of these fatty acids is of primary importance in accretion of these fatty acids in the fetus. Based on quantitation of 22:6n3 and 22:5n3 in human milk,[7] our data show that preterm infants fed their own mother's milk receive adequate amounts of long-chain polyunsaturated fatty acids, which are sufficient to meet the estimated requirements for neural tissue synthesis.[51]

Brain growth is affected by nutrition at all steps of development but may be more vulnerable during critical periods of brain growth.[46] While the mature brain is spared to great extent from the effects of malnutrition, brain content and composition are affected during malnutrition in the early developmental period, myelin-associated lipids being particularly vulnerable, resulting in impairment of myelination and synaptogenesis.[52] Although most of these studies have been carried out in animals, they might have great importance for human infants, especially those born prematurely. The high content of 22:6n3 in brain lipids and the absence of this fatty acid from infant formulas, even those specially prepared for feeding the premature, combined with good evidence for inadequate synthesis of this fatty acid from the precursor linolenic acid (18:3n3), have led to recent research aimed at adding long-chain polyunsaturated fatty acids to the diet of premature infants.

Quantitation of 22:6n3 in individual red blood cell phospholipids in infants under 32 weeks at gestation showed that 22:6n3 decreased from cord blood levels while the infants were receiving 60 kcal/kg/day from oral gastric feedings. Similar 22:6n3 quantitation at 7 weeks of age showed, however, that this fatty acid increased in infants fed preterm human milk, while it continued to decline in infants fed premature formula.[53] Studies to increase the level of 22:6n3 [docosahexaenoic acid (DHA)] by giving preterm infants fish oil (MaxEPA; Smith Kline & French) in the form of a bolus or dispersed in the formula, showed increased plasma phospholipid levels of 22:6n3 with both modes of administration. The dispersed long-chain fatty acid was, however, absorbed to a greater extent than when given as a bolus. These studies[54, 55] show that it is possible to prevent the postnatal decline in DHA and to maintain serum levels of this fatty acid at concentrations seen in preterm infants fed human milk by its careful addition to infant formulas. It might, however, be advisable to supplement infant formulas, not only with the long-chain polyunsaturated fatty acids of the n-3 series (such as DHA-22:6n3) but also those of the n-6 series,[47] in order to maintain a concentration of fatty acids similar to that in human milk, especially in the milk produced by women who deliver prematurely.[7]

High levels of DHA-22:6n3 are present in retina. Feeding of diets low in 18:3n3 during pregnancy and after birth to newborn rhesus monkeys resulted in a marked decrease of 22:6n3 content in retina and cerebral cortex (50% of control values in the retina and 25% of control values in the cerebral cortex).[56] At 22 months of age the content of 22:6n3 in these tissues doubled in the control animals, but failed to increase in the deficient group. Functionally, the deficient animals had subnormal visual acuity at 4 to 12 weeks of age and a prolonged recovery time of the dark-adapted electroretinogram after a saturating flash.[56] The very disturbing effect of this early nutritional deficiency is the irreversible nature of the damage.[57] Thus, after 9 months of fish oil feeding, despite normalization of the DHA content of the retina, abnormal retinal function appears to be a persistent effect of n-3 fatty acid deficiency during development. These studies indicate that primates, including humans, might not recover full brain function when early nutritional deficiencies are countered after the weaning period.[58] The avid uptake of polyunsaturated fatty acids by the developing brain, which increases steadily with increasing degrees of unsaturation,[59] indicates that these fatty acids have to be provided in optimal amounts for normal functional development.[60]

Carnitine, Medium-chain Fatty Acids and Ketone Bodies

Carnitine

(α-trimethylamino-β-hydroxybutyrate) is essential for the catabolism of long-chain fatty acids. All the enzymes for β-oxidation of fatty acids are localized in the matrix of the mitochondria; the inner mitochondrial membrane is, however, impermeable to fatty acids. Long-chain fatty acids are transported into the mitochondrial matrix by a system involving carnitine and several specific enzymes (carnitine palmitoyl transferase I, carnitine transferase, and carnitine palmitoyl transferase II). Carnitine is synthesized in human liver and kidney from the essential amino acids lysine and methionine; cardiac and skeletal muscle cannot synthesize carnitine and receive it from the blood. The metabolism and function of carnitine[61, 62] as well as its special role in the newborn[62] have been reviewed recently.

Because fatty acid oxidation and ketogenesis are critical to the survival of newborn infants, an adequate supply of carnitine is of major importance for the newborn. Recent studies[62] show that (1) the newborn has a critical need for carnitine, (2) plasma and tissue concentrations of carnitine are low in the newborn, (3) the biosynthesis of carnitine is not fully developed in the newborn, and (4) the lack of dietary carnitine results in significantly lower plasma carnitine concentrations.[62]

Medium-chain Fatty Acids

Medium-chain fatty acids (C8 and C10) are present in very low amounts in human milk.[7] They are mainly components of preemie formulas, where they were added because of the poor absorption of cow's milk fat. The change in formula fat to vegetable fat blends results, however, in similar absorption of long-chain or medium-chain fatty acids.[36] Medium-chain fatty acids are more easily released from triglycerides by lingual and gastric lipases and are absorbed directly through the gastric mucosa.[36] These fatty acids are preferentially oxidized (as compared to long-chain fatty acids)[63]; however, storage of C8, C10, and C12 in adipose tissue has recently been reported.[64]

Because medium-chain fatty acids can enter mitochondia without the need for carnitine-mediated transfer, they are a good source of ketone bodies.

Ketone Bodies

Ketone bodies give rise to acetoacetate. Acetoacetate is reduced by a specific inner-membrane mitochondrial β-hydroxybutyric acid dehydrogenase to yield β-hydroxybutyrate. The release of acetoacetate and hydroxybutyrate from the liver into the blood and their uptake by peripheral tissues are constant, normal processes.

Recent studies suggest that the capacity for ketone synthesis by the liver is low in the immediate neonatal period in the human and the guinea pig. Developmental changes in ketogenesis in the perinatal period have been reported also in other species.

The activity of the enzymes of ketone body utilization (such as 3-oxoacid-CoA transferase) in adult rat tissue is highest in kidney, heart, brown adipose tissue, and adrenal gland, followed by submaxillary gland, lactating mammary gland, and brain. The liver has low activity of 3-oxoacid-CoA transferase, which means that ketone bodies synthesized by the liver are not utilized by the liver but directed to peripheral tissues. The enzymes of ketone body utilization show marked changes in activity during development of the rat, and the pattern varies in different tissues. In the suckling rat, activity is very high in brain and low in heart and kidney, resulting in channeling of ketone bodies to the developing brain in the suckling rat.

Although fatty acid oxidation does not occur in adult brain, it is present in fetal and neonatal brain, contributing as much as 25% of the metabolites entering the Krebs citric acid cycle. Ketone bodies are a major source of energy for the developing brain in many species, including humans, in whom ketone bodies can be metabolized as early as 12 to 21 weeks gestation. Such activity remains high during the remainder of gestation as well as postnatally.

In rat brain, permeability for 3-hydroxybutyrate is sevenfold higher during suckling than either at birth or in the adult. Milk fatty acids are the source of ketone bodies during this period. The brain is the major ketone body–using tissue in suckling mammals; activity of the enzymes that convert ketone bodies to acetyl-CoA increases rapidly after birth, reaches peak activity before weaning, and decreases thereafter. There is a direct relationship between neurologic immaturity at birth and the extent of ketone-body utilization.

Recent studies, using stable isotopes, show that ketone bodies can account for 25% of the neonate's basal energy requirements in the 1st few days of life.[65] Ketone body production and metabolism in the fetus and neonate have been reviewed recently.[66]

NORMAL FAT REQUIREMENTS

The normal fat requirements, as suggested by the American Academy of Pediatrics, with some of my own suggestions, are listed in Table 6–8.

It is important to monitor the amount and type of dietary lipid as well as the extent of fat absorption in the infant in order to prevent deficiencies. Special attention should be given to provide sufficient essential fatty acids (linoleic acid, 0.3 g/100 cal). In light of the special role of n-3 fatty acids in neonatal brain development, and in normal nerve function at all ages, linolenic (C18:3n3) acid should be provided as well as its long-chain derivatives eicosapentaenoic and DHA. The latter should be provided because of clinical evidence of the inability of the newborn (especially the premature) infant to chain elongate and desaturate the parent compound of this fatty acid family—linolenic acid.

Although overfeeding might lead to obesity and should be avoided, it is important to remember that fats are essential for growth, not only as a source of energy, but also as cell components. Therefore, infants should not be subjected to "fat restriction" which might result in failure to thrive.

PATHOPHYSIOLOGY—DIFFERENCES BETWEEN PRETERM AND FULL-TERM INFANTS

The differences between premature and full-term infants have been discussed in this chapter when describing the various stages of fat metabolism. Because fat deposition and accretion of specific lipids occur in the last trimester of intrauterine development, very low birth weight infants are deficient both in specific metabolites (total adipose tissue mass, brain DHA and eicosapentaenoic acids, carnitine) as well as in the enzymes needed for fat digestion and metabolism (pancreatic lipase, fatty acid desaturation and elongation). Furthermore, one of the most important differences in fat metabolism is the fact that very low birth weight infants are often maintained on total parenteral nutrition for various periods of time after birth.

LIPIDS IN TOTAL PARENTERAL NUTRITION

Improvement in the clinical nutritional management of very low birth weight infants has been largely dependent on methods of nutrient delivery. The addition of lipids to

TABLE 6–8.

Fat Requirements for Newborn Infants*

Fat content	3.3–6.0 g/100 kcal (30%–54% of calories)
Fat composition	

Essential fatty acids C18:2, 0.3 g/100 kcal
Polyunsaturated fatty acids C20, C22 should be added in amounts present in human milk
Fat absorption should be at least 85% in full-term infants at 1 month of age
Cholesterol and phospholipids should be present in amounts similar to that in human milk, i.e., 10 to 20 mg/dL

* From Hamosh M: Fat needs for term and preterm infants, in Tsang RC, Nichols BL (eds): *Nutrition During Infancy.* Philadelphia, Hanley & Belfus, 1988, pp 133–159.

total parenteral nutrition has markedly advanced the growth of very tiny babies.

Lipid is administered to infants on an empirical basis; it is generally advised that it be given in amounts that do not cause lipemia (plasma triglycerides in excess of 100 to 150 mg/dL).[67] The widespread use of lipid in parenteral nutrition is in marked contrast to the limited knowledge of the enzymes and cofactors active in the lipid clearing process in low-birth-weight infants.

Recent studies indicate that infusion period and infusion rate affect the clearing of lipid in low-birth-weight infants maintained on total parenteral nutrition.[68] Furthermore, the presence of heparin in solutions prepared for intravenous (IV) use (even the low concentration of 1 U/mL IV fluid, added to prevent clotting of catheters) might affect the lipid clearing process.[68] We have recently reviewed the enzymes and cofactors active in the mechanism of lipid clearing,[26] with special emphasis on the developmental period (Table 6–9).[68, 69]

Low-birth-weight infants have lower levels of lipolytic enzymes (lipoprotein lipase) and LCAT than full-term infants.[68–70] Recent studies in weanling rats, show that intralipid infusion markedly lowers LCAT activity.[71] This is probably the reason for the hyperlipemia that develops in very low birth weight infants maintained on total parenteral nutrition with lipids in excess of 2 g/kg/day.[68, 69]

The ability to synthesize lipoprotein lipase in response to the administration of heparin seems to be well developed even in preterm infants.[68, 72] The presence of high levels of free fatty acids and triglycerides in preterm infants who clear the infused intralipid well suggests that free fatty acids are produced in excess of the infant's ability for their catabolism.

AREAS FOR FUTURE RESEARCH

Future research is needed in almost all areas of lipid metabolism in the newborn. Specific questions that need answers are:

1. Does the amount and type of fat fed to the infant affect adiposity (obesity) and atherosclerosis in later life?

TABLE 6–9.
Enzymes, Cofactors, and Sites of Lipid Clearing and Catabolism*

Enzyme	Cofactor	Substrate	Site of Activity	Function
Lipoprotein lipase	Apoprotein CII	Chylomicrons, VLDL, Intralipid	Endothelium of extrahepatic tissues	Hydrolysis to triglycerides, to free fatty acids, and monoglyceride
Hepatic lipase		VLDL, HDL	Endothelium of liver	Hydrolysis of triglycerides and phospholipids
Lecithin: cholesterol acyl transferase	Apoprotein AI	Lecithin, cholesterol	Plasma	Fatty acid (FA) transfer, synthesis of cholesteryl ester
Acyl carnitine transferase	Carnitine	Long-chain FA	Mitochondria	Transfer of FA across mitochondrial membrane for oxidation

* Data from Hamosh M, Dhanireddy R, Zaidan H, et al: Total parenteral nutrition with lipid in the newborn: The enzymes and cofactors active in the clearing of circulating lipoprotein triglyceride, in Stern L, Xanthou M, Friis-Hansen B (eds): *Physiologic Foundations of Perinatal Care.* New York, Praeger, 1985, pp 178–195. VLDL = very low density lipoproteins, HDL = high-density lipoproteins.

2. Does the absence of long-chain polyenoic acids from the diet of the formula-fed infant have long term (or even permanent) effects on brain function and retinal function?

3. What are the quantitative contributions of the different digestive lipases to fat digestion, both as a function of gestational and postnatal age?

4. What are the interactions between parenteral lipid administration and lipid-clearing enzymes? Does this mode of lipid administration change the physiological maturation of the lipid-clearing process?

Acknowledgments

The expert secretarial assistance of Barbara M. Runner is gratefully acknowledged. The author's studies are supported by NIH grants HD-10823, HD-15631, and HD-10833, and by grants from Wyeth-Ayerst, Mead Johnson Nutrition Division, and Ross Laboratories.

REFERENCES

1. Hamosh M: Fat needs for term and preterm infants, in Tsang RC, Nichols BL (eds): *Nutrition During Infancy*. Philadelphia, Hanley & Belfus, 1988, pp 133–159.
2. Hamosh M: Lipid metabolism in premature infants. *Biol Neonate* 1987; 52(suppl):50–64.
3. Patton JS: Gastrointestinal lipid digestion, in Johnson LR (ed): *Physiology of the Gastrointestinal Tract*. New York, Raven Press, 1981, pp 1123–1146.
4. Hamosh M, Bitman J, Wood DL, et al: Lipids in milk and the first steps in their digestion. *Pediatrics* 1985; 75(suppl):146–150.
5. Mehta NR, Jones JB, Hamosh M: Lipases in human milk: Ontogeny and physiologic significance. *J Pediatr Gastroenterol Nutr* 1982; 1:317–326.
6. Hamosh M: Physiological role of human milk lipases, in Lebenthal E (ed): *Gastrointestinal Development and Infant Nutrition*. New York, Raven Press, 1981, pp 473–482.
7. Bitman J, Wood DL, Hamosh M, et al: Comparison of the lipid composition of breast milk from mothers of term and preterm infants. *Am J Clin Nutr* 1983; 38:300–313.
8. Ruegg M, Blanc B: The fat globule size distribution in human milk. *Biochim Biophys Acta* 1981; 666:7–13.
9. Jensen RG, Clark RM, Ferris AM: Composition of the lipids in human milk: A review. *Lipids* 1980; 15:345–352.
10. Bitman J, Hamosh M, Wood DL, et al: Lipid composition of milk from mothers with cystic fibrosis. *Pediatrics* 1987; 80:927–932.
11. Harris WD, Conner WE, Lindsey S: Will dietary W-3 fatty acids change the composition of human milk? *Am J Clin Nutr* 1984; 40:780–785.
12. Craig-Schmidt MC, Weete JD, Faircloth SA, et al: The effect of hydrogenated fat in the diet of nursing mothers on lipid composition and prostaglandin content of human milk. *Am J Clin Nutr* 1984; 39:778–786.
13. Chappell JE, Clandinin MT, Kearney-Volpe C: Trace fatty acids in human milk lipids: Influence of maternal diet and weight loss. *Am J Clin Nutr* 1985; 42:49–56.
14. Bitman J, Hamosh M, Hamosh P, et al: Milk composition and volume during the onset of lactation in a diabetic mother. *Am J Clin Nutr* 1989; 50:1364–1369.
15. Wang CS, Illingworth DR: Lipid composition and lipolytic activities in milk from a patient with homozygous familial hypobetalipoproteinemia. *Am J Clin Nutr* 1987; 45:730–736.
16. Hamosh M, Hamosh P: Does nutrition in early life have long term metabolic effects? Can animal models be used to predict these effects in humans? in Goldman AS, Atkinson AS, Hanson LA (eds): *Human Lactation*, vol 3: *The Effect of Human Milk Upon The Recipient Infant*. New York, Plenum Publishing Corp, 1987, pp 37–55.

17. Hamosh M: Does infant nutrition affect adiposity and cholesterol levels in the adult? *J Pediatr Gastroenterol Nutr* 1988; 7:10–16.
18. Lucas A, Lucas PJ, Baum JD: Pattern of milk flow in breast fed infants. *Lancet* 1979; 2:57–58.
19. Lucas A, Lucas PJ, Baum JD: Differences in the pattern of milk intake between breast and bottle fed infants. *Early Hum Dev* 1981; 5:195–199.
20. Cavell B: Gastric emptying in infants fed human milk or infant formula. *Acta Paediatr Scand* 1981; 70:639–641.
21. Lucas A, Blackburn AM, Aynsley-Green A, et al: Breast vs. bottle: Endocrine responses are different with formula feeding. *Lancet* 1980; 1:267–269.
22. Kramer MS, Barr RG, Leduc DG, et al: Determinants of weight and adiposity in the first year of life. *J Pediatr* 1985; 106:10–14.
23. Butte NF, Garza C, Smith EO, et al: Human milk intake and growth in exclusively breast fed infants. *J Pediatr* 1984; 104:187–195.
24. Dewey KG, Heinig MJ, Rashmawi LA, et al: Growth patterns and energy intakes of breast fed infants during the first year of life: The DARLING study, in *Human Lactation,* vol 4: *Breast Feeding, Nutrition, Infection, and Infant Growth in Developed and Emerging Countries.* St John's, Newfoundland, Canada, ARTS Biomedical Publishers, 1990.
25. Eckel RH, Yost TJ: Weight reduction increases adipose tissue lipoprotein lipase responsiveness in obese women. *J Clin Invest* 1987; 80:992–997.
26. Hamosh M, Hamosh P: Lipoprotein lipase: Its physiological and clinical significance. *Mol Aspects Med* 1983; 6:199–289.
27. Yost TJ, Eckel RH: Fat calories may be preferentially stored in reduced-obese women: A permissive pathway for assumption of the obese state. *J Clin Endocrinol Metab* 1988; 67:259–264.
28. Hamosh M, Burns WA: Lipolytic activity of human lingual glands (Ebner). *Lab Invest* 1977; 37:603–608.
29. DeNigris SJ, Hamosh M, Kasbekar DK, et al: Human gastric lipase: Secretion from dispersed gastric glands. *Biochim Biophys Acta* 1985; 836:67–72.
30. Hamosh M, Hamosh P: Lingual and gastric lipase during development, in Lebenthal E (ed): *Human Gastrointestinal Development.* New York, Raven Press, 1989, pp 251–276.
31. Watkins JB: Mechanism of fat absorption and the development of gastrointestinal function. *Pediatr Clin North Am* 1975; 22:721–730.
32. Hamosh M: Lingual and breast milk lipases. *Adv Pediatr* 1982; 29:33–67.
33. Abrams CK, Hamosh M, Hubbard VS, et al: Lingual lipase in cystic fibrosis: Quantitation of enzyme activity in the upper small intestine of patients with exocrine pancreatic insufficiency. *J Clin Invest* 1984; 73:374–382.
34. Abrams CK, Hamosh M, Dutta SK, et al: Role of nonpancreatic lipolytic activity in exocrine pancreatic insufficiency. *Gastroenterology* 1987; 92:125–129.
35. Patton JS, Rigler MW, Liao TH, et al: Hydrolysis of triacylglycerol emulsions by lingual lipase—a microscopic study. *Biochim Biophys Acta* 1982; 712:400–407.
36. Hamosh M, Bitman J, Liao TH, et al: Gastric lipolysis and fat absorption in preterm infants: Effect of medium-chain triglyceride or long-chain triglyceride-containing formulas. *Pediatrics* 1989; 83:86–92.
37. DeNigris SJ, Hamosh M, Kasbekar DK, et al: Lingual and gastric lipases: Species differences in the origin of prepancreatic digestive lipases and in localization of gastric lipase. *Biochim Biophys Acta* 1988; 959:38–45.
38. Moreau H, Gargouri Y, Lecat D, et al: Screening of lipases in several mammals. *Biochim Biophys Acta* 1988; 959:247–252.
39. Carey MC, Small DM, Bliss CM: Lipid digestion and absorption. *Ann Rev Physiol* 1983; 45:651–677.
40. Freudenberg E: *Die frauenmilch Lipase.* Basel, Karger, 1953.
41. Hamosh M, Bitman J, Fink CS, et al: Lipid composition of preterm human milk and its

digestion by the infant, in Schaub J (ed): *Composition and Physiological Properties of Human Milk*. Amsterdam, Elsevier, 1985, pp 153–164.

42. Tso P, Balint JA: Formation and transport of chylomicrons by enterocytes to the lymphatics. *Am J Physiol* 1986; 250:G715–G726.

43. Glomset JA: Lecithin: Cholesterol acyltransferase. An exercise in comparative biology. *Prog Biochem Pharmacol* 1976; 15:41–46.

44. Gaull GE, Hamosh M, Hommes FA: Human biochemical development, in Faulkner F Tanner JM (eds): *Human Growth, A Comprehensive Treatise,* vol 1. New York, Plenum Publishing Corp, 1986, pp 83–113.

45. Carey EM: The biochemistry of fetal brain development and myelination, in Jones CT (ed): *Biochemical Development of the Fetus and Neonate*. New York, Elsevier Biomedical Press, 1982, pp 287–336.

46. Meisami E, Timiras PS: Normal and abnormal biochemical development of the brain after birth, in Jones CT (ed): *The Biochemical Development of the Fetus and Neonate*. New York, Elsevier, 1981, pp 759–821.

47. Feldman M, Van Aerde JE, Clandinin MT: Lipid accretion in the fetus and newborn, in Section on Lipid Metabolism in The Fetus and Newborn, M Hamosh, ed, in Polin RA, Fox WW (eds): *Neonatal and Fetal Medicine*. Philadelphia, WB Saunders (in press).

48. Carlson SE: Very long chain fatty acids in the developing retina and brain, in Section on Lipid Metabolism in The Fetus And Newborn, M Hamosh, (ed), in Polin RA, Fox WW (eds): *Neonatal and Fetal Medicine*. Philadelphia, WB Saunders (in press).

49. Clandinin MT, Chappell JE, Heim T, et al: Fatty acid utilization in perinatal de novo synthesis of tissues. *Early Hum Dev* 1981; 5:355–366.

50. Kuhn DC, Crawford M: Placental essential fatty acid transport and prostaglandin synthesis. *Prog Lipid Res* 1986; 25:345–353.

51. Clandinin MT, Chappell JE, Heim T: Do low weight infants require nutrition with chain elongation–desaturation products of essential fatty acids? *Prog Lipid Res* 1981; 20:901–904.

52. Sastry PS: Lipids of nervous tissue: Composition and metabolism. *Prog Lipid Res* 1985; 24:69–176.

53. Carlson SE, Rhodes PG, Ferguson MG: Docosohexaenoic acid status of preterm infants at birth and following feeding with human milk or formula. *Am J Clin Nutr* 1985; 44:798–804.

54. Liu CCF, Carlson SE, Rhodes PG, et al: Increase in plasma phospholipid docosahexaenoic and eicosapentaenoic acids as a reflection of their intake and mode of administration. *Pediatr Res* 1987; 22:292–296.

55. Carlson SE, Rhodes PG, Roa VS, et al: Effect of fish oil supplementation on the n3 fatty acid content of red blood cell membranes in preterm infants. *Pediatr Res* 1987; 21:507–510.

56. Neuringer M, Conner WE, Lin DS, et al: Biochemical and functional effects of prenatal and postnatal n3 deficiency on retina and brain of rhesus monkeys. *Proc Natl Acad Sci USA* 1986; 83:4021–4025.

57. Neuringer M, Conner WE, Luck SL: Omega-3 fatty acid deficiency in rhesus monkeys: Depletion of retinal docosahexaenoic acid and abnormal electroretinograms. *Am J Clin Nutr* 1985; 43:706.

58. Menon NK, Dhopeshwarkar GA: Essential fatty acid deficiency and brain development. *Prog Lipid Res* 1982; 21:309–326.

59. Anderson GJ, Connor WE: Uptake of fatty acids by the developing rat brain. *Lipids* 1988; 23:286–290.

60. Yamamoto N, Saitoh M, Moriuchi A, et al: Effect of dietary linolenate/linoleate balance on brain lipid compositions and learning abilities of rats. *J Lipid Res* 1987; 28:144–151.

61. Brennen J: Carnitine metabolism and function. *Physiol Rev* 1983; 63:1420–1460.

62. Borum PR: Carnintine. *Ann Rev Nutr* 1983; 3:233–259.

63. Putet G: Lipids as an energy source for the premature and full term neonate, in Section on Lipid Metabolism in the Fetus and Newborn, M Hamosh, ed, in Polin RA, Fox WW (eds): *Neonatal and Fetal Medicine*. Philadelphia, WB Saunders, (in press).

64. Sarda P, Lepage G, Roy CC, et al: Storage of medium chain triglycerides in adipose tissue of orally fed infants. *Am J Clin Nutr* 1987; 45:399–405.

65. Bougneres PF, Lemmel C, Ferre P, et al: Ketone body transport in the human neonate and infant. *J Clin Invest* 1986; 77:42–48.

66. Williamson DH: Ketone body production and metabolism in the fetus and newborn, in Section on Lipid Metabolism in the Fetus and Newborn, M Hamosh ed, in Polin RA, Fox WW (eds): *Neonatal and Fetal Medicine*. Philadelphia, WB Saunders, (in press).

67. American Academy of Pediatrics, Committee on Nutrition: Nutritional needs of low-birth-weight infants. *Pediatrics,* 1985; 76:976–986.

68. Stahl GE, Spear ML, Hamosh M: Intravenous administration of lipid emulsion to premature infants. *Clin Perinatol* 1986; 13:133–162.

69. Hamosh M, Berkow SE, Chowdhry P, et al: Lipid clearing in parenterally fed low birth weight infants: Enzyme status at birth and the effect of infusion regimen on lipid catabolism, in Stern L, Oh W, Friis-Hansen B (eds): *Physiologic Foundations of Perinatal Care.* New York, Elsevier, 1987, pp 72–84.

70. Papadopoulos A, Hamosh M, Chowdhry P, et al: Lecithin:cholesterol acyl transferase in the newborn: Low activity level in preterm infants. *J Pediatr* 1988; 113:896–898.

71. Amr S, Hamosh P, Hamosh M: Effect of Intralipid infusion on lecithin: Cholesterol acyl transferase and lipoprotein lipase in young rats. *Biochim Biophys Acta* 1989; 1001:145–149.

72. Rovamo L, Nikkila EA, Taskinen MR, et al: Postheparin plasma lipoprotein and hepatic lipases in preterm neonates. *Pediatr Res* 1984; 18:1104–1107.

Chapter 7

Vitamins

Brian D. Riedel, M.D.

Harry L. Greene, M.D.

Vitamins are organic compounds required in trace amounts from dietary sources for the maintenance of normal health. The estimation of daily requirements for infants has historically been based on an analysis of the vitamin content of human milk and the average milk intake of thriving term infants (Table 7–1). More concrete data derived from the measurement of intake required to maintain normal serum or tissue levels or physiologic function, particularly in the preterm infant, have until recently been lacking.

The vitamins have been traditionally classified into water-soluble and fat-soluble groups based on their chemistry, and certain generalizations are possible based on this taxonomy. The water-soluble vitamins include vitamin C, or ascorbic acid, and the B complex vitamins. They serve physiologically as prosthetic groups for enzymes involved in a broad variety of metabolic functions, including amino acid metabolism, energy production, and nucleic acid synthesis. With the exception of vitamin B_{12}, the water-soluble vitamins are not stored to any appreciable extent. This implies that dietary excesses are largely excreted in the urine and bile, while deficiencies in intake become manifest quickly as interference in vital physiologic processes due to depletion of important enzyme activities. As a result, continued intake at frequent intervals is required to avoid deficiency. Because excessive intake is excreted, the water-soluble vitamins have been considered to be extremely safe, even in doses several orders of magnitude greater than their minimum daily requirements. This has translated into generous recommendations for the supplementation of infant formulas and parenteral vitamin preparations in order to avoid the more apparent problem of vitamin deficiency (Table 7–2).[1, 2] Recently, however, it has become clear that, especially in the case of preterm infants, the usual excretory capabilities for handling large excesses of the vitamins are relatively less developed and this results in supraphysiologic levels of certain vitamins when they are given in excessive doses. The determination of appropriate enteral and parenteral vitamin intake based on scientific data regarding levels achieved in the preterm infant remains a major area requiring further urgent investigation.

The fat-soluble vitamins A, D, E, and K function in cell differentiation and growth, rather than as classical cofactors. As a group, their precise physiological roles have been more difficult to elucidate, and much work remains to be done in this area. Vitamins A, E, and K require the presence of pancreatic enzymes and bile acids in the gut for their absorption. The fat-soluble vitamins, especially vitamins A, D,

TABLE 7–1.

Vitamin Content of Human Milk and Commercial Infant Formulas

Vitamins	Human Milk* (units/100 kcal)	Standard Milk Based Formulas† (units/100 kcal)	Preterm Formulas‡ (units/100 kcal)
C, mg	7.8	8.1–9	8.6–35
Thiamine, µg	25	78–100	100–250
Riboflavin, µg	60	150–156	160–620
B_6, µg	15	60–62	60–250
Niacin, mg	0.25	0.8–1.3	4–7.5
Biotin, µg	1.0	2.2–4.4	2–37
Pantothenic acid, µg	300	315–470	400–1900
B_{12}, µg	0.15	0.2–0.25	0.3–0.55
Folate, µg	4	7.5–15.6	12.5–37
A, µg	75	90–93	100–400
E, mg	0.2	0.9–2.0	1.3–3.0
K, µg	2	8–8.6	8.6–13

* Adapted from reference 106.
† Enfamil (Mead Johnson), Similac (Ross Laboratories), SMA (Wyeth Laboratories).
‡ Enfamil Premature (Mead Johnson), Similac Special Care (Ross Laboratories), SMA Preemie (Wyeth Laboratories).

and E, are stored in the body. As a result, clinical deficiency in an adult may require months or years to develop, in marked contrast to deficiencies of the water-soluble group which may become manifest within as little as 1 month. Since excessive intake accumulates in the body, the fat-soluble vitamins carry with them the risk of toxicity, requiring more attention to the delivery of adequate, yet safe doses to infants who may have a narrower margin of tolerance to variance in either direction.

TABLE 7–2.

Current Recommendations for Infant Vitamin Intake

Vitamin	FDA Minimum† (units/100 kcal)	Enteral RDA‡ (units/day) 0–6 mos	Enteral RDA‡ (units/day) 6–12 mos	Parenteral (ASCN)* Term (units/day)	Parenteral (ASCN)* Preterm (units/kg/day)
C, mg	8	30	35	80	25
Thiamine, µg	40	300	400	1,200	350
Riboflavin, µg	60	400	500	1,400	150
B_6, µg	35	300	600	1,000	180
Niacin, mg	0.25	5	6	17	6.8
Biotin, µg	1.5§	10**	15**	20	6
Pantothenic acid, mg	0.30	2**	3**	5	2.0
B_{12}, µg	0.15	0.3	0.5	1.0	0.3
Folate, µg	4	25	35	140	56
A, µg RE)‖	75	375	375	700	500
E, mg	0.5	3	4	7	2.8
K, µg	4	5	10	200	80

* Adapted from Reference 10.
† Adapted from Reference 1.
‡ Recommended Daily Allowances; adapted from Reference 2.
§ Required only for non-milk–based formulas
‖ RE = retinol equivalent.
**Estimated safe and adequate daily dietary intake.

The recognition of clinical vitamin deficiency is often difficult, especially in infancy. Given their central roles in a broad group of metabolic processes, the early signs of any particular vitamin deficiency are often vague and nonspecific. Such signs may include irritability, anorexia, poor growth and lethargy. Vitamin deficiencies are seldom "pure," in the sense that multiple vitamin deficiencies frequently coexist with generalized protein malnutrition or marasmus. The clinician must therefore be attuned to the possibility of vitamin deficiency in the high-risk patient, and investigate when appropriate with laboratory measures.

It is now apparent that certain inborn errors of metabolism can be corrected by the administration of vitamins, in doses ranging from near physiologic to several hundred times usual requirements. The mechanisms by which vitamins are efficacious are by overcoming a defect in the absorption, transport or recycling of the vitamin, or by increasing the concentration of the vitamin for a defective apoenzyme with a decreased affinity for its cofactor. Detailed discussion of the individual defects is beyond the scope of this text and the interested reader is referred to a recent review of the subject.[3]

VITAMIN C

Biochemistry and Metabolism

Vitamin C, or ascorbic acid, is involved in a number of metabolic roles, with proposed involvement in several more. Known roles for ascorbic acid include:

1. Hydroxylation of the amino acids proline and lysine during the synthesis of collagen, which is important for the proper folding of the peptide into the triple helix that lends collagen its unique structural properties.[4] In addition, ascorbic acid has a separate stimulatory effect on collagen synthesis unrelated to its role in hydroxylation, apparently at the regulatory level of messenger ribonucleic acid (mRNA) production.[5]
2. Amino acid catabolism. Ascorbic acid acts as a reducing agent, activating the catabolism of tyrosine, as well as stimulating the production of norepinephrine from dopamine, and the serotonin precursor 5-hydroxytryptamine from tryptophan.[4]
3. Hematopoiesis. It is known that ascorbic acid enhances iron absorption from the gastrointestinal tract, while inhibiting copper uptake. It facilitates the transfer of iron from transferrin to ferritin in addition to improving iron mobilization in iron overload conditions. Furthermore, ascorbic acid contributes to a stable pool of folate metabolites by aiding in the conversion of folic acid to folinic acid, as well as by limiting its oxidation.[6]
4. Ascorbic acid has a sparing effect on several other vitamins, perhaps due to its antioxidant properties. These include the B complex vitamins, vitamin A and vitamin E.

Ascorbic acid is produced from glucose by most animals; however, humans and a few other species cannot synthesize it and therefore require it in the diet. The L isomer is the biologically active form and circulates in both reduced and oxidized dehydro- forms. Ascorbic acid is present in all tissues and accumulates against a concentration gradient through a saturable, carrier-mediated, energy-requiring process.[7, 8] Highest levels of ascorbic acid are found in the adrenals, leukocytes, brain, liver, and spleen, and average

40 to 50 times plasma levels. Human milk contains the vitamin at levels exceeding those of plasma. There is no storage of ascorbic acid. In a healthy adult, the estimated body pool of ascorbic acid is 1,500 mg and is metabolized at 3% per day. After 60 days on a deficient diet, near deficiency levels are reached, with clinical symptoms following shortly if the deficient diet persists. The size of the ascorbic acid pool in infants and children is unknown, but deficiency probably occurs more quickly.

Fetal blood levels of ascorbic acid are greater than maternal levels in both preterm and term gestations, which speaks for an active placental transport process operational up to concentrations of 2 mg/dL.[8] At higher concentrations, simple diffusion predominates. Glucose competes with ascorbic acid for transport and decreases its bioavailability. As a result, maternal hyperglycemia may decrease the supply of ascorbic acid to the developing fetus.[9]

Excretion is in the urine, with one quarter as the unchanged vitamin under conditions of normal intake. The remainder is in the form of inactive metabolites, of which oxalate comprises the majority.

Requirements

Enteral feeding with either breast milk or proprietary cow's milk formula supplies approximately 8 mg/100 kcal. The current RDA is 30 mg/day for the neonate (see Table 7–2).

Parenteral administration of 80 mg/day to term infants maintained normal plasma levels and appears to be an appropriate dose. In preterm infants weighing less than 1,500 g, doses of 52 mg/day for 28 days caused a threefold increase of plasma ascorbic acid concentrations compared with concentrations in cord blood. Based on body weight, an expert panel of the American Society for Clinical Nutrition (ASCN) suggests a dose of 25 to 31 mg/kg/day for preterm infants up to 3 kg.[10]

Measurement

The most common method of measurement in use today is the 2,4-dinitro-phenyl-hydrazine method, which detects both the reduced and dehydroascorbic acid forms of the vitamin. Acceptable plasma levels by this technique are greater than 0.60 mg/dL, while levels less than 0.20 mg/dL are usually associated with the development of clinical signs of deficiency.[4]

Deficiency

Both human milk and proprietary infant formulas are good sources of vitamin C; however, cow's milk is a poor source. Scurvy is the clinical syndrome resulting from ascorbic acid deficiency and is similar in many respects to the bone changes seen with copper deficiency.[11, 12] The infantile form may develop within 6 to 12 months in infants fed exclusively unsupplemented cow's milk. Early signs, as in many other vitamin deficiencies, are nonspecific and include anorexia, failure to thrive, and irritability. With time, a scaly dermatitis develops and is accompanied by tenderness of the extremities and hemorrhage into the skin, mucous membranes, gingiva, and under the periosteum of the long bones. A "scorbutic rosary", comprising swollen osteochondral junctions along the anterior rib cage has been described, mimicking that seen in rickets. Laboratory findings may show a normochromic, normocytic anemia due to blood loss into the tissues, as well as radiographic evidence of arrested bone growth.[4]

The chronic ingestion of megadoses of vitamin C appears to induce decreased gut absorption, increased renal clearance, and increased catabolism of the vitamin. The abrupt withdrawal of extremely large doses of ascorbic acid may precipitate overt clinical scurvy. The infant born to a mother on high doses of vitamin C may be at increased risk of deficiency during the newborn period.[13]

Toxicity

Renal clearance of ascorbic acid far exceeds doses in general use, making toxicity extremely uncommon. There is a theoretical risk of increased urinary stone formation because of increased excretion of oxalate and uric acid, although the significance and actual clinical risk are uncertain.

THIAMINE

Biochemistry and Metabolism

The primary functional form of thiamine is thiamine pyrophosphate, which serves as a cofactor for three enzyme complexes involved in carbohydrate metabolism[4]:

1. *Pyruvate dehydrogenase* catalyzes the conversion of pyruvate to acetyl coenzyme A (CoA) for entry into the Kreb's cycle.
2. *Alpha-ketoglutarate dehydrogenase* converts α-ketoglutarate to succinate at a later step in the Kreb's cycle.
3. *Transketolase* is involved in the production of ribose for the synthesis of RNA and also provides NADPH,* which is required for fatty acid synthesis.

Other roles for this vitamin include the decarboxylation of branched-chain amino acids and facilitation of nerve conduction through its influence on membrane sodium ion conductance.

Thiamine is absorbed in the small intestine in its free form by a carrier-mediated process at low concentrations (~2 μM), while passive diffusion assumes greater importance at higher levels.[14] Following absorption, thiamine is converted to the primary active cofactor thiamine pyrophosphate (TPP) chiefly in the liver in a process which consumes adenosine triphosphate. Further phosphorylation to thiamine triphosphate (TTP) occurs in the central nervous system (CNS). The specific role of TTP in neuronal tissues is not entirely clear, although some patients with depressed cerebrospinal fluid content of TTP have reportedly improved with pharmacologic doses of the vitamin.[15, 16] Both thiamine and TPP circulate in the serum, although thiamine predominates. Total body stores have been estimated in adults as 30 mg, of which 80% is TPP, 10% TTP, and the remaining fraction free thiamine and the monophosphorylated form. Amounts present in breast milk are directly proportional to intake, so that alcoholic and malnourished mothers frequently have low milk thiamine.[17] Following dephosphorylation, free thiamine is excreted in the urine as the unchanged vitamin.[4]

*The reduced form of NADP (nicotinamide-adenine dinucleotide phosphate).

Requirements

The current enteral recommendation for thiamine is 300–400 μg/day. The thiamine content of human milk and infant formula is summarized in Table 7–1.

As with many other vitamins, thiamine requirements vary with dietary content; high carbohydrate intake increases demand for thiamine. A parenteral dose of 1.2 mg/day in term infants is sufficient to prevent deficiency and is probably an appropriate dose (see Table 7–2). Preterm infants will not become deficient on 0.78 mg/kg/day; however, this dose is probably excessive. The American Society for Clinical Nutrition (ASCN) committee suggests 0.35 mg/kg body weight for the preterm infant.[10]

Measurement

The most reliable index of thiamine status is whole blood thiamine levels. Erythrocyte transketolase activity determined both with and without added TPP is a useful screening method but does not detect marginal or elevated concentrations of the vitamin. An increase of over 26% on addition of TPP indicates deficiency. The 24-hour excretion of thiamine or thiamine : creatinine ratio are alternative measures of thiamine status.[18, 19] Direct measurement of plasma thiamine and its metabolites may provide a more accurate measure of thiamine status, particularly in evaluation of parenteral needs.

Deficiency

Thiamine deficiency, or beri-beri, occurs most commonly in Asia where polished rice serves as the dietary stable, commonly with codeficiencies of riboflavin and niacin. The Wernicke-Korsakoff syndrome occurs in adult alcoholics. In infants, deficiency is more prone to occur in the context of a breast-fed infant of a malnourished mother. Onset is typically between the 2d and 5th months of life, although it may be delayed as long as 10 months. The onset is often insidious and may be triggered by an intercurrent infection. Initial signs may include edema, restlessness, insomnia, and anorexia. Later, cardiac symptoms predominate, with the development of dyspnea and cyanosis, and the chest radiograph shows increased heart size. Aphonia may be present because of paralysis of the recurrent laryngeal nerve. Death may ultimately ensue with cardiomegaly and extensive CNS degeneration. A pseudomeningitic form described in older infants is manifested by fever, convulsions, strabismus, and nystagmus. Laboratory evaluation in beri-beri will show decreased urinary excretion of thiamine and low blood levels of thiamine with simultaneous elevation of pyruvate, lactate, and α-ketoglutarate.

Certain inborn errors of metabolism have been successfully treated with large doses of thiamine, including a variant of maple syrup urine disease.[3] Subacute necrotizing encephalomyelopathy (Leigh's disease) is a rare autosomal recessive condition characterized by elevated blood levels of pyruvate and lactate and CNS lesions similar to Wernicke's encephalopathy, although they are without other signs of beri-beri. Current evidence suggests that many of these patients have an inhibitor of the enzyme required to produce TTP,[20–22] the form of the vitamin used in the CNS, and some cases have responded to doses of thiamine of up to 2 g/day.

Toxicity

Thiamine is safe even in large doses, although respiratory depression has been rarely reported with excessive administration. A rare anaphylactic reaction associated with intravenous administration of small doses of less than 100 mg may result in death or severe morbidity.

RIBOFLAVIN

Biochemistry and Metabolism

Riboflavin serves as an essential component of flavoproteins, which function as hydrogen carriers in a number of crucial oxidation-reduction reactions such as energy metabolism, glycogen synthesis, erythrocyte production, and the conversion of folate to its active coenzyme.[4] Furthermore, riboflavin has been shown to facilitate bilirubin photocatabolism.[23] It is abundantly present in milk; however, ultraviolet and visible sunlight rapidly reduce the vitamin content in a few hours.

Under normal conditions, riboflavin absorption and elimination is tightly controlled by balanced mechanisms. Uptake occurs predominantly in the proximal small intestine by means of a high-affinity, low-capacity carrier.[4] This allows for efficient absorption even at low gut concentrations while preventing excessive absorption, as the carrier is easily saturated. Operating in parallel is a high-capacity renal tubular secretory pathway to enhance riboflavin elimination.[4]

In the intestinal mucosa, riboflavin is phosphorylated to riboflavin-5'-phosphate, also known as flavin mononucleotide (FMN). Further phosphorylation produces flavin adenine dinucleotide (FAD), the other main coenzyme. Riboflavin is carried bound largely to albumin, although in fetal serum a specific high-affinity riboflavin-binding protein has been identified that may play a role in transplacental transport during gestation.[3] Riboflavin stores are small and easily depleted in as little as 2 weeks, with largest quantities being in the liver and kidney. The vitamin circulates in a labile tissue pool that can be turned over in times of increased need, as well as a highly protein bound pool that serves to maintain local tissue stores. Elimination of excess intake takes place chiefly as the unchanged vitamin in the urine, with lesser amounts eliminated in the bile.

Requirements

The minimum oral intake for infants is 60 μg/100 kcal, while the current RDA is 400 μg/day. Breast milk and formula riboflavin content is summarized in Table 7–1.

Requirements for riboflavin are related to nitrogen intake. The current parenteral recommendation of 1.4 mg/day for full-term infants is probably more than required; however, this dose appears to be safe (see Table 7–2). Preterm infants, on the other hand, have poor renal clearance of the vitamin relative to term infants, so that previously administered doses of 0.56 mg/kg/day resulted in serum levels of the vitamin which exceeded normal by as much as 100-fold.[10] A lower dose of 0.15 mg/kg/day has been recommended by the ASCN committee.[10]

Measurement

A useful screen for riboflavin sufficiency can be obtained by measuring erythrocyte glutathione reductase activity both in the presence and absence of excess added active cofactor FAD. An increase in activity of the enzyme of more than 20% indicates riboflavin deficiency, although glucose-6-phosphate dehydrogenase deficiency is a common cause for falsely normal results. A more accurate measure of riboflavin status is measurement of riboflavin and its phosphorylated cofactors FMN and FAD in plasma and erythrocytes.[24] Urinary riboflavin concentrations, coupled with blood levels, provide the best measure of riboflavin status.[25]

Deficiency

Deficiency of riboflavin usually occurs in the setting of more generalized malnutrition associated with multiple vitamin deficiencies. A particularly high-risk setting is the pregnant teenager, because as many as one half of all teenagers have been estimated to be riboflavin-deficient.[26] Oral contraceptives, other corticosteroids, and imipramine may impair riboflavin metabolism,[27] and boric acid increases renal loss of riboflavin.[28] Negative nitrogen balance, a common condition in the severely stressed infant, increases urinary excretion of the vitamin.

The principle manifestations of riboflavin deficiency are dermatologic and ophthalmologic, including angular stomatitis, cheilosis, glossitis, seborrhea, photophobia, and increased corneal vascularity. Severe deficiency has been reported to cause electrocardiographic abnormalities and developmental delay.

Certain inborn errors of metabolism may respond to riboflavin supplementation.[3]

Toxicity

There are no known toxic effects of this vitamin, although Baeckert et al. have described plasma riboflavin levels in preterm infants receiving parenteral multiple vitamins of approximately 100 times the cord blood levels. The urinary concentrations in one such infant was only slightly below that which causes precipitation of riboflavin and obstructive tubular damage.[24]

VITAMIN B$_6$

Biochemistry and Metabolism

Vitamin B$_6$ serves as a cofactor for a large number of reactions involved in the synthesis, interconversion, and catabolism of amino acids.[29] The vitamin exists in three forms which are readily converted in vivo: pyridoxal, the aldehyde, is the chief active form once it is phosphorylated to pyridoxal phosphate (PLP) in the liver; pyridoxamine, the amine, like pyridoxal, is widely available in meat, fish, and poultry, and serves as a cofactor in transaminase reactions; pyridoxine, the alcohol, is widely present in plants, although it must be converted to one of the other forms for biologic activity. The vitamin is absorbed in the dephosphorylated forms by passive diffusion in the jejunum[30] and transported to the liver where it is efficiently converted to the active forms, PLP or pyridoxamine phosphate, in reactions that require the presence of flavin.[26] From there, it is carried on albumin to tissues. Body stores of this vitamin are small, with nearly 50% of its activity tied up in muscle phosphorylase.[31] However, because of its ubiquitous supply, deficiency is uncommon even in infancy. In addition to its role in amino acid metabolism, pyridoxine is also required for the synthesis of niacin, neurotransmitters (histamine, serotonin, dopamine, norepinephrine, and gamma-aminobutyric acid), heme and prostaglandins. Ultimately the vitamin is dephosphorylated by alkaline phosphatase in the liver and degraded predominantly to 4-pyridoxic acid, which is excreted in the urine.

Requirements

Considering the central role of pyridoxine in amino acid metabolism, it is not surprising that requirements are directly proportional to protein intake. In the early days of cow's milk feeding of infants, pyridoxine deficiency was occasionally described because milk is a poor source of this otherwise abundant vitamin. Furthermore, it is extremely heat labile, so that even the small amounts present were easily inactivated in the processing of formulas or other foods. Today, commercial formulas are supplemented by pyridoxine hydrochloride, a relatively heat-stable form of the vitamin,[4] so deficiency is rarely seen (see Table 7–1). Formula-fed infants overall tend to have higher levels of this vitamin than breast-fed infants and, as with riboflavin deficiency, the single remaining setting in which deficiency is seen is the breast-fed infant of the malnourished, typically adolescent, mother.

In term infants, 1.0 mg/day given parenterally in total parenteral nutrition (TPN) as pyridoxine is sufficient to prevent deficiency (see Table 7–2). A lower dose of 0.3 mg/kg/day in preterm infants is adequate to prevent deficiency; however, serum levels measured after this dose may be excessive secondary to the relative immaturity of the preterm liver and kidneys to handle the vitamin.[10] The current recommendation of the ASCN is 0.18 mg/kg/day.

Certain drugs may increase the requirements for pyridoxine, although these are uncommonly used in infancy. Isoniazid and hydralazine form inactive metabolites with PLP, with the potential for depletion of body B_6 stores. Theophylline, which has gained widespread use in the neonatal intensive care unit (NICU), decreases levels of the active coenzyme PLP by inhibiting pyridoxal kinase.[32] Penicillamine inactivates the vitamin,[33] while corticosteroids and certain anticonvulsant medications may also increase requirements.

Measurement

Several measures of pyridoxine status are available. Plasma PLP levels may be measured directly by radioimmunoassay, although determination of erythrocyte aspartate aminotransferase activity both with and without added PLP is a useful screen for vitamin sufficiency.[34, 35] Most recently, high-performance liquid chromatography (HPLC) methods to quantitate all the vitamans in plasma and erythrocytes promise to provide the most accurate and reliable measure of vitamin B_6 status.[36]

Because of the requirement for B_6 in the normal metabolism of tryptophan, the measurement of certain urinary metabolites following a tryptophan load has been proposed as a functional test for vitamin deficiency. Greater than 50 mg xanthurenic acid/24 hours following a 2- to 5-gm tryptophan load is interpreted as evidence of deficiency.[10]

Deficiency

Due to widespread availability, deficiency of this vitamin is quite uncommon. Lactation must be viewed as a relatively deficient state. Malabsorption syndromes such as celiac disease or cystic fibrosis may result in deficiency. Inadequate intake during pregnancy has been linked to adverse gestational outcomes.[26] Deficiency in infants results in a syndrome including a hypochromic, microcytic anemia, vomiting, diarrhea, failure to thrive, irritability, and seizures. Very low levels of PLP have been reported in patients with chronic renal disease and hyperphosphatasia.[37]

A number of rare inborn errors of metabolism have been reported to respond to large doses of pyridoxine.[3]

Toxicity

Toxicity is rare and not described at the doses given in infant formulas or standard parenteral preparations. Megadoses in adults have been reported to produce a sensory neuropathy.[38]

NIACIN

Biochemistry and Metabolism

Niacin is the term used to describe two equivalent compounds, nicotinic acid and nicotinamide, which are widely available in meats and grains. Niacin is converted in the liver to the active cofactors nicotinamide adenine dinucleotide (NAD) and nicotinamide adenine dinucleotide phosphate (NADP). These cofactors play central roles in body metabolism in a wide variety of oxidation-reduction reactions including glycolysis, electron transport, and fat synthesis; as a result, a deficiency in this vitamin has diffuse manifestations. Transport to tissue sites occurs largely in erythrocytes,[26] although there is no storage form of the vitamin. Further metabolism to N^1-methyl nicotinamide and N^1-methyl-2-pyridone-5-carboxylamide allows urinary excretion of these compounds.[39]

In strict terms, niacin is not a vitamin in the sense that the active cofactors NAD and NADP can be synthesized in vivo from the amino acid tryptophan by reactions that require vitamin B_6.[4] Therefore, niacin requirements depend on the amount of dietary tryptophan available and on vitamin B_6 status.

Requirements

Enteral requirements are generally met by intakes of 0.25 mg/100 kcal for both term and low-birth-weight infants, although the current RDA is more generous at 5 mg/day (see Table 7–2).

Parenteral administration of 17 mg/day in term infants and 11 mg/day in preterm infants receiving TPN is sufficient to prevent deficiency while simultaneously avoiding excessive levels. When calculated based on total energy intake, these doses lead to the current recommendations of 6.8 mg/kg/day for preterm infants and 17 mg/day for term infants.[10] The quantities of tryptophan present in standard neonatal TPN are not sufficient to influence niacin requirements.

Measurement

The most commonly employed method of determining niacin status is the measurement of the urinary metabolite N^1-methyl nicotinamide, which declines late in niacin deficiency simultaneously with or just before the development of overt clinical signs.[40] The other major urinary metabolite, N^1-methyl-2-pyridone-5-carboxylamide, declines much earlier in the course of niacin deficiency making the ratio of these compounds a much more sensitive index of niacin status. However, difficulties in the laboratory measurement of the latter compound make this impractical. Blood niacin levels have also been used as a measure of niacin status.[10]

Deficiency

Niacin deficiency today is limited to developing areas of Central and South America, which rely heavily on corn as a dietary staple. Corn is poor in tryptophan and rich in the amino acid lysine, which interferes with niacin metabolism, while the niacin present is in a poorly absorbable form.[26] Other settings of high risk include alcoholics,[41] who often have multiple vitamin deficiencies because of malnutrition, and occasionally in isoniazid-treated patients due to vitamin B_6 depletion with its secondary effects on NAD synthesis. Infants born in these contexts are at increased risk for niacin deficiency.

Pellagra is the classic syndrome of niacin deficiency, with the four Ds of dermatitis, diarrhea, dementia, and death. The dermatologic manifestations are generally the first to appear as an erythematous sunburned appearance predominantly in areas exposed to sunlight and trauma. Gastrointestinal symptoms include glossitis, angular stomatitis, anorexia, diarrhea, malabsorption, and weight loss due to villous atrophy. Neurologic manifestations are not as easily recognized in infancy but may appear as lassitude, irritability, and eventually coma.

Toxicity

Toxicity is not described at the doses administered in TPN or standard infant formulas. Megadoses of niacin have enjoyed widespread use in the treatment of certain hyperlipidemic conditions, for which it is effective in reducing levels of low-density lipoprotein cholesterol and increasing high-density lipoprotein cholesterol.[42] At these megadoses (on the order of 2 to 4 g/day), side effects have included flushing, nausea and vomiting, dry skin, and—less commonly—elevated liver function tests and hyperuricemia. Other controversial applications have included the treatment of schizophrenia[43] and various vascular conditions.

BIOTIN

Biochemistry and Metabolism

Biotin is important for the function of four known mammalian enzymes involved in carboxylation and carbon dioxide transfer reactions.[4] These include:

1. *Propionyl CoA carboxylase,* which is involved in the degradation of valine, leucine, and methionine.
2. *3-methylcrotonyl-CoA carboxylase,* also required for leucine degradation.
3. *Pyruvate carboxylase,* which catalyzes the rate-limiting step of gluconeogenesis from alanine and pyruvate.
4. *Acetyl CoA carboxylase,* the cytosolic enzyme catalyzing the formation of methyl malonyl CoA which is the first step in fatty acid synthesis.

Biotin is also active in folate metabolism.[44] Biotin is unique among the vitamins in that it is bound covalently to the apoenzyme by a reaction requiring ATP.[3]

Intestinal absorption in man is not well studied; however, absorption in lower mammals occurs in the first half of the small intestine through mechanisms that have included either a saturable carrier or passive diffusion, depending on species.[45] In addition, intestinal flora synthesize biotin, although the importance of this source is uncertain. Biotin is widely available in a variety of foods. Once absorbed, biotin circulates bound to plasma proteins and is taken up by hepatocytes by way of a sodium-dependent carrier[46] and is converted to 5-adenylate biotin, which is used for the synthesis of carboxylase enzymes.

Biotin-containing enzymes are degraded to biocytin, from which biotin can be recovered by liver and plasma biotinidase. This mechanism of biotin conservation makes biotin deficiency extremely uncommon even with marginal intakes of the vitamin. Ultimately, biotin is excreted unchanged in the urine.

Requirements

Enteral requirements for term neonates are probably about 10 μg/day. The content of breast milk and infant formulas is summarized in Table 7–1.

Parenteral administration of 20 μg/day to term infants maintains normal plasma levels for 21 days (see Table 7–2). Parenteral doses of 12 μg/kg/day in preterm infants produced excessive levels tenfold greater than controls over 28 days.[47] A smaller dose of 6 μg/kg/day appears to be adequate.

Measurement

Urine biotin excretion can be measured, with a decline to 10% of normal occurring in deficiency states.[26]

Plasma levels depend on the method used. Available methods include bioassay or competitive binding using avidin.

Deficiency

Due to widespread availability in food and intestinal bacterial production, biotin deficiency is uncommon. Low levels are reported in pregnant women.[39] Chronic diarrhea or antibiotic use may increase requirements due to decreased availability from intestinal sources. Chronic ingestion of large amounts of raw egg whites may result in biotin deficiency because of the presence of avidin, a glycoprotein of egg albumin, which is a high affinity binder of the vitamin. Because of the mechanism of biotin conservation, isolated biotin deficiency was not noted in humans until Mock et al. described the syndrome in parenterally fed infants receiving biotin-deficient solutions for several weeks.[48] Symptoms of deficiency include alopecia, an exfoliative dermatitis, and conjunctivitis. If prolonged, progression to nausea, anorexia, and mental and neurologic symptoms occurs. Laboratory data may include anemia and elevated plasma cholesterol levels. At present, the pediatric multiple vitamin formulation has biotin included, and no infants have shown deficiency states.

Several inborn errors of metabolism affect the biotin dependent enzymes.[3, 49, 50]

Toxicity

Biotin toxicity has not been reported.

PANTOTHENIC ACID

Biochemistry and Metabolism

As signified by its name, pantothenic acid is widely distributed in plant and animal sources, including milk. The vitamin forms an important part of the ubiquitous acyl transfer group coenzyme A and, as such, is essential for the metabolism of fat, carbohydrate, and protein in reactions involved in fatty acid elongation, energy release, and gluconeogenesis.[51] Approximately half of the ingested vitamin is biologically available for absorption.[26] Intestinal flora produce pantothenate, but the importance of this source in man is unknown. Following absorption, pantothenic acid is converted to 4′-phosphopantetheine and then is covalently linked to form CoA or is bound to acyl carrier protein, the two functional forms of the vitamin. Pantothenic acid has been identified in the liver, adrenals, brain, heart, and kidneys, and circulates in the plasma as the free vitamin.[26] Excretion is in the urine predominantly as the unchanged vitamin.

Requirements

Enteral requirements of pantothenic acid for both term and preterm infants are met by an intake of 0.3 mg/100 kcal with a more liberal RDA of 2 mg/day (see Table 7–2).

Term infants given 5 mg/day parenterally maintained stable plasma levels over 21 days, and this appears to be an adequate dose. Preterm infants given 2.9 mg/kg/day parenterally have elevated plasma levels, such that a dose of 2.0 mg/kg/day should be sufficient.[10]

Measurement

Plasma levels of pantothenic acid can be measured by means of a two-stage assay that involves, first, the enzymatic cleavage of the bound vitamin, and second, bioassay or radioimmunoassay of the liberated pantothenic acid.[10] Measurement of urine pantothenic acid levels are also useful in assessing deficiency states.

Deficiency

Widespread availability make isolated deficiency of pantothenic acid rare, but deficiency of this vitamin may occur as a part of more generalized malnutrition, or under experimentally induced conditions employing a specific pantothenic acid antagonist.[52] Such experimental deficiency is characterized in adults by apathy, headache, depression, paresthesias, muscle weakness, vomiting, and intermittent diarrhea. Inborn errors involving defects in pantothenic acid metabolism have not been described.

Toxicity

Pantothenic acid toxicity has not been reported.

VITAMIN B_{12}

Biochemistry and Metabolism

Vitamin B_{12}, or cobalamin, is a cobalt-containing vitamin produced only by bacteria, which are its source in animals. The primary source for humans is through the ingestion of animal products including meat, eggs, and milk. The vitamin is not required or present in plants, so that strict vegetarians are at risk for the development of deficiency. Although the vitamin is produced in the gut by normally present flora, little of this vitamin is absorbed.

Cobalamin is present in two active forms in man[4]: methyl cobalamin and adenosyl cobalamin.

Methyl cobalamin is chiefly a cytoplasmic cofactor, and is also the form found in plasma and fluids such as breast milk. It is involved in the synthesis of methionine from homocysteine via the transfer of a methyl group from 5-methyl tetrahydrofolate. It is interference with this reaction in B_{12} deficiency, which leads to the "methyl folate trap" in which reduced folate is trapped in the 5-methyl form making it unavailable for other important reactions involved in purine and pyrimidine synthesis.[4] One manifestation of this is megaloblastic anemia.

Adenosyl cobalamin is present largely in the mitochondria of solid tissues where it is involved in the formation of myelin sheaths of neural tissue.[26]

The absorption of B_{12} occurs in the distal third of the small intestine and is a complex process requiring the presence of intrinsic factor (IF), a B_{12}-binding protein produced in the stomach. After binding to IF, the IF–B_{12} complex then binds to specific receptors on the ileal brush-border. Once absorption takes place, the vitamin circulates bound to a family of specific binding proteins, the transcobalamins. Transcobalamin II is the chief form responsible for the delivery of B_{12} to tissues and appears to serve as a membrane transferase.[4]

Vitamin B_{12} is the only water-soluble vitamin that is stored. In adults, total body stores are estimated at 2 to 5 mg, 1 mg of which is found in the liver.[4] There is an obligatory loss of approximately 0.1% of the body pool per day, so that the development of deficiency in adults occurs over years. Excretion is in the urine, bile, and milk as the unchanged vitamin, with extensive enterohepatic circulation playing a role in vitamin conservation.

Requirements

Enteral needs in term infants are 0.3 μg/day (see Table 7–2).

Parenteral administration of 1.0 μg/day (0.1 μg/100 kcal) to term infants maintained plasma levels above those of controls.[10] There is evidence that 0.75 μg/day is sufficient. Preterm infants receiving 0.65 μg/kg/day (0.85 μg/100 kcal) similarly have elevated plasma levels.[47] Therefore, 0.3 μg/kg/day should be adequate to prevent deficiency.[10]

Measurement

Plasma B_{12} levels are proportional to body stores and serve as a useful index of vitamin status. Previous microbiologic methods have been largely replaced by more specific radioimmunoassay techniques. Vitamin B_{12} deficiency yields increased urinary methylmalonic acid excretion due to decreased adenosyl cobalamin.[26] The Schilling test is a provocative test used in the evaluation of B_{12} deficiency in which a large dose of radiolabeled B_{12} is given enterally and urinary excretion of labeled B_{12} is measured both in the presence and absence of added IF. This test elucidates whether B_{12} absorption is normal, and if not, whether the defect is due to insufficient IF.

Deficiency

Due to large body stores of this vitamin and conservation due to enterohepatic circulation, development of vitamin B_{12} deficiency in normal adults may require several years of a diet deficient in vitamin B_{12}. Breast milk excretion of the vitamin, however, is proportional to maternal levels, so that infants who are born with marginal reserves due to maternal pernicious anemia, malnutrition, or dietary habits (such as seen with restrictive vegan diets), and are exclusively breast-fed may develop signs of deficiency within as little as 6 months.[53, 54] The other settings in which vitamin B_{12} deficiency may be seen include pernicious anemia; following gastrectomy or severe gastric mucosal disease due to deficient IF production; in small bowel bacterial overgrowth; in small bowel mucosal defects such as celiac disease; following ileal resection; and in pancreatic protease deficiency due to failure of proteases to inactivate competing B_{12} binding proteins (R proteins). Numerous drugs such as neomycin, chlorpromazine, potassium chloride, oral contraceptive agents, and large doses of vitamin C interfere with B_{12} absorption or metabolism.[55]

The clinical picture is characterized by weakness, megaloblastic anemia, congestive heart failure, glossitis, lemon-colored skin, and neurologic changes including peripheral neuritis, posterior and lateral column spinal cord degeneration, and paresthesias. The effects of deficiency on dividing cells such as erythrocytes are generally reversible; however, neurologic changes, especially those of the spinal cord and following deficiency of long-standing duration, may result in irreversible neuronal damage.

Inborn errors of B_{12} metabolism are summarized in a recent review by Bartlett.[3]

Toxicity

Vitamin B_{12} toxicity has not been described. The most commonly employed therapeutic form of the vitamin is cyanocobalamin, and carries with it the theoretical potential for cyanide poisoning.[26] As a result, hydroxycobalamin may be preferable in neonates, particularly if large doses will be required for treatment of inborn errors of vitamin B_{12} metabolism.

FOLATE

Biochemistry and Metabolism

Folate is a broad term referring to a group of compounds synthesized by bacteria and plants and consisting of a pteroic acid moiety conjugated to a variable number of up to 11 glutamic acid residues. Folic acid refers to pteroyl glutamic acid, the monoglutamate; however, the majority of the naturally occurring vitamin exists as polyglutamates. The glutamate tail serves in the attachment of the cofactor to the apoenzyme. As its name implies, the vitamin is widely available in leafy vegetables ("foliage"); human and cow's milk are also good sources.

Absorption of folate in the rat jejunum appears to be by way of a specific, pH-dependent, saturable carrier[56] and requires first that the polyglutamate form be hydrolyzed by an intestinal mucosal γ-carboxypeptidase.[3] Following this, the vitamin is transported across the mucosa after being transformed to reduced methyl and formyl folate. Once absorbed, folate is transported in the serum weakly bound to albumin and mostly in the 5-methyltetrahydrofolate form.[10] Specific folate-binding proteins have been identified in serum and breast milk; however, their role in normal folate metabolism has not yet been elucidated.[3] The liver contains small stores of this vitamin which are quickly exhausted at a rate of ~1%/day in adults on a deficient diet. The majority of folate accumulation by the fetus occurs during the third trimester of pregnancy, so that term infants have higher levels and are at lower risk for the development of deficiency than the preterm infant.[57, 58]

The folate content of breast milk is tightly regulated, producing constant levels even in mothers with marginal vitamin status.[59] As a result, deficiency is uncommon in the breast-fed infant, who frequently has higher folate levels than the mother herself.

Excretion of folate occurs mostly in the urine. Enterohepatic circulation does occur, however, so that interruption of this recycling mechanism may increase the risk of deficiency.[60]

The metabolic function of folate is as a cofactor in single carbon transfer reactions vital for the synthesis of nucleotides. Folate can exist in the oxidized and dihydro- or tetrahydro- reduced forms. Tetrahydrofolate is the chief coenzyme that receives single carbon units from the amino acids serine, glycine, histidine, and tryptophan. These are then transferred in the synthesis of purines, as well as thymidilic acid which is necessary for production of deoxyribonucleic acid (DNA). As a result, folate deficiency is manifest as a disturbance of DNA production which becomes most obvious in rapidly dividing tissues such as the gut and bone marrow.

Medicine has taken advantage of the central role of folate metabolism. Combination of the antibiotics trimethoprim and sulfamethoxazole interrupts folate metabolism at two sequential steps, which profoundly interferes with cell division. Because of the several-fold higher affinity of bacterial enzymes for the drugs over human equivalents, the drugs can be employed to treat bacterial infection while exerting a minimal effect on a patient.[61] Similarly, the antineoplastic agent methotrexate takes advantage of the high nucleotide synthetic rates of malignant tissues to selectively target these tissues for disruption of DNA synthesis by interfering with dihydrofolate reductase,[61] while the folate intermediate leucovorin is sometimes employed to "rescue" healthy tissues from the toxic effects of high-dose methotrexate therapy.

Requirements

Recommended dietary intake in term infants is 25 μg/day. Parenteral requirements are 140 μg/day for term infants and 56 μg/kg/day for preterm infants (see Table 7–2).[10]

Measurement

Serum and erythrocyte folate levels are both readily measurable and serve as the best indicators of folate status. Serum levels decline first, so that it is possible to have low serum levels while levels in erythrocytes and tissue remain normal.[26] Urinary excretion of formiminoglutamate, an intermediate in the metabolism of histidine to glutamate, is elevated in folate deficiency, especially after an oral histidine load; however, this measure is chiefly of historic interest today.

Deficiency

Folate deficiency is one of the more commonly occurring vitamin deficiencies. Pregnancy and lactation increase folate need, especially due to the efficient sequestration of folate by the fetus or nursing infant despite m ternal deficiency.[61] Adolescence and nutritional deficiency, commonly associated with lower socioeconomic status, are other high-risk conditions. Goat's milk is virtually free of folate, with levels of 7 µg/L compared with 52 µg/L for cow's milk,[62] necessitating routine folate supplementation for the infant exclusively fed goat's milk. Anticonvulsant therapy with dilantin, phenobarbital, and other medications is known to lower serum folate levels, and may be important for the therapeutic effect of these medications—as folate supplementation has been known to trigger convulsions in such patients. Sulfasalazine interferes with the intestinal absorption of folate and may cause deficiency. Less common causes of folate deficiency include tropical sprue and celiac disease due to malabsorption of the vitamin by diseased mucosa, although these conditions are rarely seen in the neonatal period.

The most common and important manifestation of folate deficiency is megaloblastic anemia, which may or may not be associated with glossitis, irritability, listlessness, weight loss, neuropathy, or other neuropsychiatric symptoms. In adults fed a folate-deficient diet, low serum folate levels became apparent after 3 weeks. The sequence of manifestations proceeded to hypersegmented neutrophils at 7 weeks, decreased red blood cell folate at 17 weeks, and overt anemia at 19 weeks.[63] One could expect the sequence to be compressed in infants, especially in the preterm infant.

Inborn defects in folate metabolism have been described, including impairment of intestinal and blood-brain barrier transport of the vitamin, as well as defects of specific enzymes of folate metabolism.[3]

Toxicity

Folate is remarkably free of toxicity even in the large doses (up to 60 mg/day) used to treat certain inborn errors of metabolism.[64] Hypersensitivity reactions characterized by an erythematous rash with urticaria and pruritus have been described.

VITAMIN A

Biochemistry and Metabolism

Retinol is the general term used to describe the several active forms of vitamin A, as well as being specific for the alcohol form of the vitamin. Other forms of the vitamin include retinal (the aldehyde) and retinoic acid, which are available only from animal sources, including milk. The carotenes, most notably beta-carotene, are provitamins available from plant sources which can be converted by man to active vitamin A compounds. The majority of vitamin A intake in the adult diet is in the form of carotenes and retinol esters.[26] Vitamin A is quantitated in terms of the retinol equivalent (RE) which is equal to 1.0 µg retinol or 1.83 µg retinyl palmitate. One international unit (IU) is equal to 0.3 µg retinol.

Retinol and retinal are readily interconverted. Once retinoic acid is formed from retinal, however, it is eventually conjugated in the liver and excreted in the bile.[26] As a result, retinoic acid is a less toxic form of the vitamin, but it is unable to fulfil all of the vitamin's physiologic roles.[65]

Vitamin A metabolism is quite complex. Retinyl palmitate in the diet must first be hydrolyzed by brush-border and pancreatic hydrolases in a process that requires bile acids and bile salt–stimulated lipase for maximum efficiency. The liberated free retinol is then absorbed through an active transport process,[66] following which it undergoes reesterification in the enterocyte. The retinyl ester then circulates in chylomicrons and is cleared by the liver. Vitamin E enhances the absorption of retinol, whereas protein malnutrition, pancreatic insufficiency, and cholestatic conditions impede its absorption. Dietary carotene is absorbed intact, then undergoes cleavage in the enterocyte to retinol in a reaction which is stimulated by thyroxine.[65]

Retinol binding protein (RBP) is synthesized in the liver and serves as the chief carrier protein for circulating retinol. Decreased levels of RBP have been associated with malnutrition and zinc deficiency. Placental transfer of RBP is the primary source for the developing fetus[67] and this transfer is relatively poor until the third trimester of pregnancy, resulting in lower RBP levels in prematurely born infants. Compounding this problem is the finding that RBP synthesis in the fetal rat liver is depressed until the last quarter of gestation.[68] In contrast, placental transfer of retinol and beta-carotene is by passive diffusion, and beta-carotene is rapidly converted to vitamin A in the fetal liver.[69]

The physiologic roles of vitamin A include epithelial cell integrity and differentiation, vision, bone growth, and reproductive function. Recent data suggest that retinol has a critical role in the maintenance of normal epithelial integrity and differentiation in the tracheobronchial tree of the preterm infant, and in the prevention of bronchopulmonary dysplasia (BPD).[70, 71] The pathologic findings of vitamin A deficiency and BPD are very similar and include basal cell proliferation in the conducting airways, with a loss of mucus-secreting and ciliated cells and squamous metaplasia. Furthermore, Shenai and co-workers[71] found that supplementation with intramuscular retinyl palmitate normalized plasma retinol levels and reduced the incidence of BPD from 55% in controls to 21%. Coincidental reduction in the rate of retinopathy of prematurity from 60% to 26% was also noted.

Requirements

In contrast to adults who have significant hepatic reserves of vitamin A, the term infant has very little reserve at birth and the preterm infant has virtually none.[72] Normal vitamin A levels in healthy adults are in the range of 25 to 90 μg/dL. Children and term infants with vitamin A levels 20 μg/dL or more are considered sufficient in this vitamin.[73] Term infants have mean plasma vitamin A levels of 23.9 μg/dL within 24 hours of birth,[74] although 39% of term infants had levels less than 20 μg/dL. In contrast, preterm infants (≤36 weeks) had a lower mean plasma vitamin A level of 16.0 μg/dL, with 82% having levels in the deficient range.

Enteral requirements for vitamin A for term infants are based on the retinol content of human milk (see Table 7–1). Based on an average content of 49 μg/100 mL, the typical term infant receives 420 RE/day or 1,400 IU/day.

The delivery of adequate vitamin A to parenterally fed infants has been problematic. Retinol binds to the plastic delivery sets, resulting in losses of up to 80% of the original dose of the vitamin.[75, 76] These losses can be reduced by using the palmitate ester, and further lessened by delivering the vitamin in the lipid mixture rather than the glucose and amino acid solution. Term infants receiving 700 RE/day in TPN have been shown to maintain normal plasma vitamin levels.[10] Preterm infants have been shown to have low plasma retinol levels at birth, with no increment in their levels after 4 weeks of receiving 455 RE/day in TPN. Alternate-day supplemental intramuscular doses of 400 to 450 RE/kg/day were sufficient to raise plasma levels of retinol and RBP.[71] Thus, a starting dose of 500 RE/kg/day given in the lipid component should be adequate to overcome losses during administration (see Table 7–2).[10]

Measurement

Current methods for measurement of plasma vitamin A levels include fluorometric[77] and HPLC[78] techniques. Plasma levels decline only after liver reserves have been exhausted. A level less than 20 μg/dL is considered to be deficient in children, and levels less than 10 μg/dL in children and adults are almost always associated with signs of deficiency.

Deficiency

Vitamin A deficiency is commonly a part of more generalized malnutrition. In this setting, RBP levels are low, and plasma vitamin A levels may not accurately represent the patient's vitamin status.[26] Vitamin A deficiency is often accompanied by thiamine and riboflavin deficiency. Because of large retinol losses during administration, prolonged parenteral nutrition places the infant at risk of developing vitamin A deficiency. Other high-risk scenarios include biliary atresia, cystic fibrosis, pancreatic insufficiency, malabsorption syndromes, and following extensive small bowel resection. The first apparent sign in the infant is xerosis (drying) of the cornea and conjunctiva, which may be followed by keratomalacia (softening of the cornea), ulceration, and even overt endophthalmitis, leading to destruction of the eye. Generalized hyperkeratosis characterized by a dry, scaly, pruritic dermatitis, and anemia secondary to bone marrow suppression are other signs of retinol deficiency.

Rare cases have been reported of an inborn defect in the ability to convert dietary beta-carotene to retinol, with subsequent development of vitamin A deficiency.[79] This condition is easily treated by supplementation with oral vitamin A.

Toxicity

Acute toxicity from single doses requires the intake of 3 to 10 times more vitamin A than the level required for the development of chronic toxicity when taken over months to years.[80] In monkeys, this acute LD_{50} is 168 mg/kg, equivalent to 560,000 IU/100 kcal.

Infants and children appear to be more susceptible to vitamin A toxicity, with several reported cases of toxicity with chronic intake as low as 2,000 to 3,000 IU/100 kcal.[81] For this reason, Olson[81] has offered an intake of 750 to 1,000 IU/100 kcal as a maximum safe dose.

Toxicity may occur within 1 week to 3 months in infants, and results in a reversible hydrocephalus with split sutures and vomiting. There may be periosteal bone production or inhibition of bone growth. Anemia and hepatomegaly have also been described. Most symptoms resolve quickly upon discontinuation of excessive intake, despite the persistence of elevated plasma levels for up to 6 weeks.

Retinol is a recognized teratogen,[65] and maternal ingestion of large doses of the vitamin must be avoided, especially during the first trimester of pregnancy.

Carotene is unable to induce hypervitaminosis, as its conversion to vitamin A is not sufficiently rapid.

VITAMIN E

Biochemistry and Metabolism

Vitamin E refers to a group of eight biologically active tocopherols which differ in the number and position of methyl substitutions on the chromanol ring. Alpha-tocopherol is the most potent compound and comprises 90% of the vitamin present in animal tissues. By contrast, γ-tocopherol, which is the predominant form in soy oils (including parenteral lipid emulsions such as Intralipid),[10] possesses only 10% to 20% of the activity of the α-compound. Vitamin E is widely present in all tissues, where it serves as an antioxidant and free radical scavenger. It is chiefly bound to membrane, so that it is in close proximity to both the oxidase enzymes, which generate potentially damaging free radicals, and the polyunsaturated fatty acids (PUFA) of the lipid membranes, which are the major targets of oxidative injury. The presence of the selenium-containing enzyme glutathione peroxidase complements the antioxidant role of vitamin E by protecting the cytosolic domain of the cell.

The first step in enteral absorption of vitamin E is the hydrolysis of the tocopheryl esters that comprise the majority of the dietary vitamin. This hydrolysis requires the presence of both pancreatic esterases and bile acids. Following hydrolysis, the free vitamin is solubilized into micelles by bile acids, which is critical for the passage of this extremely hydrophobic compound across the unstirred water layer. Absorption then occurs by passive diffusion, largely in the mid-jejunum.[65] Overall, 20% to 40% of dietary tocopherol is absorbed, with high dietary PUFA levels interfering with uptake. Preterm infants are less efficient at tocopherol absorption, although uptake improves after 26 weeks gestation to normal levels by 36 weeks.[82] Unlike vitamin A, tocopherol is not reesterified in the gut, but is transported in chylomicrons and very low density lipoprotein by way of the lymphatics to the liver. The vitamin is then resecreted in hepatic very low density lipoprotein and, following metabolism to low-density lipoprotein, is taken up by tissues. Ultimately, vitamin E is metabolized to water-soluble products that are excreted chiefly in the bile, with smaller quantities in the urine.

Requirements

One IU of vitamin E is that activity provided by 1.0 mg of racemic *dl*-α-tocopheryl acetate. The same weight of the most active *d*-α-tocopherol supplies 1.49 IU of activity.

Vitamin E requirements depend on dietary PUFA intake; the term, enterally fed infant generally requires 0.5 mg/kg/day. Human milk is a good source of the vitamin, providing 1.3 to 3.3 mg/L (2 to 5 IU) of vitamin E (see Table 7–1). Infants who are exclusively breast-fed have been shown to undergo increases in serum vitamin E levels to achieve adult levels over the first few weeks of life.[65] Recommendations for the preterm infant are 0.7 IU (0.5 mg) of vitamin E/100 kcal of formula, assuring an intake of 0.4 to 0.5 mg/g PUFA.

An intravenous dose of 7 mg/day of racemic α-tocopherol in term infants was sufficient to maintain plasma levels of the vitamin between 0.5 to 1.5 mg/dL and is the currently recommended dose (see Table 7–2).[10] The data for preterm infants are less secure and are clouded by the deaths of several preterm infants who received large doses (25 to 50 mg/day) of the intravenous vitamin in the early 1980s, although it remains unclear whether the deaths were directly due to vitamin E or to the emulsifier used in the preparation (see Toxicity). A dose of 2.8 mg α-tocopherol/kg/day in infants less than 1,500 g has been estimated to maintain plasma levels between 1.0 and 2.5 mg/dL, based on recent measurements in very low birth weight infants, and is the current recommendation.[10]

Measurement

Vitamin E levels vary directly with serum lipids so that values must be interpreted with caution in conditions of hyper- or hypolipidemia. It is preferable to express vitamin E levels per unit of plasma lipids, although the blood volumes required make this seldom practical in the NICU setting. The most common method employed for vitamin E determination is HPLC, which has largely supplanted spectrophotometric techniques. Levels of 0.8 mg vitamin E/g total plasma lipids are considered adequate for infants.[26] Plasma vitamin E levels of 0.5 to 1.5 mg/dL in term infants and 1.0 to 2.5 mg/dL in preterm infants appear to be adequate and are achieved by the currently recommended doses.

Several functional assays of vitamin E activity, such as hydrogen peroxide–induced hemolysis and platelet aggregation studies are available, but are chiefly of interest in patients with lipid disorders in whom plasma levels are unreliable.

Deficiency

For some time after its initial discovery, no clear human vitamin E deficiency state was recognized. This is presumably because of the large tissue stores in adults and the prolonged periods of several years required to develop deficiency. Since then, a neuromuscular syndrome characterized by posterior column and spinocerebellar tract degeneration, peripheral neuropathy, and progressive myopathy has been identified in children with chronic cholestasis.[83] Retinal ceroid deposition, abnormalities of visual evoked response, and the brown bowel syndrome are also associated with long-standing deficiency.[84] Infants, particularly preterm infants, have much more limited tissue stores both because of their smaller mass and poor transplacental transport of the vitamin.[85] In combination with generally deficient intake, relative malabsorption, greatly increased requirements for rapid growth, and the oxidative stresses of the NICU environment, the sick infant is at increased risk of developing deficiency compared with an adult. The first recognized human deficiency condition was the hemolytic anemia seen in preterm infants, particularly in association with plasma vitamin E levels of less than 0.4 mg/dL, and aggravated by the oxidative insult of iron supplementation.[26] This condition can be completely avoided by the currently recommended levels of supplementation. An area of great interest at present is the role of vitamin E in the prevention of intracranial hemorrhage. Preliminary data suggest that vitamin E supplements can prevent both the incidence and severity of intraventricular hemorrhage if given within the first 12 hours of life.[86] Another role for the vitamin in the NICU includes evidence for decreasing the severity of retinopathy of prematurity in supplemented infants.[87] A theoretical role in the prevention of bronchopulmonary dysplasia has been suggested, although the data are not yet available to support this use.

Virtually every malabsorptive state is accompanied by the risk of vitamin E deficiency. The most severe deficiencies are seen in biliary obstruction, because of the critical role of bile acids in the absorption of the vitamin. The vast majority of infants with chronic cholestasis can be demonstrated to be deficient and are often resistant to oral supplementation with the currently available oral preparation, which is an emulsified form of the fat-soluble vitamin. In these patients, it may be necessary to supplement with frequent intramuscular injections of Ephynal (Hoffman-LaRoche). A truly water soluble form of vitamin E, d-α-tocopheryl polyethylene glycol 1000 succinate, is currently under investigation for enteral use in the cholestatic patient.[88]

Recently, a rare condition of isolated vitamin E deficiency in the absence of other signs of malabsorption has been described, presumably due to a defect in the absorption or processing of the vitamin.[89] These patients generally present after infancy with the neuromuscular syndrome and respond to oral supplementation with very large doses (800 to 1,200 IU/day) of vitamin E.

Toxicity

Animal data suggest that oral vitamin E is safe even in large doses, with no mortality occurring until doses of 1,000 mg/kg/day were reached.[90] Parenteral vitamin E was somewhat more toxic, with an LD_{50} of 200 to 500 mg/kg/day.[91, 92]

Toxic effects associated with elevated vitamin E levels in adults have included increased bleeding tendency due to suppression of vitamin K–dependent clotting factors and decreased platelet aggregation.[93]

The data in infants are less clear. There is virtually no information available regarding vitamin E supplementation in term infants. The safety of parenteral vitamin E has been called into question due to the E-Ferol experience in which preterm infants receiving large doses of intravenous tocopheryl acetate with propylene glycol as a stabilizer developed progressive hepatic insufficiency, renal failure, thrombocytopenia, ascites, and death.[94] Whether this condition was due to vitamin E toxicity is still uncertain, although one infant dying with the syndrome had a plasma level of 12.9 mg/dL.[95] There are reports that oral supplementation of preterm infants with vitamin E is associated with increased risk of necrotizing enterocolitis and infection, particularly in those infants who developed vitamin E levels above 3.5 mg/dL.[96, 97] Other investigators have not found an increased risk in vitamin E–supplemented infants.[87] There has been concern over increasing the risk of intracranial hemorrhage in preterm infants with vitamin E supplementation because of the vitamin's effects on the coagulation system. Recent studies have not borne out these concerns, and rather suggest a protective effect of early vitamin E supplementation.[86]

VITAMIN K

Biochemistry and Metabolism

Vitamin K refers to a group of menadione derivatives important in normal coagulation. Vitamin K_1, or phytonadione (phylloquinone), is the naturally occurring fat-soluble vitamin that composes the majority of normal dietary intake and represents the commonly used parenteral preparation AquaMEPHYTON (Merck Sharp & Dohme). Vitamin K_2, or menaquinone, is synthesized by intestinal bacteria and possesses only 60% of the activity of vitamin K_1.[65] It is also fat-soluble and serves as the major source of vitamin K in infants after absorption in the colon.[26] A synthetic form of the vitamin, referred to as menadione, or K_3, is water soluble, which makes it useful in the treatment of various malabsorptive states. It is commercially available as Synkayvite (Roche).

The colonic absorption of vitamin K, which is produced by intestinal bacteria, is the most important source in infancy. As a result, antibiotic treatment, with resulting disruption of normal gut flora, may seriously interfere with vitamin K production and result in symptomatic deficiency in as little as 2 weeks.[65] In contrast, the intestinal source is less important in older children and adults, who rely on upper small intestinal absorption of dietary vitamin K. Absorption of the vitamin requires the presence of both bile acids and pancreatic enzymes. Data from rat gut sacs implicate an energy-requiring, saturable transporter.[65] Dietary PUFA and large doses of vitamin A may interfere with vitamin K absorption. Following absorption, vitamin K is transported by way of chylomicrons to the liver, kidney, skin, heart, and muscle. Placental transport of vitamin K in the rat occurs by facilitated diffusion.[98] Transport by the human placenta appears to be poor based on the increased risk of preterm infants to hemorrhagic disease due to vitamin K deficiency. However, maternal administration of vitamin K late in pregnancy is effective in preventing hemorrhagic disease, indicating intact transfer by the end of gestation.[99]

The physiologic role of vitamin K is in the maintenance of normal coagulation by means of its influence on the synthesis of the active forms of the "vitamin K–dependent factors" II (prothrombin), VII, IX, and X. Vitamin K serves as a cofactor for the γ-carboxylation of glutamic acid residues of the inactive precursor factors. Carboxylation is necessary for the binding of calcium and phospholipid by prothrombin.

Requirements

The American Academy of Pediatrics Committee on Nutrition recommends that all newborn infants receive 0.5 to 1.0 mg of vitamin K on the day of delivery for routine prophylaxis of hemorrhagic disease of the newborn (see Table 7–2).[100] The institution of this recommendation has virtually eliminated this condition in hospital-born infants in developed nations. The recommended daily allowance for vitamin K recently has been fixed at 5 μg/day for neonates[2]; however, the average breast-fed infant receives 0.3 μg/ kg/day from dietary sources, while the formula-fed infant receives approximately 8 μg/ kg/day.[101]

Vitamin K requirements in parenterally fed infants are met by the currently recommended doses of 200 μg/day of phylloquinone for term infants and 80 μg/kg/day for preterm infants (see Table 7–2).[10]

Measurement

Assessment of vitamin K sufficiency is most readily accomplished by the measurement of the one-stage prothrombin time. Factor VII activity is actually a more sensitive indicator of marginal deficiency,[65] declining before a prolongation of prothrombin time is detectable. Recently, HPLC measurement of plasma vitamin K levels has become possible[101, 102] but is not widely employed.

Deficiency

Deficiency of vitamin K occurs more rapidly than for the other fat-soluble vitamins because of its relatively short half-life. In adults, 60% to 70% of a parenteral dose of vitamin K is cleared in the bile and urine within 3 days.[103]

Deficiency in the neonate is manifest as hemorrhagic disease of the newborn, with spontaneous bleeding into the skin, gastrointestinal tract, lungs, and CNS posing potentially life-threatening problems. High-risk settings include the breast-fed infant, because of the poor vitamin K content of human milk; the infant of the malnourished mother, because of poor placental transfer; and the home-delivered infant who does not receive prophylactic vitamin K at birth.

Toxicity

Naturally occurring, fat-soluble vitamin K_1 is generally nontoxic, although the rapid intravenous infusion of large doses (>1 mg/kg) may result in an anaphylactic reaction. In contrast, synthetic vitamin K_3 is relatively more toxic to the newborn infant, especially the preterm infant, and its use is not recommended in the neonatal period. Doses as low as 5 mg of synthetic vitamin K may produce hemolysis, hyperbilirubinemia, and kernicterus, particularly in preterm infants, although the toxicity is generally dose-related.[104, 105]

Acknowledgment

We gratefully acknowledge the expert assistance of Kathie Williams in the preparation of this manuscript. This work is supported in part by National Institute of Health grant NIH NIDDK 26657.

REFERENCES

1. Food and Drug Administration Rules and Regulations: Nutrient requirements for infant formulas. *Federal Register* 1985; 50:45106–45108.
2. Committee on Dietary Allowances Food and Nutrition Board: *Recommended Dietary Allowances,* ed 10. Washington, DC, National Academy of Sciences, 1989.
3. Bartlett K: Vitamin-responsive inborn errors of metabolism. *Adv Clin Chem* 1986; 23:141–198.
4. Moran JR, Greene HL: Nutritional biochemistry of water-soluble vitamins, in Grand RJ, Sutphen JL, Dietz WH Jr (eds): *Pediatric Nutrition. Theory and Practice.* Boston, Butterworths, 1987, pp 51–67.
5. Tajima S, Pinell SR: Regulation of collagen synthesis by ascorbic acid. Ascorbic acid increases type I procollagen mRNA. *Biochem Biophys Res Commun* 1982; 106:632–637.
6. Wallerstein RO, Wallerstein RO Jr: Scurvy. *Semin Hematol* 1976; 13:211–218.
7. Finn FM, Johns PA: Ascorbic acid transport by isolated bovine adrenal cortical cells. *Endocrinology* 1980; 106:811–817.
8. Streeter M, Rosso P: Transport mechanisms for ascorbic acid in the human placenta. *Am J Clin Nutr* 1981; 34:1706–1711.
9. Norkus EP, Bassi JA, Rosso P: Maternal hyperglycemia and its effect on the placental transport of ascorbic acid. *Pediatr Res* 1982; 16:746–750.
10. Greene HL, Hambidge KM, Schanler R, et al: Guidelines for the use of vitamins, trace elements, calcium, magnesium and phosphorus in infants and children receiving total parenteral nutrition: Report of the Subcommittee on Pediatric Parenteral Nutrient Require-

ments from the Committee on Clinical Practice Issues of The American Society for Clinical Nutrition. *Am J Clin Nutr* 1988; 48:1324–1342.

11. Heller RM, Howard L, Greene HL: Skeletal changes of copper deficiency in infants receiving prolonged total parenteral nutrition. *J Pediatr* 1978; 92:942–949.

12. Prockop DJ, Guzman NA: Collagen diseases and the biosynthesis of collagen. *Hosp Pract* 1977; 12:61–68.

13. Herbert V: The rationale of massive-dose vitamin therapy, in *Proceedings of Western Hemisphere Nutrition Congress IV*. Littleton, Mass, Publishing Sciences Group, 1975, p 84.

14. Rindi G, Ventura U: Thiamine intestinal transport. *Physiol Rev* 1972; 52:817–821.

15. Pincus JH, Copper JR, Murphy JV, et al: Thiamine derivatives in subacute necrotizing encephalomyelopathy. A preliminary report. *Pediatrics* 1973; 51:716–721.

16. Shah N, Wolff JA: Thiamine deficiency: Probable Wernicke's encephalopathy successfully treated in a child with acute lymphocytic leukemia. *Pediatrics* 1973; 51:750–751.

17. Davis ED, Icke GC: Clinical chemistry of thiamine. *Adv Clin Chem* 1983; 23:93–140.

18. Ariaey-Nejad MR, Balaghi M, Baker EM, et al: Thiamine metabolism in man. *Am J Clin Nutr* 1970; 23:764–778.

19. Sauberlich HE: Biochemical alterations in thiamine deficiency: Their interpretation. *Am J Clin Nutr* 1967; 20:528–546.

20. Cooper JR, Itokawa Y, Pincus JH: Thiamine triphosphate deficiency in subacute necrotising encephalomyelopathy. *Science* 1969; 164:74–75.

21. Murphy JV, Craig L, Glew R: Leigh's disease: Biochemical nature of the inhibitor. *Pediatr Res* 1974; 8:392.

22. Pincus JH: Subacute necrotizing encephalomyelopathy (Leigh's disease): A consideration of clinical features and etiology. *Dev Med Child Neurol* 1972; 14:87–101.

23. Kostenbauder HB, Sanvordecker DR: Riboflavin enhancement of bilirubin photocatabolism in vivo. *Experientia* 1973; 29:282–283.

24. Baeckert PA, Greene HL, Fritz I, et al: Vitamin concentrations in very low birth weight infants given vitamins intravenously in a lipid emulsion: Measurement of vitamins A, D, and E and riboflavin. *J Pediatr* 1988; 113:1057–1065.

25. Horwitt MK: Interpretations of requirements for thiamin, riboflavin, niacin-tryptophan and vitamin E, plus comments on balance studies and vitamin B6. *Am J Clin Nutr* 1986; 44:973–985.

26. Brewster MA: Vitamins, in Kaplan L, Pesce A (eds): *Clinical Chemistry*. St Louis, CV Mosby Co, 1984, pp 656–685.

27. Pinto J, Huang YP, Rivlin RS: Inhibition of riboflavin metabolism by chlorpromazine, imipramine and amitriptyline. *J Clin Invest* 1981; 67:1500–1506.

28. Pinto J, Huang YP, McConnell R, et al: Increased urinary riboflavin excretion resulting from boric acid ingestion. *J Lab Clin Med* 1978; 92:126–134.

29. Barker BM, Bender DA: Vitamin B6, in Barker BM, Bender DA (eds): Vitamins in medicine, ed 4. London, Heinemann Medical Books, 1980, pp 348.

30. Wilson RG, Davis RE: Clinical chemistry of vitamin B6. *Adv Clin Chem* 1983; 23:1–68.

31. Sebrell WM Jr, Harris RS: *The Vitamins*. New York, Academic Press, 1968.

32. Ubbink JB, Delport R, Becker PJ, et al: Evidence of a theophylline-induced vitamin B6 deficiency caused by noncompetitive inhibition of pyridoxal kinase. *J Lab Clin Med* 1989; 113:15–22.

33. Jaffe IA: The antivitamin B6 effect of penicillamine: Clinical and immunological implications. *Adv Biochem Psychopharmacol* 1972; 4:217–226.

34. Sauberlich HE, Canham JE: The vitamins, in Goodhart RS, Shils ME (eds): *Modern Nutrition in Health and Disease,* ed 6. Philadelphia, Lea & Febiger, 1980, p 216.

35. Leklem JE, Reynolds RD: *Methods in Vitamin B6 Nutrition.* New York, Plenum Publishing Corp, 1979.

36. Ubbink JB, Schnell AM: Assay of erythrocyte enzyme activity levels involved in vitamin

B6 metabolism by high-performance liquid chromatography. *J Chromatogr* 1988; 431:406–412.

37. Spannuth CL Jr, Laken GW, Wagner C, et al: Increased plasma clearance of pyridoxal 5′-phosphate in vitamin B6-deficient uremic man. *J Lab Clin Med* 1977; 90:632–637.
38. Schaumburg H, Kaplan J, Windebank A, et al: Sensory neuropathy from pyridoxine abuse—a new megavitamin syndrome. *N Engl J Med* 1983; 309:445–448.
39. Moran JR, Greene HL: The B vitamins and vitamin C in human nutrition: II. 'Conditional' B vitamins and vitamin C. *Am J Dis Child* 1979; 133:308–314.
40. Sauberlich HE, Skala JH, Dowdy RP: *Laboratory Tests for the Assessment of Nutritional Status.* Cleveland, CRC Press, 1974.
41. Spivak JL, Jackson DL: Pellagra: An analysis of 18 patients and a review of the literature. *Johns Hopkins Med J* 1977; 140:295–309.
42. Carlson LA: Nicotinic acid and inhibition of fat-mobilizing lipolysis. Present status of effects on lipid metabolism. *Adv Exp Med Biol* 1978; 109:225–238.
43. American Psychiatric Association Task Force on Vitamin Therapy in Psychiatry: Megavitamin and orthomolecular therapy in psychiatry. Washington, DC, Publications Services Division, American Psychiatric Association, 1973.
44. National Academy of Sciences: *Recommended Dietary Allowances,* ed 8. Washington, DC, GPO, 1974.
45. Spencer RP, Brody KR: Biotin transport by the small intestine of rat, hamster and other species. *Am J Physiol* 1964; 206:653–657.
46. Rose RC, McCormick DB, Li TK, et al: Transport and metabolism of vitamins. *Fed Proc* 1986; 45:30–39.
47. Moore MC, Greene HL, Phillips B, et al: Evaluation of a pediatric multiple vitamin preparation for total parenteral nutrition in infants and children: I. Blood levels of water-soluble vitamins. *Pediatrics* 1986; 77:530–538.
48. Mock DM, DeLorimer AA, Liebman WM, et al: Biotin deficiency: An unusual complication of parenteral alimentation. *N Engl J Med* 1981; 304:820–823.
49. Wolf B, Heard GS, Weissbecker KA, et al: Biotinidase deficiency: Initial clinical features and rapid diagnosis. *Ann Neurol* 1985; 18:614–617.
50. Wolf B, Hsia YE, Sweetman L, et al: Multiple carboxylase deficiency: Clinical and biochemical improvement following neonatal biotin treatment. *Pediatrics* 1981; 68:113–118.
51. Kutsky RJ: *Handbook of Vitamins, Minerals and Hormones,* ed 2. New York, Van Nostrand Reinhold, 1981.
52. Hodges RE, Bean WB, Ohlson MA, et al: Human pantothenic acid deficiency produced by omega-methyl pantothenic acid. *J Clin Invest* 1959; 38:1421–1425.
53. Higginbottom MC, Sweetman L, Nyhan WL: A syndrome of methylmalonic aciduria, homocystinuria, megaloblastic anemia and neurologic abnormalities in a vitamin B12-deficient breast-fed infant of a strict vegetarian. *N Engl J Med* 1978; 299:317–323.
54. Specker BL, Miller D, Norman E, et al: Increased urinary methylmalonic acid excretion in breast fed infants of vegetarian mothers and identification of an acceptable dietary source of vitamin B12. *Am J Clin Nutr* 1988; 47:89–92.
55. Davis RE: Clinical chemistry of vitamin B12. *Adv Clin Chem* 1985; 24:163–216.
56. Selhub J, Rosenberg IH: Folate transport in isolated brush border membrane vesicles from rat intestine. *J Biol Chem* 1981; 256:4489–4493.
57. Ek J: Plasma and red cell folate values in newborn infants and their mothers in relation to gestational age. *J Pediatr* 1980; 97:288–292.
58. Hoffbrand AV: Folate deficiency in premature infants. *Arch Dis Child* 1970; 45:441–444.
59. Tamura T, Yoshimura Y, Arakawa T: Human milk folate and folate status in lactating mothers and their infants. *Am J Clin Nutr* 1980; 33:193–197.
60. Baker SJ, Kumar S, Swaminathan SP: Excretion of folic acid in bile. *Lancet* 1965; 1:685.
61. Davis RE: Clinical chemistry of folic acid. *Adv Clin Chem* 1986; 25:233–294.

62. Nichol DJ, Davis RE: The folate and vitamin B12 content of infant milk foods with particular reference to goat's milk. *Med J Aust* 1967; 2:212–213.
63. Goldsmith GC: Vitamin B complex. *Prog Food Nutr Sci* 1975; 1:559–609.
64. Herman RB, Stifel FB, Greene HL: Vitamin-deficient states and other related diseases, in Dietschy JM (ed): *Disorders of the Gastrointestinal Tract, Disorders of the Liver, Nutritional Disorders.* New York, Grune & Stratton, 1976, pp 380–384.
65. Moran JR, Greene HL: Nutritional biochemistry of fat-soluble vitamins, in Grand RJ, Sutphen JL, Dietz WH Jr (eds): *Pediatric Nutrition. Theory and Practice.* Boston, Butterworths, 1987, pp 69–85.
66. Loran MR, Althausen TL: Transport of vitamin A in vitro across normal isolated rat intestine and intestine subjected to "partial" resection. *Am J Physiol* 1959; 197:1333–1336.
67. Vahlquist A, Rask L, Peterson PA, et al: The concentrations of retinol-binding protein, prealbumin, and transferrin in the sera of newly delivered mothers and children of various ages. *Scand J Clin Lab Invest* 1975; 35:569–575.
68. Takahashi YI, Smith JE, Goodman DS: Vitamin A and retinol binding protein metabolism during fetal development in the rat. *Am J Physiol* 1977; 233:E263–E272.
69. Baker H, Frank O, Thomson AD, et al: Vitamin profile of 174 mothers and newborns at parturition. *Am J Clin Nutr* 1975; 28:59–65.
70. Shenai JP, Chytil F, Stahlman MT: Vitamin A status of neonates with bronchopulmonary dysplasia. *Pediatr Res* 1985; 19:185–189.
71. Shenai JP, Kennedy KA, Chytil F, et al: Clinical trial of vitamin A supplementation in infants susceptible to bronchopulmonary dysplasia. *J Pediatr* 1987; 111:269–277.
72. Olson JA, Gunning DB, Tilton RA: Liver concentrations of vitamin A and carotenoids as a function of age and other parameters of American children who died of various causes. *Am J Clin Nutr* 1984; 39:903–910.
73. O'Neal RM, Johnson OC, Schaefer AE: Guidelines for classification and interpretation of group blood and urine data collected as part of the national nutrition survey. *Pediatr Res* 1970; 4:103–106.
74. Shenai JP, Chytil F, Jhaveri A, et al: Plasma vitamin A and retinol-binding protein in premature and term neonates. *J Pediatr* 1981; 99:302–305.
75. Greene HL, Phillips BL, Franck L, et al: Persistently low blood retinol levels during and after parenteral feeding of very low birth weight infants: Examination of losses into intravenous administration sets and a method of prevention by adding to a lipid emulsion. *Pediatrics* 1987; 79:894–900.
76. Shenai JP, Stahlman MT, Chytil F: Vitamin A delivery from parenteral alimentation solutions. *J Pediatr* 1981; 99:661–663.
77. Thompson JN, Erdody P, Brian R, et al: Fluorometric determinations of vitamin A in human blood and liver. *Biochem Med* 1971; 5:67–89.
78. Bieri JG, Tolliver TJ, Catignani GL: Simultaneous determination of alpha-tocopherol and retinol in plasma or red cells by high pressure liquid chromatography. *Am J Clin Nutr* 1979; 32:2143–2149.
79. McLaren DS, Zekian B: Failure of enzymic cleavage of beta-carotene. *Am J Dis Child* 1971; 121:278–280.
80. Bauernfeind JC: *The Safe Use of Vitamin A: A Report of the International Vitamin A Consultative Group (IVACG).* New York, Nutrition Foundation, 1980.
81. Olson JA: Upper limits of vitamin A in infant formulas, with some comments on vitamin K. *J Nutr* 1989; 119:1820–1824.
82. Melhorn DK, Gross S: Vitamin E-dependent anemia in the premature infant: Relationship between gestational age and absorption of vitamin E. *J Pediatr* 1971; 79:581–588.
83. Guggenheim MA, Ringel SP, Silverman A, et al: Progressive neuromuscular disease in children with chronic cholestasis and vitamin E deficiency: Diagnosis and treatment with alpha tocopherol. *J Pediatr* 1982; 100:51–58.

84. Bauman MB, DiMase JD, Oski F, et al: Brown bowel and skeletal myopathy associated with vitamin E depletion in pancreatic insufficiency. *Gastroenterology* 1968; 54:93–100.

85. Mino M, Nishino H: Fetal and maternal relationship in serum vitamin E level. *J Nutr Sci Vitaminol* 1973; 19:475–482.

86. Sinha S, Davies J, Toner N, et al: Vitamin E supplementation reduces frequency of periventricular haemorrhage in very preterm babies. *Lancet* 1987; 1:466–471.

87. Phelps DL, Rosenbaum AL, Isenberg SJ, et al: Tocopherol efficacy and safety for preventing retinopathy of prematurity: A randomized, controlled, double-masked trial. *Pediatrics* 1987; 79:489–500.

88. Sokol RJ, Heubi JE, Butler-Simon N, et al: Treatment of vitamin E deficiency during chronic childhood cholestasis with oral *d*-alpha tocopheryl polyethylene glycol-1000 succinate. *Gastroenterology* 1987; 93:975–985.

89. Harding AE, Matthews S, Jones S, et al: Spinocerebellar degeneration associated with a selective defect of vitamin E absorption. *N Engl J Med* 1985; 313:32–35.

90. Wheldon GH, Bhatt A, Keller P, et al: *d,l*-alpha-tocopheryl acetate (vitamin E): A long term toxicity and carcinogenicity study in rats. *Int J Vitam Nutr Res* 1983; 53:287–296.

91. Phelps DL: Local and systemic reactions to the parenteral administration of vitamin E. *Dev Pharmacol Ther* 1981; 2:156–171.

92. Yasunaga T, Kato H, Ohgaki K, et al: Effect of vitamin E as an immunopotentiation agent for mice at optimal dosage and its toxicity at high dosage. *J Nutr* 1982; 112:1075–1084.

93. Bell EF: Upper limit of vitamin E in infant formulas. *J Nutr* 1989; 119:1829–1831.

94. Martone WJ, Williams WW, Mortensen ML, et al: Illness with fatalities in premature infants: Association with an intravenous vitamin E preparation E-ferol. *Pediatrics* 1986; 78:591–600.

95. Phelps DL: E-ferol: What happened and what now?. *Pediatrics* 1984; 74:1114–1116.

96. Finer NN, Peters KL, Hayek Z, et al: Vitamin E and necrotizing enterocolitis. *Pediatrics* 1984; 73:387–393.

97. Johnson L, Bowen FW Jr, Abbasi S, et al: Relationship of prolonged pharmacologic serum levels of vitamin E to incidence of sepsis and necrotizing enterocolitis in infants with birth weight 1,500 grams or less. *Pediatrics* 1985; 75:619–638.

98. Dam H, Prange I, Sondergard E: Deposition of injected massive doses of colloidal vitamin K1 in chicks, after partial blockage of the reticuloendothelial system and in pregnant rats. *Acta Pharmacol Toxicol* 1955; 11:90–93.

99. Owen GM, Nelsen CE, Baker GL, et al: Use of vitamin K1 in pregnancy: Effect on serum bilirubin and plasma prothrombin in the newborn. *Am J Obstet Gynecol* 1967; 99:368–373.

100. American Academy of Pediatrics Committee on Nutrition: Vitamin and mineral supplement needs in normal children in the United States. *Pediatrics* 1980; 66:1015–1021.

101. Haroon Y, Shearer MJ, Rahim S, et al: The content of phylloquinone (vitamin K1) in human milk, cow's milk and infant formula foods determined by high performance liquid chromatography. *J Nutr* 1982; 112:1105–1117.

102. Shearer MJ: High-performance liquid chromatography of K vitamins and their antagonists, in Giddings JC, Grushka E, Cazes J, et al (eds): *Advances in Chromatography*. New York, Marcel Dekker, 1983, pp 243–301.

103. Shearer MJ, Mallinson CN, Webster GR, et al: Clearance and excretion in urine, faeces and bile of an intravenous dose of tritiated vitamin K1 in man. *Br J Haematol* 1972; 22:579–588.

104. Meyer TC, Angus J: The effect of large doses of "Synkavit" in the newborn. *Arch Dis Child* 1956; 31:212–215.

105. Herman RH: Disorders of fat-soluble vitamins A, D, E, and K, in Suskind RM (ed): *Textbook of Pediatric Nutrition*. New York, Raven Press, 1981, pp 65–112.

106. Committee on Nutrition, American Academy of Pediatrics; Forbes GB (ed): *Pediatric Nutrition Handbook,* ed 2. Elk Grove Village, Ill, American Academy of Pediatrics, 1985.

Chapter 8

Calcium, Phosphorus, and Magnesium in the Newborn: Pathophysiology and Management

Oussama Itani, M.D.

Reginald C. Tsang, M.B.B.S.

Perinatal calcium (Ca), phosphorus (P), and magnesium (Mg) homeostasis involves an intricate system of hormones that regulate the concentrations of these minerals in the tissues of the mother, fetus, and the neonate. Understanding of the perinatal physiology of these minerals is important in the practical management of mineral disorders in the newborn. In this chapter, we review the perinatal physiology of Ca, Mg, and P metabolism in the fetus and the neonate and offer a practical approach to the pathophysiology and management of neonatal Ca, P, and Mg disorders.

PERINATAL MINERAL PHYSIOLOGY

Mineral metabolism in the newborn is closely related to gestational factors controlling maternal mineral homeostasis, as well as to postnatal factors, particularly those affecting the overall mineral balance of the newborn.

Body Mineral Content (Table 8–1)

The fetus is dependent on maternal resources to acquire Ca, P, and Mg. These minerals are actively transported across the placenta to the fetal circulation against a concentration gradient.[1-6] Numerous studies have demonstrated that total Ca concentration in cord blood at birth exceeds that in maternal blood at all times during the third trimester.[7-11] Similarly, P and Mg concentrations are higher in cord blood at birth than in corresponding maternal blood concentrations.[11] The fetal accretion rate for these minerals increases exponentially during the last trimester of pregnancy (24 to 38 weeks). The peak accretion rate is reached at 34 to 36 weeks gestation and amounts to 117 mg of Ca,

TABLE 8–1.

Neonatal Body Mineral Composition, Distribution, and Fetal Accretion*

Mineral	Fetal Accretion, 3d Trimester (mg/kg/day)	Total Body Content (g)	Distribution			
			Bone (%)	Muscle (%)	ICF† (%)	Circ‡ (%)
Calcium	117	28	98	—	—	<1
Phosphorus	74	16	80	9	—	<1
Magnesium	2.7	0.8	60	20	19	<1

* Data adapted from references 1 through 12.
† ICF = intracellular fluid.
‡ CIRC = circulation.

74 mg of P, and 2.7 mg of Mg per kilogram body weight per day.[1, 4, 5, 12, 13] The fetus acquires more than two-thirds of its body mineral content during the third trimester.

Therefore, preterm newborns are theoretically at a disadvantage for mineral homeostasis because they have not acquired their full complement of minerals antenatally. Human milk (which contains 24 to 32 mg Ca/dL and 11 to 16 mg of P/dL and standard humanized milk formulas do not provide enough Ca, P, and Mg to meet the bone mineralization rate of these rapidly growing preterm infants.[14, 15] With the increasing survival of very low birth weight (VLBW) and extremely premature infants, the incidence of bone demineralization and rickets (with or without fractures) is rising. The problem of "metabolic bone disease of prematurity" is further aggravated by other complications of prematurity that may be associated with limited mineral intake [bronchopulmonary dysplasia (BPD) patients with fluid restriction and prolonged parenteral alimentation with solutions containing insufficient mineral concentrations] or excessive mineral loss in urine (BPD patients on diuretics). Neonatologists face this challenging situation by utilizing milk formulas that are fortified with Ca, P, and Mg to meet the fetal mineral accretion rate in order to ensure an optimal mineral intake necessary for normal bone mineralization.

Total body Ca content in the newborn amounts to 28 g, most of which (98%) is in bone. Bone mineral content amounts to 4 g Ca/kg body weight in the infant, which is almost fourfold less than in an adult (19 g Ca/kg).[1, 2]

Total body P in the newborn infant is 16 g (2.4 g of P/kg body weight), 80% of which is in bone, 9% in skeletal muscle, and the remainder in the viscera and extracellular fluid.[1, 2]

Total body Mg content in the newborn amounts to 0.8 g (0.22 g mg/kg body weight). Magnesium is the second most common intracellular electrolyte and is mostly concentrated in bone (60%). Twenty percent of total body Mg is concentrated in muscle and another 20% in the intracellular compartment of other body tissues.[1, 2]

Serum Mineral Concentration (Table 8–2)

Because most of the body's mineral content is in tissues and less than 1% of Ca, P, and Mg is in the circulation, serum concentrations of these minerals do not reflect tissue concentrations. Yet serum concentrations are useful in clinical practice; fluctuations from "normal serum ranges" for these minerals often are associated with clinical symptoms.

Total serum Ca concentration normally ranges between 8 and 11 mg/dL. Up to 45%

TABLE 8–2.

Distribution of Minerals in the Circulation*

| | | % Ultrafilterable | |
Mineral	Protein Bound (%)	Ionized	Complexed
Calcium	40–45	50–55	5–10
Phosphorus	10–15	50	35–40
Magnesium	20–30	55–60	10–15

*Data adapted from Koo WWK, Tsang RC: Calcium and magnesium metabolism in health and disease, in Werner M (ed): *CRC Handbook of Clinical Chemistry*, vol II (in press).

of total serum Ca is usually bound to serum proteins, the remainder (55%) being ultrafiltrable. Eighty-five percent to 90% of the unbound serum Ca remains ionized, and the remaining 10% to 15% is complexed to anions (phosphate, lactate, and citrate).[1] Total serum Ca concentration is readily determined by atomic absorption spectrophotometry. However, serum ionized Ca determination is a better physiologic indicator of Ca homeostasis, but is not available in all centers.

Total serum Mg concentration in infancy and early childhood is 2.2 ± 0.3 mg/dL (mean ± SD). Approximately 70% to 80% of serum Mg is ultrafiltrable; 70% to 80% of ultrafiltrable Mg is ionized, and the rest is complexed to anionic phosphate, citrate, and oxalate.[1]

Serum P concentrations are higher during infancy (4 to 7.1 mg/dL) than adulthood (2.7 to 4.5 mg/dL). At least 10% of total serum P is bound to protein, 50% is present as free ions, and the remainder is complexed to Ca, Mg, and sodium salts.[1]

Hormonal Regulation of Mineral Metabolism

Parathyroid hormone (PTH), an 84-amino-acid peptide that promotes bone resorption and elevates serum Ca concentration, does not cross the placenta.[16] Because of fetal "relative hypercalcemia," the fetal parathyroid glands may be suppressed in utero. However, from recent data, the PTH or a PTH–related peptide may have a role in placental transport of Ca.[17, 18]

Calcitonin, a 22-amino-acid peptide hormone that inhibits bone resorption and decreases serum Ca concentration, may play an active role in fetal bone mineralization and modulation of placental transfer of calcium.[19] Theoretically, the relative fetal hypercalcemia stimulates thyroid C-cells to secrete calcitonin, a process that may promote bone mineralization in utero. However, the role of calcitonin is not clearly understood. In the immediate neonatal period, serum Ca concentrations decrease slowly after birth and reach a nadir by 24 to 48 hours of life, before rising gradually to approach adult concentrations by 7 days.[20–22] The drop in serum Ca is associated with a rise in PTH concentrations, possibly due to stimulation of the parathyroid glands by the hypocalcemic stimulus. Contrary to expectations, serum calcitonin rises consistently after birth, despite hypocalcemia, and reaches a peak by 7 days before drifting down to adult concentrations. Higher serum calcitonin concentrations may occur in sick and stressed infants.

The role of vitamin D metabolites in perinatal mineral homeostasis is not completely clear.[20] The major vitamin D metabolite that crosses the placenta is 25-hydroxyvitamin D [25(OH)D]. Cord blood 1,25-dihydroxyvitamin D [1,25(OH)$_2$D] concentrations are lower than adult values; the contribution of placental and maternal 1,25(OH)$_2$D sources is unclear. Nevertheless, production of $1,25(OH)_2D$ by fetal kidneys is likely to be significant. This has been demonstrated in vitro[23, 24] and is further supported by the fact that bilateral fetal nephrectomy in sheep results in lower fetal serum concentrations of $1,25(OH)_2D$ and Ca.[25] Theoretically, the constant transplacental Ca transport in utero suppresses fetal PTH secretion and renal 1α-hydroxylation. Thus, low serum $1,25(OH)_2D$ in cord blood might be expected. The role of vitamin D metabolites in fetal bone mineralization is unclear. Postnatally, serum $1,25(OH)_2D$ concentrations increase over the first 5 days of life concomitantly with the rise in PTH and calcitonin.[26] The rise in serum $1,25(OH)_2D$ concentrations postnatally theoretically may serve to enhance neonatal intestinal Ca absorption and retention.[27]

Postpartal serum Mg concentrations are variable but generally may correlate with those of Ca. Cord blood P concentrations are higher than those of the mother. Serum P concentrations decrease slightly over the first week of life but remain relatively elevated compared to adult values.

NEONATAL HYPOCALCEMIA

Definition

Neonatal hypocalcemia is generally defined as a total serum Ca concentration below 7 mg/dL as determined by atomic absorption spectrophotometry.[28] However, the serum ionized Ca concentration is a better indicator of physiologic Ca activity; it is readily quantitated with the availability of precise and stable ion-selective electrodes. Recently, the lower limit of serum ionized Ca concentrations in healthy term newborns has been proposed as 4.4 mg/dL.[29]

Etiology (Table 8–3)

Because Ca homeostasis is intricately integrated with that of P and Mg, neonatal hypocalcemia may be associated with hyperphosphatemia (serum P concentration over 8 mg/dL) or hypomagnesemia (serum Mg under 1.5 mg/dL).

On the basis of its temporal onset, hypocalcemia has been classified into early or late. It may be asymptomatic or associated with signs of exaggerated neuromuscular excitability (muscular twitches, positive Chvostek's and Trousseaus's signs), or seizures.

Early neonatal hypocalcemia often occurs within the first few days of life. Normally, serum Ca concentration attains a nadir by 24 hours of age and early neonatal hypocalcemia appears to be an exaggeration of this fall.[28] Risk factors for early hypocalcemia are cited in Table 9–3. Prematurity probably is the prime predisposing risk factor for early hypocalcemia;[26, 30] 30% to 90% of preterm neonates develop hypocalcemia, with an incidence that correlates inversely with gestational age and birth weight.[26, 31] Hypercalcitoninemia also is a major factor in early neonatal hypocalcemia.[25, 32, 33]

Birth asphyxia or hypoxia has been associated with hypocalcemia, which was described in about 30% of newborn infants who had an Apgar score below 7 at 1 minute of age.[34, 35] With modern perinatal care, hypocalcemia occurs more in association with a low 5-minute Apgar score. Infants of insulin-dependent diabetic mothers (IDM) are described to have low serum Mg concentrations, which may explain their transient neonatal hypoparathyroidism.[36] In fact, 50% of IDMs develop early neonatal hypocalcemia.[37] Intrauterine growth retardation per se does not predispose to hypocalcemia unless

TABLE 8–3.

Causes of Neonatal Hypocalcemia

Early
  Prematurity
  Asphyxia neonatorum
  Infant of diabetic mother
  Hypoparathyroidism—2° to maternal
    hyperparathyroidism
  Phototherapy
  Gestational exposure to anticonvulsants
Late
  High dietary phosphorus content:
    Cow's milk formulas
    Cereals
  Maternal factors
    Decreased vitamin D intake
    Decreased sunlight exposure
    Advanced age and parity
    Lower socioeconomic status
  Hypoparathyroidism
    Primary
      Sporadic
      Hereditary
    Secondary: Maternal hyperparathyroidism
  Hypomagnesemia
  Intestinal malabsorption
  High concentration of long-chain free fatty acid in
    blood
  Exchange transfusion with citrate-containing blood

the neonate is premature or has experienced an asphyctic insult.[31, 38] Early neonatal hypocalcemia has also been described with decreased Ca intake,[39] transient neonatal hypoparathyroidism,[40, 41] and occasionally with disordered vitamin D metabolism.[42–45]

Maternal hyperparathyroidism with hypercalcemia is thought to result in fetal hypercalcemia that suppresses the fetal parathyroid glands, ultimately causing neonatal hypoparathyroidism that manifests as early neonatal hypocalcemia.[28] Early neonatal hypocalcemia and congenital rickets have been described in infants born to mothers with intestinal malabsorption[46] or vitamin D deficiency osteomalacia.[47–50]

Neonatal hypocalcemia has also been described in neonates subjected to phototherapy[51]; the cause is unclear, and the condition has been proposed to be related to melatonin disturbance.[52] Hypocalcemia also occurs in neonates born to mothers with gestational exposure to antiepileptic medications[53]; the mechanism is not clearly understood but may be related to the effect of phenobarbital or phenytoin in enhancing accelerated metabolism of 25(OH)D by hepatic microsomal P450 oxidase activity.[53–55]

Late neonatal hypocalcemia characteristically presents as tetany by the end of the first week of life. Several predisposing factors have been identified, the most common being administration of relatively high P-containing cow milk formulas. Even modern cow milk formulas with modified Ca and P contents appear to result in hyperphosphatemia and symptomatic hypocalcemia, presumably because the P load is still higher than in human milk.[56] Similarly, ingestion of high P-containing cereals has resulted in late neonatal hypocalcemia.[57] Disturbed maternal vitamin D metabolism, from insufficient dietary intake and exposure to sunlight associated with increased maternal age and parity and lower socioeconomic status, appear to predispose to higher incidence of late neonatal hypocalcemia. Other causes include intestinal malabsorption of Ca,[58] hypomagnesemia,[59] and hypoparathyroidism.[28, 60]

A normal total serum Ca concentration may conceal a depressed serum ionized Ca concentration. Infants who undergo exchange transfusions with blood containing acid citrate dextrose or citrate phosphate dextrose as an anticoagulant are prone to have lower serum ionized Ca concentrations because of Ca chelation by citrate.[61–64] Similarly, lower serum ionized Ca concentration may be found in infants receiving parenteral lipid solutions, and the mechanism has been attributed to Ca binding to long-chain free fatty acids.[65] Finally, "iatrogenic" alkalosis resulting from mechanical hyperventilation of infants on respirators or excessive alkali administration results in increased Ca binding to plasma proteins and a decreased plasma ionized Ca fraction.[28]

Diagnosis

Identification and the etiology of hypocalcemia depend on its time of onset, clinical signs in the neonate, and maternal and family history. Early neonatal hypocalcemia is usually asymptomatic and detected only by biochemical measurements, particularly in VLBW (<1.5 kg) premature infants. It is a common practice to check serum Ca concentration in preterm newborns by 24 hours of life; in VLBW infants it may be necessary to check values at 12 hours of age. In contrast, late neonatal hypocalcemia manifests clinically with neuromuscular twitching, seizures, laryngospasms, high-pitched cry, and positive Chvostek's and Trousseau's signs. A family history of metabolic Ca disorders (DiGeorge syndrome in a sibling) or maternal history of hyperparathyroidism or drug ingestion is valuable in the "work-up" of a hypocalcemic neonate. The circumstances of birth and delivery should be investigated for any coincident asphyctic/hypoxic insult.

Serum biochemic studies are helpful in the diagnosis of neonatal hypocalcemia; these include a serum total Ca, ionized Ca (a better physiologic indicator of Ca status), P, Mg, and 25(OH)D. Hyperphosphatemia (>8 mg/dL) may be a clue to high dietary phosphate intake (cow milk formula, cereal) or hypoparathyroidism. Hypomagnesemia (serum Mg <1.5 mg/dL) may be the etiologic factor for hypocalcemia in IDMs. Low serum 25(OH)D (<10 ng/mL) points to vitamin D deficiency. Findings such as biochemical evidence of hypoparathyroidism with absence of the thymus on chest x-ray, cell-mediated immune defects, mucocutaneous candidiasis, and aortic arch anomalies are highly suggestive of DiGeorge syndrome. Measurements of corrected QT intervals on electrocardiograms may be of assistance in assessing the course of the hypocalcemia, but a prolonged QT interval is not necessarily indicative of a low serum ionized Ca.

Prevention and Treatment

Early neonatal hypocalcemia can be prevented in neonates at risk by oral[66] and parenteral[67] Ca supplementation (75 mg elemental Ca/kg/day). In some experimental trials,[68–72] prevention of neonatal hypocalcemia was achieved in large preterm infants with short-term use of moderately high doses of $1,25(OH)_2$ D, the active metabolite of vitamin D (approximately 0.5 μg/kg/day for 2 days).[71] However, VLBW neonates were responsive only at extremely high doses of $1,25(OH)_2D$ (4 μg/kg/day).[72]

Treatment of diagnosed hypocalcemia may be achieved by administration of oral or continuous intravenous Ca salts—usually Ca gluconate 10% solution; however, it is unclear whether asymptomatic hypocalcemia should be treated. Because Ca ions have a crucial physiologic role in the initiation of intracellular enzymatic processes, hypocalcemia, though asymptomatic, theoretically may have detrimental effects on cellular physiology. Administration of elemental Ca (as 10% Ca gluconate solution) at a dose of 75 mg/kg/day for 2 days usually achieves normocalcemia (ideally 8 to 10.5 mg/dL). Alternatively, Ca supplementation may be administered at gradually decreasing doses to allow a more physiologic Ca adaptation by the baby. For example, the first dose could be 75 mg/kg over the first 24 hours, followed by half the dose over the next 24 hours and a quarter of it over the next 24 hours, provided that daily serum Ca determinations exceed 8 mg/dL.

Hypertonic Ca gluconate oral solutions, such as Neo-Calglucon (Sandoz Pharmaceuticals), have been associated with increased incidence of necrotizing enterocolitis[73] and should therefore be avoided. A daily oral dose of 10% Ca gluconate solution (for intravenous use) given in 4- to 6-hour intervals is well tolerated by low-birth-weight neonates with no significant side effects. Intravenous Ca gluconate administration is also an effective means to achieve normocalcemia. Continuous infusions are preferable to intermittent pulse infusions because the latter are associated with calciuria. Continuous infusions should be administered under strict cardiac monitoring because of the risk of bradycardia and even cardiac arrest associated with an accidental increase in the rate of the infusion. Intermittent intravenous boluses of 10% Ca gluconate should be given at a rate not exceeding 2 mL/kg/10 min and under simultaneous cardiac monitoring. In infants requiring alkali therapy, sodium bicarbonate therapy should not be given through the same intravenous line as Ca gluconate because of the risk of precipitate formation.

Extravasation of Ca gluconate into cutaneous and subcutaneous tissues may be associated with skin burns and sloughing and therefore should be watched for and avoided by ensuring a patent intravenous line. Intra-arterial infusion of Ca salts is contraindicated because of the risk of necrosis of tissues supplied by the artery infused. Necrosis of intestinal tissue may occur following infusion of Ca salts into a mesenteric artery.[74]

Hypocalcemia secondary to administration of high-phosphate milk formula is best treated by institution of a low-phosphate formula. Refractory hypocalcemia suggests the possibility of Mg deficiency or hypoparathyroidism. Alkalosis-related low serum concentrations of ionized Ca are best managed by avoiding excess alkali administration and hyperventilation of infants on respirators.

NEONATAL HYPERCALCEMIA

Definition

Neonatal hypercalcemia is defined by a serum Ca concentration above 11 mg/dL or an ionized Ca concentration above 5.8 mg/dL as determined by the Radiometer ionized Ca electrode. Hypercalcemia may present early in the neonatal period or weeks or months later.

Etiology (Table 8–4)

Neonatal hypercalcemia is related to a multitude of etiologic factors that comprise maternal, hereditary, dietary, or other factors.

Prolonged maternal ingestion of high doses of vitamin D or its metabolites leads to fetal and neonatal hypercalcemia.[75] Chronic maternal hypercalcemia resulting from thy-

TABLE 8–4.

Causes of Neonatal Hypercalcemia

Nutrition-related
  Excessive maternal vitamin A and D intake
  Increased Ca content in parenteral nutrition
    solutions
  Phosphorus deficiency syndrome
Endocrine-related
  Maternal thyrotoxicosis
  Primary neonatal hyperparathyroidism
    Sporadic
    Familial
  Secondary neonatal hyperparathyroidism:
    Maternal hypoparathyroidism
    Maternal pseudohypoparathyroidism
  Congenital hypothyroidism
Renal-related
  Familial hypocalciuric hypercalcemia
  Thiazide diuretics
  Congenital hypokalemia with hypercalciuria
Miscellaneous
  Subcutaneous fat necrosis
  Idiopathic infantile hypercalcemia
  Williams syndrome
  Infantile hypophosphatasia
  Neoplasms: congenital nephroblastoma
  Bartter's syndrome

rotoxicosis,[76] vitamin A intoxication, or chronic diuretic therapy with thiazides during pregnancy,[77] apparently leads to increased bone resorption and maternal hypercalcemia, and to a high risk of fetal and possible neonatal hypercalcemia. Neonatal hyperparathyroidism may be inherited in an autosomal dominant,[78] or recessive manner[79] or may be secondary to uncontrolled maternal hypoparathyroidism.[80] Hypercalcemia has been reported before and during thyroxine therapy of infants with congenital agoitrous hypothyroidism. The mechanism of hypercalcemia in these infants is possibly the absence or dysfunction of calcitonin-producing parafollicular C-cells, resulting in deficient calcitonin response to calcium loading.[81–83]

Infantile hypercalcemia occurs in about 15% of patients with Williams syndrome,[84, 85] which comprises a characteristic elfin (pixie) facies, short stature, mild mental retardation, congenital heart disease (often supravalvular aortic stenosis), and hyperacusis. Hypercalcemia in Williams syndrome is associated with increased intestinal absorption of Ca, possibly through increased sensitivity to the effect of vitamin D metabolites. Other defects in vitamin D[86–89] or calcitonin[90] metabolism have been implicated, but reports are inconsistent in regard to the basic defect in this syndrome. Infantile hypercalcemia may occur independent of Williams syndrome, but its cause is equally elusive.[91]

Neonatal hyperparathyroidism has also been described in association with familial hypocalciuric hypercalcemia (FHH).[92, 93] This entity, inherited as an autosomal dominant disorder with a high penetrance at all ages, is characterized by variable degrees of hypercalcemia associated with decreased renal clearance of calcium. The clinical spectrum ranges from asymptomatic heterozygous subjects with mild hypercalcemia detected by blood testing, to severe life threatening hypercalcemia and neonatal hyperparathyroidism in homozygous subjects.[94] The interesting association between the two clinical entities stems from two observations. First, in several families of patients with neonatal hyperparathyroidism, other family members (e.g., a parent, sibling or cousin) had FHH.[95, 96] And secondly, several patients who underwent parathyroidectomy in infancy were found to have FHH later in life because of persistent mild to moderate hypercalcemia.[97, 98] The inheritance of FHH may be linked with a specific HLA (human leukocyte antigens) haplotype.[98, 99]

Hypercalcemia is an associated feature of the severe infantile form of hypophosphatasia, a rare autosomal recessive disorder characterized by severe bone demineralization most remarkably at growth plates, low serum alkaline phosphatase concentrations, and high urine phosphoethanolamine concentrations.[100, 101] The mechanism of hypercalcemia in hypophosphatasia is severe depression of bone mineralization in the absence of alkaline phosphatase. Most of the body's calcium is thought to be diverted into the circulation resulting in hypercalcemia, hypercalciuria, and nephrocalcinosis. A subgroup of patients may die in utero or shortly after birth because of inadequate skeletal support of the thorax and skull.[100]

Newborns who had difficult deliveries may develop subcutaneous fat necrosis over areas of increased pressure. The diagnosis is made by presence of tender, purple-colored indurated area of subcutaneous fat. These infants may develop transient hypercalcemia days or weeks later, probably because of Ca mobilization from necrosed tissues.[102, 103]

Phosphorus deficiency syndrome and hypercalcemia have been described in VLBW preterm infants who are fed human milk, which normally has low P content relative to the needs of the growing bones of these infants.[104–106]

Hypercalcemia occurs in association with congenital renal tumors, particularly mesoblastic nephroma.[107–111] The mechanism of hypercalcemia in these tumors is attributed to the production of ectopic PTH[112] or prostaglandin E[113, 114] by tumor cells. In most cases, surgical removal of the tumor restores normocalcemia.

Finally, a variant of Bartter's syndrome,[115, 116] which consists of hypokalemic alkalosis, hyperreninemia, and hyperaldosteronism, has been associated with infantile hypercalcemia.[117] These infants have prostaglandin-mediated hypercalciuria (>4 mg/kg/day) and increased intestinal Ca absorption facilitated by high serum concentrations of calcitriol. In the face of normal 25(OH)D, the mechanism of increased synthesis of calcitriol is thought to be prostaglandin E_2 (PGE_2)-mediated, which stimulates renal 1α-hydroxylase activity in vivo in thyroparathyroidectomized rats,[118] and in vitro in chick[119] and rat[120] kidney cells. Consistent with this mechanism is a significant correlation found between urinary PGE_2 and serum calcitriol concentrations and the fact that prostaglandin synthesis inhibition with indomethacin reduces urinary PGE_2, serum calcitriol concentration, hypercalciuria, and nephrocalcinosis.[117, 121]

Clinical Manifestations and Diagnosis

Signs and symptoms of hypercalcemia in the neonatal period are generally nonspecific and may include lethargy, poor feeding, vomiting, irritability, polyuria, dehydration, constipation, and failure to thrive. Hypertension, nephrocalcinosis, and corneal and conjunctival calcifications are rarely noted in neonates.

The presence of "elfin facies" and congenital heart disease suggest the diagnosis of Williams syndrome. Family history for hereditary disorders of Ca and P disorders is important in the diagnosis of hypercalcemia in the neonatal period (e.g., familial hyperparathyroidism, familial hypocalciuric hypercalcemia, hypophosphatasia). Maternal dietary and drug history is also helpful in the work-up of neonatal hypercalcemia (excessive vitamin A and D intake).

Biochemical studies should include serum Ca (total and ionized); P; alkaline phosphatase and calciotropic hormones; and urinary Ca, P, and cyclic adenosine monophosphate (cAMP) concentrations. Renal wasting with hypercalcemia and elevated urine cAMP concentration may be a clue to the possibility of hyperparathyroidism. Radiologic examination of the hands and wrists revealing subperiosteal resorption, in addition to hypercalcemia and hypophosphatemia, suggest the diagnosis of hyperparathyroidism.

Treatment

Therapy of neonatal hypercalcemia depends on the underlying cause. Excessive maternal ingestion of vitamins A and D should be discontinued, and vitamin D and Ca should be reduced in the diet. Hypercalcemia related to human milk feeding of preterm infants indicates a deficiency of P, and supplementation with P may be required. However, in this instance there is usually concomitant Ca deficiency; therefore, the appropriate treatment is supplementation with both P and Ca.

Severe hypercalcemia results in major polyuric water loss and requires prompt repletion of extracellular fluids. Volume expansion is achieved by 10 to 20 mL/kg body weight of 0.9% normal saline solution, followed by administration of a calciuretic diuretic (furosemide, 1 to 2 mg/kg/dose) to increase the clearance of Ca in urine. Sodium ethylenediaminetetraacetic acid may be administered parenterally in severe cases to chelate Ca and increase its urinary excretion. Calcitonin has been used in severe cases but is not usually recommended because of limited experience in neonates and development of antibodies to nonhuman calcitonin preparations. In chronic hypercalcemia, prednisone (2 mg/kg/day) may be used to decrease intestinal absorption of Ca.

Virtually all cases of primary hyperparathyroidism require subtotal or total parathyroidectomy, since the hypercalcemia may become life-threatening and does not respond to medical management.[97] Finally, as mentioned earlier, indomethacin therapy decreases the hypercalciuria and nephrocalinosis in a number of patients.[117]

HYPOMAGNESEMIA

Definition

Hypomagnesemia is defined as a serum Mg concentration below 1.5 mg/dL. However, tissue Mg deficiency may coexist with normal serum Mg concentrations.[122] Hypomagnesemia may cause hypocalcemia through the following mechanisms: (1) decreased Mg-dependent adenylate cyclase-mediated secretion of PTH, (2) end-organ resistance to PTH, (3) decreased intestinal Ca absorption, or (4) decreased heteroionic exchange of Ca for Mg at the bone surface.[123, 124]

Etiology (Table 8–5)

Hypomagnesemia may be due to: (1) decreased Mg supply to the infant, (2) increased body losses, (3) endocrine-related disorders, and (4) others causes.

TABLE 8-5.

Causes of Neonatal Hypomagnesemia

Decreased supply
  Primary Mg malabsorption
    Isolated
    Familial
  Maternal malabsorption
  Short bowel syndrome
  Intrauterine growth retardation
  Low Mg Content—parenteral nutrition
Increased losses
  Decreased renal tubular reabsorption
    Congenital
    Acquired:
      Diuretics (Furosemide, Thiazides)
      Aminoglycosides
      Polyuric phase of acute tubular necrosis
  Hepatobiliary disorders:
    Congenital biliary atresia
    Severe neonatal hepatitis
  Intestinal losses:
    Surgical fistulas
    Diarrhea
  Exchange blood transfusion with acid-citrated blood
Endocrine disorders
  Transient hypoparathyroidism
    Maternal hyperparathyroidism
    Maternal insulin-dependent diabetes mellitus
    Transient parathyroid dysplasia
  Persistent hypoparathyroidism
    Congenital hypoplasia or aplasia of parathyroid
      glands
      Sporadic
      Familial
    DiGeorge syndrome
    Zellweger syndrome
Miscellaneous
  Excess vitamin D ingestion
  Hyperphosphatemia (cow milk formula)
  Birth asphyxia

Decreased Mg Supply

Primary intestinal Mg malabsorption is a familial disorder that has been reported in the neonatal period between 2 to 4 weeks and usually in boys.[125-130] These neonates require Mg supplementation for life to prevent hypomagnesemia and secondary hypocalcemia. Hypomagnesemia may occur in infants born to mothers with intestinal malabsorption.[131]

Decreased intestinal surface available for Mg absorption in infants with "short bowel syndrome," especially after surgical resection of the jejunum and ileum where most of Mg absorption occurs, may lead to hypomagnesemia.[132, 133] Small-for-gestational age infants frequently have hypomagnesemia.[134, 135] A significant number of these infants are born to young, primigravida, and preeclamptic mothers who are themselves hypomagnesemic—theoretically either because of poor gestational nutrition or because of placental disease and impaired Mg transfer to the fetus.[136] In fact, maternal hypomagnesemia appears to be a possible risk factor for preeclampsia and secondary placental insufficiency.[136] Infants maintained on parenteral nutrition with low Mg content may develop hypomagnesemia. Because most fetal Mg accretion takes place in the third trimester, preterm infants are at risk of developing hypomagnesemia if not supplied with enough Mg in their diet.

Increased Mg Loss

Excessive Mg losses occur most commonly by way of the kidney and the intestines. Increased renal Mg losses can result from decreased renal tubular reabsorption as a congenital (familial or isolated) or acquired defect.[137-140] Diuretics[141, 142] (thiazides and furosemide) and aminoglycosides[143, 144] increase renal Mg losses by decreasing tubular reabsorption. The polyuric phase following recovery from acute renal tubular necrosis may lead to significant magnesuria and resulting hypomagnesemia.

Excessive intestinal Mg losses may occur with neonatal cholestasis because of congenital biliary atresia and severe neonatal hepatitis.[145] It is thought that secondary hyperaldosteronism in severe liver disease, due to decreased metabolism of aldosterone, accounts for excessive intestinal Mg wasting.[146] Severe chronic diarrhea[147] and surgically related small intestinal fistulas (short bowel syndrome)[148-150] are complicated by hypomagnesemia. Increased intestinal magnesium loss in short bowel syndrome is due to binding of Mg to unabsorbed fatty acids and the formation of intraluminal insoluble soaps, therefore resulting in decreased Mg retention.[148-150] For the same reason, hypocalcemia may occur in patients with short bowel syndrome and may further aggravate metabolic bone disease.[150]

Hypomagnesemia may be a sequela to repeated exchange blood transfusions with acid citrated blood because citrate anions complex with Mg ions, and Mg may become depleted from the circulation.[151, 152]

Endocrine Causes

Hypomagnesemia may be associated with neonatal hypoparathyroidism, which may be transient or persistent.[59] Possible mechanisms for the occasional hypomagnesemia in hypoparathyroidism are diminished PTH-induced Mg release from bone, increased renal tubular Mg loss, poor intestinal absorption, and elevated serum P concentration.[153, 154] Infants of mothers with hyperparathyroidism may develop transient neonatal hypoparathyroidism[155] manifesting as hypocalcemia and hypomagnesemia.[156-159] Maternal hypercalcemia suppresses the fetal parathyroid glands, resulting in neonatal hypoparathyroidism. An alternative explanation is based on the fact that hyperparathyroidism causes hypomagnesemia and negative Mg balance in the pregnant mother and possibly in the fetus. Consequently, the hypomagnesemic neonate may present with transient hypoparathyroidism and failure of PTH secretion. Persistent congenital hypoparathyroidism may occur as an isolated or familial X-linked recessive or autosomal dominant entity as part of the DiGeorge syndrome (hypoplastic thymus, cell-mediated immune deficiency, and aortic arch anomalies), Zellweger syndrome, or as an autoimmune disorder with mucocutaneous candidasis. In insulin-dependent diabetes mellitus, the mother may be magnesium-depleted[157-159] because of deficient insulin-dependent cellular uptake of Mg[160] and increased renal Mg clearance due to hyperglycemia.[161] Consequently, IDMs are at a higher risk of neonatal hypomagnesemia.[59, 162] Hypomagnesemia occurs also in birth asphyxia, but the cause is uncertain.

Cow milk formula, with high P content, has been reported to cause hypomagnesemic hypocalcemia associated with neonatal jitteriness and seizures.[163] Although hypocalcemia is more common than hypomagnesemia, the latter has been observed with or without concomitant hypocalcemia.[164, 165]

Clinical Signs and Diagnosis

Hypomagnesemia may be asymptomatic or may present with intractable convulsions and coma. Because less than 1% of total body Mg is present in the blood and the remaining 99% is found intracellularly, serum Mg concentrations may not reflect tissue Mg deficiency.

Awareness of predisposing factors offers the best clinical clue to the diagnosis of hypomagnesemia, especially when the clinician is faced with a case of "intractable hypocalcemia." In fact, most cases of hypomagnesemia in the literature are first misdiagnosed as cases of hypoparathyroidism.

Clinical signs of hypomagnesemia manifest with serum Mg concentrations less than 1.2 mg/dL[59] and are similar to those of hypocalcemia: tremors, irritability, hyperreflexia (with or without positive Chvostek and Trousseau signs), possibly muscle fasciculations and in severe cases, tetany and seizures. Often, biochemical testing reveals hypomagnesemia, secondary hypocalcemia and possibly hypoparathyroidism.

Treatment

The management of hypomagnesemia depends on the primary cause. Supplementation of Mg may be needed for prolonged periods in infants with congenital and hereditary, renal and hepatobiliary Mg-losing disorders. Infants with primary intestinal Mg malabsorption and those with intestinal resections and short gut syndrome require lifelong supply of high doses of Mg in their diet to prevent hypomagnesemia.

Diet intake control, such as avoiding cow milk formulas in early infancy and adjusting Mg concentration in parenteral nutrition solutions, may prevent the occurrence of hypomagnesemia.

Asymptomatic hypomagnesemia can be corrected with a 50% $MgSO_4$ solution given as an intramuscular injection of 0.2 mL/kg body weight every 8 to 12 hours until serum Mg concentration is normal. In symptomatic infants, $MgSO_4$ solution is diluted to 5% or 10% solution and given as a slow intravenous infusion over 10 minutes under continuous cardiopulmonary monitoring because of the risk of sinoatrial or atrioventricular heart block, respiratory depression, and systemic hypotension.

HYPERMAGNESEMIA

Definition

Neonatal hypermagnesemia is defined by a serum Mg concentration above 2.5 mg/dL.[59]

Etiology (Table 8–6)

Neonatal hypermagnesemia is most commonly encountered with infants of mothers who receive Mg sulfate for preterm labor.[166, 167] Because Mg sulfate is a commonly used tocolytic agent,[168] neonatal hypermagnesemia should always be anticipated and looked for in the newborn. Reduced renal function due to prematurity,[169] asphyxia,[170]

TABLE 8–6.

Causes of Neonatal Hypermagnesemia

Increased intake
Maternal MgSO$_4$ for tocolysis
High Mg content parenteral nutrition
Magnesium salt enemas
Reduced renal excretion
Prematurity
Asphyxia
Oliguric renal failure

or renal failure,[167] impairs Mg excretion and predisposes to elevated serum Mg concentrations.[59, 171] High rates of Mg administration in parenteral infusions (more than 5 to 7 mg/kg/day) may predispose to neonatal hypermagnesemia, particularly in preterm newborns. The Mg-containing enemas used in the past caused significant neonatal hypermagnesemia, and their use has been abandoned.[59]

Clinical Features

The main effects of hypermagnesemia are on the neuromuscular and cardiovascular systems. Excess magnesium exerts a curare-like effect at the motor end plate, resulting in muscle paralysis. Also, it decreases smooth muscle contraction, resulting in vasodilatation and hypotension. Hypermagnesemic newborns manifest variable degrees of neuromuscular depression with hypotonia, flaccidity, and respiratory depression that may culminate with cardiac arrest and respiratory failure at very high serum concentrations of Mg (>12 mg/dL). Variable electrocardiographic changes (increased atrioventricular and ventricular conduction times) may be seen with serum Mg concentrations above 6 mg/dL.

Elevated serum Mg concentrations suppress the parathyroid gland, resulting in low serum PTH concentrations.[172, 173] Serum Ca concentrations may be normal or elevated in hypermagnesemic newborns,[171] presumably because of heteroionic exchange of Ca for Mg at the blood–bone interface.[174]

Apgar scores, though lower in hypermagnesemic newborns, do not correlate with absolute serum Mg concentrations.[171] A significant correlation exists between neonatal neuromuscular depression and the duration of maternal therapy with Mg sulfate.[171]

Recently, there have been anecdotal reports of neonatal osseous changes and rickets attributed to prolonged maternal treatment with Mg sulfate for preterm labor.[175, 176] The mechanism of bone demineralization in these cases is thought to be due to increased flux of Mg into bone, thus replacing Ca and causing rickets.

Treatment

Usually, neonatal hypermagnesemia resolves over a few days with adequate hydration and a normal renal function. Occasionally, severe hypermagnesemia may require the use of 10% Ca gluconate infusions (0.2 to 0.3 ml/kg body weight) to counteract the inhibitory effect of Mg cations on neuromuscular excitability.[177] Loop diuretics (furosemide or ethacrinic acid) that increase Mg excretion may be given following adequate hydration. In cases of severe neuromuscular depression and respiratory failure, maintenance of cardiopulmonary support is of prime importance. Double volume "exchange" blood transfusions with citrated blood chelates Mg and helps decrease serum Mg concentrations in cases of life-threatening hypermagnesemia.[169]

RECOMMENDED DIETARY CA, MG, AND P INTAKE IN THE NEWBORN

Oral Intake

Human milk provides optimal Ca, Mg, and P content for the bone mineralization of *term* newborns and probably of preterm newborns who are at least 2 kg in body weight. Intestinal Ca absorption is lower when cow milk formula is fed to these infants, compared with human milk feeding. Therefore, cow milk formulas generally have higher Ca content (by 40%) than human milk to compensate for this intestinal absorption discrepancy and to achieve optimal mineralization of the growing bones. The recommended daily intake for these infants is about 60 mg of Ca/kg body weight, up to a total of 800 mg at 1 year of age; 8 mg of Mg/kg body weight, up to a total daily intake of about 150 mg at 1 year; and 40 mg of P/kg body weight, up to a total daily intake of about 800 mg at 1 year of age.[1]

For *preterm* infants less than 2 kg in body weight, the goal is to offer them milk formulas with higher Ca and P contents (or Ca and P fortifiers if they are fed human milk) in order to achieve in utero mineral accretion rates. Assuming retention rates of 64% for Ca and 71% for P, preterm newborns (those less than 2 kg in body weight) should receive an intake of 200 mg of Ca and 100 mg of P/kg/day to achieve optimal bone mineralization.[1]

Human milk and standard cow milk formulas provide sufficient amounts of Mg (12 to 30 mg/kg/day), almost threefold the required dietary intake to achieve intrauterine Mg accretion rate.[176]

Parenteral Intake

From our experience with parenteral nutrition solutions, optimal Ca, Mg, and P homeostasis may be achieved in large preterm and term newborns by providing the following concentrations: 60 mg of Ca, 7 mg of Mg, and 45 mg of P per deciliter, with a Ca:P ratio of 1.3:1 by weight and 1:1 by molar ratio.[179] Parenteral solutions containing these concentrations have been used successfully to promote acceptable Ca, P, and Mg homeostasis in term and near-term[179] and in preterm infants,[180] as demonstrated by normal and steady serum concentrations of $1,25(OH)_2D$ and $25(OH)D$, decreased calciuria, and normal and stable renal tubular reabsorption of P.

Smaller preterm infants require more Ca and P intakes (by roughly 25%) per kilogram body weight than larger preterm and term newborns to reach an optimal Ca and P homeostasis and bone mineralization.[181] Fortunately the fluid intake of smaller infants is generally higher per kilogram body weight; thus a higher Ca, P, and Mg intake is often achieved compared with larger infants. Required Mg intakes for small preterm infants are probably similar to larger preterm and term newborns and need not be higher to achieve adequate Mg homeostasis.

We anticipate that the use of the "mineral-enriched" parenteral solutions will achieve optimal bone mineralization and therefore prevent metabolic bone disease (rickets) in the very small premature infant.

RICKETS OF PREMATURITY

Definition

Rickets of prematurity is a disease of growing bone characterized by hypomineralization of bone matrix, leading to weak structural support and fractures from little mechanical stress.[182]

Incidence

The true incidence of rickets in preterm infants is unknown because a large number of subclinical cases remain unrecognized. It has been estimated that in VLBW (<1,500 g birth weight) preterm infants, at least 30% will show evidence of rickets.[182–184] The incidence of metabolic bone disease in preterm infants is inversely related to gestational age and directly related to the severity and chronicity of postnatal diseases, for example, chronic BPD and chronic diuretic therapy. In infants with birth weights less than 1,000 g, the incidence of rickets is much higher and has been reported to be as high as 75%.[184]

Etiology

The cause of rickets of prematurity is multifactorial: several factors have been implicated, but the most important etiologic factor is suboptimal Ca and P dietary intake (especially in VLBW preterm infants) that does not meet the requirements for bone mineralization.

Though early studies suggested an etiologic role for vitamin D, in most cases serum 25(OH)D concentrations are in the normal range[185–194] and do not suggest an etiologic role for vitamin D in the pathogenesis of rickets of preterm infants. Further, it appears from very recent clinical studies that additional dietary intake of vitamin D beyond the recommended daily intake does not prevent nor alter the course of metabolic bone disease of prematurity.[195] Because the disease is primarily related to suboptimal Ca and P intake by preterm infants, there is difficulty of providing milk formulas or parenteral solutions containing enough Ca and P to meet intrauterine mineral accretion rates. The severity of the disease may be correlated with parenteral nutrition–induced cholestasis[182, 188, 196, 197] and hypersulfatemia.[198] Aluminum-containing parenteral solutions theoretically may aggravate bone disease in preterm infants.[182] Infants with BPD may be in negative Ca and P balance (and therefore at risk for rickets) because of restricted fluid intake and increased renal losses resulting from chronic loop diuretic therapy. Some appear to have secondary hyperparathyroidism[185] and may have decreased bone mineral content as determined by photon absorptiometry.[199]

Clinical Manifestations and Diagnosis

Rickets of prematurity is most often a subclinical disease, detected incidentally on x-ray examination.[182, 200] Classically, the clinical picture of rickets comprises craniotabes, widening of costochondral junctions of the ribs ("rachitic rosary") (Fig 8–1), and thickening of the wrists and ankles. It is important to remember that the classic signs of rickets are not always present when rickets of prematurity is diagnosed.[182, 184, 192] Preterm infants with rickets may have an enlarged anterior fontanel or a rachitic rosary.[182] About 30% of preterm infants with rickets present with skeletal fractures (Fig 8–2),

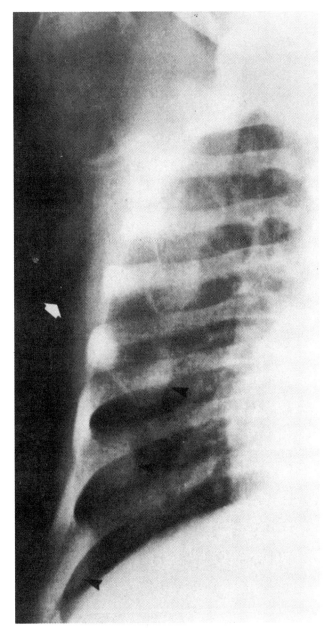

FIG 8–1.
Radiologic manifestations of rickets. Rachitic rosary *(dark arrows),* widening of costochondral junctions, and splaying of the anterior rib ends of the rachitic rosary. (From Oestreich AE, Crawford AH: *Atlas of Pediatric Orthopedic Radiology.* Stuttgart, GRF, Thieme, 1985, p 97. Used by permission.)

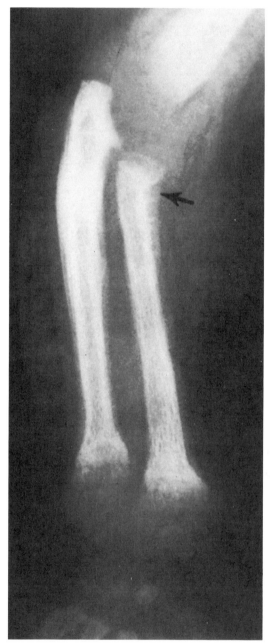

FIG 8–2.
Florid rickets. Cupping and fraying of the metaphysis; increased distance between the distal radius metaphysis and its indistinct growth centers under mineralized cortices; fracture in proximal radius *(dark arrow)*. (From Oestreich AE, Crawford AM: *Atlas of Pediatric Orthopedic Radiology,* Stuttgart, GFR, Thieme, 1985, p 97. Used by permission.)

usually involving the ribs and long bones.[182, 184, 192, 200, 201] Some infants may present with a rachitic respiratory distress syndrome characterized by gradual progressive respiratory decompensation sometimes associated with an expiratory wheeze.[187, 201, 202, 203]

Preterm infants may present with rickets from 4 weeks to 20 weeks of postnatal age, with 2 to 4 months being the most common time of diagnosis.*

In addition to the clinical and radiologic manifestations of rickets, some biochemical abnormalities may be present. However, biochemical parameters are quite variable and usually are not diagnostic of rickets: serum Ca concentration is often normal but occasionally may be low or even elevated, especially if serum P concentrations are low.† Serum P concentration is often low but may be normal.‡ Serum 25(OH)D concentration may be low, normal, or high.[182, 183, 189, 204] Serum PTH concentrations range from normal to elevated.[104, 184, 188, 204] In contrast, serum 1,25(OH)$_2$D concentrations are generally elevated in case reports of rickets of prematurity,[104, 182, 183, 188, 204] supporting the contention that there is Ca and P deficiency. Serum alkaline phosphatase activity may be increased in rickets of prematurity.[182, 183, 188, 204] However, this assay is not reliable because of the presence of non-osseous isoenzymes (cardiac, hepatic, and muscular), the variations in technical assays, and the wide "normal range" in growing infants.[182] Osteocalcin is the major noncollagenous bone protein. It contains two residues of vitamin K–dependent amino acid, gamma-carboxyglutamic acid.[205] Serum osteocalcin concentration increases with rises in serum, 1,25(OH)$_2$D,[206] with increases in serum alkaline phosphatase,[207] and with increases in bone turnover;[208] therefore, it may be a useful bone-specific marker for rickets of prematurity.

Infants with rickets of prematurity may have excessive urine Ca loss (>100 mg/day/ 1.73 m^2)[209] and very high tubular resorption of P (>95%), particularly in phosphorus-depleted infants.[104–106] Supplementation with P decreases renal Ca wasting and normalizes renal tubular P reabsorption.

Radiologic bone examinations remain the best tool for the definitive clinical diagnosis of rickets of prematurity. Histologic bone disease presumably occurs before any radiologic signs appear. The earliest x-ray signs of rickets of prematurity may be bone rarefaction, which may be observed as early as the second week of postnatal life,[210] and delayed ossification of the hamate and capitate growth centers. Metaphyseal cupping of the ends of long bones along with fraying of metaphyseal margins may be observed in older children.[182] Radiologic examination of the thoracic wall in preterm infants with rickets may show demineralization of the ribs with splaying of the anterior rib ends. Periosteal new bone formation may be noted along the inferior border of the mandible and the shafts of long bones ("mandibular mantle" sign).[203]

Recently, bone mineral content (BMC) determinations are feasible with the use of photon absorptiometry.[199] The technique has been standardized for use in term and preterm infants and BMC norms have been established. However, this method is still considered as a research tool and is available only in a few medical centers.

Prevention and Therapy

The increasing survival of extremely premature infants is expected to increase the number of subjects at high risk for rickets of prematurity. Once ex utero, these infants

---

*References 182–184, 189, 192, 201, 202.
†References 104, 106, 182, 183, 188, 189, 192, 201, 204.
‡References 104, 182, 183, 188, 189, 201, 204.

should receive sufficient amounts of Ca and P in an attempt to meet the intrauterine mineral accretion rate required for adequate bone mineralization. Human milk and standard humanized cow milk formulas do not provide optimal Ca and P concentrations (Table 8–7) to meet the requirements of preterm infants; therefore, much research has been done to prepare the most appropriate milk formula for growth of preterm infants. Preterm infant milk formulas have been manipulated to increase their Ca and P contents to insure that the infant dietary mineral intake is as close to the fetal accretion rate as possible.

During the third trimester, the daily net accretion rates for Ca and P range between 120 and 140 mg/kg and 60 to 75 mg/kg, respectively. Assuming that the intestinal absorption rates for Ca and P in the preterm infant are 65% and 85%,[211] a daily intake of elemental Ca and P of 215 mg/kg and 90 mg/kg, respectively, might be expected to supply sufficient minerals to meet the intrauterine accretion rate in the preterm infant.

The ideal Ca and P content of milk formulas to prevent rickets of prematurity is not known, especially in VLBW infants. However, several studies demonstrated improvement in bone mineralization (Figs 8–3 and 8–4), and biochemical measurements of rickets by Ca and P fortification of human milk or cow milk "standard" formulas fed to preterm infants.[212–216]

The optimal quantity of Ca and P required to treat rickets in VLBW infants is not known. In general, supplementation of 100 mg elemental Ca/kg/day and 50 mg of elemental P/kg/day (Ca:P ratio = 2:1), in addition to the standard milk feeding, may be attempted, provided the infant is not already receiving Ca and P fortified formula. Therapy with Ca and P supplementation should usually be maintained for 3 months, and biochemical measurements made (serum Ca, P, and alkaline phosphatase; if possible, serum 25(OH)D, 1,25(OH)$_2$D, and urine Ca and P concentrations) and x-ray examinations

TABLE 8–7.

Calcium, Phosphorus, and Magnesium Contents of Infant Formulas (units/100 kcal)*

	Calcium (mg)	Ca:P	Magnesium (mg)	Phosphorus (mg)
Human milk	38.89	2:1	4.86	19.44
Routine cow's milk formulas				
Enfamil (Mead Johnson)	69.00	1.5:1	7.80	47.00
PM 60/40 (Ross)	56.00	2:1	6.00	28.00
SMA (Wyeth)	63.00	1.5:1	7.00	42.00
Similac (Ross)	75.00	1.3:1	6.00	58.00
Preterm infant formulas				
Enfamil Premature (Mead Johnson)	117.00	2:1	4.90	59.00
Similac Special Care (Ross)	180.00	2:1	12.00	90.00
SMA Preemie (Wyeth)	90.00	1.8:1	8.60	50.00
Similac LBW (Ross)	90.00	1.3:1	10.00	70.00
Soy protein formulas				
ProSobee (Mead Johnson)	94.00	1.3:1	10.90	74.00
Isomil (Ross)	105.00	1.4:1	7.50	75.00
Isomil SF (Ross)	105.00	1.4:1	7.50	75.00
Nursoy (Wyeth)	90.00	1.4:1	10.00	63.00
Soyalac (Loma Linda)	94.00	1.7:1	12.00	55.00
i-Soyalac (Loma Linda)	102.00	1.4:1	11.00	71.00

*Data adapted from Koo WWK, Tsang RC: Calcium, magnesium, and phosphorus, in Tsang RC (ed): *Nutrition in Infancy.* Philadelphia, Hanley and Belfus, 1988, pp 419–424.

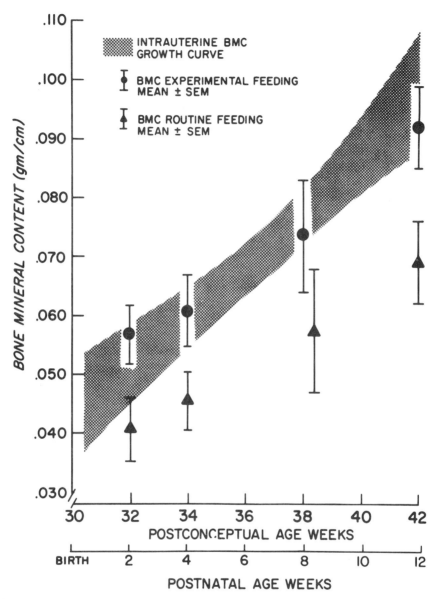

FIG 8–3.

Postnatal bone mineral content (BMC) of infants born between 28 and 32 weeks gestation receiving experimental feeding (Ca and P fortified routine formula), compared with the intrauterine bone mineralization curve (IUBMC), and to postnatal BMC of infants born between 28 and 32 weeks gestation receiving routine formula (68 Kcal/100 ml). BMC in the experimental group is not different from the IUBMC and is significantly greater than BMC in the routine feeding group at 2, 4, and 12 weeks of postnatal age, respectively. (From Steichen JJ, Gratton TL, Tsang RC: Osteopenia of prematurity: The cause and possible treatment. *J Pediatr* 1980; 96:528–534. Used by permission.)

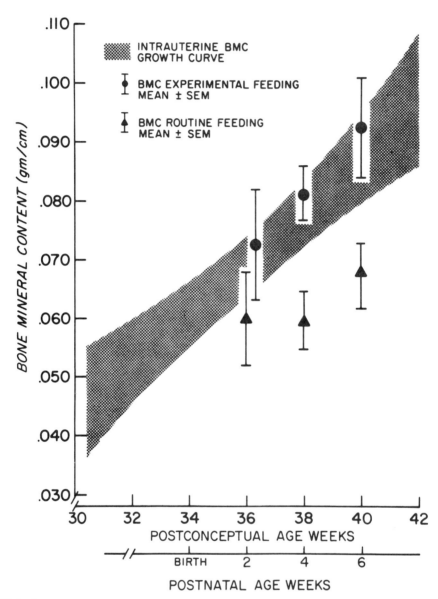

FIG 8–4.
Postnatal BMC of infants born between 33 and 35 weeks gestation receiving experimental Ca and P fortified formula compared with the intrauterine bone mineralization curve (IUBMC) and to the postnatal BMC of routine formula-fed infants born between 33 and 35 weeks gestational age. BMC in the experimental group is not different from the IUBMC and is significantly greater than BMC in the routine feeding group at 4 and 6 weeks postnatal age. (From Steichen JJ, Gratton TL, Tsang RC: Osteopenia of prematurity: The cause and possible treatment. *J Pediatr* 1980; 96:528–534. Used by permission.)

of the wrists or knees done at regular intervals. As discussed earlier, infants with rickets of prematurity have a normal vitamin D status[194] and generally do not show improvement with additional vitamin D administration beyond 400 IU/day.[195]

Conclusion

Rickets of prematurity occurs frequently among surviving small preterm infants. The most important etiologic factors in this disease appear to be deficient Ca and P dietary intake in these infants. Nutritionists and neonatologists have focused mainly on the prevention of this disease by providing Ca- and P-enriched milk formulas to meet the intrauterine mineral accretion rate. Vitamin D supplementation of 400 IU/day is probably sufficient to prevent vitamin D deficiency rickets. Additional doses of vitamin D appear to have no benefit in preventing rickets of prematurity.

Acknowledgment

This work was supported in part by NIH HD 11725, Diabetes in Pregnancy; NIH HD 07200, Research Training; and NIH 5 P5 OHD20748, Prenatal Emphasis Research Center.

REFERENCES

1. Koo WWK, Tsang RC: Calcium, magnesium and phosphorus, in Tsang RC, (ed): *Nutrition in Infancy*. Philadelphia, Hanley & Belfus, 1988, pp 175–189.
2. Greer FR, Tsang RC: Calcium, phosphorus, magnesium, and vitamin D requirements for the preterm infant, in Tsang RC (ed): *Vitamin D and Mineral Requirements in Preterm Infants*. New York, Marcel Dekker, 1985; pp 99–136.
3. Greer FR, Chesney RW: Disorders of calcium metabolism in the neonate. *Semin Nephrol* 1983; 3:100–115.
4. Ehrenkranz RA: Mineral needs of the very low birth weight infant. *Semin Perinatol* 1989; 13:142–159.
5. Sparks JW: Human intrauterine growth and nutrient accretion. *Semin Perinatol* 1984; 8:74–95.
6. Widdowson EM, Spray CM: Chemical development in utero. *Arch Dis Child* 1951; 26:205–214.
7. Wieland P, Fisher JA, Treschsel U, et al: Perinatal parathyroid hormone, vitamin D metabolites, and calcitonin in man. *Am J Physiol* 1980; 239:E385–390.
8. Steichen JJ, Tsang RC, Gratton TL, et al: Vitamin D homeostasis in the perinatal period: 1,25-dihydroxyvitamin D in maternal, cord, and neonatal blood. *N Engl J Med* 1980; 302:315–319.
9. Fleishman AR, Rosen JF, Cole J, et al: Maternal and fetal serum 1,25-dihydroxyvitamin D levels at term. *J Pediatr* 1980; 97:640–642.
10. Gertner JM, Glassman MS, Coustan DR, et al: Feto-maternal vitamin D relationships at term. *J Pediatr* 1980; 97:637–640.
11. Bouillon R, Van Assche FA, Van Baelen H, et al: Influence of the vitamin D-binding protein on the serum concentration of 1,25-dihydroxyvitamin D: Significance of the free 1,25-dihydroxyvitamin D concentration. *J Clin Invest* 1981; 67:589–596.
12. Ziegler EE, O'Donnell AM, Nelson SE, et al: Body composition of the reference fetus. *Growth* 1976; 40:320–341.
13. Widdowson EM, McCance RA: The metabolism of calcium, phosphorus, magnesium and strontium. *Pediatr Clin North Am* 1965; 12:595–614.

14. Lemons P, Stuart M, Lemons JA: Breast-feeding the premature infant. *Clin Perinatol* 1986; 13:111–122.

15. Anderson GH: Human milk feeding. *Pediatr Clinic North Am* 1985; 32:335–353.

16. Garel JM, Dumont C: Distribution and inactivation of labelled parathyroid hormone in the rat fetus. *Horm Metab Res* 1972; 4:217–221.

17. Robinson NR, Sibley CP, Mughal MZ, et al: Fetal control of calcium transport across the rat placenta. *Pediatr Res* 1989; 26:109–115.

18. Rodda CP, Kubota M, Heath JA, et al: Evidence for a novel parathyroid hormone-related protein in fetal lamb parathyroid glands and sheep placenta: Comparisons with a similar protein implicated in humoral hypercalcemia of malignancy. *J Endocrinol* 1988; 117:261–271.

19. Barlet JP: Calcitonin may modulate placental transfer in ewes. *J Endocrinol* 1985; 104:17–21.

20. Pitkin RM: Calcium metabolism in pregnancy and the perinatal period: A review. *Am J Obstet Gynecol* 1985; 151:99–109.

21. Ross R, Care AD, Taylor CM, et al: The transplacental movement of metabolites of vitamin D in the sheep, in Norman AW, Schaefer K, Coburn JW, et al (eds): *Vitamin D, Basic Research and Its Clinical Applications*. Berlin de Gruyter, 1979, pp 341–344.

22. Fenton E, Britton HG: 25-Hydroxycholecalciferol 1 alpha-hydroxylase activity in the kidney of the fetal, neonatal and adult guinea pig. *Biol Neonate* 1980; 37:254–256.

23. Ross R, Care AD, Robinson JS, et al: Perinatal 1,25(OH)$_2$D$_3$ in the sheep: Involvement of foetal 1,25(OH)$_2$D$_3$ in the maintenance of the transplacental calcium gradient, in Cohen DV, Talmage RV, Matthews JL (eds): *Hormonal Control of Calcium Metabolism*. Proceedings of the 7th International Conference on the Calcium Regulating Hormones and the 7th Parathyroid Conference. Amsterdam, Excerpta Medica, 1981, p 382.

24. Nishioka T, Yasuda T, Niimi H, et al: Evidence that calcitonin plays a role in the postnatal increase of serum 1α,25-dihydroxyvitamin D. *Eur J Pediatr* 1988; 147:148–152.

25. Hillman LS, Rojanasathit S, Slatopolsky E, et al: Serial measurements of serum calcium, magnesium, parathyroid hormone, calcitonin, and 25-hydroxyvitamin D in premature and term infants during the first week of life. *Pediatr Res* 1977; 11:739–744.

26. Venkataraman PS, Tsang RC, Chen IW, et al: Pathogenesis of early neonatal hypocalcemia: Studies of serum calcitonin, gastrin, and plasma glucagon. *J Pediatr* 1987; 110:599–603.

27. Glorieux FH, Salle BL, Delvin EE, et al: Vitamin D metabolism in preterm infants: Serum calcitriol values during the first five days of life. *J Pediatr* 1981; 99:640–643.

28. Koo WWK, Tsang RC: Neonatal hypocalcemia, in Lifshitz F (ed): *Perspectives in pediatrics: I. Pediatric Endocrinology*. New York, Marcel Dekker, 1985; pp 387–411.

29. Loughead JL, Mimouni F, Tsang RC: Serum ionized calcium concentrations in normal neonates. *Am J Dis Child* 1988; 142:516–518.

30. Tsang RC, Light IJ, Sutherland JM, et al: Possible pathogenetic factors in neonatal hypocalcemia of prematurity: The role of gestation, hyperphosphatemia, hypomagnesemia, urinary calcium loss, and parathyroid hormone responsiveness. *J Pediatr* 1973; 82:423–429.

31. Tsang RC, Oh W: Neonatal hypocalcemia in low birth weight infants. *Pediatrics* 1970; 45:773–781.

32. Romagnoli C, Zecca E, Tortorolo G, et al: Plasma thyrocalcitonin and parathyroid hormone concentrations in early neonatal hypocalcemia. *Arch Dis Child* 1987; 62:580–584.

33. David L, Salle B, Chopard P, et al: Studies on circulating immunoreactive calcitonin in low birth weight infants during the first 48 hours of life. *Helv Paediatr Acta* 1977; 32:39–48.

34. Tsang RC, Chen I, Hayes W, et al: Neonatal hypocalcemia in infants with birth asphyxia. *J Pediatr* 1974; 84:428–433.

35. Venkataraman P, Tsang RC, Chen I, et al: Elevated calcitonin in birth asphyxia and prematurity: Role in the pathogenesis of early neonatal hypocalcemia. *Pediatr Res* 1984; 18:352A.

36. Nogushi A, Eren M, Tsang RC: Parathyroid hormone in hypocalcemic and normocalcemic infants of diabetic mothers. *J Pediatr* 1980; 97:112–117.

37. Tsang RC, Kleinman L, Sutherland JM, et al: Hypocalcemia in infants of diabetic mothers: Studies in Ca, P and Mg metabolism and in parathyroid hormone responsiveness. *J Pediatr* 1972; 80:384–395.

38. Tsang RC, Gigger M, Oh W, et al: Studies in calcium metabolism in infants with intrauterine growth retardation. *J Pediatr* 1975; 86:936–941.

39. Brown DR, Tsang RC, Chen IW: Oral calcium supplementation in premature and asphyxiated neonates. *J Pediatr* 1976; 89:973–977.

40. David L, Anast CS: Calcium metabolism in newborn infants: The interrelationship of parathyroid function and calcium, magnesium, and phosphorus metabolism in normal, "sick", and hypocalcemic newborns. *J Clin Invest* 1974; 54:287–296.

41. Tsang RC, Chen IW, Friedman MA, et al: Neonatal parathyroid function: Role of gestational age and postnatal age. *J Pediatr* 1973; 83:728–738.

42. Rosen JF, Roginsky M, Nathenson G, et al: 25-hydroxyvitamin D: Plasma levels in mothers and their premature infants with neonatal hypocalcemia. *Am J Dis Child* 1974; 127:220–223.

43. Fleischman AR, Rosen JF, Nathenson G: 25-hydroxycholecalciferol for early neonatal hypocalcemia: Occurrence in premature newborns. *Am J Dis Child* 1978; 132:973–977.

44. Chan GM, Tsang RC, Chen IW, et al: The effects of $1,25(OH)_2$-vitamin D supplementation in premature infants. *J Pediatr* 1978; 93:91–96.

45. Hillman LS, Haddad JG: Perinatal vitamin D metbolism: II. Serial 25-hydroxyvitamin D concentrations in sera of term and premature infants. *J Pediatr* 1975; 86:928–935.

46. Begum R, Coutinho ML, Dormandy TL, et al: Maternal malabsorption presenting as congenital rickets. *Lancet* 1968; 1:1048–1052.

47. Ford JA, Davidson DC, McIntosh WB, et al: Neonatal rickets in Asian immigrant population. *Br Med J* 1973; 3:211–212.

48. Moncrieff M, Fadahunsi TO: Congenital rickets due to maternal rickets due to maternal vitamin D deficiency. *Arch Dis Child* 1974; 49:810–811.

49. Sann L, David L, Frederick A, et al: Congenital rickets. *Acta Paediatr Scand* 1977; 66:323–327.

50. Park W, Paust H, Kaufmann HJ, et al: Osteomalacia of the mother—rickets of the newborn. *Eur J Pediatr* 1987; 146:292–293.

51. Romagnoli C, Polidori G, Cataldi L, et al: Phototherapy induced hypocalcemia. *J Pediatr* 1979; 94:815–816.

52. Hakanson DO, Bergstrom WH: Prevention of light-induced hypocalcemia by melatonin, in Norman AW (ed): *Vitamin D, Chemical, Biochemical and Clinical Endocrinology of Calcium Metabolism.* New York, Walter de Gruyter, 1982, pp 1163–1165.

53. Hahn TJ: Drug-induced disorders of vitamin D and mineral metabolism. *Clin Endocrinol Metab* 1980; 9:107–129.

54. Markestad T, Ulstein M, Stanjord RE: Anticonvulsant drug in human pregnancy: Effects on serum concentrations of vitamin D metabolites in maternal and cord blood. *Am J Obstet Gynecol* 1984; 150:254–258.

55. Stamp TCB: Effects of long-term anticonvulsant therapy on calcium and vitamin D metabolism. *Proc R Soc Med* 1979; 67:64–68.

56. Venkataraman PS, Tsang RC, Greer FR, et al: Acute infantile tetany and secondary hyperparathyroidism in infants fed humanized cow milk formula. *Am J Dis Child* 1985; 139:664–668.

57. Pearson JD, Crawford JD: Dietary dependent neonatal hypocalcemia. *Am J Dis Child* 1972; 123:472–474.

58. Gribetz D: Hypocalcemic states in infancy and childhood. *Am J Dis Child* 1957; 94:301–312.

59. Tsang RC: Neonatal magnesium disturbances. *Am J Dis Child* 1972; 124:282–293.

60. David L, Anast CS: Calcium metabolism in newborn infants: The interrelationship of para-

thyroid function and calcium, magnesium and phosphorus metabolism in normal, 'sick' and hypocalcemic newborns. *J Clin Invest* 1974; 54:287–296.

61. Maisels MJ, Li TK, Peichocki JT, et al: The effect of exchange transfusion on serum ionized calcium. *Pediatrics* 1974; 53:683–686.

62. Wieland P, Duc G, Binswanger U, et al: Parathyroid hormone response in newborn infants during exchange transfusion with blood supplemented with citrate and phosphate: Effect of IV calcium. *Pediatr Res* 1979; 13:963–968.

63. Dincsoy MY, Tsang RC, Laskarzewski P, et al: The role of postnatal age and magnesium on parathyroid hormone responses during "exchange" blood transfusion in the newborn period. *J Pediatr* 1982; 100:277–283.

64. Dincsoy MY, Tsang RC, Laskarzewski P, et al: Serum calcitonin response to administration of calcium in newborn infants during exchange blood transfusion. *J Pediatr* 1982; 100:782–786.

65. Whitsett J, Tsang RC: In vitro effects of fatty acids on serum ionized calcium. *J Pediatr* 1977; 91:233–236.

66. Brown DR, Tsang RC, Chen I: Oral calcium supplementation in premature and asphyxiated neonates. *J Pediatr* 1976; 89:973–977.

67. Nervez CT, Shott RJ, Bergstromm WH, et al: Prophylaxis against hypocalcemia in low birth weight infants requiring bicarbonate infusion. *Pediatrics* 1975; 87:439–442.

68. Venkataraman PS, Tsang RC, Steichen JJ, et al: Early neonatal hypocalcemia in very low birth weight infants: High incidence, early onset and refractoriness to supraphysiologic doses of 1,25 dihydroxyvitamin D_3. *Am J Dis Child* 1986; 140:1004–1008.

69. Salle BL, David L, Glorieux FH, et al: Early oral administration of vitamin D and its metabolites in premature neonates. Effect on mineral homeostasis. *Pediatr Res* 1982; 16:75–78.

70. Fleishman AR, Rosen JF, Nathenson G: 25-Hydroxycholecalciferol for early neonatal hypocalcemia. Occurrence in premature newborns. *Am J Dis Child* 1978; 132:973–977.

71. Chan GM, Tsang RC, Chen IW, et al: The effect of $1,25(OH)_2$ vitamin D_3 supplementation in premature infants. *J Pediatr* 1978; 93:91–96.

72. Koo WWK, Tsang RC, Poser JW, et al: Elevated serum calcium and osteocalcin levels from calcitriol in preterm infants. A prospective randomized study. *Am J Dis Child* 1986; 140:1152–1158.

73. Willis DM, Chabot J, Radde IG, et al: Unsuspected hyperosmolality of oral solutions contributing to necrotizing enterocolitis in very low birth weight infants. *Pediatrics* 1977; 60:535–538.

74. Book LS, Herbst JJ, Stewart D: Hazards of calcium gluconate therapy in the newborn infant: Intra-arterial injection producing intestinal necrosis in rabbit ileum. *J Pediatr* 1978; 92:793–797.

75. Marx SJ, Swart EG, Hamstra AJ, et al: Normal intrauterine development of the fetus of a woman receiving extraordinarily high doses of 1,25 dihydroxy-vitamin D. *J Clin Endocrinol Metab* 1980; 51:1138–1142.

76. Burman KD, Monchik JM, Earll JM, et al: Ionized and total serum calcium and parathyroid hormone in hyperthyroidism. *Ann Intern Med* 1976; 84:668–671.

77. Mahomadi M, Bivins L, Becker KL: Effect of thiazides on serum calcium. *Clin Pharmacol Ther* 1979; 26:390–394.

78. Spiegel AM, Harrison HE, Marx SJ, et al: Neonatal primary hyperparathyroidism with autosomal dominant inheritance. *J Pediatr* 1977; 90:269–272.

79. Goldbloom RB, Gillis DA, Prasad M: Hereditary parathyroid hyperplasia: A surgical emergency of early infancy. *Pediatrics* 1972; 49:514–523.

80. Stuart C, Aceto T Jr, Kuhn JP, et al: Intrauterine hyperparathyroidism. *Am J Dis Child* 1979; 133:67–70.

81. Carey DE, Jones KL, Parthemore JG, et al: Calcitonin secretion in congenital non-goitrous cretins. *J Clin Invest* 1980; 65:892–895.

82. Carey DE, Jones KL: Hypothyroidism and hypercalcemia. *J Pediatr* 1987; 111:155–156.
83. Tau C, Garabedian M, Farriaux JP, et al: Hypercalcemia in infants with congenital hypothyroidism and its relation to vitamin D and thyroid hormones. *J Pediatr* 1986; 109:808–814.
84. Jones KL, Smith DW: The Williams elfin facies syndrome: A new perspective. *J Pediatr* 1975; 86:718–723.
85. Smith DW: Williams syndrome, in Schaffer AJ (ed): *Recognizable Patterns of Human Malformation*. Philadelphia, WB Saunders Co, 1982, pp 100–101.
86. Aarskog D, Aksnes L, Markestad T: Vitamin D metabolism in idiopathic infantile hypercalcemia. *Am J Dis Child* 1981; 135:1021–1024.
87. Taylor AB, Stern PH, Bell NH: Abnormal regulation of circulating 25-hydroxyvitamin D in the Williams syndrome. *N Engl J Med* 1982; 306:972–975.
88. Garabedian M, Jacqz E, Guillozo H, et al: Elevated plasma 1,25-dihydroxyvitamin D concentrations in infants with hypercalcemia and an elfin facies. *N Engl J Med* 1985; 312:948–952.
89. Chesney RW, DeLuca HF, Gertner JM: Increased plasma 1,25-dihydroxyvitamin D in infants with hypercalcemia and elfin facies. *N Engl J Med* 1985; 313:889–890.
90. Culler FL, Jones KL, Deftos LJ: Impaired calcitonin secretion in patients with Williams syndrome. *J Pediatr* 1985; 107:720–723.
91. Martin NDT, Snodgrass GJAI, Cohen RD: Idiopathic infantile hypercalcaemia—a continuing enigma. *Arch Dis Child* 1984; 59:605–613.
92. Marx SJ, Spiegel AM, Levine MA, et al: Familial hypocalciuric hypercalcemia: The relation to primary parathyroid hyperplasia. *N Engl J Med* 1982; 307:416–426.
93. Matsuo M, Okita K, Takemine H, et al: Neonatal primary hyperparathyroidism in familial hypocalciuric hypercalcemia. *Am J Dis Child* 1982; 136:728–731.
94. Marx SJ, Frazer D, Rapoport A: Familial hypocalciuric hypercalcemia: Mild expression of the gene in heterozygotes and severe expression in homozygotes. *Am J Med* 1985; 76:15–22.
95. Marx SJ, Attie MF, Spiegel AM, et al: An association between neonatal severe primary hyperparathyroidism and familial hypocalciuric hypercalcemia in three kindreds. *N Engl J Med* 1982; 306:257–264.
96. Fujita T, Watanabe N, Fukase M, et al: Familial hypocalciuric hypercalcemia involving four members of a kindred including a girl with severe neonatal primary hyperparathyroidism. *Miner Electrolyte Metab* 1983; 9:51–54.
97. Ross AJ, Cooper A, Attie MF, et al: Primary hyperparathyroidism in infancy. *J Pediatr Surg* 1986; 21:493–499.
98. Auwerx J, Brunzell J, Bouillon R, et al: Familial hypocalciuric hypercalcaemia–familial benign hypercalcaemia: A review. *Postgrad Med J* 1987; 63:835–840.
99. Sopwith AM, Burns C, Grant DB, et al: Familial hypocalciuric hypercalcemia: Association with neonatal primary hyperparathyroidism and possible linkage with HLA haplotype. *Clin Endocrinol* 1984; 21:57–64.
100. Fraser D: Hypophosphatasia. *Am J Med* 1957; 22:730–746.
101. Rasmussen H, Bartter FC: Hypophosphatasia, in Stanbury JB, Wyngaarden JB, Fredrickson DS (eds): *The Metabolic Basis of Inherited Disease*, ed 4. New York, McGraw-Hill Book Co, 1978; pp 1340–1349.
102. Veldhuis JD, Kulin HE, Demers LM, et al: Infantile hypercalcemia with subcutaneous fat necrosis: Endocrine studies. *J Pediatr* 1979; 95:460–462.
103. Barltrop D: Hypercalcemia associated with neonatal subcutaneous fat necrosis. *Arch Dis Child* 1963; 38:516–518.
104. Sagy M, Birenbaum E, Balin A, et al: Phosphate depletion in a premature infant fed human milk. *J Pediatr* 1980; 96:683–684.
105. Rowe JC, Wood DH, Rowe DW, et al: Nutritional hypophosphatemic rickets in a premature infant fed breast milk. *N Engl J Med* 1979; 300:293–294.

106. Rowe JC, Carey DE: Phosphorus deficiency syndrome in very low birth weight infants. *Pediatr Clinic North Am* 1987; 34:997–1017.

107. Ferraro EM, Klein SA, Fakhry J, et al: Hypercalcemia in association with mesoblastic nephroma: Report of a case and review of the literature. *Pediatr Radiol* 1986; 16:516–517.

108. Woolfield NF, Abbott GD, McRae CU: A mesoblastic nephroma with hypercalcaemia. *Aust Paediatr J* 1988; 24:309–310.

109. Rousseau-Merck MF, Nogues C, Roth A, et al: Hypercalcemic infantile renal tumors: Morphological, clinical, and biological heterogeneity. *Pediatr Pathol* 1985; 3:155–164.

110. Shanbhogue LKR, Gray E, Miller SS: Congenital mesoblastic nephroma of infancy associated with hypercalcemia. *J Urol* 1986; 135:771–772.

111. Jayabose S, Iqbal K, Newman L, et al: Hypercalcemia in childhood renal tumors. *Cancer* 1988; 61:788–791.

112. Rosseau-Merck MF, DeKeyzer Y, Bourdeau A, et al: PTH mRNA transcription analysis in infantile tumors associated with hypercalcemia. *Cancer* 1988; 62:303–308.

113. Calo L, Cantaro S, Bertazzo L, et al: Synthesis and catabolism of PGE_2 by a nephroblastoma associated with hypercalcemia without bone metastases. *Cancer* 1984; 54:635–637.

114. Vido L, Carli M, Rizzoni G, et al: Congenital mesoblastic nephroma with hypercalcemia: Pathogenic role of prostaglandins. *Am J Pediatr Hematol Oncol* 1986; 8:149–152.

115. Bartter FC, Pronove P, Gill JR, et al: Hyperplasia of the juxtaglomerular complex with hyperaldosteronism and hypokalemic alkalosis: A new syndrome. *Am J Med* 1962; 33:811–828.

116. Stein JH: The pathogenetic spectrum of Bartter's syndrome. *Kidney Int* 1985; 28:85–93.

117. Restrepo deRovetto C, Welch TR, Hug G, et al: Hypercalciuria with Bartter syndrome: Evidence for an abnormality of vitamin D metabolism. *J Pediatr* 1989; 115:397–404.

118. Yamada M, Matsumoto T, Takahashi N, et al: Stimulatory effect of prostaglandin E_2 on 1-alpha, 25-dihydroxyvitamin D_3 synthesis in rats. *Biochem J* 1983; 216:237–240.

119. Wark JD, Taft JL, Michelangeli VP, et al: Biphasic action of prostaglandin E2 on conversion of 25-hydroxyvitamin D_3 to 1,25-dihydroxyvitamin D_3 in chick renal tubules. *Prostaglandins* 1984; 27:453–463.

120. Kurose H, Sonn YM, Jafari A, et al: Effects of prostaglandin E_2 and indomethacin on 25-hydroxyvitamin D_3-1-alpha-hydroxylase activity in isolated kidney cells of normal and streptozocin-induced diabetic rats. *Calcif Tissue Int* 1985; 37:625–629.

121. Matsumoto J, Kim Han B, Restrepo deRovetto C, et al: Hypercalciuric Bartter syndrome: Resolution of nephrocalcinosis with indomethacin. *AJR* 1989; 152:1251–1253.

122. Harris I, Wilkinson AW: Magnesium depletion in children. *Lancet* 1971; 2:735–736.

123. Allen DB, Friedman AL, Greer FR, et al: Hypomagnesemia masking the appearance of elevated parathyroid hormone concentrations in familial pseudohypoparathryoidism. *Am J Med Genet* 1988; 31:153–158.

124. Allgrove J, Adami S, Fraher L, et al: Hypomagnesemia: Studies of parathyroid hormone secretion and function. *Clin Endocrinol* 1984; 21:435–449.

125. Friedman M, Hutcher G, Watson L: Primary hypomagnesemia with secondary hypocalcemia in an infant. *Lancet* 1967; 1:703–705.

126. Paunier L, Radde IC, Kooh SW, et al: Primary hypomagnesemia with secondary hypocalcemia in an infant. *Pediatrics* 1968; 41:385–402.

127. Skyberg D, Stromme JH, Nesbakken R, et al: Neonatal hypomagnesemia with selective malabsorption of magnesium: A clinical entity. *Scand J Clin Lab Invest* 1968; 21:355–363.

128. Stromme JH, Steen-Johnsen J, Harnaes K, et al: Familial hypomagnesemia. *Acta Paediatr Scand* 1969; 58:433–444.

129. Dudin KI, Teebi AS: Primary hypomagnesemia: A case report and literature review. *Eur J Pediatr* 1987; 146:303–305.

130. Abdulrazzaq YM, Smigura FC, Wettrell G: Primary infantile hypomagnesemia: Report of two cases and review of literature. *Eur J Pediatr* 1989; 148:459–461.

131. Davis JA, Harvey DR, Yu JS: Neonatal fits associated with hypomagnesemia. *Arch Dis Child* 1965; 40:286–290.

132. Atwell JD: Magnesium deficiency following neonatal surgical procedures. *J Pediatr Surg* 1966; 1:427–440.

133. Baron DN: Magnesium deficiency after gastrointestinal surgery and loss of secretions. *Br J Surg* 1960; 48:344–346.

134. Tsang RC, Oh W: Serum magnesium levels in low birth weight infants. *Am J Dis Child* 1970; 120:44–48.

135. Jukarainen E: Plasma magnesium levels during the first five days of life. *Acta Paediatr Scand [Suppl]* 1974; 222:1–58.

136. Seelig MS: Prenatal and neonatal mineral deficiencies: Magnesium, zinc, and chromium, in Lifshitz F (ed): *Pediatric Nutrition. Infant Feedings—Deficiencies–Diseases. Clinical Disorders in Pediatric Nutrition/2.* New York, Marcel Dekker, 1982, pp 167–196.

137. Booth BE, Johanson A: Hypomagnesemia due to renal tubular defect in reabsorption of magnesium. *J Pediatr* 1974; 85:350–354.

138. Michelis MF, Drash AL, Linarelli LG, et al: Decreased bicarbonate threshold and renal magnesium wasting in a sibship with distal renal tubular acidosis (evaluation of the pathophysiologic role of parathyroid hormone). *Metabolism* 1972; 21:905–920.

139. Gitelman HJ, Graham JB, Welt LG: A new familial disorder characterized by hypokalemia and hypomagnesemia. *Trans Assoc Am Physicians* 1966; 79:221–235.

140. Runeberg L, Collan Y, Jokinen EJ, et al: Hypomagnesemia due to renal disease of unknown etiology. *Am J Med* 1975; 59:873–881.

141. Koo WWK, Guan ZP, Tsang RC, et al: Growth failure and decreased bone mineral of newborn rats with chronic furosemide therapy. *Pediatr Res* 1986; 20:74–78.

142. Brickman AS, Massry SG, Coburn JW: Changes in serum and urinary calcium during treatment with hydrochlorothiazide: Studies on mechanisms. *J Clin Invest* 1972; 51:945–954.

143. Bar RS, Wilson HE, Mazzaferri EL: Hypomagnesemic hypocalcemia secondary to renal magnesium wasting. A possible consequence of high-dose gentamycin therapy. *Ann Intern Med* 1975; 82:646–649.

144. Keating MJ, Sethi MR, Bodey GP, et al: Hypocalcemia with hypoparathyroidism and renal tubular dysfunction associated with aminoglycoside therapy. *Cancer* 1977; 39:1410–1414.

145. Kobayashi A, Shiraki K: Serum magnesium level in infants and children with hepatic diseases. *Arch Dis Child* 1967; 42:615–618.

146. Cohen MI, McNamara H, Finberg L: Serum magnesium in children with cirrhosis. *J Pediatr* 1970; 76:453–455.

147. Thoren L: Magnesium deficiency in gastrointestinal fluid loss. *Acta Chir Scand (Suppl)* 1963; 306:5–65.

148. Cowan GSM, Luther RW, Sykes TR: Short bowel syndrome: Causes and clinical consequences. *Nutr Supp Serv* 1984; 4:25–32.

149. Weser E: Nutritional aspects of malabsorption: Short gut adaptation. *Am J Med* 1979; 67:1014–1020.

150. Ziegler MM: Short bowel syndrome in infancy: Etiology and management. *Clin Perinatol* 1986; 13:163–173.

151. Bajpai E, Sugden D, Stern L: Serum ionic magnesium in exchange transfusion. *J Pediatr* 1967; 70:193–197.

152. Bottini E, Ventura G, Cocciante G, et al: Serum magnesium in icteric newborns undergoing exchange transfusion with donor's blood collected in ACD solution. *Biol Neonate* 1968; 12:102–106.

153. Jones KH, Fourman P: Effects of infusions of magnesium and of calcium in parathyroid insufficiency. *Clin Sci* 1966; 30:139–150.

154. MacIntyre I, Boss S, Troughton VA: Parathyroid hormone and magnesium homeostasis. *Nature* 1963; 198:1058–1060.

155. Monteleone JA, Lee JB, Tashjian AH Jr, et al: Transient neonatal hypocalcemia, hypomagnesemia, and high serum parathyroid hormone with maternal hyperparathyroidism. *Ann Intern Med* 1975; 82:670–672.

156. Ertel NH, Reiss JS, Spergel G: Hypomagnesemia in neonatal tetany associated with maternal hyperparathyroidism. *N Engl J Med* 1969; 280:260–262.

157. Cruikshank DP, Pitkin RM, Reynolds WA, et al: Altered maternal calcium homeostasis in diabetic pregnancy. *J Clin Endocrinol Metab* 1980; 50:264–267.

158. Dooling EC, Stern L: Hypomagnesemia with convulsions in a newborn infant. *Can Med Assoc J* 1967; 97:827–831.

159. Jackson CE, Meier DW: Routine serum Mg analysis. *Ann Intern Med* 1968; 69:743–748.

160. Aikawa JK: Effect of alloxan-induced diabetes on magnesium metabolism in rabbits. *Am J Physiol* 1960; 199:1084–1086.

161. Linderman RD, Adler S, Yiengst MJ, et al: Influence of various nutrients on urinary divalent cation excretion. *J Lab Clin Med* 1967; 70:236–245.

162. Tsang RC, Strub R, Brown DR, et al: Hypomagnesemia in infants of diabetic mothers: Perinatal studies. *J Pediatr* 1976; 89:115–119.

163. Gardner LI, MacLachlan EA, Pick W, et al: Etiologic factors in tetany of newly born infants. *Pediatrics* 1950; 5:228–239.

164. Brown JK, Cockburn F, Forfar JO: Clinical and chemical correlates in convulsions of the newborn. *Lancet* 1972; 1:135–139.

165. Wong HB, Teh YF: An association between serum magnesium and tremor and convulsions in infants and children. *Lancet* 1968; 2:18–21.

166. Stone SR, Pritchard JA: Effect of maternally administered magnesium sulfate on the neonate. *Obstet Gynecol* 1970; 35:574–577.

167. Lipsitz PJ: The clinical and biochemical effects of excess magnesium in the newborn. *Pediatrics* 1971; 47:501–509.

168. Elliot J: Magnesium sulfate as a tocolytic agent. *Am J Obstet Gynecol* 1983; 147:277–284.

169. Brady JP, Williams HC: Magnesium intoxication in a premature infant. *Pediatrics* 1967; 40:100–103.

170. Engel RR, Elin RJ: Hypermagnesemia from birth asphyxia. *J Pediatr* 1970; 77:631–637.

171. Donovan EF, Tsang RC, Steichen JJ, et al: Neonatal hypermagnesemia: Effect of parathyroid hormone and calcium homeostasis. *J Pediatr* 1980; 96:305–310.

172. Buckle RM, Care AD, Cooper CW: The influence of plasma magnesium concentration on parathyroid hormone secretion. *J Endocrinol* 1968; 42:529–534.

173. Massry SG, Coburn JW, Kleeman CR: Evidence for suppression of parathyroid gland activity by hypermagnesemia. *J Clin Invest* 1970; 49:1619–1629.

174. MacManus J, Heaton FW: The influence of magnesium on calcium release from bone in vitro. *Biochem Biophys Acta* 1970; 215:360–367.

175. Lamm CI, Norton KI, Murphy RJC, et al: Congenital rickets associated with magnesium sulfate infusion for tocolysis. *J Pediatr* 1988; 113:1078–1082.

176. Cumming WA, Thomas VJ: Hypermagnesemia: A cause of abnormal metaphyses in the neonate. *Am J Radiol* 1989; 152:1071–1072.

177. Levine BS, Coburn JW: Magnesium, the mimic/antagonist of calcium. *N Engl J Med* 1984; 310:1253–1255.

178. Committee on Nutrition, American Academy of Pediatrics: Nutritional needs of low birth weight infants. *Pediatrics* 1985; 75:976–986.

179. Koo WWK, Tsang RC, Steichen JJ, et al: Parenteral nutrition for infants: Effects of high versus low calcium and phosphorus content. *J Pediatr Gastroenterol Nutr* 1987; 6:96–104.

180. Koo W, Tsang RC, Succop P, et al: Minimal vitamin D, high calcium and phosphorus requirement of preterm infants receiving parenteral nutrition. *J Pediatr Gastroenterol Nutr* 1989; 8:225–233.

181. Koo WWK, Tsang RC: Calcium and magnesium metabolism in health and disease, in

Werner M (ed): *CRC Handbook of Clinical Chemistry,* vol IV. Boca Raton, Florida, CRC Press, 1989; pp 51–91.

182. Halbert KE, Tsang RC: Rickets in the newborn period and premature infants, in Castells S, Finberg L (eds): *Metabolic Bone Disease in Children.* New York, Marcel Dekker, 1990, pp 99–150.

183. Callenbach JC, Sheehan MB, Abramson SJ, et al: Etiologic factors in rickets of very low birth weight infants. *J Pediatr* 1981; 98:800–805.

184. Koo WWK, Gupta JM, Nayanar VV, et al: Skeletal changes in preterm infants. *Arch Dis Child* 1982; 57:447–452.

185. Venkataraman PS, Han BK, Tsang RC, et al: Secondary hyperparathyroidism and bone disease in infants receiving long-term furosemide therapy. *Am J Dis Child* 1983; 137:1157–1161.

186. Davies DP, Hughes CA, Moore JR: Rickets in preterm infants. *Arch Dis Child* 1978; 53:88–90.

187. Bosley ARJ, Verrier-Jones ER, Campbell MJ: Aetiological factors in rickets of prematurity. *Arch Dis Child* 1980; 55:683–686.

188. Steichen JJ, Tsang RC, Greer FR, et al: Elevated serum 1,25-dihydroxyvitamin D concentrations in rickets of very low birth weight infants. *J Pediatr* 1981; 99:293–298.

189. McIntosh N, Livesey A, Brooke OG: Plasma 25-hydroxyvitamin D and rickets in infants of extremely low birth weight. *Arch Dis Child* 1982; 57:848–850.

190. Kovar IZ, Mayne PD, Robbe I: Hypophosphatemic rickets in the preterm infant, hypocalcemia after calcium and phosphorus supplementation. *Arch Dis Child* 1983; 58:629–631.

191. Kovar IZ, Mayne P, Wallis J: Neonatal rickets in one of identical twins. *Arch Dis Child* 1982; 57:792–794.

192. Markestad T, Aksnes L, Finne PH, et al: Plasma concentrations of vitamin D metabolites in a case of rickets of prematurity. *Acta Paediatr Scand* 183; 72:759–761.

193. Walters EG, Murphy JF, Brown RC, et al: Vitamin D metabolism in rachitic preterm infants (letter). *Lancet* 1983; 2:629.

194. Koo WWK, Sherman R, Succop P, et al: Serum vitamin D metabolites in very low birth weight infants with and without rickets and fractures. *J Pediatr* 1989; 114:1017–1022.

195. Evans JR, Allen AC, Stinson DA, et al: Effect of high-dose vitamin D supplementation on radiographically detectable bone disease of very low birth weight infants. *J Pediatr* 1989; 115:779–786.

196. Pereira GR, Sherman MS, DiGiacomo J, et al: Hyperalimentation-induced cholestasis. *Am J Dis Child* 1981; 135:842–845.

197. Callahan J, Haller JO, Cacciarelli AA, et al: Cholelithiasis in infants: Association with total parenteral nutrition and furosemide. *Radiology* 1982; 143:437–439.

198. Cole DEC, Zlotkin SH: Increased sulfate as an etiological factor in the hypercalciuria associated with total parenteral nutrition. *Am J Clin Nutr* 1983; 37:108–113.

199. Mimouni F, Tsang RC: Bone mineralization in infants: The contribution of photon absorptiometry, in Stern L (ed): *Feeding the Sick Infant.* Nestle Nutrition Workshop Series, vol 11. New York, Nestlé Ltd, Vevey/Raven Press, 1987, pp 75–100.

200. Koo WWK, Oestreich AE, Sherman R, et al: Radiological case of the month: Osteopenia, rickets and fractures in preterm infants. *Am J Dis Child* 1985; 139:1045–1046.

201. Geggel RL, Pereira GR, Spackman TJ: Fractured ribs: Unusual presentation of rickets in premature infants. *J Pediatr* 1978; 93:680–682.

202. Glasgow JFT, Thomas PS: Rachitic respiratory distress in small preterm infants. *Arch Dis Child* 1977; 52:268–273.

203. Thomas PS, Glasgow JFT: The "mandibular mantle"—a sign of rickets in very low birth weight infants. *Br J Radiol* 1978; 51:93–98.

204. Greer FR, Steichen JJ, Tsang RC: Calcium and phosphate supplements in breast milk-related rickets: Results in a very-low-birth-weight infant. *Am J Dis Child* 1982; 136:581–583.

205. Poser JW, Esch FS, Ling NC, et al: Isolation and sequence of the vitamin K-dependent

protein from human bone: Undercarboxylation of the first glutamic acid residue. *J Biol Chem* 1980; 255:8685–8691.

206. Price PA, Baukol SA: 1,25-dihydroxyvitamin D_3 increases serum levels of the vitamin K-dependent bone protein. *Biochem Biophys Res Commun* 1981; 99:928–935.

207. Pettifor JM, Stein H, Herman A, et al: Mineral homeostasis in very low birth weight infants fed either on mother's milk or pooled pasteurized preterm milk. *J Pediatr Gastroenterol Nutr* 1986; 5:248–253.

208. Delmas PD, Wahner HW, Mann KG, et al: Assessment of bone turnover in postmenopausal osteoporosis by measurement of serum bone Gla-protein. *J Lab Clin Med* 1983; 102:470–476.

209. Karlen J, Aperia A, Zetterstrom R: Renal excretion of calcium and phosphate in preterm and term infants. *J Pediatr* 1985; 106:814–819.

210. Caffey J: *Pediatric X-ray Diagnosis*. Chicago, Year Book Medical Publishers, Inc, 1972, pp 1222–1231.

211. Ziegler EF, Biga RL, Fomon SJ: Nutritional requirements of the premature infant, in Suskind RM (ed): *Textbook of Pediatric Nutrition*. New York, Raven Press, 1981, pp 29–39.

212. Gross SJ: Bone mineralization in preterm infants fed human milk with and without mineral supplementation. *J Pediatr* 1987; 111:450–458.

213. Modanlou HD, Lim MD, Hansen JW, et al: Growth, biochemical status, and mineral metabolism in very low birth weight infants receiving fortified preterm human milk. *J Pediatr Gastroenterol Nutr* 1986; 5:762–767.

214. Chan GM, Mijur L, Hansen JW: Effects of increased calcium and phosphorus formulas on bone mineralization in preterm infants. *J Pediatr Gastroenterol Nutr* 1986; 5:444–449.

215. Schanler RJ, Garza C: Improved mineral balance in very low birth weight infants fed fortified human milk. *J Pediatr* 1988; 112:452–456.

216. Greer FR, McCormick A: Improved bone mineralization and growth in premature infants fed fortified own mother's milk. *J Pediatr* 1988; 112:961–969.

Chapter 9

Trace Minerals

K. Michael Hambidge

In general, identification of the role of the trace elements[1,2] in human nutrition has come late in the study of nutrients. With the outstanding exceptions of iron and iodine, trace elements were generally thought to be of little or no practical significance in human nutrition, and it was not until the 1960s that older concepts, initially with considerable skepticism, were modified. During the past 30 years it has become apparent that life-threatening deficiencies of trace elements other than iron and iodine can occur in the human and that a multitude of factors can render individuals and population groups susceptible to disease resulting from trace element deficiencies. Despite recent progress, however, our understanding of the biologic roles, metabolism, nutritional requirements, causes, and effects of micronutrient deficiencies is very far from complete. We are even uncertain about the number of trace elements that have a role in human nutrition. A summary of those trace elements of proved or putative importance in human nutrition and human disease is given in Table 9–1. Different experts may each provide a slightly different breakdown, reflecting current uncertainties.

Any trace element that has a physiologic role should be detectable consistently in human tissues. Concentrations of the trace elements will vary from less than 1 part per billion up to many parts per 1,000 in different tissues and subcellular components. By definition, a trace element contributes less than 0.01% to the total body weight.

Though the trace elements are present in the human body in such small quantities, they are analogous to their organic counterparts, the vitamins, in that they have multiple, indispensable roles in a variety of important metabolic pathways. The best clarified of these roles are summarized in Table 9–2. The activity of many enzymes is known to be dependent on one or another trace element, as is the integrity or biological activity of other proteins of cardinal importance in intermediary metabolism. The structure as well as the function of subcellular organelles is also dependent on optimal quantities of trace elements.

As depicted in Figure 9–1, all nutrients have an optimal range of intake, with either deficiency or excess being potentially harmful. This concept of a "dose-response" for nutrients is, however, most frequently cited in the context of the trace elements. One reason for this is that, in general, there was a great deal more concern historically about toxicity than about deficiency states. For example, copper salts have long been used in suicide and homicide as well as leading to death from accidental ingestion, while only recently has the occurrence of human copper deficiency been identified. However, interest in the other end of the spectrum of the "dose-response" curve has grown rapidly in

TABLE 9–1.

Trace Elements of Biologic Interest

Importance	Element
Identified human deficiencies	Iron, iodine, zinc, copper, selenium
Limited evidence for human deficiencies	Cromium, molybdenum, manganese
Pharmacologic value	Fluorine
Other trace elements of known biological importance in the human	Cobalt
Other trace elements of established biological importance in other mammalian species	Nickel, arsenic, vanadium, boron, silicon
Other trace elements of possible biologic importance in mammals	Beryllium, tin, cadmium, lead
Examples of trace elements of toxic importance only	Aluminum, mercury

TABLE 9–2.

Overview of Biological Roles of the Trace Elements

Metalloenzymes (structural, regulatory, catalytic roles): iron, zinc, copper, manganese, molybdenum
Metal-ion activated enzymes (catalytic role): zinc, manganese
Components (in parentheses) of other metabolically important compounds and subcellular organelles, including:

Vitamins	B_{12} (cobalt)
Hormones	T_3 and T_4 (iodine)
Proteins	(Iron)
Transcription proteins	(Zinc)
Porphyrins	Heme (iron), protoporphyrin (zinc)
Subcellular organelles	Cell membrane (zinc), nucleus (zinc)

TABLE 9–3.

Factors Contributing to Trace Element Deficiencies in the Infant*

Inborn metabolic disease	Zinc, copper
Intravenous nutrition	Zinc, copper
Inadequate supply from formula or use of unmodified cow's milk	Selenium, copper,* iron, zinc*
Geochemical environment	Iodine, selenium
Diseases impairing absorption or aggravating losses	Zinc, copper
Blood loss	Iron

*Does not apply to formulas marketed in the United States in 1989.

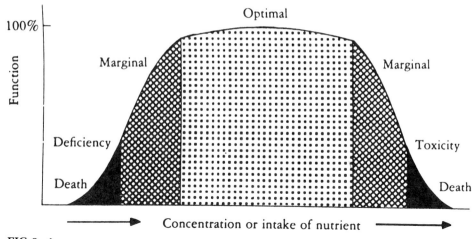

FIG 9–1.
Dependence of biologic function on tissue concentration or intake of a nutrient. (From Mertz W: The essential trace elements. *Science* 1981; 213:1330. Used by permission.)

the past 30 years, and during this time a wide variety of different circumstances have been identified that predispose to one or more trace element deficiencies. Causes of trace element deficiencies in infants and/or children are summarized in Table 9–3.

Some aspects of the causes of human deficiencies of the "newer" trace elements remain quite puzzling at this time. For example, some deficiencies occur despite evidence of well-developed homeostatic control of trace element absorption, metabolism, excretion (Table 9–4), and the ability of the body to adapt to different levels of intake. It is also known that the placenta can regulate the transport of trace elements to the fetus, though data on the placental physiology of these micronutrients are still limited. For some of the trace elements, it is apparent that the fetus can accumulate a favorable reserve in utero. However, if maternal status is compromised, the embryo or fetus does not necessarily receive an adequate supply of trace elements. For example, restriction of dietary zinc intake to the rat dam can have profound teratogenic consequences for the fetus, and it does not appear possible to mobilize zinc from maternal tissues to avert this catastrophic deficiency.[3]

TABLE 9–4.
Overview of Trace Element Homeostasis*

| Element | Intestine | | Storage | Liver Biliary Excretion | Kidney Excretion in Urine |
	Fractional Absorption	Endogenous Excretion			
Iron	++++		++		
Iodine			++		+++
Zinc	+++	++			+
Copper	+		+	+++	
Selenium					+++
Manganese	+++			+++	
Chromium	?				+
Molybdenum					+

*Plus signs indicate the relative importance on a scale of least (+) to most (++++). No plus signs indicates no importance.

TABLE 9–5.

Unique Factors That Can Affect Trace Element
Requirements in Very Low Birth Weight Infants

Factor	Examples
Neonatal stores low	Iron, copper
Rapid growth	Zinc
Immature gastrointestinal system	Zinc
Immaturity of homeostatic control	Zinc

TABLE 9–6.

Estimated Trace Element Requirements for Premature Infants, μg/kg/day

Element	Oral		Intravenous
	Formula	Human Milk	
Zinc	1,200–1,500*	500	400
Copper	120	40	20
Selenium	3.0	2.5	2.0
Manganese	10–20	1.0	1.0
Chromium	2	0.05	0.2
Molybdenum	2	0.3	0.25
Iodide	1	1.0	1.0
Iron† (BW > 1,000 g)	2,000	2,000	(200)‡
(BW < 1,000 g)	3,000–4,000	3,000–4,000	. . .
Fluoride	100	100	(100)‡

* Assuming 20% to 25% net absorption.
† Commence 2 months after delivery. BW = body weight.
‡ Use in intravenous infusate not established.

In the premature infant, homeostatic control of trace element metabolism can be immature, thus enhancing the risk of certain trace deficiencies. Other factors affecting trace element requirements that are unique to the premature infant are summarized in Table 9–5.

Current estimates of requirements, both enteral and parenteral, are summarized in Table 9–6.

ZINC

Historical Background

Zinc was demonstrated to be necessary for microorganisms in the late 19th century. Its role in mammalian nutrition was identified in the 1930s, and the commercial importance of this observation became clear in the 1950s when zinc deficiency was shown to be the cause of porcine parakeratosis. The first zinc metalloenzyme, carbonic anhydrase, was documented in 1940. In the late 1950s, abnormalities of zinc metabolism were found in association with alcoholic cirrhosis, and in the early 1960s the first cases of apparent human zinc deficiency were reported. These were subjects with the syndrome of adolescent nutritional dwarfism in Egypt and Iran. The practical importance of human zinc deficiency in North America has become increasingly apparent over the past 20 years with the identification of both severe, life-threatening zinc deficiency states occurring in special circumstances and evidence for milder zinc deficiency occurring in some sections of the free-living population.[4, 5]

Zinc Absorption, Metabolism, Excretion, and Body Distribution

Dietary zinc absorption takes place in the small intestine, though the major site of absorption within the small intestine remains unclear. The small intestine may frequently have to reabsorb more endogenous zinc, especially that from the pancreatic exocrine secretions, than is present in the diet.[6] When zinc is given as an inorganic salt in the postabsorptive state, absorption averages 60% to 70% and may be considerably higher. Absorption of zinc from composite meals averages only about 25%. While all diets, with the possible exception of human milk, have some inhibitory effect on zinc absorption, some dietary constituents, especially phytate, have a more notable effect.[7] Absorption of zinc from cow's milk and infant formulas appears to average about 30% and from soy protein formulas about 15%.[8] Absorption from human milk averages 50% to 60% but may be considerably higher. These fractional absorption figures are based primarily on the results of studies in adults. Some very recent data suggest a similar pattern in the premature infant,[9] but results of studies in premature infants prior to 36 week's postconceptional age have been conflicting. This applies both to the results of recent pilot studies using a zinc stable isotope[10] and to the results of traditional balance studies. Our own balance data in very low birth weight premature infants are summarized in Table 9–7. Mean zinc balance for formula-fed infants was slightly negative and for infants fed with their own mother's milk slightly positive. Others have reported much more extreme data, either negative or positive.

Transport of zinc across the brush-border appears to be a carrier-mediated process that probably involves interaction of the metal in a chelated form. A large number of low molecular weight binding ligands have been shown to enhance mucosal uptake. At high luminal zinc concentrations, nonmediated zinc absorption also occurs.[11]

Zinc homeostasis is governed primarily at the level of the small intestine. Fractional zinc absorption and fecal excretion of endogenous zinc vary with zinc intake and zinc status.[12] The feces are normally the major route of excretion of endogenous zinc in addition to the unabsorbed dietary zinc. The homeostatic control mechanisms are not understood but may, in part, involve metallothionein synthesis. Synthesis of this low molecular weight protein is increased in the enterocyte when zinc intake is relatively high. Binding of zinc to this protein probably slows its passage through the enterocyte and allows it to be excreted when the enterocyte is sloughed. An increase in dietary zinc also increases messenger ribonucleic acid for denovo synthesis of metallothionein in liver and some other organs.[13] Some of the absorbed zinc is retained by the liver during the

TABLE 9–7.

Zinc Balance in Very Low Birth Weight Premature Infants

Type of Feed	No. of Subjects	No. of Samples	Postpartum Age (days)	Balance μg Zn/kg/day
Own mother's milk	6	14	30 ± 4*	+ 46 ± 89
Formula	4	8	42 ± 4	− 31 ± 73

*Standard error of the mean.

first pass.[14] The concentration of zinc in the fetal liver from 20 to 40 week's gestation ranges from 100 to 300 μg Zn/g wet weight, with a small decline as gestational age advances.[15] At term, concentrations remain higher than in the adult, and the liver accounts for 20% of total term neonatal zinc compared with 2% in the adult. These higher levels are associated with a larger fraction of hepatic zinc attached to metallothionein. Thus, it appears that, contrary to earlier concepts, a modest store of hepatic zinc may be available to the neonate, especially the premature neonate. In the adult, zinc concentrations in skeletal muscle (approximately 50 μg Zn/g wet weight) are similar to those in the liver, but because of the size of muscle mass, skeletal muscle accounts for 50% to 60% of total body zinc. In contrast to the liver, zinc concentrations in muscle are lower in the premature infant than in the adult. Uptake and turnover of zinc by muscle is slow, with a half-life of approximately 300 days. Uptake by bone—in which concentrations exceed 100 μg Zn/g and account for 25% to 30% of body zinc in the adult—is even slower, and zinc is not thought to be released from bone significantly unless bone reabsorption is increased.[4]

In the plasma, over 80% of zinc is carried primarily attached to albumin, with a smaller fraction (5% to 10%) specifically bound to α-2 macroglobulin.[16] The physiologic significance of this distribution is not understood. The mean pre-breakfast plasma concentration in adults is 80 to 90 μg Zn/dL with a range from 60 to 100, though with some interlaboratory variation. Meals depress plasma zinc concentrations by about 15%, with a nadir 3 to 4 hours after eating.[17] There have been variable reports on correlations between plasma zinc and serum albumin. In our own experience, there appears to be little effect of changes in serum albumin on plasma zinc until albumin levels fall to 3 g/dL, below which plasma zinc may drop about 10 μg/dL for every 1 g/dL decline in serum albumin.[18] Plasma zinc concentrations are unusually high during the 1st week or two of postnatal life in the premature infant, averaging 100 to 110 μg Zn/dL. Subsequently, these fall quite rapidly to adult levels or often considerably lower.[19] The extent of this decline varies with the type of feeding and may be related primarily to variations in zinc nutritional status rather than to temporary physiologic changes or to low levels of serum albumin. Another factor that may have an important effect on circulating zinc concentrations in this population is bone resorption. Plasma zinc concentrations have been found to be higher in premature infants with osteopenia and bone fractures than in infants matched for postconceptional age who have no evidence of rickets.[20] Zinc concentrations in erythrocytes are unusually low in early postnatal life because the great majority of erythrocyte zinc is accounted for by the zinc present in carbonic anhydrase. Erythrocyte carbonic anhydrase activity is especially low in the premature infant.[21]

Though the primary route of endogenous zinc excretion is the intestinal tract, approximately 0.5 mg Zn/day is excreted in urine and another 0.5 mg/day in sweat in the adult. On a body weight basis, urine zinc excretion rates are unusually high (averaging about 35 μg Zn/kg/day) during the first 5 weeks of postnatal life. These rates then decline quite rapidly to the adult range of ≤10 μg Zn/kg/day by 7 to 8 weeks (K.M. Hambidge and N.F. Krebs, unpublished data). Sweat zinc losses have not been measured in the premature infant but are likely to be low.

Biologic Role

Zinc is an integral component of a wide variety of different enzymes, including at least one in every major enzyme classification. In these zinc metalloenzymes, zinc has catalytic, structural, and/or regulatory roles. Examples include many of the enzymes involved in nucleic acid metabolism, carbonic anhydrase, alkaline phosphatase, and the carboxypeptidases. Zinc-dependent enzymes necessary for nucleic acid synthesis include the rate-limiting deoxyribonucleic acid (DNA) polymerases, aspartate transcarbamylase and thymidine kinase.[4] In general, DNA synthesis and cell replication appear to be impaired by zinc deficiency to a greater extent than protein synthesis, but zinc is also necessary for cell hypertrophy and differentiation. The adverse effects of zinc deficiency on cell replication and differentiation may be mediated primarily by interference with gene expression rather than by reduced activity of any zinc-dependent enzymes. For example, zinc is necessary for the integrity and function of transcription proteins, the correct binding of which to DNA is necessary to initiate transcription.[22] "Zinc fingers," the conformation of which depends on a zinc atom at the base of the finger, play a key role in the correct positioning and binding of these transcription proteins to DNA (Fig 9–2).

Zinc also appears to play a critical physiologic role in the structure and function of biomembranes.[23] Zinc deficiency may cause oxidative damage to membranes, alter function of specific receptors and nutrient absorption sites, alter activity of membrane-bound enzymes, alter function of permeability channels and alter function of carrier and transport proteins in the membrane.[16] Membrane sodium transport is affected adversely by zinc deficiency. Zinc also appears to play a role in regulating the function of calmodulin, especially as it affects the cell microtubules and microfilaments. Microtubule polymerization may be impaired in zinc deficiency.

Though considerable progress has been accomplished in elucidating the biologic roles of zinc in subcellular and molecular levels, the biochemical correlates of the features of zinc deficiency remain ill-defined.

It has been hypothesized that the effects of zinc on gene expression are dependent on a small intracellular pool of readily exchangeable zinc and that this pool is rapidly depleted when dietary zinc is restricted. This could explain the profound and rapid effects of zinc restriction on normal growth and development when there is no measurable

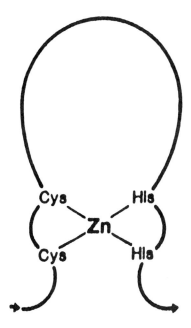

FIG 9–2.
"Zinc fingers" binding to DNA.

decrease in total tissue concentrations of zinc. The effects of zinc deficiency on growth could also be mediated in part by effects on appetite, by hormonal changes, for example, somatomedin,[17] or by local effects on the epiphyses.

Zinc and Early Development

In animal models that have included the rat, sheep, and monkey, experimental zinc deficiency is especially devastating during fetal and early postnatal development. Maternal zinc deficiency is severely teratogenic when occurring during critical periods of organogenesis.[24, 25] Later in gestation, maternal zinc deficiency has adverse effects on fetal growth,[26] development of the immune system,[27] and on subsequent brain function.[28] Zinc deficiency during the suckling and early weaning period has similar effects. Severe zinc deficiency has been identified in term and/or premature infants in three main circumstances. These are:

1. Acquired severe deficiency states. Most, but not all of these cases have been attributable at least in part to intravenous feeding without adequate addition of zinc to the infusate. This problem is less common now that it is more a universal practice to add reasonable quantities of zinc to the intravenous infusate.

2. The rare, autosomal recessive inherited disorder, acrodermatitis enteropathica. The molecular defect in this disorder awaits identification but is known to result in an impairment of the normal carrier-mediated intestinal absorption of zinc. It usually presents clinically by 2 to 3 months of age in the formula-fed infant, but clinical manifestations may be delayed until after weaning if the infant is breast-fed.

3. Failure of the mammary gland to secrete normal quantities of zinc into the milk even when the mother's zinc nutritional status is apparently normal. There have now been several case reports of this circumstance, which is analogous to the lethal milk mutation in mice. In all but one instance, the symptomatic infant has been born prematurely. An infant born at term and breast-fed for 6 months by one of the subjects remained asymptomatic, whereas a premature infant fed by the same mother developed severe symptomatic zinc deficiency by 2 to 3 months postnatal age[29] (Fig 9–3).

The hallmark of severe zinc deficiency states is the skin rash with its characteristic acro-orificial distribution (see Fig 9–3). The dermatitis also involves flexures and friction areas and may become more generalized. In premature infants, characteristic changes in the anterior neck fold may occur at an early stage, with a poorly marginated erythema in the depth of the fold which becomes well demarcated and scaling within 5 days.[30] Exematoid, psoriaform, vesiculobullous, and pustular lesions may be present.

FIG 9–3.
Infant aged 13 weeks with severe zinc deficiency. Erythematous rash is seen on face, hands, wrist; perineum, thighs, umbilicus; and foot and ankle.

Mucous membranes are characteristically involved at an early stage with dermatitis, glossitis, and conjunctivitis. Histologically, the early lesions are characterized by loss of the granular layer of the epidermis and replacement of this layer by clear cells and focal parakeratosis. If untreated, the epidermis becomes increasingly psoriaform and the parakeratosis becomes more and more confluent. Pallor of the upper part of the epidermis, attributable to the formation of balloon cells with pyknotic nuclei, is the single most typical histologic finding.[4]

Alopecia becomes prominent in poorly treated acrodermatitis enteropathica. The majority of patients exhibit diarrhea. Characteristically, there is cessation of weight gain with onset of the rash. If untreated, failure to thrive will be progressive. Depressed mood is a consistent and notable feature of severe zinc deficiency. Premature infants exhibit excessive crying and difficulty in consolation. Susceptibility to bacterial and candida infections is enhanced and is attributable to a variety of abnormalities of the immune system, especially of T-cell function. Leukocyte function is also zinc-dependent and can be impaired in zinc deficiency states. In the pre-zinc era, acrodermatitis enteropathica characteristically had a downhill course, with a fatal outcome in later infancy or early childhood.

Cases of milder zinc deficiency have been reported in premature infants. Zinc deficiency has, for example, been suggested to be a cause of edema and hypoprotenemia in premature infants,[31] although this has been disputed. In term infants and toddlers, there is considerable evidence from randomized, blinded, controlled studies of zinc supplementation that a mild, growth-limiting zinc deficiency syndrome can occur in some otherwise healthy subjects.[5] One similar study has been undertaken in premature infants with negative results, despite a dietary zinc intake of the control group that was below estimated requirements even assuming that 100% absorption could be achieved.[32] Further research will be necessary to give a clearer understanding of the occurrence of milder zinc deficiency states in the premature infant. Features of zinc deficiency are summarized in Table 9–8.

Diagnosis

The most widely accepted and utilized laboratory assay for the detection of zinc deficiency is a plasma or serum zinc concentration. There are significant limitations to this assay, including inadequate sensitivity and changes with meals that lack definition in early postnatal life when feeds are so frequent. Plasma zinc concentrations below 60 μg/dL are suggestive of zinc deficiency, though some depression of plasma zinc may

TABLE 9–8.

Features of Zinc Deficiency

Growth retardation
Acral and circumorificial dermatitis
Diarrhea
Alopecia
Increased susceptibility to infection with immune
    defects
Neuropsychiatric manifestations
Impaired appetite and possibly hypogeusia
Delayed sexual and lung maturation
Disturbance of vitamin A metabolism

---

result from acute infection and release of interleukin-1. Mild hypozincemia may also be attributable to severe hypoalbuminemia. Levels below 50 μg/dL are more clearly indicative of zinc deficiency; in severe deficiency states, levels typically decline below 30 μg/dL; in mild deficiency states, plasma zinc may remain within the normal range. If there is reason to suspect the possibility of zinc deficiency, a trial of zinc supplementation is justified.

Requirements

Zinc requirements lack clear definition even in the adult. Interpretation of balance data in the adult is complicated by the humans' apparent ability to adapt to widely varying zinc intakes with increases in fractional absorption and decreased endogenous zinc losses.[10, 26] An approximate estimate of the amount of zinc that a growing premature infant needs to absorb is given in Table 9–9. The quantity for new growth is based on in utero accumulation rates.[33] These are a good deal higher than calculated growth requirements in the term infant[34] (Fig 9–4). These calculations assume that the composition of postnatal growth is similar to that at the same postconceptional age in utero. It now appears that the premature infant may have access to some hepatic zinc stores, which could conceivably lower the requirement for exogenous zinc. Thus it is possible, though not proved, that requirements for retention of exogenous zinc may be as low as about 150 μg Zn/kg/day. Obviously, the quantity of dietary zinc required will depend on the fractional absorption. Until zinc absorption at progressive postconceptional ages and with different types of milk feeding has been further clarified, it appears advisable to make a conservative estimate of absorption (e.g., 25 to 30 true absorption or 20 to 25 net absorption for formula-fed infants). This figure is likely to be considerably higher if human milk is fed. Based on these calculations, the dietary requirement of a formula fed premature infant would be approximately 1.25 μg Zn/kg/day.

Factorial calculations for the intravenously fed infant are simpler because the vexing problem of fractional absorption is avoided.[35] Fecal losses average 25 μg Zn/kg/day in the intravenously fed infant,[36] though it is possible that, as in the adult, gastrointestinal losses may be much higher in the presence of abnormal gastrointestinal fluid losses. Urine zinc losses have been found to vary very substantially depending on the commercial source of amino acids used in the infusate. Thus, with Aminosyn (Abbott laboratories) urine zinc losses were found to be no greater than in the enterally-fed premature infant. However, when Freamin 3 (American McGaw) and Vamin (Kavi-Butrum) were used as the source of the amino acids, urine zinc losses in preterm infants averaged 150

TABLE 9–9.

Factorial Estimate of Zinc Requirements in the Premature Infant, μg/kg/day

Factor	Enteral*	Parenteral
Growth	250	250
Urine	40	40†
Feces (endogenous)	75	25
Integumental	(?) 10	(?) 10
Total	375‡	325

* Requirement for absorption.
† Can be much higher.
‡ Corresponding figure for net absorption = 300.

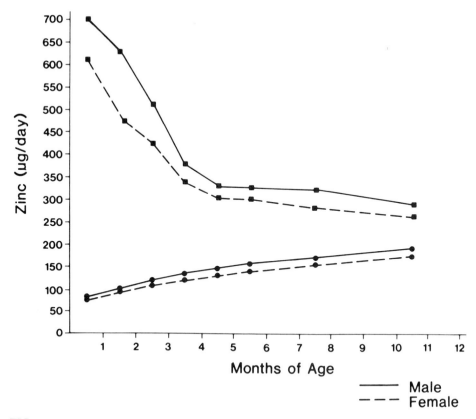

FIG 9-4.
Longitudinal calculations of zinc required for growth (*squares*) and of zinc losses in urine and sweat (*circles*) in infancy. (From Krebs NF, Hambidge KM: Zinc requirements and zinc intakes of breast-fed infants. *Am J Clin Nutr* 1986; 43:288–292. Used by permission.)

to 200 µg/kg/day (K.M. Hambidge and N.F. Krebs, unpublished data). Such losses make a very substantial difference to estimated requirements, and these are difficult to account for until more complete data on the effect of different amino acids infusates are available. The recommended figure of 400 µg Zn/kg body weight/day[35] provides some margin for excessive urine zinc losses. The results of studies based on balance data and on plasma zinc data give some support to this factorial calculation. Thus, premature infants were found to retain 240 µg Zn/kg/day when given 450 µg Zn/kg/day intravenously.[36] Low-birth-weight premature infants were also found to have a decrease in plasma zinc with intakes of 200 µg/kg/day of zinc, but this was not observed with intravenous intakes of 400 µg/kg/day.[37]

Treatment of Zinc Deficiency

A standard recommendation for treatment of suspected mild zinc deficiency is 1 to 2 mg/kg/day of zinc. One milligram of the zinc ion (Zn^{++}) is equivalent to 4.5 mg zinc sulfate ($ZnSO_4$). In cases of severe zinc deficiency attributable to a defect in mammary zinc secretion, human milk can be supplemented with 2 to 4 mg/kg/day of zinc. Increase this dose if necessary. Skin rash should resolve in 2 to 3 days. Zinc supplements can be discontinued when other zinc-containing foods are introduced into the diet. However, in

the treatment of classic acrodermatitis enteropathica, permanent zinc therapy is necessary to achieve and maintain a complete clinical remission. Doses of 20 to 30 mg zinc
are likely to be needed in infants.

Toxicity

Zinc does interfere with copper absorption at the level of the intestinal mucosal
cell.[38] The quantities of zinc used in the treatment of severe zinc deficiency states may
be sufficient to at least mildly impair copper status.[39] Monitoring of serum copper or
ceruloplasmin concentrations is recommended.

Future Research

A great deal of clinically relevant research is clearly needed. Three priority areas
are suggested:

1. Reliable, quantitative data on fractional zinc absorption and endogenous losses
   of zinc in the feces on different feeds and at progressive postconceptional ages.
2. Improved techniques for assessing zinc nutritional status and detecting mild
   zinc deficiency and application of these techniques to define the extent of this
   problem in premature infants.
3. Investigation of the effects of zinc deficiency on intermediary metabolism and
   postnatal growth and development.

COPPER

Copper is thought to be one of the first trace elements to have been incorporated
into biologic systems during evolution and has a vitally important role in many redox
reactions in the body.

Absorption, Metabolism, and Excretion of Copper

In the adult, approximately one third of ingested copper is absorbed in the stomach
and small intestine.[40] Percentage absorption is inversely related to the quantity ingested
and is increased in copper deficiency states. Fractional absorption also depends on the
chemical form and on other dietary constituents. Ascorbic acid inhibits copper absorption, probably by reducing cupric ions to cuprous ions. Copper absorption is enhanced
by fructose. Zinc, iron, and cadmium can interfere with copper absorption at the level of
the intestinal mucosa. Absorbed copper is transported in the portal circulation attached
to albumin and is taken up by the hepatocytes, in which it may be temporarily stored
attached to metallothionein. Large hepatic stores of copper are accumulated by the fetus
during the third trimester.[41] Within the hepatocytes, copper is used for the synthesis of
cuprous proteins, especially ceruloplasmin, which is released 3 days later into the systemic circulation. Because of its chemical reactivity, it appears that copper must be
transported in the circulation tightly bound to this cuproprotein. The rate of ceruloplasmin synthesis is low in the term neonate, gradually increasing to an adult level by about
3 months of age. Circulating levels of ceruloplasmin, and hence of plasma copper, are
correspondingly low. Synthesis of ceruloplasmin in the premature infant is exceptionally

low and increases only slowly so that at 40 weeks postconception, circulating levels of copper and ceruloplasmin are similar to those at delivery in the term infant. In order for copper to be released when ceruloplasmin attaches to its peripheral receptor sites, cupric ions must be reduced to cuprous ions, primarily by ascorbic acid. This may be the reason why the bone lesions of scurvy are so similar to those of copper deficiency.

The term neonate contains about 17 mg copper, of which half to two-thirds is in the liver.[42] Neonatal hepatic copper concentrations are of the order of 200 to 400 μg Cu/g dry weight or 10 to 20 times that of the adult liver. Two-thirds of the neonatal hepatic copper is in a special storage form attached to metallothionein.[42] During the third trimester, the fetus accumulates 50 μg Cu/kg body weight/day. Two-thirds of this copper is located in the liver.

The major route of excretion of endogenous copper is the bile. Copper is complexed in a form that renders it unavailable for reabsorption. Copper excretion in urine of the premature infant is less than 5 μg Cu/kg/day.

Biologic Role

Copper has a major role in aerobic metabolism as an essential component of cytochrome oxidase, the terminal oxidase in the electron transport chain which plays a crucial role in the electron shuttle of aerobic metabolism. Cytochrome oxidase catalyzes the oxidation of reduced cytochrome C by molecular oxygen, which is itself reduced to water. This enzyme is thus necessary for the production of most of the energy of metabolism. Copper-containing monoamine oxidases, including lysyl oxidase, are necessary for the cross-linking of collagen and elastin. Lysyl oxidase catalyzes the oxidative deamination of epsilon amino groups of lysine, a necessary step in the synthesis of desmosine. Dopamine beta hydoxylase is another copper-containing enzyme necessary for the synthesis of catecholamines. Tyrosinase, which catalyzes the first two steps in the oxidation of tyrosine to melanin, is another example of an oxidative cuproenzyme. Both mitochondrial and cytosolic superoxide dismutase enzymes contain copper. These enzymes catalyze the dismutation of superoxide-free radical ions with the formation of molecular oxygen and hydrogen peroxide. Thus, while the cupric ion and some copper enzymes are pro-oxidant, others are very important physiologic antioxidants.

Because it is so highly reactive, copper must be transported through the circulation tightly bound to ceruloplasmin, a glycoprotein that contains 6 copper atoms per molecule (0.32% copper).[43] Ceruloplasmin also appears to have several other roles including ferroxidase activity. In this capacity, ceruloplasmin and another copper enzyme, ferroxidase 2, catalyzes the oxidation of stored ferrous iron to ferric iron, a step that is necessary before binding to transferrin for transport to the bone marrow.

Copper Deficiency

The premature infant is at risk from copper deficiency because of the limited hepatic copper stores. Clinical manifestations of copper deficiency may be evident by 2 to 3 months following delivery.[44, 45] The risk of copper deficiency in premature infants in North America appears to have been greatly diminished by steps to provide adequate copper supplements in formulas consumed by premature infants. Several case reports have cited clinical copper deficiency in infants fed intravenously without the addition of copper to the infusate.[46] Chronic diarrhea or fat malabsorption aggravates the risk of copper deficiency. Characteristically, infants with Menkes' steely-hair syndrome, an X-linked inborn error of copper metabolism, are born prematurely.

The principle features of copper deficiency are an hypochromic anemia that is unresponsive to iron therapy, neutropenia, and osteoporosis. The bone marrow exhibits megaloblastic changes and vacuolization of the erythroid series. Iron deposits may be seen by electron microscopy in mitochondria and in some of the cytoplasmic vacuoles in red blood cell precursors. Iron stores in the intestinal mucosa, reticuloendothelial system, and liver are increased. The anemia is initially hypoferremic, but later becomes hyperferremic because of a decreased uptake of transferrin-bound iron by the developing erythrocytes. Anemia is attributed in part to lack of copper-containing ferroxidases, including ceruloplasmin. There is maturation arrest of the granulocytic series.

The third major feature of copper deficiency is the bone lesions[47] attributed to a lack of copper-containing amine oxidases necessary for the cross-linking of bone collagen. Early radiologic findings are osteoporosis and retarded bone age. Findings in the established case are increased density of the provisional bone of calcification and cupping, with sickle-shaped spurs in the metaphyseal region. Other features include periosteal layering and submetaphyseal and rib fractures. Reported clinical findings of copper deficiency in premature infants also include pallor, decreased pigmentation of skin and hair, prominent superficial veins, skin lesions similar to those of seborrheic dermatitis, failure to thrive, diarrhea, and hepatosplenomegaly. Features suggestive of central nervous system involvement are hypotonia, a lack of interest in outside surroundings, psychomotor retardation, lack of visual responses, and apneic episodes. The incidence of various clinical manifestations in one recent report are depicted in Figure 9–5.[48]

In Menkes' steely-hair syndrome, there is an inherited defect in the intracellular transport of copper, affecting most if not all tissues apart from the liver.[49] This results in

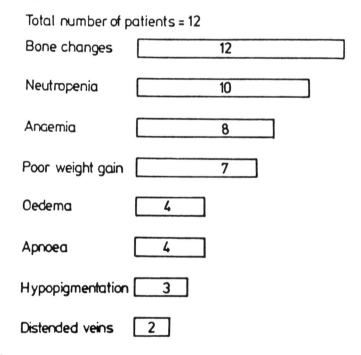

Total number of patients = 12

Bone changes	12
Neutropenia	10
Anaemia	8
Poor weight gain	7
Oedema	4
Apnoea	4
Hypopigmentation	3
Distended veins	2

FIG 9–5.
Clinical features of copper deficiency in the preterm infant. (From Sutton AM: Copper deficiency in the preterm infant of very low birthweight. *Arch Dis Child* 1985; 60:644–651. Used by permission.)

a profound copper deficiency disorder that cannot be corrected by the parenteral administration of copper. These infants have severe and progressive neurologic disease, which becomes clinically apparent by about the 2d month of postnatal life. Both the neurologic disease and hypothermia have been attributed to decreased activity of cytochrome oxidase. A variety of defects of connective tissue are also apparent, including aneurysms of the aorta and bladder diverticular. For unexplained reasons, anemia and neutropenia are not characteristic features.

Diagnosis

The differential diagnosis of copper deficiency includes findings of scurvy, rickets, and nonaccidental trauma. With more advanced skeletal changes, copper deficiency can be differentiated from rickets by the increased density of the provisional zone of calcification and the absence of metaphyseal fraying. Differentiation of the metaphyseal fractures of copper deficiency from those of nonaccidental trauma includes the symmetric nature of the fractures of copper deficiency and other radiologic signs.

Laboratory confirmation of suspected copper deficiency in the premature infant is problematic. Erythrocyte superoxide dismutase activity remains a research tool at this time. Plasma copper concentrations are normally very low in the premature infant, averaging about 35 μg/dl prior to 35 weeks' postconception, 40 to 45 μg/dl for 35 to 38 weeks; 50 to 59 μg/dl from 39 to 42 weeks; 65 μg/dl at 43 to 44 weeks, and 75 μg/dl at 45 weeks. Levels that are even lower than these may be seen in association with copper deficiency.[48]

Copper Requirements

Calculations of copper requirements in early postnatal life are complicated by inadequate understanding of the rate of release and efficiency of utilization of neonatal hepatic copper stores.[50] These stores are effective in protecting the term infant from copper deficiency for several months even when intake is very low. The lower the gestational age at delivery, the smaller are the hepatic stores. However, even at 26 to 28 weeks gestation, 1 to 2 mg of hepatic storage copper is probably present, and the very premature infant does not appear to be at any risk of copper deficiency until 2 months or so of postnatal age. Because of the more limited copper stores in the premature infant and because of evidence of poor absorption (10% to 15%) of copper from formulas, it is recommended that the premature infant receive 100 to 120 μg Cu/kg/day. The premature infant fed with own mother's milk will probably ingest only 30 to 40 μg Cu/kg/day; however, because of superior absorption, this is quite adequate.

Calculations of intravenous copper requirements for the premature infant are given in Table 9–10.[35] The major uncertainty is again the amount of copper supplied from hepatic stores. In practice, however, 20 μg/kg/day appears to be quite adequate, and should be reduced or withheld in the presence of cholestatic disease. Once again, the cupric ion is a highly reactive pro-oxidant which, when given in the intravenous infusate, is introduced into the systemic circulation without being tightly bound to ceruloplasmin. Hence, there should be considerable caution with the administration of intravenous copper.

Nutritional copper deficiency in premature infants can be treated with 200 to 600 μg Cu/day provided as a 1% solution of copper sulfate.

TABLE 9–10.

Estimate of Intravenous Copper Requirement for Premature Infant (μgCu/kg/day)

Copper accumulation by fetus in utero*	60
Copper stored in liver*	40
Therefore requirements for growth*	20
urine losses = 5	
fecal losses = 10†	
Total endogenous losses§	15
physiological requirement (20+15)§	35
Assumed minimal supply from	15
fetal hepatic stores‡	

*During third trimester.
†Higher in cases of biliary drainages or jejunostomy.
‡Estimated, for example, as follows: 26-week fetal liver contains 3 mg copper; assumed that two thirds is storage copper which is released over 2-month period and that there is 50% utilization of released copper. This particular example would provide 17 μg/Cu/day. Corresponding figures at 32 weeks are approximately 5 mg copper in fetal liver, providing 28 μg/Cu/day.
§Intravenous Cu requirement.

Toxicity

Acute ingestion of quantities of copper that are 1,000 times the daily requirement can have a fatal outcome. Copper intoxication has occurred from consumption of contaminated drinking water with a copper concentration of 2 to 8 mg/L. Contamination of cow's milk with copper from brass containers has been cited as the major environmental factor in the cause of Indian childhood cirrhosis. It has been calculated that cow's milk stored in brass utensils would supply approximately 400 μg/kg/day of copper to an infant.[51] This disease may be an example of a genetic–nutrient interaction. Acute copper poisoning has toxic effects on the liver, kidneys, heart, and central nervous system, and causes intravascular hemolysis. These changes may all be attributable to oxidative damage from the free cupric ion. Chronic copper toxicity may cause cirrhosis.

Formulas providing 300 μg Cu/100 kcal have been fed to premature infants without evidence of adverse effects. However, it is advisable to restrict the copper content of formulas to no more than 200 μg/100 kcal.[52] In practice, this is considerably more than is ever needed.

Future Research Needs

The features of copper deficiency now recognized in the human are not necessarily the only ones of importance. For example, chronic mild copper deficiency in the rat dam before and during the reproductive cycle and then maintained in the offspring after weaning results in histologic lesions in the aorta that are indistinguishable from those of atherosclerosis.[51] The copper deficiency is sufficiently mild that plasma copper concentrations do not drop below the normal range. It is not known if this observation has any parallel in the human, though there is some concern that copper intakes in the adult, including the pregnant and lactating woman, may not be optimal. This is an important area for future research.

Among other research needs are improved laboratory indices of copper status. In particular, the value of superoxide dismutase activity should be more clearly defined.

SELENIUM

Interest in the biologic role of selenium did not develop until this century and then initially focused on selenium toxicity, with the discovery of both acute and chronic forms of selenosis in grazing animals in Nebraska and Wyoming. It was not until 1958 that selenium deficiency was shown to be responsible for muscular dystrophy in lambs and calves, a problem that occurs in many areas of the world. Within the past decade, human selenium deficiency has been identified.

Selenium Metabolism

Fractional absorption of dietary selenium is relatively high, averaging about 60%.[53] From some foods, for example, human milk, absorption is as high as 80%. Absorption and bioavailability depend on the chemical form. For example, when selenium is added as a supplement to formula, bioavailability is greatest from selenite and least favorable from selenomethionine and selenocysteine[54]; in contrast, in the postabsorptive state, absorption of selenomethionine is greater. Distribution of selenomethionine within the body is different, with a considerably greater percentage being taken up by skeletal muscle. As the biologic significance of this difference in distribution is poorly understood, it is advisable to use the selenite or selenate form both enterally and intravenously.[53] Homeostasis of selenium metabolism is controlled by the kidney. Urine selenium excretion reflects recent selenium intake. Highest body selenium concentrations are found in liver, tooth enamel, and nails, but the majority of selenium is in skeletal muscle. The total adult body content of selenium in North America is about 15 mg, but in New Zealand, where selenium intakes are lower, body content is only about 6 mg.

Biologic Roles

The one clearly established biologic role for selenium is as an essential component of glutathione peroxidase (GPX), which catalyzes the reduction of hydrogen peroxide to water by the addition of reducing equivalents derived from glutathione.[55] This enzyme is also capable of catalyzing the reduction of a wide range of lipid hydroperoxides to the corresponding hydroxy acids. This becomes important when peroxides of unsaturated fatty acids are released from the cell membrane by the action of phospholipase A_2. In the absence of dietary selenium, when GPX levels are low, accumulation of fatty acid peroxide will lead to the formation of fatty acid peroxyl radicals or oxy radicals under the catalytic activity of iron. Thus selenium is an important nutrient in the body's defenses against free radicals.[56]

Selenium Deficiency

Selenium deficiency is now recognized as the major etiologic factor in Keshan disease, an often fatal dilated (congestive) cardiomyopathy, affecting children and young women in China a large geographic area from the northeast toward the southwest.[57] Histologically, there are focal areas of myocyte loss and fibrous replacement scattered throughout the ventricular subepicardium. The incidence and severity of Keshan disease have been dramatically reduced following public health measures to provide selenium supplementation in the affected geographic areas.[58] A few similar case reports concern patients maintained on long-term intravenous nutrition in North America.[59] Skeletal my-opathies have also been attributable to selenium deficiency in these circumstances.[60] Milder cases of selenium deficiency have been reported recently in parenterally fed infants and children.[61] Clinical manifestations were a macrocytosis and loss of hair pigment. Selenium deficiency may also have been an important cause of morbidity in some infants suffering from protein energy malnutrition.[62]

It was suggested more than 10 years ago that selenium deficiency may contribute to hemolytic anemia in premature infants.[63] Selenium intakes and selenium concentrations are generally lower in formula-fed infants[58] and have been reported to be very low in infants fed special formulas for inborn errors of metabolism.[64] The practical significance of these observations is not certain, but there is currently increasing concern that selenium deficiency may be of practical importance in the premature infant. Selenium concentrations in serum and erythrocytes from cord blood of preterm infants do not differ from those of infants born at term. However, in very low birth weight infants, selenium concentrations dropped very rapidly within 72 hours of delivery.[65] Particularly, low plasma selenium concentrations, which persist for many weeks, have been found in premature infants who develop bronchopulmonary dysplasia. However, it is not known whether selenium deficiency may contribute to the onset or severity of the disease processes resulting from oxygen damage in the very low birth weight premature infant.

Diagnosis

Whole blood, erythrocyte, and plasma (serum) selenium concentrations are depressed in selenium deficiency states. Activity of GPX in erythrocytes and serum is also reduced. These laboratory parameters of selenium status vary widely according to age and geographical location (i.e., geochemical environments). Representative values are depicted in Table 9–11. Though average adult blood selenium levels in North America vary by 100% between populations with "medium" and "high" selenium exposure, whole blood GPX activity is the same. On the other hand, GPX activity is lower in New Zealand, where it is positively correlated with blood selenium.[66] Plasma selenium in cord blood averages 40 to 50 ng/mL (0.5 to 0.63 μM). In breast-fed infants, or in infants fed a formula containing a similar quantity of selenium (i.e., about 20 μg/L) in North America, levels increase to an average of 75 to 100 mg/mL by 6 to 12 months.[53, 67] However, in some countries, selenium intake and selenium levels are much lower[68] and GPX activity correlates with plasma selenium levels.[69] Many plasma selenium levels below 40 ng/mL and even below 10 ng/mL have been documented in subjects who have had no overt signs of selenium deficiency. However, selenium levels below 40 ng/mL and especially below 10 ng/mL have also been associated with clinical evidence of selenium deficiency.

TABLE 9–11.

Representative Examples of Plasma Selenium Concentrations (ng/ml)

Normal adults (USA)	100
Normal adults (New Zealand)	60
Premature infants*	40–80
Macrocytosis; hair changes	35–40
Cardiomyopathy (Keshans Disease)	<10

*Depends on selenium intake.

Requirements

Selenium requirements have been especially difficult to define in adults because of the outstanding extent to which long-term adaptation can take place to low selenium intakes. Thus, adults in New Zealand, though exhibiting lower blood selenium levels, have no recognized ill-effects from selenium intakes that are extremely low by standards in most parts of the world, including North America. It has been calculated that North Americans require about 70 μg Se/day, whereas only 20 μg Se/day is needed to maintain balance in young New Zealand women. However, from studies in China, including measurements of glutathione peroxidase activity, it has been concluded that the minimal requirement for adults is 50 μg Se/day.[70] In infants, requirements have been calculated at 2.5 to 3.0 μg Se/kg/day.

Selenium intake of fully breast-fed infants in North America averages about 20 μg Se/day in a country where maternal intakes are neither exceptionally high nor low. Intakes moderately lower than this (1.4 μg Se/kg/day) are associated with depressed plasma selenium concentrations. Selenium intakes have been reported to be lower in preterm infants, with an average intake of only 7 μg/day at 3 months postnatal age.[71] It seems likely that most formulas in North America will be supplemented routinely with selenium in the very near future.

Because of the high absorption of selenium, estimates for intravenous requirements are only a little lower than those for oral requirements. Recommendations for infants fed intravenously are 2 μg Se/kg/day. If renal function is impaired, it may be judicious to lower this level. Selenate is probably the chemical form of choice for intravenous administration.

Toxicity

Although excess selenium can cause serious economic consequences in agriculture, chronic toxicity of selenium does not appear to be a major problem in humans. Loss of hair, brittleness of fingernails, garlic odor, a high incidence of dental caries, increased fatigue, and irritability were reported to be signs of selenosis in an early survey of South Dakota in which urinary selenium excretion was elevated.

Research Needs

Research is required to determine the clinical significance of selenium deficiency in free radical–mediated damage in the premature infant in the first few days and weeks of postnatal life. Meanwhile, there does not appear to be any logical reason to delay in supplementing formulas with selenium up to the level found in human milk in this country.

IODIDE

Historical Background

Endemic cretenism and its association with goiter have been known in Europe for many centuries. Iodine was first employed for the treatment of goiter early in the 19th century. At the end of that century iodine was discovered in the thyroid gland from which thyroxine was crystallized early in the 20th century. Also early in this century, it was shown that small amounts of iodine prevented endemic goiter. More recently the full spectrum of fetal iodine deficiency disorders has been more clearly recognized,[72, 73] and in the 1970s transient neonatal hypothyroidism[74] was first identified.

Iodine Metabolism

Iodine is rapidly reduced to iodide in the gut, and at least 50% of iodide is absorbed in the upper small bowel. Absorbed iodide is cleared from the plasma primarily by the thyroid gland and the kidney. In the thyroid gland, iodide is oxidized and is attached to tyrosyl residues of thyroglobulin. Monoiodotyrosine and di-iodotyrosine are converted to iodothyronine through another oxidative step. The thyroid gland normally stores enough hormone to last several months. In conditions of iodide deficiency, secretion of thyrotropic hormone (TSH) by the pituitary is increased. This promotes iodide uptake by the thyroid and may lead to hyperplasia and hypertrophy of the gland. Iodide is excreted by way of the kidneys. Shortly after birth, circulating levels of TSH temporarily increase and, in response, levels of T_4 and T_3 also increase. Levels of T_4 and T_3 are lower in the cord blood of the premature infant, and these postnatal changes are of smaller magnitude. Levels remain in the hypothyroid range in the first weeks of postnatal life and then increase, corresponding to increased synthesis of thyroid-binding globulin.

Biologic Role

The only clearly demonstrated function of iodide is as a component of the thyroid hormones. Iodide may have a direct role in early fetal development; however, effects thought to be attributable to iodide may be attributable to maternal thyroid hormones.[75] The physiologic effects of the thyroid hormones are primarily due to T_3. Most of the T_3 that appears in the plasma is derived from peripheral deiodination of T_4.

Fetal Iodine Deficiency

It is now known that maternal iodine deficiency during pregnancy can have a spectrum of adverse effects on fetal development that can be prevented by treating maternal iodine deficiency prior to pregnancy. Endemic goiter occurs in the offspring when maternal iodine intake is less than 20 μg/day. Some cases of endemic goiter have evidence of classic endemic cretinism. Maternal iodine excretion (intake) is less than 15 μg/day for this to occur. There are two well-defined clinical presentations of endemic cretinism, neurological and hypothyroid or myxedematous (Table 9–12). The myxedematous form is typically seen in Zaire and used to be seen in various European countries. Some cases[76] in China are of this type. In a number of other geographic areas, deaf-mutism and cerebral dyplegia occur as characteristic manifestations of the neurologic form. Milder impairment of brain development, especially motor function, appear to be much more common in areas of endemic goiter than in frank endemic cretinism. The pathogenesis of the neurologic disorder remains unclear, and the possibility of a direct effect of iodine deficiency on the fetus during the 3d trimester has been considered. Endemic cretinism no longer exists in North America, but on a global basis is still a major public health problem. It occurs especially in isolated mountainous regions where the iodine has been leached from the soil. China, Indonesia, the Indian subcontinent, and certain South American countries are prominent among those that have still not developed adequate preventive programs.

TABLE 9–12.

Features in Neurologic and Hypothyroid Cretinism

Feature	Neurologic Cretin	Hypothyroid Cretin
Mental retardation	Present, often severe	Present, often severe
Deaf-mutism	Usually present	Absent
Cerebral diplegia	Often present	Absent
Stature	Usually normal, occasionally slight growth retardation	Severe growth retardation
General features	No physical signs of hypothyroidism	Coarse dry skin, protuberant abdomen with umbilical hernia; large tongue
Reflexes	Excessively brisk	Delayed relaxation
Electrocardiogram	Normal	Small voltage QRS complexes and other abnormalities of hypothyroidism
X-ray limbs	Normal	Epiphyseal dysgenesis
Effect of thyroid hormones	No effect	Improvement

Neonatal Hypothyroidism

In regions of endemic goiter, milder degrees of iodine deficiency in utero and after delivery may have detrimental effects on growth and intellectual development. Levels of T_3 and T_4 are lower in young infants from endemic goiter areas than from nonendemic goiter areas even when there is no evidence of goiter. Levels in the preterm infant are lower than those of the term infant, both in endemic goiter and nonendemic goiter areas.

Neonatal primary hypothyroidism can sometimes be transient. This condition appears to be extremely rare in North America but is a good deal more common in several European countries where iodide intakes are not as high as those in North America. The majority of the isolated case reports in North America have been secondary to the administration of maternal antithyroid drugs or of iodine medications. Maternal iodine overload is a recognized cause of neonatal hypothyroidism. Temporary neonatal hypothyroidism occurs most commonly in premature infants, especially those who are acutely ill with the respiratory distress syndrome. In European studies, serum levels of TSH and of thyroid hormone were normal in core blood. Hormonal levels dropped quickly after birth, however, together with markedly elevated TSH concentrations. This appears to be a multifactorial syndrome resulting both from immaturity of the newborn thyroid gland and from external factors including iodine deficiency or iodine excess. It is recommended that if this condition is diagnosed it should be treated promptly with iodide and T_3 therapy. In Germany, it has been reported that T_4 and T_3 administration on admission to the neonatal intensive care unit significantly lowered mortality rates.[77] This was thought to result from accelerated production of surfactant in the lungs.

Requirements

Oral requirements of iodide in the infant, including the premature infant, are no more than 2 to 4 μg iodide/day. Both human milk and cow's milk in North America contain very substantial quantities of iodide, and neither breast-fed nor formula-fed premature infants are at risk from iodide deficiency. When hypothyroidism occurs it is due to a metabolic abnormality in the thyroid gland rather than to iodine deficiency. Hence, while thyroid replacement therapy may be required in some neonates, iodine supplements are not indicated.

In general, it appears that the intravenously fed infant acquires sufficient iodide accidentally from dressings, antiseptic lotions used on the skin, and so forth. However, biochemical evidence of iodide deficiency has been reported in an infant on long-term parenteral nutrition, and it is advisable to supplement the intravenous infusate with 1 to 2 μg iodide/kg/body weight/day.

Toxicity

Though iodide intakes of up to 1,000 μg/day in children have found to be devoid of harmful effects, there has been recent concern about the potential dangers of excess iodide. It appears that 4% of individuals are particularly sensitive to iodide excess, which can cause hypothyroidism.

FLUORIDE

Fluoride is of established value in the prevention of dental carries and may also have beneficial effect on the skeletal system. No specific recommendations for fluoride supplementation have been made for premature infants. However, prematurity is associated with an increased incidence of dental caries, and there appears to be particular reason for ensuring adequate fluoride supplementation in premature infants. It is not clear to what extent, if any, that fluoride will exert a beneficial effect on nonerrupted teeth, or what if any benefits can be conferred by systemic fluoride as opposed to the local effect in the oral cavity. However, it is prudent to provide 0.1 mg fluoride/kg body weight/day up to a maximum of 0.25 mg fluoride/day[78] to premature infants, other than those who are fed with formula that has been made up with water in a fluoridated area. Infant formulas and packaged water marketed for making up powdered formula provide less than 0.3 mg fluoride per liter.

MANGANESE

Historical Background

The need of manganese in mammals was demonstrated in 1931 when it was shown to be necessary for growth in mice and reproduction in rats. Manganese was one of the first of the "newer" trace elements to be added to synthetic formulas and intravenous infusates, although human manganese deficiency has not been convincingly documented.

Metabolism

Adults absorb only about 3% of an ingested dose of isotopically labeled $MnCl_2$, and this low level does not change when the quantity of carrier is altered. Ten days later 1.5% of the ingested dose is retained by adults, but newborns retain 8% and premature infants 16%.[79] Manganese absorption is especially high in very early postnatal life in the mouse, and little manganese is excreted at that stage.[80] Dietary manganese absorption does depend on the level of manganese intake and also on the type of diet. When various milks and infant formulas are fed to adults, the percentage absorption ranged from 1% when given with soy formula up to 9% with human milk. Absorption from cow's milk and from humanized cow's milk formulas ranged from 3% to 6% but dropped to 1.5% with iron-fortified formulas.[81] Much higher percentage absorption of manganese from milks and formulas has been observed in rat pups with manganese retention from human milk exceeding 80%. Comparable data for the human infant are lacking.

Manganese is excreted almost entirely through the bile. When manganese intake is increased, there is a decrease in the percentage absorption and an increase in biliary excretion. Intestinal mucosa and the liver together provide effective homeostatic control of manganese status in normal circumstances, although it is not clear that this pertains to premature infants.

Physiologic Role

Mitochondrial superoxide dismutase and pyruvate carboxylase are manganese metalloenzymes. Manganese is required for the synthesis of mucopolysaccharides through the manganese-dependent enzymes polymerase and galactotransferrase. Manganese deficiency in various animal species leads to impaired skeletal development and ataxia. The latter is due to defective formation of the otoliths in fetal life. Abnormalities in carbohydrate and liver metabolism have also been documented.

Manganese Deficiency

Human manganese deficiency has not been described convincingly apart from a case of one volunteer on an experimental synthetic diet from which manganese was inadvertently omitted. Features attributed to manganese deficiency in this case were hypercholesterolemia, depressed levels of clotting proteins in the plasma, weight loss, and slow growth of hair and nails. The lack of evidence of manganese deficiency in circumstances in which many other trace elements have been identified, especially intravenous nutrition, may be attributable to the widespread use of manganese supplements from an early stage in the history of synthetic diets and formulas. No established laboratory criteria are available for the assessment of manganese status. Low serum manganese levels have been reported in some diabetic and epileptic children, and a negative manganese balance has been observed in children with pancreatic insufficiency. The clinical significance of these observations is obscure.

Manganese Requirements

Manganese intake of the fully breast-fed infant is approximately 0.5 μg Mn/kg/day.[82] Because of differences in fractional absorption, it is likely that the manganese requirements of the formula-fed infant are an order of magnitude higher than this. Many formulas provide even more manganese, and this applies especially to soy formulas with which a higher concentration of manganese is naturally associated. Soy formulas are likely to provide approximately 50 μg Mn/kg/day. Though no toxic effects have been observed on these higher intakes, no careful examination of the safety of such intakes in premature infants has been reported. In view of the evidence for a higher fractional absorption in premature infants and the indications from an animal model that excretion may be very limited, considerable care is recommended in providing manganese to very low birth weight premature infants. Pending further information, a maximum figure of

50 μg/kg/day from a soy formula and 10 μg/kg/day from a cow's milk–based formula is suggested.

A supplement sufficient to provide 1 μg Mn/kg/day intravenously appears to be adequate for patients fed parenterally. Larger quantities than this are discouraged in the premature infant. In parenterally fed patients who develop cholestatic liver disease marked hypermanganesemia has been documented.[83] In the face of cholestatic liver disease, suspension of intravenous manganese supplement is recommended. The background manganese contamination in the infusate is sufficient to maintain serum manganese concentrations over a period of many months.

CHROMIUM

Trace quantities of chromium in rat diets were found in the 1950s to be necessary for normal glucose tolerance. The results of subsequent research were consistent with the hypothesis that chromium acted as a cofactor for insulin while facilitating the initial attachment of insulin to peripheral receptors. However, chromium has not been detected in these receptors.

The results of several studies in the 1960s and 1970s suggested that human chromium deficiency may be a cause of impaired glucose tolerance, especially in the elderly and in patients on prolonged parenteral nutrition. Chromium deficiency was also reported in infants with protein energy malnutrition. In general, more recent studies have failed to confirm earlier observations, and the importance of chromium in human nutrition remains uncertain.

Results of earlier tissue analyses indicated that tissue chromium concentrations are relatively high in the term neonate and decrease progressively during the life cycle. Relatively low chromium concentrations were observed in the plasma and hair of infants born prematurely and those with intrauterine growth retardation. More recent advances in analytical techniques for the measurement of chromium in biologic samples has led to major revisions in normal values for tissue chromium concentrations. Unfortunately no data are available on the premature infant or in changes in tissue chromium concentrations through the life cycle using modern analytic methodology.

There have been two careful studies of zinc concentrations in human milk with modern analytic techniques. The concentration averaged 0.3 μg Cr/L, and the range is quite small. Thus the chromium intake of the breast-fed infant is approximately 0.05 μg Cr/kg/day. In reaching tentative estimates of chromium requirements of the formula-fed infant, it is advisable to assume that absorption is considerably less than from human milk. Thus the recommended intake of 2.5 μg Cr/kg/day.

MOLYBDENUM

Molybdenum enzymes that have been identified in the human are xanthine oxidase, which is involved in purine metabolism, and sulfite oxidase. One case of human molybdenum deficiency has been described in an adult on long-term total parenteral nutrition. Features included tachycardia, tachpnea, vomiting, and central scotomas, with rapid progression to coma. There was intolerance to infused amino acids, and methionine levels were elevated. Serum uric acid and urine excretion of sulphate were decreased. The clinical and biochemical response to 2.5 μg Mo/kg/day in the infusate was excellent.

The concentration of molybdenum in human milk is about 2 μg/L. Thus the infant receiving human milk has an intake of approximately 0.3 μg Mo/kg/day. This level of intake is probably adequate for the premature infant as well as the term infant. However, data on tissue concentration and fetal accumulation are inadequate. Intravenously, an intake of 0.25 μg Mo/kg/day is probably adequate. Intravenous molybdenum supplements are recommended only with long-term intravenous nutrition. Excess molybdenum interferes with copper metabolism.

ALUMINUM

Aluminum is not thought to have any physiologic role. However, there has been considerable recent concern about aluminum toxicity, particularly in dialysis patients, but also, more recently, in association with intravenous feeding.[84] Some concern has also been expressed about aluminum concentrations in infant formulas. Though these concerns are unsubstantiated, the kidneys of the premature infant may be especially limited in their ability to excrete this metal. Hence, the premature infant may be especially vulnerable to aluminum toxicity.

Aluminum contamination of dialysis fluids has been a major cause of encephalopathy and osteomalasia and also has been implicated as a cause of microcytic hypochromic anemia. Intravenous infusates are contaminated with aluminum to variable extents, and marked aluminum accumulation in bone has occurred after as little as 3 weeks of parenteral nutrition in infants. Aluminum concentrations vary widely among the different components of intravenous infusates and among lots from different manufacturers. Components of the parenteral infusate that have been found to be associated with high levels of aluminum include calcium and phosphorus salts. Twenty-five percent albumin has also been found to contain considerable aluminum. Until standards for aluminum contamination of these products are enforced, the potential for aluminum toxicity will remain, especially in the premature infant, the infant or child with impaired renal function, and the patient on prolonged parenteral nutrition.

IRON

The vulnerability of the premature infant to anemia has been recognized since the 1920s. In general this anemia is more pronounced than occurs in the term infant. In contrast to the 3d-trimester fetus in utero, erythropoiesis decreases abruptly after birth in the premature infant, and the hemoglobin concentration declines at a rate of approximately 1 g/dL/wk during the first 1 to 3 months of postnatal life.[85] The extent of the early "physiologic anemia of prematurity" depends on the gestational age. This decline is considered to reflect decreased needs because of improved tissue oxygenation in the extrauterine environment. This early anemia is not affected by the administration of iron. After 1 to 3 months, postnatal erythropoiesis commences and total body hemoglobin increases. Because of a rapidly expanding blood volume, this may not be reflected in an immediate increase in circulating hemoglobin concentrations. If adequate iron is not given postnatally, late anemia of prematurity will start to develop sometime after 2 months of postnatal life.[85] Iron depletion will be reflected by a decrease in serum ferritin and disappearance of stainable iron from the bone marrow. Red cell protoporphyrin concentrations increase and mean cell volume will decrease. This will be followed by a decline in hemoglobin concentration.

Effects of Iron Deficiency

Effects of iron deficiency are not limited to those of iron deficiency anemia.[86] In addition to its key role in hemoglobin and myoglobin, iron-dependent enzymes are involved in several key metabolic pathways including DNA synthesis, mitochondrial electron transport, catecholamine metabolism, neurotransmission, and detoxification.

Rats deprived of iron during early life have reduced amounts of non-heme iron in the brain. There is accumulation of serotonin and 5-hydroxyindol compounds, which have been reported to produce drowsiness and decreased attentiveness. The history of studies of cognitive development and attentiveness in infants and toddlers as related to iron status is complex. There is evidence, however, that impaired cognitive development can be attributed not only to iron deficiency anemia but to milder degrees of iron deficiency in subjects who are not yet anemic.

The role of iron in resistance to infection is complex. On the one hand, free iron is essential for the multiplication of all bacteria and excess iron is thought to enhance the risk of gram-negative septicemia. On the other hand iron is necessary for the normal development and functional integrity of the immune system. There is some evidence that iron deficiency impairs immune responses mediated by the lymphocytes and granulocytes.

Other functional deficits resulting from iron deficiency[86] include decreased exercise tolerance. Anorexia and failure to thrive appear to be other possible complications of iron deficiency.

Iron Requirements

Factors determining iron requirements and the risk of iron deficiency in infants include:

1. Birth weight. The fetus contains approximately 75 mg Fe/kg body weight.
2. Initial hemoglobin. The bulk of the fetal iron is present as hemoglobin. One gram of hemoglobin contains 3.4 mg Fe. If the initial hemoglobin is 17 g/dL, hemoglobin iron will account for 58 mg Fe/kg body weight. A substantial percentage of this hemoglobin will be released and stored during the first 2 months of postnatal life.
3. Initial iron stores. Iron stores in the liver and spleen at birth amount to approximately 10 mg/kg. The remaining body iron, (7 mg/kg) is in the tissues.
4. Rate of postnatal growth.
5. Postnatal blood losses.
6. Infections. Even a mild infections can increase iron requirements.

Premature infants weighing 1,000 to 2,000 g require 2 mg supplemental iron per kilogram body weight as soon as the birth weight has doubled, that is, at about 2 months of postnatal age. This iron may be administered either as ferrous sulfate or given in an iron-fortified formula. The supplement should be continued for 12 to 15 months. If the birth weight is less than 1,000 g, this supplement should be increased to 3 to 4 mg Fe/kg/day. If the initial hemoglobin is less than 17 g/dL or a substantial blood loss has occurred without replacement, the iron supplement should be started at 2 to 4 weeks. However, unless there are specific indications, it is recommended strongly that an iron-supplemented formula or an iron supplement not be commenced before the birth weight is doubled.

Iron has powerful oxidant properties and can enhance the demand for antioxidants, especially vitamin E. The vitamin E status of premature infants is especially liable to be precarious unless vitamin E supplements are given. It is important to give a vitamin E supplement with these iron supplements if the infant is fed with human milk.

Iron requirements for the intravenously fed premature infant have been calculated at approximately 200 μg Fe/kg/day. Again, this is not generally necessary before 2 months of postnatal age. A diluted form of inferon has been used in TPN infusates in doses of 1 to 2 mg/L in some centers for several years. However, there have been no detailed reports of compatibility with the other constituents of the infusate. Such additions of iron should therefore be made with considerable caution pending more detailed evaluation.

Acknowledgment

Unpublished data included in this chapter were gained under support of the National Institutes of Health grant DK-12432 and RR69.

REFERENCES

1. Underwood EJ, Mertz W, Smith JC Jr, et al: *Trace Elements in Human and Animal Nutrition,* ed 5, vol 1, San Diego, Academic Press, 1987.
2. Hambidge KM, Casey CE, Krebs NF, et al: *Trace Elements in Human and Animal Nutrition,* ed 5, vol 2, Orlando, Academic Press, 1986.
3. Shyy-Hwa T, Hurley LS: Effect of dietary calcium deficiency during pregnancy on zinc mobilization in intact and parathyroidectomized rats. *J Nutr* 1975; 105:220–225.
4. Hambidge KM, Krebs NF, Walravens A: Growth velocity of young children receiving a dietary zinc supplement. *Nutr Res* 1985; 1:306–316.
5. Walravens PA, Koepfer DM, Hambidge KM: Zinc supplementation in infants with a nutritional pattern of failure to thrive: a Double blind controlled study. *Pediatrics,* 1989; 83:532–538.
6. Matsehe JW, Phillips SF, Malagelade JR, et al: Recovery of dietary iron and zinc from the proximal intestine of healthy man: Studies of different meals and supplements. *Am J Clin Nutr* 1980; 33:1946–1953.
7. Turnlund JR, King JC, Keyes WR, et al: A stable isotope study of zinc absorption in young men: Effects of phytate and x-cellulose. *Am J Clin Nutr* 1984; 40:1071–1077.
8. Sandstrom B, Cederblad A, Lonnerdal B: Zinc absorption from human milk, cow's milk, and infant formulas. *Am J Dis Child* 1983; 137:726–729.
9. Ehrenkranz RA, Gettner PA, Nelli CM, et al: Zinc and copper nutritional studies in very low birthweight infants: Comparison of stable isotopic extrinsic tag and chemical balance methods. *Pediatr Res* 1989; 26:298–307.
10. Peirce PL, Hambidge KM, Fennessey PV, et al: Zinc absorption in premature infants, in Hurley LS (ed): *Trace Elements in Man and Animals,* No 6. New York, Plenum Publishing Corp, 1988, pp 215–218.
11. Cousins RJ: Absorption, transport, and hepatic metabolism of copper and zinc: Special reference to metallothionein and ceruloplasmin. *Physiol Rev* 1985; 65:238–309.
12. Jackson MF, Jones DA, Edwards RHT: Zinc homeostasis in man: Studies using a new stable isotope-dilution technique. *Br J Nutr* 1984; 51:199–208.

13. McCormick CC, Menard MP, Cousins RJ: Induction of hepatic metallothionein by feeding zinc to rats of depleted zinc status. *Am J Physiol* 1981; 240:E414–E421.

14. Wastney ME, Aamodt RL, Rumble WF, et al: Kinetic analysis of zinc metabolism and its regulation in normal humans. *Am J Physiol* 1986; 251:R398–R408.

15. Widdowson EM, Chan H, Harrison GE, et al: Accumulation of Cu, Zn, Mn, Cr and Co in the human liver before birth. *Biol Neonate* 1972; 20:360–367.

16. Foote JW, Delves HT: Albumin bound and alpha-2 macroglobulin bound zinc concentrations in the sera of healthy adults. *Clin Pathol* 1984; 37:1050–1054.

17. Hambidge KM, Goodall M, Stahl C, et al: Post-prandial and daily changes in plasma zinc. *J of Trace Elements in Health and Disease.* 1989; 3:55–57.

18. Hambidge KM, Krebs NF, Lilly JR, et al: Plasma and urine zinc in infants and children with extrahepatic biliary atresia. *J Pediatr Gastroenterol Nutr* 1987; 6;872–877.

19. Hambidge KM: Zinc deficiency in the premature infant. *Pediatr Rev* 1985; 6:209–216.

20. Koo W, Hambidge KM: Serial serum alkaline phosphatase and zinc concentrations in very low birth weight infants with radiographic rickets and fractures during infancy. *J Am Coll Nutr* 1987; 6:432.

21. Kleinman LI, Petering HG, Sutherland JM: Blood carbonic anhydrase activity and zinc concentration in infants with respiratory-distress syndrome. *N Engl J Med* 1967; 277:1157–1162.

22. Evans RM, Hollenberg ST: Zinc fingers: Guilt by association. *Cell* 1988; 52:1–3.

23. Bettger WJ, O'Dell BL: A critical physiological role of zinc in the structure and function of biomembranes. *Life Sci* 1981; 28:1425–1438.

24. Hurley LS: Teratogenic aspects of manganese, zinc, and copper nutrition. *Physiol Rev* 1981; 61:249–295.

25. Dreosti IE: Zinc in prenatal development, in Prasad A (ed): *Clinical Applications of Recent Advances in Zinc Metabolism.* New York, Alan R. Liss, 1982, pp 19–38.

26. Solomons NW, Helitzer-Allen DL, Villar J: Zinc needs during pregnancy. *Clin Nutr* 1986; 5:63–71.

27. Beach RS, Gershwin ME, Hurley LS: Nutritional zinc deprivation in mice: Persistence of immunodeficiency for three generations. *Science* 1982; 218:469–471.

28. Halas ES: Behavioral changes accompanying zinc deficiency in animals, in Droesti IE, Smith RM (eds): *Neurobiology of the Trace Elements,* vol 1. Clifton, New Jersey, Humana Press, 1983, pp 213–244.

29. Zimmerman AW, Hambidge KM, Lepow ML, et al: Acrodermatitis in breast-fed premature infants: Evidence for a defect of mammary zinc secretion. *Pediatrics* 1982; 69:176–183.

30. Arlette JP, Johnston MM: Zinc deficiency dermatosis in premature infants receiving prolonged parenteral alimentation. *J Am Acad Dermatol* 1981; 5:37–42.

31. Kumar SP, Anday EK: Edema, hypoproteinemia, and zinc deficiency in low-birth weight infants. *Pediatrics* 1984; 73:327–329.

32. Haschke F, Singer P, Baumgartner D, et al: Growth, zinc and copper nutritional status of male premature infants with different zinc intake. *Ann Nutr Metab* 1985; 29:95–102.

33. Shaw JCL: Trace elements in the fetus and young infant: II. Zinc. *Am J Dis Child* 1979; 133:1260.

34. Krebs NF, Hambidge KM: Zinc requirements and zinc intakes of breast-fed infants. *Am J Clin Nutr* 1986; 43:288–292.

35. Greene HL, Hambidge KM, Schanler R, et al: Guidelines for the use of vitamins, trace elements, calcium magnesium and phosphorus in infants and children receiving total parenteral nutrition. Report of Subcommittee, Committee on Clinical Practice Issues of the American Society for Clinical Nutrition. *Am J Clin Nutr* 1988; 48:1324–1342.

36. Zlotkin SH, Buchanan BE: Meeting zinc and copper intake requirements in the parenterally fed pre-term and full-term infant. *J Pediatr* 1983; 103:441–446.

37. Lockitch G, Godolphin W, Pendray MR, et al: Serum zinc, copper, retinol-binding protein, prealbumin, and ceruloplasmin concentrations in infants receiving intravenous zinc and copper supplementation. *J Pediatr* 1983; 102:304–307.

38. Festa MD, Anderson HL, Dowdy RP, et al: Effect of zinc intake on copper excretion and retention in men. *Am J Clin Nutr* 1985; 41:285–292.
39. Hambidge KM, Walravens PA, Neldner KH: Zinc, copper and fatty acids in acrodermatitis enteropathica, in Kirchgessner M (ed): *Trace Element Metabolism in Man and Animals—3*, Weihenstephan, Arbeitskreis fier Tierernahrungs-forschung, 1978, pp 413–417.
40. Solomons NW: Biochemical, metabolic, and clinical role of copper in human nutrition. *J Am Coll Nutr* 1985; 4:83–105.
41. Widdowson EM, Dauncey J, Shaw JCL: Trace elements in foetal and early postnatal development, in Naismith DJN (ed): *Trace Elements and Nutrition, Proceedings of the Nutrition Society,* vol 33. Cambridge, England, Cambridge University Press, 1974, pp 275–284.
42. Baaka A, Webb M: Metabolism of zinc and copper in the neonate: Changes in the concentration and contents of thionein-bound Zn and Cu with age in the livers of the newborn of various mammalian species. *Biochem Pharmacol* 1981; 30:721–725.
43. Frieden E: Ceruloplasmin: A multi-functional cupro-protein of vertebrate plasma, in Sorenson JRJ (ed): *Inflammatory Diseases and Copper.* Clifton, New Jersey, Humana Press, 1982, pp 159–169.
44. Seely JR, Humphrey GB, Matter BJ: Copper deficiency in a premature infant fed an iron-fortified formula. *New Engl J Med* 1972; 286:109–110.
45. Al-Rashid RA, Spangler J: Neonatal copper deficiency. *N Engl J Med* 1971; 285:841.
46. Tokuda Y, Yokoyama S, Tsuji M, et al: Copper deficiency in an infant on prolonged total parenteral nutrition. *J Parenter Enteral Nutr* 1986; 10:242–244.
47. Ashkenazi A, Levin S, Djaldetti M, et al: The syndrome of neonatal copper deficiency. *Pediatrics* 1973; 52:525–533.
48. Sutton AM, Harvie A, Cockburn F, et al: Copper deficiency in the preterm infant of very low birthweight. *Arch Dis Child* 1985; 60:644–651.
49. Danks DM: Hereditary disorders of copper metabolism in Wilson's disease and Menkes' disease, in Stanbury JB, Wyngaarden JB, Fredrickson DS, et al (eds): *The Metabolic Basis of Inherited Disease,* ed 5. New York, McGraw-Hill Book Co, pp 1251–1256.
50. Casey CE, Hambidge KM: Trace element requirements, in Tsang R (ed): *Vitamin and Mineral Requirements of Preterm Infants.* New York, Marcel Dekker, 1985, pp 153–184.
51. Hunsaker HA, Morita M, Allen KGD: Marginal copper deficiency in rats: Aortal morphology of elastin and cholesterol values in first-generation adult males. *Atherosclerosis* 1984; 51:1–19.
52. Levander OA: Selenium, in Mertz W: *Trace Elements in Human and Animal Nutrition,* vol 2, Orlando, Fla, Academic Press, 1986, pp 209–279.
53. Levander OA: The importance of selenium in total parenteral nutrition, in *Proceedings: Working Conference on Parenteral Trace Elements II.* New York, New York Academy of Science, 1984, pp 144–155.
54. McGuire MK, Burgert SL, Picciano MF, et al: Selenium nutriture of infants fed human milk or bovine milk-based formula with or without added selenium. *FASEB J* 1989; 3:1309.
55. Hoekstra WG: Biochemical function of selenium and its relation to vitamin E. *Fed Proc* 1975; 34:2083–2089.
56. Machlin LF, Bendich A: Free radical tissue damage: Protective role of antioxidant nutrients. *FASEB J* 1987; 1:441–445.
57. Keshan Disease Research Group: Epidemiologic studies on the etiologic relationship of selenium and Keshan disease. *Chin Med J [Engl]* 1979; 92:477–482.
58. Keshan Disease Research Group: Observations on effect of sodium selenite in prevention of Keshan disease. *Chin Med J [Engl]* 1979; 92:471–476.
59. Johnson RA, Baker SS, Fallon JT, et al: An occidental case of cardiomyopathy and selenium deficiency. *N Engl J Med* 1981; 304:1210–1212.
60. Kien CL, Ganther HE: Manifestations of chronic selenium deficiency in a child receiving total parenteral nutrition. *Am J Clin Nutr* 1983; 37:319–328.
61. Vinton NE, Dahlstrom KA, Strobel CT, et al: Macrocytosis and pseudoalbinism: Manifestation of selenium deficiency. *J Pediatr* 1987; 111:711–717.

62. Golden MHN, Ramdath D: Free radicals in the pathogenesis of kwashiorkor, in Taylor TG, Jenkins NK (eds): *Proceedings of the XIII International Congress of Nutrition.* London, John LIbbey, 1985, pp 597–598.

63. Gross S: Hemolytic anemia in premature infants: Relationship to vitamin E, selenium, glutathione peroxidase, and erythrocyte lipids. *Semin Hematol* 1976; 13:187–199.

64. Smith AM, Picciano MF, Milner JA: Selenium intakes and status of human milk and formula fed infants. *Am J Clin Nutr* 1982; 35:521–526.

65. Lombeck I, Kasperek K, Harbisch HD, et al: The selenium state of children: II. Selenium content of serum. Whole blood, hair and the activity of erythrocyte glutathione peroxidase in dietetically treated patients with phenylketonuria and maple-syrup-urine disease. *Eur J Pediatr* 1978; 128:213–223.

66. Lockitch G, Jacobson B, Quigley G, et al: Selenium deficiency in low birthweight neonates: An unrecognized problem. *J Pediatr* (in press).

67. Whanger PD, Beilstein MA, Thomson CD: Blood selenium and glutathione peroxidase activity of populations in New Zealand, Oregon, and South Dakota. *FASEB J* 1988; 2:2996–3002.

68. Kumpulainen J, Salmenpera L, Siimes MA: Formula feeding results in lower selenium status than breast-feeding or selenium supplemented formula feeding: A longitudinal study. *Am J Clin Nutr* 1987; 45:49–53.

69. van Callie-Bertrand M, Degenhart HJ, Fernandes J: Influence of age on the selenium status in Belgium and The Netherlands. *Pediatr Res* 1986; 20:574–576.

70. Yang G, Ge K, Chen J, et al: Selenium-related endemic diseases and the daily selenium requirement of humans. *World Rev Nutr Diet* 1988; 55:98–152.

71. Friel JK, Gibson RS, Balassa R, et al: Selenium and chromium intakes of very low birthweight pre-term and normal birthweight full-term infants during the first twelve months. *Nutr Res* 1985; 5:1175–1184.

72. Hetzel BS, Potter BJ: Iodine deficiency and the role of thyroid hormones in brain development, in Droesti IE, Smith RM (eds): *Neurobiology of the Trace Elements,* vol 1. Clifton, New Jersey, Humana Press, 1983, pp 45–70.

73. From endemic goitre to iodine deficiency disorders. *The Lancet* 1983; 1:1121–1122.

74. Delange F, Bourdoux P, Ketelbant-Balasse P, et al: Transient primary hypothyroidism in the newborn, in Dussault JH, Walker P (eds): *Congenital Hypothyroidism.* New York, Marcel Dekker, 1983, pp 275–301.

75. Del Ray FE, Pastor R, Mallol J, et al: Effects of maternal iodine deficiency on the *t*-thyroxine and 3,5,3′-triiodo-L-thyronine contents of rat embryonic tissues before and after onset of fetal thyroid function. *Endocrinology* 1986; 118:1259–1265.

76. Report of the Subcommittee for the Study of Endemic Goitre and Iodine Deficiency of the European Thyroid Association: Goitre and iodine deficiency in Europe. *Lancet* 1985; 1:1289–1292.

77. Schonberger W, Grimm W, Emrich P, et al: Thyroid administration lowers mortality in premature infants. *Lancet* 1979; 2:1181.

78. Committee on Nutrition: Fluoride supplementation: Revised dosage schedule. *Pediatrics* 1979; 63:150–152.

79. Mena I: Manganese, in Bronner F, Coburn JW (eds): *Disorders of Mineral Metabolism,* vol 1. New York, Academic Press, 1981, pp 233–270.

80. Miller ST, Cotzias GC, Evert HA: Control of tissue manganese: Initial absence and sudden emergence of excretion in the neonatal mouse. *Am J Physiol* 1975; 229:1080–1084.

81. Davidson L, Cederblad A, Lonnerdal B, et al: Manganese absorption from human milk, cow's milk and infant formulas, in Hurley LS (ed): *Trace Elements in Man and Animals—6.* New York, Plenum Publishing Corp, 1988, pp 511–512.

82. Casey CE, Hambidge KM, Neville MC: Studies in human lactation: Zinc, copper, manganese and chromium in human milk in the first month of lactation. *Am J Clin Nutr* 1985; 41:1193–1200.

83. Hambidge KM, Sokol RJ, Fidanza SJ, et al: Plasma manganese concentrations in infants and children receiving parenteral nutrition. *Parenter Enteral Nutr* 1989; 13:168–171.
84. American Academy of Pediatrics, Committee on Nutrition: Aluminum toxicity in infants and children. *Pediatrics* 1986; 78:1150–1154.
85. Oski FA: Iron requirements of the premature infant, in Tsang RC (ed): *Vitamin and Mineral Requirements in Preterm Infants.* New York, Marcel Dekker, 1985, pp 9–22.
86. Vyas D, Chandra RK: Functional implications of iron deficiency, in Stekel A (ed): *Iron Nutrition in Infancy and Childhood.* New York, Raven Press, 1984, pp 45–59.

PART III

Nutrient Mixtures and Methods of Feeding

Chapter 10

Intravenous Feeding

William C. Heird, M.D.

Sudha Kashyap, M.D.

The introduction, some 50 years ago, of protein hydrolysates suitable for parenteral administration heralded the modern era of parenteral nutrition. When infused with 5% to 10% glucose, these products permitted achievement of a positive nitrogen balance. However, consistent achievement of weight gain was not possible until some 20 years later when a cottonseed oil emulsion suitable for intravenous administration became available, making possible the delivery of greater energy intakes.

The first account of a pediatric patient managed successfully with parenteral nutrition appeared in 1944.[1] The patient was a 5-month-old boy with severe marasmus. He was given alternate infusions by peripheral vein of a mixture of 50% glucose and 10% casein hydrolysate and a noncommercial olive oil–lecithin homogenate. The regimen provided 130 kcal/kg/day; total volume was 150 mL/kg/day. After 5 days, "the fat pads of the cheek had returned, the ribs were less prominent, and the general nutritional status was much improved."[1]

Most subsequent attempts to administer nutrients parenterally were not as successful. The cottonseed oil emulsion that initially seemed so promising proved unstable, and its use resulted in such numerous undesirable problems that the product was removed from the market in the mid-1960s.* This resulted in some enthusiasm for the use of ethanol as an alternative parenteral source of energy. Indeed, peripheral vein infusions of a mixture of protein hydrolysate, glucose, and ethanol, along with electrolytes, minerals, and vitamins, permitted achievement of weight gain and general improvement in nutritional and clinical status.[3] However, maintenance of the infusions required considerable effort and, even with this effort, infusion could not be maintained consistently for more than 10 to 14 days. In addition, the amount of ethanol tolerated by individual patients proved to be both variable and unpredictable. Infusion of large volumes of less-concentrated mixtures of glucose and protein hydrolysate, with administration of diuretics to

---

*These quasi-successful efforts at parenteral nutrition during the 1940s, 1950s, and early 1960s were preceded by even less successful efforts spanning several centuries.[2] In fact, since the possibility ingested nutrients' being absorbed from the intestine into the blood stream was first suspected, physicians have reasoned that intravenous administration of nutrients would prevent starvation of patients who cannot eat. Thus, sporadic reports of the technically successful but otherwise disastrous infusion of such substances as wine, honey, milk, and various oils have appeared.

maintain fluid balance, was popular for a while but was soon abandoned because of the severe plasma electrolyte and acid–base disturbances that frequently ensued.

Parenteral nutrition therapy, more or less as practiced today, was first reported in the late-1960s.[4] The major difference between the technique described in this report and in those preceding it was that a hypertonic nutrient infusate was infused continuously through a catheter inserted into the superior vena cava (SVC)—where the high blood flow immediately dilutes the hypertonic infusate—rather than directly into a peripheral vein. Wilmore and Dudrick,[5] using this technique to deliver a hypertonic mixture of glucose, protein hydrolysate, electrolytes, minerals, and vitamins, demonstrated that it was possible to maintain normal growth and development for several months in an infant with multiple atresias of the small intestine.

This dramatic demonstration was the stimulus for the now widespread use of total parenteral nutrition (TPN) in pediatric patients, most frequently in infants requiring multiple operative procedures for correction of congenital or acquired anomalies of the gastrointestinal tract, and in infants and children with intractable diarrhea. In fact, successful parenteral nutrition undoubtedly is a major factor in the currently high survival rate of infants with these conditions compared with the dismally low survival rate 25 years ago.[6]

Low-birth-weight (LBW) infants probably comprise the largest group of pediatric patients who receive parenteral nutrients. Such infants account for about 7% of all births in the United States, and many, particularly the smaller ones [those weighing < 1,500 g at birth (in excess of 1% of all births)], are unable to tolerate adequate amounts of enterally delivered nutrients for several weeks. Because the endogenous nutrient stores of these infants are limited (e.g., the 1,000-g infant has fat stores of ~1% of body weight, or ~10 g) and their rate of ongoing energy expenditure is relatively high (~60 cal/kg/day), these infants theoretically are at great risk for development of malnutrition or actual starvation within the first few days of life. For example, the total endogenous nutrient stores of the 1,000-g infant are sufficient to support survival without exogenous nutrients for only about 5 days.

Despite these theoretical considerations and the fact that the survival rate of LBW infants has improved dramatically over the past 2 decades, it is not clear that use of parenteral nutrition has contributed to this improved survival. During this time, there have been a number of improvements in other aspects of neonatal care, which may have contributed as much or more to this improved survival as the ability to provide nutrients exogenously.

Regardless of the exact role of TPN in improving survival of certain groups of pediatric patients, the therapy appears to be firmly established. In major pediatric centers, from 5% to 10% of the total patient population on any one day is receiving parenteral nutrients either by central vein or by peripheral vein infusion. Virtually all infants who weigh less than 1,500 g at birth receive at least some, if not all, of their total nutrient intake for the first several days of life by the parenteral route. In addition, a rapidly increasing number of pediatric patients are receiving parenteral nutrition at home.

Despite this widespread use and the fact that the overall efficacy of the technique in nutritional management of infants who cannot tolerate enteral nutrients is unquestioned, a number of aspects of the technique remain poorly understood. Since it is likely that a more thorough understanding of all aspects of the technique will further enhance efficacy, several aspects of the TPN technique are discussed in some detail in this chapter. Unsolved problems related to the technique are emphasized, but a number of practical aspects of the therapy that tend to enhance its efficacy are also discussed.

TECHNIQUES OF PARENTERAL NUTRITION THERAPY

The basic concept of parenteral nutrition therapy is infusion of a hypertonic nutrient solution at a constant rate into a vessel with rapid blood flow, usually through an indwelling catheter, the tip of which is in the SVC just above the right atrium. In infants, the catheter is usually placed through a surgical cutdown in either the internal or external jugular vein. In older children and adolescents, it is often placed percutaneously through the subclavian vein. Regardless of the route of placement, the proximal portion of the catheter is tunneled subcutaneously to exit some distance from the site of insertion, usually the anterior chest, and this exit site is covered by an occlusive dressing. The channeling of the catheter to a point distant from the phlebotomy site is thought to be important with respect to protecting the catheter from both inadvertent dislodgement and contamination by microorganisms. It also makes maintenance and care of the catheter exit site easier.

The inferior vena cava also is a large vessel with rapid flow, and catheters placed in this vessel just below the right atrium should be equally effective. However, introduction of a catheter through a cutdown in the groin area, in theory, increases the risk of infection and, for this reason, inferior vena cava catheters are not as popular as SVC catheters. On the other hand, some argue that such catheters, if tunneled subcutaneously to an exit site on the abdominal wall or the thigh, represent no greater risk with respect to infection than the usual SVC catheters.[7] Unfortunately, no firm data are available to substantiate this argument.

In general, Silastic rather than polyvinyl catheters are preferred. The latter have a tendency to become very rigid when in place for a only short period of time. In recent years, use of Silastic catheters with a polyvinyl cuff on the portion that is tunneled subcutaneously has become quite popular. The cuff promotes fibroblast proliferation, which helps secure the catheter in place, thereby considerably increasing the life of a single catheter. Such catheters are particularly useful for home parenteral nutrition.

Before the nutrient infusion is begun, radiographic confirmation of correct catheter position is mandatory; otherwise, the hypertonic nutrient infusate may be infused into an undesired site. Regular and meticulous care of the central vein catheter also is essential for prolonged, safe, complication-free use. Attention to this detail seems to be the most important factor in preventing infection. It is recommended that the occlusive dressing at the catheter exit site be changed at least three times a week. Each time, the skin area should be cleaned with both a defatting agent and an antiseptic agent, and an antiseptic ointment as well as a fresh occlusive dressing applied. Unnecessary use of the catheter for purposes other than delivery of the nutrient infusate, particularly for blood transfusions and blood sampling, is discouraged. With meticulous care, a single catheter, particularly one with a polyvinyl cuff, can be used safely for months, perhaps years.

Although the complications of central vein delivery of concentrated nutrient mixtures (see Complications of Parenteral Nutrition, later in this chapter) can be reduced to an acceptable level, doing so requires considerable effort, personnel, and expense. Thus, parenteral nutrition regimens that can be infused by peripheral vein are advocated by some. Of necessity, the glucose concentration of such regimens cannot be much greater than 10%, and the nutrient intake that can be delivered by peripheral vein without excessive fluid intake is limited. Use of parenteral lipid emulsions helps compensate for this drawback, but if fluid intake is limited to a total volume of 150 mL/kg/day and intravenous lipid intake is limited to 3 g/kg/day, the maximum energy intake that can be delivered is approximately 80 kcal/kg/day.[3] Obviously, the growth achievable with such an intake is less than with conventional central vein parenteral nutrition regimens. Despite this limitation of peripheral vein regimens, there are a number of patients for whom such regimens may be preferable (discussed in section on "Indications for Parenteral Nutrients").

The idea that parenteral nutrient delivery by peripheral vein is easier and less time-consuming than successful delivery by central vein is not supported by fact. The supervision required for successful peripheral vein delivery is certainly equal to that required for successful central vein delivery. In addition, because a single infusion site rarely lasts for more than 24 hours, considerable time and effort are required to maintain peripheral vein infusions. Further, the complications per day of therapy associated with the two routes of delivery, although different in nature and seriousness, are similar.[8] Thus, it seems reasonable to base the choice of delivery route for parenteral nutrients on an individual patient's clinical condition and nutritional needs rather than on the perceived ease or difficulty of a particular technique.

INDICATIONS FOR PARENTERAL NUTRIENTS

Most agree that any infant who is unable to tolerate sufficient enteral feedings for a significant period of time will benefit from either central or peripheral vein TPN. There is less agreement, however, concerning the definition of "significant period of time" and the indications for central vs. peripheral vein delivery. A reasonable guideline is to gauge the extent to which an infant's endogenous nutrient stores are likely to be eroded if nutrient intake is inadequate. For example, a large infant who must forego enteral feedings for only a few days is unlikely to experience serious erosion of endogenous nutrient stores, whereas a small infant or a large infant with preexisting nutritional depletion is likely to experience further depletion of already limited endogenous stores with even a short period of starvation.

Peripheral vein parenteral nutrition regimens almost certainly maintain existing body composition; therefore, this route of delivery is a reasonable choice for a normally nourished infant who is likely to tolerate an adequate enteral regimen within 1 to 2 weeks. On the other hand, central vein delivery is a more reasonable choice for an infant who is likely to be intolerant of enteral feedings for longer than 2 weeks. This distinction is based both on the practical consideration of the difficulty in maintaining peripheral vein infusions for more than 2 weeks and the fact that more nutrients can be delivered by central vein infusion.

Most infants require parenteral nutrients as their sole source of nutrition for no longer than 10 to 18 days (e.g., for intolerance of enteral feedings, postoperative complications, necrotizing enterocolitis, many surgically correctable lesions, intractable diarrhea). Thus, when choosing between peripheral and central vein delivery, it is difficult, frequently impossible, to use as criterion how long the patient is expected to require therapy. Factors such as nutritional status, duration of illness, and clinical course prior to beginning parenteral nutrition must be considered. The nutritional status of a larger infant who becomes intolerant of enteral feedings within the first few days of life (e.g., the term infant with a surgically correctable lesion of the intestine) is likely to be reasonable; such an infant, therefore, might reasonably be assigned to a peripheral vein regimen. On the other hand, central vein delivery is a more reasonable choice for a smaller neonate who requires parenteral nutrition for the same condition (e.g., a small-for-gestational age infant with the same surgically correctable lesion). Similarly, an infant who requires parenteral nutrition after the first 1 to 2 weeks of life following a complicated clinical course characterized by inadequate nutritional intake (e.g., the infant with intractable diarrhea or some infants with necrotizing enterocolitis) is likely to require central vein delivery. In such an infant, it is unlikely that peripheral infusions can be maintained for an additional 2 weeks; such an infant also is likely to be nutritionally depleted.

INFUSATE COMPOSITION AND DELIVERY

The parenteral nutrition infusate, whether delivered by central or peripheral vein, should include a nitrogen source as well as adequate energy, electrolytes, minerals, and

TABLE 10–1.

Composition of a Nutrient Infusate Suitable for Both Central Vein and Peripheral Vein Infusions

Component	Central Vein (amount/kg/day)	Peripheral Vein (amount/kg/day)
Crystalline amino acids, g	3–4	2.5–3.0
Glucose, g	20–30	15
Lipid emulsion, g	0.5–3.0	0.5–3.0
Sodium, mEq	3–4	3–4
Potassium,* mEq	2–4	2–4
Calcium, mg	40–80	40–80
Magnesium, mEq	0.25	0.25
Chloride, mEq	3–4	3–4
Phosphorus, mmol*	1.4	1.4
Zinc, μg	200	200–400
Copper, μg	20	
Other trace minerals†	. . .	. . .
Iron‡	. . .	. . .
Vitamins (MVI-Pediatric)§	. . .	. . .
Total volume	120–130	150

*Hyperphosphatemia frequently develops if phosphorus intake exceeds 1.4 mmol/kg/day, the amount given with a daily potassium intake of 2 mEq/kg as a mixture of KH_2PO_4 and K_2HPO_4; if a potassium intake of more than 2 mEq/kg/day is required, the additional potassium should be given as KAC.

†See text and Table 11–4.

‡Iron Dextran (Imferon, Fisons Corp., Bedford, Mass) can be added to the infusate of patients requiring prolonged parenteral nutrition therapy; we arbitrarily limit the dose to 0.1 mg/kg/day. Alternatively, the indicated intramuscular dose can be used intermittently, either as the sole source of iron or as an additional dose.

§MVI-Pediatric (Armour Pharmaceutical Co., Chicago, Ill) is a lypholized product. When reconstituted as directed, 5 mL added to the daily infusate provides 80 mg vitamin C, 700 μg vitamin A, 10 μg vitamin D, 1.3 mg thiamine, 1.4 mg riboflavin, 1.0 mg pyridoxine, 17 mg niacin, 5 mg pantothenic acid, 7 mg vitamin E, 20 μg biotin, 140 μg folic acid, 1 μg vitamin B_{12}, and 200 μg vitamin K_1.

vitamins. Peripheral and central vein infusates suitable for most pediatric patients are shown in Table 10–1.

One of several crystalline amino acid mixtures (Table 10–2) is usually used as the nitrogen source. The amount of amino acids provided ranges from 2 to 4 g/kg/day; an intake of 2.5 to 3.0 g/kg/day results in nitrogen retention comparable to that observed in enterally fed, healthy term infants but, in LBW infants, higher intake may be required to achieve a rate of nitrogen retention equal to the intrauterine rate.

Glucose is the major energy source of most parenteral nutrition regimens. An intake greater than 15 g/kg/day is rarely tolerated by any infant on day 1 of therapy, and the amount tolerated by LBW infants is frequently less. However, intake usually can be increased by 2 to 5 g/kg/day until the desired intake is achieved. Any patient who receives a fat-free parenteral nutrition regimen will develop essential fatty acid deficiency within a relatively short period of time (preterm and nutritionally depleted infants do so within days, particularly if growth is rapid)[9]; therefore, sufficient amounts of a parenteral lipid emulsion to prevent this deficiency (i.e., 0.5 to 1.0 g/kg/day) are indicated. The maximum intakes recommended are 2 g/kg/day for the LBW infant and 3 g/kg/day for the older infant.[10]

Convenient additive preparations of electrolytes, minerals, and vitamins have been available for many years. Because the requirements for these nutrients vary from patient to patient, the amounts shown in Table 10–1 cannot be interpreted as absolute requirements. The amount of calcium suggested almost certainly is inadequate for optimal skeletal mineralization, but inclusion of more calcium without decreasing the amount of phosphate is likely to result in precipitation of calcium phosphate. The amounts of vitamins listed in Table 10–1 are particularly tenuous but can be provided conveniently us-

TABLE 10–2.

Composition of Available Parenteral Amino Acid Mixtures (mmols/2.5g)

Amino Acid	Aminosyn (Abbott)	Aminosyn-PF (Abbott)	FreAmine III (McGaw)	Neopham (Cutter)	Travasol (Travenol)	TrophAmine (McGaw)
Threonine	1.090	1.080	0.840	1.160	0.910	0.883
Valine	1.710	1.390	1.420	1.180	0.980	1.675
Leucine	1.795	2.267	1.730	2.050	1.180	2.671
Isoleucine	1.375	1.458	1.325	0.930	0.910	1.567
Lysine	1.235	1.156	1.740	1.475	0.790	1.396
Methionine	0.670	0.300	0.890	0.335	0.970	0.571
Cystine	0	0	0.050	0.410	0	0.050
Histidine	0.485	0.510	0.455	0.520	0.705	0.771
Phenylalanine	0.665	0.650	0.855	0.630	0.935	0.729
Tyrosine	0.120	0.088	0	0.110	0.055	0.333*
Tryptophan	0.195	0.220	0.185	0.265	0.220	0.246
Arginine	1.410	1.760	1.361	0.910	1.490	1.742
Serine	1.000	1.181	1.400	1.395	0	0.904
Proline	1.870	1.789	2.430	1.875	0.945	1.492
Glycine	4.265	1.280	4.667	1.075	6.910	1.200
Alanine	3.595	1.966	1.985	2.720	5.820	1.517
Aspartate	0	1.000	0	1.190	0	0.608
Glutamate	0	1.411	0	1.860	0	0.854
Taurine	0	0.171	0	0	0	0.057

*Mixture of L-tyrosine and N-acetyl-tyrosine.

ing currently available products. Zinc and copper deficiency develop relatively frequently if these nutrients are not provided, so these trace minerals should be added to the infusate of any patient likely to require parenteral nutrients for more than 1 to 2 weeks. Inclusion of other essential trace minerals (e.g., chromium,[11] selenium,[12] molybdenum[13]) should be considered in patients who require parenteral nutrients exclusively for a longer period of time.

Recommendations for parenteral vitamin and trace mineral intakes have been revised recently. The most recent recommendations are summarized in Tables 10–3 and 10–4.

The nutrient infusate should be delivered at a constant rate using one of several available constant infusion pumps. Use of a 0.22-μm membrane filter between the catheter and the administration tubing is advocated by some, including the authors; others feel that this precaution is not necessary.

Many patients tolerate the same infusate for the total duration of parenteral nutrition. Others, however, require more frequent adjustment of the intake of one or more nutrients. For this reason, ability to change the composition of the infusate in response to clinical and chemical monitoring or to increase the volume in response to diarrheal and other ongoing losses is important.

TABLE 10–3.

Suggested Parenteral Intakes of Vitamins*

Vitamin	Preterm Infants (amount/kg/day)†	Term Infants and Children (amount/day)‡
Vitamin A, μg	280	700
Vitamin E, mg	2.8	7
Vitamin K, μg	80	200
Vitamin D, μg	4	10
IU	160	400
Ascorbic acid, mg	25	80
Thiamin, mg	0.48	1.2
Riboflavin, mg	0.56	1.4
Pyridoxine, mg	0.4	1.0
Niacin, mg	6.8	17
Pantothenate, mg	2.0	5
Biotin, μg	8.0	20
Folate, μg	56	140
Vitamin B_{12}, μg	0.4	1.0

*From Greene HL, Hambidge KM, Schanler R, et al: Guidelines for the use of vitamins, trace elements, calcium, magnesium, and phosphorus in infants and children receiving total parenteral nutrition: Report of the subcommittee on pediatric parenteral nutrient requirements from the committee on clinical practice issues of the American Society for Clinical Nutrition. *Am J Clin Nutr* 1988; 48:1324–1342. Used by permission.

†Total daily dose should not exceed that recommended for term infants and children. A dose of 2 mL of reconstituted MVI-Pediatric provides the recommended amount/kg/day of all vitamins except ascorbic acid.

‡These amounts are provided by 5 mL of reconstituted MVI-Pediatric (Armour Pharmaceutical Co.).

TABLE 10–4.

Recommended Parenteral Intakes of Trace Minerals*†

Trace Mineral	Preterm Infants (µg/kg/day)	Term Infants (µg/kg/day)
Zinc	400	250‡
Copper	20	20
Selenium	2.0	2.0
Chromium	0.20	0.20
Manganese	1.0	1.0
Molybdenum	0.25	0.25
Iodide	1.0	1.0

*From Greene HL, Hambidge KM, Schanler R, et al: Guidelines for the use of vitamins, trace elements, calcium, magnesium, and phosphorus in infants and children receiving total parenteral nutrition: Report of the subcommittee on pediatric parenteral nutrition from the committee on clinical practice issues of the American Society for Clinical Nutrition. *Am J Clin Nutr* 1988; 48:1324–1342. Used by permission.
†If parenteral nutrients are used as a supplement for tolerated enteral feedings or as the sole source of nutrients for < 4 weeks, only zinc is needed.
‡100 mg/kg/day for infants > 3 mo of age.

RATIONALE FOR RECOMMENDED PARENTERAL NUTRIENT INTAKES

The parenteral requirements for various nutrients depend on the endpoints to be achieved with the parenteral nutrition regimen and any peculiarities of metabolism of specific nutrients incident to route of administration. The requirements for normal growth, and certainly those for normal growth plus catch-up growth, are considerably greater than the requirements for merely preserving existing body composition. Although the requirements for achieving either goal have not been studied extensively, considerable information is available concerning, particularly, the requirements for protein and energy. Much less information is available concerning special requirements imposed by parenteral vs. enteral delivery of nutrients.

Rationale for Parenteral Amino Acid Intake

According to Zlotkin et al.,[14] the amino acid intake necessary to result in the intrauterine rate of nitrogen accretion (i.e., ~ 300 mg/kg/day), at an average energy intake of about 80 kcal/kg/day is approximately 3 g/kg/day. This combination of amino acid and energy intakes also results in a rate of weight gain approximating the intrauterine rate (i.e., about 15 g/kg/day). An even higher rate of nitrogen retention, but not weight gain, can be achieved with an amino acid intake of 4 g/kg/day with the same energy intake. The rates of both nitrogen retention and weight gain of infants who received amino acid intakes of 3 and 4 g/kg/day at an energy intake of 50 kcal/kg/day were lower than the intrauterine rate.

Anderson et al.[15] studied LBW infants who received a regimen providing an energy intake of 60 kcal/kg/day with an amino acid intake of 2.5 g/kg/day during the 1st week of life vs. a control group of infants who received the same energy intake with no amino acids. The former were in positive (178 mg/kg/day) and the latter were in negative

(−132 mg/kg/day) nitrogen balance, but neither group gained weight. However, changes in weight during the 1st week of life are difficult to interpret because of marked shifts in fluids. Since others[14] studying older LBW infants have reported either lack of weight loss or slow rates of weight gain with similar intakes, it is likely that these intakes are close to maintenance requirements.

The quality of the amino acid intake also must be considered in defining the parenteral requirement for amino acids. Both Duffy et al.[16] and Helms et al.[17] observed differences in nitrogen utilization between groups of infants receiving isonitrogenous and isocaloric parenteral nutrition regimens in which only the quality of the nitrogen source differed. Duffy et al.[16] found that nitrogen retention was greater in infants who received a regimen containing a crystalline amino acid mixture than in those who received to a regimen containing casein hydrolysate; in addition, protein synthesis accounted for a greater percentage of total nitrogen flux in those who received the crystalline amino acid regimen. Helms et al.[17] observed more efficient nitrogen retention in infants who received a regimen in which the nitrogen source was a parenteral amino acid mixture designed for infants (i.e., 78% of intake) than in infants who received an isocaloric regimen in which the nitrogen source was a general-purpose parenteral amino acid mixture (i.e., 66% of intake).

Neither of these studies provide insight into the reason for the better utilization of one regimen over the other. The more efficiently utilized regimen studied by Helms et al.[17] contained more cyst(e)ine and tyrosine, both considered indispensable amino acids for the infant[18]; thus, the investigators suggested that the reason for the greater nitrogen retention was provision of more optimal intakes of these two amino acids. This is an unlikely explanation for the more efficient nitrogen utilization observed by Duffy et al.[16]; in that study, the less efficiently utilized nitrogen source provided more tyrosine and cyst(e)ine.

Cystine and tyrosine are insoluble, and cysteine is unstable in aqueous solution; hence, no currently available parenteral amino acid mixture contains appreciable amounts of these amino acids. Presumably as a result of inadequate intake, plasma cyst(e)ine and tyrosine concentrations of infants receiving these amino acid mixtures are quite low. Moreover, greater intakes of methionine and phenylalanine do not result in greater plasma concentrations, respectively, of cyst(e)ine and tyrosine.

Hepatic activity of cystathionase, which is required for endogenous conversion of methionine to cysteine (Fig 10–1), is known to be low at birth and for some time postnatally.[19, 20] This developmental deficit is an acceptable explanation for the low plasma cyst(e)ine concentrations of infants receiving cyst(e)ine-free parenteral nutrition regimens. Since there appears to be no developmental delay in hepatic phenylalanine hydroxylase activity,[21] the low plasma tyrosine concentrations of infants receiving tyrosine-free parenteral nutrition regimens is not explicable on this basis.

According to Chawla et al.,[22] adults receiving cyst(e)ine-free and tyrosine-free parenteral nutrition regimens have lower plasma concentrations of cyst(e)ine and tyrosine than patients receiving a cyst(e)ine- and tyrosine-free elemental enteral diet. In addition, those receiving the parenteral regimen have lower plasma concentrations of taurine, which is synthesized endogenously from cysteine, as well as lower plasma concentrations of carnitine, creatine, and choline, all of which require a methyl group from S-adenosyl-methionine for endogenous synthesis. These differences in plasma concentrations between patients receiving similar enterally vs. parenterally administered regimens led the investigators to suggest that parenterally delivered methionine is metabolized by a pathway other than the transsulfuration pathway by which methionine is con-

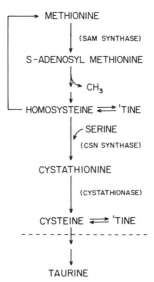

FIG 10–1.

Key steps of the transsulfuration pathway by which methionine is converted to cyst(e)ine. Rate-limiting enzymes catalyzing the various steps are shown in *parentheses*.

verted, first, to S-adenosyl-methionine and, subsequently, through a number of steps to cyst(e)ine and, then, to taurine (see Fig 10–1). The specific reason for the apparent requirement for tyrosine is less clear but a similar mechanism seems reasonable.

In both adults and infants, then, it appears that parenterally administered methionine and phenylalanine may not be metabolized by the usual pathways and, hence, are not effectively converted, respectively, to cyst(e)ine and tyrosine. Although evidence is lacking that other amino acids are metabolized differently when delivered parenterally vs. enterally, the strong possibility that this is true for methionine and phenylalanine suggests that the same may also be true for other amino acids.

Cysteine hydrochloride is soluble and also is reasonably stable for short periods of time; thus, it is possible to supplement parenteral nutrition infusates with cysteine. However, trials of cysteine supplementation[23, 24] have not shown a beneficial effect of parenteral cysteine intake on nitrogen retention, perhaps because the tyrosine content of the control regimens of these studies also was low and any beneficial effect of cysteine intake on nitrogen retention was masked by concurrent tyrosine deficiency. One of the newer parenteral amino acid mixtures contains N-acetyl-L-tyrosine (see Table 10–2), which is soluble. Although the absolute efficacy of this tyrosine derivative has not been determined, infants receiving this mixture have higher plasma tyrosine concentrations than infants receiving other mixtures.[25] If N-acetyl-L-tyrosine proves to be an efficacious source of tyrosine, it should be possible to define the need for both tyrosine and cyst(e)ine in infants requiring parenteral nutrition.

Rationale for Parenteral Energy Intake

Theoretically, an energy intake approximating the resting energy expenditure (50 to 60 kcal/kg/day) is sufficient for maintenance (i.e., prevention of weight loss provided amino acid intake is adequate), whereas an energy intake in excess of resting energy expenditure is necessary to achieve weight gain. This theoretical consideration, in fact, is confirmed by the finding of Zlotkin et al.[14] mentioned earlier and discussed in this section.

Because of genetic differences as well as differences in other factors affecting energy expenditure, the resting energy requirement varies considerably from infant to infant. Obviously, the total energy intake necessary to produce a specific rate of weight gain will be greater in infants with higher resting energy expenditures. For example, the resting energy expenditure of infants with bronchopulmonary dysplasia is about 10% greater than that of infants without bronchopulmonary dysplasia.[26] Such infants will require a greater energy intake than infants without bronchopulmonary dysplasia both to meet resting needs and to result in the same rate of weight gain. The same is likely to be true for infants with other conditions as well.

According to Zlotkin et al.,[14] LBW infants who receive an energy intake of 80 kcal/kg/day with a concomitant amino acid intake of 3 g/kg/day gain weight at a rate approximating the intrauterine rate. Theoretically, those who receive a greater energy intake will experience an even greater rate of weight gain. However, this greater rate of weight gain most likely will represent only deposition of additional adipose tissue. Hence, if the rate of weight gain of a LBW infant receiving 80 kcal/kg/day is at or near the intrauterine rate, it is unlikely that a greater energy intake will be particularly desirable unless it is accompanied by a greater amino acid intake, thereby supporting greater rates of deposition of both protein and adipose tissue. Unfortunately, there are no data concerning this theoretical consideration.

In addition to the absolute energy requirements for maintenance and growth, the relationship between energy intake and nitrogen utilization must be considered. The usual concept, developed primarily in animals and adults, is that utilization of any protein intake increases with increases in energy intake until the protein rather than the energy intake becomes limiting.[27] In infants, Zlotkin et al.[14] observed greater nitrogen retention in infants receiving amino acid intakes of either 3 or 4 g/kg/day with a concomitant energy intake of 80 vs. 50 kcal/kg/day. However, Pineault et al.[28] observed a minimal effect of an energy intake of 80 vs. 60 kcal/kg/day on nitrogen retention of LBW infants receiving an amino acid intake of 2.7 g/kg/day. These two sets of data suggest that an amino acid intake of 2.7 g/kg/day is reasonably well utilized, although perhaps not maximally utilized, if accompanied by an energy intake of 60 kcal/kg/day, whereas an amino acid intake of 3 g/kg/day is not.

The effect of distribution of energy intake between glucose and lipid on amino acid utilization also may be important. In general, the nitrogen-sparing effect of carbohydrate in the absence of nitrogen intake is not shared by fat, but the effect of parenterally administered glucose vs. lipid on utilization of concomitantly administered amino acids is less well understood. Studies in adults suggest both that the two energy substrates are equal in this regard[29] and that lipid exerts no such effect unless glucose provides at least 85% of the resting energy requirement.[30] This apparent discrepancy may reflect differences in the patient populations of the two studies (depleted adults in the former; burn patients in the latter). In infants, Pineault et al.,[28] studying the effects of high (3 g/kg/day) and low (1 g/kg/day) parenteral lipid intakes at total energy intakes of both 60 and 80 kcal/kg/day, found that the higher carbohydrate regimens, regardless of total energy intake, resulted in somewhat lower plasma concentrations of most amino acids, suggesting better amino acid utilization. However, at each energy intake, the rates of nitrogen retention with the two regimens did not differ significantly.

Rationale for Recommended Parenteral Lipid Intakes

Parenteral lipid emulsions containing soybean oil (e.g., Intralipid and Liposyn III) and a mixture of safflower and soybean oils (e.g., Liposyn II) are currently available (Table 10–5). The emulsifying agent of all emulsions is egg yolk phospholipid, and the emulsion particles of all are roughly the size of chylomicrons or very low density lipoprotein. After infusion, the triglyceride portion of these particles is hydrolyzed by endothelial lipoprotein lipase and the free fatty acids and glycerol released are metabolized by the usual mechanisms.[31] The ability to hydrolyze the infused emulsion particles increases with increasing gestational age and, at any gestational age, the capacity for hydrolysis is less in the infant who is small for gestational age vs. the infant whose size is appropriate for gestational age.[32] A number of clinical conditions (such as infection, surgical stress, or malnutrition) adversely affect the hydrolysis step,[31] but less information is available concerning the factors that affect metabolism of free fatty acids and glycerol.

Theoretically, dramatic changes in plasma triglyceride concentrations are unlikely, as long as the rate of lipid infusion is less than or equal to the rate of hydrolysis. However, if the rate of lipid infusion exceeds the rate of hydrolysis, plasma triglyceride concentration will rise, and the adverse effects of elevated triglyceride concentrations on pulmonary diffusion[33, 34] and polymorphonuclear leukocyte function[35, 36] may be seen. In either situation, if the rate of hydrolysis exceeds the rate at which the released free fatty acids are oxidized, the plasma concentration of free fatty acids will increase. Since free fatty acids displace bound bilirubin from albumin,[37] this possibility is of some concern in infants with hyperbilirubinemia. Unfortunately, the concentration of free fatty acids likely to result in displacement of albumin-bound bilirubin in vivo is not known.

As discussed earlier, it has been suggested that low plasma carnitine concentrations, commonly observed in infants and adults receiving carnitine-free parenteral nutrition regimens,[22, 38] may inhibit fatty acid oxidation. However, only one trial of the effect of

TABLE 10–5.

Composition (Amount/Lr) of Representative Parenteral Lipid Emulsions

Component	Soybean Oil Emulsion*	Soybean/ Safflower Oil Emulsion†
Soybean oil, g	100+	50‡
Safflower oil, g	. . .	50‡
Egg yolk phospholipid, g	12	Up to 12
Glycerol, g	22.5	25
Fatty acids, % of total		
16:0	10	8.8
18:0	3.5	3.4
18:1	26	17.7
18:2	50	65.8
18:3	9	4.2
Particle size, (nm)	0.5	0.4

*Intralipid, Kabi-Vitrum, Sweden.
†Liposyn II, Abbott Laboratories, North Chicago, Ill.
‡Twenty percent emulsions also are available; these contain twice as much of the oils but roughly the same amounts of all other ingredients.

carnitine supplementation on fatty acid oxidation has shown an effect on fatty acid oxidation.[39, 40] One exception is the study of Helms et al.[41] showing that carnitine supplementation following a prolonged period of carnitine-free parenteral nutrition improves fatty acid oxidation.

Based on the linoleic acid content of soybean oil, the amount of the soybean oil emulsions necessary to prevent essential fatty acid deficiency (i.e., 2% to 4% of total energy intake) is approximately 0.5 g/kg/day, a dose that is likely to be tolerated by almost all infants. Because the linoleic acid content of safflower oil (~75%) is higher than that of soybean oil (~50%), an even smaller dose of the safflower plus soybean oil emulsion should provide the linoleic acid requirement. Although a previously available pure safflower oil emulsion, which contains no linolenic acid, resulted in linolenic acid deficiency,[42] this is unlikely to be a problem with any of the currently available emulsions. However, as the requirement for linolenic acid is unknown, it is not clear that a dose of 0.5 g/kg/day of either emulsion, in fact, provides a sufficient amount of this fatty acid.

Perhaps the most prudent approach for use of the currently available lipid emulsions is to limit intake initially to 0.5 g/kg/day in those infants likely to experience difficulties in hydrolyzing parenteral lipid emulsions as well as those with hyperbilirubinemia. Subsequently, as tolerance of the emulsion is demonstrated and/or hyperbilirubinemia resolves, the amount can be increased. This approach is common in clinical practice but appears to be based on the assumption that slow introduction of the lipid emulsion increases the recipient infant's ability to utilize the infused lipid. The data of Brans et al.,[43] however, do not support this assumption; rather, they demonstrate that the plasma triglyceride and free fatty acid concentrations of LBW infants receiving parenteral lipid emulsions, regardless of the method or duration of lipid infusion, is a function of the amount of emulsion administered over a given time. Plasma triglyceride and free fatty acid concentrations remained within an acceptable range as long as the dose of emulsion did not exceed 0.08 to 0.12 g/kg/hr (i.e., 2 to 3 g/kg/24 hr). Thus, in infants who are likely to tolerate the recommended dose, there is little reason to gradually increase the dose of lipid emulsion over several days. On the other hand, more gradual introduction may be more prudent in the smaller infant, the small-for-gestational age infant, or the infant who is infected or is experiencing other complications associated with delayed triglyceride hydrolysis. In such infants, the graded introduction permits assessment of lipid tolerance before the next increase in dose.

Rationale for Recommended Parenteral Intakes of Other Nutrients

Early parenteral nutrition regimens providing the same electrolyte intakes as infants receiving maintenance parenteral fluid therapy (approximately 3 mmols/kg/day of sodium and chloride and approximately 2 mmols/kg/day of potassium) were found to be appropriate for most infants, and parenteral infusates used subsequently have provided the same electrolyte intakes.[44] However, because of immature renal function, very small LBW infants may require greater intakes of sodium in order to maintain a normal plasma sodium concentration. Nutritionally depleted infants may require greater potassium intakes to maintain a normal plasma potassium concentration. In all infants, frequent monitoring of plasma electrolyte concentrations and appropriate reformulation of the nutrient infusate to maintain normal plasma electrolyte concentrations are recommended, particularly during the first few days of parenteral nutrition.

The recommended parenteral intakes of phosphorus (2 mmols/kg/day) and magnesium (0.25 mmol/kg/day) were established in the same manner as the recommended electrolyte intakes. These intakes, too, appear to be adequate for most infants, but frequent monitoring of the plasma concentration of both and, if indicated, appropriate reformulation of the infusate are recommended.

In contrast, most commonly used parenteral nutrition regimens do not provide an adequate calcium intake, largely because of the insolubility of calcium phosphate. Hence, osteopenia, rickets, and collapsed vertebra have been reported in both LBW and term infants who require parenteral nutrition as their sole source of nutrient intake for prolonged periods.[45, 46]

Whereas the fetus deposits about 100 mg/kg/day of calcium[47] during the last trimester of gestation, parenteral nutrition regimens usually provide no more than 40 to 60 mg (1 to 1.5 mmol/kg/day). If phosphorus intake is decreased, more calcium can be provided, but this frequently results in hypophosphatemia.

The lower pH of some of the newer amino acid mixtures allows provision of more calcium without sacrificing phosphorus intake. Using this approach to maximize calcium phosphate solubility, Koo et al.[48] studied the effects of regimens providing either 0.5 mmols/dL of both calcium and phosphorus or 1.5 to 2.0 mmol/dL of both; the vitamin D content of both regimens was 25 IU/dL. Serum 1,25-dihydroxyvitamin D concentrations of the high calcium/phosphorus group were stable and within the normal range; tubular reabsorption of phosphorus also was stable and consistently less than 90%. Serum 1,25-dihydroxyvitamin D concentrations of the low calcium/phosphorus group, on the other hand, were high, and tubular reabsorption of phosphorus was consistently greater than 90%. It appears, therefore, that delivery of calcium and phosphorus intakes approaching those required to achieve intrauterine accretion rates produce minimal stress to calcium and phosphorus homeostatic mechanisms, whereas delivery of smaller intakes stresses these mechanisms. Whether the higher intakes result in more optimal skeletal mineralization is less clear; serum alkaline phosphatase activity of the two groups did not differ.

Another peculiarity of calcium phosphate is its greater solubility at cooler temperatures than at room or body temperature. This peculiarity of calcium phosphate raises serious concerns about the overall safety of recently advocated three-in-one or complete parenteral nutrient infusates that contain glucose, amino acids, and the lipid emulsion in the same bottle with required electrolytes, minerals, and vitamins. Because these infusates must be administered without an in-line filter, and the presence of lipid in the infusate obscures any precipitate of calcium phosphate that may occur either on removal from refrigeration and warming prior to administration or during the time of infusion, their use in LBW infants seems unwise, particularly when efforts are being made to maximize calcium and phosphate intakes.

Mixtures of vitamins for parenteral use have been available since the early days of parenteral nutrition, and these mixtures have been used to formulate parenteral nutrition infusates. Hence, the amounts provided were (and are) determined by the multivitamin preparations available. Trace mineral preparations suitable for parenteral use were not available until several years after the advent of parenteral nutrition. During the early years of this therapy, it was thought that frequent plasma and/or blood transfusions provided needed trace minerals. Reports of zinc and copper deficiencies, even in infants who had received these transfusions, demonstrated the inadequacy of this approach and led to the availability of zinc and copper additives. Today, additives of all trace minerals for which a deficiency has been demonstrated in patients (usually adults) receiving parenteral nutrition are available.

To date, little definitive information is available concerning the parenteral requirements of either trace minerals or vitamins. Research concerning the parenteral requirements of these nutrients by infants is, of course, hindered by the difficulties both of measuring plasma concentrations of both groups of nutrients using small volumes of plasma and of interpreting plasma concentrations. Accurate studies of nutrient retention are also notoriously difficult. The most recent recommendations for parenteral vitamin and trace mineral intakes (see Tables 10–3 and 10–4)[49] are based on the most reliable information available, much of it theoretical, rather than data from randomized trials of various intakes.

COMPLICATIONS OF PARENTERAL NUTRITION

Two general categories of complications are associated with parenteral nutrition: those related to the technique, particularly the presence of an indwelling catheter (catheter-related complications), and those related to the infusate (metabolic complications).

The major catheter-related complication is infection. Although many of the infusate components support growth of various microorganisms,[50, 51] a contaminated infusate rarely is the underlying cause of infection. Rather, most infections appear to result from improper care of the catheter, particularly failure to follow meticulously the requirement for frequent changes of the catheter exit site dressing. Other catheter-related complications include malposition, dislodgement, thrombosis, and SVC (or inferior vena cava) thrombosis. Malposition can be avoided by radiographic confirmation of the location of the catheter tip prior to infusion of the hypertonic nutrient infusate and reconfirmation as indicated thereafter. The other catheter-related complications cannot be completely avoided; however, most believe that careful attention to all procedures involving the catheter will reduce their incidence to an acceptable level.

Complications associated with peripheral vein infusion of nutrients include thrombophlebitis as well as skin and subcutaneous sloughs secondary to infiltration of the hypertonic infusate. Infection is much less common with peripheral vein delivery than with central vein delivery and, if it occurs, is more likely to result from a contaminated infusate.

The metabolic complications of parenteral nutrition and their presumed cause are summarized in Table 10–6. These causes include two general categories: those related to the patient's limited metabolic capacity for the various components of the infusate and those related to the infusate per se. Because the infusates delivered by central vein and peripheral vein are qualitatively similar, the latter group of complications should be similar regardless of the route of delivery. The metabolic complications related to the patient's metabolic tolerance of the infusate, on the other hand, are likely to be less with the less-concentrated peripheral vein regimens. Certainly, glucose intolerance is less frequent with peripheral vein delivery, which limits glucose intake to 15 g/kg/day. With both routes of delivery, electrolyte and mineral disorders usually result from provision of either too much or too little of the particular nutrient. Electrolyte disorders, however, can result from hyperglycemia and attendant osmotic diuresis.

Some of the early complications related to composition of the amino acid mixtures are no longer problems. Metabolic acidosis, which was common with early crystalline amino acid mixtures, was related to the use of hydrochloride salts of the cationic amino acids,[52] a practice that has since been abandoned. However, some of the currently available amino acid mixtures may produce mild metabolic alkalosis.[53] Hyperammonemia,

TABLE 10–6.

Metabolic Complications of Parenteral Nutrition and Their Most Common Causes

Disorder	Most Common Cause
Disorders related to metabolic capacity of patient	
Hyperglycemia	Excessive intake (either excessive concentration or excessive infusion rate; *e.g.*, pump dysfunction); change in metabolic state (*e.g.*, infection)
Hypoglycemia	Sudden cessation of infusion
Azotemia	Excessive nitrogen intake
Electrolyte, mineral (major and trace), and vitamin disorders	Excessive or inadequate intake
Disorders related to infusate composition	
Abnormal plasma aminograms	Amino acid pattern of nitrogen source
Hypercholesterolemia/phospholipidemia	Characteristics of lipid emulsion
Abnormal fatty acid pattern	Characteristics of lipid emulsion or its route of metabolism
Hepatic disorders	Unknown

another early metabolic problem in patients who received protein hydrolysates[54] and one of the early crystalline amino acid mixtures,[55] also is no longer a serious problem. This complication, at least in infants receiving the crystalline amino acid mixture, was related to inadequate arginine intake (<0.5 mmol/kg/day).[55] All currently available parenteral amino acid mixtures contain at least this amount of arginine (see Table 10–2). In the authors' experience, any parenteral nutrition regimen causes an increase in blood ammonia concentration; however, when arginine intake is greater than 0.5 mmol/kg/day, symptomatic hyperammonemia does not occur.

The major concern with respect to the metabolic consequences of currently available amino acid mixtures is that none results in a completely normal plasma amino acid pattern.[56] This concern is based, in part, on the long-recognized coexistence of mental retardation and elevated plasma concentrations of specific amino acids in patients with various inborn errors of metabolism (e.g., hyperphenylalaninemia in patients with phenylketonuria). However, in patients receiving parenteral nutrition, the plasma concentrations of many amino acids are low rather than high, suggesting that the intake of these amino acids may be inadequate. As discussed earlier, plasma concentrations of the possibly indispensable amino acids cyst(e)ine and tyrosine are quite low, presumably because these amino acids are either unstable or insoluble in aqueous solution and, therefore, are not included in appreciable amounts in most available parenteral amino acid mixtures.

From studies in animals it is clear that the abnormal plasma amino acid pattern associated with administration of parenteral nutrition regimens is accompanied by an abnormal tissue amino acid pattern.[57] Although this relationship is not necessarily direct, the abnormal plasma and tissue amino acid patterns are of concern with respect to possible adverse effects on ongoing protein synthesis. They also raise concerns regarding the concentration of various neurotransmitters within the central nervous system. Unfortunately, these areas have not been studied sufficiently to warrant major concern or to allay fears.

Many of the metabolic abnormalities related to the composition and/or metabolism of available parenteral lipid emulsions are better understood than those related to available parenteral amino acid mixtures.[31] Perhaps the most pressing concern is related to the fatty acid pattern of serum and tissue lipids associated with use of available parenteral lipid emulsions. While all available emulsions contain adequate amounts of linoleic and linolenic acid, the parent fatty acids, respectively, of the n-6 and n-3 fatty acid families, none contains the longer-chain, more unsaturated fatty acids of either family (see Table 10–5). Because the infant may be unable to elongate and desaturate the parent fatty acids,[58] this lack gives rise to two concerns.

First, arachidonic acid, an elongated and desaturated derivative of linoleic acid, is a precursor of many prostaglandin series. Thus, if it cannot be formed from linoleic acid, infants receiving available lipid emulsions may, in theory, develop arachidonic deficiency and, in turn, derangements in prostaglandin production. Indeed, the arachidonic content of serum lipids decreases in infants receiving available emulsions, and in these infants, urinary excretion of a stable metabolite of prostaglandin E is very low.[59] Although not associated with clinical abnormalities, this association is disturbing; unfortunately, it has received very little attention.

Second, since appreciable amounts of the longer-chain, more unsaturated members of both the n-3 and n-6 fatty acid families accumulate during development,[60, 61] particularly in the developing central nervous system (Table 10–7), the possibility that the infant cannot convert the parent fatty acids of either family to these longer-chain, more unsaturated derivatives gives rise to concern regarding the fatty acid pattern of tissue lipids. Currently, this is purely a theoretical concern. Whether the fatty acid pattern of lipids deposited by infants receiving only parenteral nutrients is abnormal as well as whether such an abnormal pattern, if it occurs, is associated with functional abnormalities remains unknown.

MONITORING REQUIREMENTS FOR PARENTERAL NUTRITION

Adequate monitoring to detect both metabolic and catheter-related complications is obviously necessary for successful parenteral nutrition. In addition, the actual parenteral intake of various nutrients and the clinical results of this intake must also be monitored carefully if the full potential of the technique is to be realized. Adequate clinical monitoring usually requires considerable nursing time. The observation time necessary to

TABLE 10–7.

Accretion of n-6 and n-3 Fatty Acids in the Developing Human Brain*

Fatty Acid	Fetal Period (mg/wk)	Postnatal Period (mg/wk)
Total n-6	31	78
18:2	<1	2
20:4	19	45
Total n-3	15	4
18:3	<1	<1
Total	181	149

*From Clandinin MT, Chappell JE, Leong S, et al: Intrauterine fatty acid accretion in infant brain; duplications for fatty acid requirements. *Early Hum Dev* 1980; 4:121–129, and Extrauterine fatty acid accretion in infant brain: Implications for fatty acid requirements. *Early Hum Dev* 1980; 4:131–138. Used by permission.

prevent infiltration of the nutrition infusate delivered by peripheral vein and to assure long-term function of the central vein catheter frequently cannot be provided in the usual clinical setting. Adequate monitoring also requires personnel who are familiar with the intricacies of the intravenous infusion apparatus, including the many varieties of constant infusion pumps that are an absolute necessity both for central vein and peripheral vein delivery.

A suggested schedule for chemical monitoring is shown in Table 10–8. This schedule allows detection of metabolic complications in sufficient time to permit correction by altering the infusate. Instead of routine monitoring of blood glucose concentration, as suggested by some, checking the urine regularly for the presence of glucose (at least three times daily, perhaps even more frequently during the first few days of the technique) and determining blood glucose concentrations only when glucosuria is present appear to be adequate. If the urine is free of glucose, it is safe to assume that the blood glucose concentration is not sufficiently high to cause problems. Determinations by use of reagent strips are useful in monitoring for hypoglycemia (e.g., following either infiltration of a peripheral vein infusion or sudden cessation of a central vein infusion), but this method is not sufficiently accurate to detect troublesome degrees of hyperglycemia.

In the absence of hyperglycemia, plasma osmolality can be estimated sufficiently accurately as twice the plasma sodium concentration. Thus, it is not necessary, as frequently suggested, to monitor osmolality, per se.

The derangements of the plasma amino acid pattern incident to use of available parenteral amino acid mixtures are predictable from the pattern of the mixture of amino

TABLE 10–8.

Suggested Monitoring Schedule During Parenteral Nutrition

Variables to be Monitored	Suggested Frequency (per wk)*	
	Initial Period	Later Period
Growth variables		
Weight	7	7
Length	1	1
Head circumference	1	1
Metabolic variables		
Blood or plasma		
Electrolytes	2–4	1
Calcium, magnesium, potassium	2	1
Acid–base status	2	1
Urea nitrogen	2	1
Albumin	1	1
Liver function studies	1	1
Lipids†	. . .	. . .
Hemoglobin	2	1
Urine glucose	2–6/day	2/day
Prevention and detection of infection		
Clinical observations (activity, temperature)	Daily	Daily
White blood cell count and differential	As indicated	As indicated
Cultures	As indicated	As indicated

*"Initial Period" refers to the time before full intake is achieved as well as any period during which metabolic instability is present or suspected (e.g., postoperative, presence of infection). "Later period" refers to the time during which the patient is in a metabolic steady state.
†See text.

acids used.[56] This expensive and difficult-to-obtain determination, therefore, is rarely helpful.

The consequences of the hepatic dysfunction that develops during the course of parenteral nutrition in many patients[62] are not known. Nonetheless, the fact that such dysfunction occurs and, in a few patients, progresses to cirrhosis and death mandates careful assessment and monitoring of hepatic function. The indices listed in Table 10–8 are adequate for this purpose.

The monitoring required to insure safe and efficacious use of intravenous fat emulsions is more problematic. The usual clinical practice, if any, is periodic visual or nephelometric inspection of the plasma for presence of lipemia. However, neither method is effective for detecting elevated plasma triglyceride and free fatty acid concentrations.[63] Rather, adequate monitoring requires actual chemical determinations of both triglyceride and free fatty acid concentrations. But because microtechniques for these assays are not routinely available or, if available, are performed only two or three times per week, such monitoring is not practical. A reasonable compromise is to inspect the plasma frequently, either visually or by nephelometry, and to determine actual triglyceride and free fatty acid concentrations once or twice weekly. This is particularly important during the initial period of parenteral nutrition and when the patient develops a clinical condition likely to interfere with hydrolysis. Other serum lipid abnormalities associated with use of parenteral lipid emulsions (e.g., hypercholesterolemia, hyperphospholipidemia, deranged free fatty acid patterns of serum and tissue lipids) are predictable, perhaps unavoidable, and/or of questionable clinical relevance; thus, monitoring to detect these is not necessary.

EXPECTATIONS OF PARENTERAL NUTRITION

Clinical Results

There is little doubt that parenteral nutrition regimens delivered by central vein produce normal growth of infants and children and regrowth of depleted adults. In infants, a regimen delivering 2.5 to 3.0 g/kg/day of amino acids and 100 kcal/kg/day reliably produces a weight gain of 10 to 15 g/kg/day and nitrogen retention of 200 to 300 mg/kg/day. Increases in length also occur in infants receiving these parenteral nutrition regimens but, in the authors' experience, the increase in length may lag behind the increase in weight, so that weight for length soon exceeds the 50th percentile. Since it is possible to produce proportionate growth (i.e., to maintain weight for length at or around the 50th percentile), it is likely that the disproportionate growth is a result of somewhat excessive energy intake. Disproportionate growth, of course, is only a problem in patients who are dependent on parenteral nutrients for months rather than weeks. In the usual patient, weight for length is frequently low when parenteral nutrition is started; thus, the disproportionate increase in weight is not undesirable.

Gastrointestinal Function During Parenteral Nutrition

Because the one unquestioned clinical indication for use of parenteral nutrition is to maintain or restore the nutritional status of patients with deranged gastrointestinal function, there has been considerable interest in the consequences of this therapy with respect to gastrointestinal function. In healthy animals, parenteral nutrition, like starvation, results in an appreciable decrease in enteric mucosal mass.[64–66, 68] However, parenteral nutrition following a period of starvation prevents a further decrease in mucosal mass but does not support regrowth of the enteric mucosa as occurs in animals that are refed with chow.[67] The effect of parenteral nutrition on mucosal enzyme activities is unclear. Some studies suggest that the specific activity of several disaccharidases decreases relative to that of control animals,[64] but others suggest that the specific activity of these enzymes do not differ between control animals and animals treated with parenteral nutrition.[66] These discrepancies may be related to the nature of the diet consumed by the control animals of the various studies.

The few available clinical studies of the effects of parenteral nutrition on intestinal tract structure and function do not demonstrate morphological involution.[69, 70] On the other hand, disaccharidase activities, which usually are low when parenteral nutrition begins, are not fully restored until enteral intake is reinstituted.[70]

Two recent studies in LBW infants suggest that infants who receive seemingly negligible amounts of enterally delivered nutrients during the period of parenteral nutrition are more easily weaned from parenteral to enteral nutrients.[71, 72] The mechanism of this apparent effect is not known but may be related to the different pattern of release of enteric hormones between fed and unfed (i.e., parenterally fed) infants.[73]

REFERENCES

1. Helfrick FW, Abelson NM: Intravenous feeding of a complete diet in a child: A report of a case. *J Pediatr* 1944; 25:400–403.
2. Wretlind A: Total parenteral nutrition. *Surg Clin North Am* 1978; 58:1055–1070.
3. Heird WC: Parenteral nutrition, in Grand RJ, Sutphen JL, Dietz WH Jr (eds): *Pediatric Nutrition: Theory and Practice*. Boston, Butterworths, 1987, pp 747–761.
4. Dudrick SJ, Wilmore DW, Vars HM, et al: Long term parenteral nutrition with growth, development, and positive nitrogen balance. *Surgery* 1968; 64:134–142.
5. Wilmore DM, Dudrick SJ: Growth and development of an infant receiving all nutrients by vein. *JAMA* 1968; 203:860–864.
6. Heird WC: Nutritional support of the pediatric patient, in Winters RW, Greene HL (eds): *Nutritional Support of the Seriously Ill Patient*. New York, Academic Press, 1983, pp 157–179.
7. Mulvihill SJ, Fonkalsrud EW: Complication of superior versus inferior vena cava occlusion in infants receiving central total parenteral nutrition (abstract). *J Pediatr Surg* 1984; 19:752.
8. Jacobowski D, Ziegler MD, Perreira G: Complications of pediatric parenteral nutrition: Central versus peripheral administration (abstract). *J Parenter Enteral Nutr* 1979; 3:29.
9. Friedman Z, Danon A, Stahlman MT, et al: Rapid onset of essential acid deficiency in the newborn. *Pediatrics* 1976; 58:640–649.
10. Committee on Nutrition, American Academy of Pediatrics: Use of intravenous fat emulsions in pediatric patients. *Pediatrics* 1981; 68:738–743.
11. Jeejeebhoy KN, Chu RC, Marliss EB, et al: Chromium deficiency, glucose intolerance, and neuropathy reversed by chromium supplementation, in a patient receiving long-term total parenteral nutrition. *Am J Clin Nutr* 1977; 30:531–538.
12. Kien CL, Ganther HE: Manifestations of chronic selenium deficiency in a child receiving total parenteral nutrition. *Am J Clin Nutr* 1983; 37:319–328.
13. Abumrad NN, Schneider AJ, Steel D, et al: Amino acid intolerance during prolonged total parenteral nutrition reversed by molybdate therapy. *Am J Clin Nutr* 1981; 34:2551–2559.
14. Zlotkin SH, Bryan MH, Anderson GH: Intravenous nitrogen and energy intakes required to duplicate in utero nitrogen accretion in prematurely born human infants. *J Pediatr* 1981; 99:115–120.

15. Anderson TL, Muttart C, Bieber MA, et al: A controlled trial of glucose vs. glucose and amino acids in premature infants. *J Pediatr* 1979; 94:947–951.

16. Duffy B, Gunn T, Collinge J, et al: The effect of varying protein quality and energy intake on the nitrogen metabolism of parenterally fed very low birth weight (1,600 g) infants. *Pediatr Res* 1981; 15:1040–1044.

17. Helms RA, Christensen ML, Mauer EC, et al: Comparison of a pediatric versus standard amino acid formulation in preterm neonates requiring parenteral nutrition. *J Pediatr* 1987; 110:466–472.

18. Snyderman SE: The protein requirements of the premature infant, in Jonxis JHP, Visser HKA, Troelsta JA (eds): *Metabolic Processes in the Fetus and Newborn Infant*. Leiden, Stenfert Kruesse, 1971, pp 128–141.

19. Sturman JA, Gaull GA, Räihä, NCR: Absence of cystathionase in human liver: Is cystine essential? *Science* 1970; 169:74–76.

20. Zlotkin SH, Anderson GH: The development of cystathionase activity during the first year of life. *Pediatr Res* 1982; 16:65–68.

21. Räihä NCR: Phenylalanine hydroxylase in human liver during development. *Pediatr Res* 1973; 7:1–4.

22. Chawla RK, Berry CJ, Kutner MH, et al: Plasma concentrations of transsulfuration pathway products during nasoenteral and intravenous hyperalimentation of malnourished patients. *Am J Clin Nutr* 1985; 42:577–584.

23. Zlotkin SH, Bryan MH, Anderson GH: Cysteine supplementation to cysteine-free intravenous feeding regimens in newborn infants. *Am J Clin Nutr* 1981; 34:914–923.

24. Malloy MH, Rassin DK, Richardson CJ: Total parenteral nutrition in sick preterm infants: Effects of cysteine supplementation with nitrogen intakes of 240 and 400 mg/kg/d. *J Pediatr Gastroenterol Nutr* 1984; 3:239–244.

25. Heird WC, Hay W, Helms RA, et al: Pediatric parenteral amino acid mixture in low birth weight infants. *Pediatrics* 1988; 81:41–50.

26. Weinstein MR, Oh W: Oxygen consumption in infants with bronchopulmonary dysplasia. *J Pediatr* 1981; 99:958–961.

27. Munro HN: General aspects of the regulation of protein metabolism by diet and hormone, in Munro HN (ed): *Mammalian Protein Metabolism*, vol I. *Biochemical Aspects of Protein Metabolism*. New York, Academic Press, 1964, pp 381–481.

28. Pineault M, Chessex P, Bisaillon S, et al: Total parenteral nutrition in the newborn: Impact of the quality of infused energy on nitrogen metabolism. *Am J Clin Nutr* 1988; 47:298–304.

29. Jeejeebhoy KN, Anderson GK, Nakhooda AF, et al: Metabolic studies in total parenteral nutrition with lipid in man: comparison with glucose. *J Clin Invest* 1976; 57:125–136.

30. Long JM III, Wilmore DW, Mason AD Jr, et al: Effect of carbohydrate and fat intake on nitrogen excretion during total intravenous feeding. *Ann Surg* 1977; 185:417–422.

31. Heird WC: Lipid metabolism in parenteral nutrition, in Fomon SJ, Heird WC (eds): *Energy and Protein Needs During Infancy*. New York, Academic Press, 1986, pp 215–229.

32. Andrew G, Chan G, Schiff D: Lipid metabolism in the neonate: I. The effect of intralipid infusion on plasma triglyceride and free fatty acid concentrations in the neonate. *J Pediatr* 1976; 88:273–278.

33. Greene HL, Hazlett D, Demaree R: Relationship between intralipid-induced hyperlipidemia and pulmonary function. *Am J Clin Nutr* 1976; 29:127–135.

34. Perreira GR, Fox WW, Stanley CA, et al: Decreased oxygenation and hyperlipidemia during intravenous fat infusions in premature infants. *Pediatrics* 1980; 66:26–30.

35. Loo LS, Tang JP, Kohl S: The inhibition of leukocyte cellular cytotoxicity to herpes simplex virus in vitro and in vivo by intralipid. *J Infect Dis* 1982; 146:64–70.

36. Cleary TC, Pickering LK: Mechanisms of intralipid effect on polymorpho-nuclear leukocytes. *J Clin Lab Immunol* 1983; 11:21–26.

37. Odell GB, Cukier JO, Ostrea EM Jr, et al: The influence of fatty acids on the binding of bilirubin to albumin. *J Clin Med* 1977; 89:295–307.

38. Penn D, Schmidt-Sommerfeld E, Pascu F: Decreased carnitine concentration in newborn infants receiving total parenteral nutrition. *Early Hum Dev* 1979; 4:23–28.
39. Schmidt-Sommerfeld E, Penn D, Wolf H: Carnitine deficiency in premature infants receiving total parenteral nutrition: Effect of L-carnitine supplementation. *J Pediatr* 1983; 102:931–935.
40. Orzali A, Donzelli F, Enzi G, et al: Effect of carnitine on lipid metabolism in the newborn: I. Carnitine supplementation during total parenteral nutrition in the first 48 hours of life. *Biol Neonate* 1983; 43:186–190.
41. Helms RA, Whitington PF, Mauer EC, et al: Enhanced lipid utilization in infants receiving oral L-carnitine during long-term parenteral nutrition. *J Pediatr* 1986; 109:984–988.
42. Holman RT, Johnson SB, Hatch TF: A case of human linolenic acid deficiency involving neurological abnormalities. *Am J Clin Nutr* 1982; 35:617–623.
43. Brans YW, Andrew DS, Carrillo DW, et al: Tolerance of fat emulsions in very-low-birth-weight neonates. *Am J Dis Child* 1988; 142:145–152.
44. Heird WC, Winters RW: Total parenteral nutrition: The state of the art. *J Pediatr* 1975; 86:2–16.
45. Koo WWK, Tsang RC: Bone mineralization in infants. *Prog Food Nutr Sci* 1984; 8:229–302.
46. Koo WWK, Tsang RC: Rickets in infants, in Nelson NM (ed): *Current Therapy in Neonatal Perinatal Medicine*. Philadelphia, BC Decker, 1985, pp 299–304.
47. Ziegler EE, O'Donnell AM, Nelson SE, et al: Body composition of the reference fetus. *Growth* 1986; 40:329–341.
48. Koo WWK, Tsang RC, Steichen JJ, et al: Parenteral nutrition for infants: Effect of high versus low calcium and phosphorus content. *J Pediatr Gastroenterol Nutr* 1987; 6:96–104.
49. Greene HL, Hambidge KM, Schanler R, et al: Guidelines for the use of vitamins, trace elements, calcium, magnesium, and phosphorus in infants and children receiving total parenteral nutrition: Report of the subcommittee on pediatric parenteral nutrient requirements from the committee on clinical practice issues of the American Society for Clinical Nutrition. *Am J Clin Nutr* 1988; 48:1324–1342.
50. Goldman DA, Martin WT, Worthington JW: Growth of bacteria and fungi in total parenteral nutrition solutions. *Am J Surg* 1973; 126:314–318.
51. McKee KT, Melly MA, Greene HL, et al: Gram-negative bacillary sepsis associated with use of lipid emulsion in parenteral nutrition. *Am J Dis Child* 1979; 133:649–650.
52. Heird WC, Dell RB, Driscoll JM JR, et al: Metabolic acidosis resulting from intravenous alimentation mixtures containing synthetic amino acids. *N Engl J Med* 1972; 827:943–948.
53. Heird WC: Studies of pediatric patients receiving Aminosyn as the nitrogen source of total parenteral nutrition, in *Current Approaches to Nutrition of the Hospitalized Patient*. Chicago, Abbott and Ross Laboratories, 1977, pp 45–49.
54. Johnson JD, Albritton WL, Sunshine P: Hyperammonemia accompanying parenteral nutrition in newborn infants. *J Pediatr* 1972; 81:154–161.
55. Heird WC, Nicholson JF, Driscoll JM Jr, et al: Hyperammonemia resulting from intravenous alimentation using a mixture of synthetic L-amino acids: A preliminary report. *J Pediatr* 1972; 81:162–167.
56. Winters RW, Heird WC, Dell RB, et al: Plasma amino acids in infants receiving parenteral nutrition, in Greene HL, Holliday MA, Munro HN (eds): *Clinical Nutrition Update: Amino Acids*. Chicago, American Medical Association, 1977, pp 147–154.
57. Heird WC, Malloy MH: Brain composition of beagle puppies receiving total parenteral nutrition, in Itka V (ed): *Nutrition and Metabolism of the Fetus and Infant*. The Hague, Martinus Nijhoff, 1979, pp 365–375.
58. Clandinin MT, Chappell JE, Heim PR, et al: Fatty acid utilization in perinatal de novo synthesis of tissues. *Early Hum Dev* 1981; 5:355–366.
59. Friedman Z, Frolich JC: Essential fatty acids and the major urinary metabolites of the E prostaglandins in thriving neonates and in infants receiving parenteral fat emulsions. *Pediatr Res* 1979; 13:926–932.

60. Clandinin MT, Chappell JE, Leong S, et al: Intrauterine fatty acid accretion rates in human brain: Implications for fatty acid requirements. *Early Hum Dev* 1980; 4:121–129.
61. Clandinin MT, Chappell JE, Leong S, et al: Extrauterine fatty acid accretion in infant brain: Implications for fatty acid requirements. *Early Hum Dev* 1980; 4:131–138.
62. Merritt RJ: Cholestasis associated with total parenteral nutrition. *J Pediatr Gastroenterol Nutr* 1980; 5:9–22.
63. Schreiner RL, Glick MR, Nordschow CD, et al: An evaluation of methods to monitor infants receiving intravenous lipids. *J Pediatr* 1979; 94:197–200.
64. Levine GM, Deren JJ, Steiger E, et al: Role of oral intake in maintenance of gut mass and disaccharidase activity. *Gastroenterology* 1974; 67:975–982.
65. Johnson LR, Copeland EM, Dudrick SJ, et al: Structural and hormonal alterations in the gastrointestinal tract of parenterally fed rats. *Gastroenterology* 1975; 68:1177–1183.
66. Feldman EJ, Dowling RH, McNaughton J, et al: Effects of oral versus intravenous nutrition on intestinal adaptation after small bowel resection in the dog. *Gastroenterology* 1976; 70:712–719.
67. Mones RL, Heird WC, Rosensweig SN: Unpublished data.
68. Heird WC, Tsang HL, MacMillan R, et al: Effect of total parenteral alimentation on rat small intestine (abstract). *Pediatr Res* 1974; 8:107.
69. Shwachman H, Lloyd-Still JD, Khaw KT, et al: Protracted diarrhea of infancy treated with intravenous alimentation: II. Studies of small intestinal biopsy results. *Am J Dis Child* 1973; 125:365–368.
70. Greene HL, McCabe DR, Merenstein GB: Intractable diarrhea and malnutrition in infancy: Changes in intestinal morphology and disaccharidase activities during treatment with total intravenous nutrition or oral elemental diets. *J Pediatr* 1975; 87:695–704.
71. Dunn L, Hulman S, Weiner J, et al: Beneficial effects of early hypocaloric enteral feeding on neonatal gastrointestinal function: Preliminary report of a randomized trial. *J Pediatr* 1988; 112:622–629.
72. Slagle TA, Gross SJ: Effect of early enteral substrate on subsequent feeding tolerance. *J Pediatr* 1988; 113:526–531.
73. Lucas A, Bloom SR, Aynsley-Green A: Metabolic and endocrine effects of depriving preterm infants of enteral nutrition. *Acta Paediatr Scand* 1983; 72:245–249.

Chapter 11

Secretion and Composition of Human Milk*

Margaret C. Neville, Ph.D.

In the past decade there has been an upsurge of interest among physicians and scientists in the nutrient and anti-infection properties of human milk. The recognition that many of these properties are not duplicated in milks of animal origin has led to the recommendation that infants be breast-fed whenever possible.[1] This recommendation is often extended to preterm infants, with many authorities suggesting that these infants receive their own mother's milk whenever feasible.[62] Successful initiation of breast-feeding in the term infant requires motivated mothers and often assistance from knowledgeable health care personnel.[43] The mother of the premature infant faces additional emotional and technical problems in providing milk for her hospitalized infant. A thorough understanding of milk secretion and its regulation is important if she is to be given useful assistance in overcoming these problems. This chapter, therefore, begins with a discussion of the physiology of lactation in the mother of the full-term infant. Milk secretion in the mother of the preterm infant is dealt with more briefly; it is clear that milk from these mothers differs in composition,[35] and often volume,[2] from milk of mothers of term infants. However, our knowledge of the physiologic factors involved is rudimentary. Finally some comments are made about the growth of the breast-fed term infant. It is not possible in a chapter of this scope to deal in depth with the experimental basis of the principles described. The interested reader is, therefore, referred to several books[34, 41, 48, 51] and articles[18, 43, 62] that provide excellent reviews of all aspects of mammary gland biology, lactation, and breast-feeding management. For more specific articles on human lactation and milk the reader is referred to the three-volume series sponsored by the International Society for Research in Human Milk and Lactation.[19, 21, 29]

*Research described from the author's laboratory was supported by NIH grant HD19547, NIH contract HD 22801, and grant RR-69 from the General Clinical Research Centers Program of the Division of Research Resources.

DEVELOPMENTAL ANATOMY OF THE HUMAN MAMMARY GLAND

The mammary gland is a compound tubuloalveolar organ embedded in a cushion of adipose tissue[7, 34] (Fig 11–1). A rudimentary ductal system, present at birth, is developmentally quiescent until puberty, when growth of both the mammary fat pad and the ductile system is stimulated by the rising levels of estrogen.[3] With the onset of menses the cyclic production of progesterone brings about limited formation of alveolar complexes. Mammary development is completed during pregnancy with extensive growth of the alveoli that form the site of future milk secretion. The alveoli are lined with a single layer of cuboidal epithelial cells surrounded by a basket-like complex of myoepithelial cells. After the birth of the infant the epithelial cells assume a secretory morphology with a basally placed nucleus surrounded by rough endoplasmic reticulum, extensive Golgi complexes with expanded terminal cisterna, and large secretory vesicles within which casein micelles can be seen surrounded by a clear area (Fig 11–2).[56] The cells rest on a basement membrane and show extensive invagination of their basal and lateral surfaces. Near the luminal surface adjacent cells are joined by prominent junctional complexes (see Fig 11–2). The apical surface has a fuzzy plasma membrane, reflecting an extensive mucopolysaccharide coat, and extensive microvilli. Milk fat globules can occasionally be observed protruding from the apical surface. The lumen of the lactating gland contains casein micelles and cellular elements as well as milk fat globules. As weaning occurs, the capacity of the gland to produce milk decreases; with complete weaning, the secretory elements involute to a quiescent state similar to that found prior to pregnancy.[7, 56] The hormonal control of this developmental sequence will be considered after a description of the function of the mature mammary gland.

FIG 11–1.
Camera lucida drawing of a thick section of a breast from a woman who was never pregnant. Four of the 15 to 20 ducts originating at the nipple are shown coursing through the stroma of the breast to terminate in bunches of tubuloalveolar complexes that are particularly prevalent in the distal regions. (From Dabelow A: Die postnatale Entwicklung der menschlichen Milchdruse und ihre Korrelationen. *Morphol J* 1941; 85:361–416. Used by permission.)

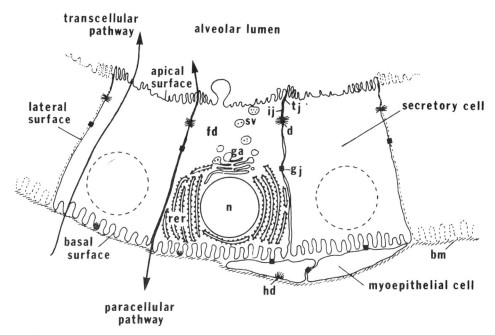

FIG 11–2.
Diagram of the mammary epithelium showing secretory pathways and associations between cells. The basal surface shows extensive infolding and rests on a basement membrane *(bm)*. The lateral surfaces of adjacent cells are joined at intervals by tight junctions *(tj,* zonulae occludentes), intermediate junctions *(ij,* zonulae adhaerentes), and desmosomes *(d).* Gap junctions *(gj)* allow communication between adjacent epithelial cells as well as between secretory and myoepithelial cells. Within one cell the basally placed nucleus *(n),* the rough endoplasmic reticulum *(rer),* the Golgi apparatus *(ga),* secretory vesicles *(sv),* and fat droplets *(fd)* are illustrated. Note the microvilli and budding fat droplet at the apical surface. (From Mather IH, Keenan TW: Function of endomembranes and the cell surface in the secretion of organic milk constituents, in Mepham TB (ed): *Biochemistry of Lactation.* Amsterdam, Elsevier, 1983. Used by permission.)

MECHANISMS OF MILK SECRETION AND EJECTION

The production of milk can be divided into two distinct processes: secretion and ejection.[46] *Milk secretion* is continuous and results in the accumulation of milk in the mammary alveoli and ducts near the cells that secrete it. The composition of the milk is not altered by storage in the alveoli or passage through the ducts[36] and is, therefore, entirely determined by the mammary epithelial cells. *Milk ejection,* also called "letdown", is the process by which the mammary secretion is discharged from the alveoli through the ducts to the nipple, where it becomes available to the suckling infant. Although nipple stimulation leads to the secretion of hormones that influence both ejection and secretion, the mechanisms and regulation of the two processes are distinct and are dealt with separately.

Milk Ejection

Milk ejection is the result of a neuroendocrine reflex initiated by suckling or other nipple stimulation. Afferent impulses are carried by sensory fibers to the hypothalamus where they directly stimulate the release of oxytocin by magnocellular neurons whose processes terminate in the posterior pituitary.[45] Oxytocin is transported through the blood stream to the breast, where it interacts with receptors on myoepithelial cells surrounding the alveoli and smaller mammary ducts. When these cells contract they force milk from the alveoli into the duct system and out the nipple. The let-down reflex is essential to removal of milk from the breast. The reflex is easily conditioned—so that it can occur when the mother hears the infant cry, or even at the sight of a picture of the infant. Strong emotions and pain interfere with the reflex[53]; for this reason, maternal anxiety may impede breast feeding.

Milk Composition

Milk is a complex fluid whose major constituents are the proteins casein, α-lactalbumin, secretory IgA, lactoferrin, and lysozyme; the milk sugar lactose; monovalent and divalent ions; and triacylglycerol and other lipids present as a *milk fat globule* surrounded by a specialized plasma membrane. Minor components include a wide variety of cells, enzymes, trace elements, vitamins, growth factors, mucins, and free amino acids.[5, 18] Because small amounts of cytoplasm may be enclosed within the milk fat globule membrane, all cytoplasmic constituents may be present at small concentrations in milk. Milk provides complete nutrition as well as a measure of protection for the infant from birth to 4 to 6 months of age.[1, 34]

Cellular Mechanisms of Milk Secretion

The cellular mechanisms that result in milk secretion are illustrated in Figure 11–3. A number of distinct pathways are present.[46] Pathway *I,* the exocytotic pathway, is responsible for secretion of most of the components of the aqueous fraction of milk. Like all secreted proteins, caseins and α-lactalbumin are synthesized on ribosomes, inserted across the membrane of the rough endoplasmic reticulum into the lumen, and transported to the Golgi, where they participate in specialized reactions that result in formation of at least two milk-specific components, lactose and the casein micelle. Alpha-lactalbumin serves as a coenzyme with galactosyl transferase in the synthesis of the milk-specific sugar, lactose. Calcium pumped into the terminal cisternae of the Golgi initiates aggregation of the casein into complex micellar structures which package protein, calcium, and phosphate into an elegant structure capable of conveying the large amounts of these substances necessary for growth.*

Other substances that have been shown to be secreted by this pathway include phosphate and citrate. It can be inferred that sodium, potassium, and chloride are all present in the fluid of the secretory vesicles that carry the aqueous fraction of milk from the Golgi to the plasma membrane.

Pathway *II* is a unique pathway for secretion of lipid from cells, found only in the mammary epithelium. Triacylglycerols are synthesized in the mammary alveolar cell from fatty acids and glycerol derived either from the plasma or from endogenous synthesis.[12] Lipid droplets accumulate in the cytoplasm of the mammary alveolar cell and migrate from the basal to the apical surface of the cell. This process is distinct from the exocytotic process by which lipids are secreted by enterocytes and hepatocytes.[40] When they reach the apical membrane the lipid droplets interact with a mammary-specific apical membrane protein, butyrophilin.[39] The fat droplet eventually becomes encapsulated in membrane and is extruded from the cell with a membrane coat that appears to serve

---

*Human milk, adapted to the relatively slow growing human infant, contains relatively little casein (2 to 4 g/L) compared with cow's milk (28 g/L) or rodent milk (up to 100 g/L).[9]

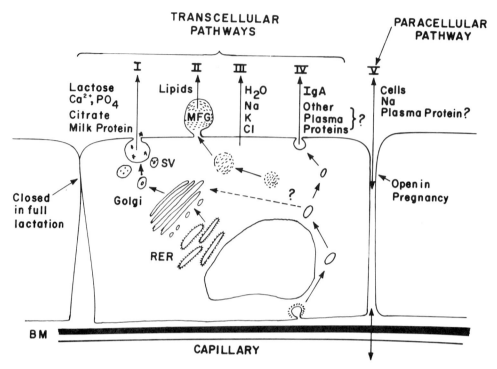

FIG 11–3.
Pathways for synthesis and secretion of milk components from mammary alveolar cell. *I*, exocytosis of milk protein and lactose in Golgi-derived secretory vesicles. *II*, milk lipid secretion via membrane-bound milk fat globule. *III*, passage of water and monovalent ions across apical membrane; these substances likely find their way across the Golgi and secretory vesicle membranes to be secreted by exocytosis as well. *IV*, secretion of IgA by transcytosis from the basolateral membrane to the apical membrane. *V*, paracellular pathway, open during pregnancy, mastitis, and after weaning, but closed during lactation. This pathway is likely the route taken by lymphocytes and macrophages in their passage into milk. (From Neville MC, Neifert MR: *Lactation: Physiology, Nutrition, and Breastfeeding.* New York, Plenum Publishing Corp, 1983. Used by permission.)

two purposes: it provides phospholipids to the infant, and it prevents the fat droplets from coalescing within the alveolar lumen, thus aiding their secretion.

The apical membrane of the mammary alveolar cell contains channels or transporters for a very few milk components, namely sodium, potassium, chloride[54] and glucose[13] (pathway *III*). It is not entirely clear to what extent this pathway is important in determining milk composition, as the concentrations of these milk components may be adjusted within the Golgi apparatus and secretory vesicles.

Pathway *IV* provides an interesting mechanism for the secretion of immunoglobulins, specifically IgA, into milk.[61] Dimeric IgA is made by plasma cells, primarily in the interstitial spaces of the mammary gland. The IgA is bound to a specific receptor on the lateral membranes of the mammary alveolar cells and transferred across the mammary cell to the apical membrane by transcytosis. At the apical membrane the receptor is cleaved proteolytically, and the resulting monomer, called *secretory component*, remains associated with the immunoglobulin. The association of secretory component with IgA (now called secretory IgA) protects the protein from digestion, possibly allowing it to perform a protective function within the infant's digestive system.

It is important to note that during full lactation only transcellular pathways are of importance in determining the concentrations of most milk components. Cellular components consist of sloughed alveolar cells and a variety of white blood cells that probably enter milk by a paracellular pathway. A variety of measurements indicate that this paracellular pathway is closed by the tight junctions during lactation but is "leaky" in pregnancy, during mastitis, and after involution. Under these conditions the concentrations of plasma components, particularly sodium and chloride, in the mammary secretion increase, and milk components such as lactose are free to pass into the blood stream.

REGULATION OF MAMMARY GLAND DEVELOPMENT AND LACTATION

Mammary gland development can be divided into four stages: mammogenesis, lactogenesis, lactation, and involution.[45] Each stage is subject to complex regulatory mechanisms that are not yet completely understood. *Mammogenesis* refers to the development of the mammary gland. Some authors have made a distinction between stage I lactogenesis, occurring during pregnancy when the gland becomes competent to secrete milk, and stage II lactogenesis, occurring after parturition.[14, 22] *Lactogenesis* will be used here to refer to the onset of copious milk secretion during the first 4 days following delivery. *Lactation* refers to the period of continuing milk production, sometimes called galactopoiesis in the dairy literature, and *involution,* to the return of the gland to the prepregnancy state after weaning.

Mammogenesis

Mammogenesis occurs in two stages: the first at puberty, and final development completed during pregnancy. Pubertal growth has been studied in detail in the mouse, where implantation of permeable capsules containing hormones and growth factors is beginning to give a picture of the complex regulatory mechanisms involved.[8] Although it is clear that the increasing levels of estrogen present at puberty initiate the developmental process, current evidence makes it unlikely that this hormone acts directly on the mammary epithelium.[25] Rather, the effects of estrogen appear to be mediated by growth factors secreted either by distant organs such as the liver, pituitary, or salivary gland, or locally by the mammary stroma.[10] The important role of the stroma in mammary development is illustrated by the observation that the normal epithelial anlage of the mammary gland will grow into normal duct structures if transplanted into a mammary fat pad but not into other locations in the body.[8] A fascinating story of local developmental regulation is beginning to emerge, but the details are not yet sufficiently clear to allow expansion here.

During pregnancy, lobulo-alveolar development results in full development of the secretory epithelium. The hormones of pregnancy—progesterone, prolactin, and placental lactogen—have all been implicated as regulators of this developmental stage, but the precise mechanisms are not yet fully known.[45, 63] The gland becomes competent to secrete milk around midpregnancy when stable levels of alpha-lactalbumin appear in the blood[45]; after this point parturition is usually followed by the onset of milk secretion. During pregnancy small amounts of a yellowish fluid, the *prepartum secretion,* can often be expressed from the breast. However, milk secretion is inhibited until after parturition by the high levels of circulating sex steroids, particularly progesterone.[30, 31] In goats,[63] mammary development and subsequent milk production are proportional to the degree of stimulation by placental lactogen. If this is true in humans as well, then it seems likely that full mammary development may not be achieved until the gland has been subjected to the high levels of placental lactogen (also called human chorionic so-matomammotropin) observed near term. The consequence could be that the mammary epithelium of mothers of premature infants may not be sufficiently developed to produce normal volumes of milk. There is currently no direct evidence bearing on this point. However, the ability of the magnetic resonance imager to distinguish epithelial and stro-mal tissue in the breast presents an opportunity for investigation of the problem.[44]

Lactogenesis

The onset of copious milk secretion—or *lactogenesis,* as the process has been termed by dairy scientists—is delayed until about 48 hours postpartum in women.[49] This delay is unusual; in all animals except guinea pigs, lactogenesis occurs within hours of parturition. For example, in the goat, lactogenesis precedes birth of the kids by a day or two; in the cow it appears to coincide with parturition.[55] Lactogenesis is per-ceived by most women as a more or less abrupt feeling of fullness or engorgement of the breasts. At this time the milk is said to "come in." However, this feeling of en-gorgement may or may not coincide with the actual increase in milk volume, which nor-mally occurs between 48 and 96 hours postpartum (Fig 11–4) and is associated with

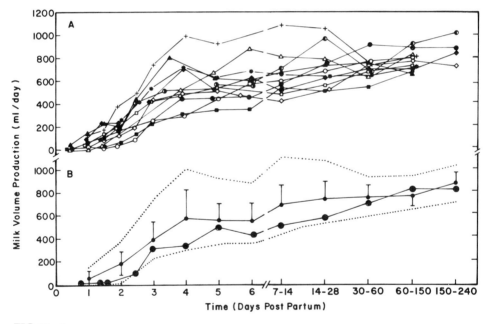

FIG 11–4.
A, milk volumes during lactogenesis in 12 fully breast-feeding mothers of full-term infants. Infants were test-weighed before and after each breast-feed for the 1st week postpartum and thereafter at weekly or monthly intervals until partial weaning occurred. Note the wide divergence between women in the amount of milk pro-duced in the 1st month. All women showed a substantial increase in milk production between 48 and 96 hours postpartum. All these women were exclusively breast-feeding at 3 months and were producing between 580 and 920 mL/day at that time. **B,** mean milk volumes from the women depicted in Fig 11–5 *(small circles),* with range of values *(dotted line)* compared to milk volumes produced by the mother of a full-term infant who pumped her breasts for the first 14 days *(large circles).* Milk volumes in this woman fell within the range of the fully breast-feeding women. (From Neville MC, Keller R, Seacat J, et al: Studies in human lactation: Milk volumes in lactating women during the onset of lactation and full lactation. *Am J Clin Nutr* 1988; 48:1375–1386. Used by permission.)

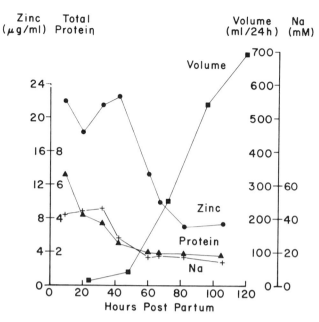

FIG 11–5.
Changes in milk composition during the early postpartum period in a single subject. Changes in sodium, protein, and zinc content preceded the rapid increase in milk volume that occurred between 48 and 120 hours postpartum.

significant changes in the composition of the mammary secretion product (Fig 11–5).

Two physiologically and temporally distinct changes in the mammary epithelium occur at lactogenesis. First, the junctional complexes between the cells close, leading to a fall in the concentrations of sodium, chloride, and protein in the milk (see Fig 11–5); this process is nearly complete by 48 hours postpartum. Second, once the junctions have closed there is a more or less abrupt increase in the synthesis and secretion of all milk components, leading to the increase in milk volume depicted in Figures 11–4 and 11–5. Over the first 4 days postpartum, then, the mammary secretion goes from a solution containing high concentrations of sodium, chloride, and protein, and low concentrations of lactose and fat (Table 11–1),[32] to a solution containing low concentrations of sodium, chloride, and protein, and high concentrations of lactose and fat. Zinc is un-

TABLE 11–1.

Postpartum Interval and the Composition of the Mammary Secretion*

Milk Component	Prepartum	Postpartum Day					
		1	5	21	60	120	180
Volume, mL/day	. . .	50	600	700	700	725	800
Lipid, %	2	3.2	4	4.7	4.0	4.5	5.6
Sodium, mmol	60	35	18	9	7.0	6.1	6.0
Chloride, mmol	60	45	22	15	13	12	13
Protein, g/dL	5.4	4.7	1.8	1.2	1.0	0.9	1.0
Lactose, mmol	80	90	160	176	184	189	191
Calcium, mmol	6.2	4.2	8.0	7.7	7.5	7.1	6.3
Zinc, μmol	121	83	72	55	27	20	17

*Unpublished compositional data from the longitudinal study described in reference 49. Data represent extrapolated values from a detailed study of 13 multiparous Caucasian women in Denver who practiced exclusive breast-feeding 6 months or longer. The standard error of the mean is <10% of the mean for all values.

usual in that it shows a biphasic response with an increase during the first 2 days post-partum followed by a decrease in concentration.[6] These changes are not understood. The mammary secretion product during the first 4 days postpartum is often called "co-lostrum." However, because this secretion has a constantly changing composition it is preferable to refer to it as *early milk* and actually specify the day on which it was col-lected.

The major initiator of lactogenesis in most or all species appears to be the fall in progesterone that occurs around parturition.[30, 31] Lactogenesis is delayed in women (and guinea pigs) because progesterone falls relatively slowly after parturition, taking 5 days to return to basal levels.[45] In women, estrogen has long been known to be inhibitory to milk secretion,[16] but as estrogen falls in parallel with progesterone, it is possible that it also plays a role in the timing of lactogenesis. However, placental retention has been associated with delayed lactogenesis,[42] and as isolated placental fragments could be ex-pected to secrete progesterone but not estrogens, it seems likely that progesterone plays the major role. Prolactin levels at parturition average about 200 μg/mL, about 20 times the level in the nonpregnant, nonlactating woman, and remain in that high range for 2 to 3 weeks postpartum, even in the non-breast-feeding woman.[38] Inhibition of prolactin se-cretion by such drugs as bromocriptine prevents lactogenesis,[4] revealing an absolute re-quirement for prolactin if lactogenesis is to occur. In summary, lactogenesis in women is initiated by the postpartum fall in progesterone in the presence of maintained high levels of prolactin.

It is often suggested that infants should be put to the breast as soon as possible after birth, with the implication that this procedure aids lactogenesis. There is no hard evi-dence that the physiologic onset of milk secretion is indeed altered by early suckling, as important as this may be in establishing a good breast-feeding relation between mother and infant.[43] What little evidence there is, in fact, suggests the opposite. Thus, Wool-ridge and colleagues, studying the onset of lactation in Thai women, found no correla-tion between milk transfer to the infant and the time at which they were first suckled.[66] Moreover, milk composition changes in the first 3 days postpartum are similar in breast-feeding and non-breast-feeding women (Fig 11–6), suggesting that it is the hormonal changes in the early postpartum period that lead to lactogenesis rather than suckling or milk removal. Once milk secretion has been initiated, however, milk removal is of cru-cial importance. Thus, as seen in Figure 11–6, the composition of the milk returns quickly to that of the prepartum secretion if suckling is not initiated by the 4th postpar-tum day.[32]

Lactation

By 5 days postpartum the mean milk volume is about 600 mL/day and the compo-sition has tended to stabilize. Milk from days 5 to 10 of lactation has been designated in the past as transitional milk, and after 10 days as mature milk. However, detailed stud-ies (References 18, 62, and M.C. Neville, unpublished data) have shown that milk com-position changes continuously during lactation. For this reason it is preferable to refer to the period of exclusive breast-feeding from day 5 to the onset of weaning as *full lacta-tion*. Again, the actual time at which lactation or milk composition is evaluated should be stated.

Milk volume through the course of lactation is shown in Figure 11–7. There is an increase from day 5 to day 21 of about 100 mL (see Table 11–1). Thereafter milk vol-ume increases at a rate of about 1 mL/day to 8 months postpartum. These values seem

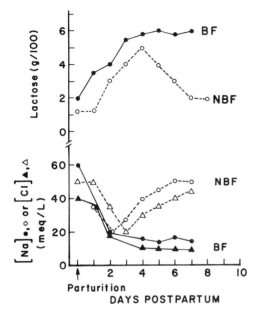

FIG 11–6.

Milk composition in breast-feeding *(BF)* and non-breast-feeding *(NBF)* women during the early postpartum period. (Data replotted from Kulski JK, Hartmann PE: Changes in human milk composition during the initiation of lactation. *Aust J Exp Biol Med Sci* 1981; 59:101–114. Used by permission.)

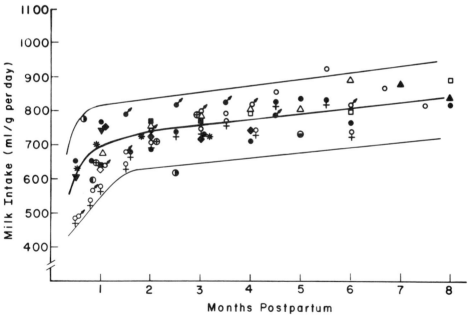

FIG 11–7.

Milk intake in exclusively breast-fed infants. *Heavy line* indicates the mean values for the women depicted in Figure 11–4; *light lines* indicate one standard deviation on either side of the mean. Symbols represent published values from all studies available in which milk volume transfer was determined by test-weighing the infant and in which the postpartum interval was specified. The sources of these data are given in reference 49. The symbols represent data from the U.S., Sweden, Finland, Kenya, U.K., Canada, and the Gambia. (From Neville MC, Keller R, Seacat J, et al: Studies in human lactation: Milk volumes in lactating women during the onset of lactation and full lactation. *Am J Clin Nutr* 1988; 48:1375–1386. Used by permission.)

FIG 11–8.

Effect of removal of residual milk by breast pump on total milk production. Subjects were five exclusively breast-feeding women 4 to 5 months postpartum who emptied their breasts with an electric breast pump after 3 feeds daily. (From Neville MC, Oliva-Rasbach J: Is maternal milk production limiting for infant growth during the first year of life in breast-fed infants?, in Goldman A, Atkinson SA (eds): *Human Lactation 3: Effect of Human Milk on the Recipient Infant.* New York, Plenum Publishing Corp, 1987, pp 123–133. Used by permission.)

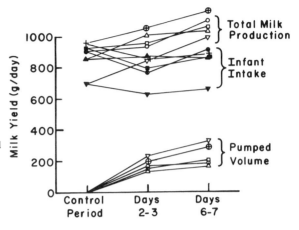

to pertain worldwide. Thus, similar milk intake values were obtained in affluent populations in the United States, Britain, and Sweden, and in less privileged areas such as Kenya and the Gambia. Studies by Hartmann and colleagues[24] in Perth, Australia, suggest that infant intakes in his study population are higher. However, data in those studies were obtained by test-weighing the mother, a process that may be associated with increased error due to insensible weight loss during the feed. Changes in milk composition during lactation (see Table 11–1) include decreases in sodium, chloride, protein, zinc, and calcium, and increases in lactose and possibly, fat.*

Regulation of Milk Volume Secretion

In the past few years it has become clear that infant demand is the most important variable regulating milk secretion.[11, 52] In general, milk production has not been found to correlate with maternal nutritional status or the capacity of the gland to secrete milk.[37, 60] High parity (> 9) was associated with diminution in both milk volume and fat content in Gambian women.[58] Women are able to increase their milk production by regular pumping of the milk remaining after breast-feeding. For example, we found that exclusively breast-feeding women 5 months postpartum increased their milk production by 30% in 7 days when they extracted all residual milk from their breasts with a breast pump three times a day[52] (Fig 11–8). Similar results have been obtained by Dewey and colleagues.[11]

Increasing the milk volume as described in the preceding paragraph requires several days of extraction of residual milk. On a day-to-day basis, milk production is matched to infant demand. Thus if milk is removed by breast pump at hourly intervals, once residual milk has been removed, the rate of milk secretion is equivalent to the mean rate of infant intake.[49] Two mechanisms have been proposed for regulation of the volume of milk production: hormonal regulation by prolactin, and autocrine control by locally secreted factors. The rate of prolactin secretion is generally proportional to suckling by the infant.[45] Since prolactin stimulates milk production by mammary epithelial cells, it has

---

*Data on total milk lipid content must be approached with caution. Thus, milk lipid increases significantly from the beginning to the end of the feed and varies from one feed to the next, depending on the amount of residual milk.[50] The most accurate values are probably obtained when pooled milk obtained by breast pump from several consecutive feeds is used. However, few laboratories have used this procedure, and highly variable concentrations of milk fat have been published.[28]

been postulated that it may play a primary role in regulating the rate of milk production. However, prolactin levels vary widely from woman to woman and tend to decrease during the course of lactation as milk secretion increases, suggesting that some other mechanism is responsible for the "fine tuning" of milk volume. Based largely on studies in lactating goats, Wilde and associates have postulated that milk secretion is under autocrine control.[65] That is, a substance secreted into milk by the epithelial cells themselves interacts with these cells to inhibit milk production. There is good evidence for the existence of such an inhibitory protein in goat[65] and human milk,[59] but the identity of the substance has not yet been published, and the mechanism of its action is not known. If it were to work by regulating prolactin receptors on mammary epithelial cells, an integration of the two hypotheses would be possible.

In summary, it is clear that residual breast milk has an inhibitory effect on milk secretion. To what extent autocrine factors within such milk play a role in the regulation of milk production is currently unknown.

Weaning and Involution

Involutional changes in the mammary gland take place during or after weaning. Total weaning results in rapid changes in milk composition—consisting of an increase in sodium, chloride, and protein (especially IgA and lactoferrin) and a decrease in lactose.[23] Gradual weaning, usually carried out in western societies by decreasing the feed frequency, occurs with minimal change in milk composition.[17, 47] However, changes similar to those that occur with abrupt weaning are seen once feed frequency drops to once per day or daily milk volume below 100 mL (M.C. Neville and J.C. Allen, unpublished data). It is not clear whether the reduction in milk production during weaning is the result of a decrease in the secretory activity of existing mammary epithelial cells or the reduction in the number of such cells. Again use of magnetic resonance imaging during weaning could resolve this problem.

Once the infant is totally weaned, the alveolar complexes are gradually resorbed and the gland regresses to the prepregnancy condition.[7] Only after menopause is there complete involution of the breast, a process that may involve both parenchyma and adipose tissue.

LACTOGENESIS IN MOTHERS OF PRETERM INFANTS

The period of lactogenesis has not been studied in detail in mothers of preterm infants. However, there is extensive documentation of the composition of their milk during the first month of lactation when there are statistically significant differences from the milk of mothers of term infants.[35, 62] By and large these differences, which include increased protein, sodium, chloride and possibly iron (Fig 11–9), are in the direction that potentially enhances infant growth. For this reason milk from their own mothers is preferred over banked milk for preterm infants. The reasons for the compositional differences are unclear. They could result from delayed maturation of the mammary epithelium or the pathologic processes responsible for the preterm birth itself. Most important, however, may be the emotional burden of having a hospitalized premature infant who cannot be cared for in the normal way and for whom milk must be obtained by breast pump. Under these circumstances the let-down response may be inhibited and residual

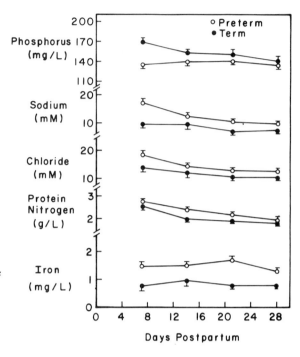

FIG 11-9.
Changes in composition of preterm milk during first postpartum month. (Data plotted from Lemons JA, Moye L, Hall D, et al: Differences in the composition of preterm and term human milk during lactation. *Pediatr Res* 1982; 16:113–117. Used by permission.)

milk may accumulate, with a consequent decrease in milk production and associated composition changes.

In a preliminary attempt to sort out these alternatives, we measured the total volume of pumped milk in four mothers of hospitalized infants, taking milk samples at intervals for analysis of several milk components. The daily milk volumes and sodium content of the milks are shown in Figure 11–10, where they are compared with data on our reference group of full-term, breast-fed infants.[49] Two of the mothers had infants that were clearly preterm, weighing less than 2,500 g with estimated gestational ages of 30 weeks *(top two graphs)*. The onset of milk volume secretion appeared to occur only slightly later than milk secretion in the reference group.[49] Milk volumes achieved with the breast pump were at the low end of the normal range, but fell off in one of the two mothers. Sodium concentrations were within the normal range in both women. These preliminary observations suggest that prematurity in and of itself does not alter either the closure of the junctional complexes or the onset of volume secretion.

The increase in milk volume secretion associated with lactogenesis did appear to be delayed until day 5 in a mother with gestational diabetes *(third row,* Fig 11–10), and volumes achieved were low. This infant was only slightly premature. It is our impression and the impression of others (Ferris A., personal communication) that a delay in lactogenesis often occurs in diabetic mothers. In our subject the initial sodium concentrations were again within normal limits but rose on day 5 to reach a peak on day 6. The increase in sodium was accompanied by a significant increase in chloride, protein, and calcium, and a decrease in lactose, potassium, and glucose, all changes that occur in mastitis and are also seen in preterm milk. An accompanying low fever and "flulike" syndrome virtually confirmed the diagnosis of mastitis at this time.[33] A similar condition may have been responsible for the rise in sodium on day 14, also accompanied by changes in the components listed. This example illustrates the point that mastitis or a mastitis-like condition may be responsible for differences in milk composition similar to

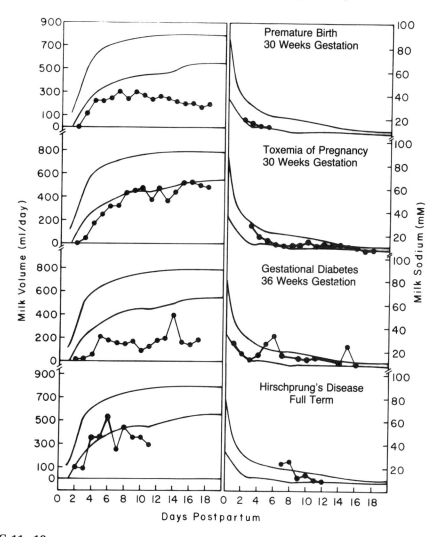

FIG 11–10.
Milk volumes and sodium concentrations in milk from mothers of hospitalized infants. All mothers pumped their breasts three to seven times per day to obtain milk for their infants. No infant was put to the breast during the period of the study. *Top row:* premature birth; cesarian section due to toxemia of pregnancy; birth weight, 1,392 g. *Second row:* premature birth; induced vaginal delivery due to rupture of membranes; birth weight, 1,092 g. *Third row:* gestational diabetes; infant complications required hospitalization; birth weight, 3,460 g. *Fourth row:* full-term infant with Hirshbrung's disease; birth weight, 4,016 g. All pumped volumes were measured and recorded by the mothers, who also provided milk samples on a regular basis. (Neville MC, Klingbeil H, unpublished data.)

those observed, on a population basis, in mothers of premature infants. We also see such composition changes in the milk of mothers who are weaning their infants and producing milk volumes below 100 mL/day (M.C. Neville and J.C. Allen, unpublished data). Gross et al.[20] did observe that the sIgA concentration in the milks of preterm mothers was inversely proportional to milk volume, providing additional evidence for a linkage between low milk volumes and the composition differences between preterm and term milks.

The last row in Figure 11–10 illustrates the principle that pumping in and of itself does not lead to changes in lactogenesis. Here a mother with a hospitalized full-term infant obtained milk for that infant by breast pump. Similarly to the subject shown in Figure 11–4,B, lactogenesis was not delayed and she was able to obtain sufficient volumes for her infant with ease.

Based on these preliminary results and our understanding of the composition of term milk, the differences between preterm and term milk may result from insufficient extraction of residual milk from the breast and would be more likely to occur in mothers producing small milk volumes and mothers with mastitis. If this hypothesis can be confirmed by more detailed longitudinal studies, it may be possible, although not necessarily desirable from the standpoint of infant nutrition, to improve extraction of residual milk by improved pumping techniques or possibly the use of nasal oxytocin to improve let-down.[49]

LACTATION AND THE GROWTH OF THE BREAST-FED INFANT

The rate of weight gain of breast-fed boys and girls in the Denver study described by Neville et al.[49] is shown in Figure 11–11. The mean growth rate in these infants peaked at about 4 weeks at an incremental weight gain of about 40 g per day or 10 g/day/kg. This rate is significantly higher than the rates observed both by Fomon et al.[15] in a large group of bottle-fed infants (Table 11–2) and the growth rate predicted by the

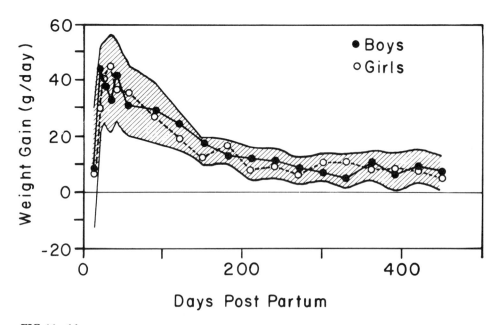

FIG 11–11.
Growth rates of breast-fed boys and girls. Graph shows mean daily weight gains of the 7 girls and 6 boys whose milk intake is depicted in Figure 11–4. All infants were exclusively breast-fed for at least 6 months and in general did not receive more than 100 kcal/day beikost until after 9 months. Data at 12 months represent 4 girls and 4 boys. By 450 days only 2 girls and 1 boy remained in the study. (Neville MC, Oliva-Rasbach J, unpublished data.)

TABLE 11–2.

Growth and Protein Intake in Breast and Bottle-fed Infants*

Category	Birth	Postpartum Interval (days)				
		7–14	15–29	30–60	61–90	91–180
Breast-fed (no. = 13)*						
Weight at end of interval, g	3,333	3,658	4,260	5,158	5,863	7,071
Incremental weight gain, g/day		37.1	42.3	31.1	21.4	13.3
Incremental weight gain, g/kg/day		10.1	9.9	6.6	3.9	2.1
Protein intake, g/day		8.2	8.8	8.3	7.6	7.8
Protein intake, g/kg/day		2.2	2.7	1.6	1.3	1.4
Bottle-fed (no. = 142)†						
Weight at end of interval, g	3,375	3,630	4,170	5,113	5,871	7,510
Incremental weight gain, g/day		31.0	39.0	34.0	30.0	20.3
Incremental weight gain, g/kg/day		8.5	9.3	6.6	5.1	2.7
Protein intake, g/day		8.9	10.7	11.6	12.3	NA
Protein intake, g/kg/day		2.4	2.6	2.4	2.1	NA

*Data from Denver longitudinal study described in reference 49.
†Data from Foman et al.[15] except for the 90- to 180-day values taken from the National Center for Health Statistics standards. NA = not available.
Although there were differences in weight gain between boys and girls in both studies, the values do not affect the differences between breast-fed and bottle-fed infants. The data have, therefore, been lumped for clarity. The standard errors are <15% for all values.

National Center for Health Statistics (NCHS) standards. The growth rate fell to about 30 g/day during the 2d month, a rate similar to that of the bottle-fed infants. After the 2d month the growth rate decreased more rapidly in the breast-fed infants than in the bottle-fed control infants, so that by 6 months of age the growth rate in the breast-fed infants was less than 70% of that achieved by bottle-fed infants (see Table 11–2). Similar observations have been made in many groups of fully breast-fed infants.[18, 26, 27, 64] Height comparison between the breast-fed infants in our study and bottle-fed infants also showed a trend of rapid growth during the first 2 to 3 months postpartum followed by slower growth thereafter (M.C. Neville et al., unpublished data).

It is not surprising that breast-fed infants, who obtain a fluid expected to be entirely adapted to their needs, grow more rapidly than bottle-fed infants during the first 2 months postpartum. The surprising thing is that the growth rate is slower during the subsequent months. We and others have ruled out insufficient maternal milk production[11, 52] as an explanation for this phenomenon except possibly in rare cases. Clearly, breast-fed infants ingest less protein than the bottle-fed infants in the Fomon study (see Table 11–2). However, very low birth weight infants are able to sustain a growth rate of about 20 g/day/kg, twice the growth rate observed in the full-term infants, on a protein intake of about 3 g/kg/day.[57] This is not much greater than the protein intake of the breast-fed infants during the 1st month. Many questions can be asked about this phenomenon. What is the optimal growth rate for infants after the first 2 months of life? Why does breast milk stimulate infant appetite less than formula? Does the greater protein concentration in formula contribute to the increased growth rate in the breast-fed infants? To what extent does the changing composition of breast milk contribute to the decrease in growth rate after the 3d month? To what extent do breast-fed infants practice "catch-up" growth after weaning? Does the growth rate of breast-fed infants actually represent an optimal rate? Is later development affected? Answers to these and similar questions may provide us with some interesting insights into growth regulation in general.* Further research in this area is clearly warranted.

CONCLUSIONS

Lactation is the result of a complex developmental process in the woman that takes place in several stages during late childhood and as an adult. The result is the elaboration of a fluid that is capable of providing complete nourishment for the term infant for the first several months of life. However, the composition of this fluid is not static. It is likely that milk secreted in early lactation—with its higher concentrations of protein, calcium, zinc, and possibly other essential nutrients—is better able to support rapid infant growth and development than milk from later lactation. Additional research is needed to determine to what extent lactogenesis proceeds normally in the mother of the preterm infant. The relation of human milk composition to the growth of the breast-fed infant is also an area badly in need of further research.

Acknowledgments

The able assistance of Heidi Klingbeil, M.D., and Jean Rasbach, R.D., in collecting the data on preterm infants and growth in term infants, respectively, is gratefully acknowledged, as is the cooperation of the mothers involved.

REFERENCES

1. American Academy of Pediatrics Committee on Nutrition: Encouraging breast-feeding. *Pediatrics* 1980; 65:657–658.
2. Anderson DM, Williams FH, Merkatz RB, et al: Length of gestation and nutritional composition of human milk. *Am J Clin Nutr* 1983; 37:810–814.
3. Anderson RR: Embryonic and fetal development of the mammary apparatus, in Larson BL (ed): *Lactation IV: The Mammary Gland/Human Lactation/Milk Synthesis*. New York, Academic Press, 1978, pp 3–39.
4. Brun del Re R, del Pozo E, de Grandi P, et al: Prolactin inhibition and suppression of puerperal lactation by Br-ergo cryptine (CB154). A comparison with estrogen. *Obstet Gynecol* 1973; 41:884–890.
5. Casey CE, Hambidge KM: Nutritional aspects of human lactation, in Neville MC, Neifert MA (eds): *Lactation: Physiology, Nutrition and Breast-feeding*. New York, Plenum Publishing Corp, 1983, pp 199–248.
6. Casey CE, Hambidge KM, Neville MC: Studies in human lactation: Zinc, copper, manga-

*It should be made clear that, although the growth rate of breast-fed infants appears to be substantially slower than that of bottle-fed infants after the 4th month of life, such infants have usually gained sufficient weight during the first 2 postpartum months that they remain within normal limits for growth until at least 4 months, and often 6 months, postpartum. Concern should be taken for breast-fed infants who grow very slowly during the first 2 months postpartum, as normal breast-milk supplies and a normal nursing relation between mother and child should promote a rate of growth not less than the NCHS standards during this time interval (M.R. Neifert and J.M. Seacat, personal communication).

nese and chromium in human milk in the first month of lactation. *Am J Clin Nutr* 1985; 41:1193–1200.

7. Dabelow A: Die postnatale Entwicklung der menschlichen Milchdruse und ihre Korrelationen. *Morphol J* 1941; 85:361–416.

8. Daniel CW, Silberstein GB: Postnatal development of the rodent mammary gland, in Neville MC, Daniel CW (eds): *The Mammary Gland*. New York, Plenum Publishing Corp, 1987, pp 3–36.

9. Davies DT, Holt C, Christie WW: The composition of milk, in Mepham TB (ed): *Biochemistry of Lactation*. Amsterdam, Elsevier, 1983,

10. Dembinski TC, Shiu RPC: Growth factors in mammary gland development and function, in Neville MC, Daniel CW (eds): *The Mammary Gland*. New York, Plenum Publishing Corp, 1987, pp 355–382.

11. Dewey KG, Lonnerdal B: Infant self-regulation of breast milk intake. *Acta Paediatr Scand* 1986; 75:893–898.

12. Dils RR: Milk fat synthesis, in Mepham TB (ed): *Biochemistry of Lactation*. Amsterdam, Elsevier, 1983, pp 141–157.

13. Faulkner A, Peaker M: Regulation of mammary glucose metabolism in lactation, in Neville MC, Daniel CW (eds): *The Mammary Gland*. New York, Plenum Publishing Corp, 1987, pp 536–562.

14. Fleet IR, Goode JA, Hamon MH, et al: Secretory activity of goat mammary glands during pregnancy and the onset of lactation. *J Physiol* 1975; 251:763–773.

15. Fomon SJ, Thomas LN, Filer LJ Jr, et al: Food consumption and growth of normal infants fed milk-based formulas. *Acta Paediatr Scand [Suppl]* 1971; 223:3–31.

16. Foss GL, Phillips P: The suppression of lactation by oral estrogen therapy. *Br Med J [Clin Res]* 1938; 2:887–890.

17. Garza C, Johnson CA, Smith EO, et al: Changes in the nutrient composition of human milk during gradual weaning. *Am J Clin Nutr* 1983; 37:61–68.

18. Garza C, Schanler RJ, Butte NF, et al: Special properties of human milk. *Clin Perinatol* 1987; 14:11–32.

19. Goldman AS Atkinson SA: *Human Lactation 3: Effect of Human Milk on the Recipient Infant*. New York, Plenum Publishing Corp, 1987.

20. Gross SJ, Buckley RH, Wakil SS, et al: Elevated IgA concentration in milk produced by mothers delivered of preterm infants. *Pediatrics* 1981; 99:389–393.

21. Hamosh M Goldman AR: *Human Lactation 2: Maternal and Environmental Factors*. New York, Plenum Publishing Corp, 1986.

22. Hartmann PE: Changes in the composition and yield of the mammary secretion of cows during the initiation of lactation. *J Endocrinol* 1973; 59:231–247.

23. Hartmann PE, Kulski JK: Changes in the composition of the mammary secretion of women after abrupt termination of breast feeding. *J Physiol* 1978; 275:1–11.

24. Hartmann PE, Kulski JK, Rattigan S, et al: Lactation in Australian women. *Proc Nutr Soc Aust* 1980; 5:104–110.

25. Haslam SZ: Role of sex steroid hormones in normal mammary gland function, in Neville MC, Daniel CW (eds): *The Mammary Gland*. New York, Plenum Publishing Corp, 1987, pp 499–535.

26. Hitchcock NE, Gracey M, Gilmour AI: The growth of breast-fed and artifically fed infants from birth to twelve months. *Acta Paediatr Scand* 1985; 74:240–245.

27. Hoffmans MDAF, Obermann-deBoer GL, Florack EIM, et al: Determinants of growth during infancy. *Hum Biol* 1988; 60:237–249.

28. Jensen RG: *The Lipids of Human Milk*. Boca Raton, Fla, CRC Press, 1989.

29. Jensen RG, Neville MC: *Human Lactation. 1: Milk Components and Methodologies*. New York, Plenum Publishing Corp, 1985.

30. Kuhn NJ: Progesterone withdrawal as the lactogenic trigger in the rat. *J Endocrinol* 1969; 44:39–54.

31. Kuhn NJ: The biochemistry of lactogenesis, in Mepham TB (ed): *Biochemistry of Lactation.* Amsterdam, Elsevier, 1983, pp 351–380.

32. Kulski JK, Hartmann PE: Changes in human milk composition during the initiation of lactation. *Aust J Exp Biol Med Sci* 1981; 59:101–114.

33. Lawrence RA: Breastfeeding and medical disease. *Med Clin North Am* 1989; 73:583–603.

34. Lawrence RA: *Breastfeeding: A guide for the medical profession,* 3 ed. St Louis, CV Mosby, 1989.

35. Lemons JA, Moye L, Hall D, et al: Differences in the composition of preterm and term human milk during early lactation. *Pediatr Res* 1982; 16:113–117.

36. Linzell JL, Peaker M: The effects of oxytocin and milk removal on milk secretion in the goat. *J Physiol* 1971; 216:717–734.

37. Lonnerdal B: Effects of maternal nutrition on human lactation, in Hamosh M, Goldman AS (eds): *Human Lactation: Maternal and Environmental Factors.* New York, Plenum Publishing Corp, 1986, pp 301–392.

38. Martin RH, Glass MR, Chapman C, et al: Human alpha-lactalbumin and hormonal factors in pregnancy and lactation. *Clin Endocrinol* 1980; 13:223–230.

39. Mather IH: Proteins of the milk-fat-globule membrane as markers of mammary epithelial cells and apical plasma membrane, in Neville MC, Daniel CW (eds): *The Mammary Gland: Development, Regulation and Function.* New York, Plenum Publishing Corp, 1987, p 268.

40. Mather IH, Keenan TW: Function of endomembranes and the cell surface in the secretion of organic milk constituents, in Mepham TB (ed): *Biochemistry of Lactation.* Amsterdam, Elsevier, 1983.

41. Mepham TB: *Physiology of lactation.* Milton Keynes, England, Open University Press, 1987.

42. Neifert MR, McDonough SL, Neville MC: Failure of lactogenesis associated with placental retention. *Am J Obstet Gynecol* 1981; 140:477–478.

43. Neifert MR, Seacat JM: Medical management of successful breastfeeding. *Pediatr Clin North Am* 1986; 33:743–762.

44. Nelson TR, Pretorius DH, Schiffer LM: Menstrual variation of normal breast: NMR relaxation parameters. *J Comput Assist Tomogr* 1985; 9:875–879.

45. Neville MC: Regulation of mammary development and lactation, in Neville MC, Neifert MR (eds): *Lactation: Physiology, Nutrition and Breast-feeding.* New York, Plenum Publishing Corp, 1983, pp 103–140.

46. Neville MC, Allen JC, Watters C: The mechanisms of milk secretion, in Neville MC, Neifert MR (eds): *Lactation: Physiology, Nutrition and Breast Feeding.* New York, Plenum Publishing Corp, 1983, pp 49–102.

47. Neville MC, Casey CE, Keller RP, et al: Changes in milk composition after six months of lactation: The effects of duration of lactation and gradual weaning, in Hamosh M, Goldman A (eds): *Human Lactation 2: Effects of Maternal and Environmental Factors.* New York, Plenum Publishing Corp, 1986, pp 141–154.

48. Neville MC, Daniel CW: *The Mammary Gland: Development, Regulation and Function,* New York, Plenum Publishing Corp, 1987.

49. Neville MC, Keller R, Seacat J, et al: Studies in human lactation: Milk volumes in lactating women during the onset of lactation and full lactation. *Am J Clin Nutr* 1988; 48:1375–1386.

50. Neville MC, Keller RP, Seacat J, et al: Studies on human lactation: I. Within-feed and between-breast variation in selected components of human milk. *Am J Clin Nutr* 1984; 40:635–646.

51. Neville MC, Neifert MR: *Lactation: Physiology, Nutrition and Breastfeeding.* New York, Plenum Publishing Corp, 1983.

52. Neville MC, Oliva-Rasbach J: Is maternal milk production limiting for infant growth during the first year of life in breast-fed infants?, in Goldman A, Atkinson SA (eds): *Human Lactation 3: Effect of Human Milk on the Recipient Infant.* New York, Plenum Publishing Corp, 1987, pp 123–133.

53. Newton N, Newton M: Psychologic aspects of lactation. *N Engl J Med* 1967; 277:1179–1183.

54. Peaker M: Secretion of ions and water, in Mepham TB (ed): *Bichemistry of Lactation*. New York, Elsevier, 1983, pp 285–307.

55. Peaker M, Linzell JL: Citrate in milk: Harbinger of lactogenesis. *Nature* 1975; 253:464–465.

56. Pitelka DR, Hamamoto ST: Ultrastructure of the mammary secretory cell, in Mepham TB (ed): *Biochemistry of Lactation*. Amsterdam, Elsevier, 1983, pp 29–43.

57. Polberger SKT, Axelsson IA, Räihä NCE: Growth of very low birth weight infants on varying amounts of human milk protein. *Pediatr Res* 1989; 25:414–419.

58. Prentice A: The effect of maternal parity on lactational performance in a rural African community, in Hamosh M, Goldman AS (eds): *Human Lactation 2: Maternal and Environmental Factors*. New York, Plenum Publishing Corp, 1986, pp 165–174.

59. Prentice A, Addey CP, Wilde CJ: Evidence for local feedback control of human milk secretion. *Biochem Soc Trans* 1989; 16:122.

60. Prentice AM, Paul A, Prentice A, et al: Cross-cultural differences in lactational performance, in Hamosh M, Goldman AS (eds): *Human Lactation: Maternal and Environmental Factors*. New York City, Plenum Publishing Corp, 1986, pp 13–50.

61. Solari R, Kraehenbuhl J-P: Receptor-mediated transepithelial transport of polymeric immunoglobulins, in Neville MC, Daniel CW (eds): *The Mammary Gland*. New York, Plenum Publishing Corp, 1987, pp 269–300.

62. Steichen JJ, Krug-Wispé SK, Tsang RC: Breastfeeding the low birth weight preterm infant. *Clin Perinatol* 1987; 14:131–171.

63. Thordarson G, Talamantes F: Role of the placenta in mammary gland development and function, in Neville MC and Daniel CW (eds): *The Mammary Gland*. New York, Plenum Publishing Corp, 1987, pp 459–498.

64. Whitehead RG: Growth charts and the assessment of infant feeding practices in the western world and in developing countries. *Early Hum Dev* 1984; 9:187–207.

65. Wilde CJ, Addey CVP, Casey MJ, et al: Feed-back inhibition of milk secretion: The effect of a fraction of goat milk on milk yield and composition. *Q J Exp Physiol* 1988; 73:391–397.

66. Woolridge MW, Greasley V, Silpisornkosol S: The initiation of lactation: The effect of early versus delayed contact for suckling on milk intake in the first week post-partum. A study in Chiang Mai, Northern Thailand. *Early Hum Dev* 1985; 12:269–278.

Chapter 12

Lactation

Pamela K. Lemons, M.S., N.N.P.

Joan K. Sharda, M.D.

James A. Lemons, M.D.

HISTORICAL PERSPECTIVES

Since the beginning of historic time, wide variations in cultural and social traditions have been noted in trends of infant feeding practices. With the transition of human society from preliterate-tribal through rural-agricultural to present day urban-industrial form, the definitions of mothering have changed, particularly with respect to patterns of breast-feeding. Nature has endowed the female anatomy with an organ intended to provide optimal infant nutrition, but the breast has been ascribed alternate roles of aesthetic and/or pleasurable character superceding this resourceful dimension.

Human milk was the staple in infant nutrition until the latter part of the 19th century. Yet, forms of artificial feeding (dry nursing) were also attempted even in the earliest eras, as evidenced by the discovery of infant feeding vessels in Egyptian tombs (25 B.C.). In the 1600s infants were fed with various mixtures of broths, animal milks, and starch gruels.[9, 36] However, infant mortality was prohibitive in virtually all artificial modes of feeding, with fatal diarrhea endemic in the 18th and early 19th centuries. Breast-feeding remained an essential and natural art for the survival of the human race.

William Cadogan, M.D. (1711–1797), a pioneer in infant hygiene, stated in his *Essay Upon Nursing* (1748):

> If I could prevail, no Child should ever be crammed with any unnatural mixture, til the Provision of Nature was ready for it . . . . Nature seems to direct this.[9]

Nineteenth century physicians advocated breast milk over "hand-fed" methods, as the belief was that nature should prevail. A medical treatise in 1805 proclaimed,

> Nothing can shew the disposition which mankind have to depart from nature more than their endeavouring to bring up children without the breast. The mother's milk, or that of a healthy nurse, is unquestionably the best food for an infant. Neither art nor nature can afford a proper substitute for it.[9]

Wet nurses (selected with scrutiny) were preferable sources of human milk for orphaned or illegitimate infants rather than artificial forms of nutrition. During periods of cultural affluence (e.g., ancient Spartas), many women made use of wet nursing or artificial feeding in spite of royal dictates that mandated breast-feeding.[36] In fact, breast-feeding often had the force of biblical injunction, as women were dutifully instructed to nurse.

A complex matrix of features during the 17th through 19th centuries resulted in a declining trend in the incidence of breast-feeding. With the advent of scientific technology, urbanization, and sociologic changes within the family structure, the impetus for a perfected infant formula became stronger. Discoveries in bacteriology, infant metabolism, and biochemical analysis of milk composition led to refinements in the production of a safe, proprietary form of infant feeding. Pasteurization, refrigeration, and curd homogenization of milk, along with improved sanitation measures, allowed such a product to be maintained in stable form without attendant risk of milkborne diseases. Indeed, the first 60 years of the 20th century saw a mass production of paraphernalia suited for formula feeding, paralleling a downward spiral in breast-feeding that became accentuated in the 1960s. Although concern was expressed about this alarming trend, only in the 1970s did a resurgence of breast-feeding occur.[3, 28] Public awareness, feminist consciousness, and "return to nature" attitudes promoted the swing of the pendulum. From 1971 to 1982, the number of breast-feeding women in America increased from 25% to 60% and has plateaued since. This breast-feeding population tends to be middle class, better-educated, white women who provide good prenatal care and have few obligations outside the home. In contrast, the lower-income, young, unmarried, non-white women have generally opted for formula feeding.[14, 15, 21] The 1970s and 1980s also witnessed a dramatic increase in the survival of preterm infants, who only recently have been included in the breast-fed population.

Of contemporary concern is the declining incidence of breast-feeding in Third World countries secondary to promotional advertising and economic pressures of the infant-food industry. Perhaps former cultural associations of breast-feeding with the lower class and slavery have drawn these Third World inhabitants to the formula alternative as a sign of the affluent. The World Health Organization (WHO) has begun to address this problem by encouraging governments to design more effective breast-feeding promotional programs, as declared by the WHO International Code of Marketing of Breast Milk Substitutes.[14, 15, 20]

Cultural mores through the ages have often supported different breast-feeding practices. Ancient societies utilized unrestricted feeding rather than rigidly scheduled patterns, as the mother was always proximal to (carrying) the child and therefore readily accessible to the baby's needs.[9, 36] This promoted frequent feeding and communicative cues between mother and infant. "Insufficient milk syndrome" has become an urban problem resulting in part from the disruption of unrestricted mothering and of the behavioral interaction between mother and infant associated with close contact. Milk insufficiency may also be related in part to neurohumoral inhibition from psychosocial stress in the contemporary world.[14, 15, 20]

Of great importance in the maternal–infant dyad is the ability of both to receive and process interactive cues in an appropriate fashion. Infant behavior encompasses a broad spectrum of subtle changes in state, which remained undefined prior to Brazelton's descriptive work (the Neonatal Behavioral Assessment Scale, 1960). A newborn was not ascribed any particular feature of unique personality until the recent decade. However, in recent years it became apparent that with the increased frequency of physical contact afforded by breast-feeding, a mother can learn to recognize her baby's individual behavioral cues and provide the appropriate intervention. The Brazelton Scale, when shared with parents, is an effective tool for relating to an infant's behavior and thus promoting neurobehavioral maturation.[1]

Anticipatory guidance provided during pregnancy will assist in optimizing medical and psychological preparedness for the role of parenting. As a mother approaches term, readily available sources of information are essential in order to implement effective and satisfying choices.

PRACTICAL ASPECTS OF BREAST-FEEDING

Prenatal Assessment

Choice of a method of infant feeding generally occurs in the prenatal period and involves careful scrutiny of a variety of factors, including historic and current trends within families, societal norms, and environmental pressures. The recent trend toward breast-feeding as the preferred method of feeding may leave many young families with conflicting emotions. Their parents and grandparents are products of the bottle-feeding era, and thus may be unfamiliar with and wary of the art of breast-feeding. Breast-feeding peers as role models are often lacking for young families. Employment outside the home, single-parent status, and economic constraints may further contribute to a growing feeling of uncertainty regarding breast-feeding.

The first step in overcoming these obstacles is to engage the prenatal client in active discussion of the pros and cons of breast vs. bottle feeding. Mothers are particularly receptive to information regarding infant care practices as they proceed through the 3d trimester and prepare for active role transition into motherhood. Care should be taken to allow the mother autonomy over the ultimate feeding decision, however, as the establishment of lactation requires commitment and perseverance.

The prenatal approach to the assessment of lactation involves a thorough history and physical examination of the mother. The history may uncover previous successes or failures with breast-feeding attempts and will alert the physician to potential problems (e.g., primary lactation failures, slow-to-gain infants). Adequate weight gain during pregnancy (20 to 25 lb) is another important historical factor, as energy for milk production is dependent on mobilization of fat stores as well as maternal intake of calories. Assessment of social support systems and financial stressors during the pregnancy may allow for modification of these potential barriers to successful lactation.

Breast examination should begin by a general observation of the breast mass and nipples. The mother should normally experience a substantial increase in her breast size during pregnancy, changes reflective of lobuloalveolar and ductal growth.[31] The absence of breast changes during pregnancy may be an early indicator of subsequent lactation failure. Further examination may reveal scarring, consistent with breast augmentation, reduction, or surgical excision of a mass. While such procedures may not be absolute contraindications to lactation, they are often associated with insufficient lactation. Those procedures that involve the nipple–areola complex, with associated interruption of innervation or the continuity of the ducts and sinuses, are the most problematic.[22]

The breast should be palpated and inspected for masses, and the nipple assessed for protractility by the application of gentle pressure on opposite poles of the nipple[25] (Fig 12–1). Although manipulation of the nipple is generally discouraged prior to term (because of the risk of inducing premature labor mediated by oxytocin release), gentle compression of the lactiferous sinus should be performed. Unusual discharge, such as serosanguinous or bloody exudate, requires prompt evaluation prior to the onset of lactation.

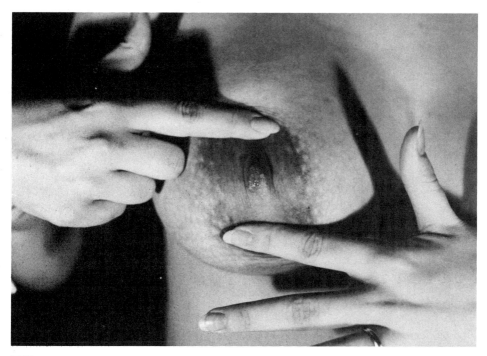

FIG 12–1.
Breast protractility assessment.

The presumptive diagnosis under these conditions is intraductal carcinoma until proved otherwise.

General educational approaches that involve the prenatal client in her plan of care are likely to be the most successful for those women who elect breast-feeding.[36] Normalizing expectations for the frequency of infant feedings, explaining the physiology and onset of lactation, and increasing the awareness of infant wake-sleep cycles, among other topics, will allow the mother to anticipate the early postpartum days and ultimately enhance the lactation experience.

Initiation of Lactation

There are three major stages of activity of hormonal control of lactation:

1. Mammary growth, beginning in the embryo and culminating during pregnancy
2. Initiation of milk production
3. Maintenance of lactation, which begins 72 to 96 hours postpartum and continues as long as there is a stimulus.

At delivery, with the loss of the placenta, there is a sharp decline in serum estrogen and progesterone. The fall in levels of these and other hormones triggers the onset of lactation. The continuation of lactation is dependent on prolactin production and release under the stimulus of suckling.[22] The afferent nerve impulse ascending to the hypothalmus controls pituitary release of prolactin and oxytocin. Prolactin stimulates the synthesis and secretion of milk. Oxytocin causes milk ejection by contraction of the myoepithelial cells lining the alveoli and milk ducts, and propulsion of the milk through the lactiferous ducts and sinuses. This process is known as "let-down." Because milk ejection involves both neural afferent and endocrine efferent pathways, this response may be inhibited by a number of factors such as pain, stress, or fatigue.

The milk supply is directly related to the amount of stimulation supplied to the breast and to the level of prolactin and oxytocin secretion. In the presence of appropriate levels of these hormones, the breast must also be serially emptied or the process of lactation will be suppressed, due to the reduced capillary blood flow from the pressure of the retained milk.[23] Failure of lactation results from the absence of either factor.

To establish a good lactation response in the early postpartum period, the infant should be allowed to nurse on a "demand" schedule. The baby should be put to the breast as soon as possible after delivery, remain for at least 5 minutes on each breast, and then be fed every 2 to 3 hours (eight to ten times daily). Breast-feeding should ideally take place within the 1st hour after delivery (Fig 12–2) if no complications have arisen, for several reasons:

1. The suckling reflex may be most intense during the first one hour following birth.
2. Early breast-feeding may enhance interest in subsequent feedings.
3. Suckling initiates oxytocin release and facilitates uterine contraction, thus minimizing maternal blood loss.
4. Maternal/infant attachment is enhanced during this sensitive time when the infant is in the alert state.

The colostrum the infant receives during these feedings varies in amount, and provides approximately 67 kcal/100 mL in a 24-hour period.[22] Colostrum is a viscous fluid, rich in protein and minerals. It contains a high concentration of immunoglobulins, especially secretory IgA, which provides antibodies against a wide array of bacterial and vi-

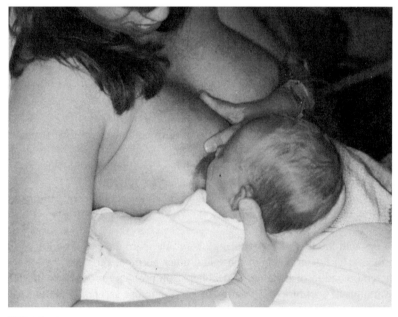

FIG 12–2.
Breast feeding soon after delivery.

ral organisms. The presence of secretory IgA antibodies in human milk, which act against possible pathogens in the mother's environment, provides an environmentally specific milk.[33]

Feeding Intervals

Since gastric emptying time in breast-fed infants is typically 1 to 2 hours, the infant should be fed around the clock at frequent intervals. Hospital routines that schedule infant feedings on a 3- to 4-hour basis socialize mothers into anticipating that infants should be fed according to the clock, rather than according to their physiologic and neurologic cues. Behaviors that cue the mother to initiate feedings are increased states of arousal (active alert state leading to crying); hand-to-mouth activity; and active sucking on the tongue, and/or evidence of rooting or searching for a nipple[1, 2] (Fig 12–3). Feedings offered when the infant indicates readiness to take the nipple will promote total breast emptying. Breast emptying can be further enhanced by continuous massage of the breast during feeding as well as by alternating the breast that is offered first. The duration of the feeding session will vary with different infants, but the breast is usually emptied in 7 to 8 minutes. Suckling beyond this interval is generally non-nutritive. Frequent and shorter experiences at the breast in the early postpartum period are generally associated with decreased postpartum engorgement and increased milk yield.[10]

Breast Care

Nipple soreness is the most frequent cause for discontinuation of breast-feeding, and the most common cause of soreness is improper positioning of the infant on the breast. To maximize skin integrity, the infant should grasp as much of the nipple and areola as possible, and be positioned to facilitate a posterior nipple placement in the

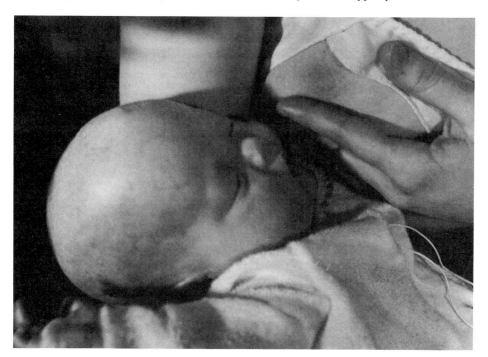

FIG 12–3.
Note premature infants weak rooting behavior, semi-drowsy state, and general hyptonia.

mouth (Fig 12–4). Suction should be released before removing the infant from the breast by placing a finger into the side of the infant's mouth and gently pressing downward. Varying the position of the baby's head in relation to the breast will also help to prevent or treat skin trauma. The reverse infant holds (such as the football carry) are particularly helpful as they allow the mother good control of the infant's head and visualization of the mouth and tongue prior to insertion of the nipple (Figs 12–5,A through H).

Breast hygiene can be accomplished by daily bathing, excluding the use of soap to the breast. Montgomery's glands, present on the areola, secrete a liquid that both protects and lubricates the nipple. Skin integrity is promoted by leaving this sebacious secretion on the breast. The breast milk that remains on the nipple after feeding should be air-dried with a commercial blow dryer. This method seems to give good relief to sore nipples and promotes skin healing in general. Breast pads with plastic liners should be avoided, as they diminish air flow around the nipple and may become intermittently saturated with milk, causing excoriation. If leakage of milk occurs the infant should be placed at the breast so that the spontaneous let-down of milk coincides with nursing sessions. Over the 1st month of lactation, the lactiferous ducts enlarge considerably and the let-down reflex will no longer be associated with such copious milk leakage.

A supporting brassiere is necessary throughout the lactation experience to minimize contour changes of the breast. Breasts engorged with milk may become pendulous and prone to injury. The ligaments of Cooper, the fibrous bands that connect the breast to the chest wall, provide some natural protection against gravitational pull. Damage to these ligaments is prevented by constraining the breast toward the chest wall. Ideally, the brassiere chosen should contain no underwire and allow easy entry of the hand between the bra and axilla. An ill-fitting brassiere may cause obstruction of milk flow and predispose the woman to breast infection.

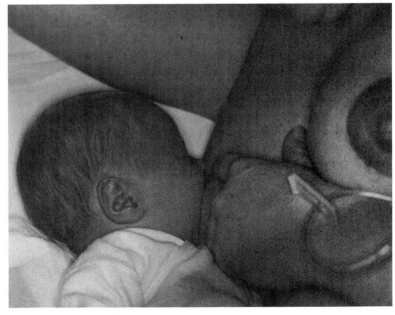

FIG 12–4.
Posterior placement of infant on nipple, to avert nipple soreness.

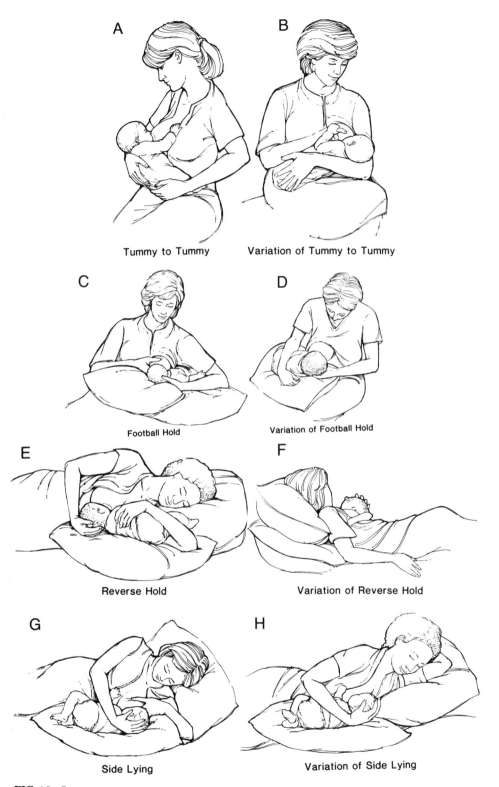

A   B

Tummy to Tummy   Variation of Tummy to Tummy

C   D

Football Hold   Variation of Football Hold

E   F

Reverse Hold   Variation of Reverse Hold

G   H

Side Lying   Variation of Side Lying

FIG 12–5.
A–H, varying placement on the infant as a means of reducing maternal breast soreness.

Milk Production

The caloric requirement of the lactating mother is commensurate with that of pregnancy and requires little adjustment in the postpartum period. Dietary recommendations include approximately 2,300 to 2,500 kcal/24 hr, with increases in protein, calcium, and phosphorus intake.[17] As milk production is also dependent on mobilization of energy from tissue stores, poor weight gain during pregnancy may be mirrored in the postpartum period by reduced milk production. In this instance the mother's caloric requirement will exceed these standard recommendations. Fluid intake should be generous and should minimally include 1 to 2 L of fluid daily. Routine prenatal vitamin supplementation should be continued throughout lactation.

Milk volume will approximate 600 to 750 mL/day in the first postpartum month, peaking at 800 to 1000 mL/day at 4 to 5 months, and diminishing gradually as feedings become less frequent. Infants may lose up to 10% of their birth weight in the 1st week of life but should regain this weight by the 2d to 3d week of age. Weight gain thereafter should approximate 15 to 40 g/day. Failure to regain birth weight or a suboptimal weight gain in the 1st month of life suggests limited milk volume and requires prompt investigation. The majority of women with poor milk yields will respond with increased production if they are encouraged to increase the frequency of feedings, while avoiding infant supplementation with water or proprietary formulas.

Routine supplementation of breast-feeding with formula should be discouraged, as unnecessary supplementation may lead to early discontinuation of breast-feeding. While some controversy persists regarding the role of supplementation,[16] common sense would indicate that routine bottle feeding of formula will decrease infant demand for nursing and therefore jeopardize continued lactation.[19] Nonetheless, supplementation for specific reasons may be necessary in the immediate newborn period, in some instances. It is essential that the mother have a clear understanding of the rationale for and the duration of these supplemental feedings. Commercial discharge packs that contain bottle feeding supplies may accelerate the discontinuation of breast-feeding, as these materials may reinforce the need for supplements as well as suggest that the maternal milk volume and/or milk quality may be inadequate.[13]

Maintenance

Counseling and Education

Breast-feeding beyond 1 month of age is positively correlated with maternal counseling and educational preparation.[21] This emphasizes the importance of instruction in the antepartum as well as postpartum periods. Prior to discharge, each mother should have the basics of breast-feeding reviewed and, additionally, be taught methods of assessing her newborn for adequate intake. As previously stated, the infant should be fed eight to ten times in a 24-hour period and be awakened for feeds if he or she fails to demand at this rate. Infants should be in the quiet or active alert states prior to the initiation of feedings. The infant should feed 5 to 10 minutes from both breasts in each nursing session and be brought back to wakefulness between breasts by diaper change, socialization, or unswaddling. Infant satiety is reflected by increasingly smooth cycles between sleep and wakefulness, which correspond to more predictable feeding times. Reasonable urine output will result in soaked diapers occurring with every feeding, or six to eight times for a daily minimum. Frequent stooling, as often as every feeding, also suggests that the intake is adequate. Absent or infrequent stooling in the early postpartum period is an abnormal finding that requires further evaluation.

Between 3 and 4 weeks of age, many infants go through a stage of "fussiness," particularly in the evening hours. This is probably a function of a rapidly developing central nervous system that must cope with increasing environmental stimulation as the infant spends more time in the alert state. This fussiness is interpreted as "colic" in the bottle-fed infant and as "hunger" in the breast-fed baby. Counseling during this period is particularly helpful in the prolongation of breast-feeding, as this maturational spurt is self-limited and will usually resolve spontaneously. Frequent feedings in conjunction with alternate methods of infant consolation can be employed:

1. Movement—rocking, walking, car rides
2. Visual and auditory stimuli—singing or talking to infant, music, motion of a mobile
3. Environmental modifications—feeding in low-traffic areas, protection from sensory bombardment, reduced lighting, and so forth.

If the infant is gaining at the expected rate, maternal reassurance and reinforcement are potent contributors to the continuation of lactation.

Vitamin and mineral requirements in term infants are generally met by breast milk; however, supplemental vitamin D, fluoride, and iron are frequently prescribed.[17] Breast milk is adequate nutrition for the 1st year of life, but cultural norms have influenced the introduction of solid foods, commencing at approximately 5 to 6 months. Regression of the extrusion reflex is a behavioral indication of the readiness to begin spoon feedings. Pureed baby foods are generally offered one at a time, with the exclusion of wheat, citrus, and egg white products for the 1st year of life.

Posthospitalization Management

Federal budget cuts and increasing hospital costs have promoted a trend of early home discharge from obstetric units across the nation. In 1955, the length of stay for an uncomplicated vaginal delivery was approximately 6 days. In 1970 the hospital stay decreased to 4.1 days, and in 1980 the duration of hospitalization was only 3.6 days.[26] Current obstetric hospitalizations last for approximately 24 to 48 hours. The 1990s may well witness the development of outpatient facilities that are completely geared to the delivery process itself, and maternal and infant assessment will be the responsibility of the primary health care provider.

Although this trend in practice may have a deleterious effect on the establishment and maintenance of lactation, this is not a natural consequence of early discharge. In Sweden, early home discharge has not had a negative effect on breast-feeding because women are actively managed following discharge with three to four home visits by a midwife in the 1st week of their child's life.[40] While socialized medicine makes this intervention approach a viable option, the economic and time constraints of western society often preclude frequent home visits. An alternative approach to the management of the early breast-feeding experience would be systematic use of a telephone call *survey* to assess and manage the mother and infant. This *survey* (Appendix) could be implemented by the primary care provider within 24 hours after hospital discharge. Clients who screen as "abnormal" could be seen at home (by a nurse/clinician) or be assessed during an office visit. The condition of infants who screen as "suspect" could be reevaluated by telephone in the next 24 to 48 hours and corresponding recommendations made. The majority of infants (particularly those whose mothers are breast-feeding for the first time) should be seen for full evaluation in the physician's office between 7 and 10 days following birth.

Weaning

Lactation is well established by 4 weeks postpartum with the let-down reflex experienced at each feeding session. If the mother wishes to offer the baby a supplemental feeding intermittently after this time, her milk volume will not be radically altered. As stated previously, milk volume reaches its peak at about 5 months, the same point in time when many mothers begin to offer solid food, and thus a gradual weaning will naturally take place as the infant decreases the frequency of breast-feedings. As the child matures, the mother may also begin to offer sips of milk and juice from a cup.

Weaning prior to the introduction of solids is best accomplished by deleting one nursing session each 5 to 7 days and replacing this feeding with proprietary formula. The mother may wish to save the feeding that she enjoys the most (e.g., the early morning feeding) as the last to be discontinued. Gradual weaning helps prevent the acute engorgement that is associated with precipitous discontinuation of breast-feeding.

Weaning will occasionally be accompanied by the onset of maternal depression, appearing much like the "postpartum blues." Although true psychotic breakdowns are rare, childbirth does have a documented role in precipitating psychiatric disease.[22] Warning the mother ahead of time that weaning from the breast may be accompanied by unusual and disturbing feelings will normalize the perception of her own behavior and facilitate further discussion if the "blues" become a clinical depression.

COMMON PROBLEMS OF LACTATING WOMEN

Engorgement

The stimulus for milk production occurs through the action of prolactin on the mammary alveoli beginning 24 to 96 hours after delivery. Breast engorgement can occur during this time in both lactating and nonlactating women, because of (1) an increase in venous and lymphatic stasis in the surrounding breast tissue, and (2) an accumulation of milk within the alveoli and duct systems. Early nursing after delivery and flexible feeding during the first postpartum days may significantly decrease breast engorgement. This is particularly important because breast engorgement is not only painful, but is also associated with a higher rate of breast infection and lactation failure.

If engorgement becomes a problem, it is often advantageous to apply heat—by warm showers or hot packs—to the breast just prior to nursing. The use of mild analgesics may alleviate pain and can be given immediately after a feeding. If engorgement impedes nipple protractility, milk should be expressed from both breasts by manual or pump techniques until the infant can grasp the nipple easily. The baby should then be permitted to nurse until completion, during which time the mother should massage the breasts thoroughly. Reassurance should be provided to the mother that breast engorgement is normal and temporary and will not interfere with the subsequent success of the breast-feeding experience (if appropriate interventions are offered early in the course) (Table 12-1).

The electric breast pump provides an efficient method for emptying the engorged breast in the postpartum period. The pump can be utilized by placing the breast shield over the nipple area and holding it firmly against the breast to ensure a good seal. The

TABLE 12–1.

Common Problems in Breast-feeding

Engorgement
  Heat application 10 min prior to emptying
  Increase feeding/pumping frequency (every 2 to 3 hr)
  Circular breast massage and milk expression
  Analgesic medications as needed at termination of feed
Nipple soreness
  Vary infant–mother positioning at each feed
  Lean infant into the breast
  Allow breast milk to dry on nipple area
  Air dry nipple with blow dryer 5 min every feed
Cracked or bleeding nipples
  Apply milk or nontoxic lubricants to nipple area
  Unilateral pumping with contralateral feeding
  Keep infant off affected side 24 to 48 hr
  Offer affected side last when breast is reintroduced
Galactocele
  Intervene as per engorgement
  Monitor for superinfection by observation and palpation every feed
Mastitis
  Milk sampling for culture and sensitivity
  Institution of broad-spectrum antibiotic therapy
  With systemic illness, temporary interruption of feedings with artificial milk expression
  Antipyretic/analgesic relief as needed
Jaundice
  Exclude pathologic causes of hyperbilirubinemia
  Increase feeding frequency to a minimum of seven to eight times daily
  Consider 24° interruption of breast milk feeds
  Monitor serum levels during resolution
Drug precautions
  Establish medical indication for drug
  Crosscheck against contraindicated/cautioned drugs
  Consider pharmacokinetics and infant's metabolic capacity
  Administer drug immediately after feeding
  If drug is potentially toxic, temporarily express and discard milk

pump should be started at the minimum vacuum setting and increased only if the flow of milk is inadequate. The electric pump generates suction intermittently at approximately 48 cycles per minute in a rhythmic pattern that simulates the actual suckling of an infant at the breast. The breast shield should be kept in place continuously, with breast massage techniques used throughout, until the milk flow slows to a drip. The pump can then be turned off, the breast shield switched to the opposite side, and the same procedure repeated. Some women find it advantageous to switch sides a number of times during the pumping session. Total pumping time should not exceed 20 minutes in length, and both breasts should be equally stimulated. There are double collection systems currently available that allow the mother to pump both breasts simultaneously. The use of these systems will halve the time required for pumping and may improve milk production by stimulating increased prolactin secretion.[32]

For posthospitalization milk expression, many commercially available hand-held pumps can be purchased for $25 to $30. These hand pumps are either manual, battery powered, or electric, and provide women easy access to efficient methods of milk expression. If milk let-down is not experienced during pumping or nursing by 7 to 10 days postpartum, oxytocin (Syntocinon) nasal spray may be used to augment this reflex arc. Galactagogues, such as metoclopramide, are not currently recommended for bolstering low milk yields.[30]

Cracked and/or Fissured Nipples

Although some nipple soreness is anticipated at the onset of breast-feeding, severe nipple trauma will be prevented by proper positioning at the breast (see Fig 12–5,A–H). Improper positioning of the infant on the breast is the most common cause of significant nipple trauma. With cracked and bleeding nipples, it may be necessary to limit the infant's access to the damaged nipple temporarily (for 24 to 48 hours), while maintaining milk production with a pump. Because nipple breakdown is usually a unilateral problem, the infant can be placed on the opposite breast while pumping takes place on the affected side. This will facilitate milk let-down and enhance milk yield.

Methods to promote skin integrity that have been explained earlier in this chapter may also be employed. The frequent application of breast milk to the affected area is particularly helpful. The infant can be gradually reintroduced to the affected nipple by offering feedings intermittently over the next 24 hours as tolerated by the patient. Full resumption of feedings can usually take place in 48 to 72 hours. Nipple injury is a predisposing factor to breast infection and requires prompt and effective treatment. (see Table 12–1).

Galactocele/Mastitis

As already detailed, engorgement is a frequent and normal occurrence during the first days of lactation. Prevention of excessive engorgement is usually possible with proper instruction and breast care. Early frequent feedings to stimulate milk production and promote breast emptying are necessary. The infant should be fed on demand every 2 to 3 hours during the first postpartum days. Thorough massaging of the breast should be performed regularly during nursing to maintain patency of milk ducts throughout the gland.

Should a milk duct become obstructed with inspissated milk in the postpartum period, it may present as an area of localized tenderness, erythema, and swelling. The galactocele thus formed may be treated effectively by the application of moist heat in conjunction with breast massage during nursing or milk expression. Occasionally, analgesics are required for relief of associated discomfort. Should superinfection within the galactocele be suspected, antistaphylococcal antibiotics may be prescribed (see Table 12–1).

Severe mastitis with generalized infection of the breast parenchyma is a relatively rare complication that usually occurs after the first 2 to 3 weeks of lactation. It is the result of bacterial invasion (usually coagulase-positive *Staphylococcus aureus* or *Streptococcus*) into the breast by way of cracked or fissured nipples. Some degree of engorgement often precedes the actual infection, which is heralded by acute systemic symptoms. High fever and chills with hardening and tenderness of the entire involved breast are characteristic. Appropriate management includes expression of milk for culture and sensitivity testing, and institution of appropriate antibiotic therapy. Continued expression of milk from the infected breast is mandatory and can be accomplished by continued nursing, or in severe illness by temporarily interrupting breast-feedings on the infected side with concurrent use of efficient breast pumps (see Table 12–1).

Jaundice

Breast milk jaundice is an entity whose existence and significance have been the subject of controversy through the years.[38] This nonhemolytic hyperbilirubinemia is characterized by an increase in the indirect fraction of bilirubin after 3 to 4 days of age. Evidence suggests that the presence of 5α-pregnane-3α,20β-diol in breast milk may inhibit the conjugation of bilirubin through interference with the hepatic enzyme production of glucuronyl transferase.[4] In addition, jaundice may be accentuated in the 1st week of life due to relative starvation in early lactation (i.e., inadequate caloric intake in the initial postpartum days). A third mechanism that may contribute to protracted hyperbilirubinemia may be maternal milk lipase, which results in increased levels of free fatty acids in the infant and, possibly, in impaired bilirubin conjugation.[18] Regardless of the cause, breast milk jaundice is relatively common, may be associated with bilirubin levels in excess of 20 mg/dL in the first 1 to 2 weeks of life, and may result in protracted jaundice with bilirubin elevations for several weeks.

It is important to exclude other causes of unconjugated hyperbilirubinemia in breast-fed babies, as is customary in any jaundiced infant. Breast milk jaundice is suspected as the cause of pronounced hyperbilirubinemia in an infant when, after abstention from breast-feeding for a period of 24 to 36 hours, a prompt and significant fall in the bilirubin level occurs. A partial rebound phenomenon may take place after resuming breast milk feedings, but bilirubin levels should not approach previous peak levels. If temporary interruption of breast-feeding is indicated, milk expression should be continued and the mother reassured that her breast milk is not harmful.[24]

Protracted hyperbilirubinemia must be followed after hospital discharge (through at least 14 days of life) in the otherwise healthy infant to be certain other diagnoses are not applicable. With current trends in early discharge, the onset of jaundice may not be detected. Because breast milk jaundice can be delayed to day 4 or 5 and peak at 10 to 14 days, close follow-up and instruction to the parents regarding signs of jaundice should be implemented (see Table 12–1).

Medication/Drugs

In this era of modern medicine, it is commonplace for patients to be utilizing a multiplicity of drugs and medications that are readily accessible as over-the-counter or prescription remedies. Pregnant women normally take five to eight drugs in the peripartum period.[22] Against the backdrop of alarm raised by the teratogenic and embryopathic effects of such drugs as thalidomide and diethylstilbesterol, strict regulations for safe and effective drug use were established in the early 1960s. These guidelines also address the potential hazards of drug ingestion concurrent with breast-feeding. Clinically, it is important to rely on clear medical indication(s) for prescribing/recommending a drug in the breast-feeding mother. Considerations should include relative risk of maternal illness vs. drug effect, and the potential sequelae of drug ingestion in the breast-fed infant. Recommendations should then be made to the mother regarding the advisability of breast-feeding her infant if such a drug is to be taken.

Few data are available documenting metabolism and safety for most medications during lactation. A general recommendation is to err on the side of safety and abstain from breast-feeding during the period when a required but questionably adverse agent is taken, or to substitute a drug with documented safety. Judicious use of any drug in reasonable doses is warranted in all situations. If a mother requires a specific medication that is of minimal potential hazard to the nursing infant, drug dosing and timing can be optimized to allow the least possible passage into the milk. Generally, the mother should take the medication immediately after a breast-feeding session. Long-acting forms of a drug should be avoided to prevent accumulation in the infant. In all such instances, the infant should be carefully monitored for potential drug effects during the medicated period[22] (see Table 12–1).

Health professionals caring for a breast-feeding maternal–infant dyad must have an accessible fund of knowledge pertaining to drug metabolism in breast milk. The pharmacokinetic properties that promote passage of a drug into the milk include lipid solubility, low molecular weight, nonionized chemical structure, basic (nonacidic) pH, and low protein binding. The route, dose, and timing of ingestion relative to the amount and frequency of feeding are crucial. In addition, an often ignored set of variables is the ability of the infant to absorb, metabolize, detoxify, and excrete the portion of the drug ingested by the mother and passed into the milk. A number of comprehensive references in the literature provide specific recommendations regarding individual drugs and drug classes.[6–8, 22, 34] Those drugs which are clearly contraindicated during breast-feeding,

TABLE 12–2.

Drugs in Breast Milk

Contraindicated	Cautioned
Antipsychotics	Nicotine, amphetamine
Narcotic analgesics (heroin)	
Antineoplastics	Antimalarial agents
Ergot alkaloids	Barbiturates (benzodiazepines)
Iodides	Phenytoin
Antithyroid (most)	Salicylates
Chloramphenicol	Caffeine
Erythromycin	Atropine
	Isoniazid
Tetracycline	Ethanol
Metronidazole	Narcotic agents
Radioactive isotopes	Meprobamate
Anticoagulants (phenindione)	Dextropropoxyphene
	Warfarin
Lithium	Methadone
Gold	Sulfonamides
Isotretinoin	Diuretics
Marijuana	Cimetidine
Cocaine	Codeine
Hallucinogens	Steroids
Others	Oral contraceptives (estrogenic)
	Others

as well as those which may be consumed on a cautionary basis with continued effective monitoring, are shown in Table 12–2.

The effects of occupational hazards, environmental toxins, and contaminants are an ongoing concern as modern technologic advances produce foreign by-products. Historically, caution has been exercised with such pollutants as pesticides (e.g., DDT), polybromylbiphenyls, and polychlorinated biphenyls; other exposures continue to be questioned with regard to potential adverse effects through breast milk. Experts tend to agree that breast-feeding should continue whenever possible, as the benefits confer advantages that outweigh risks of exposure to low levels of these toxins.

SPECIAL NEEDS OF MOTHERS AND BABIES

Infections

Current recommendations and precautions concerning the compatibility of breast-feeding with specific maternal infections can be found in several references,[17, 35] and are summarized in the following sections.

Cytomegalovirus.—The transmission of cytomegalovirus (CMV) occurs transplacentally in utero, vaginally during delivery, and postnatally by blood transfusions or by ingestion of infected breast milk. Because of the ubiquitous nature of the virus, up to 60% of infants will acquire CMV postnatally in the 1st year of life, but for the majority their symptoms are minimal and there are no chronic sequelae. Transmission of CMV can occur silently through virus-positive breast milk, and is associated with passive transfer of maternal antibody and chronic shedding of the virus. Thus, infection can be a type of natural immunization with minimal morbidity; breast-feeding is clearly more advantageous than hazardous. Caution is exercised for mothers with identified *primary* CMV infection in the acute phase of the illness. Milk infected with CMV may be more virulent in the premature or CMV-negative infant, who is typically deficient in specific transplacental antibodies.[12, 39] The American Academy of Pediatrics currently recommends biologically related milk donors and cautions against use of banked milk from heterologous donors.

Hepatitis A.—There is neither a contraindication to breast-feeding nor recommendation for the use of immunoglobulin in the infant of a mother who is positive for hepatitis A. If during the acute phase of the illness the mother has jaundice, nursing may be temporarily withheld.

Hepatitis B.—Transplacental transmission is frequent in the third trimester and intrapartum. Surface antigen is found in breast milk, but infants restricted from breast-feeding remain prone to acquiring both the virus and antibodies from affected mothers. Immunoprophylaxis of infants born to mothers positive for the surface antigen diminishes the risk of neonatal infection. A vaccination schedule is also initiated at birth. Breast-feeding is not precluded by maternal seropositivity. In the absence of active disease at the time of the infant's birth, the mother may reasonably exercise this option.

Herpes Simplex Virus.—Breast-feeding is acceptable during active maternal infection if careful attention is paid to proper hygiene, and if no vesicular herpetic lesions are present on the breast. Adequate covering of cutaneous lesions must be observed until they are dried. A mother with herpes labialis or stomatitis (cold sore) should wear a mask until lesions are crusted. A case of postnatal acquisition of herpes simplex type I infection was traced to the mother's milk[11]; however, in general the mode of transmission tends to be through contact with skin and other infectious material.

Human Immunodeficiency Virus.—Although the human immunodeficiency virus (HIV) has been isolated from cultured cell-free portions of breast milk, no case of acquired immune deficiency syndrome (AIDS) from breast milk has been documented. A large multicenter European study on the perinatal transmission of HIV has shown a negligible incremental risk of infection in breast-fed infants.[29] As it is difficult to distinguish intrauterine, intrapartum, and postnatal infection using current laboratory methods, the relative contribution of breast-feeding to HIV transmission is undeterminable and in all likelihood small. Case reports suggesting vertical postnatal transmission have involved breast-feeding mothers infected by postnatal blood transfusion. By the same token, there have been instances of mothers infected antepartum who breast-fed for prolonged periods and did not transmit HIV.[27]

Current guidelines from the Centers for Disease Control and U.S. Public Health Service recommend that HIV-infected women abstain from breast-feeding.[35] In developed countries where formula is a safe and ready alternative, this can be effectively implemented. However, as the World Health Organization has maintained, when sanitation and nutrition factors are suboptimal, as in Third World countries, breast-feeding may well continue to be the method of choice in spite of HIV seroconversion. The immunologic advantages of breast milk are of sufficient merit to confer a beneficial effect in the infant subjected to a deprived environment where artificial feeds may be hazardous, and HIV antibody transmitted from the mother may be potentially protective for the nursing infant.

The future demands more prospective longitudinal studies by means of surveillance of AIDS dissemination patterns. Perhaps "breast is best," but in the current controversy on health practices related to AIDS, more investigation is required regarding the impact of breast-feeding on HIV transmission.

Failure to Thrive

Health professionals caring for a breast-feeding maternal–infant dyad must be knowledgeable and supportive in their efforts to promote, preserve, and enhance the breast-feeding relationship. Misconceptions often prevail, resulting in less than optimal feeding practices with a rising incidence of critical failure-to-thrive infants. Whether this outcome is based on simple mismanagement problems or true organic deficiencies, early evaluation and intervention are essential.

Failure to thrive is defined as a pattern of retarded growth in weight and/or length over a period of time which consistently corresponds to at least two standard deviations below the mean values for age. An infant who fails to gain weight or continues to lose weight after the 10th day of life, or has not regained birth weight by 3 weeks of age, is suspect for the diagnosis. Weight loss in excess of 15% to 25% of birth weight by 2 weeks of age can occur.[22]

The infant often presents with a subtle peripartum abnormality (prematurity, mild birth depression, excessive early weight loss), and with an inexperienced mother. As the infant incurs a significant trend of delayed growth (within 7 to 10 days of lactation), the parent(s) may still perceive the child as adequately fed and content—a "good baby".

Loss of over 20% to 30% of birth weight may thus occur unnoticed over the first 10 to 14 days of breast-feeding. This syndrome of acute failure to thrive affects all social and educational strata. Cases in the literature describe the unfortunate consequences of hypernatremic dehydration, critical weight loss, and malnutrition.[37] The practitioner's responsibility is that of deciphering organic vs. nonorganic pathologic conditions, and maternal vs. infant causes.

Nonorganic Causes

Insufficient lactation frequently accompanies failure to thrive. The mother may have poor let-down of milk due to inadequate diet, medical illness, ingested medication, stress, and/or fatigue. A vicious cycle of feeding problems ensues, aggravated by mounting maternal anxiety and continued inhibition of milk secretion through a depressed oxytocin release reflex. In addition, ill-informed mothers may adopt inappropriate and rigid feeding schedules, which result in unrelieved engorgement and partial involution of lactation secondary to pressure atrophy of the glandular secreting cells. Babies who are allowed to sleep 8 to 10 hours or for prolonged intervals between daytime feeds, by virtue of their undemanding nature, are at risk for failure to thrive. Modern-day maternal separation patterns tend to disrupt a more unrestricted mode of breast-feeding.[22]

Introduction of water or formula supplements prior to the establishment of lactation contributes to nipple confusion and possibly to inadequate suckling. Improper positioning, unilateral breast feeding, tandem nursing (breast-feeding siblings simultaneously), and other suboptimal breast-feeding techniques may also impair the lactation experience.

Organic Causes

Mothers may exhibit a genuine disease state that manifests itself by failure to lactate. This category includes primary prolactin deficiency, disrupted neurohumoral pathways, retained placental fragments, hypoplastic breast/insufficient mammary glandular tissue, and surgical reconstruction of the breast that has disrupted the lactiferous ducts. Nipple abnormalities not amenable to corrective measures might also preclude lactation.[31]

The infant may fail to thrive due to intrinsic features of anatomic or physiologic deficiency. Intake may be limited because of inadequacy of the suckling mechanism, as in "flutter sucking," or because of anomalies such as cleft lip/palate or micrognathia that interfere mechanically with feeding prowess. When intake itself is satisfactory, an infant may fail to thrive because of net nutritional losses secondary to intestinal problems, metabolic diseases, or infection. In addition, infants with some neurologic disorders, congenital heart disease, or growth retardation may expend surplus energy beyond the nutritional yield provided, thus losing weight.[22]

Intervention must involve close scrutiny of the maternal–infant interaction during a breast-feeding session, after proper evaluation has been carried out to eliminate primary maternal or infant disease. A follow-up visit is recommended within 7 to 10 days of discharge from the hospital (for the newly breast-feeding mother). Careful history taken may elicit essential information about the mother's lifestyle as it influences lactation, and the infant's feeding, elimination, and activity patterns. The infant's weight should be monitored serially, and growth parameters (weight, length, head circumference) plotted sequentially to follow percentile status. The mother must be instructed in normal voiding, stooling, and feeding patterns in a breast-feeding infant. Eight to ten feedings per day should be encouraged.

If an increased feeding schedule fails to improve weight gain, supplementation with proprietary formulas is indicated. These supplements can be offered as an adjunct to feeding at the breast. In all cases the health care provider can continue to reinforce and support the breast feeding relationship effectively.

Adoption/Relactation

Special circumstances may arise in which a nonbiologic mother expresses a desire to nurse her adopted infant, or a mother who has given birth wishes to breast-feed after initial deferment of the option. Such requests have led, respectively, to methods for induced lactation and relactation.

The adoptive mother should approach the lactation experience with a goal of establishing a close maternal-infant bond that may also, incidentally, provide some benefits of nutrition. Thus, the emphasis is on a nurturing relationship rather than focusing on the volume of milk produced. An adoptive mother who plans to breast-feed should be counseled about the process of induced lactation as she anticipates the arrival of the infant. Preparation of the breast and manual stimulation of the nipple are explained, as well as the somewhat similar physiologic changes (breast size, menstrual pattern, and weight) which may occur. Stress reactions that may surface during the adoptive process may render a mother unable to generate a good ejection reflex. Again, the emphasis should be placed on mothering rather than milk volume per se.[22]

There is no specific protocol by which to induce lactation except effective breast stimulation by systematic pumping or manual expression, and frequent suckling. Supplemental sources of nutrition (donor human milk or formula) are esential, especially during the 1- to 6-week period of onset of lactation. The Lact-Aid Nursing Trainer System* can be an invaluable asset and avoids nipple confusion. Drugs that induce lactation (galactagogues) by simulation of the natural process of hormonal influences that occur in pregnancy are not currently recommended. Intranasal administration of oxytocin may enhance let-down and therefore production of milk. The composition of milk produced by induction of lactation is comparable to that of the puerperium.

Relactation in the biologic mother is established in similar fashion, but with the advantage that the breast has been primed by pregnancy and merely experiences a delay in providing nourishment for the infant. If the woman has received the prolactin inhibitor bromocriptine (Parlodel), lactation can be induced by the active stimulation of the breast during suckling and pumping. Supplementation is again advisable and may be weaned as breast milk quantities become sufficient. In a retrospective study of relactating mothers, the overall success rate was encouraging, with 75% breast-feeding beyond 6 months, and 50% discontinuing supplements when the child was 1 month of age.[5]

Working Mothers

In an age where it is imperative that many mothers work outside of the home, measures are essential to insure that breast-feeding and employment are not mutually exclusive. Obviously this is a disciplined effort mandating high motivation and effective

*Lact-Aid International, Inc., Athens Tennessee, 80206.

scheduling on the part of the mother, and requiring adaptation from employers and family members.

Work that disrupts maternal–infant proximity for any duration of time demands some flexibility for a mother to maintain an adequate milk supply for her infant. She should begin to express and freeze surplus milk between feedings, approximately 1 week prior to returning to work. Sterilized plastic receptacles for collection should each contain the volume of one feeding. Although the infant may resist bottle feeding of breast milk from the mother, alternate caretakers are usually successful in these bottle feedings.

Expression of milk at the work place requires facilities for privacy and for proper refrigeration of milk. Electric pump(s) provided in this setting may be of major benefit to the lactating employee. A breast-feeding mother must remember to eat regularly and drink additional fluids while at work. It is essential to time the milk let-down reflex to the pumping episodes, and to pump at regular intervals. Reverse-cycle nursing (increased frequency at night) is recommended, and the importance of special times reserved for quality mothering and close contact should not be underestimated.

Employee support groups and professional breast-feeding advocates are helpful in advising the working mother who chooses to breast-feed. The stresses and fatigue inherent in the mother's multiple roles may threaten successful lactation, but informed and careful planning will optimize the outcome.

Milk Banking/Storage

The storage of human milk by procedural milk banking has been in effect for over half a century. In the past, multiple unrelated heterologous donors provided pooled milk after careful screening and controls were implemented. Such pooling is no longer acceptable because of safety concerns.[17] Nonbiologic, individual milk donors must be screened for maternal serology (syphilis, hepatitis B surface antigen, HIV, tuberculosis, CMV), medication consumption, and other factors that might impair milk purity. The American Academy of Pediatrics currently recommends biologic donors *only* for the hospitalized newborn.

Proper hygienic techniques of collection and processing must be observed to avoid bacterial contamination, while preserving potential immunologic and nutritional benefits of the milk. Harsh heat treatments (such as Holder pasteurization) inactivate pathogens but also alter the putative host-defense factors in the milk. The relative merits of freezing make it the preferred alternative for effective inactivation of contaminants. Milk is safely refrigerated for a period of 24 hours, and can be frozen for 2 to 3 months. Thawing is best accomplished by placing the container under tepid running water. It is prudent to avoid long exposure of milk to room temperature and subjecting it to hot water or microwave methods of thawing. Once thawed, milk should not be refrozen.[17]

Support Groups/Community Resources/Lactation Consultants

The promotion of breast-feeding extends beyond prenatal preparation and the peripartum into the crucial time after discharge from the hospital. After a woman has made the informed decision to breast-feed, she must be fully supported by a network of health care professionals, employment associates, family members, and peers. "Mothering the mother" is a beneficial approach to postpartum care of the breast-feeding patient.[22]

In this age of isolation of the nuclear family by urbanized society, various support groups have provided nursing mothers with information, moral support, and counseling, all of which tend to boost confidence and reinforce normalcy through the dynamics of group interactions. The sisterhood concept of rooming-in units also tends to promote breast-feeding by means of the conversational interchange that occurs naturally between mothers.[22]

Of key importance is the need for a perceived visibility of the medical profession at the core of all support personnel involved. In the efforts to educate mothers and promote breast-feeding, ongoing re-education of health care providers is essential. Lactation counselors must demonstrate appropriate qualifying credentials beyond those of mere personal experience. Counselors ideally undergo a period of intensive training that encompasses the adoption of special personal qualities that are conducive to the role. They must also possess an adequate fund of current information in the science and practice of human lactation, but provision of medical advice should be deferred to the physician.

When lactation counselors and visiting nurses are integrated into and supervised within the medical framework as part of a team, their role can be extremely effective in nurturing the breast-feeding mother.[41] Ready availability of such personnel at the bedside during the peripartum and after discharge from the hospital is invaluable, and enhances the link of communication with the physician providing care. Telephone counseling is a most useful tool (see the Appendix).

SUMMARY

In conclusion, the art of breast-feeding and the science of lactation have advanced through the years. By virtue of its nurturing as well as nourishing advantages, breast-feeding should remain the cornerstone of early infant nutrition worldwide. Professionals in the realm of maternal-child health care must take an active role in the promotion of breast-feeding, by serving as advocates in the dissemination of appropriate information and support at all levels.

REFERENCES

1. Als H: A synactive model of neonatal behavioral organization. *Phys Occup Ther Pediatr* 6(2–3):3–53, 1986.
2. Als H, Brazelton TB: Assessment of behavioral organization in a preterm and a full term infant. *J Am Acad Child Psychiatry* 1981; 20:239.
3. American Academy of Pediatrics: Policy statement: The promotion of breast-feeding. *Pediatrics* 1982; 69:654–661.
4. Arias IM, et al: Prolonged neonatal unconjugated hyperbilirubinemia associated with breast-feeding and steroid pregnane-3,20-diol in maternal milk that inhibits glucuronide formation in vitro. *J Clin Invest* 1964; 43:2037.
5. Auerbach K, Avery J: Relactation-a study of 366 cases. *Pediatrics* 1980; 65:236.
6. Beall MH: Advising the nursing mother about her medications. *Contemp Pediatr* 2/88, 67–80.
7. Briggs GG, Freeman RK, Yaffe SJ: *Drugs in Pregnancy and Lactation*, ed 2. Baltimore, Williams & Wilkins, 1986.
8. Committee on Drugs: The transfer of drugs and other chemicals into human breast milk. *Pediatrics* 1983; 72:375–383.
9. Cone TE: *200 Years of Feeding Infants in America*. Columbus, Ohio, Ross Laboratories, 1976.

10. DeCarvalho M, Robertson S, Friedman A, et al: Effect of frequent breast-feeding on early milk production and infant weight gain. *Pediatrics* 1983; 72:307–311.
11. Dunkle LM, Schmidt RR, O'Connor DM: Neonatal herpes simplex infection possibly acquired via maternal breast milk. *Pediatrics* 1979; 63:250–251.
12. Dworsky M, Yow M, Stagno S, et al: Cytomegalovirus infection of breast milk and transmission in infancy. *Pediatrics* 1983; 72:295–299.
13. Frank DA, Wirtz SJ, Sorenson JR, et al: Commercial discharge packs and breast-feeding counseling: Effects on infant-feeding practices in a randomized trial. *Pediatrics* 1987; 80:845–854.
14. Garfield E: Breast is best: 1 Merits of mother's milk. *Curr Contents,* May 1986; 19:3–11.
15. Garfield E: Breast is best: 2 Factors affecting breast-feeding worldwide. *Curr Contents,* May 1986; 26:3–13.
16. Gray-Donald K, Kramer MS, Munday S, et al: Effect of formula supplementation in the hospital on the duration of breast-feeding: A controlled clinical trial. *Pediatrics* 1985; 75:514–518.
17. *Guidelines for Perinatal Care,* ed 2, Elk Grove Village, Ill, American Academy of Pediatrics and American College of Obstetricians and Gynecologists, 1988.
18. Hargreaves T: Effect of fatty acids on bilirubin conjugation. *Arch Dis Child* 1973; 48:446–450.
19. Herrera AJ: Supplemented versus unsupplemented breast-feeding. *Perinatol-Neonatol* 1984; May/June: 70–71.
20. Kocturk T, Zetterstrom R: Breast-feeding and its promotion. *Acta Paediatr Scand* 1988; 77:183–190.
21. Kurinij N, Shiono PH, Rhoads GG: Breast-feeding incidence and duration in black and white women. *Pediatrics* 1988; 81:365–371.
22. Lawrence RA: *Breast-feeding: A Guide for the Medical Profession.* St Louis, CV Mosby Co, 1985.
23. Lemons P, Stuart M, Lemons JA: Breast-feeding the premature infant. *Clin Perinatol* 1986; 13:111–122.
24. Lemons PK, Kochanczyk M, Lemons JA: Breast-feeding the newborn. *J Ind St Med Assoc* 1980; 73:373–378.
25. Lemons PK: Breast-feeding the premature newborn. *Perinatal Press* 1983; 7:83–88.
26. *Length of Stay in PAS Hospital, 1965–1980.* Ann Arbor, Mich, Commission on Professional and Hospital Activities, 1982.
27. Lifson AR: Do alternate modes for transmission of human immunodeficiency virus exist? A review. *JAMA* 1988; 259:1353–1356.
28. Martinez GA, Nalezienski JP: The recent trend in breast-feeding. *Pediatrics* 1979; 64:686–692.
29. Mok JQ, et al: Infants born to mothers seropositive for HIV—preliminary findings from a multicenter European study. *Lancet* 1987; 1:1164.
30. Neifert MR, Seacat JM: Practical aspects of breast-feeding the premature infant. *Perinatol-Neonatal* 1988; Jan/Feb:24–31.
31. Neifert MR, Seacat JM: A guide to successful breast-feeding. *Contemp Pediatr* 1986; 3:26–45.
32. Neifert MR, Seacat JM: Milk yield and prolactin rise with simultaneous breast pumping, abstract. Presented at the Annual Meeting of the Ambulatory Pediatric Association, Washington, DC, May 1985.
33. Ogra SS, Ogra PL: Immunologic aspects of human colostrum and milk. *J Pediatr* 1978; 92:546.
34. Reisner SH, Eisenberg NH, Stahl B, et al: Maternal medications and breast-feeding. *Dev Pharmacol Ther* 1983; 6:285–304.
35. Report of the Committee on Infectious Diseases, ed 21. Elk Grove Village, Ill, American Academy of Pediatrics, 1988.

36. Riordan J, Countryman BA: Basics of breast-feeding. J Obstet Gynecol Neonatal Nurs 1980; July/Aug:207–213; Sept/Oct:273–283; Nov/Dec:357–360, 1980.
37. Roddey O, Martin E, Swetenburg R: Critical weight loss and malnutrition in breast-fed infants. *Am J Dis Child* 1981; 135:597–599.
38. Schneider AP: Breast milk jaundice in the newborn—a real entity. JAMA 1986; 255:3270–3274.
39. Stagno S, Reynolds DW, Pass RF, et al: Breast milk and the risk of cytomegalovirus infection. *N Engl J Med* 1980; 302:1073–1076.
40. Waldenstrom U, Sundelin C, Lindmark G: Early and late discharge after hospital birth: Breast-feeding. *Acta Paediatr Scand* 1987; 76:727–732.
41. Winikoff B, Myers D, Laukaran VH, et al: Overcoming obstacles to breast-feeding in a large municipal hospital—applications of lessons learned. *Pediatrics* 1987; 80:423–433.

APPENDIX

BREAST-FEEDING TELEPHONE SURVEY

Name:_____   Prior Breast-Feeding Experience: Yes___ No___

Age:____ G____ T____ P____ LC____ AB____   Support Person:_____

Delivered At:_____   Telephone #:_____

Type of Delivery:_____   Insurance Co.:_____

Telephone #:_____   Occupation:_____

Complications:_____

	Normal	Abnormal	Suspect

1. Milk has come in (milk leaking from oppos. side, let-down).
2. Demands to feed a minimum 7-8 per day/7-10 min each side.
3. Baby produces 6-8 soaked diapers a day.
4. Baby has had at least 1 stool in past 24 hours.
5. Sleeps at least 1-2 hrs between feedings.
6. Baby awakens for feedings. Sleep/wake cycle?
7. Baby appears jaundiced.
8. Sore or reddened areas on breasts or nipples?
9. Other:_____
   _____
   _____

Initial Phone Log @ 24 Hours

Time_____ Date_____   Phone Action: Initial_____ Follow-up_____

Consultant:_____   Follow-up Visit:_____

Status:_____   Recall in 24 Hrs:_____

_____   Office/Home Visit:_____

Follow-up Phone Log @ 48-72 Hours   Home/Office Visit:_____

Time_____ Date_____   Recommendations:_____

Consultant:_____   _____

Status:_____   _____

_____   _____

_____   _____

Chapter 13

Infant Formulas for Enteral Feeding*

Richard J. Schanler, M.D.

Shyh-Fang Cheng, M.D.

During the early 19th century in London, only 10% of infants who were not breast-fed survived their 1st year.[1] Subsequent changes in sanitation and medical care, and the recognition that milk had to be pasteurized, provided a basis for the development of human milk substitutes.[1]

When human milk is unavailable, substitutes provide an artificial nutrient source. The ideal human milk substitute should meet the nutrient needs of healthy infants, be well tolerated without inducing metabolic stress or biochemical abnormality, and not result in short-term or long-term morbidity.[2] In the construction of the ideal formula from nonhuman milk components, one should account for the bioavailability, digestibility, and biological value of the nutrients, all of which may differ from those in human milk.[2] Nevertheless, in the manufacture of human milk substitutes, the major goal appears to be the formulation of a product that is nutritionally as close to human milk as possible.[3]

A 1984 survey of feeding practices (Table 13–1) indicated a high prevalence of breast-feeding at 1 week postpartum. At 2, 4, and 6 months postpartum, however, the incidence of breast-feeding had declined by 45%, 35%, and 26%, respectively, and prepared formula feeding had increased by 63%, 72%, and 74%, respectively.[4] Prevalence rates of breast and formula feeding have remained relatively stable since that time.

The type of feeding selected for the first 6 months of infant life is of primary importance. The Committee on Nutrition of the American Academy of Pediatrics (CON/ AAP) states that "nutrient requirements are most critical in this period, during which nutritional deficiencies can have lasting effects on growth and development."[5] Recent reports suggest that breast-feeding beyond 6 months of life may reduce the risk of developing childhood malignancies.[6] In addition, a negative relationship between diabetes and breast-feeding has been reported.[6] Such reports must be substantiated further and

*This work is a publication of the USDA/ARS Children's Nutrition Research Center, Department of Pediatrics, Baylor College of Medicine and Texas Children's Hospital, Houston, Texas. This project has been funded in part with federal funds from the U.S. Department of Agriculture, Agricultural Research Service under Cooperative Agreement number 58-7MN1-6-100. The contents of this publication do not necessarily reflect the views or policies of the U.S. Department of Agriculture, nor does mention of trade names, commercial products, or organizations imply endorsement by the U.S. government.

TABLE 13–1.

Infants (%) at 1 Week of Age Receiving Various Milks and Formulas

Feeding Preference	Year									
	1955	1960	1965	1970	1975	1980	1981	1982	1983	1984
Human milk*	29.2	28.4	26.5	24.9	33.4	54.0	56.4	60.5	59.9	61.0
Evaporated milk	45.9	40.0	17.3	3.0	0.7	0.2	0.2	0.2	0.2	0.2
Bovine milk	4.1	2.8	1.5	0.6	0.3	0.1	0.1	0.1	0.0	0.0
Infant formula	23.2	34.9	59.0	74.9	69.2	50.6	48.5	45.3	45.8	45.0
Totals†	102.4	106.1	104.3	103.4	103.6	104.9	105.2	106.0	105.9	106.2

*Includes supplemental bottle-feeding (i.e., formula in addition to breast-feeding).
†Modified, with permission, from Martinez GA, Krieger FW: 1984 Milk-feeding patterns in the United States. *Pediatrics* 1985; 76:1004–1008.

the causes of specific diseases must be evaluated; nevertheless, these studies emphasize the value of a considered decision in the selection of the type of infant feeding.

HISTORICAL DEVELOPMENT OF INFANT FORMULAS

Breast-feeding alternatives can be traced back to biblical times. One of the most primitive infant feeding methods used instead of suckling was premastication, which probably was introduced by the Egyptians 1,500 years ago.[7] An early reference to an infant formula came from Isaiah (VII:15), "butter and honey shall he eat." The prophet Ezekiel mentioned fine flour and olive oil as nutrient sources for infants.[7] Biblical references can be found for a variety of animal milks used to feed infants (e.g., goat, ass, horse, camel, pig, and deer).[7]

The first commercially marketed preparation, a mixture of wheat flour, bovine milk, and malt flour cooked with potassium bicarbonate, was made in 1865 by the German chemist Justus von Liebig, who called his formula the "perfect infant food."[1, 7, 8] Because this product deteriorated in liquid form, it was later prepared and sold as a powder. Liebig's formulation was similar to other preparations of that time, which were essentially carbohydrates. Despite Liebig's argument that the formulation was similar to mother's milk, many physicians reported that it was indigestible.[8] In the late 19th century, William Newton developed the process of condensing milk by evaporation.[7] Evaporated milk came into use as a base for infant feeding in 1856 when Gail Borden developed a method to concentrate raw bovine milk by vacuum evaporation and preserve the concentrate with sugar. This product is still commercially available as Eagle Brand Condensed Milk.[1, 7] Myenberg, in 1883, developed a procedure to sterilize (93° C to 116° C) unsweetened milk concentrate.[1] This technological advance preserved the unsweetened evaporated milk and modified the casein to a finer curd.[1] By 1930, evaporated milk became the most widely used ingredient for infant formula. It was inexpensive, did not require refrigeration, and assured sterility at a time when the purity of bovine milk supplies was questioned.[1] The first single complete infant formula in modern times was prepared in 1915 by Gerstenberger.[1] The artificial milk was adapted to simulate the 4.6% fat content of human milk by replacing bovine fat with fat derived from cod liver oil and beef tallow.[8] This product was called SMA for "synthetic milk adapted."[1] The letters SMA have remained, but the formulation has been modified extensively. The fat blend has been replaced with vegetable oils, lactose has been added, and the vitamin and mineral composition has been modified.

HUMAN VS. BOVINE MILK

We have come almost full circle since the pioneering efforts of von Liebig. He believed his product to be equal to that of mother's milk, and the aim of manufacturers today is to make their products as similar to human milk as possible.[8] The rationale for this effort is described in many reviews that identify the differences between human and bovine milks.[9, 10] The differences are evidenced in the nutrient compositions and bioavailabilities of the various milks. Hansen et al.[3] stated recently that the protein, vitamin, and mineral contents of infant formula usually are higher than the average levels found in human milk, to ensure adequate nutrient intake by all infants consuming the product. Additional quantities of nutrients are added to infant formulas to account for variabilities in processing and storage. These "overages" are added to ensure that the appropriate nutrient contents are present at the end of shelf life.[3]

Profound differences in functional immunologic outcomes are observed between infants fed formula and those fed human milk.[11] Fewer episodes of respiratory and gastrointestinal illness occur in breast-fed infants.[12] Episodes of neonatal sepsis and necrotizing enterocolitis occur less frequently in preterm infants from high-risk populations when they are fed human milk.[10, 12] The feeding of human milk also creates an environment in the intestine that facilitates the growth of beneficial, nonpathogenic flora, compared with pathogenic species of anaerobes and coliforms that predominate in the feces of infants fed formula.[13] The quantities of host defense proteins, lactoferrin and secretory IgA, are smaller in the feces and urine of formula-fed infants, possibly suggesting impaired host protection.[10, 12] Whereas both milks contain whey proteins, bovine milk differs qualitatively because β-lactoglobulin is the major whey protein, rather that the secretory IgA and lactoferrin that are found in human milk.[9] A "humanized" bovine milk–based formula does not include the host defense proteins that provide human local gastrointestinal tract protection.

Feeding human milk to the preterm infant poses a controversy. Although impaired host defense is common and human milk may be beneficial in that regard, multicenter feeding trials have shown that optimal growth patterns and shorter periods of hospitalization occur only when preterm infants are fed preterm commercial formula as compared with human milk.[14–16] The differences in infant outcome described in reports of these trials should be considered when a choice of nutrient sources is to be made.

TYPES OF FORMULAS

Human milk is recommended for feeding healthy infants during the 1st year of life whenever possible.[17] Manufacturers of infant formulas have focused their efforts on the development of products that simulate human milk composition. Whether further refinements of their products will be more beneficial remains uncertain.

When infant formulas are substituted for human milk, they should provide protein of appropriate biological value at 7% to 16% of calories and fat at 30% to 54% of calories (including linoleic acid at 2% to 3% of calories); carbohydrate should account for the remainder of calories (29% to 63%).[1, 5, 18] The selection of ingredients to meet formula composition requirements depends on the digestive capabilities and particular needs of the infant and the bioavailability of the nutrient source.[1] Levels of nutrients required in infant formulas by the Infant Formula Act of 1980 (PL 96-359) are shown in Table 13–2.[1, 5, 18]

Infant formulas generally may be categorized as bovine milk–based, soy-based, and protein hydrolysate–based. Several formulas are available for specialized indications. All formulas discussed in the following sections have the manufacturer's listing in the Tables.

TABLE 13–2.

Nutrient Levels of Infant Formulas*

Nutrient	Requirements (per 100 kcal) of the Infant Formula Act of 1980	
	Minimum	Maximum
Protein, g	1.8†	4.5
Fat, g (% kcal)	3.3 (30.0)	6.0 (54.0)
Linoleic acid, mg (% kcal)	300.0 (2.7)	. . .
Vitamins		
A, IU	250.0‡	750.0§
D, IU	40.0	100.0
K, μg	4.0	. . .
E, IU	0.7‖	
Ascorbic acid, mg	8.0	. . .
Thiamin, μg	40.0	. . .
Riboflavin, μg	60.0	. . .
Pyridoxine, μg	35.0¶	. . .
B_{12}, μg	0.15	. . .
Niacin, μg	250.0	. . .
Folic acid, μg	4.0	. . .
Pantothenic acid, μg	300.0	. . .
Biotin, μg	1.5#	. . .
Choline, mg	7.0#	. . .
Inositol, mg	4.0#	. . .
Minerals		
Calcium, mg	50.0**	
Phosphorus, mg	25.0**	
Magnesium, mg	6.0	. . .
Iron, mg	0.15	. . .
Iodine, μg	5.0	. . .
Zinc, mg	0.5	. . .
Copper, μg	60.0	. . .
Manganese, μg	5.0	. . .
Sodium, mg	20.0	60.0
Potassium, mg	80.0	200.0
Chloride, mg	55.0	150.0

*Data from References 1, 5, and 18.
†The source of protein shall be at least nutritionally equivalent to casein.
‡75 μg retinol equivalents.
§225 μg retinol equivalents.
‖0.7 IU/g linoleic acid.
¶15 μg/g of protein.
#Required to be included in this amount only in formulas that are not milk-based.
**Ca:P ratio >1.1 and ≤2.0.

TABLE 13–3.
Bovine Milk–based Formulas for Full-term Infants, 20 kcal/oz (67 kcal/dL)

Formula	Manufacturer	Protein Source	g/100 kcal* (g/dL)	Carbohydrate Source	g/100 kcal* (g/dL)	Fat Source	g/100 kcal* (g/dL)
Casein-dominant							
Similac	Ross†	Non-fat milk, taurine	2.2 (1.5)	Lactose	10.7 (7.2)	Soy, coconut oil	5.4 (3.6)
Portagen‡	Mead Johnson§	Sodium caseinate, taurine	3.5 (2.3)	Corn syrup solids, sucrose	11.5 (7.7)	Medium-chain triglycerides, corn oil, L-carnitine	4.8 (3.2)
Advance (54 kcal/dL)	Ross	Non-fat milk, soy protein	3.7 (2.0)	Corn syrup, lactose	10.2 (5.5)	Soy, corn oil	5.0 (2.7)
Whey-dominant							
Enfamil	Mead Johnson	Non-fat milk demineralized whey, taurine	2.2 (1.5)	Lactose	10.3 (6.9)	Corn, coconut oil	5.6 (3.7)
SMA	Wyeth‖	Non-fat milk, demineralized whey, taurine	2.2 (1.5)	Lactose	10.6 (7.1)	Oleo, coconut, oleic, soybean oil	5.3 (3.5)
Similac PM 60/40	Ross	Whey protein concentrate, taurine, sodium caseinate	2.3 (1.6)	Lactose	10.2 (6.8)	Soy, coconut oil; L-carnitine	5.6 (3.7)

*Concentrations are provided per 100 kcal and per dL for comparison.
†*Ross Laboratories Product Handbook 1988* (Ross Laboratories, Columbus, OH 43216).
‡Reconstituted from powder; not available as liquid preparation.
§*Pediatric Products Handbook 1990* (Mead Johnson & Company, Evansville, IN 47721).
‖*Wyeth Hospital Infant Feeding System 1986* (Wyeth Laboratories, Philadelphia, PA 19101).

Milk-based Formulas

Milk-based formulas (Table 13–3) are prepared from bovine milk. A comparison of the composition of milk-based formula with those of human milk, whole bovine milk, and various bovine milk products is shown in Table 13–4. Note that the protein composition of whole bovine milk and its derivatives (skim milk, 2% milk, ½% milk, and evaporated milk) contain excessive quantities of protein (20% to 40% of calories) when compared with infant formula and human milk. The bovine milks provide an unbalanced fat composition and excessive minerals. The elevated protein and mineral contents result in an increased renal solute load. An infant fed whole bovine milk, or its derivative milks, potentially would develop dehydration and evidence of protein and electrolyte toxicity.

Bovine milk–based formulas, however, are designed to overcome these serious limitations. The composition of these formulas is within the guidelines for appropriate caloric distribution (9% protein, 49% fat, and 42% carbohydrate) and has a mineral content that will not impose undue stress on the maturing renal capacity of an infant (see Tables 13–3 and 13–4).

There are two broad categories of bovine milk–based formulas for full-term infants: casein-dominant and whey-dominant. Bovine milk protein is approximately 80% casein and 20% whey, and the formulas derived from this non-fat milk are termed "casein-dominant." "Whey-dominant" formulas have been developed to provide a protein composition more like that of human milk. The "humanized" formulas are prepared by combining non-fat bovine milk with demineralized whey, a by-product in the manufacture of

TABLE 13–4.
Comparison of Infant Formula vs. Human and Bovine Milks*

Component	Infant Formula	Human Milk†	Whole Bovine Milk	Skim Milk	2% Milk	½% Milk	Evaporated Milk, Undiluted
Energy, kcal/dL	67	68	65	36	59	38	137
Protein							
g/100 kcal	2.2	1.5	5.4	10.0	7.1	8.9	5.1
g/dL	1.5	1.0	3.5	3.6	4.2	3.3	7.0
% Calories	9%	6%	22%	40%	28%	36%	20%
Carbohydrate							
g/100 kcal	10.4	10.2	7.5	14.2	10.1	12.2	7.1
g/dL	7.0	7.0	4.9	5.1	6.0	4.6	9.6
% Calories	42%	41%	30%	57%	40%	49%	28%
Fat							
g/100 kcal	5.4	5.9	5.4	0.3	3.4	1.1	5.8
g/dL	3.6	4.0	3.5	0.1	2.0	0.4	7.9
% Calories	49%	53%	48%	3%	31%	10%	52%
Selected minerals and vitamins (units/dL)							
Calcium (Ca), mg	47	26	118	121	143	100	252
Phosphorus (P), mg	33	15	93	95	112	79	205
Sodium, mg	17	17	50	52	61	54	119
Potassium, mg	67	51	144	145	175	142	303
Iron, mg	0.14	Trace	0.04	0.04	0.05	0.04	0.12
Ca/P ratio, mg/mg	1.4	1.7	1.27	1.26	1.28	1.26	1.23

*From Adams CF: *Nutritive Value of American Foods,* Agriculture Handbook no. 456. Washington, DC, Agricultural Research Service, U.S. Department of Agriculture, 1975.
†See references 17, 20, and 21.

cheese. Because of the lower carbohydrate content of whole bovine milk, lactose is added to milk-based formula to provide a more appropriate ratio of protein to energy (see Table 13–4). When non-fat bovine milk is used, vegetable oils are added as the milk-based fat source, because they are more easily digested. Bovine milk–based formulas are available for full-term (see Table 13–3) and preterm (Table 13–5) infants and are in ready-to-feed form.

Bovine milk–based formulas (Similac, Enfamil, and SMA) (see Table 13–3) are suitable for routine infant feeding. Current state-of-the-art selections available for preterm infants include Similac Special Care, Enfamil Premature Formula, and Preemie SMA (see Table 13–5). Although listed as infant formula, Advance is marketed for older infants as a means to restrict their intake because of actual or potential obesity. In this regard, other considerations that foster sound nutritional practices should be encouraged; for example, such infants could be fed a reduced quantity of a routine formula.

Soy-based Formulas

Soy-based formulas (Table 13–6) originally were made from soy flour, which contained the nondigestible carbohydrates raffinose and stachyose. Because of these carbohydrates, the recipient infants tended to have loose, foul-smelling stools.[1, 18, 22] The use of water-soluble soy protein isolates, now purified to over 90% protein, overcame these problems.[1, 18, 22] Soy protein isolate is deficient in methionine, which is thus added to soy-based formulas.[22] All proteins do not have the same nutritional value; soy-based formulas contain approximately 30% more protein than bovine milk–based formulas. Corn syrup and sucrose are the carbohydrate sources in soy-based formulas. These formulas do not contain lactose. The osmolality of soy formulas is low, because of the substitution of longer chain polymers for lactose.

The indications for the use of soy formulas (Table 13–7) generally are related more to the carbohydrate composition of the formula rather than its soy protein composition. When the recommendation of a non-lactose-containing formula seems appropriate, a soy-based formula is often substituted.[22] Lactose intolerance, either secondary after a severe diarrheal illness, or primary, as in congenital lactose intolerance, is a clinical situation in which soy formulas are indicated. A short course of soy-based formula in situations either following the cessation of diarrhea or occasionally during the acute phase is appropriate.[22, 23] Because lactose is a disaccharide comprised of glucose-galactose monosaccharides, the dietary management of infants with galactosemia, a defect in the utilization of galactose, requires the provision of a nonlactose formula.[22] Soy-based products contain no bovine milk products, and thus are suitable for vegetarian families and meet Kosher dietary requirements for a nondairy product.

The use of soy protein in infant feeding and the relationship between soy protein and allergy are subject to considerable debate.[22, 24, 25] Initially, soy-based formulas were recommended in cases of allergy to bovine milk protein. The incidence of certain allergic conditions, asthma and rhinitis, reportedly was reduced in infants whose families had a strong allergy history when the index infant was fed soy-based vs. bovine milk–based formula (18% vs. 50% incidence).[24] The author noted that the 18% incidence of atopy in infants fed soy-based formula was greater than that reported for breast-fed infants. Not all allergic conditions responded to soy-based formula; eczema was such an example. Other investigators found that the immunogenicity of soy and bovine milk proteins was similar and that sensitivity to both proteins coexisted.[22, 25] When an infant has an allergy to bovine milk protein, the gastrointestinal uptake of intact pro-

TABLE 13–5.
Bovine Milk–based Formulas for Preterm Infants, 24 kcal/oz (81 kcal/dL)

Formula	Manufacturer	Protein Source	Protein g/100 kcal* (g/dL)	Carbohydrate Source	Carbohydrate g/100 kcal* (g/dL)	Fat Source	Fat g/100 kcal* (g/dL)
Casein-dominant							
Similac 24 LBW	Ross[†]	Non-fat milk, taurine	2.7 (2.2)	Hydrolyzed cornstarch, lactose	10.5 (8.5)	Medium-chain Triglycerides (MCT), soy, coconut oil, L-carnitine	5.5 (4.5)
Whey-dominant							
Similac Special Care	Ross	Non-fat milk, whey protein concentrate, taurine	2.7 (2.2)	Hydrolyzed cornstarch, lactose	10.6 (8.6)	MCT, soy, coconut oil; L-carnitine	5.4 (4.4)
Similac Natural Care	Ross	Non-fat milk, whey protein concentrate, taurine	2.7 (2.2)	Hydrolyzed cornstarch, lactose	10.6 (8.6)	MCT, soy, coconut oil; L-carnitine	5.4 (4.4)
Enfamil Premature Formula	Mead Johnson[‡]	Whey protein concentrate, non-fat milk, taurine	3.0 (2.4)	Corn syrup solids, lactose	11.0 (8.9)	Soy, MCT, coconut oil	5.1 (4.1)
SMA Preemie	Wyeth[§]	Non-fat milk, whey protein contentrate, taurine	2.4 (1.9)	Maltodextrins, lactose	10.5 (8.5)	Coconut, oleo, oleic, soy, MCT oil	5.4 (4.4)

*Concentrations are provided per 100 kcal and per dL for comparison.
[†]*Ross Laboratories Product Handbook 1988* (Ross Laboratories, Columbus, OH 43216).
[‡]*Pediatric Products Handbook 1990* (Mead Johnson & Company, Evansville, IN 47721).
[§]*Wyeth Hospital Infant Feeding System 1986* (Wyeth Laboratories, Philadelphia, PA 19101).

TABLE 13–6.
Soy-Based Formulas for Infants, 20 kcal/oz (67 kcal/dL)

Formula	Manufacturer	Protein		Carbohydrate		Fat	
		Source	g/100 kcal* (g/dL)	Source	g/100 kcal* (g/dL)	Source	g/100 kcal* (g/dL)
ProSobee	Mead Johnson[†]	Soy protein isolate, L-methionine, taurine	3.0 (2.0)	Corn syrup solids	10.0 (6.7)	Corn, coconut oil; L-carnitine	5.3 (3.5)
Isomil	Ross[‡]	Soy protein isolate L-methionine, taurine	2.7 (1.8)	Corn syrup, sucrose	10.1 (6.8)	Soy, coconut oil; L-carnitine	5.5 (3.6)
Isomil SF	Ross	Soy protein isolate, L-methionine, taurine	2.7 (1.8)	Hydrolyzed cornstarch	10.1 (6.8)	Soy, coconut oil; L-carnitine	5.5 (3.6)
Nursoy	Wyeth[§]	Soy protein, L-methionine	3.1 (2.1)	Sucrose	10.2 (6.8)	Oleo, coconut, soybean oil; L-carnitine	5.3 (3.5)
Soyalac	Loma Linda[‖]	Soybean solids, L-methionine, taurine	3.1 (2.1)	Sucrose, corn syrup solids	10.0 (6.7)	Soy oil, L-carnitine	5.5 (3.5)
i-Soyalac	Loma Linda	Soy protein isolate, L-methionine, taurine	3.1 (2.1)	Sucrose, tapioca, starch, dextrins	10.0 (6.7)	Soy oil, L-carnitine	5.5 (3.5)

*Concentrations are provided per 100 kcal and per dL for comparison.
[†]*Pediatric Products Handbook 1990* (Mead Johnson & Company, Evansville, IN 47721).
[‡]*Ross Laboratories Product Handbook 1988* (Ross Laboratories, Columbus, OH 43216).
[§]*Wyeth Laboratories Product Handbook 1986* (Wyeth Laboratories, Philadelphia, PA 19101).
[‖]*Loma Linda Handbook 1987* (Loma Linda, Riverside, CA 92515).

TABLE 13−7.

Indications for Soy-Based Formulas

Lactose intolerance
Secondary to diarrheal disease
Primary
Galactosemia
Strict vegetarian families
Potentially atopic infants; those with strong family
history, who have not demonstrated allergy

teins is likely. Potentially, this might cause a similar allergic response to soy protein.[22] Available evidence, however, tends to favor the hypothesis that withholding bovine milk in atopic families may reduce the risk of certain allergic diseases.[24]

Colic, the symptom complex of severe crying and abdominal pain in young infants, is occasionally treated with soy-based formulas.[22] A randomized study of colic, in which bovine milk−based formulas were used, suggested that in a number of cases, recovery from the symptom complex occurred after a ˉ switch to a protein hydrolysate−based formula, but not to a soy-based formula.[26] A large number of infants had adverse reactions to both bovine milk−based and soy based-formulas. At present, there appears to be no indication for soy-based formulas in young infants with colic.

Soy-based formulas are not indicated for the feeding of preterm infants, for the dietary management of documented bovine milk protein and/or soy protein allergy, or for the management of colic.[22] Both nitrogen and mineral metabolism are altered in preterm infants after the prolonged feeding of soy-based formulas.[22] When similar infants were fed either soy-based or bovine milk−based formulas, those receiving the soy formulas had lower retention of nitrogen and absorption of phosphorus, lesser weight gain, and lower serum albumin concentrations.[27] Hall and associates[28] reported that preterm infants fed soy-based formula gained less weight, the weight gained had a lower caloric efficiency, and serum albumin and total protein values were lower than those of infants fed whey-dominant formula. Preterm infants, therefore, should not receive soy-based formulas for prolonged periods.

Protein Hydrolysate−based Formulas

To meet the needs of infants with true hypersensitivity to bovine milk protein and infants with protein digestion difficulties, hydrolyzed casein formulations have been developed (Table 13−8). Casein is isolated and incubated with enzymes to produce hydrolysis products. Occasionally, the hydrolysates are charcoal-treated to remove larger proteins. The average peptide molecular weight in the hydrolysate fraction is 200 daltons; less than 1% of isolated peptides have molecular weights greater than 500 daltons, and none are detectable above 1,200 daltons.[3] The crude hydrolysate is tested for antigenicity before its acceptability for use in infant formulas. Free amino acids can be added, either to compensate for those removed during processing (L-cystine, L-tyrosine, L-tryptophan) or to produce a more elemental formulation. Because protein hydrolysate−based formulas contain peptides and amino acids, they have greater osmolality than formulas that contain intact proteins. Newer preparations contain hydrolysates derived from bovine whey protein fractions. For atopic infants, those with severe colic, or those with severe malabsorption problems, the protein hydrolysate−based formulas are particularly well-advised.[29]

TABLE 13–8.
Protein Hydrolysate–based Formulas for Infants, 20 kcal/oz (67 kcal/dL)

Formula	Manufacturer	Protein Source	Protein g/100 kcal* (g/dL)	Carbohydrate Source	Carbohydrate g/100 kcal* (g/dL)	Fat Source	Fat g/100 kcal* (g/dL)
Nutramigen	Mead Johnson[†]	Casein: enzymatically hydrolyzed and charcoal-treated; L-cystine, L-tyrosine, L-tryptophan, taurine	2.8 (1.9)	Corn syrup solids, modified cornstarch	13.4 (9.0)	Corn oil, L-carnitine	3.9 (2.6)
Pregestimil[‡]	Mead Johnson	Casein: enzymatically hydrolyzed and charcoal-treated; L-cystine, L-tyrosine, L-tryptophan, taurine	2.8 (1.9)	Corn syrup solids, modified tapioca starch, glucose	10.3 (6.9)	Medium-chain Triglycerides (MCT), corn, safflower, oleic oil; L-carnitine	5.6 (3.7)
Alimentum	Ross	Casein: enzymatically hydrolyzed and charcoal-treated; L-cystine, L-tyrosine, L-tryptophan, taurine	2.75 (1.9)	Sucrose, modified tapioca starch	10.2 (6.9)	MCT, safflower, soy oil; L-carnitine	5.5 (3.7)
Good Start H.A.	Carnation§	Whey: enzymatically hydrolyzed and demineralized whey protein concentrate; taurine	2.4 (1.6)	Maltodextrins, lactose	11.0 (7.4)	Oleo, oleic, coconut oil; L-carnitine	5.1 (3.4)

*Concentrations are provided per 100 kcal and per dL for comparison.
[†]*Pediatric Products Handbook 1990* (Mead Johnson & Company, Evansville, IN 47721).
[‡]Mead Johnson letter January, 1989 (Mead Johnson Nutritionals). Powder form only; to make normal dilution (20 kcal/oz), add 9.7 g of powder to each 60 mL of water.
§*Carnation Handbook 1988* (Carnation, Fairview, NJ 07022).

Specialized Formulations

Unique formulations are available for a variety of conditions including inborn errors of metabolism and carbohydrate intolerance (Tables 13–9 and 13–10). Essentially, these preparations are mixtures of casein hydrolysates and/or free amino acids, with specific amino acids removed if necessary. Unique partial or modular formulas are avail-

TABLE 13–9.

Specialized Formulations for Metabolic Disease

Indication	Formula	Comments
Phenylketonuria	Lofenalac (Mead Johnson)	Casein hydrolysate with reduced phenylalanine; corn syrup solids
	Analog XP (Ross)	Amino acids, no phenylalanine; corn syrup solids (infants)
	Maxamaid XP (Ross)	Amino acids, no phenylalanine; sucrose (children 1–8 yrs)
	Maxamum XP (Ross)	Amino acids, no phenylalanine; sucrose (children >8 yr and adults)
	Phenyl-Free (Mead Johnson)	Amino acids, no phenylalanine; sucrose
Maple syrup urine disease	MSUD Diet Powder (Mead Johnson)	Amino acids, no leucine, valine, isoleucine; corn syrup solids
	Analog MSUD (Ross)	Amino acids, no leucine, valine, isoleucine (infants)
	Maxamaid MSUD (Ross)	Amino acids, no leucine, valine, isoleucine (children 1–8 yr)
	Maxamum MSUD (Ross)	Amino acids, no leucine, valine, isoleucine (children >8 yr and adults)
Tyrosinemia	Low PHE/TYR Diet Powder (Mead Johnson)	Casein hydrolysate, no phenylalanine and tyrosine; corn syrup solids
	Analog XPHEN,TYR (Ross)	Amino acids, no phenylalanine and tyrosine (infants)
	Maxamaid XPHEN,TYR (Ross)	Amino acids, no phenylalanine and tyrosine (children 1–8 yr)
	Analog XPEN,TYR,XMET (Ross)	Amino acids, no phenylalanine, tyrosine, methionine (infants)
Homocystinuria	Low Methionine Diet Powder (Mead Johnson)	Soy protein without added methionine; corn syrup solids
	Analog XMET (Ross)	Soy protein without added methionine (infants)
Hypermethioninemia	Maxamaid XMET (Ross)	Soy protein without methionine (children >1 yr)
Methylmalonic and propionic acidemia	Analog XMET, THRE, VAL, ISOLEU [Maxamaid] (Ross)	Amino acids without valine, threonine, methionine, and low in isoleucine (infants [children])
Hypoglycemia, leucine-sensitive	Wyeth S-14	Dilution of all amino acids in standard formula by 73%
Low renal solute load	Wyeth S-29 (Wyeth S-44)	Ca:16, P:19, Na:1 mg/dL (S-29 without vitamins)
Malnutrition	PediaSure (Ross)	Bovine milk; corn syrup solids, sucrose; safflower, soy, medium-chain triglyceride oils; 100 kcal/dL (Children 1–6 yr)

TABLE 13-10.

Modular Formulations

RCF (Ross Carbohydrate-Free), Ross (concentrated liquid)
    Soy protein isolate, soy and coconut oil
    Must add carbohydrate source
Mono- and Disaccharide-Free Diet Powder (Product 3232A), Mead Johnson
    Casein hydrolysate, tapioca starch (stabilizer), medium-chain triglycerides and corn oil
    Must add carbohydrate source
Protein Free Diet Powder (Product 80056), Mead Johnson
    Corn syrup solids, tapioca starch, corn oil
    Must add protein source
ProViMin, Ross.
    Casein (73%); complete vitamin and mineral preparation
    Must add fat and carbohydrate sources
Enfamil Human Milk Fortifier, Mead Johnson (powder)
    For mixture with human milk: 4 packets/100 mL
    Per 4 packets:*
        14 kcal
        0.7 g protein (60% whey, 40% casein)
        2.7 g carbohydrate (75% corn syrup solids, 25% lactose)
        90 mg calcium
        45 mg phosphorus
        7 mg sodium
        0.7 mg zinc
        80 μg copper

*800 IU vitamin A, 208 IU vitamin D, 3.4 IU vitamin E, 9.2 μg vitamin K, 188 μg thiamin, 248 μg riboflavin, 192 μg pyridoxine, 0.2 μg vitamin B_{12}, 3,120 μg niacin, 23 μg folic acid, 800 μg pantothenate, 0.8 μg biotin, 24 mg vitamin C.

TABLE 13-11.

Dietary Supplements*

Supplement (Type) [Manufacturer]†	kcal	g/tbsp	Composition and Comments
Dextrose (P)	4.0/g	10	Corn syrup sugar; monosaccharide
Sucrose (P)	4.0/g	12	Cane or beet sugar; disaccharide
Fructose (P)	4.0/g	10	Fruit sugar; monosaccharide
Corn syrup (L)	4.0/mL	20	Light corn syrup; vanilla, 1.5 mg/g sodium
Moducal (P) [Mead Johnson]	3.8/g	6	100% maltodextrins
Polycose (P) (L) [Ross]	3.8/g	6	Glucose polymers from hydrolyzed corn starch:
	2.0/mL	15	(P) 94%, (L) 50% glucose polymers
Pro Mod (P) [Ross]	5.6/g	4	100% bovine whey protein
			Minerals: Ca = 9 mg/g, P = 7 mg/g, Na = 3 mg/g, K = 13 mg/g
Casec (P) [Mead Johnson]	3.7/g	4.7	88% bovine Ca caseinate; Ca = 16 mg/g, P = 8 mg/g, Na = 1.5 mg/g
MCT oil (L) [Mead Johnson]	8.3/g	14	Derived from coconut oil; fatty acids: C8, 67%,
	7.7/mL	15	C10, 23%, <C8, <6%, >C10, 4%
Corn oil (L)	8.4/mL	14	Corn; polyunsaturated fatty acids
Safflower oil (L)	8.4/mL	14	Safflower; polyunsaturated fatty acids
Infant cereal (P)	4.3/g	3.6	Rice: used to thicken feedings, 1 tbsp/oz; primarily carbohydrate source (1 g/g) Fe = 0.05 mg/g, P = 1 mg/g
Instant non-fat and dry milk (P)	3.6/g	6	40% bovine protein; protein (0.4 g/g) carbohydrate (0.5 g/g) supplement, Ca = 13 mg/g, P = 10 mg/g, Na = 5 mg/g

*Modified from *Texas Children's Hospital Reference Guide for Infant Formulas, Nutritional Supplements, and Parenteral Nutrition,* 1988.
†P = powder; L = liquid.

able that allow incremental addition of carbohydrate as monosaccharide, disaccharide, or glucose polymers. Incremental addition of protein or the addition of specific amino acid sources is also possible. Dietary supplements for use in modular formulas are shown in Table 13–11. Several of the formulations described in Tables 13–9 and 13–10 are indicated for older infants, but are included here for completeness and to provide a basis on which to continue nutritional support in unique circumstances.

WHOLE BOVINE MILK

Although not considered as infant formula, whole bovine milk is occasionally given to young infants. The CON/AAP recommends that whole bovine milk not be fed until after the child is 6 months of age, and preferably after 1 year.[30]

Problems (Table 13–12), such as occult gastrointestinal bleeding and iron deficiency anemia, arise when whole bovine milk or unmodified bovine milks are fed to infants.[31] Such problems are alleviated by the processing of milk to produce infant formulas.[32] Manifestations of iron deficiency anemia in infants fed unprocessed bovine milk also were reported in the second 6 months of life and iron supplements were recommended.[33] Evaporated milk formula, used historically and for economic reasons, is prepared by mixing 100 mL (3 oz) vitamin D–fortified evaporated milk, 130 mL (4.5 oz) water, and 10 mL (2 tsp) corn syrup.[30] In addition, the infant should receive vitamin C (20 mg) and iron (7 mg) supplements each day.

NUTRITIONAL CONSIDERATIONS

Protein

The protein content of bovine milk (3.1 g/dL) is greater than that of human milk (0.9 g/dL).[9] The quality of bovine and human milk protein also differs.[9, 10] The caseins, those proteins precipitated by acid to form large curds, represent approximately 82% of bovine milk and 28% of human milk proteins. Because infant formulas are heat-treated, the curds are smaller than those in unprocessed milk.[3] The supernatant or whey fraction, that contains the soluble proteins, forms smaller curds and also is used in the manufacture of cheese. The whey fraction of human milk is 72% of the total protein and is much larger than that of bovine milk (18% of total protein). In an attempt to mimic the protein quality of human milk, the infant formula industry has "humanized" bovine milk by marketing formulas containing 60% whey and 40% casein. The processing of this whey-

TABLE 13–12.

Potential Problems With the Use of Whole Canned Milk in Infancy*

Dehydration secondary to high renal solute load
Hypocalcemic tetany due to high phosphate load
Casein curd obstruction
Vitamin deficiency (rickets, scurvy)
Iron deficiency anemia

*Modified with permission from Lucas A: Infant feeding, in Roberton NRC (ed): *Textbook of Neonatology*. Edinburgh, Churchill Livingstone, 1986, pp 178–210.

dominant product involves mixing equal parts of whey protein and bovine milk protein.[3] The quantity of protein in bovine milk–based formulas is approximately 2.2 g/100 kcal (1.5 g/dL). Current preparations also contain cystine and taurine to improve the nutritional quality of the protein. As described in the discussion of protein hydrolysate–based formulas, additional amino acids are added to these formulations to account for inadequate quantities. Soy protein is nutritionally inadequate unless methionine is supplemented.

The benefits of whey-dominant vs. casein-dominant formulas have been evaluated in full-term and preterm infants. Theoretically, whey-dominant formulas may be more easily digested because of smaller curd size. Plasma amino acid imbalances are lessened through a more appropriate blend of amino acids (lower methionine, phenylalanine, and tyrosine). Despite attempts to provide protein quality similar to that found in human milk, bovine whey protein differs significantly from human whey protein. Whereas human whey contains proteins necessary for host defense—secretory IgA, lactoferrin, and lysozyme—the predominant bovine whey protein is lactoglobulin, a protein with no role in host defense.[10] Plasma amino acid patterns and relationships to indices of nitrogen utilization have been reported[34] to differ significantly in preterm infants fed isonitrogenous and isocaloric quantities of either human milk or whey-dominant formula. Despite the potential advantages of feeding a whey-dominant formula, the differences between bovine and human whey proteins must be considered.

Experimental evidence tends to favor the use of whey-dominant formulas in preterm infants. Low-birth-weight infants fed a whey-dominant formula (60% whey) had greater weight gain, greater nitrogen absorption, and lesser urea excretion than similar infants fed casein-dominant formulas.[35] Azotemia, metabolic acidosis, and amino acid imbalances (phenylalanine, tyrosine, methionine, cystine, taurine) occurred more frequently when preterm infants were fed casein-dominant formulas with the same protein content as whey-dominant formulas.[14, 17, 36] Specialized milk-based formulas for preterm infants (Enfamil Premature Formula, Similac Special Care, and Preemie SMA) are whey-dominant. One formula for preterm infants, Similac LBW, is casein-dominant.

The whey fraction also includes those compounds containing nonprotein nitrogen (NPN). The relatively large proportion of NPN in human milk is not duplicated in bovine milk. Some of the components, such as urea, may be utilized as a nitrogen source.[37] The free amino acid taurine is another example, and is the most recent amino acid addition to infant formulas. Although feeding taurine-supplemented infant formula affected the taurine concentrations in urine and plasma,[38, 39] the functional significance of these differences remains unclear.[39, 40] The controversy over the use of the NPN fractions has caused investigators to reevaluate protein needs of full-term and preterm infants.

Studies in full-term infants fed soy-based formulas have illustrated the problems with the nutritional quality of protein. The growth rates and weight gain per unit energy consumed of infants fed soy-based formula were lower than those of infants fed bovine milk–based formula.[22, 30] Preterm infants retain less nitrogen when fed soy-based compared with bovine milk-based formulas.[22]

The nutritional quality of a protein is related to the quantity and quality of its amino acids. The protein equivalency ratio (PER) assay generally is used to compare the quality of protein sources.[3] By this method, rats are fed reference or test proteins and their growth is monitored. Casein is the official reference source. The CON/AAP and the Food and Drug Administration (FDA) recommend that infant formula protein have a PER of not less than 70% of casein and that at least 1.8

g/100 kcal of protein with a PER 100% of casein be supplied.[3, 5] Dietary protein supplements are shown in Table 13–11.

Energy

Manufacturers' labels include the energy content of the formula. Generally, the energy value, referred to as metabolizable energy, is calculated from actual nutrient contents using classical Atwater factors, 4 kcal/g (16.7 kJ/g) for protein and carbohydrate and 9 kcal/g (37.7 kJ/g) for fat (Table 13–13). The amount of energy (gross energy) in a food is ideally determined by burning a sample and measuring the amount of heat released in a bomb calorimeter.[41] The measurement of energy lost in feces and urine can be obtained similarly. The energy contained in excreta is subtracted from gross energy to determine the energy available to the body for metabolism, the metabolizable energy. The derivation of Atwater factors was performed in adults and has not been validated for infants.[42] Nevertheless, because of variability among preterm infants, and the different diets fed to this population, Atwater factors provide a rough guide by which to compute metabolizable energy intakes.[41] Gross energy can be obtained using the heats of combustion of various fuels (kcal/g) published by the Food and Agricultural Organization of the World Health Organization (FAO/WHO): glucose, 3.75; lactose, 3.95; sucrose,

TABLE 13–13.

Commonly Used Conversion Factors and Formulas

Energy
   1 kcal = 4.184 kJ
Gross energy (kcal/g)
   Protein = 5.65
   Carbohydrate = 3.95
   Fat = 9.25
Metabolizable energy (kcal/g)
   Protein = 4
   Carbohydrate = 4
   Fat = 9
Protein
   Total protein (g/dL) = total nitrogen (g/dL) × 6.25
Vitamins
   1 IU vitamin A = 0.3 retinol equivalents
             = 0.3 µg retinol
             = 1.8 µg β-carotene
   400 IU vitamin D = 10 µg vitamin D
   1 IU vitamin E = 1 mg dl-α-tocopherol
Minerals
   1 mEq Na = 1 mmol Na = 23 mg Na
   1 mEq K = 1 mmol K = 39 mg K
   1 mEq Cl = 1 mmol Cl = 35 mg Cl
   2 mEq Ca = 1 mmol Ca = 40 mg Ca
   1 mmol P = 31 mg P
Osmolarity (mOsm/L) = osmolality (mOsm/kg H_2O)
   × kg H_2O/L solution
Renal solute load (mOsm/dL) = [protein (g/dL)] × 4
           + [Na + K + Cl (mEq/dL)]
Potential renal solute load (mOsm/dL) = [protein
   (g/dL)] × 5.7 + [Na + K + Cl (mEq/dL)] + [P
   (mg/dL)/31]

3.95; dextrins, 4.10; long-chain triglycerides, 9.30; medium-chain triglycerides, 8.30; and bovine milk casein, 5.65. The energy content of various formulas is similar to the average value reported for human milk, 67 kcal/dL. Formulas designed for preterm infants contain 81 kcal/dL. Dietary energy supplements are shown in Table 13–11.

Carbohydrates

The concentration of lactose, the predominant carbohydrate in human milk and infant formula, averages 6 to 7 g/dL. The lactose concentration of bovine milk is 4 to 5 g/dL.[10] Primarily an energy source, lactose may enhance mineral absorption. Lactase enzyme activity in preterm infants, although less than that in full-term infants, is adequate for lactose metabolism. Approximately 1% to 5% of the lactose present in heat-treated liquid formulas is converted to lactulose. Lactulose may enhance the growth of beneficial, nonpathogenic fecal flora.[18] Sucrose is the chief carbohydrate source used in formulas for conditions such as primary or secondary lactase deficiency.

An approach often used in the design of formulas for preterm infants is to reduce the lactose content and replace the carbohydrate with glucose polymers (see Table 13–5). In this manner, the osmolarity of the preparation is reduced without a loss of net energy. Polymers of glucose, derived from the hydrolysis of cornstarch polysaccharides (Fig 13–1), are well-tolerated by preterm infants who have intestinal glycosidases necessary for polymer metabolism.[43] When an infant is deficient in disaccharidase, glucose polymers tend to be appropriate carbohydrate choices for feeding. From the hydrolysis of cornstarch, various polymers, depending on their chain length, are available as carbohydrate sources. Figure 13–1 depicts the hydrolysis of cornstarch. Starch, containing 20 to 2,500 glucose units per molecule, can be used as a fat stabilizer in the formula and as a nutritional source.[44] The first step in the reaction produces dextrins, polysaccharides of 10 to 20 glucose units per molecule. Maltodextrins are oligosaccharides comprising 5

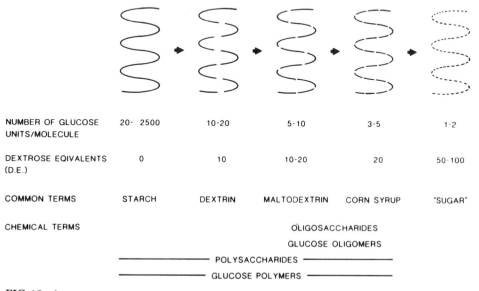

NUMBER OF GLUCOSE UNITS/MOLECULE	20- 2500	10-20	5-10	3-5	1-2
DEXTROSE EQIVALENTS (D.E.)	0	10	10-20	20	50-100
COMMON TERMS	STARCH	DEXTRIN	MALTODEXTRIN	CORN SYRUP	'SUGAR'

CHEMICAL TERMS   OLIGOSACCHARIDES
                                                         GLUCOSE OLIGOMERS
                              ―――――――――――― POLYSACCHARIDES ――――――――――
                              ―――――――――― GLUCOSE POLYMERS ――――――――――

FIG 13–1.
Hydrolysis of starch into smaller and smaller units can be regulated to derive carbohydrate molecules of varying size. (From Hansen JW, Cook DA, Cordano A, et al: Human milk substitutes, in Tsang RC, Nichols BL (eds): *Nutrition During Infancy*. Philadelphia, Hanley & Belfus, 1988, pp 378–398. Used by permission.)

to 10 glucose units per molecule. Corn syrup contains oligosaccharides of 3 to 5 glucose units per molecule. The final products are monosaccharides and disaccharides. Dietary carbohydrate supplements are shown in Table 13–11.

Fat

Fat is the major source of energy in human and bovine milks and infant formula, approximately 50% of calories. The quality of fat contained in milk preparations, however, differs. The composition of fat depends on fatty acid chain length (medium or long chain), degree of saturation (number of double bonds), quantity of essential fatty acids (linoleic, linolenic acid), and inclusion of cofactors for fat metabolism (e.g., carnitine, cholesterol).[45]

Vegetable oils and bovine milk fats are used as fat sources for infant formulas (Table 13–14). Corn and soy oils, which are commonly used in infant formulas, are rich sources of linoleic and linolenic acids, respectively.[3] Oleo and safflower oil are the most abundant sources of polyunsaturated fatty acids (PUFA). Large amounts of PUFA are not present in human milk and may not be beneficial to preterm infants unless the infants are vitamin E sufficient. Coconut oil, palm oil, and bovine milk fat provide highly unsaturated fatty acids in infant formulas. Usually coconut oil is used in a blend with PUFA to provide short-chain and medium-chain fatty acids, which creates a fat composition comparable to that in human milk. Bovine milk, similar to human milk, contains monoglycerides esterified with palmitic acid in the 2 position. Fats derived from vegetable oils, however, do not share this similarity.[18]

One of the most frequently discussed aspects of milk fat composition is the quantity of medium-chain triglycerides (MCT) in the formulation. The MCTs contain fatty acids C8 to C12. Early studies that compared animal fats and MCTs reported that the latter were associated with improved fat absorption. The digestion of medium-chain fatty acids is passive; bile salts are not involved. The preterm infant, therefore, whose bile acid pools are immature, is a suitable candidate for the use of MCT. Improvements in cal-

TABLE 13–14.

Fatty Acid Composition (%) of Various Cooking Oils and Fats*

Type	Fatty Acid	Sesame Oil	Corn Oil	Coconut Oil	Cottonseed Oil	Olive Oil	Peanut Oil	Safflower Oil	Soybean Oil	Cocoa Butter	Butter	Cow's Milk
	4:0											3.6
	6:0			0.8							2.0	0.9
	8:0			5.4							0.5	0.8
	10:0			8.4							2.3	2.5
Lauric	12:0			45.4					0.2		2.5	3.3
	14:0		1.4	18.0	1.4	Trace			0.1		11.1	10.4
Palmitic	16:0	9.1	10.2	10.5	23.4	6.9	8.3	6.8	9.8	24.4	29.0	32.0
	18:0	4.3	3.0	2.3	1.1	2.3	3.1		2.4	33.4	9.2	14.5
	20:0	0.8		0.4	1.3	0.1	2.4		0.9		2.4	
	16:1		1.5		2.0				0.4		4.6	2.7
Oleic	18:1	45.4	49.6	7.5	22.9	84.4	56.0	18.6	28.9	38.1	26.7	23.4
Linoleic	18:2	40.4	34.3	Trace	47.8	4.6	26.0	70.1	30.7	2.1	3.6	3.5
Linolenic	18:3							3.4	6.5			0.8
	Other			1.3	0.1	1.7	4.2	1.1	0.1		2.5	5.2

*From Hamosh M: Fat needs for term and preterm infants, in Tsang RC, Nichols BL: *Nutrition During Infancy*. Philadelphia, Hanley & Belfus, 1988, pp 133–159. Used by permission.

cium, magnesium, and nitrogen absorption also have been reported after MCTs were used.[45-47] Improved mineral absorptions, however, were not found in a similar study of two groups of preterm infants fed formulas containing either 60% MCT or 5% MCT.[48] When similar formulas that had either 40% or 80% fat as MCTs were compared, Okamoto and co-workers[49] found better fat absorption in the latter group, but no growth advantage. Whyte and associates[50, 51] reported no advantages in weight gain, nitrogen retention, or energy expenditure and storage when preterm infants were fed a formula containing 46% vs. 4% MCT. Infants who were fed the 46% MCT diet had greater urinary dicarboxylic acid excretion. The significance of this finding was unclear. Ketone body formation, however, may be enhanced when high-MCT formulas are fed.[52] Portagen is a formula that contains a high percentage (85%) of short-chain and medium-chain fatty acids, and is commonly used in infants with fat malabsorption from impaired liver function.

Essential fatty acid deficiency (skin lesions) was reported in infants fed bovine milk–based formulas that contained low levels of linoleic acid.[53] The lesions disappeared when 1% to 2% of calories in the infant's diet were provided as linoleic acid. Current formulas contain 2% to 20% of calories as linoleic acid.[1, 5, 18] Bovine milk contains only 20% as much linoleic acid as human milk.[1] Human milk and formula, however, contain similar quantities of linoleic acid.[10] Either excessive or deficient intakes of essential fatty acids arouse concern, because both may result in altered prostaglandin metabolism.[54] The minimal level of dietary linoleic acid is 1% of calories, which is exceeded in most infant formulas (range, 1% to 3% of calories).[55] Dietary fat supplements are shown in Table 13–11.

Carnitine plays a major role in fatty acid utilization and ketone body formation.[56] Preterm infants are unable to synthesize carnitine. Bovine milk–based formulas contain similar or greater quantities of carnitine than human milk.[57] All soy-based formulas are supplemented with carnitine, which generally is lower in foods of plant origin than animal origin.[22, 58]

Vitamins

The vitamin composition of infant formulas manufactured in the United States is shown in Table 13–15. Conversion factors for the units of certain vitamins are shown in Table 13–13. Current formulations, actually those developed after 1960, are adequately fortified with vitamins. Historically, there has been a progression of knowledge regarding vitamin needs and vitamin fortification of formulas. Bovine milk has low levels of vitamin D; thus, bovine milk–based formulas require fortification with vitamin D. Infants in the 1950s who received soy formulas prepared with defatted soy flour manifested vitamin A deficiency.[1] Vitamin A also was absent in protein hydrolysate–based milks.[1] Under unusual circumstances (diarrhea or antibiotic therapy), infants who received protein hydrolysate–based formulas developed retinal and epidermal bleeding that responded to the administration of vitamin K.[1] Vitamin K is added to all infant formulas that contain less than 4 μg/100 kcal.

Because infant formulas are prepared with polyunsaturated fatty acids, vitamin E needs are increased and vitamin E supplements must be added to the formulas. Formulas contain approximately 1 to 3 mg/dL of vitamin E, but its bioavailability in formula differs from that in human milk.

Pyridoxine may be destroyed at high temperatures or prolonged heating.[1] This phenomenon was demonstrated in a rather disheartening circumstance in the 1950s. Infants

TABLE 13–15.

Vitamin Contents (Units/dL) of 20 kcal/oz Infant Formulas (unless specified 16, 24 kcal/oz)

Formula	A (IU)	D (IU)	E (IU)	K (µg)	Thiamin (µg)	Riboflavin (µg)	B6 (µg)	B12 (µg)	Niacin (µg)	Folate (µg)	Pantothenate (µg)	Biotin (µg)	C (mg)
Bovine milk–based, casein-dominant													
Similac (Ross)	203	41	2.0	5.4	68	101	41	0.17	710	10	304	3.0	6.0
Similac 24 LBW (Ross)	244	49	2.4	6.5	102	122	49	0.20	853	12.2	365	3.6	10.0
Portagen (Mead Johnson)	527	53	2.1	10.5	105	127	142	0.42	1420	10.5	710	5.3	5.5
Advance-16 (Ross)	200	40	2.0	5.4	65	92	40	0.16	702	10.3	302	2.4	5.4
Bovine milk–based, whey-dominant													
Enfamil (Mead Johnson)	210	42	2.1	5.8	53	105	42	0.16	845	10.5	318	1.6	5.5
SMA (Wyeth)	200	40	1.0	5.5	67	100	42	0.13	500	5	210	1.5	5.5
Similac PM 60/40 (Ross)	203	41	2.0	5.4	68	101	41	0.17	710	10	304	3.0	6.0
Similac Special and Natural Care-24 (Ross)	552	122	3.2	10.0	203	503	203	0.45	4060	30.0	1543	30.0	30.0
Enfamil Premature Formula-24 (Mead Johnson)	974	220	3.7	10.6	203	284	203	0.24	3248	28.4	974	1.6	28.4
SMA Preemie-24 (Wyeth)	240	48	1.5	7.0	80	130	50	0.2	630	10	360	1.8	7.0
Soy-based													
Isomil, Isomil SF (Ross)	203	41	2.0	10.0	41	61	41	0.3	913	10	507	3.0	6.0
ProSobee (Mead Johnson)	210	42	2.1	10.5	53	64	42	0.21	845	10.5	318	5.3	5.5
Nursoy (Wyeth)	200	40	0.95	10.0	67	100	42	0.2	500	5.0	300	3.5	5.5
Soyalac, i-Soyalac (Loma Linda)	210	43	1.55	5.3	64	64	58	0.21	845	15.5	317	6.4	8.1
Protein hydrolysate–based													
Nutramigen (Mead Johnson)	210	42	2.1	10.5	53	64	42	0.21	845	10.5	318	5.3	5.5
Pregestimil (Mead Johnson)	252	50	2.5	12.6	53	64	42	0.21	845	10.5	318	5.3	7.9
Alimentum (Ross)	203	41	2.0	10.0	41	61	41	0.30	913	10	507	3.0	6.0
Good Start H.A. (Carnation)	202	41	0.8	5.5	41	91	51	0.15	507	6.1	304	1.5	5.4

who were fed commercially prepared liquid formula manifested hyperirritability and developed seizures.[1] The infants had received no other feedings or vitamins.[59] No adverse responses were reported in infants fed the powdered form of the formula.[59] By 1953, a heat-stable form of pyridoxine hydrochloride was added to formulas and resolved the deficiency state.[1] Soy products contain low amounts of thiamin, the concentration of which is reduced further by processing.[1] Low levels of folic and ascorbic acids in bovine milk have resulted in deficiencies of these vitamins.[1]

Minerals

The mineral composition of infant formulas manufactured in the United States is shown in Table 13–16, and conversion factors for minerals are shown in Table 13–13. Speculation, early in the manufacture of infant formulas, that a large sodium intake during infancy would result in adult-onset hypertension led to the limitation of sodium in infant formulas.[1] The CON/AAP recommended that the molar ratio of sodium to potassium not exceed 1.0 and that the ratio of (Na + K)/Cl be at least 1.5.[1, 5, 18] Ideally, the ratios should be similar to those in human milk, 0.5 and 1.0, respectively.[1, 5, 18]

The minimum levels of calcium and phosphorus required in infant formulas has been shown in Table 13–2. Late neonatal hypocalcemia, classic neonatal tetany, was reported in infants fed unprocessed bovine milk.[60] Infants affected with this disorder were unable to excrete the high phosphorus load in bovine milk (see Table 13–4). Compared with unprocessed bovine milk, commercially prepared formulas have lower concentrations of phosphorus. To approximate the proportions in human milk, the recommended ratio (wt/wt) of calcium to phosphorus is between 1.1 to 2.0:1, with an optimal ratio of 1.5:1.[17, 18] Classic neonatal tetany is treated by removing unprocessed bovine milk from the diet and feeding milk with a low phosphorus content and a high ratio of calcium to phosphorus. Human milk, if available, or a formula such as Similac PM 60/40 is indicated in this circumstance. Usually, if either human milk or Similac PM 60/40 is used in this manner, additional calcium is provided.

The provision of adequate calcium and phosphorus in formulas designed for preterm infants poses certain difficulties. The bioavailability of calcium and phosphorus salts also has been questioned.[61] The calcium and phosphorus contents of formulas designed for preterm infants, Similac Special Care and Enfamil Premature Formula, are significantly greater than the contents of other available formulas. These formulas provide adequate mineral concentrations and enable the preterm infant to achieve nearly optimal calcium and phosphorus status.[17, 28, 43] Mineral homeostasis is impaired in human milk-fed preterm infants.[61] The infant formula industry recently has introduced complete formulas (Similac Natural Care; see Table 13–5) or partial modular formulas (Enfamil Human Milk Fortifier; see Table 13–10) that can be mixed with human milk to augment its mineral composition.

Disordered mineral homeostasis is reported in infants fed soy-based formulas.[22, 27] Calcium and phosphorus absorption may be impaired by contaminants (phytates) in the processing of soy protein.[22] Radial bone mineral content was lower in full-term infants fed soy-based formula than in infants fed bovine milk–based formula.[62] Subsequent studies indicated no difference in humeral bone mineral content between infants fed a soy-based formula containing a new mineral suspension and infants fed soy-based and bovine milk–based formulas.[63]

Soy-based formulas have been suggested to provide less than sufficient quantities of calcium and phosphorus for preterm infants.[22] Hypophosphatemia and deficiencies in mineral absorption that might lead to reduced bone mineral content have been reported in preterm infants fed soy-based formulas for prolonged periods.[22, 27, 28]

Technical problems have been reported with the delivery of formulas containing high levels of calcium and phosphorus designed specifically for preterm infants.[64, 65] Various methods have been described to prevent precipitation and settling-out of the minerals.[64]

Zinc is absorbed more readily from human milk than from infant formulas. To ensure adequate absorption, the zinc content of infant formulas is greater than that of human milk. The bioavailability of trace elements may also be reduced in soy-based formulas.[66] The addition of zinc to soy-based formula resulted in no increment in zinc absorption, although its addition to bovine milk increased zinc absorption. The addition of phytate to bovine milk reduced zinc absorption from 30% to 16%. The authors concluded that phytate may inhibit zinc absorption from soy-based formulas.[66] Iron also is more available from human milk than infant formulas. Iron-fortified formulas are now available and are the choice for feeding infants (see Table 13–16).

PHYSICAL CHARACTERISTICS OF FORMULAS

In addition to nutrient information, other ingredients are reported on the labels affixed to infant formulas. Additives used as emulsifiers, thickening agents, antioxidants, and pH adjusting compounds are regulated by the FAO/WHO.[18]

Infant formulas contain emulsifiers (lecithin and mono- and diglycerides) to hold fat in a homogenized dispersion, which prevents its separation from milk.[18] With prolonged storage, separated fat becomes too firm to get back into suspension.[1] Protein agglomeration, manifested as gel formation or protein precipitation, may occur with excessive storage time.

Thickening and stabilizing agents (carrageenan and modified cornstarch) are used frequently to provide a uniform consistency and to prolong the stability of liquid formulations.[18] Thickeners are hydrophilic colloids (usually called gums). These long-chain, high molecular weight polysaccharides derived from plants disperse in water to give a thickening and sometimes a geling effect.[67] Carrageenans and agar are thickeners derived from seaweed; guar and locust bean are derived from plant seed gums. Although these substances have been approved for use in the United States, the European Society for Paediatric Gastroenterology and Nutrition (ESPGAN) recommended in 1977 that they not be used for infants less than 4 months of age.[1, 18]

Osmolality is another important physical characteristic of infant formulas. Defined as a measure of the depression of the freezing point or vapor pressure of the solute, per kilogram of water, osmolality is often confused with osmolarity, which refers to the depression produced by the solute per liter of solution.[1, 68] The formula for the conversion of osmolality to osmolarity is given in Table 13–13. The difference between these terms becomes important when one considers concentrated solutions such as infant formulas, where osmolarity is only 80% of the osmolality. Carbohydrates and minerals are the main determinants of osmolality.[1, 3] When present as peptides, protein contributes to the osmolality. The feeding of milk with a high osmolality may cause diarrhea, dehydration, and electrolyte abnormalities. An association between hyperosmolar preparations and necrotizing enterocolitis has been reported.[69] Because of these concerns, the CON/AAP recommends that formulas for healthy infants have osmolarities no greater than

TABLE 13–16.

Mineral Contents (units/dL) of 20 kcal/oz Infant Formulas (unless specified 16, 24 kcal/oz)

Formula	Ca (mg)	P (mg)	Zn (mg)	Mg (mg)	Mn (μg)	Cu (μg)	I (μg)	Na (mg)	K (mg)	Cl (mg)	Fe (mg)	Ca/P (mg/mg)
Bovine milk–based, casein-dominant												
Similac (Ross)	51	39	0.51	4.1	3.4	61	10	19	73	45	0.15 (1.2)*	1.3:1
Similac 24 LBW (Ross)	73	57	0.8	8.1	4.1	81	12.2	33	122	79	0.3	1.3:1
Portagen (Mead Johnson)	64	47	0.64	13.5	85	105	4.7	37	85	58	1.2	1.4:1
Advance-16 (Ross)	51	39	0.49	4.1	3.2	59	9.7	19	79	48	1.0	1.3:1
Bovine milk–based, whey-dominant												
Enfamil (Mead Johnson)	47	32	0.53	5.3	10.5	64	4	18	73	42	0.11 (1.2)*	1.5:1
SMA (Wyeth)	42	28	0.5	4.5	15	47	6	15	56	38	0.15 (1.2)*	1.5:1
Similac PM 60/40 (Ross)	38	19	0.5	4.1	3.4	61	4	16	58	40	0.15	2.0:1
Similac Special Care-24 (Ross)	146	73	1.2	10	10	203	5	35	105	66	0.3 (1.5)	2.0:1
Similac Natural Care-24 (Ross)	170	85	1.2	10	10	203	5	35	105	66	0.3	2.0:1
Enfamil Premature Formula-24 (Mead Johnson)	134	67	1.3	6.1	10.6	105	6.4	32	83	69	0.2 (1.5)*	2.0:1
SMA Preemie-24 (Wyeth)	75	40	0.8	7.0	20	70	8.3	32	75	53	0.3	1.9:1
Soy-based												
Isomil, Isomil SF (Ross)	71	51	0.51	5.1	20	51	10	30	73	42	1.2	1.4:1
ProSobee (Mead Johnson)	64	50	0.53	7.4	17	64	6.9	24	82	56	1.2	1.3:1
Nursoy (Wyeth)	60	42	0.5	6.7	20	47	6.0	20	70	38	1.1	1.4:1
Soyalac, i-Soyalac (Loma Linda)	69	47	0.53	7.4	32	79	5.2	28	79	53	1.3	1.5:1
Protein hydrolysate–based												
Nutramigen (Mead Johnson)	64	42	0.53	7.4	21	64	4.7	32	74	58	1.2	1.5:1
Pregestimil (Mead Johnson)	64	42	0.63	7.4	21	64	4.7	26	74	58	1.2	1.5:1
Alimentum (Ross)	71	51	0.51	5.1	20	51	10	30	80	54	1.2	1.4:1
Good Start H.A. (Carnation)	43	24	0.51	4.5	47	54	5.4	16.2	66	40	1.0	1.7:1

*Value for formula "with iron" is in parentheses.

400 mOsm/L.[5] Most infant formulas have osmolarities well below this maximum value, usually around 300 mOsm/L.

The mineral and protein contents of a formula determine its solute load. The renal solute load (RSL) of a formula (i.e., the soluble waste products that remain after nutrients are metabolized and which must be excreted) is an important determinant of the quantity of water excreted by the kidney.[1, 70] If the formula solute load is excessive, dehydration or solute toxicity may occur. Most formulas provide a relatively low RSL, but when prepared formulas are supplemented with minerals injudiciously, the solute load may be enhanced. The estimation of RSL is based on full-term infants fed bovine milk–based formula. Because rapidly growing preterm infants use a portion of the solute load for growth, not all nitrogen and electrolytes will be available for renal excretion. The potential renal solute load (PRSL), therefore, is a more appropriate term for preterm infants because it includes all solutes of dietary origin regardless of whether they are excreted or utilized for growth.[70] The formulas for the calculation of RSL and PRSL are found in Table 13–13.

ADVERSE REACTIONS

The infant formula industry has a remarkable safety record, considering the number of infants that have been served. Adverse reactions are reported infrequently and arise either from improper processing, new formulations, or anomalous infant responses. Bacteriologic safety is monitored, and to prevent contamination, common formulations are available as a "ready-to-feed" product.

Comments are made frequently about infant gastrointestinal "tolerance" of a particular formulation. When discussing intolerance of a particular milk, the agents in question may be the carbohydrate, fat, or protein components; a combination of factors; or none of the nutrients. It is important to define the particular clinical symptoms and the response to the index formula before the condition is designated as true milk intolerance. Congenital lactase deficiency is rare. Transient lactase deficiency may result after a lengthy bout of gastrointestinal illness. Bovine milk protein intolerance is characterized as a hypersensitivity reaction, manifested by gastrointestinal bleeding, abdominal distention, and anaphylactic shock. The particular selection of an infant formula occasionally is made on claims of tolerance, which makes it important to document responses objectively.

Specific adverse reactions to high-density preterm infant formulas have been reported. A survey of the literature has shown that a number of preterm infants fed casein-dominant formulas developed gastrointestinal symptoms (abdominal distention, emesis, bloody stools, diarrhea, abdominal mass, gastric perforation) suggesting lactobezoars.[71] The cause of lactobezoar formation is unclear and probably multifactorial. Several factors reported in association with lactobezoars have been postnatal age, delayed gastric emptying, large curd formation, diminished gastric acid secretion, method of feeding, selection of formulas with large quantities of medium-chain triglycerides, and use of concentrated formulas.[71–73] Cases of lactobezoar formation in infants fed human milk or whey-dominant formula are rare.[74, 75]

The addition of commercial mineral supplements, such as those used to supplement human milk, also may cause adverse reactions similar to those described for lactobezoars. Koletzko et al.[65] reported three cases of intestinal milk bolus obstruction associated with the use of calcium–phosphorus supplements.

Processing errors have resulted in nutrient omission and/or destruction. Infants fed a specific soy-based formula that is no longer marketed (Neo-Mull-Soy, Syntex) were noted to manifest poor weight gain and metabolic alkalosis.[76] Soy formulas have a lower chloride content than human milk.[77] A technical error led to an even lower chloride content of the formula. Addition of chloride to the infant's diet resulted in correction of the alkalosis and improved weight gain.[77] Heat processing destroyed vitamin B_6 when it was originally added to infant formula. Pyridoxine deficiency in infants that was corrected with vitamin supplementation has been reported in formula-fed infants.[59]

Concern has been expressed recently about the aluminum content of infant formulas and parenteral solutions. Aluminum contamination of infant formulas has been reported.[78, 79] More heavily processed formulas (protein hydrolysates, soy-based formulas) have greater contamination. The implications of these findings are unclear.

SELECTION OF APPROPRIATE FORMULA

The selection of an appropriate infant formula is complicated because of the variety of infant formulas now available. Knowledge of formula composition, however, can simplify the decision. In addition, certain factors should be considered in the selection or change of formulas.[80] Common parental complaints that influence formula recommendations made by physicians are spitting up, colic, rash, and mild diarrhea. These minor complaints usually result in a change from standard, bovine milk–based formulas to soy-based formulas. Although casual formula changes are not harmful, conclusions derived from such changes may be misleading and potentially cause problems.[80] Milk protein sensitivity, for example, does not manifest as emesis, nonspecific rash, mild diarrhea, and only rarely, as infant colic. Milk protein sensitivity, although rare, when documented should be treated by change to a protein-hydrolysate formula. Carbohydrate intolerance is a common indication for switching an infant's formula. In such situations, a change from a lactose- to a non-lactose-containing formula is recommended. Infant obesity, although a controversial subject, may be a factor in formula selection. Advance, a formula available for older infants, has a reduced energy content that results in an unbalanced energy density. Rather than a recommendation to feed Advance ad libitum to "obese" infants, a recommendation that might encourage better dietary habits would be to feed a routine formula at a lesser volume.[80]

QUALITY ASSURANCE

Legislation

The FDA regulates the manufacture of infant formula through the Code of Federal Regulations. Many approved food items, including food additives such as stabilizers and emulsifiers, are listed by the FDA as Generally Recognized As Safe. In 1980, the United States Congress passed the Infant Formula Act (PL 96-359), which defined an infant formula as "a food which purports to be or is represented for special dietary use solely as a food for infants by reason of its simulation of human milk or its suitability as a complete or partial substitute for human milk."[1, 18] The Act enabled the FDA to establish quality control procedures for formula manufacture and to stipulate nutrient composition based on recommendations of the CON/AAP.[1] The Act enabled the Secretary of the Department of Health and Human Services to revise the listing and the required levels of nutrients and to establish requirements for the quality of nutrients and procedures for quality control. All current and new formulations for healthy infants must meet standards for nutrient composition, quality of components, and processing methods. Special formulas, such as those for preterm infants or for infants with inborn errors of metabolism, are currently exempt from the Act.

The Infant Formula Council is a voluntary, nonprofit, trade association of infant formula manufacturers that determines various guidelines for the manufacture of infant formula.[1] The Codex Alimentarius Commission is a joint FAO/WHO Food Standards Program that recommends international standards for foods for infants and children. Several pediatric organizations are recognized authorities in infant nutrition, and their recommendations constitute the goals for infant feeding. The CON/AAP and the ESPGAN Committees on Nutrition provide recommendations for infants and children. Nutritional recommendations for infancy through adulthood are provided, under the auspices of the National Academy of Sciences and Public Health Service, by the Food and Nutrition Board of the National Research Council, as Recommended Dietary Allowances.

Formula Testing

The specifications of the Infant Formula Act require that new formulas, reformulations and/or changes in the processing of formulas must be submitted to the FDA, and that when major changes are planned, formula testing must be implemented. There are many levels of testing, such as product stability, preclinical nutritional studies, or formal clinical testing. Clinical testing may be accomplished by metabolic balance studies, growth trials, acceptance and tolerance studies, measurements of body composition, and determination of serum biochemical indices of nutritional status. The FDA has initiated steps to provide guidelines that regulate all formulas, for full-term and preterm infants.

Marketing

The decision to use commercial formula or to breast-feed is often based on sociological and economic factors. Social pressure from one's peer group or constraints imposed on the working mother may be major factors in the decision.[81] Manufacturer's strategies often are mentioned as an influence in the choice. The receipt of a sample packet of infant formula before discharge from the hospital has been a factor that has favored the selection of formula feeding over breast-feeding.[81] The relationship between the receipt of a sample packet and subsequent formula feeding was strengthened when the mothers were less educated or ill.[81] The cost of formula also has been considered as a factor in feeding choice. In the United States, a 1981 estimate of the cost of infant formula was $200 to $300 per year.[81] In developing nations, such as India and Ethiopia, that cost was $51 and $140 per year, respectively. Related to per capita gross national product (GNP), however, such costs were prohibitively expensive, and amounted to 15% to 30% of the GNP in the Philippines and 50% to 140% of the GNP in Ethiopia.[81]

FUTURE CHANGES IN INFANT FORMULAS

Immune Components

A comparison of the immune components in human and bovine milks identifies their differences most markedly. Significantly more IgA, lactoferrin, and lysozyme are present in human milk.[9, 10] Attempts are in progress to provide immune factors in bovine milk. Scientists have hyperimmunized cows against a variety of human conditions, coliforms, tetanus, and rotavirus.[18, 82, 83] After successful immunization with rotavirus, bovine milk rotavirus–specific IgG has been isolated and used successfully in the treatment of infant diarrhea.[82, 83] Raw bovine milk, but not pasteurized milk or formula, has been found to possess antibody activity against human rotavirus.[84] Alterations may be required in the processing of new generation milks to allow for the inclusion of host defense factors.

Cholesterol

Because cholesterol is present in greater quantities in human than in bovine milk, there is concern that its omission in infant formula may be detrimental. No advantages to growth and metabolism were noted, however, when preterm infants were fed bovine milk–based formula supplemented with cholesterol.[85]

Nucleotides

Bovine milk contains high concentrations of orotic acid and low concentrations of adenosine, cytidine, guanosine, inosine, uridine monophosphates, and uridine diphosphate.[86] The addition of these nucleotides to, and the reduction of orotic acid levels in, bovine milk–based formula fed to full-term infants resulted in greater omega-6 and omega-3 polyunsaturated fatty acids in red blood cell phospholipids.[86, 87] The speculation is that these nucleotides potentially play a role in essential fatty acid chain elongation.

Docosahexaenoic Acid

The long-chain essential fatty acid, docosahexaenoic acid (22:6n3), is an important constituent of brain gray matter, retinal membranes, and red blood cell membranes.[88] The composition of 22:6n3 is between 0.1% and 0.3% of total fatty acids in human milk and is undetectable in formula. Preterm infants fed bovine milk–based formula had declining concentrations of docosahexaenoic acid by 7 weeks compared with similar infants fed human milk.[88] The use of fish oil, particularly high in 22:6n3 fatty acids, in infant formulas was feasible and maintained adequate red blood cell phospholipid patterns.[89]

Human Milk Fat Component System

The superior fat absorption noted in human milk–fed infants prompted Alemi et al.[90] to add human milk to infant formula to study fat absorption. The authors found an increase in fat absorption after the mixture was fed. They hypothesized that either the particular configuration of human milk fat, the fat globule, or the endogenous lipase enzymes mediated the improved fat absorption. The practical significance of the increased fat absorption is unclear.

SUMMARY

If parents have decided not to breast-feed, there are a variety of infant formulas from which to choose. Normally, healthy full-term infants who are not breast-fed should receive a bovine milk–based formula (Enfamil, Similac, SMA). The use of any other formula should be determined by the specific needs of the full-term infant. Preterm infants should receive one of the specialized whey-dominant bovine milk–based formulas.

When the millions of exclusively formula-fed infants are considered, one realizes that the formula industry has performed in an exemplary manner in meeting the needs of infants. Support of further research into novel areas of nutrition should continue.

Acknowledgment

We thank A. Cavese for secretarial assistance and E.R. Klein for editorial advice.

REFERENCES

1. Anderson SA, Chinn HI, Fisher KD: History and current status of infant formulas. *Am J Clin Nutr* 1982; 35:381–397.
2. Lucas A: Infant feeding, in Roberton NRC (ed): *Textbook of Neonatology*. Edinburgh, Churchill Livingstone, 1986, pp 178–210.
3. Hansen JW, Cook DA, Cordano A, et al: Human milk substitutes, in Tsang RC, Nichols BL (eds): *Nutrition During Infancy*. Philadelphia, Hanley & Belfus, 1988, pp 378–398.
4. Martinez GA, Krieger FW: 1984 Milk-feeding patterns in the United States. *Pediatrics* 1985; 76:1004–1008.
5. Committee on Nutrition, American Academy of Pediatrics: Commentary on breast-feeding and infant formulas, including proposed standards for formulas. *Pediatrics* 1976; 57:278–285.
6. Davis MK, Savitz DA, Graubard BI: Infant feeding and childhood cancer. *Lancet* 1988; 1:365–368.
7. Radbill SX: Infant feeding through the ages. *Clin Pediatr* 1981; 20:613–621.
8. Widdowson E: Preparations used for the artificial feeding of infants. *Postgrad Med J* 1978; 54:176–179.
9. Hambraeus L: Proprietary milk versus human breast milk in infant feeding, a critical appraisal from the nutritional point of view. *Pediatr Clin North Am* 1977; 24:17–35.
10. Schanler RJ: Human milk for preterm infants: Nutritional and immune factors. *Semin Perinatol* (in press).
11. Jason JM, Nieburg P, Marks JS: Mortality and infectious disease associated with infant-feeding practices in developing countries. *Pediatrics* 1984; 74(part 2):702–727.
12. Schanler RJ, Goldblum RM, Garza C, et al: Enhanced fecal excretion of selected immune factors in very low birth weight infants fed fortified human milk. *Pediatr Res* 1986; 20:711–715.
13. Roberts AK: Prospects for further approximation of infant formulas to human milk. *Hum Nutr Appl Nutr* 1986; 40A:27–37.
14. Raiha NCR, Heinonen K, Rassin DK, et al: Milk protein quantity and quality in low-birthweight infants: I. Metabolic responses and effects on growth. *Pediatrics* 1976; 57:659–674.

15. Gross SJ: Growth and biochemical response of preterm infants fed human milk or modified infant formula. *N Engl J Med* 1983; 308:237–241.
16. Lucas A, Gore SM, Cole TJ, et al: Multicentre trial on feeding low birthweight infants: Effects of diet on early growth. *Arch Dis Child* 1984; 59:722–730.
17. Committee on Nutrition, American Academy of Pediatrics: Nutritional needs of low-birth-weight infants. *Pediatrics* 1985; 75:976–986.
18. Packard VS: Infant formula composition, formulation, and processing, in Packard VS (ed): *Human Milk and Infant Formula.* New York, Academic Press, 1982, pp 140–176.
19. Adams CF: *Nutritive Value of American Foods,* Agriculture Handbook no. 456. Washington, DC, Agricultural Research Service, United States Department of Agriculture, 1975.
20. Schanler RJ, Oh W: Composition of breast milk obtained from mothers of premature infants as compared to breast milk obtained from donors. *J Pediatr* 1980; 96:679–681.
21. Butte NF, Garza C, Johnson CA, et al: Longitudinal changes in milk composition of mothers delivering preterm and term infants. *Early Hum Dev* 1984; 9:153–162.
22. Committee on Nutrition, American Academy of Pediatrics: Soy-protein formulas: Recommendations for use in infant feeding. *Pediatrics* 1983; 72:359–363.
23. Santosham M, Foster S, Reid R, et al: Role of soy-based, lactose-free formula during treatment of acute diarrhea. *Pediatrics* 1985; 76:292–298.
24. Burr ML: Does infant feeding affect the risk of allergy? *Arch Dis Child* 1983; 58:561–565.
25. Taitz LS: Soy feeding in infancy. *Arch Dis Child* 1982; 57:814–815.
26. Lothe L, Lindberg T, Jakobsson I: Cow's milk formula as a cause of infantile colic: A double-blind study. *Pediatrics* 1982; 70:7–10.
27. Shenai JP, Jhaveri BM, et al: Nutritional balance studies in very low-birth-weight infants: Role of soy formula. *Pediatrics* 1981; 67:631–637.
28. Hall RT, Callenbach JC, Sheehan MB, et al: Comparison of calcium- and phosphorus-supplemented soy isolate formula with whey-predominant premature formula in very low birth weight infants. *J Pediatr Gastroenterol Nutr* 1984; 3:571–576.
29. Cordano A, Cook DA: Preclinical and clinical evaluations with casein hydrolysate products, in Lifshitz F (ed): *Nutrition for Special Needs in Infancy: Protein Hydrolysates.* New York, Marcel Dekker, 1985, pp 119–130.
30. Fomon SJ, Filer LJ, Anderson TA, et al: Recommendations for feeding normal infants. *Pediatrics* 1979; 63:52–59.
31. Oski FA: Is bovine milk a health hazard? *Pediatrics* 1985; 75(part 2):182–186.
32. Heppell LMJ, Cant AJ, Kilshaw PJ: Reduction in the antigenicity of whey proteins by heat treatment: A possible strategy of producing a hypoallergenic infant milk formula. *Br J Nutr* 1984; 51:29–36.
33. Tunnessen WW, Oski FA: Consequences of starting whole cow milk at 6 months of age. *J Pediatr* 1987; 111(part 1):813–816.
34. Schanler RJ, Garza C: Plasma amino acid differences in very low birth weight infants fed either human milk or whey-dominant cow milk formula. *Pediatr Res* 1987; 21:301–305.
35. Berger HM, Scott PH, Kenward C, et al: Curd and whey proteins in the nutrition of low birth weight babies. *Arch Dis Child* 1979; 54:98–104.
36. Kashyap S, Okamoto E, Kanaya S, et al: Protein quality in feeding low birth weight infants: A comparison of whey-predominant versus casein-predominant formulas. *Pediatrics* 1987; 79:748–755.
37. Heine W, Tiess M, Wutzke KD: ^{15}N tracer investigations of the physiological availability of urea nitrogen in mother's milk. *Acta Paediatr Scand* 1986; 75:439–443.
38. Gaull GE, Rassin DK, Raiha NCR, et al: Milk protein quantity and quality in low-birth weight infants: III. Effects on sulfur amino acids in plasma and urine. *J Pediatr* 1977; 90:348–355.
39. Okamoto E, Rassin DK, Zucker MS, et al: Role of taurine in feeding the low-birth weight infant. *J Pediatr* 1984; 104:936–940.
40. Michalk DV, Tittor F, Ringeisen R, et al: The development of heart and brain function in

low-birth-weight infants fed with taurine-supplemented formula. *Adv Exp Med Biol* 1987; 217:139–145.

41. De Curtis M, Senterre J, Rigo J: Estimated and measured energy content of infant formulas. *J Pediatr Gastroenterol Nutr* 1986; 5:746–749.

42. Schutz Y, Decombaz J: Metabolisable energy estimates in infants. *J Pediatr Gastroenterol Nutr* (letter to the editor). 1987; 6:477–478.

43. Shenai JP, Reynolds JW, Babson SG: Nutritional balance studies in very-low-birth-weight infants: Enhanced nutrient retention rates by an experimental formula. *Pediatrics* 1980; 66:233–238.

44. Shulman R, Wong WW, Irving CS, et al: Utilization of dietary cereal by young infants. *J Pediatr* 1983; 103:23–28.

45. Hamosh M: Fat needs for term and preterm infants, in Tsang RC, Nichols BL: *Nutrition During Infancy*. Philadelphia, Hanley & Belfus, 1988, pp 133–159.

46. Tantibhedhyangkul P, Hashim SA: Medium-chain triglyceride feeding in premature infants: Effects on calcium and magnesium absorption. *Pediatrics* 1978; 61:537–545.

47. Roy CC, Ste-Marie M, Chartrand L, et al: Correction of the malabsorption of the preterm infant with a medium-chain triglyceride formula. *J Pediatr* 1975; 86:446–450.

48. Huston RK, Reynolds JW, Jensen C, et al: Nutrient and mineral retention and vitamin D absorption in low-birth-weight infants: Effect of medium-chain triglycerides. *Pediatrics* 1983; 72:44–48.

49. Okamoto G, Muttard CR, Zucker CL, et al: Use of medium-chain triglycerides in feeding the low-birth-weight infant. *Am J Dis Child* 1982; 136:428–431.

50. Whyte RK, Campbell D, Stanhope R, et al: Energy balance in low birth weight infants fed formula of high or low medium-chain triglyceride content. *J Pediatr* 1986; 108:964–971.

51. Whyte RK, Whelan D, Hill R, et al: Excretion of dicarboxylic and omega-1 hydroxy fatty acids by low birth weight infants fed with medium-chain triglycerides. *Pediatr Res* 1986; 20:122–125.

52. Wu PYK, Edmon J, Auestad N, et al: Medium-chain triglycerides in infant formulas and their relation to plasma ketone body concentrations. *Pediatr Res* 1986; 20:338–341.

53. Hansen AE, Wiese HF, Boelsche AN, et al: Role of linoleic acid in infant nutrition: Clinical and chemical study of 428 infants fed on milk mixtures varying in kind and amount of fat. *Pediatrics* 1963; 31:(part 2)171–192.

54. Friedman Z, Seyberth H, Frolich J, et al: Effect of dietary variation in linoleic acid content on the major urinary metabolites of the E prostaglandins (PGE-M) in infants. *Adv Prostaglandin Thromboxane Leukotriene Res* 1980; 8:1799–1805.

55. Friedman Z: Polyunsaturated fatty acids in the low-birth-weight infant (review). *Semin Perinatol* 1979; 3:341–361.

56. Penn D, Schmidt-Sommerfeld E, Wolf H: Carnitine deficiency in premature infants receiving total parenteral nutrition. *Early Hum Dev* 1980; 4:23–34.

57. Schmidt-Sommerfeld E, Nova KM, Penn D, et al: Carnitine in the development of newborn adipose tissue. *Pediatr Res* 1978; 12:660–664.

58. Borum PR, York CM, Broquist HP: Carnitine content of liquid formulas and special diets. *Am J Clin Nutr* 1979; 32:2272–2276.

59. Bessey OA, Adam DJD, Hansen AE: Intake of vitamin B_6 and infantile convulsions: A first approximation of requirements of pyridoxine in infants. *Pediatrics* 1957; 20:33–44.

60. Pierson JD, Crawford JD: Dietary dependent neonatal hypocalcemia. *Am J Dis Child* 1972; 123:472–474.

61. Schanler RJ, Abrams SA, Garza C: Mineral balance studies in very low birth weight infants fed human milk. *J Pediatr* 1988; 113:230–238.

62. Steichen JJ, Tsang RC: Bone mineralization and growth in term infants fed soy-based or cow milk-based formula. *J Pediatr* 1987; 110:687–692.

63. Hillman LS: Bone mineral content in term infants fed human milk, cow milk-based formula, or soy-based formula. *J Pediatr* 1988; 113:208–212.

64. Bhatia J, Fomon SJ: Formulas for premature infants: Fate of the calcium and phosphorus. *Pediatrics* 1983; 72:37–40.

65. Koletzko B, Tangermann R, von Kries R, et al: Intestinal milk-bolus obstruction in formula-fed premature infants given high does of calcium. *J Pediatr Gastroenterol Nutr* 1988; 7:548–553.

66. Lonnerdal B, Cederblad A, Davidsson L, et al: The effect of individual components of soy formula and cows' milk formula on zinc bioavailability. *Am J Clin Nutr* 1984; 40:1064–1070.

67. Glicksman M: Food applications of gums, in Lineback DR, Linglett GE (eds): *Food Carbohydrates.* Westport, Conn, AVI Publishing Co, 1982, pp 270–295.

68. Tomarelli RM: Osmolality, osmolarity, and renal solute load of infant formulas. *J Pediatr* 1976; 88:454–456.

69. Book LS, Herbst JJ, Atherton SO, et al: Necrotizing enterocolitis in low-birth-weight infants fed an elemental formula. *J Pediatr* 1975; 87:602–605.

70. Bergmann KE, Ziegler EE, Fomon SJ: Water and renal solute load, in Fomon SJ (ed): *Infant Nutrition.* Philadelphia, WB Saunders Co, 1974, pp 245–266.

71. Schreiner RL, Brady MS, Franken EA, et al: Increased incidence of lactobezoars in low birth weight infants. *Am J Dis Child* 1979; 133:936–940.

72. Erenberg A, Shaw RD, Yousefzadeh D: Lactobezoar in the low-birth-weight infant. *Pediatrics* 1979; 63:642–646.

73. Levkoff AH, Gadsden RH, Hennigar GR, et al: Lactobezoar and gastric perforation in a neonate. *J Pediatr* 1970; 77:875–877.

74. Yoss BS: Human milk lactobezoars. *J Pediatr* 1984; 105:819–822.

75. Schreiner RL, Brady MS, Ernst JA, et al: Lack of lactobezoars in infants given predominantly whey protein formulas. *Am J Dis Child* 1982; 136:473–479.

76. Roy III S, Arant BS: Hypokalemic metabolic alkalosis in normotensive infants with elevated plasma renin activity and hyperaldosteronism: Role of dietary chloride deficiency. *Pediatrics* 1981; 67:423–429.

77. Garin EH, Geary D, Richard GA: Soybean formula (Neo-mull-soy) metabolic alkalosis in infancy. *J Pediatr* 1979; 95:985–987.

78. Weintraub R, Hams G, Meerkin M, et al: High aluminum content of infant milk formulas. *Arch Dis Child* 1986; 61:914–916.

79. Koo WWK, Kaplan LA: Aluminum and bone disorders: With specific reference to aluminum contamination of infant nutrients. *J Am Coll Nutr* 1988; 7:199–214.

80. Hansen RC, Elsberry VA, Blazovich JL: A physician's guide to infant formula feeding. *Ariz Med* 1977; 5:325–330.

81. Simopoulos AR, Grave GD: Factors associated with the choice and duration of infant-feeding practice. *Pediatrics* 1984; 74(part 2):603–614.

82. Brussow H, Hilpert H, Walther I, et al: Bovine milk immunoglobulins for passive immunity to infantile rotavirus gastroenteritis. *J Clin Microbiol* 1987; 25:982–986.

83. Hilpert H, Brussow H, Mietens C, et al: Use of bovine milk concentrate containing antibody to rotavirus to treat rotavirus gastroenteritis in infants. *J Infect Dis* 1987; 156:158–166.

84. Yolken RH, Losonsky GA, Vonderfecht S, et al: Antibody to human rotavirus in cow's milk. *N Engl J Med* 1985; 312:605–610.

85. Jarvenpaa A-L, Raiha NCR, Rassin DK, et al: Feeding the low-birth-weight infants: I. Taurine and cholesterol supplementation of formula does not affect growth and metabolism. *Pediatrics* 1983; 71:171–178.

86. DeLucchi C, Pita ML, Faus MJ, et al: Effects of dietary nucleotides on the fatty acid composition of erythrocyte membrane lipids in term infants. *J Pediatr Gastroenterol Nutr* 1987; 6:568–574.

87. Gil A, Pita M, Martinez A, et al: Effect of dietary nucleotides on plasma fatty acids in at-term neonates. *Hum Nutr Clin Nutr* 1986; 40:185–195.

88. Carlson SE, Rhodes PG, Ferguson MG: Docosahexaenoic acid status of preterm infants at birth and following feeding with human milk or formula. *Am J Clin Nutr* 1986; 44:798–804.

89. Liu CC, Carlson SE, Rhodes PG, et al: Increase in plasma phospholipid docosahexaenoic and eicosapentaenoic acids as a reflection of their intake and mode of administration. *Pediatr Res* 1987; 22:292–296.

90. Alemi B, Hamosh M, Scanlon JW, et al: Fat digestion in very low-birthweight infants: Effect of addition of human milk to low-birthweight formula. *Pediatrics* 1981; 68:484–489.

Chapter 14

Techniques of Enteral Feeding in the Preterm Infant

Joseph Kaempf, M.D.

Neonatology has been critiqued as a medical specialty that has relied too heavily on uncontrolled clinical trials and anecdotal observations in the pursuit of improved patient care. Iatrogenic disease and therapeutic misadventures are unfortunate consequences.[1] Within neonatology nowhere has this been more true than with methods of enteral feeding. There has been a surprising lack of prospective, controlled, randomized clinical trials addressing such fundamental issues in nutrition as route of milk delivery, hormonal effects of feeding, and the cardiorespiratory response to enteral feeds. Despite this, major advances in neonatal nutrition have occurred over the past 4 decades that have greatly contributed to the improved care and survival of high-risk neonates. The purpose of this chapter is to review the practice of delivering food enterally to the sick neonate, particularly the premature neonate. Several controversial issues and unanswered clinical questions are reviewed to provide the reader with a background in those areas of enteral nutrition that deserve increased attention by investigators, both in the laboratory and at the bedside.

HISTORICAL BACKGROUND

The development and practice of providing enteral nutrition to sick and/or premature infants have been critical to the advancement of neonatal care over the past century. Premature infants do not develop a coordinated suck and swallow until about 32 to 34 weeks postconception, so it was imperative for early practitioners to develop alternative methods of feeding these neonates, especially as they did not have the option of intravenous nutrition. To overcome the difficulties of feeding premature "weaklings," Marchant introduced the technique of orogastric gavage feeding to the Academy of Medicine in Paris in 1850.[2] This method involved the use of a 14-Fr rubber catheter passed into the infant's stomach for the infusion of milk. Gavage feeding and simple principles of thermal support were largely responsible for the marked improvement in survival of prematurely born infants during the late 19th and early 20th centuries, as popularized by Pierre Budin.[3] Other techniques used to feed premature or sick infants involved trickling milk into the infant's mouth with a dropper or spoon, which was time-consuming, dangerous, and less effective than gavage feeding. Nasal spoons were developed for the installation of milk directly into the nares, but this curious practice was largely abandoned by the start of the 20th century.[2]

Intermittent orogastric and nasogastric feeds were widely used through the first half of the 20th century to feed infants too sick or too premature to suckle the nipple. There were several drawbacks to this type of feeding. It was moderately time-consuming, the feeding tube could be accidently placed in the trachea, and there was always the risk of pharyngeal, esophageal, and/or gastric irritation or perforation when a feeding tube was repeatedly placed into an infant for each feeding. To overcome some of these limitations to gavage feeding, Royce, in 1951, introduced the use of the chronically indwelling nasogastric tube to feed premature infants.[4] This technique has been widely accepted and is commonly used in neonatal intensive care units (NICU) today. During the 1960s and 1970s, improved clinical care and medical technology resulted in far more survivors with birth weights less than 1,500 g. To overcome problems with poor gastric motility, abdominal distention, and aspiration, continuous nasogastric feeds were first described by Valman and associates in 1972.[5] As an alternative method to surmount feeding intolerance in the very low birth weight (VLBW) infant, Rhea introduced nasojejunal (transpyloric) feeding in 1970; this was the first recommendation for bypassing the stomach when providing enteral nutrition to the premature infant.[6]

Important research today in enteral nutrition focuses not only on the route of delivery of milk but also on complex issues such as the relationship of feedings to gut hormone secretion, the pathophysiology of necrotizing enterocolitis, and various cardiorespiratory consequences of feeding. The remainder of this chapter concerns these and related topics.

METHODS OF MILK DELIVERY

Prior to the 1950s intermittent gavage feeding (orogastric or nasogastric) was the method of choice for delivering milk to infants too sick or premature to suckle. Subsequently, major strides were made in neonatal care with the result of ever increasing numbers of surviving VLBW infants weighing less than 1,500 g. These infants were thought by many clinicians to be too fragile and unstable to warrant feeding in the first 24 to 96 hours of life. "Starvation" was recommended in the care of these premature infants to avoid complications such as abdominal distention, edema, and aspiration.[7] This practice of withholding feeds from premature infants was challenged by several investigators in the 1960s, when it was suggested that delayed feeding was associated with poorer neurologic outcome than the practice of infant gavage feeding from day 1 of life onward.[8, 9]

It was, and is, a great challenge to provide milk to the sick or premature infant too feeble or premature to suck and swallow. Intermittent orogastric or nasogastric feeding enables the clinician to deliver milk to the infant's stomach, bypassing the physiologic limitations of neurologic immaturity or pulmonary disease. However, intermittent gavage feeding has drawbacks that limit its universal application. Gavage feeding tubes can be accidently placed into the trachea, causing possible aspiration, and frequently are responsible for gagging and vagal responses such as apnea and bradycardia when they are passed into the stomach. To overcome these limitations, Royce first described the practice of intermittent nasogastric milk feeds in premature infants by use of a chronically indwelling polyethylene tube.[4] Many clinicians prefer the use of orogastric tubes because most infants are obligate nose breathers and nasal feeding tubes can increase upper airway resistance; such tubes also can promote purulent rhinitis, nasal septum erosion, and/or otitis media.[10]

Unfortunately, intermittent bolus feeding is not always tolerated by sick VLBW infants, who may experience abdominal distention, gastric residuals, and pulmonary aspiration related to the bolus of milk. To circumvent these problems, Valman and co-workers introduced the technique of continuous nasogastric feeding of premature infants.[5] This method is widely used today, although again, many clinicians prefer the use of orogastric tubes for continuous infusion, rather than nasogastric, for the reasons cited earlier.

Another approach to feeding the premature infant is use of the gastrostomy tube. This method was advocated by some clinicians in the 1960s as a way of avoiding the attendant problems of orogastric or nasogastric tube placement (vagal stimulation, tracheal intubation, dislodgement). However, a controlled trial comparing premature infants fed with gastrostomy tubes with those fed by intermittent gavage or dropper showed higher mortality rates and increased infectious complications in the infants with gastrostomy tubes.[11] Gastrostomy tubes are not currently recommended for routine use, and are reserved for infants with specific surgical indications or severe neurologic impairment.

Transpyloric feeding methods for premature infants were introduced by Rhea and Kilby.[6] Nasoduodenal and nasojejunal routes of milk administration were touted effective means to achieve high volumes of enteral feeds quite early after birth, avoiding the problems of poor gastric motility, reflux, and aspiration common to sick, premature infants. Milk is delivered in a continuous fashion, with necessary close monitoring of the infant's abdomen and overall clinical status. Transpyloric feeds were introduced and popularized during a period in neonatology when it was being recognized that the VLBW infant had considerable fluid and nutrient requirements that were often impossible to fulfill by conventional enteral routes. Gavage feedings could not always surmount the problems of poor gastric motility, abdominal distention, reflux, and aspiration. Two important developments greatly curtailed the popularity and utility of transpyloric feeds in the mid to late 1970s. First, a series of case reports was published that linked transpyloric feeding tubes to duodenal perforation.[12] This probably resulted from use of polyvinyl chloride feeding tubes, which stiffen considerably after 72 to 96 hours in situ. Other reported complications were abdominal distention, vomiting, diarrhea, malabsorption of nutrients, accidental dislodgement, small bowel intussusception, tube obstruction with proteinaceous clots, pyloric stenosis, and alteration of small bowel microbial flora.[13-16] The second important development was the refinement of intravenous amino acid, fat, and carbohydrate solutions, which enabled the clinician to provide adequate nutrition by vein while gavage and/or nipple feeds could be advanced appropriately. Hyperalimentation fluids lessened the great urgency to provide large amounts of enteral feeds early in the sick neonate's life. Transpyloric feeds are used today in a minority of infants in the NICU, and are most useful for those babies with documented severe gastroesophageal reflux and/or aspiration, or babies with particularly poor gastric motility complicated by large feeding residuals. Only soft, Silastic-type feeding catheters that do not stiffen should be used for transpyloric feeding.

No one method of delivering milk to sick or premature infants is perfect for every patient in every clinical situation. Each feeding technique has its own particular strengths and weaknesses. The advantages and disadvantages of each of the common methods used to feed neonates are summarized in Table 14-1.[17] Several investigators

TABLE 14−1.

Advantages and Disadvantages of the Common Methods of Enteral Feeding

Method	Advantages	Disadvantages
Nipple	Simple; physiologic hormonal, digestive, neurologic benefits	Consumes energy and time; possible air swallowing, gagging, aspiration; impossible in ventilated patients
Orogastric-nasogastric	Suck-swallow not required; decreased aspiration and gagging; quick, relatively simple to place catheter; conserves energy; can use with intubated and ventilated patients	Vagal stimulation with possible gagging and aspiration; inadvertent tracheal intubation; increased nasal airway resistance, nasal erosion, purulent rhinitis, otitis media
Intermittent-bolus	Simple, minimal equipment; mimics nipple feeds with possible enteric hormone benefits; can combine with non-nutritive sucking	Vagal stimulation; gastric residuals, reflux, abdominal distention; possible aspiration
Constant infusion	Avoids overdistention in infants with decreased gastric emptying time; possibly greater total milk intake over time	More equipment needed; constant monitoring needed; decreased cyclic enteric hormone response; loss of nutrients in syringe tubing
Transpyloric	Greater milk intake in infants with poor gastric emptying time; less reflux/aspiration in some infants	More equipment, constant monitoring, increased radiography needed; catheter easily displaced; duodenal perforation, malabsorption, altered microbial flora; unphysiologic, decreased cyclic enteric hormone response
Gastrostomy	Surgical indications (e.g., fundiplication), severe neurologically damaged patients with long-term inability to suck/swallow	Morbidity/mortality of procedure; increased infectious complications

*Modified from Dweck HS: Feeding the premature born infant. *Clin Perinatol* 1975; 2:183−202.

have published studies reporting faster growth in a few premature infants fed with transpyloric tubes as compared with the nasogastric route.[18, 19] However, several larger, controlled studies have not shown any advantage to transpyloric feeds in terms of feeding tolerance or rate of growth[20−23] (Fig 14−1). These studies demonstrate the increased expense, difficulties, and complications of transpyloric feeding that make it an undesirable method to feed premature infants in most circumstances. Therefore, most infants too sick or premature to suckle their feeds should be fed intermittently by the orogastric or nasogastric route. Feedings should be advanced slowly—with careful attention paid to the infant's overall clinical status, abdominal examination, and tolerance of previous feedings. Table 14−2 is a suggested guideline for feeding the premature infant.[24]

ENTERIC HORMONES

The importance of various enteric hormones in neonatal gastrointestinal growth and maturation is receiving increasing attention. Lucas et al.[25] have shown that even minimal nasogastric feeds in premature infants elicits a surge of several enteric hormones

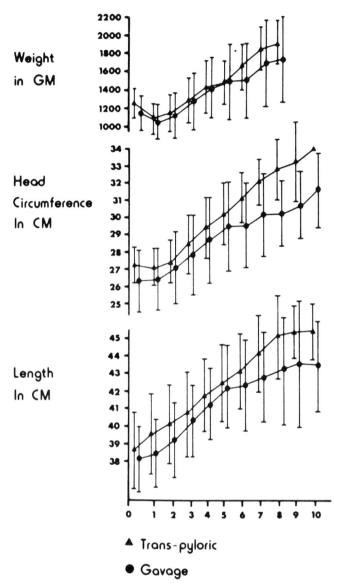

FIG 14–1.
Growth patterns in two groups of premature infants fed either by transpyloric means *(triangles)* or intermittent gavage *(circles).* (From Pereira G, Lemons J: Controlled study of transpylor and intermittent gavage feedings in the small preterm infant. *Pediatrics* 1981; 67:68–72. Used by permission.)

that mimics the response seen in healthy, nursing, term infants (Fig 14–2). A key issue is how these hormonal responses are affected by the method of milk delivery. Aynsley-Green and associates[26] compared two groups of premature infants, one fed human milk by the intermittent nasogastric route, the other by continuous nasogastric infusion. Both types of feeding induced postprandial increases in several enteric hormones, but the infants fed by intermittent bolus had much more marked cyclical surges in these hormones. The importance of meal-related surges in enteric hormones and other fundamental questions such as the relationship of hormone secretion to site of delivery and volume of milk feedings await further research.

TABLE 14–2.

Suggested Guidelines for Feeding the Preterm Infant*

Weight (g)	Day of Feeding	Type of Food	Volume (mL)	Frequency (hr)
<1,000	1	B or 10 kcal/oz F	2	q 2
	3–4	B or 20 kcal/oz F	4	q 2
	7–8	B or 20 kcal/oz F	8	q 2
	10–12	B or 20–24 kcal/oz F (± suppl)	10–15	q 2
1,000–1,500	1	B or 20 kcal/oz F	2	q 2
	3–4	B or 20 kcal/oz F	6	q 2
	7–8	B or 20 kcal/oz F	10–12	q 2
	10–12	B or 20–24 kcal/oz F (± suppl)	15–30	q 2–3
1,500–2,000	1	B or 20 kcal/oz F	4–5	q 2–3
	3–4	B or 20 kcal/oz F	10–15	q 2–3
	5–7	B or 20–24 kcal/oz F (± suppl)	25–40	q 2–3

*From Kaempf JW, Bonnabel C, Hay WW: Neonatal nutrition, in Merenstein GB, Gardner SL, (eds): *Handbook of Neonatal Intensive Care,* ed 2. St Louis, CV Mosby Co, 1989. p 199. Used by permission. B = breast milk, F = formula, suppl = supplements.

NECROTIZING ENTEROCOLITIS

The precise pathophysiology of necrotizing enterocolitis (NEC) is incompletely understood. Because it is almost always seen in enterally fed premature infants, various investigators have tried to link its occurrence to the rate and volume of milk feedings. Brown and Sweet[27] reported that NEC has become rare in their NICU since the introduction of a slow, cautious feeding regimen. Goldman[28] has reported that NEC in their NICU was virtually absent until the introduction of a "fast" feeding regimen associated with rapid milk volume increases.

Several prospective, controlled clinical trials have addressed the issue of whether early feeding or rapid advancement of enteral feeds increases the risk of NEC in premature infants. These studies have involved relatively small numbers of patients, but none has shown that early enteral feeds, or increasing volumes of feeds, increases the risk of NEC.[29–32] Following a period of recovery from birth stress or asphyxia (approximately 24 to 48 hours) and assuming stable cardiopulmonary function, the vast majority of premature infants can tolerate the cautious introduction of enteral feeds at an early age. Slow, careful advancement with close observance of the infant's physical condition is usually safe and probably beneficial for the infant (see Table 14–2).

CARDIORESPIRATORY RESPONSES TO FEEDING AND GASTROESOPHAGEAL REFLUX

Feeding the sick or premature infant who is mechanically ventilated or recovering from pulmonary disease can have significant cardiorespiratory consequences. Several studies have shown that infants recovering from respiratory distress syndrome can have a pronounced, acute drop in arterial oxygen pressure (tension) (Pao_2) after an enteral feed (Fig 14–3).[33, 34] The mechanism underlying this change in oxygen level has not been demonstrated.

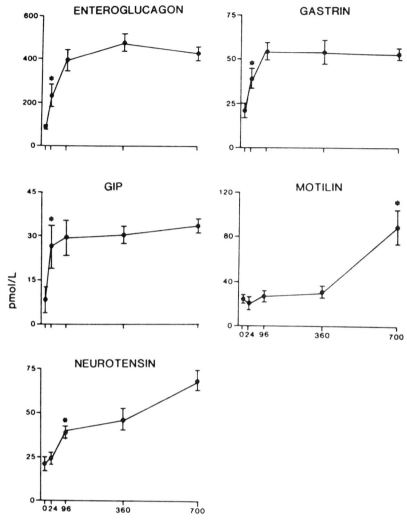

FIG 14–2.
Mean plasma concentrations of enteroglucagon, gastrin, gastric inhibitory peptide *(GIP),* motilin, and neuro-tensin (pmol/L ± SE) are plotted against the total cumulative enteral feed volume (mL) in newborn premature infants. (From Lucas A, Bloom S, Aynsley-Green: Gut hormones and minimal enteral feeding. *Acta Paediatr Scand* 1986; 75:719–723. Used by permission.)

Gastroesophageal reflux (GER) with aspiration in mechanically ventilated infants who are being fed is a frequent cause of respiratory compromise that is probably under-diagnosed. Hopper et al.[35] measured lactose in the tracheas of premature infants who were mechanically ventilated and receiving milk feedings by either orogastric, nasogas-tric, or nasojejunal routes. Sixty percent of these infants had evidence of aspiration, in-cluding those who were fed with nasojejunal catheters. It is not entirely clear just how much GER and aspiration of milk contributes to chronic lung disease, but problems of apnea, bradycardia, hypoxia, and inability to wean from mechanical ventilation in pre-mature infants should alert the clinician to consider reflux and its complications. Prema-ture infants with chronic lung disease who are being enterally fed are at high risk for GER and aspiration because they have decreased lower esophageal sphincter tone, fre-

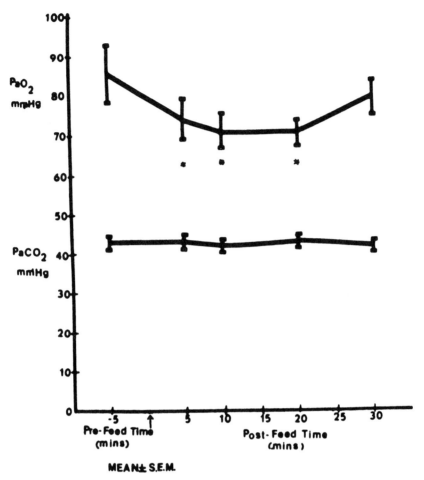

FIG 14–3.
Change in arterial oxygen tension and arterial carbon dioxide tension after feeding in 15 newborn infants recovering from respiratory disease (*Asterisks* indicate significant differences from prefeed values; $P = .05$.) (From Patel B, Dinwiddle R, Kumar S, et al: The effects of feeding on arterial blood gases and lung mechanics in newborn infants recovering from respiratory disease. *J Pediatr* 1977; 90:435–438. Used by permission.)

quently have slow gastric emptying time, and cannot protect their airway by glottic closure with an endotracheal tube in place.

Therapy for GER and/or aspiration should consist of cautiously advancing milk feedings while paying close attention to the infant's physical condition and clinical status. Extremely low birth weight infants (<1,000 g) often tolerate continuous nasogastric feeds better than bolus regimens. Transpyloric feedings are rarely required except in the most severe cases of GER and, unfortunately, do not always prevent the problem.[35] It is vital to minimize excessive disturbance of VLBW infants, especially because multiple examinations, repositioning, endotracheal tube suctioning, and chest physiotherapy may promote GER and aspiration. Certain medications such as theophylline and beta-sympathomimetics may exacerbate GER. These agents are sometimes used with questionable clinical benefits and should not be given to the premature infant without a documented, sustained, salutary effect. Infants should be kept in the prone, head-elevated position after feeding; this procedure has been demonstrated to reduce GER.[36] Thickened feedings have not been shown convincingly to reduce GER.[37] Metaclopramide, an agent used to improve gastric emptying and reduce GER in adults, has not been shown to be efficacious in infants, and may, in fact, have several undesirable side effects.[38]

NON-NUTRITIVE SUCKING

Although premature infants less than 32 weeks post-conception do not have a coordinated suck and swallow that allows oral feedings, they will often readily suck on a

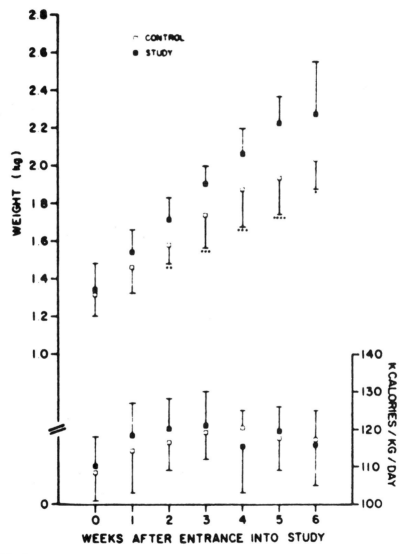

FIG 14–4.
Weight gain in two groups of premature infants, one group allowed non-nutritive sucking during tube feeding *(solid boxes)*. * means $P < .05$; ** means $P < .02$; *** means $P < .01$; **** means $P < .001$. Lower graph shows no significant differences in caloric intake throughout the study. (From Bernbaum J, Pereira G, Watkins J, et al: Nonnutritive sucking during gavage feeding enhances growth and maturation in premature infants. *Pediatrics* 1983; 71:41–45. Used by permission.)

nipple or pacifier. The benefits of this have been suspected by clinicians for years but only recently documented in bedside studies. Premature infants who are allowed to suck on a pacifier during tube feedings learn to suck and swallow their feedings earlier, gain weight faster, and are discharged from the hospital sooner than matched control infants who are not allowed a pacifier (Fig 14–4).[39] The mechanism underlying these benefits are speculative at this time, but may involve decreased energy expenditure by infants who are allowed a pacifier, or perhaps improved nutrient digestion and absorption.

The structure and milk flow characteristics of nipples used for bottle feeds have received scant scientific attention. Nipples designed for use by premature babies are smaller, softer, and more distensible to allow for greater milk flow at lower sucking pressures. Nuk™-type nipples have been designed to simulate the shape of the human nipple to allow for more efficient milk flow during sucking. However, there is wide variability in milk flow characteristics not only between different nipple types but also within the same type.[40] No generalizations about how an infant will do with a particular nipple can be made, as there is product variability rather than standardization.

MILK TEMPERATURE

Warming milk to body temperature before feeding infants is a long-standing tradition in child care. It seems logical, then, that artificial milk should be given to the infant at a temperature similar to that of naturally suckled breast milk. Most nurseries warm formula (or stored human milk) to approximately 37° C before feeding infants, and seldom give milk that is colder than room temperature (20° C to 24° C). As with so many "routine" procedures in neonatal medicine, the subject of ideal milk temperature has received remarkably little scientific study. Gibson published the first study to look at the effect of cold formula feeds (5° C) on healthy, term infants. He reported that the acceptance rate of the cold feeds was high, the growth of the infants was normal, and that there were no obvious harmful effects from nippling refrigerated milk.[41] Holt and co-workers[42] published the first study in premature infants that compared one group of babies who received warm formula (37°C) with another group who received cold formula (4° C). There were no differences between the two groups in weight gain, food intake, sleep patterns, motility, vocalization, or vomiting. The authors concluded that warming formula to body temperature offered no advantages to the healthy premature infant.

Eckburg and associates[43] studied the effects of formula temperature on the thermogenic response to gavage feeding in premature infants. Skin, rectal, and stomach temperatures dropped more after room-temperature feeds than after body-temperature feeds, but the metabolic rate rose comparably in these infants regardless of the temperature of the feedings (24° C vs. 37° C). Until more investigations are conducted with premature infants that study the effect of varying milk temperatures on growth and metabolism, it seems prudent to provide enteral feedings at room temperature or, preferably, body temperature.

ALTERATIONS OF MILK DURING DELIVERY

In a perfect world all premature infants would breast-feed from their mothers, thereby being provided a consistent, natural, safe source of nutrition. Regrettably, prematurity and various disease states necessitate the use of elaborate feeding systems consisting of various pumps, syringes, filters, tubing, and feeding catheters. Infectious complications and alterations in nutrients can occur with the use of these systems.

Fresh formula is normally negative for microorganisms. However, formula delivered over 12 to 24 hours from a standard pump and tubing apparatus has been shown to have a high rate of contamination with various gram-positive and gram-negative bacteria. The source of these organisms is thought to be the skin flora from nursing personnel who handled the formula and tubing systems.[44] Similarly, fresh breast milk given by continuous infusion over 6 to 8 hours to premature infants has been shown to have a significant increase in the colony count of *Staphylococcus epidermidis*.[45] One study suggested that the occurrence of feeding intolerance and suspected sepsis in premature infants could be significantly correlated with continuous infusions of breast milk that had high colony counts of gram-negative bacilli.[46]

No standards or recommendations exist for the bacteriologic monitoring of formula or breast milk given by bottle or infusion. However, some guidelines may be used to reduce infectious complications when delivering milk to premature infants in the NICU (Table 14–3).

The nutrient content of milk can vary when delivered through mechanical pump and tubing systems. The fat content of human milk can drop by one third during a continu-

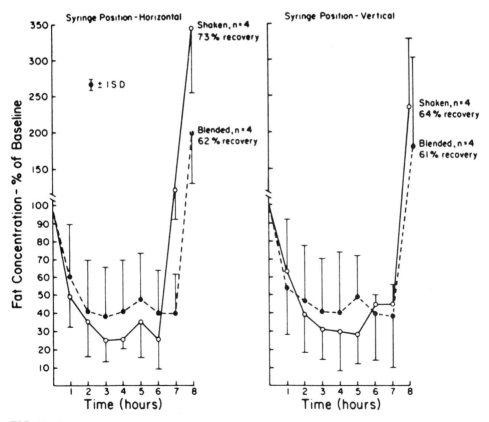

FIG 14–5.

Changes in fat concentration of human milk *(shaken* or *blended)* during continuous infusion with Harvard syringe pump in two different positions. (From Greer F, McCormick A, Loker J: Changes in fat concentration of human milk during delivery by intermittent bolus and continuous mechanical pump infusion. *J Pediatr* 1984; 105:745–749. Used by permission.)

TABLE 14–3.

Guidelines for Reducing Infectious Complications
Associated With Breast Milk or Formula Feeds

Careful monitoring for contamination by infectious
organisms should precede the use of any donor
(nonmaternal) human milk

Breast pump collection devices should be clean and
sterilized for each use

Breast milk should be immediately frozen if not used
shortly after it is collected

Strict hand-washing guidelines for nursing personnel
who prepare milk feedings should be emphasized

Continuous feeds should not be used routinely in the
neonatal intensive care unit, only in those babies
with specific indications

The continuous feeding apparatus (syringe, tubing,
milk) should be changed every 4 to 6 hours to
prevent bacterial overgrowth when breast milk is
being administered

ous infusion, probably because the lighter (cream) portion of the milk rises to the top of the syringe and/or adheres to the syringe and tubing (Fig 14–5). This fat loss can be avoided by using bolus feeds instead of continuous infusions.[47] Specialized premature formulas with high mineral contents can have serious precipitation problems when delivered by continuous infusion, with subsequent loss of calcium and other nutrients.[48] This can be remedied by frequent agitation of the formula, which is inconvenient, or better yet, use of bolus feedings.

REFERENCES

1. Silverman WA: *Human Experimentation: A Guided Step Into the Unknown*. Oxford, UK, Oxford University Press, 1985.
2. Cone TE: *History of the Care and Feeding of the Premature Infant*. Boston, Little, Brown & Co, 1985, pp 32–35.
3. Budin P: *The Nursling: The Feeding and Hygiene of Premature and Full-Term Infants*. London, Caston Publishing Co, 1907.
4. Royce S, Tepper C, Watson W, et al: Indwelling polyethylene nasogastric tube for feeding premature infants. *Pediatrics* 1951; 8:79–81.
5. Valman H, Heath C, Brown R: Continuous intragastric milk feeds in infants of low birth weight. *Br Med J [Clin Res]* 1972; 3:547–550.
6. Rhea J, Kilby J: A nasojejunal tube for infant feeding. *Pediatrics* 1970; 46:36–40.
7. Smith C, Yudkin S, Young W, et al: Adjustment of electrolytes and water following premature birth. *Pediatrics* 1949; 3:34–48.
8. Davies P, Russell H: Later progress of 100 infants weighing 1,000 to 2,000 g. at birth fed immediately with breast milk. *Dev Med Child Neurol* 1968; 10:725–735.
9. Lubchenco L, Delivaria-Papadopoulos M, Butterfield L, et al: Long-term follow-up studies of prematurely born infants: I. Relationship of handicaps to nursery routines. *J Pediatr* 1972; 80:501–508.
10. Stocks J: Effect of nasogastric tubes on nasal resistance during infancy. *Arch Dis Child* 1980; 55:17–21.
11. Vengusamy S, Pildes R, Raffensperger J, et al: A controlled study of feeding gastrostomy in low birth weight infants. *Pediatrics* 1969; 43:815–820.

12. Boros S, Reynolds J: Duodenal perforation: A complication of neonatal nasojejunal feeding. *J Pediatr* 1974; 85:107–108.
13. Heird W: Nasojejunal Feeding: A Commentary. *J Pediatr* 1974; 85:111–112.
14. Challacombe D, Richardson J, Anderson C: Bacterial microflora of the upper gastrointestinal tract in infants without diarrhoea. *Arch Dis Child* 1974; 49:264–269.
15. Roy R, Pollnitz R, Hamilton J, et al: Impaired assimilation of nasojejunal feeds in healthy low-birth-weight newborn infants. *J Pediatr* 1977; 90:431–434.
16. Raine R, Goel K, Young D, et al: Pyloric stenosis and transpyloric feeding. *Lancet* 1982; 2:821–822.
17. Dweck HS: Feeding the premature born infant. *Clin Perinatol* 1975; 2:183–202.
18. Wolfsdorf J, Makarawa S, Fernandes C, et al: Transpyloric feeding in small preterm infants. *Arch Dis Child* 1975; 50:723–726.
19. Wells D, Zachman R: Nasojejunal feedings in low-birth-weight infants. *J Pediatr* 1975; 87:276–279.
20. Drew JH, Johnston R, Finocchiaro C, et al: A comparison of nasojejunal with nasogastric feeding in low-birth-weight infants. *Med J Aust* 1979; 15:98–100.
21. Pereira G, Lemons J: Controlled study of transpylor and intermittent gavage feeding in the small preterm infant. *Pediatrics* 1981; 67:68–72.
22. Whitfield M: Poor weight gain of the low birth weight infant fed nasojejunally. *Arch Dis Child* 1982; 57:597–601.
23. Laing I, Lang M, Callaghan O, et al: Nasogastric compared with nasoduodenal feeding in low birth weight infants. *Arch Dis Child* 1986; 61:138–141.
24. Kaempf JW, Bonnabel C, Hay WW Jr: Neonatal Nutrition, in Merenstein GB, Gardner LS (eds): *Handbook of Neonatal Intensive Care,* ed 2. St Louis CV Mosby Co, 1989, p 199.
25. Lucas A, Bloom S, Aynsley-Green A: Gut hormones and minimal enteral feeding. *Acta Paediatr Scand* 1986; 75:719–723.
26. Aynsley-Green A, Adrian T, Bloom S: Feeding and the development of enteroinsular hormone secretion in the preterm infant: Effects of continuous gastric infusions of human milk compared with intermittent boluses. *Acta Paediatr Scand* 1982; 71:379–383.
27. Brown E, Sweet A: Preventing necrotizing enterocolitis in neonates. *JAMA* 1978; 240:2452–2454.
28. Goldman H: Feeding and necrotizing enterocolitis. *Am J Dis Child* 1980; 134:553–555.
29. Book L, Herbst J, Jung A: Comparison of fast- and slow-feeding rate schedules to the development of necrotizing enterocolitis. *J Pediatr* 1976; 89:463–466.
30. LaGamma E, Ostertag S, Birenbaum H: Failure of delayed oral feedings to prevent necrotizing enterocolitis. *Am J Dis Child* 1985; 139:385–389.
31. Ostertag S, LaGamma E, Reisen C, et al: Early enteral feeding does not affect the incidence of necrotizing enterocolotis. *Pediatrics* 1986; 77:275–280.
32. Dunn L, Weiner J, Kliegman R: Beneficial effects of early hypocaloric enteral feeding on neonatal gastrointestinal function: Preliminary report of a randomized trial. *J Pediatr* 1988; 112:622–629.
33. Wilkinson A, Yu V: Immediate effects of feeding on blood-gases and some cardiorespiratory function in ill newborn infants. *Lancet* 1974; 1:1083–1085.
34. Patel B, Dinwiddle R, Kumar S, et al: The effects of feeding on arterial blood gases and lung mechanics in newborn infants recovering from respiratory disease. *J Pediatr* 1977; 90:435–438.
35. Hopper A, Kwong L, Stevenson D, et al: Detection of gastric contents in tracheal fluid of infants by lactose assay. *J Pediatr* 1983; 102:415–418.
36. Orenstein S, Whitington P: Positioning for prevention of infant gastroesophageal reflux. *J Pediatr* 1983; 103:534–537.
37. Bailey D, Andres J, Danek G, et al: Lack of efficacy of thickened feeding as treatment for gastroesophageal reflux. *J Pediatr* 1987; 110:187–189.
38. Machida H, Forbes D, Gall D, et al: Metaclopramide in gastroesophageal reflux of infancy. *J Pediatr* 1988; 112:483–487.

39. Bernbaum J, Pereira G, Watkins J, et al: Nonnutritive sucking during gavage feeding enhances growth and maturation in premature infants. *Pediatrics* 1983; 71:41–45.
40. Mathew O: Nipple units for newborn infants: A functional comparison. *Pediatrics* 1988; 81:688–691.
41. Gibson J: Reaction of 150 infants to cold formulas. *J Pediatr* 1958; 52:404–406.
42. Holt L, Daview E, Hasselmeyer E, et al: A study of premature infants fed cold formulas. *J Pediatr* 1962; 61:556–561.
43. Eckburg J, Bell E, Rios G, et al: Effects of formula temperature on postprandial thermogenesis and body temperature of premature infants. *J Pediatr* 1987; 111:588–592.
44. Schreiner R, Eitzen H, Gfell M, et al: Environmental contamination of continuous drip feedings. *Pediatrics* 1979; 63:232–237.
45. Lemons P, Miller K, Eitzen H, et al: Bacterial Growth in Human Milk During Continuous Feeding. *Am J Perinatol* 1983; 1:76–80.
46. Botsford K, Weinstein R, Boyer K, et al: Gram-negative bacilli in human milk feedings: Quantitation and clinical consequences for premature infants. *J Pediatr* 1986; 109:707–710.
47. Greer F, McCormick A, Loker J: Changes in fat concentration of human milk during delivery by intermittent bolus and continuous mechanical pump infusion. *J Pediatr* 1984; 105:745–749.
48. Antonson D, Smith J, Nelson R, et al: Stability of vitamin and mineral concentrations of a low-birth-weight infant formula during continuous enteral feeding. *J Pediatr Gastroenterol Nutr* 1983; 2:617–621.

Chapter 15

Non-nutritive Sucking

Martha J. Miller, M.D., Ph.D.

The sucking patterns of human infants are as intriguing to the babies' parents as to the psychologists and physiologists who investigate these phenomena. Significant clinical benefits to the preterm infant, including improvement in weight gain, have been attributed to this behavior.[1-3] The phylogeny, characteristic descriptive features, and physiologic effects of non-nutritive sucking are explored in an effort to determine how this aspect of human behavior could affect somatic growth.

CHARACTERISTIC TEMPORAL PATTERN OF NON-NUTRITIVE SUCKING

Young infants will display one of two types of sucking when provided with a nipple in the mouth: *nutritive* or *non-nutritive*. Nutritive sucking occurs when a liquid supply is available through the nipple, and non-nutritive sucking may occur when no liquid is forthcoming. Non-nutritive sucking, as defined by Wolff, consists of a regular alternation of bursts and rest periods (Fig 15–1), with a rhythm of about 4 to 6 cycles/min (one burst of sucking and one rest period constitute one cycle).[4] Approximately one suck occurs every 0.5 seconds during a sucking burst, and these sucking bursts may occupy on average 28 min/hr when a pacifier is provided.[5] Light or sound stimulation presented to the infant may alter the frequency of these sucking bursts, but will not inhibit the behavior.[6] In addition, alteration in the infant's metabolic status due to hypoglycemia may result in a decreased frequency of sucking (see Fig 15–1,C). Non-nutritive sucking is not dependent on presence of an object in the mouth, for rhythmic mouthing movements resembling non-nutritive sucking may be observed from 4% to 32% of the time in a drowsy or sleeping infant even when no sucking object is available.[4, 7]

Non-nutritive sucking can be distinguished from nutritive sucking by the difference in the burst-pause patterns observed. In the nutritive mode, the term infant initially sucks continuously at a rate of 0.8 to 1.2 sucks/sec for 2 to 3 minutes at the onset of a feeding. Toward the latter part of a feeding, the continuous sequence of sucking is broken into segments of variable duration, which become less frequent as the feeding comes to an end.[8, 9] In term or in older premature infants non-nutritive and nutritive sucking are clearly distinguishable behaviors (Table 15–1), with nutritive sucking occurring at a consistently lower sucking rate. The lower sucking rate observed during a

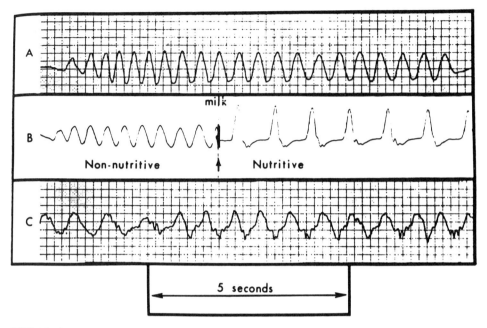

FIG 15–1.

Sucking patterns in 4-day-old infants, as detected by oral pressure transmitted to a pacifier in the infant's mouth. **A,** a single long burst of non-nutritive sucking in a healthy waking infant. **B,** a shift from non-nutritive to nutritive sucking that occurs with the onset of milk flow. **C,** non-nutritive sucking of infant with hypoglycemia, characterized by a long peak interval time. (From Wolff PH: The serial organization of sucking in the young infant. *Pediatrics* 1968; 42:943–956. Used by permission.)

feeding may reflect the inhibitory effect of frequent swallows on the central pattern generation of sucking bursts.

Wolff[9] has speculated that the presence of two distinct modes of sucking may be a unique characteristic of the human species. When sucking patterns with and without a nutrient supply were compared in a number of hand-raised mammalian species, including primates,[9] the nutritive rates of sucking were found to be characteristic for each species. Although animals continue to suck when presented with a nipple from which no fluid can be obtained (non-nutritive),[10, 11] *no* species over 1 week of age has been found to display the burst–pause cycles of non-nutritive sucking characteristic of human infants. Wolff has speculated that differences in the organization of sucking behavior be-

TABLE 15–1.

Comparison of Non-nutritive and Nutritive Sucking Rates*

| | | Mean Frequency/sec | | | |
| | Number of Infants | Non-nutritive | | Nutritive | |
Age		Mean	Range	Mean	Range
37–38 wk prematures	3	1.7	1.7–1.8	0.92	0.86–0.96
4–6 days	10	2.1	1.9–2.3	1.0	0.8–1.2
14–60 days	10	2.2	2.0–2.6	1.3	1.1–1.5
7–9 mo	5	2.7	2.4–2.7	1.5	1.3–1.6

*From Wolff PH: The serial organization of sucking in the young infant. *Pediatrics* 1968; 42:943–956. Used by permission.

tween humans and other mammals may reflect a qualitative change in the central control of the sucking reflex.[9] This species specificity may seriously hinder the development of an animal model with which to study the metabolic effects of non-nutritive sucking.

Even in the absence of swallowing, sucking requires complex sensory-motor coordination of numerous muscles of the face and lips, tongue, and soft palate. The activities of these muscle groups are regulated by nuclei in the medulla, which are functionally linked to other nearby nuclei involved in the control of respiration.[12] The origin of the burst–pause cycles characteristic of non-nutritive sucking is at present unknown. Cyclic patterning of other behaviors controlled by areas in the brain stem and medulla does occur, as exemplified by periodic breathing.[13] A hypothetical scheme for production of non-nutritive sucking bursts might first involve activation of sensory receptors in the oropharynx by insertion of a pacifier.[14] Then, afferent sensory input from these receptors to the brain stem would trigger a burst of sucking. The pause that occurs between non-nutritive sucking bursts could be produced by decay of afferent sensory activity, or by reciprocal inhibition deriving from other central nuclei. Normal organization of higher cortical areas of the brain may, in fact, not be necessary for this pattern of behavior, for Wolff has observed that infants with anencephaly may suck on a pacifier in a characteristic non-nutritive fashion.[4]

BEHAVIORAL CONSEQUENCES OF NON-NUTRITIVE SUCKING

Non-nutritive sucking may have important effects on the infant's motor activity. Indeed, the calming effect of providing an infant with a pacifier has been well known to generations of mothers. Kessen and Leutzendorff observed that within 5 seconds of insertion of a blind nipple into an infant's mouth, movement and crying both decreased.[15] Sucking also rendered the sleeping infant less responsive to an external stimulus, for the usual burst of diffuse motility occurring in infants during sleep in response to tickling is suppressed during sucking on a pacifier.[16] Non-nutritive sucking may, in addition, alter the central control of active and quiet sleep. Both preterm and term infants exhibit characteristic changes in sleep state and motor activity when supplied with a pacifier. Woodson et al. found that the time spent in both active and quiet sleep increased during non-nutritive sucking, and that the frequency of sleep state changes as well as the time spent in motor activity decreased.[17] Field and Goldson also observed that the opportunity to suck on a pacifier appeared to act as a "sedative" during heelstick blood drawing, decreasing arousal from deep sleep to an alert state as well as fussing and crying.[18] Thus, non-nutritive sucking may simultaneously inhibit other forms of motor behavior. The increase in sleep with concomitant decrease in motor activity that results from non-nutritive sucking could decrease the overall metabolic requirements of the infant, a hypothesis which will be further explored in relation to the effects of non-nutritive sucking on growth and weight gain.

POSTNATAL DEVELOPMENT OF NON-NUTRITIVE SUCKING

Non-nutritive sucking behavior is affected by both the postconceptional and postnatal age of the infant. Wolff has reported that the pattern of non-nutritive sucking before 33 weeks postconceptional age is "less organized" than after 33 to 34 weeks,[4] and that premature infants of 36 to 38 weeks postconceptional age have a higher rate of non-nutritive sucking than a comparable group of premature infants at 35 to 36 weeks (Table 15–2). Dubignon and associates have also documented steady postnatal maturation of non-nutritive sucking patterns in growing premature infants.[19] Furthermore, Wolff observed that the rate of sucking (rate per second per burst) increased between 1 and 6 months of age, then appeared to be extinguished after 6 months in approximately 55% of term infants, with the remainder continuing to suck in the non-nutritive mode into the 2d year of life.[7] In adult life, this behavior is entirely extinguished, with the possible exception of patients with profound neurologic injury accompanied by loss of voluntary motor control.[4]

Non-nutritive sucking behavior does not appear to be dependent on nutritive sucking experience. Lepecq and co-workers have compared the amount of non-nutritive sucking exhibited by two groups of infants, one group provided normal sucking experiences, and a study group fed only by parenteral nutrition.[20] Despite the fact that the study group had a higher incidence of severe gastrointestinal and other medical conditions, the proportion of time spent in non-nutritive sucking during waking and sleep did not differ between the groups. This observation supports the suggestion of Wolff that nutritive and non-nutritive sucking are two functionally independent patterns of oral behavior in human infants.

Nutritive sucking behavior in the immediate postnatal period can be affected by maternal barbiturate therapy prior to delivery. Kron et al. observed that the rate of nutritive sucking, sucking pressure, and milk consumption between 24 and 72 hours of life was greater in infants not exposed to barbiturates in utero.[21] The effect of barbiturates on non-nutritive sucking has not been reported. However, in light of the observations of Kron and associates it is possible that non-nutritive sucking may also be suppressed by maternal analgesia.

Non-nutritive sucking thus emerges as a pattern of behavior distinct from nutritive sucking, possibly unique to the human species. This sucking behavior alters the general motor activity of the infant and may, itself, be altered by post conceptional age, postnatal age, and possibly by drug therapy given to the mother. We will next examine evidence for the effects of non-nutritive sucking on respiration and gastrointestinal function.

ALTERATION OF RESPIRATION DURING NON-NUTRITIVE SUCKING

In 1978 Burroughs et al. first reported an effect of non-nutritive sucking on transcutaneous oxygen tension in preterm infants, observing that infants on assisted ventilation

TABLE 15–2.

Non-nutritive Sucking Rates of Premature Infants Tested in 1st Week After Birth*

Gestational Age	Number of Infants	Mean Frequency/sec		Standard Deviation	
		Mean	Range	SD	Range
33–35 wk	16	1.67±†	1.4–2.0±	0.42†	0.22–0.51
36–38 wk	19	1.87±†	1.5–2.3±	0.19‡	0.11–0.35

*From Wolff PH: The serial organization of sucking in the young infant. *Pediatrics* 1968; 42:943–946. Used by permission.
†$P < .01$.
‡$P > .10$. Significance of difference from normal full-term infants. As tested by Mann Whitney U-test.

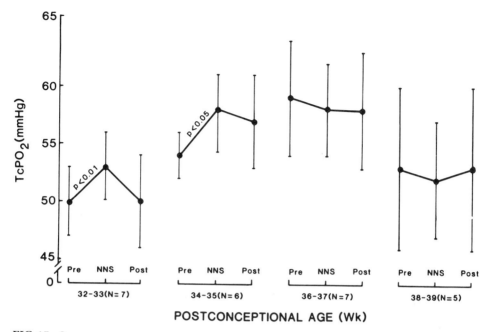

FIG 15–2.
Change in transcutaneous oxygen pressure (tcPO$_2$) in premature infants during non-nutritive sucking. (From Paludetto R, Robertson S, Hack M, et al: Transcutaneous oxygen tension during non-nutritive sucking in preterm infants. *Pediatrics* 1984; 74:539–542. Used by permission.)

exhibited a mean increase in transcutaneous oxygen pressure (tcPO$_2$) of 2 mm Hg during an 8-minute period of non-nutritive sucking.[22] Paludetto et al. confirmed these observations in a group of healthy preterm infants,[23] noting an increase in tcPO$_2$ of 3 to 4 mm Hg in infants of 33 to 34 and 34 to 35 weeks postconceptional age, but not in infants of 36 to 39 weeks (Fig 15–2). The origin of this small improvement in oxygenation is unclear. Paludetto et al. also found an increase in respiratory rate from 49 to as high as 72 breaths/min during non-nutritive sucking bursts of less than 6 seconds' duration (89% of non-nutritive sucking bursts were of this length). Higher respiratory frequency could be one mechanism by which oxygenation is improved during non-nutritive sucking. This observation was confirmed by Mathew et al.,[24] who noted an increased respiratory rate and decreased tidal volume during the intervening pause between non-nutritive sucking bursts, and speculated that pressure fluctuation within the upper airway stimulates receptors in the airway wall, resulting in a reflex increase in respiratory rate.

The *increase* in tcPO$_2$ and respiratory rate noted during non-nutritive sucking is in contrast to the *decrease* in tcPO$_2$ and respiratory rate during nutritive sucking observed in term and preterm infants[25, 26] (Fig 15–3). Stimuli related to the presence of liquid in the upper airway or to repetitive swallowing may be responsible for the relative inhibition of ventilation noted during nutritive sucking. The contributions of alteration in sleep pattern, decrease in spontaneous movement, and upper airway reflexes to the change in oxygenation during non-nutritive sucking have not been separated. It appears unlikely that the very small change in transcutaneous oxygen noted during brief bursts of non-nutritive sucking could, as an isolated effect, so alter the infant's metabolic balance as to significantly improve weight gain.

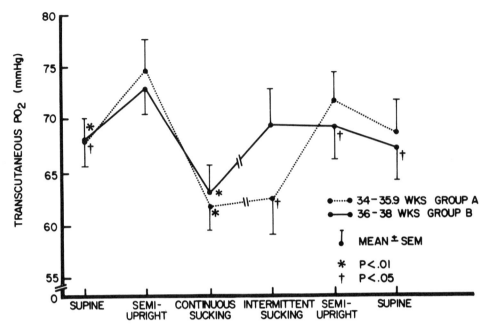

FIG 15–3.

Transcutaneous oxygen pressure (tcPO$_2$) before, during, and after nutritive sucking in premature infants of 34 to 36 weeks and 36 to 38 weeks postconceptional age. The tcPO$_2$ was significantly lower in both groups of infants during continuous sucking. (From Shivpuri C, Martin RJ, Carlo WA, et al: Decreased ventilation in preterm infants during oral feeding. *J Pediatr* 1983; 103:285–289. Used by permission.)

EFFECTS OF NON-NUTRITIVE SUCKING ON GASTROINTESTINAL FUNCTION

Considerable interest has recently focused on the effects of non-nutritive sucking on digestion. Measel and Anderson initially reported that preterm infants who were allowed the opportunity to suck on a pacifier during nasogastric feedings could be discharged from hospital at an earlier date.[1] In 1982, Field et al. reported further evidence of the effects of non-nutritive sucking on preterm infants who were less than 1,800 g in weight and less than 35 weeks postconceptional age.[2] In their study, a treatment group, which sucked on a pacifier during feedings through a nasogastric tube, was compared with a control group of infants without non-nutritive sucking experience. Each infant in the treatment group gained, on average, 2.8 g per day more than the control group; was able to bottle feed 3 days earlier; required 27 fewer tube feedings during hospitalization; and

TABLE 15–3.

Clinical Outcome Variables*

Parameter	Treatment	Control	P
Days of tube feeding	26 ± 21	29 ± 18	.01
No. of tube feedings	219 ± 191	246 ± 171	.05
Average daily weight gain, g	19.3 ± 4.9	16.5 ± 5.5	.05
Length of hospital stay, days	48 ± 21	56 ± 18	.05
Hospital cost	$16,800 ± $13,959	$20,294 ± $11,339	.01

*Values are means ± SD. From Field T, Ignatoff E, Stringer S, et al: Non-nutritive sucking during tube feedings: Effects on preterm neonates in an intensive care unit. *Pediatrics* 1982; 70:381–384. Used by permission.

was discharged on average 8 days sooner than controls, at a savings of $3,500 in hospital costs (Table 15-3). All of these outcome variables were related by the authors to improved weight gain. In 1983, Bernbaum et al.[3] also evaluated the effects of non-nutritive sucking on growth of premature infants. When allowed to suck on a pacifier during gavage feeding, infants exhibited more sucks per burst of non-nutritive sucking, a mean improvement in weight gain of 8.6 g per infant per day by the 2d week of study, and an 8% reduction in intestinal transit time from mouth to rectum[3] (Fig 15-4). Decreases in total time of oral feeding and average length of hospital stay were also noted.

On the basis of these studies, it has been suggested that provision of a pacifier during gavage feeding be employed so as to improve infants' weight gain. However, a number of questions about the observed effects of non-nutritive sucking remain to be answered. Curiously, despite the increase in weight gain that occurred, growth in head circumference, and length, and the quantity of gastric residuals were not altered by non-nutritive sucking experience.[3] This discrepancy has not been explained. In addition,

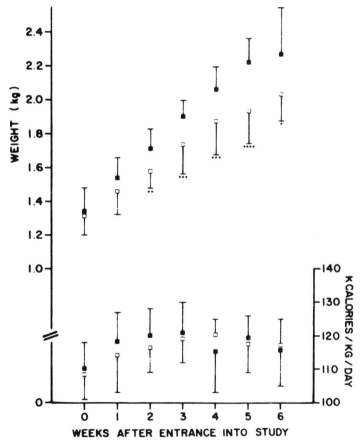

FIG 15-4.
Weight and caloric intake in the study group provided with a pacifier during feeding, and control infants. Weight gain significantly increased during the 2d week after entrance into the study in the group of infants in which non-nutritive sucking was encouraged. *Open squares* = control infants; *filled squares* = infants provided with non-nutritive sucking; *one dot* = P < 0.05; *two dots* = P < 0.02; *three dots* = P < 0.01; *four dots* = P < 0.001. (From Bernbaum JC, Pereira GR, Watkins JB, et al: Nonnutritive sucking during gavage feeding enhances growth and maturation in premature infants. *Pediatrics* 1983; 71:41-45. Used by permission.)

confounding differences in nursing or physician behavior that could have yielded improved weight gain in the treated group cannot be ruled out, for these studies could not be performed in a blinded fashion. Finally, because non-nutritive sucking patterns exhibit dependence on postconceptional age, the utility of this therapy in infants of less than 30 weeks gestation remains to be demonstrated.

By what mechanisms could non-nutritive sucking improve weight gain in premature infants? Theoretical possibilities that have been proposed include a decrease in caloric expenditure for movement; stimulation of vagal efferent activity, leading to the release of insulin and gastrointestinal hormones; improved intestinal absorption of foodstuffs; and a decrease in gastric emptying time. Premature infants do appear to have a decreased hormonal response to ingestion of formula, without the normal rise in growth hormone, gastrin, and enteroglucagon observed in the term infant.[27] However, Marchini et al.[28] noted a significant increase in the plasma level of insulin in term infants and a lesser (non-significant) increase in preterm infants after non-nutritive sucking on a pacifier prior to a meal (Fig 15–5). Plasma gastrin and somatostatin levels, in contrast, were not significantly altered during non-nutritive sucking. Vagal activation due to sham feeding in dogs and humans has been reported to cause a release of insulin and gastrin.[28–31] Marchini and co-workers have suggested that activation of this same pathway in human infants during non-nutritive sucking could lead to the increase in insulin levels that they described.[28] An increase in circulating insulin, in turn, could improve glucose utilization during feedings accompanied by non-nutritive sucking and may contribute to the increase in weight gain noted.

The effects of non-nutritive sucking on gastric emptying and intestinal transit time are somewhat controversial. Hypothetically, more rapid gastric emptying could allow the preterm infant to tolerate larger feedings and achieve better weight gain. Bernbaum et al. observed an 8% decrease in mouth to rectum transit time during non-nutritive sucking, but no effect on gastric residuals.[3] Widstrom et al. reported a decrease in somatostatin levels in infants at 3 hours after feedings which was not, however, accompanied by a significant change in gastric retention.[32] Szabo et al. also found no effect of non-nutritive sucking on gastric emptying up to 30 minutes following a gavage feed,[33] and DeCurtis et al. observed no effect of non-nutritive sucking on intestinal transit time.[34] The variation in results between these studies could be due to a number of technical differences, including time of sampling after feeding. At present, the weight of evidence does not support a pronounced effect of non-nutritive sucking on either gastric emptying or intestinal transit time. Thus the effects of non-nutritive sucking on these

FIG 15–5.
Plasma insulin concentrations in full-term infants before and during non-nutritive sucking (n = 12). *Upper bracket with arrows denotes time for* sucking. The rise from basal to 5-minute value is significant; $P < .01$. Insulin concentrations ranged from 10 to 20 μU/mL plasma. (From Marchini G, Lagercrantz H, Feuerberg Y, et al: The effect of non-nutritive sucking on plasma insulin, gastrin, and somatostatin levels in infants. *Acta Paediatr Scand* 1987; 76:573–578. Used by permission.)

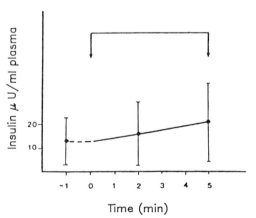

parameters alone appear unlikely to account for improvement in weight gain in premature infants.

If non-nutritive sucking significantly increases daily weight gain, one would expect energy, fat, or nitrogen balances to be altered by this behavior. The only information available on this question derives from the study of DeCurtis et al. in 1986.[34] Fat, total nitrogen, and energy content of milk, stools, and urine were measured over 3-day periods during which infants were gavage fed with or without non-nutritive sucking experience. Non-nutritive sucking did not alter energy or nitrogen balance, net nitrogen utilization, or fat absorption. The lack of a positive effect of non-nutritive sucking on these aspects of metabolism could have been due to the short duration of the study (3 days), for, as the authors point out, Bernbaum et al. noted no significant effect of non-nutritive sucking on weight gain during the first 2 weeks of their study.[3] The relatively small effect of non-nutritive sucking on daily weight gain may, itself, be an obstacle to such metabolic studies. Because non-nutritive sucking has been reported to produce only a 2- to 8-g average increase in weight gain per day in infants of 1,300 to 1,800 g weight,[2, 3] measurement of the effects of this very small weight change on daily energy balance may require proportionally larger group sizes to avoid a type II statistical error.

In summary, at present no incontrovertible evidence has been found for a single, significant effect of non-nutritive sucking on any particular aspect of metabolism other than serum insulin level in term infants. It is possible that the individual, relatively small effects of non-nutritive sucking on transcutaneous oxygen tension, serum insulin level, and motor activity may act in concert to produce the improvement in weight observed.[2, 3] Further exploration of the effects of sucking behavior on diverse phenomena such as intestinal hormone release; absorption of carbohydrate, fat, and protein; or induction of enzymes within the intestinal villi may be required before we can fully describe the mechanisms by which non-nutritive sucking may alter weight gain in premature infants.

REFERENCES

1. Measel CP, Anderson GC: Non-nutritive sucking during tube feedings: Effect upon clinical course in premature infants. *J Obstet Gynecol Neonatal Nurs* 1979; 8:265–272.
2. Field T, Ignatoff E, Stringer S, et al: Non-nutritive sucking during tube feedings: Effects on preterm neonates in an intensive care unit. *Pediatrics* 1982; 70:381–384.
3. Bernbaum JC, Pereira GR, Watkins JB, et al: Non-nutritive sucking during gavage feeding enhances growth and maturation in premature infants. *Pediatrics* 1983; 71:41–45.
4. Wolff PH: The serial organization of sucking in the young infant. *Pediatrics* 1968; 42:943–956.
5. Koepke JE, Barnes P: Amount of sucking when a sucking object is readily available to human newborns. *Child Dev* 1982: 53:978–983.
6. Sameroff A: Non-nutritive sucking in newborns under visual and auditory stimulation. *Child Dev* 1967; 38:443–452.
7. Wolff PH: The causes, controls, and organization of behavior in the newborn. *Psychol Issues, monograph,* vol V, no. 1. New York, International Universities Press, 1966.
8. Kaye H: Infant sucking behavior and its modifications, in Lipsett LP, Spiller CC (eds): *Advances in Child Development,* vol 3. New York, Academic Press, 1968, pp 1–52.
9. Wolff PH: Sucking patterns of infant mammals. *Brain Behav Evol* 1968; 1:354–367.
10. Koepke JE, Pribram KH: Effect of milk on maintenance of sucking behavior in kittens from birth to six months. *J Comp Physiol Psychol* 1971; 75:363–377.
11. Blass EM, Teicher MH: Suckling. *Science* 1980; 210:15–22.

12. Sumi T: Coordination of neural organization of respiration and deglutition: Its change with postnatal maturation, in Bosma JF (ed): *Oral Sensation and Perception.* Springfield, Ill, Charles C Thomas, 1972, pp 145–157.

13. Cherniak NS: Respiratory dysrhythmias during sleep. *N Engl J Med* 1981; 305:325–330.

14. Munger B: Specificity in the development of sensory receptors in primate oral mucosa, in Bosma JF, Showacre J (eds): *Development of Upper Respiratory Anatomy and Function. Implications for Sudden Death Syndrome,* Washington, US Government Printing Office, 1975, pp 96–119.

15. Kessen W, Leutzendorff AM: The effect of non-nutritive sucking on movement in the human newborn. *J Comp Physiol Psychol* 1963; 56:69–72.

16. Wolff P, Simmons MA: Non-nutritive sucking and response thresholds in young infants. *Child Dev* 1967; 38:631–638.

17. Woodson R, Drinkburn J, Hamilton C: Effects of non-nutritive sucking on state and activity: Term-preterm comparisons. *Infant Behav Dev* 1985; 8:435–441.

18. Field T, Goldson E: Pacifying effects of non-nutritive sucking on term and pre-term neonates during heelstick procedures. *Pediatrics* 1984; 74:1012–1015.

19. Dubignon JM, Campbell D, Partington MW: The development of non-nutritive sucking in premature infants. *Biol Neonate* 1969; 14:270–278.

20. Lepecq JC, Regoard MT, Salzarulo P: Spontaneous non-nutritive sucking in continuously fed infants. *Early Hum Dev* 1985; 12:279–284.

21. Kron RE, Stein M, Goddard KE: Newborn sucking behavior affected by obstetric sedation. *Pediatrics* 1966; 37:1012–1016.

22. Burroughs AK, Asonye OU, Anderson-Shanklin GC, et al: The effect of non-nutritive sucking on transcutaneous oxygen tension in noncrying, preterm neonates. *Res Nurs Health* 1978; 1:69–75.

23. Paludetto R, Robertson SS, Hack M, et al: Transcutaneous oxygen tension during nonnutritive sucking in preterm infants. *Pediatrics* 1984; 74:539–542.

24. Mathew OP, Clark ML, Pronske MH: Breathing pattern of neonates during non-nutritive sucking. *Pediatr Pulmonol* 1985; 1:204–206.

25. Shivpuri CR, Martin RJ, Carlo WA, et al: Decreased ventilation in preterm infants during oral feeding. *J Pediatr* 1983; 103:285–289.

26. Mathew OP, Clark ML, Pronske M, et al: Breathing pattern and ventilation during oral feeding in term newborn infants. *J Pediatr* 1985; 106:810–813.

27. Lucas A, Bloom SR, Aynsley-Green A: Metabolic and endocrine events at the time of the first feed of human milk in preterm and term infants. *Arch Dis Child* 1978; 53:731–736.

28. Marchini G, Lagercrantz H, Feuerberg Y, et al: The effect of non-nutritive sucking on plasma insulin, gastrin, and somatostatin levels in infants. *Acta Paediatr Scand* 1987; 76:573–578.

29. Nilsson G, Uvnas-Wallenstein K: Effect of teasing, sham feeding, and feeding on plasma insulin concentrations in dogs, in *Radioimmunoassay: Methodology and Applications in Physiol and Clinical Studies,* Commemorative issue for Solomon A. Berson, Supplement series, vol 5. Stuttgart, Thieme, 1974.

30. Uvnas B, Uvnas-Wallenstein K, Nilsson G: Release of gastrin on vagal stimulation in the cat. *Acta Physiol Scand* 1975; 94:167–176.

31. Feldman M, Walsh J: Acid inhibition of sham feeding—stimulated gastrin release and gastric acid secretion: Effects of atropine. *Gastroenterology* 1980; 78:772–776.

32. Widstrom A-M, Marchini G, Mathiesen AS, et al: Non-nutritive sucking in tube fed premature infants: Effects on gastric motility and gastric contents of somatostatin. *J Pediatr Gastroenterol Nutr* 1988: 7:517–523.

33. Szabo JS, Hellemeier AC, Oh W: Effect of non-nutritive and nutritive suck on gastric emptying in premature infants. *J Pedaitr Gastroenterol Nutr* 1985; 4:348–351.

34. DeCurtis M, McIntosh N, Ventura V, et al: Effect of non-nutritive sucking on nutrient retention in preterm infants. *J Pediatr* 1986; 109:888–890.

PART IV

Disorders

Chapter 16

Nutritional Requirements of the Extremely-Low-Birth-Weight Infant

William W. Hay, Jr., M.D.

The extremely low-birth-weight (ELBW) infant weighs less than 1,000 g and has a gestational age less than 28 weeks. At birth many are small for gestational age and appear under nourished. More than 10 years ago, such infants very rarely survived. Today ELBW infants represent somewhat less than 1% of all deliveries. While the mortality rate is still high, the survival rate over the past 10 years has improved dramatically from approximately 50% to nearly 80% in the 750 to 1,000 g group and from approximately 10% to nearly 50% in the 500 to 750 g group. Much of the recent improvement in survival has been accomplished with the aid of selective nutritional management, following earlier successful treatment of temperature instability, dehydration, profound hypoglycemia, and acidosis. Cardiorespiratory problems (particularly pulmonary insufficiency), neurologic disasters (especially intracranial hemorrhage), and sepsis continue to cause most morbidity and the majority of deaths.

The vulnerability of the ELBW infant to inadequate nutritional intake and thus part of the reason for the successful treatment of such infants with improved nutritional management is illustrated in Figure 16–1.[1] The less than 1,000 g ELBW infant has an endogenous energy reserve, defined arbitrarily as the sum of all nonprotein reserves plus one third of protein reserves, of only about 200 kcal. Even at an extremely low estimate of energy expenditure of 50 to 60 kcal/day/kg, such reserves could maintain energy balance for only 3 to 4 days without an exogenous energy supply. Increased fat and glycogen stores as well as increased muscle mass (protein reserve) relative to organs with high metabolic rates (brain, liver, heart) allow a longer estimated survival period for older and larger infants.

The addition of exogenous nutrients of all kinds to such infants now is standard medical practice, not only extending survival but achieving growth and preventing or ameliorating many nutritional deficiencies that otherwise caused general ill health as well as specific diseases. Empirical success, however, does not answer directly the question, "What are the nutritional requirements of the ELBW infant," and is a weak measure of the optimal nutrition that should be provided for such infants. There have been few attempts to quantify nutritional intakes in such infants or to measure the rates

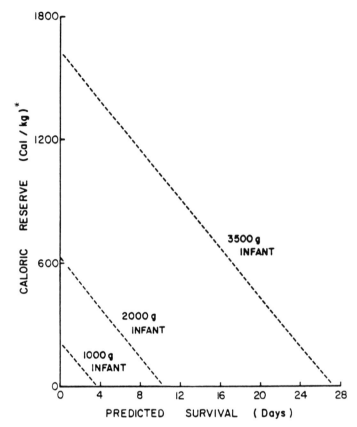

FIG 16–1.
Estimated survival time of starved infants weighing 1,000, 2,000, and 3,500 g at birth, assuming no nutritional supply and energy derived only from all nonprotein plus one third of protein reserves. (From Kashyap S: Nutritional management of the extremely-low-birth-weight infant, in Cowett RM, Hay WW Jr (eds): *The Micropremi: The Next Frontier.* Report of the 99th Ross Conference on Pediatric Research. Columbus, Ohio, Ross Laboratories, 1990; pp 115–119. Reproduced with permission.)

of metabolism and growth that the nutrients serve. Even comparison of nutrients with respect to nutrient balance or growth has not been accomplished. Thus, a rational basis for nutritional management of the ELBW is not available, except by rather tenuous extrapolation from larger, older, more mature infants. The following discussion will present a theoretical basis for some aspects of nutrition of the ELBW infant, and will focus also on some more recent practical attempts to assess what matters in feeding the ELBW infant.

I. BIOLOGIC BASES OF NUTRITIONAL REQUIREMENTS IN THE ELBW INFANT

Compared with older, more mature preterm infants, ELBW infants are increasingly different in those biologic factors that determine nutritional requirements: body composition, growth rate, metabolic rate, and the capacity for metabolic regulation. Nevertheless, in 1977, the American Academy of Pediatrics stated that the major goal of nutrition of low birth weight, preterm infants should be "the optimal diet . . . that supports a rate of growth approximating that of the third trimester of intrauterine life, without imposing stress on the developing metabolic and excretory system."[2] This statement is important but emphasizes an unfounded, even if attractive, goal. Importantly, it fails to address two important questions: (1) what are the nutritional requirements of these infants that contributed to their apparent in utero growth rate; and (2) what are the unique body compositions, growth rates, metabolic rates, and metabolic capacities of these infants at different developmental stages? Answers to these questions are largely unknown for ELBW human infants. One approach to answering them is to consider comparative fetal data from animals and cross-sectional data obtained from infants born prematurely, even though there is no ideal fetal animal model to represent human development, and ELBW preterm infants may or may not represent the results of normal intra-uterine nutrition, metabolism, or growth.

Several experimental methods with animal models and "representative" ELBW, preterm infants have been used to study nutritional requirements in fetal and neonatal life.[3] One method involves estimating nutritional requirements of ELBW infants from measurements of accretion rates of selected nutrients that are part of the "normal" fetal in utero accretion rate. This approach is limited because it provides only a minimum estimate of nutrient requirements; it does not measure or quantify those nutrient requirements that are necessary to process the accretion of nutrients, and it does not take into account the possibility that those nutrients involved in accretion can also contribute to energy production and metabolic turnover process. A second method involves measuring the provision of nutrients at "normal" net uptake rates by the umbilical circulation.

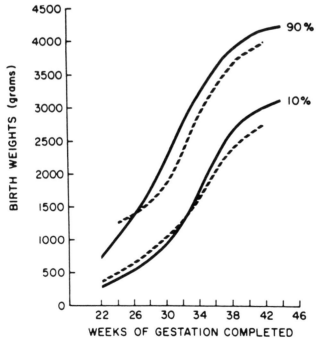

FIG 16–2.
Birth-weight percentiles for gestational age. *Solid line* represents California total single live births, 1970–1976; *dotted line* represents Colorado General Hospital live births, 1948–1960. (Modified by Creasy RK, Resnik R: Intrauterine growth retardation, in Creasy RK, Resnik R (eds): *Maternal-Fetal Medicine*, ed 2. Philadelphia, WB Saunders Co, 1989, pp 549–564; from Williams RL, Creasy RK, Cunningham GC, et al: *Obstet Gynecol* 1982; 59:624. Reproduced with permission.)

This measurement more closely measures the fetal requirements for nutrient accretion plus utilization rates but does not distinguish between these rates. A third method involves measuring the supply of nutrients at normal fetal net utilization rates; the difference between utilization and uptake will determine fetal contributions to fetal nutritional requirements such as nutrient substrate cycling within the placenta, substrate cycling between the placental and fetal tissues, and substrate cycling within fetal tissues such as with glycogenesis/glycogenolysis. Finally, studies can be conducted in the newborn infant quantifying the nutrient requirements according to the normal rate of intake of nutrients from "normal" human milk in "normal" infants.

Fetal Growth Rates to Estimate Those of ELBW Infants

Most estimates of fetal growth rate are based on cross-sectional measurements of weights of live born, preterm, term and post-term infants (Fig 16–2).[4] More recently,

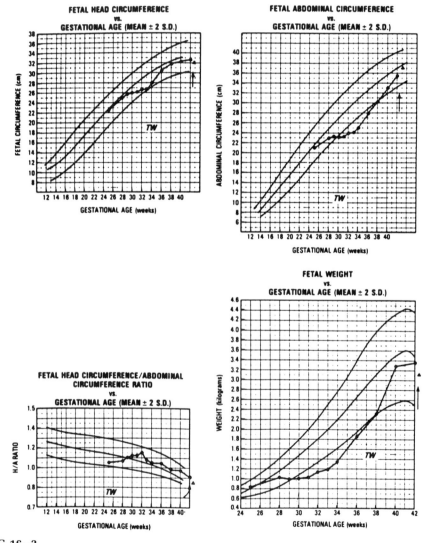

FIG 16–3.
Median growth rate curves for single and multiple births in California, 1970–1976. (From Williams RL, Creasy RK, Cunningham GC, et al: *Obstet Gynecol* 1982; 59:624. Reprinted with permission.)

incremental changes in estimated fetal weight have been assessed using ultrasound measurements of fetal size at different gestational ages coupled with weight at birth (Fig 16–3).[5] Both Figures 16–2 and 16–3 document a sigmoidal growth curve for the fetus with a maximal incremental rate (g/gestational age) in the 22 to 34-week period. When expressed as a velocity of growth (g/day) at different gestational ages (Fig 16–4), the low velocity in the mid-gestational period is approached once again as the fetus approaches term. Animal data are similar.[6] On a weight-specific basis, however, fetal growth rate actually declines with gestational age (Fig 16–5). Thus, nutritional requirements for growth, when estimated from the specific weight of the fetus, are actually much higher in the early fetus (Table 16–1).[7, 8] The implication that similar higher weight-specific requirements apply to the postnatal ELBW infant seems logical but only indirectly has been tested by noting empirically that higher weight-specific nutrient intakes are necessary to produce growth in such infants compared to older, more mature infants. For example 3 to 4 g/day/kg of protein appears necessary to support the estimated in utero growth rate in healthy, growing ELBW infants compared to 1.5 to 2.5 g/day/kg for term infants.[9] The relatively high growth promoting protein requirement of the fetus in utero has led to development of protein-enriched formulas containing 2 or more g/100 ml, while term infants do well with milk that contains only 1.3 to 1.5 g/100 ml.

Weight-specific growth also follows different percentiles across the population of fetuses in early gestation. Table 16–2 presents results from four studies showing an average of 3.2 g/day/kg difference in the specific growth rate of tenth percentile small for gestational age (SGA) infants compared with that of the ninetieth percentile large for

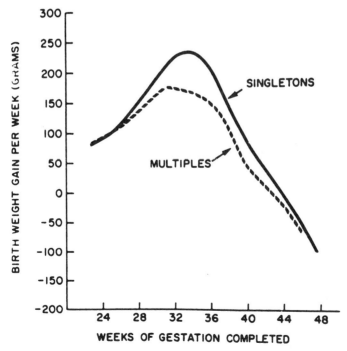

FIG 16–4.

Serial fetal body measurements in a mother with severe ulcerative colitis. Note that fetal growth begins to decrease markedly in mid-gestation but returns to normal following the initiation of central hyperalimentation at approximately 28 to 30 weeks. (From Creasy RK, Resnik R: Intrauterine growth retardation, in Creasy RK, Resnik (eds): *Maternal-Fetal Medicine,* ed 2. Philadelphia, WB Saunders Co, 1989, pp 549–564. Reproduced by permission.)

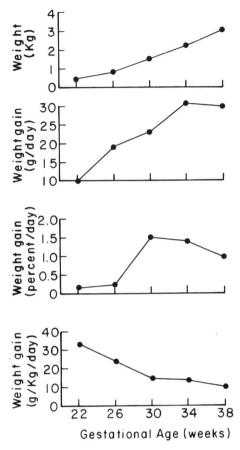

FIG 16–5.

Mean changes in weight and weight gain over the second half of gestation in human infants based on cross-sectional data at birth. Weight gain is progressive but the percent gain peaks at about 30 weeks and the weight-specific gain decreases progressively over this half of gestation. (Adapted from data of Widdowsown EM: Changes in body proportion and composition during growth, in Davis JA, Dobbing J (eds.): *Scientific Foundations of Paediatrics*. Philadelphia, WB Saunders Co, 1974, pp 44–45.).

gestational age (LGA) infants.[10–14] The implication from such data is that SGA infants require approximately 22% more nutrient intake per body weight than do LGA infants. This implication has not been tested, although recent studies in more mature SGA infants and appropriate for gestational age (AGA) controls show a higher leucine disposal rate in the SGA infants (measured with leucine tracer methodology), implying a higher protein requirement in the SGA infants. Consideration of nutritional requirements for ELBW infants also should reflect the unique body chemical and structural composition of ELBW infants (Table 16–3). For example, body water content and the distribution of water between the extracellular space (ECF) and the intracellular space (ICF) change markedly (decrease) in the fetus over the second half of gestation.[6] This is not due to changes in renal function or transepidermal water loss alone (obviously the fetus is growing in utero in the "humidified" environment of the amniotic fluid), but also, at least in part, to an increase in the extracellular matrix content of glycoproteins and mucopolysaccharides. The extracellular matrix is probably the most active area of the fetal body for tissue synthesis, specifically glycoproteins and mucopolysaccharides. The fur-

TABLE 16–1.

Body Composition: Accretion of Selected Components in the Extremely-Low-Birth-Weight and the Low Birth Weight Infant*

Accretion	24th to 25th Week Average Body Weight 730 g	30th to 31st Week Average Body Weight 1,570 g
Total body weight g/day/kg	16.6	15.6
Protein g/100 g	10.9	12.4
Lipid g/100 g	4.7	11.8
Calcium mg/100 g	535	626
Sodium mg/100 g	182	170

*Adapted from MacLean WC: What matters in feeding the extremely-low-birthweight infant?, in Cowett RM, Hay WW Jr (eds): *The Micropremi: The Next Frontier*. Report of the 99th Ross Conference on Pediatric Research. Columbus, Ohio, Ross Laboratories, 1990, pp 115–119. Calculated from data from Zeigler EE, O'Donnell AM, Nelson SE, et al: *Growth* 1976; 40:329–341.

TABLE 16–2.

Specific Growth Rate for Fetuses Growing Along Different Percentiles (g/day/kg)*

Author	10th Percentile	50th Percentile	90th Percentile
Lubchenko et al[11]	15.6	14.4	12.6
Kloosterman[12]	16.6	15.1	14.7
Babson et al[13]	18.9	16.0	13.9
Keen and Pearce[14]	18.0	16.1	15.3

*Adapted from Wharton BA (ed): *Nutrition and Feeding of Preterm Infants*. Oxford, Blackwell Scientific Publications, 1987, p 10.

TABLE 16–3.

Body Components (Expressed as Percent Body Weight) of the Premature and Full-Term Infant at Birth, Compared With the Fetus*

	Fetus (0.1 kg)	Fetus (0.5 kg)	Preterm (1.0 kg)	Preterm (1.5 kg)	Full-Term (3.3 kg)
Water	90.0	86.6	85.0	82.7	70.9
Fat	0.6	1.2	2.3	4.0	13.5
Protein	6.3	8.6	8.6	9.0	11.9
Calcium	0.3	0.5	0.6	0.7	0.8
Phosphorus	0.2	0.3	0.3	0.4	0.5
Sodium	0.26	0.22	0.21	0.19	0.18
Potassium	0.16	0.16	0.17	0.17	0.17
Chloride	0.27	0.25	0.23	0.22	0.17

*Adapted from Widdowsown EM: Changes in body proportion and composition during growth, in Davis JA, Dobbing J (eds): *Scientific Foundations of Paediatrics*. Philadelphia, WB Saunders Co, 1974, pp 44–45.

ther loss of ECF and decrease in the ECF/ICF distribution after birth accentuates the developmental pattern. These postnatal changes appear to be persistent, reducing the weight of the fetus but not altering the growth rate.

Another aspect of fetal body composition that changes over the second half of gestation but is unique to the human infant is the deposition of white fat adipose tissue. All mammalian fetuses deposit brown fat, approximately to the same fraction of body weight, but the major difference in body fat composition occurs in those species that transport lipids across the placenta. The human placenta is the most capable of transporting fat; as a result the human fetus produces about 18 to 20 percent of body weight as fat at term.[9] There is no evidence that fetal white fat adipose tissue deposition serves a useful purpose, in spite of several teleological explanations including thermoregulation and energy storage. However, the normal infant who consumes only milk continues to lay down white fat over the first several months of life, actually increasing the percent of body weight as fat to as high as 25%, suggesting that even postnatally fat deposition may have some biologic purpose.[15]

Fat deposition does not occur uniformly among infants. Some infants are fat-deficient (thin) and some have excessive fat deposition, appearing, in fact, obese. Figure 16–6 (left panel) suggests that such patterns are present as growth rates in utero but it must be appreciated that such data come from cross sectional, body composition studies at birth.[15] The same growth curves for body fat composition during fetal life apply also to body structure (see Fig 16–6, right panel), reflecting nitrogen balance and non-fat dry weight.[15] Whether or not diet should be modified to achieve or maintain one form or another of such growth patterns that are based on body composition at birth rather than true in utero growth rates will require more definitive information about the value of fat in the body or the value of being large or small. Growth patterns must be interpreted with respect to how a specific baby should grow, not necessarily with respect to how big or how fat, how small or how thin they can be made to grow either with over-feeding or under-feeding.

Another determinant of fetal and perhaps ELBW infant nutritional requirements is fetal metabolic rate. To study metabolic rate and the metabolism of specific infants in early gestation, Battaglia and Meschia recently developed a model of catheterization of vessels in the placental cotyledons of fetal sheep at 70 to 80 days or about 50% of term gestation.[16] Such fetuses weigh about 150 to 250 g or about 5% of term weight. This technical approach broadens the period of gestation in which direct measurements can be made of normal in utero growth and metabolism. Figure 16–7 presents results of measurements of net fetal oxygen consumption vs. gestational age.[17] The increase in absolute oxygen consumption with gestational age appears to be exponential. On a wet weight-specific basis, however, there is no significant change in oxygen consumption per g of body weight over the second half of gestation. On a dry-weight specific basis, there is a dramatic decrease in the metabolic rate. This change in metabolic rate indicates that comparable changes must take place for nutrient turnover and thus for nutrient requirements.

Glucose is the major nonprotein caloric source for fetal oxidative metabolism and at 75 days or about 50% of gestation glucose consumption per wet weight is about twice that near term (9.4 vs. 4.9 mg/min/kg wet weight).[18] On a dry weight basis, glucose consumption rate in mid-gestation is about three and a half to four times as great as that near term (82.5 vs 23.0 mg/min/kg dry weight), consistent with the higher dry weight-specific oxygen consumption rate at mid-gestation and thus the necessity for having a larger energy supply earlier in gestation.

Given a high metabolic rate in early fetal life and a high rate of glucose utilization, it might be expected that insulin sensitivity would be greater than that at term. Insulin infusions and insulin-glucose clamp experiments in fetal sheep have demonstrated an increase in fetal glucose utilization rate (GUR) which was statistically significant and positive in every case.[19] The GUR response to insulin on a wet weight basis was greater near term but on a dry weight basis, the increase in glucose utilization rate in response to an increase in insulin concentration at mid-gestation was several fold greater than that near term. Insulin receptors on fetal cells are quite high early in fetal life, decreasing somewhat near term before falling to much lower levels characteristic of older infants and adults.[20] In the human preterm neonate, insulin sensitivity has been variably re-

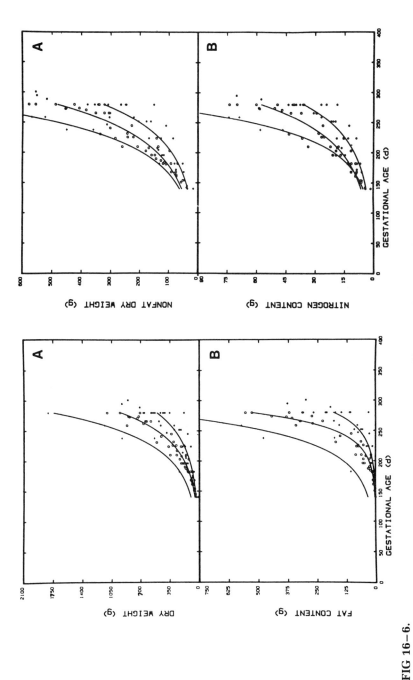

FIG 16–6.

Cross-sectional data of body composition of "normal" infants at birth at different gestational ages. It is not apparent, however, that these cross-sectional data depict in utero growth curves. Also, the preponderance of small-for-gestational-age infants (*lower curve*) vs. large-for-gestational-age infants (*upper curve*) suggests that these infants were not as "normal" as indicated.

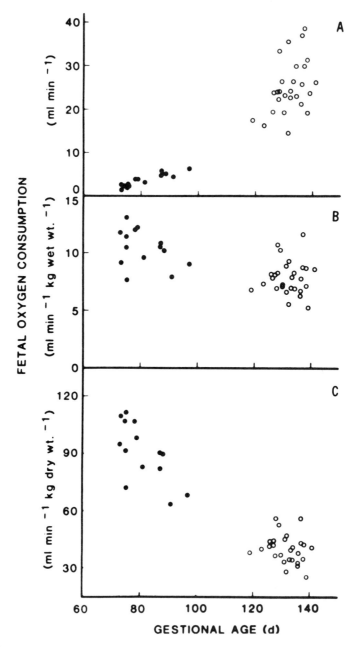

FIG 16–7.
Oxygen consumption ($\dot{V}\ O_2$) in chronic, unstressed fetal sheep at different gestational ages plotted in absolute values **(A),** wet-weight-specific values **(B),** and dry-weight-specific values **(C)** at 73–97 days *(closed circles)* and 119–141 days *(open circles)*. The decrease in dry-weight-specific $\dot{V}\ O_2$ with gestational age is consistent with a decreasing protein synthetic rate (see Fig 16–8) and a decrease in the relative proportion of body weight contributed by high-$\dot{V}\ O_2$ organs (brain, heart, liver, kidney, etc.). (From Bell AW, Kennaugh JM, Battaglia FC, et al: Metabolic and circulatory studies of fetal lamb at midgestation. *Am J Physiol* 1986; 250:E538–E544. Reproduced by permission.)

ported to be "sluggish," "normal," or "brisk."[21, 22, 23] Probably much of this variability is due to immeasurable but significant effects of counter-regulatory hormones (e.g., glucagon, cortisol, growth hormone, and epinephrine). Thus it remains to be determined whether current trials to supplement intravenous nutrient infusions with insulin infusions in ELBW infants, allegedly to promote energy balance, protein (nitrogen) balance, growth, and normoglycemia, will justify insulin infusion in more infants than those whose glucose concentrations are considered dangerously high.[22, 24] Certainly there are many potential adverse effects of insulin infusion, including tachycardia, hypoxemia, increased metabolic rate, fatty infiltration of the liver, electrolyte imbalance, severe hypoglycemia, and the potential interference with other growth hormones.[24–26]

Lipid metabolism in the early gestation fetus, and by inference in the ELBW infant, is probably limited.[27] Most mammals do not transport lipid across the placenta to the fetus in any appreciable amount.[28] Fetal lipid deposition in such cases is produced by fetal synthetic processes from glycerol, lactate, acetate, and glucose.[29] In the human, placental lipid transfer (fatty acids, and particularly essential fatty acids) is much greater, but at mid-gestation, there is very little net lipid deposition. Over the second half of gestation, however, lipid deposition increases markedly, accounting for up to about 50% of caloric requirements.[9] Essential fatty acid (EFA) stores increase proportionate to total lipid uptake and deposition. From 26 to 40 weeks, a typical infant would deposit 550 g (~5000 kcal) of lipid into adipocytes that increase in size and number over gestation. Factors stimulating and regulating the development of adipocytes are not known. Relative carnitine deficiency appears to limit total fatty acid oxidation in the fetus and ELBW infants.[30] Carnitine facilitates the transport of long-chain fatty acids across the mitochondrial membrane. Carnitine is synthesized in the body but synthesis in the fetus and preterm infant appears limited. In preterm infants not supplemented with carnitine, carnitine concentration falls even in the presence of adequate precursor amino acid concentrations. There clearly is sufficient carnitine in term infants to promote fatty acid oxidation, evidenced by a dramatic postnatal decrease in RQ in response to stress-induced lipolysis.[31] This process has not been studied in preterm ELBW infants in whom fatty acid clearance is diminished. These observations indicate that while fatty acids (and especially essential fatty acids) are necessary for normal fetal growth, much remains to be learned about their role in oxidative metabolism and their requirements for lipid synthesis.

Fetal protein metabolism also demonstrates unique relations to metabolic rate and nutrient turnover in early gestation. For example, protein accretion rate or protein growth rate estimated from the fractional rate of growth (Fig 16–8, data in fetal sheep) decreases with gestation but not nearly as rapidly as does the protein synthetic rate (shown in Figure 16–8 as the fractional protein synthetic rate).[32, 33] Such a high protein synthetic rate relative to growth rate indicates a similarly high rate of protein catabolism, providing yet another measure of why there is a higher weight-specific oxygen consumption rate in the early fetus and why this weight-specific oxygen consumption rate decreases over gestation in a normal fashion. However, the decrease in weight-specific metabolic rate over gestation is due not just to intrinsic changes in protein synthetic rate, but to a decrease in the relative amount of high metabolic rate tissues that are in the body. For example, liver, kidney, brain, and heart have relatively high fractional protein synthetic and oxygen consumption rates; the fractional protein synthetic rate and oxygen consumption rate of skeletal muscle is relatively low (Table 16–4).[28, 34] As development proceeds during gestation, the mass of skeletal muscle increases relative to that of the more metabolically active organs, thereby reducing the proportion of body mass

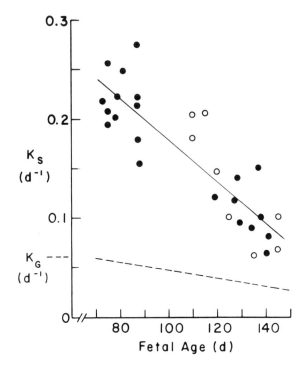

FIG 16–8.
Fractional protein synthetic rate (K_S) in fetal sheep decreases with gestational age at a greater rate than does fractional growth rate (K_G). *Closed circles* represent data derived from leucine tracer, *open circles* represent data derived from lysine tracer. Consistent with oxygen-consumption data, K_S data indicate much higher amino acid/nitrogen requirements in earlier gestation and provide a more sensitive and accurate indication of nutritional needs than does growth rate, even though both define a much different metabolism in the earlier fetus. (From Meier PR, Peterson RG, Bonds DR, et al: Rates of protein synthesis and turnover in fetal life. *Am J Physiol* 1981; 240:E320–E324. Reproduced with permission.)

with the higher metabolic rate and the higher protein synthetic rate (Table 16–5).[28]

Figure 16–9 shows data from fetal sheep collected by Lemons and associates in which the net umbilical (fetal) uptake of selected amino acids are compared with their carcass (tissue accretion) requirements.[36] These data show quite a large difference between the umbilical uptakes and the carcass requirements for nearly all of the individual

TABLE 16–4.

Fractional Synthesis Rate*

Organ	Young (%/day)	Adult (%/day)
Liver	57	54
Kidney	50	51
Brain	17	11
Heart	19	11
Skeletal/muscle	15	5

*Data from Waterlow JC, Garlick PJ, Millard DJ: *Protein Turnover in Mammalian Tissues and in the Whole Body.* Amsterdam, Elsevier/North Holland Biomedical Press, 1978; as presented in Battaglia FC, Meschia G: *An Introduction to Fetal Physiology.* Orlando, Florida, Academic Press, 1986, p 119. Used by permission.

TABLE 16–5.

Organ Weight as Percent of Body Weight*

	50% Gestation	67% Gestation	90% Gestation
Liver	6.5	5.1	3.1
Kidneys	1.6	1.2	0.7
Heart	0.9	0.8	0.8
Brain	3.4	2.9	1.7
Hindquarters	14.5	15.1	22.0

*From Bell AW, Battaglia FC, Meschia G: *J Nutr*, 1987; 117:1181–1186. Used by permission.

amino acids demonstrating a large rate of amino acid utilization other than for protein accretion. Reasonably, this utilization above accretion rate must be an oxidative rate because the uptake of other potential energy sources (glucose, lactate, lipid) cannot account for all of the oxygen consumed by the fetus.[37] Similar data have been obtained from mid-gestation fetuses.[18, 32] Thus, as early as 70 days or 50% of gestation there is a portion of umbilical amino acid uptake that is converted to energy rather than to net protein accretion. In fact, energy balance (or at least the supply of non-protein energy

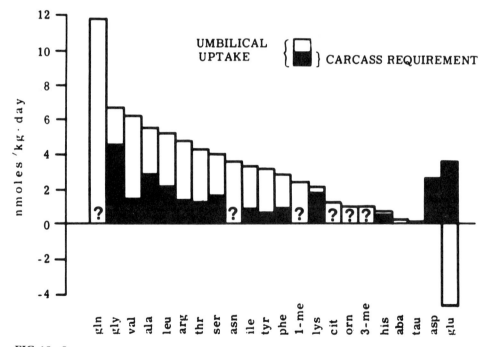

FIG 16–9.
Net umbilical uptake rates of selected amino acids in near-term fetal sheep (*total height of bar*) exceed net carcass accretion rates for most of the amino acids (*shaded portion of bar*). The difference (*open portion of bar*) represents a different metabolic rate, most likely oxidation, producing energy and CO_2 and contributing to the high fetal urea excretion rate. *Ala* = alanine, *Arg* = arginine, *Asn* = asparagine, *Asp* = aspartic acid, *Gln* = glutamine, *Glu* = glutamic acid, *Gly* = glycine, *His* = histidine, *Ile* = isoleucine, *Leu* = leucine, *Lys* = lysine, *Phe* = phenylalanine, *Ser* = serine, *Thr* = threonine, *Tyr* = tyrosine, *Val* = valine. (From Lemons JA, Adcock EW III, Jones MD Jr, et al: Umbilical uptake of amino acids in the unstressed fetal lamb. *J Clin Invest* 1976; 58:1428–1434. Reproduced with permission.)

substrates) appears to regulate this partition of amino acids into oxidation vs. protein synthesis. As shown in Figure 16–10, the oxidation-to-disposal-rate ratio for leucine (measured with leucine tracer methodology) doubles with fasting-induced hypoglycemia and hypoinsulinemia.[38] Such observations are consistent with the hypothesis that amino acid metabolism is regulated to a significant extent by the supply of non-protein energy substrates such as glucose. A similar conclusion can be drawn from two sets of experiments in pregnant rats. In the first set, protein catabolism increased in fetal rat pups whose dams underwent relative short-term fasting with hypoglycemia.[39] In contrast, in the second set, protein synthesis was decreased as well as catabolism, but only after prolonged starvation in which amino acid as well as glucose supply to the fetuses was reduced.[40]

Finally, it appears that in relation to large changes in glucose utilization rate, glucose oxidation rate, and amino acid oxidation rate, the metabolic rate of the fetus is relatively constant. For example, insulin, glucose, or both maximally double glucose utilization and oxidation in fetal sheep,[41, 42] while the leucine oxidation/disposal rate ratio nearly doubles with the opposite energy balance condition, i.e., fasting-induced hypoglycemia and hypoinsulinemia. In either case, however, there is only about a 10% to

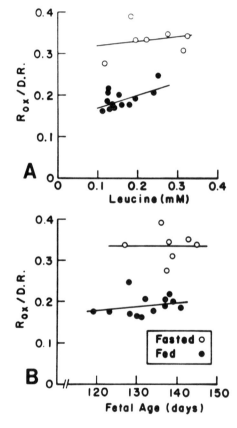

FIG 16–10.
With use of ^{14}C-U-leucine tracer in fetal sheep, the leucine oxidation/disposal rate ratio (R_{OX}/DR) nearly doubles with fasting, demonstrating a reciprocal relationship between amino acid oxidation and energy supply. (From VanVeen LCP, Teng C, Hay WW Jr, et al: Leucine disposal and oxidation rates in the fetal lamb. *Metabolism* 1987; 36:48–53. Reproduced with permission.)

20% change in fetal metabolic rate (measured as the rate of oxygen consumption). Thus, there can be large changes in glucose oxidation and large subsequent changes in protein oxidation when there is a much smaller change in fetal metabolic rate. This observation indicates that there is a reciprocal relationship between the oxidation of amino acids and the oxidation of non-protein energy substrates. The regulation of this reciprocal relationship remains to be determined. The influence of fatty acid oxidation in humans also may play a role in this process, but the effect of fatty acids has not been studied. How such substrates and hormones act, and at what gestational ages certain developmental processes allow this reciprocal substrate oxidation to occur, are not known.

Summary and Conclusion

The first part of this chapter has focused on certain aspects of early fetal body composition, growth rate, metabolic rate, and metabolic capacity that should have direct implications for nutrition of the fetus when born very early as an ELBW infant. Of course, many other aspects of fetal life may contribute to the unique nutrition of the fetus and its unique body composition, growth, and metabolism. Such aspects unique to fetal life will not be present postnatally and it remains to be determined to what extent mimicking fetal conditions and fetal development postnatally can be, or even should be achieved or used as a nutritional goal. The bias presented in this review clearly directs efforts towards providing at least those nutritional requirements that are based on body composition, growth rate, and metabolic properties intrinsic to the fetus and therefore present in the ELBW infant.

II. PRACTICAL NUTRITION OF THE ELBW INFANT: WHAT MATTERS IN FEEDING THESE INFANTS?

The literature is essentially devoid of solid, experimentally tested information about the appropriate (let alone optimal) nutritional requirements of the ELBW preterm infant. For the most part, successful nutrition of these infants has been extrapolated, with due caution in most cases, from data and experience in older, larger, more mature infants. Such data and experience are hardly solid or well-founded experimentally; thus it remains encouraging as well as remarkable that the extrapolated nutritional management of the ELBW infant is successful at all.

This part of the chapter will focus on practical aspects of nutrition for the ELBW infant. Several goals have been proposed.[7] The first goal, of course, is that those unique features of such infants described in Part I. must be recognized, understood, and accounted for. For example, ELBW infants have unique body compositions (e.g., high water content, low glycogen and fat stores, high organ/muscle mass ratio, high plasma amino acid concentrations, etc.), growth rates (e.g., high rates of protein synthesis, catabolism, and oxidation; high rates of protein accretion and body growth), metabolic rates (e.g., high rates of oxygen consumption, glucose utilization, transepidermal water evaporation, and urinary flow), and metabolic capacities (e.g., possibly increased dry weight-specific insulin sensitivity, lower fatty acid oxidation rate, high rates of glycogen and lipid synthesis).

A second goal is to promote normal development. Whether this should be according to normal intrauterine development or to some other model remains to be determined. The postnatal environment, diseases and other physical stresses, handling, mode of nutrition, etc., all impose unique changes in the infant (slow or absent initial growth rate, lower water content and extracellular/intracellular water distribution ratio, dry skin, high oxidant conditions, excessive use of certain organs, etc.) that produce an infant with unique features quite different from, even if based on, its intrauterine counterpart.

A third goal is to accelerate the gestational development of those organs that suffer diseases or must be used prematurely to promote survival and health. Examples include hormonal therapy to accelerate endogenous pulmonary surfactant production and secretion and "minimal enteral feeding" to promote gut motility, enzymatic development, and villous hypertrophy.

A fourth goal is to prevent complications that result from premature birth. Examples include vitamin E to prevent intracranial hemorrhages and ophthalmologic oxidant injury, vitamin A to prevent epithelial damage (or promote epithelial repair) and to thus diminish the severity of bronchopulmonary dysplasia, thyroid hormone to prevent neurologic impairment, and calcium plus phosphorous to prevent rickets.

Water

Water is quantitatively the most important nutrient for newborn infants, particularly those who are extremely small and immature. Furthermore, without adequate water intake and body water content, all other systems in the body fail.

Factors determining water requirements (Table 16–6):

1. *Growth.* Initially, the ELBW infant does not grow. No additional water is necessary until growth starts or at least is imminent. In utero, water accumulates at 70% to 90% of weight gain;[6, 28] the higher figure is more appropriate for the mid-gestation fetus and thus the ELBW preterm infant. Postnatally, however, water has been shown to account for only about 50% to 70% of growth in older preterm infants who have a disproportionate increase in body fat content.[43–46] If a similar growth pattern is produced in the ELBW infant, then the lower estimate of water required for growth is acceptable and usually can be accounted for by the endogenous water from nutrient oxidation ($\sim$ 12 ml/100 Kcal oxidized).

2. *Water loss in feces.* Unless diarrhea occurs, water lost in the feces is about 5 to 10 ml/kg/day. The lower figure is more appropriate (even to zero) in the early postnatal period in ELBW infants who stool less frequently and initially are not fed very much.

3. *Evaporative water loss.* This is the most variable of water fluxes from the

TABLE 16–6.

Water Requirements (ml/hr/kg) in the ELBW Infant Under Usual Conditions (Incubator, "Thermoneutral" Environmental Temperature, 80% Relative Humidity)

Evaporative loss	4–6**†
Gastrointestinal loss	0–0.5
Renal loss	3–5**
Growth	0–0.5

*Adapted from Costartino AT, Baumgart S: *Pediatr Clin N Am* 1986; 33:153–180.
**May need to be 1–2 ml/hr/kg higher in certain infants, and with addition of radiant heat.
†May be reduced if infant on positive pressure ventilator using humidified air/oxygen.

ELBW infant, reflecting regulation by body weight (>4–5 ml/hr/kg [100 to 125 ml/day/kg] for infants <1,000 g), gestational age (>4 ml/hr/kg [>100 ml/day/kg] for infants less than 27 weeks gestation), postnatal age, body temperature vs. ambient temperature, environmental relative humidity, body activity, and convection flow of air across the infant's exposed skin.[47–55] Also, the ELBW infant's surface area is very high (six times the surface area of an adult, twice that of a 1,500 g infant), they have an excess of extracellular fluid (two thirds of total body water), and their skin is extremely thin and permeable to water without a protective keratin layer.[56] Estimates of 4 to 8 ml/hr/kg (100 to 200 ml/day/kg) are appropriate for the ELBW infant (Fig 16–11), the higher range used for infants exposed to high air flow and supplemental radiant heat.[56] Baumgart's data in six infants, 575 to 835 g was 6.6 ± 0.7 ml/hr/kg (~160 ml/day/kg).[57] A lower figure, by about 1 ml/hr/kg (25 ml/day/kg), should be used for infants ventilated with 100% humidified air/oxygen by positive pressure.

4. *Renal water loss.* The ELBW infant does not restrict urinary water flow very well.[58] This is due primarily to a low renal interstitial medullary solute concentration, usually less than 400 to 500 mosmol/kg H_2O, and to a low (6.0 ml/min/1.73m²) GFR. Because of these factors, dehydration from evaporative losses will not lead to a reduction in urine flow sufficient to maintain hydration, resulting in further dehydration, hypernatremia, hyperosmolality, uremia and acidosis. Hypernatremia is compounded by tubular insufficiency which does not allow excretion of excess sodium load even when the high urine flow rate produces an obligatory natruresis.

Practically, water should be added to account for a urine flow rate of 4 to 6 ml/hr/kg

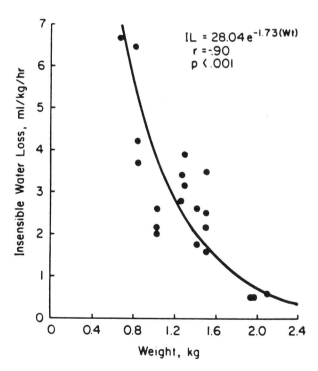

$$IL = 28.04\,e^{-1.73(Wt)}$$
$$r = -.90$$
$$p < .001$$

FIG 16–11.
Exponential increase in insensible water loss *(IL)* with decreasing body size in extremely low birth weight and larger preterm infants. (From Costartino AT, Baumgart S: Modern fluid and electrolyte management of the critically ill premature infant. *Pediatr Clin N Am* 1986; 33:153–180. Reproduced by permission.)

(100 to 150 ml/day/kg) and adjusted up or down along with water for evaporative losses to maintain body weight. Body weight should be measured at least daily and often at more frequent intervals, particularly as total fluid intake exceeds 200 ml/day/kg. A slight reduction in body weight, not to exceed about 15% birth weight, is used to determine total water supplement. Occasional checks on urine osmolality as solute load increases with advancing nutrient intake (particularly sodium and protein) should help maintain water intake sufficient not only to prevent dehydration but also to keep urinary solute concentration <200 mosmol/kg H_2O.

Energy

Based on fetal studies in the lamb (see Part I) and caloric accretion data in humans, energy requirements in a "healthy," growing ELBW infant ought to be considerably different from more mature infants. Resting metabolic rate may be about the same as in near term infants on a wet weight specific basis, but energy requirements for activity and thermoregulation are probably lower, and energy requirements for synthesis of tissue variably different: higher for the increased rate of protein synthesis, lower for the limited rate of fat accretion. The relative contribution of these factors and their effects on energy balance and requirements are not known for the ELBW infants. The one major factor determining an increased energy requirement is the high rate of evaporative water loss. Usually this is met by increasing the supply of energy as heat (convection incubator or radiant warmer) and reducing evaporative loss with a high humidity environment. Nevertheless, an increase in non-protein calories is usually necessary to maintain thermoregulation and achieve growth in these ELBW infants. At adequate or excessive protein intakes, however, excess energy intake (e.g., of glucose or lipid) may serve only to increase the growth of fat and extracellular salt plus water rather than lean tissue, length, or head circumference (Fig 16–12).[59, 60] Furthermore, developmental and physiologic problems often limit energy substrate supply. Hyperglycemia is a common disorder in these infants,[62] probably arising from stress-induced glucose production and limitations to tissue glucose uptake (e.g., by epinephrine, cortisol, glucagon, and growth hormone) as well as a sluggish insulin response. Furthermore, lipid clearance is reduced, probably the result of lower levels of lipoprotein lipase (and perhaps lecithin cholesterol acyltransferase). Lipid oxidation may be limited by reduced cellular levels of carnitine.[30] In the presence of limited fatty acid oxidation and sluggish insulin response, hyperglycemia may be necessary to supply glucose by mass action for even normal rates of energy metabolism.

Protein

Based on data in ELBW infants, Kashyap and associates have estimated that ELBW infants lose approximately 180 mg/day/kg of nitrogen during the early neonatal period (birth to 1 to 2 weeks).[60] This occurs when such infants are receiving glucose as the only nonprotein caloric source providing approximately 30 kilo calories/day/kg. This loss of nitrogen is approximately 1% of total body nitrogen stores in such infants and is about 40% greater than occurs in very low or low birthweight infants. Based on this and similar data, many clinicians have considered the ELBW infant during the early postnatal period to be in a catabolic state. This is a reasonable assumption based on the very low non-protein caloric intake which would not provide sufficient calories for maintaining nitrogen balance in any infant. Furthermore, in this period stress related hormones

GROWTH RATES WITH VARYING PROTEIN AND ENERGY INTAKES

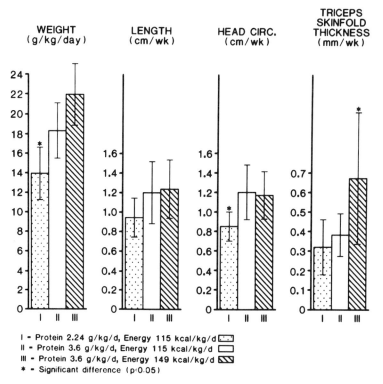

I = Protein 2.24 g/kg/d, Energy 115 kcal/kg/d ▫
II = Protein 3.6 g/kg/d, Energy 115 kcal/kg/d □
III = Protein 3.6 g/kg/d, Energy 149 kcal/kg/d ▨
* = Significant difference (p<0.05)

FIG 16–12.
The graphs show growth rates with varying protein and energy intakes. The protein intake has a major effect on promoting growth in preterm human infants. Additional calories add slightly to weight gain and significantly to triceps skinfold thickness, perhaps representing an increase in body fat. I (□) = protein 2.24 grams/kg/d, energy 115 kcal/kg/d; II (□) = protein 3.6 grams/kg/d, energy 115 kcal/kg/d; III (□) = protein 3.6 grams/kg/d, energy 149 kcal/kg/d. Significant difference, P < .05. (Adapted from Kashyap S, Shulze KF, Forsyth M, et al: Growth, nutrient retention, and metabolic response in low birth weight infants fed varying intakes of protein and energy. *J Pediatr* 1988; 113:713–721; from original data in Kennaugh JM, Hay WW Jr: Nutrition of the fetus and newborn. *Western J Med* 1987; 147:435–448. Reproduced with permission.)

such as glucagon, cortisol, and epinephrine may actively promote proteolysis and amino acid conversion to glucose adding to the negative nitrogen balance induced by the low non-protein caloric intake. As a result most clinicians have been reluctant to start intravenous amino acid feedings early for fear of producing metabolic acidosis and high plasma urea concentrations. More recently, however, Kashyap showed that administering approximately 2 g/day/kg of amino acids intravenously to ELBW infants starting as early as the second day of life increased urinary nitrogen excretion only minimally.[1] Furthermore there were no changes in blood urea nitrogen concentration and plasma amino acid concentrations were within the 95% confidence limits determined from cord plasma of normal term newborn infants. In these same infants, nitrogen balance was much less negative, and positive nitrogen balance with weight gain occurred earlier in the postnatal course. Based on these results by Kashyap and based on the information provided from early gestation fetal lamb studies showing a very high protein synthesis rate and high protein accretion rate,[32] it may be assumed that ELBW infants should be provided a much higher protein intake and that this protein intake should be administered much earlier in the neonatal course. Estimates of greater than 3 g/100 kcal/day therefore may be only minimally adequate. At such high rates of protein administration, however, most investigators including Kashyap et al[60] have noted increased concentrations of blood urea nitrogen and metabolic acid. It remains to be determined, however, whether this amount of protein is too much for the simultaneous non-protein energy administration or whether other factors are limiting. For example, the neonate may not be receiving certain unknown factors provided to the fetus through the umbilical circulation which are essential for optimal protein metabolism and accretion. Furthermore, the internal milieu of the neonate's plasma may be considerably different than that of the fetus with significant alterations in nutrient substrates, minerals, vitamins, trace elements, and hormones. Thus as shown by Kashyap, amino acids may be tolerated and may in fact be beneficial earlier in the neonatal course than previously supposed for ELBW infants, but at the same time higher levels of amino acid infusion may be poorly tolerated and should be avoided. Clearly the influence of substrate concentrations, co-factors and hormones during the early post-neonatal period on amino acid utilization and protein synthesis needs considerably more investigation before specific clinical recommendations can be made.

Lipids

Lipid absorption from the gut of the ELBW infant is limited relative to that of older and more mature infants.[62] In large part this decreased absorption of lipids occurs because of a decrease in pancreatic lipase secretion,[63-65] a decrease in bile salts secretion,[66-68] and in some cases a lower level of lingual lipase secretion,[69] especially in infants who do not suck such as those fed intravenously or by tubes.[70] On the other hand there is considerable difference among lipids for absorptive capacity even from the gut of the ELBW infants. Free fatty acids esterified in the 2 position (beta position) are less readily hydrolyzed than those esterified in the 1 and 3 positions (alpha positions). Because monoglycerides are better absorbed than free fatty acids, milk fat with 98% lipid as triacylglycerol esterified with palmitate at the 2 position is better absorbed than bovine milk lipid or formula lipid which contain approximately 30% triacylglycerol.[71]

While relative steatorrhea in ELBW infants may limit caloric intake by the enteral route, it is less certain that this steatorrhea has a significant effect on malabsorption of lipid soluble vitamins, particularly vitamins A and D,[72] although there is more certain evidence for malabsorption of vitamin E.[73] Similarly, contribution of relative steatorrhea to calcium malabsorption may be less certain than previously supposed and due to factors other than fat malabsorption alone.[74-76] Finally, there appears to be no advantage to feeding fat at greater than 9 g/day/kg (7 g/100 day/kcal) because absorption plateaus at just less than these intake rates.[77, 78] Higher intake rates of lipid may lead in fact not just to steatorrhea but to the formation of lactobezoars and diarrhea.

Some improvement in gastrointestinal absorption of lipids has been obtained by feeding diets enriched with medium change triglycerides (MCT).[79] MCTs do not necessarily require micellar formation and can be absorbed more efficiently by the direct route. Furthermore, recent studies have suggested that they are readily oxidized and can contribute to enhancement of glucose production.[80] Because they are not a normal part of breast milk some concern remains about the incorporation of such lipids into membranes, particularly in the developing central nervous system. For this reason MCTs should not be greater than 40% of the lipid intake.

As described above ELBW infants have less than one third of term infants' heparin releasable lipoprotein lipase activity.[81] This would suggest a decreased capacity for lipid clearance; however, there remains a poor correlation between lipoprotein lipase activity and lipid tolerance. Other factors such as the effect of insulin on glucose uptake by fat cells and the variable amount of fat stores[82] may contribute to the variable lipid clearance as well as the concentration and activity of other enzymes essential for fat clearance such as lecithin cholesterol acyltransferase.[83] Additionally, with intravenous lipid infusion there is recent evidence that 10% intravenous lipid emulsion, for a fixed amount of triacylglycerol, contains two to four times the amount of phospholipid-rich liposomes which can impede the removal of triglycerides from the plasma, likely competing with the emulsion particle for binding to lipase sites, thus slowing triglyceride hydrolysis.[84, 85] These phospholipid-rich liposomes also pull free cholesterol out of membranes, thus decreasing membrane cholesterol[86] and increasing plasma cholesterol. The consequences of these effects have not been readily determined although it seems prudent at this point to recommend 20% lipid emulsion for ELBW infants who already have difficulty clearing lipids from their plasma.

Carbohydrate

The administration of adequate glucose and carbohydrates to ELBW infants is even more important than in term infants. ELBW infants have limited capacity for sustained glucose production rate, a very high brain to body weight ratio, and may be more susceptible to neurological injury from hypoglycemia even of modest degree. Recent evidence shows that even modest acute hypoglycemia can lead to abnormal brain evoked potential responses[87] and additionally recurrent moderate hypoglycemia has been shown to correlate directly with significant developmental and intellectual handicaps.[88] In both of the latter studies, deviation below normal in terms of neurological function occurs at approximately 45 mg/dl of plasma suggesting this value as a reasonable choice for a lower limit for maintaining blood plasma glucose concentration in low birthweight infants.

Excessive intake of glucose, however, rapidly leads to hyperglycemia as described as above. Additionally, excess lipid formation under conditions of high glucose entry rate probably leads to an excess production of carbon dioxide which may aggravate respiratory conditions.[89] At the same time, fatty infiltration of major organs, particularly the liver, occurs.[90]

It also remains controversial which complex carbohydrate should be fed entrally to ELBW infants. Glucose alone produces an excessive osmotic load leading to hyperperistalsis, intestinal acidosis, and acidic diarrhea. Complex starches, either natural (dextromaltose from corn syrup) or synthetic (e.g., Polycose) help avoid the high osmotic load of simple glucose and appear to be reasonably well tolerated. Initially such complex carbohydrates were provided in premature infant formulas in preference to lactose, assuming that insufficient lactase would be present in the intestinal villi of the ELBW infants. Recent studies suggest that lactose is in fact well tolerated and that the mild acidic diarrhea that may occur with this carbohydrate is not of major significance.[91] Furthermore, the provision of galactose from lactose hydrolysis more directly and effectively produces glycogen.[92] The formation of glycogen in low-birth-weight infants from a feeding is essential for providing normal glucose homeostasis as the diet is switched from continuous to intermittent feedings.

Feeding Regimens and Feeding Guidelines

The success of intravenous methods of providing selective or total nutrition has taken the pressure off to feed ELBW infants aggressively in the early postnatal period. As a result, most centers do not see very frequently what used to be more common consequences of feeding too much, too fast, too early: lactobezoars, stasis, regurgitation, distension that obstructs breathing, etc. Some centers also have seen a reduction in the incidence of necrotizing enterocolitis (NEC).[93]

On the other hand, there is increasing evidence that early, small feedings (0.5 to 1.0 ml/hr by bolus or continuous drip intragastrically) can promote gut development, characterized by increased gut growth, villous hypertrophy, digestive enzyme secretion, and "feeding tolerance," perhaps representing enhanced motility. This approach has been called "minimal enteral feeding."[94, 95] It has not been associated with an increase in NEC or other gastrointestinal disturbances and it does shorten the time to achieving full enteral feedings. The reasons for the success of minimal enteral feedings are not clearly defined. Of primary interest are the surges in plasma concentration of several growth and development-regulating peptides that occur after birth, especially with feeding. Primary peptides include enteroglucagon, gastrin, gastric inhibitory polypeptide (GIP), motilin, and neurotensin.[94] Figure 16–13 shows data from one study documenting increased plasma concentrations of these peptides in preterm infants that were well or had respiratory distress syndrome (RDS) but were fed, compared with a group unfed and with values from both groups at birth. The absence of gut hormone surges in the unfed 6-day-old infants demonstrated that plasma hormone elevation after birth was likely to be related to feeding itself rather than postnatal age. The volume of feeding in the well or RDS infants averaged only 0.5 ml/hr/kg over 5 days. It is not yet established, however, what is the optimal rate of minimal enteral feeding, composition of the feeding, or the best time to start.

Clinical trials of minimal enteral feeding in ELBW infants are encouraging but largely anecdotal. Perhaps the most encouraging observation has been the increase in postprandial motor activity following early introduction of feedings. Although such motor activity is largely developmentally determined, and few infants at extreme immaturity have been studied, recent evidence (Fig 16–14) clearly defines the volume of bolus feeding and the duration of enteral feeding as key variables in the maturation of gut peristalsis in low birthweight, preterm infants.[96]

Neurodevelopmental Outcome

The most important question in preterm infant nutrition, not only with respect to individual nutrients but also for whole diets, is whether early feeding practices have long-term neurodevelopmental consequences. For example, Goldman et al studied 304 infants who weighed less than 2,000 g at birth who had been randomized to receive 2% or 4% protein diets providing, respectively, 3.0 to 3.6 g protein/day/kg and 6.0 to 7.2 g/day/kg.[97] Infants below 1,300 g in the high protein intake group had a markedly higher incidence of low IQs (below 90) by Stanford-Binet score at 5 years of age. The incidence of strabismus in infants below 1,700 g fed a high protein intake also was in-

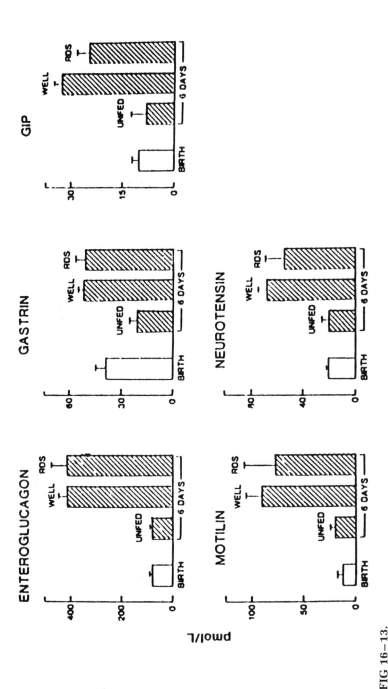

FIG 16—13.
Mean plasma concentrations of enteroglucagon, gastrin, gastric inhibitory polypeptide (GIP), motilin and neurotensin (pmol/l + SE) at birth (venous cord blood levels, n = 6), and at 6 days postnatal age in infants who had received no enteral feeds since birth ("unfed," n = 10), in "well" enterally-fed infants (n = 45), and in those infants with respiratory distress syndrome (RDS) who were restricted in enteral intake (n = 12). (From Lucas A, Bloom SR, Aynsley-Green A: Gut hormones and "minimal enteral feeding." *Acta Paediatr Scand* 1988; 75:719—723. Reproduced with permission.)

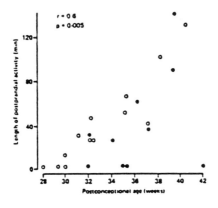

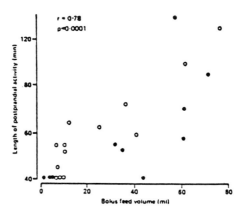

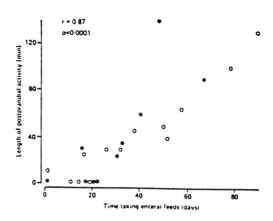

FIG 16–14.

Top, the length of postprandial motor activity compared with the postconceptional age in 23 infants. *Middle,* the length of postprandial motor activity plotted against the volume of bolus feed in 23 infants. *Bottom,* plot of length of postprandial motor activity against the length of time on enteral feed in 23 infants. *Open circles* denote those born <29 weeks gestation, and *closed circles* those born ≥29 weeks. (From Bisset WM, Watt J, Rivers RPA, et al: Postprandial motor response of the small intestine to enteral feeds in preterm infants. *Arch Dis Child* 1989; 64:1356–1361. Reproduced with permission.)

creased. It has been suggested that transient hyperaminoacidaemia (especially tyrosine) on high protein intakes might have been responsible for these adverse outcomes, but currently the explanation is uncertain.[98] These data emphasize that there are upper as well as lower safe limits for protein intake. Similar concerns apply to other selected nutrients as well.

Evidence linking neurodevelopmental outcome with early nutrition has come from many sources. For example, early malnutrition associated with certain disease states may lead to abnormal neural development. One example is infantile hypertrophic pyloric stenosis which is associated with later deficits in attention and memory.[100] A second example is the occurrence of developmental deficits from iron deficiency.[100]

General malnutrition also has been associated with neurodevelopmental problems. In human infants dying of severe malnutrition, the total number of brain cells has been found at autopsy to be reduced by 15% to 20% and by 60% in infants who weighed less than 2,000 g at birth.[101] Functional impairment in survivors of infancy malnutrition also has been observed but interpretation of results are complicated because many cultural and socioeconomic influences confounded the data.[102–104] In animal models, results are more straightforward. In rats, whose offspring are very neurodevelopmentally immature at birth, early postnatal malnutrition results in a marked loss of brain cells (not correctable completely by subsequent nutritional supplement) and impaired performance in learning tasks and discrimination tests.[105]

In human preterm infants, the most comprehensive recent study of the effect of di-

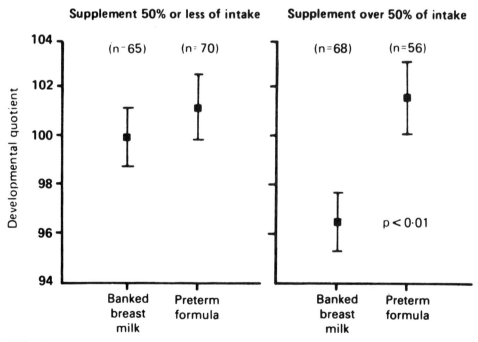

FIG 16–15.
Mean developmental quotient at 9 months after the expected date of delivery in preterm infants randomly assigned to receive either banked breast milk or preterm formula as supplements to their mothers' milk. Mean (+/− SEM) values from babies for whom this supplement was 50% or less of intake are shown on the *left,* and for those for whom it was over 50% are shown on the *right.* (From Lucas A, Morley R, Cole TJ, et al: Early diet in preterm babies and developmental status in infancy. *Arch Dis Child* 1989; 64:1570–1578. Reproduced with permission.)

etary intake on neurodevelopmental outcome was performed by Lucas et al.[106] Their study was conducted in preterm infants whose average birth weight was about 1,380 g at 31 weeks gestation. Based on delivery and care at one of 4 centers, 502 infants were randomly assigned for a median of 30 days, to receive a preterm formula or unfortified donor breast milk as sole diets or as supplements to their mothers' expressed milk. At 9 months post-expected date of delivery, developmental quotient was significantly lowest in those infants fed banked breast milk alone and was highest in those infants fed preterm formulas (Fig 16–15). The difference between these two groups, 5.3 DQ points, is probably of clinical significance. Whether such a dramatic correlation between intake and development outcome will apply to ELBW infants, or be even greater, remains to be determined. Based on the results of these studies, however, and the biological high requirement for nutrient intake, it is clear at this point that ELBW infants need nutritional intake as importantly as any other aspect of their medical care.

Feeding Guidelines

Table 16–7 presents a brief and somewhat personal approach to feeding ELBW infants after birth. Guidelines for these suggested practices are tenuously based on very limited data. In general, however, in infants who are very immature and or sick (or at least physiologically unstable), it is undesirable and often impossible to begin even modest enteral feeds in the first few days after birth and intravenous nutrition must be used. The immediate aim of this nutrition is to meet requirements for water, glucose and electrolytes providing for cellular viability and normal cellular and extra-cellular biochemical homeostasis. The decision about when to add other nutrients and to commence enteral feeding will be based on age, weight, severity of illness or pathophysiology, and tolerance to arbitrary attempts to increase nutrient intake and start minimal enteral feedings.

TABLE 16–7.
Feeding Regimens and Feeding Guidelines

I. Birth to stabilization (0–2 days)
   IV glucose, 4–10 mg/min/kg to maintain plasma glucose concentration >60 <120 mg/dl
   IV H_2O 100–150 ml/day/kg, to maintain weight with no greater than a 10% loss over 3 days and to maintain urine flow rate >2 ml/hr/kg, maintain temperature at 37° C, maximize environmental humidity; late in period start Na^+, K^+, Cl, HCO_3^- per urine loss
II. Stabilization period (1–4 days)
   IV glucose 6–10 mg/min/kg, plasma glucose concentration 60–120 mg/dl
   IV amino acids 1–2 g/day/kg
   IV lipid (towards end of period) 0.5–1.0 g/day/kg
   Feeding: begin minimal enteral feedings as early as possible via indwelling gauge, 0.5 ml/hr, bolus or continuous, advancing to bolus over several days.
   Diet: colostrum, preterm breast milk, term breast milk, elemental formula, regular formula
III. Stabilization to growth onset (1–3 weeks)
   Maintain full peripheral IV feeding
   Progressively but slowly advance enteral feeding to bolus feedings; total volume balanced with IV to maintain weight and keep urine volume and Ac^- flow relatively high; advance to 24 cal/oz "premature" infant formula or supplemented breast milk (supplements of protein, calcium, phosphorus, sodium, potassium and lipid are most important)

REFERENCES

1. Kashyap S: Nutritional management of the extremely-low-birth-weight infant, in Cowett RM, Hay WW Jr (eds): *The Micropremi: The Next Frontier*. Report of the 99th Ross Conference on Pediatric Research. Columbus, Ohio, Ross Laboratories, 1990; pp 115–119.
2. American Academy of Pediatrics Committee on Nutrition: Nutritional needs of low-birth-weight infants. *Pediatrics* 1977; 60:519–530.
3. Hay WW Jr: Nutrition of the fetus and premature infant: State of the art. *Perinatology-Neonatology*. 1985; 92:19–29 (part 1); 1985; 92:23–33 (part 2).
4. Williams RL, Creasy RK, Cunningham GC, et al: Fetal growth and perinatal viability in California. *Obstet Gynecol* 1982; 59:624–632.
5. Creasy RK, Resnik R: Intrauterine growth retardation, in Creasy RK, Resnik R (eds): *Maternal-Fetal Medicine,* ed 2. Philadelphia, WB Saunders Co, 1989, pp 549–564.
6. Widdowsown EM: Changes in body proportion and composition during growth, in Davis JA, Dobbing J (eds.): *Scientific Foundations of Paediatrics*. Philadelphia, WB Saunders Co, 1974, pp 44–45.
7. MacLean WC: What matters in feeding the extremely-low-birth-weight infant?, in Cowett RM, Hay WW Jr (eds): *The Micropremi: The Next Frontier*. Report of the 99th Ross Conference on Pediatric Research. Columbus, Ohio, Ross Laboratories, 1990, pp 115–119.
8. Ziegler EE, O'Donnell AM, Nelson SE, et al: Body composition of the reference fetus. *Growth* 1976; 40:329–341.
9. Sparks JW, Girard JR, Battaglia FC: An estimate of the caloric requirements of the human fetus. *Biol Neonate* 1980; 38:113–119.
10. Wharton BA (ed): *Nutrition and Feeding of Preterm Infants*. Oxford, Blackwell Scientific Publications, 1987; p 10.
11. Lubchenko LO, Hansman C, Dressler M et al: Intrauterine growth as estimated from live born birth weight data at 24 to 42 weeks gestation. *Pediatrics* 1963; 32:793–800.
12. Kloosterman GJ: On intrauterine growth. *Int J Gynecol Obstet* 1970; 8:895–912.
13. Babson SG, Behrman RE, Lessel R: Fetal growth: Liveborn birthweights for gestational age of white middle class infants. *Pediatrics* 1970; 45:937–944.
14. Keen DV, Pearse RG: Birth weight between 14 and 42 weeks gestation. *Arch Dis Child* 1985; 60:440–446.
15. Sparks JW: Human intrauterine growth and nutrient accretion. *Semin Perinatol* 1984; 8:74–93.
16. Bell AW, Battaglia FC, Meschia G: Methods for chronic studies of circulation and metabolism in the sheep conceptus at 70–80 days gestation, in Nathanielsz PW (ed): *Animal Models in Fetal Medicine VI,* Ithaca, NY, Perinatology Press, 1987, pp 38–54.
17. Bell AW, Battaglia FC, Meschia G: Relationship between metabolic rate and body size in the ovine fetus. *J Nutr* 1987; 117:1181–1186.
18. Bell AW, Kennaugh JM, Battaglia FC, et al: Metabolic and circulatory studies of fetal lamb at midgestation. *Am J Physiol* 1986; 250:E538–E544.
19. Molina RD, Hay WW Jr: Ontogeny of insulin effect on ovine fetal glucose metabolism. *Pediatr Res* 1989; 25(56A):323.
20. Kappy MS, Plotnick LP, Milley JR, et al: Ontogeny of erythrocyte insulin binding in the sheep. *Endocrinology* 1981; 109:611–617.
21. Goldman SL, Hirata T: Attenuated response to insulin in very low birthweight infants. *Pediatr Res* 1980; 14:50–53.
22. Binder ND, Raschko PK, Banda GI, et al: Insulin infusion with parenteral nutrition in extremely low birth weight infants with hyperglycemia. *J Pediatrics* 1989; 114:273–280.
23. Hay WW Jr: Fetal and neonatal glucose homeostasis and their relation to the small for gestational age infant. *Semin Perinatol* 1984; 8:101–116.
24. Ogata E: Problems of glucose metabolism in the extremely-low birth-weight infant, in Cowett RM, Hay WW Jr (eds): *The Micropremi: The Next Frontier*. Report of the 99th

Ross Conference on Pediatric Research. Columbus, Ohio, Ross Laboratories, 1990; pp 115–119.

25. Carson BS, Philipps AF: Simmons MA, et al: Effects of a sustained insulin infusion upon glucose uptake and oxygenation of the ovine fetus. *Pediatr Res* 1980; 14:147–152.

26. Hay WW, Jr, Meznarich HK: The effect of hyperinsulinemia on glucose utilization and oxidation and on oxygen consumption in the fetal lamb. *Quart J Exp Physiol* 1986; 71:689–698.

27. Yoshioka T, Roux JF: In vitro metabolism of palmitic acid in human fetal tissues. *Pediatr Res* 1972; 6:675–681.

28. Battaglia FC, Meschia G: *An Introduction to Fetal Physiology*. Orlando, FL, Academic Press, 1986, p 119.

29. Vernon RB, Clegg RA, Flint DJ: Metabolism of sheep adipose tissue during pregnancy and lactation. *Biochem J* 1981; 200:307–314.

30. Novak M, Monkus EF, Chung D, et al: Carnitine in the perinatal metabolism of lipids. *Pediatrics* 1981; 67:95–100.

31. Solomon JW, Swyer PR, Jequier E: Thermic effects of glucose, amino acid and lipid in the term newborn. *Biol Neonate* 1979; 35:8–16.

32. Kennaugh JM, Bell AW, Teng C, et al: Ontogenetic changes in the rates of protein synthesis and leucine oxidation during fetal life. *Pediatr Res* 1987; 22:688–692.

33. Meier PR, Peterson RG, Bonds DR, et al: Rates of protein synthesis and turnover in fetal life. *Am J Physiol* 1981; 240:E320–E324.

34. Waterlow JC, Garlick PJ, Millward DJ: Protein turnover in mammalian tissues and in the whole body. Amsterdam, Elsevier/North-Holland Biomedical Press, 1978.

35. Arnal M: Muscle protein turnover in lambs throughout development, in *Protein Metabolism and Nutrition: Proceedings of the International Symposium on Protein Metabolism and Nutrition,* ed 2. Holland, Flevohof, 1977; pp 38–40.

36. Lemons JA, Adcock EW III, Jones MD Jr, et al: Umbilical uptake of amino acids in the unstressed fetal lamb. *J Clin Invest* 1976; 58:1428–1434.

37. Sparks JW, Hay WW Jr, Meschia G, et al: Partition of maternal nutrients to the placenta and fetus in the sheep. *Europ J Obstet Gynecol Repord Biol* 1983; 14:331–340.

38. VanVeen LCP, Teng C, Hay WW Jr, et al: Leucine disposal and oxidation rates in the fetal lamb. *Metabolism* 1987; 36:48–53.

39. Johnson JD, Dunham T, Skipper BJ, et al: Protein turnover of the rat fetus following maternal starvation. *Pediatr Res* 20:1252–1257.

40. Johnson JD, Dunham T: Protein turnover in tissue of the rat after prolonged maternal malnutrition. *Pediatr Res* 1988; 25:534–538.

41. Hay WW Jr, Meznarich HK, DiGiacomo JE, et al: Effects of insulin and glucose concentrations on glucose utilization in fetal sheep. *Pediatr Res* 1988; 23:381–387.

42. Hay WW Jr, DiGiacomo JE, Meznarich HK, et al: Effects of glucose and insulin on fetal glucose oxidation and oxygen consumption. *Am J Physiol* 1989; 256:E704–E713.

43. Whyte RK, Haslam R, Vlainic C, et al: Energy balanced and nitrogen balance in growing low birth weight infants fed human milk or formula. *Pediatr Res* 1983; 17:891–898.

44. Reichman B, Chessex P, Putet G, et al: Diet, fat accretion and growth in premature infants. *N Engl J Med* 1981; 305:1495–1500.

45. Reichman B, Chessex P, Verrellen G, et al: Dietary composition and macronutrient storage in preterm infants. *Pediatrics* 1983; 72:322–328.

46. Putet G, Senterre J, Rigo J, et al: Nutrient balance, energy utilization and composition of weight gain in very low birth weight infants fed pooled human milk or a preterm formula. *J Pediatr* 1984; 105:79–85.

47. Rutter N, Hull D: Water loss from the skin of term and preterm babies. *Arch Dis Child* 1979; 54:858–868.

48. Fanaroff AA, Wald M, Gruber HS, et al: Insensible water loss in low birth weight infants. *Pediatrics* 1972; 49:236–245.

49. Hammarlund K, Sedin G: Transepidermal water loss in newborn infants: III relation to gestational age. *Acta Paediatr Scand* 1979; 68:795–801.

50. Hammarlund K, Sedin G: Transepidermal water loss in newborn infants. VI. Heat exchange with the environment in relationship to gestational age. *Acta Paediatr Scand* 1982; 71:191–196.

51. Wilson DR, Maibach HI: Transepidermal water loss in vivo. Premature and term infants. *Biol Neonate* 1980; 37:180–185.

52. Hammarlund K, Nilsson GE, Oberg PA, et al: Transepidermal water loss in newborn infants. II: Relation to activity and body temperature. *Acta Paediatr Scand* 1979; 68:371–376.

53. Hammarlund K, Nilsson GE, Oberg PA, et al: Transepidermal water loss in newborn infants. I. Relation to ambient temperature and site of measurement and estimation of total transepidermal water loss. *Acta Paediatr Scand* 1977; 66:553–562.

54. Bell EF, Gray JC, Weinstein MR, et al: The effects of thermal environment on heat balance and insensible water loss in low-birth-weight infants. *J Pediatr* 1980; 96:452–459.

55. Baumgart S: Water metabolism in the extremely-low-birth-weight infant, in Cowett RM Hay WW, Jr (eds): *The Micropremi: The Next Frontier.* Report of the 99th Ross Conference on Pediatric Research, Columbus, Ohio, Ross Laboratories, 1990; pp 83–89.

56. Baumgart S: Radiant energy and irreversible water loss in the premature newborn infant nursed under a radiant warmer. *Clin Perinatol* 1982; 9:483–503.

57. Costartino AT, Baumgart S: Modern fluid and electrolyte management of the critically ill premature infant. *Pediatr Clin N Am* 1986; 33:153–180.

58. Arant BS: Developmental patterns of renal functional maturation compared in the human neonate. *J Pediatr* 1979; 92:705–712.

59. Kennaugh JM, Hay WW Jr: Nutrition of the fetus and newborn. *Western J Med* 1987; 147:435–448.

60. Kashyap S, Shulze KF, Forsyth M, et al: Growth, nutrient retention, and metabolic response in low birth weight infants fed varying intakes of protein and energy. *J Pediatr* 1988; 113:713–721.

61. Pildes RS, Pyati SP: Hypoglycemia and hyperglycemia in tiny infants. *Clin Perinatol* 1986; 13:351–375.

62. Katz L, Hamilton JR: Fat absorption in infants of birthweight less than 1300 g. *J Pediatr* 1974; 85:608–614.

63. Zoppi G, Andreotti G, Pajo-Ferrara F, et al: Exocrine pancreatic function in premature and full-term neonates. *Pediatr Res* 1972; 6:880–886.

64. Geschwind Von R: Das Verhalten de Pancreasenzyme bei Fruhgebornen. *Ann Pediatr* 1950; 157:176.

65. Lebenthal E, Lee PC: Development of functional response in human exocrine pancreas. *Pediatrics* 1980; 66:556–560.

66. Norman A, Strandvik B, Ojamae O: Bile acids and pancreatic enzymes during absorption in the newborn. *Acta Paediatr Scand* 1972; 61:571–576.

67. Signer E, Murphy GM, Edkins S: Role of bile salts in fat malabsorption of premature infants. *Arch Dis Child* 1974; 49:174–180.

68. Watkins JB, Szczepanik P, Gould JB, et al: Bile salt metabolism in the human premature infant. *Gastroenterology* 1975; 69:706–713.

69. Hamosh M, Sivasubramanian KN, Salzman-Mann C, et al: Fat digestion in the stomach of premature infants. *J Pediatr* 93:674–679.

70. *Development of Mammalian Absorptive Process.* Ciba Foundation Symposium No 70. Amsterdam, Excerpta Medica, 1979.

71. Jensen RG, Hagerty MM, McMahon KE: Lipids of human milk and infant formulas: A review. *Am J Clin Nutr* 1978; 31:990–1016.

72. Morales S, Chung AW, Lewis JM, et al: Absorption of fat and vitamin A in premature infants. *Pediatrics* 1950; 6:86–92.

73. Melhorn DK, Gross S: Vitamin E dependent anaemia in the premature infant. II. Relationships between gestational age and absorption of vitamin E. *J Pediatr* 1971; 79:581–588.

74. Senterre J, Salle B: Calcium and phosphorus economy of the preterm infant and its interaction with vitamin D and its metabolites. *Acta Paediatr Scand* 1982; 296:85–92.

75. Shaw JC: Evidence for defective skeletal mineralization in low-birth-weight-infants: The absorption of calcium and fat. *Pediatrics* 1976; 57:16–25.

76. Lewis CT, Dickson JAC, Swain WAJ: Milk bolus obstruction in the neonate. *Arch Dis Child* 1977; 52:68–71.

77. Brooke OG: Energy balance and metabolic rate in preterm infants fed with standard high-energy formulas. *Br J Nutr* 1980; 44:13–23.

78. Hanmer OJ, Houlsby WT, Thorn H, et al: Fat as an energy supplement for preterm infants. *Arch Dis Child* 1982; 57:503–506.

79. Huston RK, Reynolds JW, Jensen C, et al: Nutrient and mineral retention and vitamin D absorption in low-birth-weight infants: Effect of medium-chain triglycerides. *Pediatrics* 1983; 72:44–48.

80. Vileisis R, Cowett RM, Oh W: Glycemic response to lipid infusion in the premature neonate. *J Pediatr* 1982; 100:108–112.

81. Zaidan H, Dhanireddy R, Hamosh M, et al: Lipid clearing in premature infant during continuous heparin infusion: role of circulating lipases. *Pediatr Res* 1985; 19:23–25.

82. Berkow SE, Spear ML, Stahl GE, et al: Total parenteral nutrition with intralipid in premature infants receiving TPN with heparin: Effect on plasma lipolyte enzymes, lipids, and glucose. *J Pediatr Gastroent Nutrit* 1987; 6:581–588.

83. Papadopoulus A, Hamosh M, Chowdhry P, et al: Lecithin-cholesterol acyltransferase in newborn infants: Low activity level in preterm infants. *J Pediatr* 1988; 113:896–898.

84. Haumont DM, Deckelbaum RJ, Carpentier YA: Approaches to improved tolerance of intravenous lipid emulsions, in Cowett RM, Hay WW Jr (eds): *The Micropremi: The Next Frontier*. Report of the 99th Ross Conference on Pediatric Research. Columbus, Ohio, Ross Laboratories, 1990, pp 115–119.

85. Haumont D, Deckelbaum RJ, Richelle M, et al: Plasma lipid and plasma lipoprotein concentrations in low birth weight infants given parenteral nutrition with twenty or ten percent lipid emulsion. *J Pediatr* 1989; 115:787–793.

86. Haumont D, Richelle M, Deckelbaum RJ, et al: Excess liposomal phospholipid content of intravenous fat emulsions impairs lipid clearance and alters lipoprotein patterns in low birth weight infants. *Pediatr Res* 1989; 25:291A.

87. Koh THHG, Aynsley-Green A, Tarbit M, et al: Neural dysfunction during hypoglycemia. *Arch Dis Child* 1988; 63:1353–1358.

88. Lucas A, Morley R, Cole TJ: Adverse neurodevelopmental outcome of moderate neonatal hypoglycemia. *Br Med J* 1988; 297:1304–1308.

89. Yunis KA, Oh W: Effects of intravenous glucose loading on oxygen consumption, carbon dioxide production, and resting energy expenditure in infants with bronchopulmonary dysplasia. *J Pediatr* 1989; 115:127–132.

90. Chang S, Silva S: Fatty liver produced by hyperalimentation in rats. *Am J Gastroenterol* 1974; 62:410–418.

91. Kien CL, Liechty EA, Mullett MD: Effects of lactose intake on nutritional status in premature infants. *J Pediatr* 1990; 116:446–449.

92. Sparks JW, Lynch A, Glinsmann WH: Regulation of rat liver glycogen synthesis and activities of glycogen cycle enzymes by glucose and galactose. *Metabolism* 1976; 25:47–55.

93. Dunn L, Hulman S, Weiner J, et al: Beneficial effects of early hypocaloric enteral feeding on neonatal gastrointestinal function: preliminary report of a randomized trial. *J Pediatr* 1989; 112:622–629.

94. Lucas A, Bloom SR, Aynsley-Green A: Gut hormones and "minimal enteral feeding." *Acta Paediatr Scand* 1988; 75:719–723.

95. Slagle TA, Gross SJ: Effect of early low-volume enteral substrate on subsequent feeding tolerance in very low birth weight infants. *J Pediatr* 1988; 113:526–531.

96. Bisset WM, Watt J, Rivers RPA, et al: Postprandial motor response of the small intestine to enteral feeds in preterm infants. *Arch Dis Child* 1989; 64:1356–1361.

97. Goldman HI, Freudentha R, Holland B, et al: Clinical effects of two different levels of protein intake of low birth weight infants. *J Pediatr* 1969; 74:881–889.

98. Goldman HI, Gold JS, Kaufman I, et al: Large effects of early dietary protein intake on low birth weight infants. *J Pediatr* 1974; 85:764–769.

99. Klein PS, Forbes GB, Nadar PR: Effects of starvation in infancy (pyloric stenosis) on subsequent learning abilities. *J Pediatr* 1975; 87:8–15.

100. Ankett MA, Parks YA, Scott PH, et al: A treatment with iron increases weight gain and psychomotor development. *Arch Dis Child* 1986; 61:849–857.

101. Winick M: Malnutrition and brain development. Oxford, Oxford University Press, 1976, p 115.

102. Chavez A, Martinez C: Neurological maturation and performance on mental tests, in Dobbing J (ed): *Early Nutrition and Later Development*. London, Academic Press, 1987, pp 138–139.

103. Freeman HE, Klein RE, Townsend JW, et al: Nutrition and cognitive development among rural Guatemalan children. *Am J Public Health* 1980; 70:1277–1285.

104. Sinisterra L: Studies on poverty. Human growth and development: the Cali experience, in Dobbing J (ed): *Early Nutrition and Later Development*. London, Academic Press, 1987; pp 208–233.

105. Smart JL, Dobbing J, Adlard BPF, et al: Vulnerability of developing brain: relative effects of growth restriction during the fetal and suckling periods on behavior and brain composition of adult rats. *J Nutr* 1973; 103:1327–1338.

106. Lucas A, Morley R, Cole TJ, et al: Early diet in preterm babies and developmental status in infancy. *Arch Dis Child* 1989; 64:1570–1578.

Chapter 17

The Metabolism and Endocrinology of Intrauterine Growth Retardation*

R.M. Kliegman, M.D.

V.L. Johnston, M.D.

Intrauterine growth retardation (IUGR) is a significant perinatal problem associated with serious morbidities and substantial mortality.[1, 2] By definition, IUGR is present in infants who are small for gestational age (SGA) (i.e., those weighing less than a defined weight standard for a given population at a given gestational age). This deviation from the normal growth parameter may be defined as weighing less than the 5th or 10th percentile or less than 2 standard deviations below the mean. Nonetheless, this definition will not include all growth-retarded infants because population standards may not be sensitive enough to enable detection of reduced growth in every situation. For example, patients with congenital rubella syndrome are not always designated as SGA when using population standards[1]; however, if weights of the affected infants are compared with the birth weights of their unaffected siblings, all congenital rubella syndrome infants are growth retarded.

The epidemiology of IUGR is similar to that for low-birth-weight (LBW) infants in general (premature and/or IUGR infants <2,500 g), as many of the identifiable risk factors are noted in both patient populations (Table 17–1).[1, 2] Indeed IUGR may also be present in 20% to 30% of premature infants. In countries where the LBW rate exceeds 10% (e.g., developing Third World countries), the majority of these LBW infants are growth retarded, while in developed nations the proportion of IUGR among LBW infants is lower. IUGR may also be present in infants born at term who weigh more than 2,500 g.

Many of the epidemiologic variables associated with IUGR affect the fetus by one or more of a few hypothesized mechanisms. Poor nutrition, for example, may reduce the availability of oxidizable fuels and precursors for macromolecule synthesis, thus reducing intrauterine growth. Predisposing factors such as poor diet, chronic illness, drug abuse, infection, poverty, poor education, poor prenatal care, low prepregnancy weight,

*This work was supported by NIH grant HD 20851.

TABLE 17–1.

Epidemiologic Risk Factors for Intrauterine Growth Retardation*

Demographic	*Prepregnancy*
Poverty	Low prepregnancy
Black race	weight
Third World birth	Maternal growth
Pregnancy	retardation at her
Twins, triplets,	birth
multiple births	Previous birth of
Concurrent chronic	growth-retarded
medical diseases	infant
Preeclampsia	Poor nutrition
Infection	*Behavioral*
Placental lesions	Cigarette, alcohol, drug
Poor weight gain	abuse
Poor nutrition	Poor prenatal care
Medications/teratogens	Poor education
Uterine anomalies	Unmarried
	Fetal
	Congenital
	malformation
	syndromes
	Genetic, chromosomal
	disorders
	Infection (TORCH)†
	Oligohydramnios

*Adapted from Kliegman R, Hulman S: Intrauterine growth retardation: Determinants of aberrant fetal growth, in Fanaroff A, Martin R (eds): *Neonatal-Perinatal Medicine, Disease of the Fetus and Infant,* ed 4. St Louis, CV Mosby Co, 1987.
†*Toxoplasmosis, other (e.g., syphillis), rubella, cytomegalovirus, and herpes simplex.*

and poor weight gain during pregnancy may be indicator-markers for reduced nutrient availability for the mother and potentially the fetus.[1, 3]

Another mechanism of IUGR is reduced blood supply to the fetus and placenta, resulting in uteroplacental insufficiency.[1, 2] Predisposing variables such as chronic hypertension, renal disease, diabetic vasculopathy, preeclampsia, and cigarette smoking may reduce uterine blood flow and hence placental perfusion, resulting in IUGR. Acquired or innate defects of fetal growth potential may also result in reduced fetal weight. Congenital anomalies, TORCH infections (see Table 18–1), chromosomal or genetic diseases, drug teratogens, and other unknown mechanisms may interfere with fetal growth, resulting in IUGR.[4] Each mechanism will function at a different time of fetal development (Table 17–2). Onset of IUGR during the 1st trimester is often associated with acquired or innate cellular defects that limit both intrauterine and postnatal growth. However, during the 1st trimester the small fetus with relatively small growth requirements usually receives sufficient nutrients and oxygen for growth, even in the presence of poor maternal nutritional status or poor placental perfusion. In contrast, onset of growth retardation during the 3d trimester is usually noted when the larger requirements for nutrients or oxygen of a rapidly growing fetus become rate-limiting because of the poor nutritional status of the mother or uteroplacental insufficiency (see Table 17–2). When these infants are removed from the suboptimal growth conditions in utero, catch-up growth is possible if the infants are provided sufficient nutrients after birth.

TABLE 17–2.

Growth Variables and Fetal Development

1st Trimester	3d Trimester
Dependence on fetal genome	Dependence on placental transfer
Expression of growth factors	Oxygen
Expression of growth factor receptors	Nutrients
Less dependent on maternal nutrition	Partial dependence on fetal genome
Early-onset growth retardation	Late-onset growth retardation
Symmetric body growth	Asymmetric body growth
Low-profile growth pattern	Late flattening growth pattern
Reduced cell number	Reduced cell size
Catch-up growth improbable	Catch-up growth probable
Examples	Examples
Teratogens (drugs, infectious agents); fetal genetic or metabolic disorders; malformation syndromes	Maternal vascular disease; malnutrition

In many instances of IUGR the underlying pathophysiology is not identified. Furthermore, the basic mechanism of IUGR at the cellular level has not been precisely defined. For some infants with IUGR, the reduction of in utero growth may be an appropriate adaptive response to an abnormal in utero environment. In others (e.g., associated with placental insufficiency), IUGR may be associated with the added risk of intrauterine fetal demise or perinatal asphyxia. Another group of patients with IUGR from teratogenic, genetic, or chromosomally mediated events may represent aberrant regulation of cell growth at a molecular level, rather than the mechanism of reduced placental supply which may be operational in the two previously noted examples. Nonetheless, whatever the initiating factor, the net final result of reduced intrauterine growth must affect the molecular mechanisms that regulate cell growth. The translation of reduced fetal nutrient or oxygen availability into aberrant fetal growth must eventually be manifested at the cellular level. The various initiating mechanisms such as teratogens, altered growth factor profiles, proto-oncogene expression, and uteroplacental insufficiency produce adaptive responses in somatic growth, growth factor expression, in utero and postnatal intermediary metabolism, and—more seriously—abnormal cardiopulmonary responses to hypoxia and stress, which results in the many morbidities and the significant mortality of infants with IUGR. Thus, a basic understanding of the normal and aberrant mechanisms of fetal growth provides a broader rationale for the therapy of infants with IUGR before and after birth.

DIET, TERATOGENS, AND CONGENITAL MALFORMATIONS

Maternal prepregnancy weight (reflecting previous nutritional status) and weight gain during pregnancy (reflecting nutrition during pregnancy) are both directly correlated with fetal weight and fetal weight gain.[1] These are independent variables, as women with reduced prepregnancy weight for height can improve eventual fetal birth weight by increasing maternal weight gain during pregnancy. Furthermore, obese women who gain little weight during pregnancy have large babies and a reduced incidence of SGA infants as compared with lean women with adequate weight gain during pregnancy. In addition to these observations, women who themselves were SGA tend to have a higher incidence of IUGR in their offspring.[5] This may reflect poor intrauterine growth of the mother, affecting her subsequent reproductive potential (uterine size, placental transport) in the next generation, or it may reflect a genetic predisposition. The genetic hypothesis seems less likely because population studies have shown a nongenetic pattern. The intergenerational effect is noted in the children of sisters, but not sisters-in-laws (children of brothers), of the index growth-retarded mother. In animal genetics, cross-breeding studies between animals of different sizes also suggest that a nongenetic factor produces uterine constraint.

Further evidence related to the role of maternal nutrition and fetal growth has come from pregnancies complicated by anorexia nervosa[6] or famine[3] and those benefitted by nutritional supplementation.[3] During World War II, the Dutch famine and the Leningrad famine resulted in IUGR in infants of women affected by poor food intake during the 3d trimester. Infants exposed to maternal famine during the 1st trimester, but with subsequent access to food in the last trimester, were not SGA. In addition, nutritional supplementation studies in Gambia and Guatemala have been associated with enhanced fetal birth weight with the provision of additional calories.[1, 3]

Various hypotheses have been proposed to explain reduced fetal growth during maternal nutritional deprivation. The most obvious is that the fetus did not receive sufficient nutrients to support growth. However, poor nutrition may have additional secondary effects on fetal growth. Maternal blood flow to the uterus may become reduced if the pregnant woman cannot expand her blood volume, which is the normal pattern in well-nourished pregnancies. The net result may be reduced placental blood flow. In addition, placental growth and function may be directly attenuated by poor nutrition. This could result in a poor placental nutrient transfer mechanism and decreased fetal growth.[1] Furthermore, the fetus may respond to decreased availability of nutrients with down regulation of growth factors or factor receptor expression, thus reducing the final signal for cell proliferation. Another mechanism for aberrant fetal growth on a nutritional basis relates to the concept of fuel-mediated teratogenesis. Traditionally a teratogen is thought of as an agent, factor, or substance having the potential to interfere with normal growth patterns of specific tissues, producing a malformation. Teratogenesis, from whatever cause, is often associated with IUGR. In fact, IUGR may represent one type of expression of teratogenesis.[7]

Fuel-mediated teratogenesis has been proposed as one of the mechanisms of anomalies or IUGR in fetuses exposed to ketones during maternal starvation or diabetes, or to excessive glucose during diabetes during pregnancy.[8, 9] Various fuels such as D-mannose and D- or L-beta-hydroxybutyrate have been associated with anomalies in experimental animals. Poor diabetic control and maternal hyperglycemia during the 1st trimester are associated with congenital malformations among infants of diabetic mothers (IDMs). Fuel-mediated teratogenesis may result from excessively high ambient levels of specific fuels, which then inhibit normal metabolic pathways associated with cellular energy production or synthesis of deoxyribonucleic acid (DNA). Normal concentrations of these fuels are readily metabolized; it is the excessive amounts present at a vulnerable developmental period which then inhibit important metabolic pathways.

The paradox of fuel-mediated teratogenesis and the IDM requires further explanation. Traditionally, the IDM is not growth retarded but is large for gestational age. This usually is due in part to excessive fetal glucose availability, subsequent fetal hyperinsulinemia and augmented fetal growth (discussed later). Nonetheless it has become increasingly evident that early fetal (7th week to 20th week) growth retardation is a risk for associated congenital anomalies in both the diabetic and nondiabetic pregnancy.[10-14] This may be identified by a reduced crown-rump length noted by ultrasound as early as

7 to 14 weeks gestation. Identification of early growth retardation in the IDM may predict subsequent anomalies, IUGR, or both when the infant is born. The reduced growth may cause the malformation as a result of poor regulation of cell growth responses. Alternatively, the IUGR and malformation may result from the same adverse factor that interfered with both organogenesis and growth.

Congenital malformations not associated with diabetes, but with various other teratogenic or genetic factors, are noted in Table 17–3. These agents may function at many regulatory points involved with uteroplacental function and cell growth.[7, 15] The net result may be IUGR, anomalies, or both. In population studies, the occurrence of IUGR among infants with congenital malformations is as high as 22%. The incidence of IUGR increases as the number of serious congenital anomalies increases in a particular patient.[4] In addition, the incidence of IUGR varies with the particular congenital malformation: for example, 83% with trisomy 18; 73% with anencephaly; 55% with renal agenesis; and 31% with trisomy 21. In these patients IUGR may be due to disturbed growth from the actual malformation, such as poor hemodynamics from congenital heart disease. Alternatively IUGR may predispose to congenital malformations, or IUGR and the malformations may coexist because of a common cause, such as congenital rubella

TABLE 17–3.

Congenital Malformations Associated With
Intrauterine Growth Retardation

Chromosome
  Trisomy 8, 13, 18, 21
  XO (one sex chromosome)
  Deletion syndromes (4p- 5p-)
  Triploidy
Infections
  Rubella
  Cytomegalovirus
  Toxoplasmosis
  Varicella
  Lyme disease
Drugs
  Antimetabolites
  Ethanol
  Phenytoin
  Methylmercury
  Polychorinated biphenyls
  Warfarin
  Valproic acid
Syndrome complexes
  Cornelia de Lange's syndrome
  Potter's syndrome
  VATER, VACTERL*
  Prune-belly syndrome
  Rubinstein-Taybi syndrome
  Russell-Silver syndrome
  Dubowitz syndrome
  Seckel's syndrome

*VATER = vertebral defects, imperforate anus, tracheoesophageal fistula, and radial and renal dysplasia. VACTERL = vertebral, anal, cardiac, tracheal, esophageal, renal, and limb.

syndrome. Rubella as a teratogen produces congenital anomalies (patent ductus arteriosus), placental inflammation (villitis), and fetal endovascular disease (obliterative endarteritis), while intracellular viral replication causes cytolysis.[1] The latter three mechanisms can reduce placental nutrient transfer, interfere with fetal tissue perfusion, and directly reduce cell number, respectively.

Fetal growth may occasionally be enhanced as part of a congenital malformation syndrome complex. This is exemplified by the Beckwith-Wiedemann syndrome which is characterized by somatic gigantism, omphalocele, macroglossia, organomegaly, hypoglycemia with pancreatic beta cell hyperplasia, and an increased incidence of tumors such as Wilms' tumor, adrenal cancer, and nephroblastoma.[16] Beckwith-Wiedemann syndrome is thought to be a contiguous gene syndrome and is an example of how genetic organization on a chromosome may effect growth through developmental genes.[17] In some but not all patients with Beckwith-Wiedemann syndrome there is an obvious duplication of 11p15. This area of chromosome 11 contains the genes for insulin, insulin-like growth factor II (IGF II), Wilms' tumor, and the Harvey ras proto-oncogene. Duplications of this area have also been found in Wilms' tumor tissue in patients without Beckwith-Wiedemann syndrome. Although not yet proved, it is logical to hypothesize that the enhanced fetal growth and susceptibility to tumor formation result from increased expression of insulin, IGF II, or the products of the proto-oncogene during embryogenesis, fetal life, and postnatal life.

GROWTH FACTORS AND FETAL GROWTH

A reproductively resting but metabolically active cell is stimulated to enter the replicative cell cycle by various growth-promoting factors.[18] Cells leave the quiescent G_o stage and enter the G_I phase in the presence of competence growth factors such as platelet-derived growth factor (PDGF) (Fig 17–1). Progression growth factors such as insulin, IGF I and II or epidermal growth factor (EGF) induce the cell to enter the S phase where chromosomal DNA replication occurs.[19–22] Next the cell enters the G_2 and M (mitotic cell division) phases (see Fig 17–1). The various peptide growth factors may effect growth by endocrine, paracrine, or autocrine mechanisms. Endocrine regulation results from a hormone being produced in a distant tissue by a specific signal. The hormone circulates to another tissue where a new cellular action is initiated by the hormone after binding to a specific receptor in another cell type. An example is glucose-stimulated pancreatic insulin release resulting in insulin-mediated muscle glucose uptake. It should be noted that the presence of a hormone in peripheral blood does not define an endocrine mechanism for that peptide. Paracrine regulation is due to local production of a hormone by one cell with subsequent peptide receptor binding in another cell in that region. Autocrine regulation is the production of a growth factor by the same cell that also contains that hormone's receptor. Various peptide growth factors function with both paracrine and autocrine mechanisms. Nerve growth factor and various hematopoietic growth factors are examples of paracrine function, while IGF I or II may function by autocrine-mediated regulation.

The regulation of the synthesis of peptide growth factors during human development is not well defined. As with the synthesis of any polypeptide, regulation begins with DNA transcription, processing of ribonucleic acid (RNA), and subsequent translation (Fig 17–2). The gene's protein product may initiate activation or inactivation of another gene. The protein may be a peptide growth factor responsible for stimulating

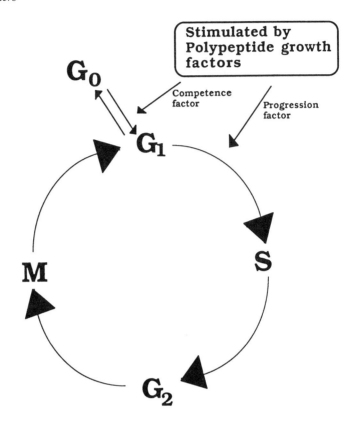

S phase = chromosome (DNA) replication
M phase = mitosis
G0 phase = quiescent cell, no growth but metabolically active
G1 phase = gap between mitosis and S phase
G2 phase = gap between S phase and mitosis

FIG 17–1.
Cell growth cycle.

cell proliferation as a competence or a progression factor, or it may enhance cell differentiation and maturation (see Fig 17–2). Alternatively, the product of gene transcription may be a polypeptide ligand receptor rather than a protein growth factor. Following transmembrane signaling (ligand binding and intracellular processing), cell metabolism, DNA synthesis, and so forth may be stimulated (see Fig 18–2).[18, 21, 23]

Peptide growth factor action, whether mediated by endocrine, paracrine, or autocrine mechanisms, requires a ligand to specifically bind to a receptor (Fig 17–3). Insulin, IGF I, PDGF, and EGF are examples of growth factors which bind to a receptor subunit that has specific and selective ligand binding properties (specificity and affinity). The initial binding occurs in the ectodomain or the extracellular domain of the receptor (see Fig 18–3). For most peptide growth factors this extracellular ligand binding subunit is heterogeneous, thus conferring ligand-binding specificity to the receptor complex.[23] The extracellular domain is anchored to the cell membrane by the transmembrane domain. After binding the mechanistic sequence of peptide growth factor, signaling (for insulin, IGF I, PDGF, and EGF) then involves the cytoplasmic domain of the receptor

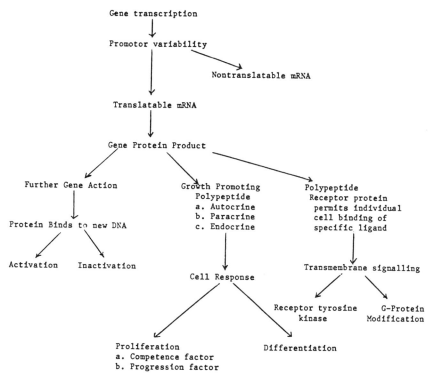

FIG 17−2.
Functional sequence of growth factor activity.

subunit. For these peptide hormones the cytoplasmic domain subunit of the receptor is much more homologous and consists of a receptor tyrosine kinase (RTK). Phosphorylation of the receptor itself (autophosphorylation) and/or of extracellular tyrosine-containing ligands by RTK results in pleiotropic cellular responses depending on the target tissue and the recognition of the original individual growth factor (see Fig 17−3). The net result may be activation of gene transcription and new protein synthesis as depicted in Figure 17−3. Transformational mutagenesis of a proto-oncogene to an oncogene in this system may result in the production of a structurally altered RTK which may be ligand independent or constitutive, thus resulting in unregulated cell proliferation.

Other growth factors may initiate transmembrane signaling through the guanosine triphosphate G protein system, which usually produces a much more rapid cell response, often mediated by ion fluxes (see Fig 17−3).[18, 19, 23−25]

Most traditional hormones affecting postnatal growth have relatively little effect on fetal growth (Table 17−4). Thus growth hormone−deficient infants are born with normal body weight—as are hypothyroid infants, as well as those fetuses with panhypopituritary lesions.[20, 26] Indeed, growth hormone receptors are not present in some fetal tissues until after birth. Despite these facts there is good evidence to suggest that various peptide growth factors have an effect on normal, reduced, and enhanced somatic tissue growth in the mammalian fetus.[20, 26]

Insulin in particular is thought to be an important fetal "growth hormone," functioning with an endocrine mechanism of cell regulation.[20, 21, 26] Insulin has anabolic effects, which result in cellular glucose and amino acid uptake, enhanced protein synthesis and inhibited protein degradation, glycogen and triglyceride synthesis, glucose oxidation,

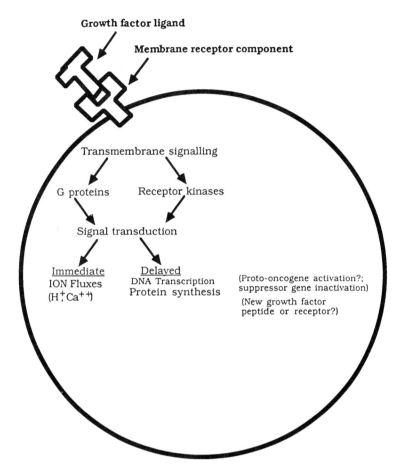

FIG 17–3.
Growth factor binding, transmembrane signaling, and intracellular action.

and DNA synthesis and transcription. Insulin does not cross the placenta and, like most peptide growth factors, is of fetal origin. Insulin excess in the fetus is associated with overgrowth syndromes or macrosomia, while reduced or absent insulin production or effect is associated with intrauterine growth retardation (Table 17–5).

Insulin receptor number and affinity are increased in neonatal tissue.[27] The action of insulin may be mediated following binding to the high-affinity insulin receptor or the lower-affinity IGF I receptor. The insulin receptor is a heterotetramer consisting of a 2 alpha-chain 135 kd specific ligand binding site (extracellular domain) and a 2 beta-chain cytoplasmic domain, 95 kd protein with RTK activity. The IGF I receptor has a similar alpha-beta RTK configuration but has low binding affinity for insulin. The IGF II receptor is a single polypeptide with minimal to no insulin-binding capacity.[20, 23, 26] Following binding to the insulin receptor, insulin may directly effect cell metabolism and growth. If insulin action is blocked because of insulin resistance at the receptor level, as in leprechaunism, IUGR will be present.[20, 26, 28]

Insulin may act synergistically with other growth factors such as PDGF, IGF I, or EGF, as insulin action may be potentiated by these peptide growth factors. Because insulin is a progression growth factor, PDGF or others may be needed as competence factors to initiate cell proliferation. Although insulin may act independent of other growth fac-

TABLE 17–4.

Endocrine Effects on Human Fetal Growth

Hormone	Effect
Growth hormone (GH)	Paucity of fetal GH receptors; fetal GH deficiency does not effect growth
Thyroid	Fetal thyroid deficiency does not effect growth; thyroid deficiency retards osseous maturation
Insulin	Stimulates growth by binding to insulin or insulin-like growth factors (IGF I) receptors, or by stimulating IGF production; excess insulin (infants of diabetic mothers) produces growth acceleration; absent insulin (pancreatic agenesis) retards growth; insulin resistance (leprechaunism) retards growth
Placental lactogen (PL)	Possible stimulation of growth by direct binding to hPL (human PL) receptor and/or stimulation of IGF production
Insulin-like growth factor I (IGF I)/somatomedin C	Present in early and late fetal life; IGF I messenger ribonucleic acid and receptor present in many tissues; endocrine, autocrine, paracrine functions; deficient IGF I in Laron dwarfs
Insulin-like growth factor II (IGF II)/multiplication-stimulating activity (MSA)	MSA is elevated in rat but not human fetus compared with adult serum
Platelet-derived growth factor (PDGF)	Present in early embryo; absent fibroblast response to PDGF noted in Werner syndrome (IUGR)
Epidermal growth factor	Mitogen plus induction of differentiation

tors, insulin may also indirectly enhance fetal growth by modulating IGF I levels.[20, 29] Insulin is one hormone that has been demonstrated to increase fetal serum levels of IGF, thus suggesting that the growth-promoting effect of insulin may, in part, be indirectly mediated by increased IGF expression. Indeed some investigations have demonstrated significant positive relationship between serum insulin and IGF I concentrations in the macrosomic IDM and in the IUGR fetus.[20] Because growth hormone does not seem to serve as a fetal growth factor, and because in postnatal life the action of growth hormone is mediated at the tissue level by local production of IGF I, it is possible that insulin, or other hormones, may regulate IGF I production and control of cell metabolism or proliferation.

Both IGF I and IGF II were previously named somatomedins and are thought to be the local tissue mediators of growth hormone action in postnatal mammals. In the somatomedin system, pituitary growth hormone circulates to local tissues (usually liver), binds to a growth hormone receptor, and stimulates somatomedin production. Somatomedins have no specific target tissue, but require binding to individual IGF I or

TABLE 17–5.

Insulin Excess and Reduction/Absence in Human Fetal Growth

Overgrowth	Growth Retardation
Infant of diabetic mother	Pancreatic agenesis
Beckwith-Wiedemann	Islet cell agenesis
Nesidioblastosis	Neonatal diabetes mellitus
	Leprechaunism

IGF II receptors to initiate metabolic or mitotic proliferation cellular responses. In contrast, other peptide growth factors such as nerve growth factor have a specific target tissue (e.g., nerve). IGF I is now named as the peptide factor previously called somatomedin C, while IGF II in the rat model was previously called multiplication stimulation activity.[20]

IGF I is composed of an alpha and beta chain, which requires processing from a larger precursor molecule.[30] These chains have 45% similarity to insulin. It is possible that a duplication of the insulin gene resulted in the IGF gene.[31, 32] The IGF I gene is on chromosome 12, while the IGF II gene is close to the insulin gene on chromosome 11. Neither IGFs cross the placenta, but are present in the fetal placenta, fetal blood, and most fetal tissues during embryogenesis and fetal life.[21, 26, 29, 30, 33–39] Expression of the IGFs in fetal tissues is detected by the presence of the peptide growth factor, and the specific precursor mRNA throughout gestation. Indeed insulin and IGF have been detected in the morulae, blastocyst, and preimplantation embryo stage.[40, 41] In addition these same tissues express IGF receptors as early as preimplantation stages, thus suggesting an autocrine mechanism for the control of fetal tissue growth by IGFs. It is important to note that serum levels of IGF I may not reflect tissue activity and that data on serum levels in various disease states must be interpreted with caution. Serum levels may also be modulated by IGF carrier proteins or circulating IGF receptor complexes.

The structural composition of the IGF I receptor is similar to that of the insulin receptor and consists of a heterotetramer with two alpha chain subunits in the ligand (IGF I) binding extracellular domain and an RTK subunit with two beta chains in the intracellular domain.[20] This receptor has low affinity for insulin but high affinity for IGF I and less affinity for IGF II. The IGF II receptor is not similar to that of the insulin and IGF I receptors, as it lacks RTK activity.[20, 24, 42] It has no affinity for insulin and much greater affinity for IGF II than IGF I. The receptor is a single polypeptide, exists 90% in an extracellular domain, and has been proposed to be similar to or identical to the mannose-6-phosphate receptor.[24, 42] The IGF II receptor causes calcium to enter the cell and stimulates DNA synthesis.[19] IGF II stimulates a peptide-sensitive calcium channel and increases the permeability of this cation channel. In addition to DNA synthesis, IGF II may enhance amino acid uptake and glycogen synthesis.[24, 42]

The relationship of IGF expression and fetal growth is confusing. In humans, IGF I and IGF II levels are lower in cord blood than adult blood in some studies.[21] In some human studies, somatomedin or IGF I cord blood levels have correlated with birth weights.[34, 43, 44] In animal models, low serum IGF I concentrations correlated with reduced fetal weight in addition to the presence of neonatal hypoglycemia and hypoinsulinemia.[45] Further evidence of the role of IGF and growth are noted in patients with leprechaunism, whose tissues bind IGF I poorly[28]; in Laron dwarfs, who lack the growth hormone receptor and thus do not produce somatomedins; and in Pygmies, who fail to produce IGF I.[32, 46] In another study, IGF I and another poorly characterized growth factor which stimulates cellular thymidine incorporation were assayed. Reduced growth factor activities were associated with IUGR.[47, 48] Using percutaneous umbilical blood sampling, these investigators identified low fetal growth-promoting activity in IUGR fetuses. Furthermore catch-up growth was associated with an increment of IGF I levels to control values.

The regulation of IGF synthesis may not be independent and probably is controlled by various modulating influences such as blood glucose and insulin concentrations and human placental lactogen (hPL) levels (Fig 17–4).[26] Human placental lactogen (chori-

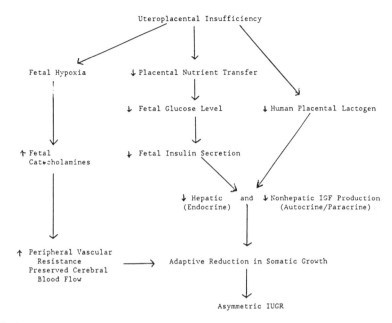

FIG 17–4.
Hypothesized scheme of regulation of growth factors during intrauterine growth retardation. Glucose may directly stimulate IGF production while hPL may directly effect fetal growth by binding to specific hPL cell receptors. Insulin may also directly effect fetal growth by binding to high-affinity insulin receptors or to the low-affinity IGF I receptor.

onic somatomammotropin) is a growth hormone–like peptide produced by the placenta throughout gestation. It had previously been used as a marker for fetal well-being because low maternal blood concentrations were associated with IUGR.[49] The hPL affects maternal metabolism by inducing a metabolic state of relative insulin resistance with enhanced lipolysis, higher blood glucose concentrations, and greater insulin release to a glucose challenge.[49] The net result is provision of fuels for fetal rather than maternal tissue utilization. In the fetus there are specific hPL receptors which, following stimulation by hPL, cause amino acid uptake, glycogen synthesis, and polyamine production.[49] The hPL is more effective in stimulating these fetal anabolic responses than is growth hormone. The hPL also stimulates fetal synthesis of IGF II, whereas growth hormone has no effect on IGF II levels in the fetus (in contrast to the adult).[31, 49] Therefore it remains uncertain if the effects of hPL are direct or if hPL produces anabolic changes in the fetus by stimulating local production of IGF II. A combination of these two mechanisms (i.e., both direct and indirect effects of hPL on fetal tissue growth) has been proposed. The immediate direct effects of hPL may stimulate amino acid uptake, while the delayed indirect effects may increase expression of IGF II, which then augments DNA synthesis.[50] Despite these data, the role of these various growth factors in fetal growth or IUGR remains speculative. It currently remains undetermined if a primary deficiency of IGF I, IGF II, or hPL is the cause of IUGR, or if the reduced levels of these growth factors noted in the IUGR infant is an adaptive response to a growth-limiting fetal environment. Nevertheless, the net effects translate to reduced fetal growth, as depicted in Figure 17–4.

Although insulin, IGFs, and hPL have been the growth factors investigated in most studies, other peptide growth factors may have a role in embryonic and fetal growth. For example, the mRNA for PDGF has been detected in embryonic tissue and even in the ovum.[51] The latter observation suggests that PDGF of maternal origin is present in the early embryo and has some important role in the early proliferation of cells.[51] This PDGF may consist of a homodimer of either two alpha or two beta chains, or it may be a heterodimer (α,β). The receptor for PDGF is similar to the insulin and IGF I receptors, as it contains an RTK subunit in the cytoplasmic domain region. PDGF inhibits cell differentiation but promotes progenitor cell division (mitogenesis) in various systems.[22, 52] It also induces competence of the cell's growth cycle. Other growth factors noted in the embryo or fetus include EDF, fibroblast growth factor, and transforming growth factor.[51] These factors may contribute to rapid cell division and the regulation of cell differentiation. An example of the importance of PDGF and fibroblast growth factor is noted in Werner syndrome, where reduced responsiveness to these growth factors may be responsible for the poor growth and premature aging noted in this syndrome.[53]

Embryonic and fetal growth are associated with rapid cell division and have some similarities to rapidly growing malignant cells and retroviral transformed cells. Proto-oncogenes are normal cell genes involved in the regulation of cell division, and hence normal growth. Proto-oncogene products may be normal peptide growth factors or receptors for growth factors (Table 17–6). Alternatively polypeptide growth factors may stimulate the expression of proto-oncogene mRNA.[18, 22, 52, 54–56] A hypothetical scheme of proto-oncogene regulation of normal growth is noted in Figure 17–5. If a mutation occurs in the regulation of the proto-oncogene, it may become an oncogene and stimulate uncontrolled cell proliferation by the mechanisms noted in Figure 17–5.[56] The relationship between reduced proto-oncogene expression and IUGR is undetermined and remains hypothetical, but should be an important area of research. It remains to be determined whether proto-oncogene expression is operational and regulatory for fetal growth, and if gene expression is the primary cause of IUGR or the secondary effect of an aberrant fetal environment.

TABLE 17–6.

Relationships of Growth Factors and Proto-Ongogenes

Factor	Proto-Oncogene Variable
Platelet-derived growth factor B	c-*sis* gene product
Platelet-derived growth factor	Stimulates c-*myc* and c-*fos* gene expression
Epidermal growth factor	EGF receptor similar to c-*erb* B gene product
Guanosine triphosphate–binding protein	c-*ras* gene product
Undetermined	n-*myc,* 1-*myc,* and c-*myc* expressed in fetus
Macrophage growth factor (CSF-1)*	CSF-1 receptor similar to c-*fms* gene product
Receptor tyrosine kinases	Stimulates c-*myc* and c-*fos* expression

*Colony-stimulating factor.

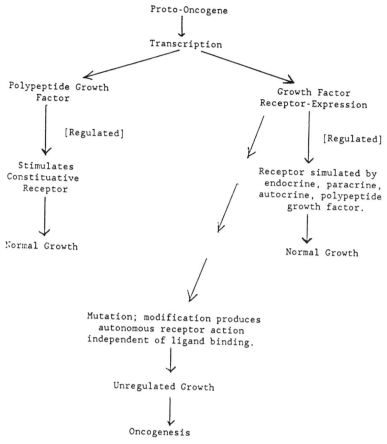

FIG 17–5.
Hypothetical scheme of proto-oncogene regulation of growth.

FETAL AND NEONATAL METABOLISM

Fetal tissue receives a continuous supply of nutrients during placental transport or diffusion of maternal substrates.[57] These fuels are required to support oxidative metabolism and also function as precursors for macromolecule synthesis such as proteins, triglycerides, complex glycolipids, DNA, and RNA. Macromolecule synthesis consists of two components: replacement of the normal turnover of macromolecules, and new tissue growth. Both processes, in addition to the processes of maintaining electrophysiologic gradients in such tissues as nerves and muscles, consume energy in the final form of adenosine triphosphate hydrolysis. During periods of decreased availability of oxidizable fuels, growth processes become attenuated and energy is utilized for maintenance activities.

Under normal conditions the fetus oxidizes glucose, amino acids, lactate, ketones, and perhaps acetate. These fuels (especially glucose) are universally of maternal origin in basal conditions and contribute to both energy-producing pathways and synthetic processes.[58, 59] These various fuels are precursors for macromolecules, in that glucose is a precursor for some hepatic glycogen and most triglyceride synthesis, amino acids are precursors for proteins (except IgG, which is actively transported across the placenta), lactate may be a precursor for hepatic glycogen and triglyceride synthesis, while ketones may be precursors for lipids. Essential fatty acids must be transported across the placenta, as the fetus cannot synthesize essential fatty acids. Under conditions of poor maternal nutrition the availability of various nutrients declines, resulting in alterations of fetal oxidative and synthetic substrates. During fasting, maternal blood glucose levels decline faster than that in nulliparous women (e.g., the "accelerated starvation of pregnancy"). Because glucose crosses the placenta by facilitative diffusion and thus down a concentration gradient, fetal glucose levels decline whenever maternal blood glucose concentrations decrease. Therefore during the accelerated starvation of pregnancy, fetal glucopenia could result in reduced availability of an important oxidative fuel. Depending on the species, amino acids (sheep), ketones (man, rat, dog), or lactate (sheep, dog) may serve as temporary alternative fuels and contribute to fetal oxidative metabolism. Indeed under some conditions fetal gluconeogenesis may be initiated from 3-carbon precursors and increase fetal glucose availability. Nonetheless, as maternal fasting continues, fetal oxidative metabolism and tissue synthesis decline and fetal growth becomes attenuated, or the fetus actually loses weight as fetal glycogen, and proteins are utilized for energy production.

During maternal starvation fetal hypoglycemia results in a concomitant fetal hypoinsulinemia.[60, 61] The relationship between the hypoinsulinemia, reduced fetal glucose utilization, and IUGR have not been well defined. The fetus may be relatively insulin resistant (compared with adults), suggesting that fetal glucose uptake is more dependent on fetal blood glucose level and availability rather than insulin-mediated effects.[62, 63] Insulin has no direct effect on placental transfer of glucose.[64, 65] In some studies the effects of insulin on fetal glucose uptake may relate to the resulting hypoglycemia or hyperglycemia, thus increasing or decreasing the maternal fetal gradient, with subsequent increased or decreased fetal glucose uptake, respectively.[60, 63, 66, 67] Nonetheless, in investigations which prevented fetal hypoglycemia, insulin increased fetal glucose uptake only twofold compared with basal fetal levels.[64] In addition to the small effects (compared with adults) of insulin on fetal glucose utilization, glucose alone can have an effect on fetal glucose utilization.[63] In hypoinsulinemic fetal sheep, the administration of exogenous glucose has resulted in an increase of fetal glucose utilization.[63]

These investigations have relevance to the various proposed mechanisms of IUGR and even more so to potential therapy of the fetus with IUGR. If fetal hypoinsulinemia is a primary cause rather than a secondary response to IUGR, increasing the glucose availability to the fetus should increase fetal glucose utilization, oxidative metabolism, and—possibly—growth. This is possible because the fetus may be able to utilize glucose independent of insulin. If fetal hypoinsulinemia is a secondary adaptive response to maternal–fetal hypoglycemia, provision of glucose to the mother should reverse the fetal hypoinsulinemia and hypoglycemia, and should restore fetal glucose utilization, energy production, and growth. Unfortunately, in some circumstances the provision of supplemental glucose to either the mother or the fetus may have adverse metabolic and cardiovascular effects for the fetus. Infusion of glucose to the normal sheep fetus has been noted to produce fetal hyperglycemia and hyperinsulinemia, in addition to fetal hypoxia, hypercarbia, and acidosis.[68–70] Fetal hypercarbia with hyperglycemia correlated with an increase in fetal oxygen consumption.[69] Fetal insulin infusion also results in fetal hypoxia, in addition to an increase in the umbilical arteriovenous glucose gradient, and increased fetal glucose uptake.[71] Further studies have suggested that fetal hyperglycemia and hypoxic acidosis may result from a reduction of umbilical blood flow.[68] Although this has not been demonstrated in the human fetus, the increased incidence of intrauterine fetal demise in the IDM is also suggestive of an adverse effect of fetal hyperglycemia/hyperinsulinemia on the fetal umbilical circulation. Furthermore, intravenous glucose given to the laboring mother has been noted to cause fetal hyperinsulinemia and lactic acidosis, in addition to reduced ketone bodies in cord blood.[72] After birth, this maternal glucose infusion has induced fetal hyperinsulinemia, which has been associated with neonatal hypoglycemia, while the reduction of ketone body levels may limit the availability of alternative fuels for neonatal metabolism.

Following birth, the pattern of fuels used for neonatal energy metabolism changes from that during fetal life. After the umbilical cord is cut and the newborn is delivered into a cold environment, the infant mobilizes the fuels that were deposited in utero, to support oxygen consumption. At birth there is a release of various counter-regulatory hormones such as epinephrine, norepinephrine, thyroid-stimulating hormone, thyroxine, and glucagon. This is associated with a marked rise in serum free fatty acids and glycerol levels, a slight reduction in blood glucose concentration, and an increase of serum triglyceride and ketone levels.[73] Blood glucose levels and systemic glucose production are initially derived from hepatic glycogenolysis.[74] With increased duration of fasting, the neonate becomes capable of gluconeogenesis as a source of ongoing hepatic glucose production. In addition to the mobilization of glycogen, enhanced lipolysis at birth results in increased availability of free fatty acids (FFAs).[74] This results in an increasing proportion of neonatal oxygen consumption from FFA oxidation, as depicted by the postnatal decline of the respiratory quotient from values as high as 1.0 (purely glucose) to values a low as 0.8 (predominantly FFAs) within 3 hours of birth.[73, 74] The relationship between glucose and FFA metabolism is depicted in Figure 17–6. As both substrates are metabolized to acetyl-CoA, either glucose or FFA can be utilized as a precursor for this intermediate. When FFA are available, they will contribute to the acetyl-CoA pool and thus spare glucose utilization. In the presence of FFA oxidation, glycogenolysis can result in hepatic glucose production, rather than hepatic glucose utilization. If glycogen stores are depleted, FFA oxidation can spare pyruvate, which will be directed toward oxaloacetate and gluconeogenesis rather than to acetyl-CoA and energy production. In the absence of FFA oxidation, glucose oxidation is not spared, and hypoglycemia may develop.[73–75]

Neonatal hypoglycemia is a common problem among IUGR infants during the 1st day after birth.[1, 2, 76–81] The cause of neonatal hypoglycemia may be multifactorial and probably relates to a state of substrate deficiency more than any other factor (Table 17–7). Substrate deficiency has been associated with reduced rates of endogenous fasting neonatal glucose production in hypoglycemic IUGR dogs.[73] This may be due to reduced hepatic glycogen stores, reduced gluconeogenesis from 3-carbon precursors (lactate, alanine), reduced FFA availability, and absence of glucose-sparing or attenuated counterregulatory hormone action (see Table 17–7).[73, 81–83] The fatty acid–glucose relationship is especially relevant to the hypoglycemia noted in IUGR neonates (see Fig 17–6). Free fatty acid oxidation can spare glucose utilization, provide the nicotinamide adenine dinucleotide (NADH) needed for gluconeogenesis, and spare pyruvate oxidation, diverting this 3-carbon precursor of gluconeogenesis to gluconeogenic metabolic pathways. The relationship between FFA availability, their oxidation, and hypoglycemia has been highlighted by studies in animal models and humans which confirmed the importance of FFAs.[81, 82] Provision of triglycerides increased serum FFA and ketone levels and increased blood glucose levels in these studies.

Another proposed theoretical mechanism of hypoglycemia relates to the brain spar-

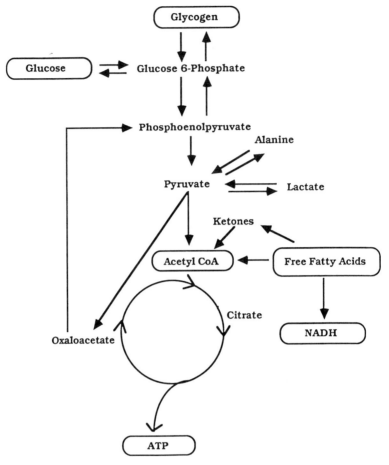

FIG 17–6.
Glucose–fatty acid metabolic interrelationship.

ing noted in IUGR. There may be an imbalance between cerebral glucose needs and the ability of the relatively small glycogen-depleted liver to provide sufficient glucose for brain metabolism. There is, however, additional evidence which suggests that this mechanism is not necessarily functional. First the neonatal brain is capable of using fuels for oxidative metabolism other than glucose. These alternative fuels include ketones, lactate, and endogenous cerebral amino acid pools such as glutamate, alanine, glutamine, and gamma aminobutyrate.[84, 85] Furthermore, when exposed to chronic glucopenia, cerebral glucose transporter activity probably increases, thus enhancing the extraction of glucose by the brain.[84, 86] In addition, in recent studies, the neonatal canine brain has been demonstrated to use only 37% of systemic glucose production rather than the much higher estimates of 70% to 90% in previous calculations.[87] In this model, newborn IUGR pups did not use a greater percentage of systemic glucose production for cerebral metabolism despite relatively larger brains and smaller livers.[87] The avidity of brain tissue for glucose in the IUGR puppies was increased, again suggesting that cerebral glucose extraction is greatest at the lower blood glucose concentrations.[84, 87] Thus a disproportionate size between brain and liver in IUGR dogs was not associated with neonatal hypoglycemia.

TABLE 17–7.

Potential Mechanisms of Neonatal Hypoglycemia in Intrauterine Growth Retardation

Mechanism	Effect
Decreased hepatic glycogen stores	Reduced precursor for hepatic glucose production
Decreased gluconeogenic precursors (e.g., alanine, lactate)	Decreased hepatic glucose production from gluconeogenesis
Decreased counterregulatory hormones (e.g., epinephrine, glucagon)	Decreased mobilization of glycogen, triglycerides; decreased gluconeogenesis
Decreased availability of free fatty acids	Increased glucose clearance, reduced alternate fuel oxidation, reduced ketogenesis and gluconeogenesis
Hyperinsulinism; decreased neonatal insulin resistance	Enhanced tissue glucose uptake; reduced glycogenolysis, gluconeogenesis, lipolysis
Chronic fetal glucopenia induced; translocation of glucose transporters to cell plasma membrane	Increased glucose clearance, extraction, and tissue avidity for glucose
Delayed induction of gluconeogenic enzymes (phosphoenolpyruvate carboxykinase)	Decreased hepatic glucose production from gluconeogenesis
Brain–liver disproportion (brain sparing with small liver)	Imbalance between cerebral glucose utilization and hepatic production

INTRAUTERINE DIAGNOSES, AND MANAGEMENT OF INTRAUTERINE GROWTH RETARDATION

The clinical diagnosis of IUGR should be suggested by relevant maternal risk factors (Tables 17–1 and 17–8) such as size vs. dates discrepancy on palpation of the gravid uterus, and should be confirmed by various ultrasonographic determinations of fetal size and congenital malformations (Tables 17–8 and 17–9).[88–90] As discussed earlier, it is imperative to determine if the fetus with IUGR has congenital malformations as part of a chromosome, genetic, or idiopathic malformation syndrome complex because the prognosis is more serious and subsequent management may be modified.

Fetal size can be determined by real-time fetal ultrasonographic examination (see Table 17–9).[91–93] Assessment of the fetal biparietal diameter, crown-rump length, head circumference, abdominal circumference, femur length, ratio of head to abdominal circumferences, ratio of femur length to abdominal circumferences, and qualitative amniotic fluid volume less than 2 cm all permit the biometric analysis of fetal growth parameters. Use of a system incorporating more than one of these parameters will yield a more accurate prediction of IUGR.[93, 94] A formula incorporating head circumference *(HC)*, femur length *(FL)*, and abdominal circumference *(AC)* has an excellent predictive value:

Log Predicted Birth Weight = 1.6961 + 0.02253 *HC* + 0.01645 *AC* + 0.06439 *FL*

The usefulness of head:abdominal circumference ratio relates to the head (brain) sparing effect of IUGR, with concomitant abdominal wasting of organ (liver) and adipose tissues. Indeed the infants with IUGR who are at high risk for fetal problems also have body wasting as determined by an abnormal ponderal index [weight (g) ÷ length (cm^3) × 100], or as identified by the ratio of the mid-arm to head circumference.[95, 96] These risks include both asphyxia and postnatal hypoglycemia.

If biometric analysis of fetal growth is combined with Doppler assessment of fetal blood flow (velocimetry), the prediction of the fetus with IUGR becomes even more ac-

TABLE 17–8.

Clinical Evaluation of the Growth-Retarded Fetus

Maternal variables
    Blood pressure
    Nutrition
    Age
    Infectious diseases
    Teratogen exposure
Fetal diagnosis
    Cordocentesis (percutaneous umbilical blood
      samples)
      Oxygen
      Lactate
      Hemoglobin
      Glucose
      Karyotype (rapid)
      TORCH evaluation (titers, culture)
Biophysical profile
    Fetal breathing movements
    Gross body movements
    Fetal tone
    Reactive fetal heart rate
    Qualitative amniotic fluid volume
Fetal diagnostic ultrasonography
    Gross multiple congenital anomalies
    Syndrome complex identification
    Symmetric vs. asymmetric growth pattern
    Fetal vascular resistance (Systolic/diastolic ratio or
      Pulsatility Index)
Fetal heart rate patterns
    Antepartum late heart rate deceleration
    Baseline heart rate variability

TABLE 17–9.

Ultrasonographic Evaluation of Growth Retardation

Methodology
    Real-time biometry
    Pulse Doppler velocimetry
Diagnostic
    Crown-rump length
    Biparietal diameter
    Abdominal circumference
    Head/abdomen ratio
    Total intrauterine volume
    Femur length
    Epiphyseal ossification
    Identification of fetal malformations
    Oligohydramnious
    Systolic/diastolic umbilical artery blood flow
    Pulsatile index ratio of umbilical and carotid
      arteries
Detection of fetal distress
    Doppler flow studies (velocity waveform)
      Umbilical vessels
      Thoracic aorta
      Descending aorta
      Middle cerebral artery
      Internal carotid artery
Placental grading

curate.[97, 98] In many patients with IUGR there is an abnormal blood flow pattern in the fetal umbilical artery or vein, and in the fetal aorta.[98-103] This can be detected with either continuous or pulsed Doppler ultrasonography. Indeed this ultrasonographic evidence of increased fetal vascular resistance may be present before obvious signs of distress are detected by nonstress tests or biophysical profiles.[104] The Doppler study determines flow in the specific artery (aorta, umbilical) during systolic and diastolic phases. The pulsatility index (PI) = (systolic–diastolic)/mean and the S/D ratio are two methods to express the relationship between systolic and diastolic flow.[104] With IUGR one can detect decreased diastolic flow or even absent or reverse diastolic flow. These changes suggest that fetal vascular resistance is increased and that this increased vascular resistance is due to fetal hypoxia or another cause of fetal distress (e.g., anemia, infection) (see Table 17–9). In some patients with IUGR the umbilical artery (or aortic) diastolic flow may be greatly reduced; however, the diastolic flow in the internal carotid artery may be normal.[90] These data suggest that the fetal circulation was redistributed during fetal distress and resulted in shunting of blood to the brain. This phenomenon could explain the brain growth–sparing effect in patients with placental insufficiency and IUGR. In some cases of IUGR this redistribution was evident before signs of growth disturbances, suggesting that the changes in vascular resistance associated with fetal distress may precede the onset of IUGR.[102]

Disturbed fetal growth, abnormal fetal vascular resistance in the umbilical circulation, and preservation of brain blood flow are usually manifested prior to evidence of fetal hypoxia or acidosis as determined by nonstress testing or the biophysical profile. Uteroplacental insufficiency of sufficient magnitude to produce these disturbances early in the development of IUGR is not detectable by routine biophysical surveillance of the fetus. Cordocentesis (percutaneous umbilical blood sampling) has confirmed the observations that subclinical fetal hypoxia is present in patients with IUGR (Table 17–10).[105-108] Cordocentesis in IUGR but otherwise asymptomatic fetuses has documented fetal hypoxia, hypercarbia, hypoglycemia, and lactic acidosis. The net effect of subclinical hypoxia and increased fetal vascular resistance is depicted in Table 17–10.

TABLE 17–10.

In Utero Consequences of Preclinical Uteroplacental Insufficiency

---

Respiratory
  Hypoxia
  Hypercarbia
  Acidosis
Cardiovascular
  Reduced descending aorta blood flow
  Reduced umbilical blood flow
  Increased vascular resistance
  Preserved (relative) cerebral blood flow
Metabolic
  Hypoglycemia
  Lactic acidosis
  Probably reduced placental amino acid transport
Hematologic
  Elevated erythropoietin levels
  Normoblastemia
  Polycythemia
Renal
  Oligohydramnios

The diagnostic and therapeutic approachs to the fetus with suspected IUGR should begin with the procedures noted in Table 17–8. This will help identify the potential cause(s) of IUGR; the association with syndromes, teratogens, and genetic disorders; the risk of intrauterine fetal demise from uteroplacental insufficiency; and the appropriate timing and management of labor and delivery.[88, 89, 91, 109]

Therapy of the fetus with IUGR is limited but has included the use of tocolysis prior to delivery to prevent fetal acidosis from myometrical contractions,[110] and the use of platelet inhibitors in women with recurrent IUGR and associated placental infarction.[111] Provision of oxygen to the mother in an attempt to improve fetal oxygenation has been successful in a small number of patients.[107] Maternal hyperoxygenation with 55% oxygen improved fetal hypoxia as determined by cordocentesis in five patients with increased vascular resistant IUGR. In addition, fetal blood flow velocity improved in the fetal thoracic aorta during maternal hyperoxygenation. Growth velocity did not improve; however, slow fetal growth was sustained in each pregnancy. The mechanism for the beneficial effects of maternal hyperoxia may be due to improved placental function (active transport). Hyperoxia may also improve fetal oxygenation and reverse hypoxic vasoconstriction. These preliminary data need to be confirmed before chronic maternal hyperoxia can be recommended for all pregnancies complicated by IUGR. Nonetheless, short-term oxygen administration during labor and delivery is an important therapy for women with a stressed, growth-retarded fetus.

POSTNATAL PROBLEMS AND INTRAUTERINE GROWTH RETARDATION

The most significant problems of the infant with IUGR are noted in Table 17–11. Congenital malformations due to TORCH,* teratogens, chromosome or genetic causes, and idiopathic malformation complexes have added problems related to the specific organ system involved, and the requirement for surgery, special diets, other therapies, and rehabilitation.[1, 112]

Fetal compromise and distress due to uteroplacental insufficiency places the newborn infant with IUGR at increased risk for hypoxic-ischemic organ injury because of intrapartum asphyxia, meconium aspiration pneumonia, persistent fetal circulation, or polycythemia-hyperviscosity syndrome.[1, 2, 89] Those infants at greatest risk for hypoxic-ischemic injury are those who demonstrate increased vascular resistance in fetal blood vessels, absent diastolic blood flow, head sparing–body wasting, and an abnormal fetal ponderal index. These infants have asymmetric IUGR, and often develop IUGR late in gestation because of a "hostile," nonpermissive uterine environment such as that during chronic uteroplacental insufficiency. This late-onset IUGR with growth arrest is often noted in women with preeclampsia, diabetes with vasculopathy, and chronic hypertension. The severity of fetal involvement is related to the degree of elevation of the maternal diastolic blood pressure as well as the duration of the hypertension. Increased vascular resistance can be demonstrated by Doppler flow studies in the uterine arteries, and end-artery disease other than the uterus will be noted in other maternal arterial beds such as the retina, kidney, or heart. Chronic antihypertensive medication may improve uteroplacental blood flow; however, careful assessment of fetal well being and adjuvant therapy with oxygen or expediant delivery for signs of severe distress may be indicated for

*Toxoplasmosis, other (syphillis, hepatitis, Zoster), rubella, cytomegalovirus, and herpes simplex.

TABLE 17–11.

Immediate Perinatal Problems and IUGR

Problem	Pathogenesis	Prevention/Treatment
Fetal demise	Placental insufficiency	Biophysical profile, vessel velocimetry, cordocentesis, maternal oxygen, early delivery
Asphyxia	Chronic and acute fetal hypoxia, acidosis; placental insufficiency	Antepartum, intrapartum monitoring; efficient neonatal resuscitation
Meconium aspiration pneumonia	Hypoxic stress	Pharyngeal-tracheal aspiration
Fasting hypoglycemia	↓ Hepatic glocogen, ↓ gluconeogenesis, ↓ Counterregulatory hormones, cold stress, asphyxia	Early oral or intravenous alimentation
Alimented hyperglycemia	Starvation diabetes	Glucose infusion not to exceed 8 mg/kg/min except if hypoglyecmic
Polycythemia/hyperviscosity	Placental transfusion Fetal hypoxia	Neonatal partial exchange transfusion
Temperature instability	Cold stress, poor fat stores, catecholamine depletion, hypoxia, hypoglycemia, reduced fasting oxygen consumption	Neutral thermal environment; early alimentation
Dysmorphology	TORCH (see text), syndrome complexes, chromosome disorders, teratogen exposure	Disease-specific therapy/prevention

individual patients (see Table 17–8). If asphyxia, hypoglycemia, or pulmonary problems are prevented, these IUGR infants do well and demonstrate catch-up growth once provided with sufficient calories. Those infants who have symmetrical growth retardation, and who do not have evidence of genetic, chromosomal, or congenital malformation syndromes, usually do much better than infants with asymmetric IUGR. These infants often have mothers who themselves were SGA at birth, thus representing decreased growth potential rather than an abnormal environment in utero. After birth, these infants have little problems but continue to be small and do not demonstrate catch-up growth.

The long-term outcome for infants with IUGR depends on the cause (presence or absence of TORCH), malformations (teratogens), immediate perinatal complication (asphyxia, hypoglycemia, pneumonia), and socioeconomic status of the family. The high rate of intrauterine fetal demise has been reduced because of intensive fetal surveillance; nonetheless, the mortality (excluding that due to anomalies) is 10 times that for AGA infants.[1, 112–114] Hypoxic-ischemic injury places these infants at risk for cerebral palsy, while as many as 35% fail to achieve normal growth after birth, and remain small. The poor postnatal growth and intellectual function are particularly more common among SGA preterm infants and those who demonstrate reduced growth in the 1st or 2d trimester of pregnancy as depicted by a reduced crown-rump length or biparietal diameter.[112]

Acknowledgment

The authors express their appreciation for the expert preparation of the manuscript by Vicki Bancroft.

REFERENCES

1. Kliegman R, Hulman S: Intrauterine growth retardation: Determinants of aberrant fetal growth, in Fanaroff A, Martin R (eds): *Neonatal Perinatal Medicine: Diseases of the Fetus and Newborn,* ed 4. St Louis, CV Mosby, 1987, pp 69–100.
2. Kliegman R, Behrman R: The fetus and the neonatal infant, in Behrman R, Vaughan V (eds): *Nelson Textbook of Pediatrics,* ed 13. Philadelphia, WB Saunders Co, 1987, pp 358–435.
3. Winick M: Maternal nutrition and fetal growth. *Perinatal-Neonatal* 1986; 10:28–34.
4. Khoury MJ, Erickson JD, Cordero JF, et al: Congenital malformations and intrauterine growth retardation: A population study. *Pediatrics* 1988; 82:83–90.
5. Klebanoff MA, Yip R: Influence of maternal birth weight on rate of fetal growth and duration of gestation. *J Pediatr* 1987; 111:287–292.
6. Van de Spuy ZM, Steer PJ, McCusker M, et al: Outcome of pregnancy in underweight women after spontaneous and induced ovulation. *Br Med J* 1988; 296:962–965.
7. Friedman JM: Teratogens and growth. *Growth: Genetics and Hormones* 1987; 3:6–8.
8. Buchanan TA, Freinkel N: Fuel-mediated teratogenesis: Symmetric growth retardation in the rat fetus at term after a circumscribed exposure to D-mannose during organogenesis. *Am J Obstet Gynecol* 1988; 158:663-669.
9. Hunter III ES, Sadler TW, Wynn RE: A potential mechanism of DL-B-hydroxybutyrate-induced malformations in mouse embryos. *Am J Physiol* 1987; 253(16):E72–E80.
10. Pedersen JF, Molsted-Pedersen L: Early fetal growth delay detected by ultrasound marks increased risk of congenital malformation in diabetic pregnancy. *Br Med J* 1981; 293:269–271.
11. Iffy L, Jacobovits A, Westlake W, et al: Early intra-uterine development. I: The rate of growth of caucasian embryos and fetuses between the 6th and 20th weeks of gestation. *Pediatrics* 1975; 56:173–186.
12. Spiers PS: Does growth retardation predispose the fetus to congenital malformation? *Lancet* 1982; ii:312–314.
13. Pederson JF, Molsted-Pedersen L: Early foetal growth delay detected by ultrasound marks increased risk of congenital malformation in diabetic pregnancy. *Br Med J* 1981; 283:269–271.
14. Pedersen JF: Fetal size in early pregnancy and congenital malformation. *Am J Obstet Gynecol* 1983; 145:641–643.
15. Rogan WJ, Gladen BG, Hung J-L: Congenital poisoning by polychlorinated biphenyls and their contaminants in Taiwan. *Science* 1988; 241:334–336.
16. Engstrom W, Lindham S, Schofield P: Wiedemann-Beckwith Syndrome. *Eur J Pediatr* 1988; 147:450–457.
17. Schmickel RD: Contiguous gene syndromes: A component of recognizable syndromes. *J Pediatr* 1986; 109:231–241.
18. Nurse P: Cell reproduction. *Br Med J* 1987; 295:1037–1038.
19. Matsunaga H, Nishimoto I, Kojima I: Activation of a calcium-permeable cation channel by insulin-like growth factor II in BALB/c 3T3 cells. *Am J Physiol* 1988; 255(24):C442–C446.
20. Hill DJ, Milner RDG: Insulin as a growth factor. *Pediatr Res* 1985; 19:879–886.
21. Johnson JD: Regulation of fetal growth. *Pediatr Res* 1985; 19:738–740.
22. Deuel TF: Polypeptide growth factors: Roles in normal and abnormal cell growth. *Am Rev Cell Biol* 1987; 3:443–492.

23. Yarden Y, Ullrich A: Molecular analysis of signal transduction by growth factors. *Biochem* 1988; 27:3113–3119.
24. Roth RA: Structure of the receptor for insulin-like growth factor II: The puzzle amplified. *Science* 1988; 239:1269–1271.
25. Allende JE: GTP-mediated macromolecular interactions: The common features of different systems. *FASEB J* 1988; 2:2356–2367.
26. Underwood L, D'Ercole AJ: Insulin and insulin-like growth factors/somatomedins in fetal and neonatal development. *Clin Endo Metab* 1984; 13:69–89.
27. Thorsson AV, Hintz RI: Insulin receptors in the newborn: Increase in receptor affinity and number. *N Engl J Med* 1977; 297:908–912.
28. Geffner ME, Kaplan SA, Bersch N, et al: Leprechaunism: In vitro insulin action despite genetic insulin resistance. *Pediatr Res* 1987; 22:286–291.
29. Hill DJ, Milner RDG: Increased somatomedin and cartilage metabolic activity in rabbit fetuses injected with insulin in utero. *Diabetologia* 1980; 19:143–147.
30. Shen S-J, Daimon M, Wang C-Y, et al: Isolation of an insulin-like growth factor II cDNA with a unique 5' untranslated region from human placenta. *Proc Natl Acad Sci* 1988; 85:1947–1951.
31. Adams SO, Nissley SP, Handwerger S, et al: Developmental patterns of insulin-like growth factor-I and -II synthesis and regulation in rat fibroblasts. *Nature* 1983; 302:150–153.
32. Froesch ER, Schmid C, Schwander J, et al: Actions of insulin-like growth factors. *Ann Rev Physiol* 1985; 47:443–467.
33. Smith EP, Sadler TW, D'Ercole AJ: Somatomedins/insulin-like growth factors, their receptors and binding proteins are present during mouse embryogenesis. *Development* 1987; 101:73–82.
34. D'Ercole AJ, Hill DJ, Strain AJ, et al: Tissue and plasma somatomedian-C/insulin-like growth factor I concentrations in the human fetus during the first half of gestation. *Pediatr Res* 1986; 20:253–255.
35. Han VKM, D'Ercole AJ, Lund PK: Cellular localization of somatomedin (insulin-like growth factor) messenger RNA in the human fetus. *Science* 1987; 236:193–197.
36. Sara VR, Hall K, Misaki M, et al: Ontogenesis of somatomedin and insulin receptors in the human fetus. *J Clin Invest* 1983; 71:1084–1094.
37. Han VKM, Hill DJ, Strain AJ, et al: Identification of somatomedin/insulin-like growth factor immunoreactive cells in the human fetus. *Pediatr Res* 1987; 22:245–249.
38. Han VKM, Lund PK, Lee DC, et al: Expression of somatomedin/insulin-like growth factor messenger ribonucleic acids in the human fetus: Identification, characterization, and tissue distribution. *J Clin Endocrinol Metab* 1988; 66:422–429.
39. Wang C-Y, Daimon M, Shen S-J, et al: Insulin-like growth factor-I messenger RNA in the developing human placenta and in term placenta of diabetics. *Molecular Endocrinology* In press.
40. Mattson BA, Rosenblum IY, Smith RM, et al: Autoradiographic evidence for insulin and insulin-like growth factor binding to early mouse embryos. *Diabetes* 1988; 37:585–589.
41. Bassas L, Lesniak MA, Serrano J, et al: Developmental regulation of insulin and type I insulin-like growth factor receptors and absence of type II receptors in chicken embryo tissues. *Diabetes* 1988; 37:637–644.
42. Sporn MB, Roberts AB: Peptide growth factors are multifunctional. *Nature* 1988; 332:217–218.
43. Vileisis RA, D'Ercole AJ: Tissue and serum concentrations of somatomedin-C/insulin-like growth factor I in fetal rats made growth retarded by uterine artery ligation. *Pediatr Res* 1986; 20:126–130.
44. Gluckman PD, Brinsmead MW: Somatomedin in cord blood: Relationship to gestational age and birth size. *J Clin Endocrinol Metab* 1976; 43:1378–1381.
45. Foley TP Jr, DePhilip R, Perricelli A, et al: Low somatomedin activity in cord serum from infants with intrauterine growth retardation. *J Pediatr* 1980; 96:605–610.

46. Merimee TJ, Zapf J, Hewlett B, et al: Insulin-like growth factors in pygmies. *N Engl J Med* 1987; 316:906–911.

47. Thieriot-Prevost G, Daffos F, Forestier F, et al: Serum growth-promoting activity in normal and hypotrophic fetuses at midpregnancy. *Pediatr Res* 1987; 22:39–40.

48. Thieriot-Prevost G, Boccara JF, Francoual C, et al: Serum insulin-like growth factor 1 and serum growth-promoting activity during the first postnatal year in infants with intrauterine growth retardation. *Pediatr Res* 1988; 24:380–383.

49. Handwerger S: Human placental lactogen and fetal growth. *Growth, Genetics and Hormones* 1988; 4:4–6.

50. Hill DJ, Crace CJ, Strain AJ, et al: Regulation of amino acid uptake and deoxyribonucleic acid synthesis in isolated human fetal fibroblasts and myoblasts: Effect of human placental lactogen somatomedin-C, multiplication-stimulating activity, and insulin. *J Clin Endo Metab* 1986; 62:753–760.

51. Mercola M, Melton DA, Stiles CD: Platelet-derived growth factor A chain is maternally encoded in *Xenopus* embryos. *Science* 1988; 241:1223–1225.

52. Beckmann MP, Betsholtz C, Heldin CH, et al: Comparison of biological properties and transforming potential of human PDGF-A and PDGF-B. *Science* 1988; 241:1346–1349.

53. Bauer EA, Silverman N, Busiek DF, et al: Diminished response of Werner's syndrome fibroblasts to growth factors PDGF and FGF. *Science* 1986; 234:1240–1243.

54. Velu TJ, Beguinot L, Vass WC, et al: Epidermal growth factor-dependent transformation by a human EGF receptor proto-oncogene. *Science* 1987; 238:1408–1410.

55. Zimmerman KA, Yancopoulos GD, Collum RG, et al: Differential expression of myc family genes during murine development. *Nature* 1986; 319:780–783.

56. Travers MT, Barrett-Lee PJ, Berger U, et al: Growth factor expression in normal, benign, and malignant breast tissue. *Br Med J* 1988; 297:1621–1624.

57. Boyd RH: Placental transport: Diversity and complexity. *Arch Dis Child* 1987; 62:1205–1206.

58. Gilfillan CA, Tserng K-Y, Kalhan SC: Alanine production by the human fetus at term gestation. *Biol Neonate* 1985; 47:141–147.

59. Menon RK, Sperling MA: Carbohydrate Metabolism. *Seminars Perinatol* 1988; 12:157–162.

60. Bloch CA, Banach W, Landt K, et al: Effects of fetal insulin infusion on glucose kinetics in pregnant sheep: A compartmental analysis. *Am J Physiol* 1986; 251:E448–E456.

61. Hay WW, Sparks JW, Wilkening RB, et al: Fetal glucose uptake and utilization as functions of maternal glucose concentration. *Am J Physiol* 1984; 246:E237–E242.

62. Milley JR, Papacostas JS, Tabata BK: Effect of insulin on uptake of metabolic substrates by the sheep fetus. *Am J Physiol* 1986; 251:E349–E356.

63. Bloch CA, Menon RK, Sperling MA: Effects of somatostatin and glucose infusion on glucose kinetics in fetal sheep. *Am J Physiol* 1988; 255:E87–E93.

64. Hay WW, Meznarich HK, Sparks JW, et al: Effect of insulin on glucose uptake in near-term fetal lambs. *Proc Soc Exp Bio Med* 1985; 178:557–564.

65. Hay WW, Sparks JW, Gilbert M, et al: Effect of insulin on glucose uptake by the maternal hindlimb and uterus, and by the fetus in conscious pregnant sheep. *J Endocr* 1984; 100:119–124.

66. Phillips AF, Rosenkrantz TS, Grunnet ML, et al: Effects of fetal insulin secretory deficiency on metabolism in fetal lamb. *Diabetes* 1986; 35:964–972.

67. Hay WW, Meznarich HK: Use of fetal streptozotocin injection to determine the role of normal levels of fetal insulin in regulating uteroplacental and umbilical glucose exchange. *Pediatr Res* 1988; 24:312–317.

68. Crandell SS, Fisher DJ, Morriss FH: Effects of ovine maternal hyperglycemia on fetal regional blood flows and metabolism. *Am J Physiol* 1985; 249:E454–E460.

69. Phillips AF, Porte PJ, Stabinsky S, et al: Effects of chronic fetal hyperglycemia upon oxygen consumption in the ovine uterus and conceptus. *J Clin Invest* 1984; 74:279–286.

70. Phillips AF, Dubin JW, Matty PJ, et al: Arterial hypoxemia and hyperinsulinemia in the chronically hyperglycemic fetal lamb. *Pediatr Res* 1982; 16:653–658.

71. Carson BS, Phillips AF, Simmons MA, et al: Effects of a sustained insulin infusion upon glucose uptake and oxygenation of the ovine fetus. *Pediatr Res* 1980; 14:147–152.

72. Philipson EH, Kalhan SC, Riha MM, et al: Effects of maternal glucose infusion on fetal acid-base status in human pregnancy. *Am J Obstet Gynecol* 1987; 157:866–873.

73. Kliegman RM, Miettinen EL, Adam PAJ: Fetal and neonatal responses to maternal canine starvation: Circulating fuels and neonatal glucose production. *Pediatr Res* 1981; 15:945–951.

74. Kliegman RM, Morton S: The metabolic response of the canine neonate to twenty-four hours of fasting. *Metabolism* 1987; 36:521–526.

75. Miettinen E-L, Kliegman RM: Fetal and neonatal responses to extended maternal canine starvation. II. Fetal and neonatal liver metabolism. *Pediatr Res* 1983; 17:639–644.

76. Mestyan J, Schultz K, Horvath M: Comparative glycemic responses to alanine in normal term and small-for-gestational-age infants. *J Pediatr* 1974; 85:276–278.

77. Haymond MW, Karl IE, Pagliara AS: Increased gluconeogenic substrates in the small-for-gestational-age infant. *N Engl J Med* 1974; 291:322–328.

78. Le Dune MA: Response to glucagon in small-for-dates hypoglycaemic and non-hypoglycaemic newborn infants. *Arch Dis Child* 1972; 47:754–759.

79. Le Dune MA: Intravenous glucose tolerance and plasma insulin studies in small-for-dates infants. *Arch Dis Child* 1972; 47:111–114.

80. Collins JE, Leonard JV: Hyperinsulinism in asphyxiated and small-for-dates infants with hypoglycemia. *Lancet* 1984; 2:311–313.

81. Sabel K-G, Olegard R, Mellander M, et al: Interrelation between fatty acid oxidation and control of gluconeogenic substrates in small-for-gestional-age (SGA) infants with hypoglycemia and with normoglycemia. *Acta Paediatr Scand* 1982; 71:53–61.

82. Ferre P, Pegorier J-P, Marliss EB, et al: Influence of exogenous fat and gluconeogenic substrates on glucose homeostasis in the newborn rat. *Am J Physiol* 1978; 234(2):E129–E136.

83. Ogata ES, Bussey ME, LaBarbera A, et al: Altered growth, hypoglycemia, hypoalaninemia, and ketonemia in the young rat: Postnatal consequences of intrauterine growth retardation. *Pediatr Res* 1985; 19:32–37.

84. Kliegman RM: Cerebral metabolic response to neonatal hypoglycemia in growth-retarded dogs. *Pediatr Res* 1988; 24:649–652.

85. Kliegman RM: Cerebral metabolic intermediate response following severe canine intrauterine growth retardation. *Pediatr Res* 1986; 20:662–667.

86. McCall AL, Fixman LB, Fleming N, et al: Chronic hypoglycemia increases brain glucose transport. *Am J Physiol* 1986; 251(14):E442–447.

87. Huang MME, Kliegman RM, Trindade C, et al: Allocation of systemic glucose output to cerebral utilization as a function of fetal canine growth. *Am J Physiol* 1988; 254(17): E579–E587.

88. Carlson DE: Maternal diseases associated with intrauterine growth retardation. *Seminars Perinatol* 1988; 12:17–22.

89. Brar HS, Rutherford SE: Classification of intrauterine growth retardation. *Seminars Perinatol* 1988; 12:2–10.

90. Brar HS, Platt LD: Reverse end-diastolic flow velocity on umbilical artery velocimetry in high-risk pregnancies: An ominous finding with adverse pregnancy outcome. *Am J Obstet Gynecol* 1988; 159:559–561.

91. Horenstein J: Ultrasound assessment of fetal growth and fetal measurements. *Seminars Perinatol* 1988; 12:23–30.

92. Peilet BW, Sabbagha RE, MacGregor SN, et al: Ultrasonic prediction of birth weight in preterm fetuses: Which formula is best? *Am J Obstet Gynecol* 1987; 157:1411–1414.

93. Divon MY, Guidetti DA, Braverman JJ, et al: Intrauterine growth retardation—a prospec-

tive study for the diagnostic value of real-time sonography combined with umbilical artery flow velocimetry. *Obstet Gynecol* 1988; 72:611–614.

94. Rosendahl H, Kivinen S: Routine ultrasound screening for early detection of small for gestational age fetuses. *Obstet Gynecol* 1988; 71:518–521.

95. Georgieff MK, Sasanow SR, Mammel MC, et al: Mid-arm circumference/head circumference ratios for identification of symptomatic LGA, AGA, and SGA newborn infants. *J Pediatr* 1986; 109:316–321.

96. Patterson RM, Pouliot MR: Neonatal morphometrics and perinatal outcome: Who is growth retarded? *Am J Obstet Gynecol* 1987; 157:691–693.

97. Gaziano E, Knox GE, Wager GP, et al: The predictability of the small-for-gestational-age infant by real-time ultrasound-derived measurements combined with pulsed Doppler umbilical artery velocimetry. *Am J Obstet Gynecol* 1988; 158:1431–1439.

98. Berkowitz GS, Mehalek KE, Chitkara U, et al: Doppler umbilical velocimetry in the prediction of adverse outcome in pregnancies at risk for intrauterine growth retardation. *Obstet Gynecol* 1988; 71:742–746.

99. Wladimiroff JW, Noordam MJ, Wijngaard van den JAGW, et al: Fetal internal carotid and umbilical artery blood flow velocity waveforms as a measure of fetal well-being in intrauterine growth retardation. *Pediatr Res* 1988; 24:609–612.

100. Berkowitz GS, Chitkara U, Rosenberg J, et al: Sonographic estimation of fetal weight and Doppler analysis of umbilical artery velocimetry in the prediction of intrauterine growth retardation: A prospective study. *Am J Obstet Gynecol* 1988; 158:1149–1153.

101. Laurin J, Lingman G, Marsal K, et al: Fetal blood flow in pregnancies complicated by intrauterine growth retardation. *Obstet Gynecol* 1987; 69:895–902.

102. Arduini D, Rizzo G, Romanini C, et al: Fetal blood flow velocity waveforms as predictors of growth retardation. *Obstet Gynecol* 1987; 70:7–10.

103. Wladimiroff JW, Wijngaard JA, Degani S, et al: Cerebral and umbilical arterial blood flow velocity waveforms in normal and growth retarded pregnancies. *Obstet Gynecol* 1987; 69:705–709.

104. Reuwer PJHM, Sijmons EA, Rietman GW, et al: Intrauterine growth retardation: Prediction of perinatal distress by Doppler ultrasound. *Lancet* 1987; ii:415–418.

105. Cox WL, Daffos F, Forestier F, et al: Physiology and management of intrauterine growth retardation: A biologic approach with fetal blood sampling. *Am J Obstet Gynecol* 1988; 159:36–41.

106. Soothill PW, Nicolaides KH, Campbell S: Prenatal asphyxia, hyperlacticaemia, hypoglycaemia, and erythroblastosis in growth retarded fetuses. *Br Med J* 1987; 294:1051–1053.

107. Nicolaides KH, Campbell S, Bradley RJ, et al: Maternal oxygen therapy for intrauterine growth retardation. *Lancet* 1987; i:942–945.

108. Cetin I, Marconi AM, Bozzetti P, et al: Umbilical amino acid concentrations in appropriate and small for gestational age infants: A biochemical difference present in utero. *Am J Obstet Gynecol* 1988; 158:120–126.

109. Koren G, Edwards MB, Miskin M: Antenatal sonography of fetal malformations associated with drugs and chemicals: A guide. *Am J Obstet Gynecol* 1987; 156:79–85.

110. Patriarco MS, Viechnicki BM, Hutchinson TA, et al: A study on intrauterine fetal resuscitation with terbutaline. *Am J Obstet Gynecol* 1987; 157:384–387.

111. Wallenburg HCS, Rotmans N: Prevention of recurrent idiopathic fetal growth retardation by low-dose aspirin and dipyridamole. *Am J Obstet Gynecol* 1987; 157:1230–1235.

112. Petersen MB, Pedersen SA, Greisen G, et al: Early growth delay in diabetic pregnancy: Relation to psychomotor development at age 4. *Br Med J* 1988; 296:598–600.

113. Chessex P, Reichman B, Verellen G, et al: Metabolic consequences of intrauterine growth retardation in very low birthweight infants. *Pediatr Res* 1984; 18:709–711.

114. Wennergren M, Wennergren G, Vilbergsson G: Obstetric characteristics and neonatal performance in a four-year small for gestational age population. *Obstet Gynecol* 1988; 72:615–620.

Chapter 18

The Infant of the Diabetic Mother*

Richard M. Cowett, M.D.

From a developmental standpoint the normal newborn is in a transitional state relative to glucose homeostasis. The fetus is completely dependent on his or her mother for glucose delivery. The adult is considered to have precise control of glucose homeostasis, as plasma glucose concentration is regulated to a fine degree[1]; in contrast, maintenance of glucose homeostasis may be a major problem even in the healthy newborn.[2] The newborn must provide for energy (particularly for the brain, which consumes 70% of glucose production per kilogram body weight per minute) and for growth. At the same time, the newborn must maintain a balance between glucose deficiency and excess. The dependence of the conceptus on the maternal organism for continuous substrate delivery contrasts with the variable and intermittent exogenous oral intake by the neonate. Development of homeostasis results from a balance between substrate availability and developing hormonal (insulin and contrainsulin effects), sympathomimetic, neural, and enzymatic systems. The precarious nature of this situation is emphasized by the numerous morbidities producing or associated with neonatal hypoglycemia and hyperglycemia during this time period. The infant of the diabetic mother (IDM) can be utilized to document not only how far we have come in understanding the pathophysiology of the metabolic disequilibrium that may exist, but also how far we need to go. From the discussion that follows, it will be apparent that much work needs to be accomplished to fully understand the mechanisms that are operative. The topic of the IDM has been evaluated previously in extensive reviews.[3-7]

Although many IDMs have an uneventful perinatal course, there is still an increased risk for complications. This discussion highlights many of the metabolic difficulties that an IDM may encounter, analyzes the pathophysiologic basis for their occurrence, and outlines specific rationale for treatment. Nonmetabolic untoward effects have been recently reviewed elsewhere,[5, 6] and are not discussed.

*Supported in part by grant NIH-NICHHD 1-550 HD 11343. During the period of the studies reported here, Dr. Cowett was the recipient of an RCDA 1-K04 HD 00308 grant from the NIH-NICHHD.

PATHOGENESIS OF THE EFFECTS OF MATERNAL DIABETES ON THE FETUS

No single pathogenic mechanism has been clearly defined to explain the diverse problems observed in IDMs. Nevertheless, many of the effects can be attributed to maternal metabolic (glucose) control. Pedersen originally emphasized the relationship between maternal glucose concentration and neonatal hypoglycemia[8] (Table 18–1). His simplified hypothesis recognized that maternal hyperglycemia was paralleled by fetal hyperglycemia, which stimulated the fetal pancreas, resulting in islet cell hypertrophy and beta cell hyperplasia with increased insulin content. Upon separation of the fetus from the mother, the former no longer was supported by placental glucose transfer which resulted in neonatal hypoglycemia.

Hyperinsulinemia in utero affects diverse organ systems, including the placenta. Insulin acts as the primary anabolic hormone of fetal growth and development, resulting in visceromegaly (especially heart and liver) and macrosomia. In the presence of excess substrate (glucose), increased fat synthesis, and deposition occur during the 3d trimester. Fetal macrosomia is reflected by increased body fat, muscle mass, and organomegaly but not in increased size of the brain or kidneys.[9, 10] After delivery there is a rapid fall in plasma glucose with persistently low concentrations of plasma free fatty acids (FFA), glycerol, and β-hydroxybutyrate. In response to an intravenous glucose stimulus, plasma insulin-like activity is increased, as are plasma immunoreactive insulin (determined in the absence of maternal insulin antibodies) and plasma C-peptide.[11] The insulin response to intravenous arginine is also exaggerated in infants of gestationally diabetic mothers.[12]

The response to an oral glucose load results in an earlier plasma insulin rise in IDMs compared with healthy infants, although the area under the insulin curve is similar.[13] During the initial hours after birth, the response to an acute intravenous bolus of glucose in IDMs is a rapid rate of glucose disappearance from the plasma.[14] In contrast, the rise in plasma glucose concentration following stepwise hourly increases in the rate of continuously infused glucose results in elevations even at normal rates (i.e., 4 to 6 mg/kg/min).[15, 16] The latter may be attributed to a persistence of hepatic glucose output which is similar to that of the healthy infant.

Alterations of plasma glucocorticoids and growth hormone have not been significant in IDMs. Definitive studies of the somatomedins (insulin-like growth factors IGF I and IGF II) are being conducted at present. In contrast, urinary excretion of catecholamines is diminished, especially in infants with low plasma glucose concentration (supra infra).[17]

TABLE 18–1.*

Observations for the Hypothesis of "Hyperinsulinism" in Infants of Diabetic Mothers

---

Islet hyperplasia and β-cell hypertrophy
Obesity and macrosomia
Hypoglycemia with low free fatty acid levels
Rapid glucose disappearance rate
   Higher plasma insulin-like activity after glucose
   Umbilical vein immunoinsulin increase
C-peptide and proinsulin elevated

---

*Modified from Pedersen J: *The Pregnant Diabetic and Her Newborn*, ed 2. Baltimore, Williams & Wilkins, 1977.

In addition, plasma glucagon levels are less elevated after delivery in comparison with those of healthy infants.[18]

Recent studies of insulin receptors on fetal monocytes isolated from placental blood of infants of gestationally diabetic mothers (IGDM) at delivery indicated that IGDMs had more receptor sites per monocyte than nondiabetic adults or healthy infants.[19] Monocytes from both healthy infants and IGDMs showed greater affinity for insulin than did those of adults. Furthermore, in the presence of increased ambient levels of plasma insulin, monocytes of the IGDM seem to develop increased (not decreased) concentrations of insulin receptors as well as increased affinity for the hormone. The significance of these observations for the physiologic effects of insulin are unclear; however, there are implications regarding the competition of insulin and its antibodies for receptor sites and resultant cell metabolism of insulin-sensitive tissues.

In a recent evaluation, the role of insulin receptors in macrosomia and the tendency to hypoglycemia was studied in the IDM and infants born to control mothers between 3 and 14 days of age. The IDMs were macrosomic. Plasma free insulin concentrations in cord blood were 15-fold higher in the IDMs than in controls, and threefold higher in peripheral venous blood. Hypoglycemia was noted in 12 of 17 IDMs but none of the control infants. In umbilical blood, binding of insulin to erythrocytes was not different between the groups, but decreased during the first weeks at a more rapid rate in the IDM. This was the result of decreased receptor affinity and receptor concentration in the IDM. Thus, insulin binding is similar in spite of gross hyperinsulinemia in the IDM, the latter resulting in macrosomia and hypoglycemia which decrease early on in the neonatal period.[20]

KINETIC ANALYSIS OF THE INFANT OF THE DIABETIC MOTHER

Application of in vivo kinetic analysis has been utilized by numerous investigators to evaluate the IDM metabolically. An early study using stable nonradioactive isotopes was reported by Kalhan et al. (using [1-^{13}C]glucose and the prime constant infusion technique).[21] The authors measured systemic glucose production rates in 5 nondiabetic infants and 5 infants of insulin-dependent diabetics at 2 hours of age. As expected, the IDMs had a lower glucose concentration during the study than infants of nondiabetic mothers. For the first time the authors reported that the IDM had a lower systemic glucose production rate. They suggested that decreased glucose output was related to inhibited glycogenolysis. They speculated that increased insulin and decreased glucagon and catecholamine responses would have resulted in decreased systemic output. What was of interest in this report was that for the time studied (late 1970s) the diabetic women were considered to be in excellent control, having been hospitalized during the last 4 weeks of the pregnancy to achieve strict metabolic control (maternal blood glucose between 50 and 150 mg/dL). Yet the systemic glucose production rates of these infants were lower than those of the control infants.

A further evaluation of the IDM was accomplished by the same group 5 years later (1982).[22] Again focusing on infants of mothers in "strict control," the authors evaluated systemic glucose production in 5 infants of insulin-dependent mothers, 1 infant of a gestational diabetic, and 5 infants born to nondiabetic mothers. The blood glucose measurements were in a range similar (36 to 164 mg/dL) to that of the previous series, and the mothers were controlled in a hospital setting for 3 to 4 weeks prior to delivery. In this series systemic glucose production rates were similar in the diabetics compared with the controls. However, the authors, similar to other groups,[23] carried their investigation a critical step further. They infused exogenous glucose, which in the nondiabetic adult can diminish endogenous glucose production because of the precise control of endogenous production known to be the hallmark of the adult. The IDMs did not evidence as great a suppression of endogenous glucose production as the adult. The authors concluded that altered regulation of glucose production may be secondary to intermittent maternal hyperglycemia, even in strictly controlled women.

These studies parallel the work of the Brown University group who have studied glucose kinetics in the newborn. Using 78% enriched D[U-^{13}C]glucose, 9 IDMs (4 insulin-dependent and 5 chemical-dependent) were compared with 5 infants of nondiabetic women. All mothers were evaluated relative to control by utilization of hemoglobin A_{1C} and maternal plasma glucose and or cord vein glucose at delivery. None of the women was maintained in the hospital prior to study. There was a similarity between glucose production rates in the infants studied. The authors concluded that good metabolic control of the maternal diabetic state would help maintain euglycemia.[24] However, in a subsequent analysis in which infants received glucose exogenously to maintain euglycemia a heterogeneity existed in the ability of the infant to depress endogenous glucose production.[25] These latter data parallel other work from the same group which reflect the transitional nature of glucose metabolism in the term and preterm infant.

The realization that neonatal glucose homeostasis is in a transitional state is further supported by studies in which maternal control was evaluated in a group of gestationally diabetic women relative to the birth weights of the infants.[26] If the Pedersen hypothesis were correct, birth weights of the infants should correlate with the degree of control of the mother during the pregnancy. There was a lack of correlation between birth weight and mean maternal plasma glucose concentration during the 3d trimester of pregnancy in this group of gestational diabetics. This lack of correlation further supports the heterogeneity of the diabetic state and suggests that while control of glucose is multifactorial, control of fetal growth is likewise. Similar conclusions led Freinkel, Milner and others

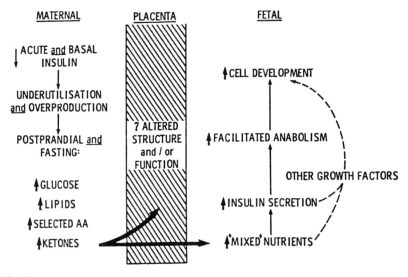

FIG 18–1.
Fetal development in insulinogenic diabetic pregnancy utilizing maternal mixed nutrients as controlling factors. (From Freinkel N: Of pregnancy and progeny, Banting lecture. *Diabetes* 1980; 29:1023–1035. Used by permission.)

to conclude that mixed nutrient (amino acids, free fatty acids, and so forth) other than glucose are important in fetal-neonatal metabolic control, as noted in Figure 18–1).[27, 28] This concept is an important one for ongoing research.

Support for this concept has recently been provided by Kalkhoff et al.,[29] who studied the relationship between neonatal birth weight and maternal plasma amino acid profiles in lean and obese nondiabetic women and in type I diabetic pregnant women. Hemoglobin A_1, plasma glucose, and total amino acid profiles were elevated in diabetic subjects compared with levels in controls. No differences were present between obese and lean control groups. Plasma glucose concentrations and profiles of HbA$_1$ did not correlate with relative weights of the newborns, while average total plasma amino acids concentrations did. The authors concluded that maternal plasma amino acid profiles may influence fetal weight generally and affect the development of neonatal macrosomia.[29]

Finally, Small et al. have suggested that macrosomia remains comparatively common in pregnancies complicated by insulin-dependent diabetic mothers. Factors other than maternal hyperglycemia must contribute to its cause.[30]

CONGENITAL ABNORMALITIES

While most morbidity and mortality data for the IDM has shown definite improvement with time, congenital anomalies remain a major unresolved problem. The threefold to fourfold increase in the incidence of congenital anomalies in the offspring of diabetic women has continued to be noted in most centers and remains the most frequent contributor to perinatal mortality.[31–34] This comes at a time when centers are reporting perinatal mortalities in offspring of insulin-dependent diabetic women that are no different from nondiabetics after correction for deaths resulting from congenital anomalies.[35, 36]

The pathogenesis of the increase in congenital anomalies among IDMs has remained obscure, although several etiologies have been proposed to account for these. They include (1) hyperglycemia, either preconceptional or postconceptional; (2) hypoglycemia; (3) fetal hyperinsulinemia; (4) uteroplacental vascular disease; and/or (5) genetic predisposition. While there are data to support each proposal, currently the evidence is best for the postconceptional hyperglycemia cause.

If a preconceptional influence of hyperglycemia or hypoglycemia or a genetic predisposition for congenital anomalies were operative, then one might anticipate that offspring of diabetic fathers and nondiabetic mothers would have an increased incidence of anomalies. This assumes, of course, that the sperm and egg would be equally affected by the physiologic and biochemical permutations of the maternal diabetes. In a careful hospital chart review by Neave of 1,262 offspring of diabetic fathers, only a slight increase in anomalies of questionable significance was found when compared with matched controls.[37] In this same study, however, a marked increase in anomalies was found in IDMs compared with both the offspring of the diabetic fathers and an independent control group.

Increasingly, studies of normalization of blood glucose concentration before conception in diabetic women have been reported. One large European (Karlsburg, German Democratic Republic) diabetic population, which included nonpregnant women cared for in an ongoing diabetic outpatient program whose objectives included normalization of blood glucose concentration, had a markedly lower incidence of congenital anomalies compared with a simultaneously studied group of women who had no such therapeutic diabetic regimen applied before they knew they were pregnant.[38]

Similar findings were recently reported by Dicker et al., who noted that congenital anomalies were 0.65% among a group of women who were not recipients of preconceptional diabetic counseling compared with no anomalies in a group who received counseling.[39]

There are scant human data on the association of hyperglycemia and anomalies. This may be due in part to the fact that organogenesis is taking place at a time during pregnancy when many diabetic women are not usually carefully evaluated for hyperglycemia. Hemoglobin A_{1C}, which reflects ambient plasma glucose concentrations over the previous 4 to 6 weeks, has the potential advantage of offering one indicator of integrated "chronic" blood glucose control. A report of initial-visit, 1st-trimester maternal HbA_{1C} values in a group of insulin-dependent subjects found higher values in those diabetic women giving birth to babies with anomalies.[40]

In recent years, multiple studies have strongly associated the concept of preconceptional testing and control with a marked diminution in the incidence of congenital anomalies. In one report 44 of 75 patients with insulin-dependent juvenile-onset diabetes were followed.[41] Glycemic control was obtained by intensified insulin therapy. They were compared with a control group who were not seen preconceptually. There were no congenital malformations in the intensively followed group compared with 9.6% congenital anomalies in the control group. These results parallel other reports suggesting that later control after the 1st trimester did not result in a fall in the incidence of congenital malformations, although other morbidity did decrease. In fact, the neonatal malformation rate rose and was not influenced by maternal age or diabetic class.[42]

In a recent report Mills et al.[43] studied 347 diabetic and 389 control women who were enrolled in a study within 21 days of conception, and 279 diabetic women who enrolled later. Major malformations were 4.9% in the infants of the early entry group, 2.1% in those of the controls, and 9.0% in those of the late entry group. Mean blood glucose concentration and glycosylated hemoglobin levels were not significantly higher in women whose infants were malformed, nor was hypoglycemia. The authors suggested that not all malformations can be prevented by good glycemic control, although the efforts in this regard justify the attempts.[43] However, in subsequent comments on this report there were major concerns relative to the definition and classification of major malformations and the grouping of infants with all malformations into a uniform group.[44]

Hypoglycemia may also play a teratogenic role in the diabetic pregnancy. Symptomatic hypoglycemia during the 1st trimester is a frequently observed symptom in insulin-dependent diabetics, although quantification has been difficult. Although the injection of insulin into chick embryos has induced rumplessness,[45] current data indicate that the primate placenta probably acts as a total barrier to maternal insulin from midgestation onward.[46] The failure of insulin to cross the placenta in the rat during the critical period of organogenesis has been evaluated by Widness et al. using ^{113}I insulin.[47]

The increase in anomalies with increasing duration and severity (White's classification) of diabetes has been interpreted to indicate the degree to which maternal vascular disease may play a role.[8] Although anomalies in IDMs tend to encompass a spectrum of organ systems rather than a specific, discrete syndrome, some individual patterns tend to occur more frequently. Thus, major congenital heart disease; musculoskeletal deformities, including the caudal regression syndrome; and central nervous system deformities (anencephaly, spina bifida, hydrocephalus) have been reported. Based on these findings, the critical period of teratogenesis for the pregnant diabetic has been inferred to take place before the 7th week following conception. A recent report has highlighted the use of ultrasound for the early diagnosis of congenital anomalies; specifically, the regression syndrome at 18 to 20 weeks of gestation.[48]

One rare congenital defect that is increased in IDMs is the small left colon syndrome.[49] The cause of this deformity is obscure. With conservative medical management, the condition usually resolves spontaneously within the neonatal period.

While the IDM is known to have signs of congestive heart failure, the spectrum of cardiomyopathy ranges from congestive to hypertrophic cardiomyopathy. A number of recent reports have evaluated the presence of hypertrophic cardiomyopathy in infants of poorly controlled diabetic women. In a recent report, 11 IDMs were followed for 30 to 40 months after presenting with signs of respiratory distress; they all had septal hypertrophy on echocardiograms.[50] The natural history appeared to be resolution of symptoms within 2 to 4 weeks and of the hypertrophy within 2 to 12 months. In another study, 34 infants of diabetic mothers were found to have hypertrophy of the interventricular septum and walls of the right and left ventricles.[51] The presence of hypertrophy was seen predominantly in infants whose mothers were under poor diabetic control. Similar conclusions were reached in a third series, in which septal hypertrophy was noted in 6 of 18 IDMs, all of whom had profound hypoglycemia after birth in contrast to infants without hypertrophy.[52] These findings were consistent with the metabolic effects of neonatal hyperinsulinism also present in the fetus. It was suggested that fetal hyperinsulinism contributes directly to the septal hypertrophy. Primary fetal hyperinsulinemia in rhesus fetus has been found by Susa et al. to be associated with significant muscular hypertrophy and cardiomegaly.[10]

Although cardiac hypertrophy apart from congenital heart disease has been recognized in autopsies of IDMs for the past 3 decades, it has only been in the past 5 years that attention has been directed to a peculiar form of subaortic stenosis similar to the idiopathic hypertrophic subaortic stenosis found in adults.[53] This particular entity may be associated with symptomatic congestive heart failure. As with the adult variant, in these infants, therapy with digoxin is contraindicated, as the resultant increased myocardial contractility has been reported to be deleterious. Propranolol appears to be the therapeutic drug of choice. Clinically, this disorder resolves spontaneously over a period of weeks to months, with correction of the echocardiographic features as well.

Recently, an epidemiologic study was conducted evaluating a series of 2,587 newborn IDMs between 1926 and 1983. An overall malformation rate of 6.6% was found. The series was divided into five consecutive periods of 500 infants each. During the final period of study, between 1979 and 1983, a decrease in severity and frequency of congenital malformations was noted. Interestingly, the authors suggested that fetuses that are statistically smaller than normal in early pregnancy carry a higher risk of being malformed. They also concluded that preconceptional metabolic control is necessary for optimal fetal outcome.[54]

HYPOGLYCEMIA

A rapid fall in plasma glucose concentration following delivery is characteristic of the IDM. Values less than 35 mg/dL in term infants and less than 25 mg/dL in preterm infants are abnormal and may occur within 30 minutes after clamping the umbilical vessels. Factors that are known to influence the degree of hypoglycemia include previous maternal glucose homeostasis and maternal glycemia during delivery.[2] An inadequately controlled pregnant diabetic will have stimulated the fetal pancreas to synthesize excessive insulin, which may be readily released. Administration of intravenous dextrose during the intrapartum period, which results in maternal hyperglycemia (> 125 mg/dL) will be reflected in the fetus and will exaggerate the infant's normal postdelivery fall in plasma glucose concentration. In addition, hypoglycemia may persist for 48 hours or may develop after 24 hours.

As noted previously, fetal hyperinsulinemia is associated with suppressed levels of plasma free fatty acids and/or diminished hepatic glucose output. Other factors that may contribute to the development of hypoglycemia include defective counterregulation by catecholamines and/or glucagon.

The neonate exhibits transitional control of glucose metabolism, which suggests that a multiplicity of factors affect homeostasis. Many of the factors are similar to those influencing homeostasis in the adult. What is different neonatally are the various stages of maturation that exist for each. Previous work in conjunction with glucose infusion studies can be summarized to suggest that there is blunted splanchnic (hepatic) responsiveness to insulin in the newborn—IDMs, of the diabetic as preterm, and term infants— compared with response in the adult.[25] What has not been studied, but what is also of particular interest, are the many contra-insulin hormones that influence metabolism. If insulin is the primary glucoregulatory hormone, then contra-insulin hormones assist in balancing the effect of insulin and other factors.

CONTRA-INSULIN STIMULATION

One should evaluate all of the contra-insulin hormones but those of particular interest in the IDMs have been of the sympathoadrenal neural axis. Many studies have examined epinephrine and norepinephrine concentrations in IDMs, with quite variable results. An early study involved 11 infants of diabetic mothers, only 2 of whom were gestational. Urinary excretion of catecholamines was measured and compared with levels in 10 infants of nondiabetic mothers. Urinary norepinephrine and epinephrine levels did not increase in the infants of diabetic women who were severely hypoglycemic, but did rise in infants whose mothers were mildly hypoglycemic.[17]

These results parallel investigations of Stern et al.,[55] who suggested that hypoglycemia may be secondary to an adrenal medullary exhaustion phenomenon. This would be secondary to long-standing hypoglycemia in the IDM (presumably fetal secondary to poor control of maternal diabetes).[55] In further studies, however, Keenan et al. noted normal plasma glucose elevations, plasma insulin declines, and free fatty acid elevations in response to exogenous administration of epinephrine.[56] This confirmed the exhaustion theory. A parallel explanation was given by Young et al. to explain the high plasma norepinephrine concentrations in IDMs whose degree of euglycemic control was not reported except that some of the infants were borderline large for gestational age.[57] They speculated that the IDM exposed to excessive quantities of glucose may be subject to chronic sympatho-adrenal stimulation.

In another series, Artel et al.[58] measured plasma epinephrine and norepinephrine levels in IDMs. Elevated levels of both hormones were found in the IDM, although the variation was markedly increased in the IDM subjects. The authors speculated that hypoglycemia after birth may be secondary to adrenal exhaustion, producing temporary depletion later in the newborn period. This temporary depletion might account for the appearance of hypoglycemia noted clinically by others.[58]

A recent series by Broberger et al.[59] evaluated sympathoadrenal activity in the first 12 hours of after birth in IDMs (9 of type 1 diabetes and 13 of insulin-treated gestational diabetes). Failure to observe differences in plasma epinephrine and norepinephrine levels between IDMs and control infants was felt to be secondary to good metabolic control of the diabetic mother.[59]

However, other factors related to sympathoadrenal activity in the newborn may be of importance. Recently, in a continuing evaluation of the transitional nature of neonatal glucose metabolism, both of insulin and contra-insulin factors, epinephrine was infused in two doses (50 mg or 500 mg/kg/min in a newborn lamb model and glucose kinetics [turnover]) were measured with [6-^{3}H]glucose. The newborn lamb showed a blunted response to the lower dose of epinephrine infused. We speculated that the newborn lamb evidenced blunted responsiveness to this important contra-insulin stimulus. It is possible that if this can be observed in the diabetic state, this would partially account for the presence of hypoglycemia noted clinically.[60, 61]

THERAPY

The IDM is a prime example of the potential of glucose disequilibrium in the newborn. Because of the transitional nature of glucose homeostasis in the newborn period in general, accentuation of disequilibrium may be enhanced in the IDM secondary to metabolic alterations present in the maternal diabetic. A great deal of work is necessary to fully appreciate the physiology of the IDM.

Most IDMs are asymptomatic, even with relatively low plasma glucose levels. This may reflect their initial brain stores of glycogen; however, the exact biochemistry is as yet undefined. Signs and symptoms that may be observed in symptomatic infants are nonspecific and include tachypnea, apnea, tremulousness, sweating, irritability, and seizures. These infants may require parenteral treatment for maintenance of carbohydrate homeostasis. Early administration of oral feeds at 3 to 4 hours of age may be beneficial to maintain plasma glucose levels that are not severely depressed.

Therapy is preventive, including rigid maternal control of blood glucose levels during pregnancy and delivery. Plasma glucose values should be obtained at delivery from the umbilical vein. Subsequently, the infant should be screened by a rapid bedside technique (probably the use of a visual strip recording such as Dextrostix [Ames]) at one-half to 1, 2, and 4 hours and then prior to each feeding until the plasma glucose concentration is in the euglycemic range consistently. Abnormal glucose values require verification by chemical analysis. This is especially so if one uses a glucose reflectance meter. Recent evaluations of glucose reflectance meters indicate they probably should not be used with the capillary heelstick blood, as such readings are neither accurate nor reliable.[62]

The hypoglycemic infant (<40 mg/dL at 4 hours of age or less in both the term and preterm) may be treated intravenously with 0.25 g/kg of 25% dextrose as a bolus administered over 2 to 4 minutes and must be followed by a continuous infusion at 4 to 6 mg/kg/min. Lilien et al. have reported successful treatment with a "minibolus" infusion of 2 mL/kg of 10% dextrose in water (200 mg/kg) given over 1 minute followed by a continuous infusion of dextrose at rate of 8 mg/kg/min.[63] Bolus injections alone without subsequent infusion will only exaggerate the hypoglycemia by a rebound mechanism and are contraindicated. Once the plasma glucose stabilizes above 45 mg/dL, the infusion may be slowly decreased while oral feeds are initiated and advanced. If symptomatic hypoglycemia persists, higher glucose rates of 8 to 12 mg/kg/min or more may be necessary.

Glucagon has been administered within 15 minutes after delivery to prevent hypoglycemia. Because the majority of infants are asymptomatic, this does not appear warranted. Furthermore, glucagon may stimulate insulin release, which may exaggerate the tendency to hypoglycemia.

Prompt recognition and treatment of the hypoglycemic infant has minimized sequelae. No specific late central nervous system complications have been attributed to neonatal hypoglycemia per se in IDMs.[64]

Recent investigations in Denver, Cleveland, and elsewhere have focused on the use of enteric galactose alimentation for feeding the newborn in general and the IDM in particular.[65, 66] While the risk of hereditary galactose intolerance must always be considered because of the potential untoward effects, investigations have supported the use of enteric galactose as an optimal probable source for neonatal tissue glycogen synthesis. This is because galactose elimination neither requires insulin nor stimulates insulin secretion. There is one report in which galactose was used in the treatment of hyperinsulmenia in the IDM. Utilizing galactose for half the glucose in the intravenous solution, investigators noted increased glucose and decreased insulin concentration in the neonates.[67] Further work in this area is required before this treatment can be utilized routinely.

SUMMARY

Although there has been continuing improvement in outcome for infants born to diabetic mothers, they remain a high-risk population. Optimal results are obtained when meticulous medical-obstetric care throughout pregnancy is combined with expert neonatal supervision. Many of the risks of metabolic abnormalities can be treated if anticipated appropriately. Further work remains to be accomplished to understand the pathophysiologic causes of the specific metabolic components discussed as well as their treatment.

Acknowledgments

We express our appreciation to Alison Richards for her expert secretarial assistance.

REFERENCES

1. Wolfe RR, Allsop J, Burke JF: Glucose metabolism in man: Responses to intravenous glucose. *Metab Clin Exp* 1979; 28:210–220.
2. Cowett RM: Pathophysiology, diagnosis and management of glucose homeostasis in the neonate. *Current Problems in Pediatrics* 1985; 15:1–43.
3. Schwartz R, Cowett RM, Widness JA: Infants of diabetic mothers, in Brodoff BN, Bleicher SJ (eds): *Diabetes Mellitus and Obesity*. Baltimore, Williams & Wilkins Co, 1980, pp 601–610.
4. Cowett RM, Schwartz R: The infant of the diabetic mother, in Oh W (ed): Symposium on the Newborn. *Pediatr Clin North Am* 1982; 29:1213–1231.
5. Cowett RM: The metabolic sequelae in the infant of the diabetic mother, in Jovanovic L (ed): Controversies in diabetes and pregnancy, in Cohen MP, Foa PP (eds): *Endocrinology and Metabolism*. New York: Springer-Verlag, 1988, pp 149–171.

6. Cowett RM: The infant of the diabetic mother, in Sweet A, Brown E (eds): *Medical and Surgical Complications of Pregnancy: Effects on the Fetus and Newborn*. In press.
7. Hay WW Jr: Fetal metabolic consequences of maternal diabetes, in Jovanic L, Peterson CM, Fuhrmann K (eds); *Diabetes and Pregnancy: Teratology, Toxicity, and Treatment*. New York, Praeger Publishers, 1986, pp 185–221.
8. Pedersen J: *The Pregnant Diabetic and Her Newborn,* ed 2. Baltimore, Williams & Wilkins Co, 1977.
9. Naeye RL: Infants of diabetic mothers: A quantitative morphologic study. *Pediatrics* 1965; 35:980–988.
10. Susa JB, McCormick KL, Widness JA, et al: Chronic hyperinsulinemia in the fetal rhesus monkey. Effects on fetal growth and composition. *Diabetes* 1979; 28:1058–1063.
11. Block MD, Pildes RS, Mossabhou NA, et al: C-peptide immunoreactivity (CRP): A new method for studying infants of insulin-treated diabetic mothers. *Pediatrics* 1974; 53:923–928.
12. King KC, Adam PAJ, Yamaguchi K, et al: Insulin response to arginine in normal newborn infants and infants of diabetic mothers. *Diabetes* 1974; 23:816–820.
13. Pildes RS, Hart RJ, Warrner R, et al: Plasma insulin response during oral glucose tolerance tests in newborns of normal and gestational diabetic mothers. *Pediatrics* 1969; 44:76–82.
14. Isles PE, Dickson M, Farquhar JW: Glucose intolerance and plasma insulin in newborn infants of normal and diabetic mothers. *Pediatr Res* 1966; 2:198–208.
15. Adam PAJ, King KC, Schwartz R: Model for investigation of intractable hypoglycemia. Insulin glucose interrelationships during steady state infusion. *Pediatrics* 1968; 41:91–105.
16. King KC, Adam PAJ, Clements GA, et al: Infants of diabetic mothers: Attenuated glucose uptake without hyperinsulinemia during continuous glucose infusions. *Pediatrics* 1969; 44:381–392.
17. Light IJ, Sutherland JM, Loggie JM, et al: Impaired epinephrine release in hypoglycemic infants of diabetic mothers. *N Engl J Med* 1967; 277:394–398.
18. Bloom SR, Johnston DT: Failure of glucagon release in infants of diabetic mothers. *Br Med J [Clin Res]* 1972; 4:453–454.
19. Kaplan SA, Neufeld ND, Lippe BM, et al: Maternal diabetes and the development of the insulin receptor, in Merkatz IR, Adam PAJ (eds): *The Diabetic Pregnancy. A Perinatal Perspective*. New York, Grune & Stratton, 1979, pp 169–173.
20. Lautala P, Puukka R, Knip M, et al: Postnatal decrease in insulin binding to erythrocytes in infants of diabetic mothers. *J Clin Endocrinol Metab* 1988; 66:696–701.
21. Kalhan SC, Savin SM, Adam PAJ: Attenuated glucose production rate in newborn infants of insulin-dependent diabetic mothers. *N Engl J Med* 1977; 296:375–376.
22. King KC, Tserng KY, Kalhan SC: Regulation of glucose production in newborn infants of diabetic mothers. *Pediatr Res* 1982; 16:608–612.
23. Cowett RM, Susa JB, Giletti B, et al: Variability of endogenous glucose production in infants of insulin dependent diabetic mothers. *Pediatr Res* 1980; 14:570.
24. Cowett RM, Susa JB, Giletti B, et al: Glucose kinetics in infants of diabetic mothers. *Am J Obstet Gynecol* 1983; 146:781–786.
25. Cowett RM, Oh W, Schwartz R: Persistent glucose production during glucose infusion in the neonate. *J Clin Invest* 1983; 71:467–473.
26. Widness JA, Cowett RM, Coustan DR, et al: Neonatal morbidities in infants of mothers with glucose intolerance in pregnancy. *Diabetes* 1985; 34(suppl 2):61–65.
27. Freinkel N: Of pregnancy and progeny, Banting lecture. *Diabetes* 1980; 29:1023–1035.
28. Milner RDG: Amino acids and beta cell growth in structure and function, in Merkatz IR, Adam PAJ (eds): *The Diabetic Pregnancy. A Perinatal Perspective*. New York, Grune & Stratton, 1979, pp 145–153.
29. Kalkhoff RK, Kandaraki, E, Morrow PG, et al: Relationship between neonatal birth weight and maternal plasma amino acid profiles in lean and obese nondiabetic women and in type I diabetic pregnant women. *Metabolism* 1988; 37:234–239.

30. Small M, Cameron A, Lunan CB, et al: Macrosomia in pregnancy complicated by insulin-dependent mellitus. *Diabetes Care* 1987; 10:594–599.

31. Kitzmiller JL, Cloherty JP, Younger MD, et al: Diabetic pregnancy and perinatal morbidity. *Am J Obstet Gynecol* 1978; 131:560–568.

32. Cocilovo G, Guerra S, Colla F, et al: Glycosylated hemoglobin (HbA$_1$) assay as a test for detection and surveillance of gestational diabetes. A reappraisal. *Diabetes Metab* 1987; 13:426–430.

33. Kucera J: Rate and type of congenital anomalies among offspring of diabetic women. *J Reprod Med* 1971; 7:61–70.

34. Pedersen LM, Tygstrup I, Pedersen J: Congenital malformations in newborn infants of diabetic women. Correlation with maternal diabetic vascular complication. *Lancet* 1964; 1:1124–1126.

35. Jovanovic L, Druzin M, Peterson CM: Effects of eugylcemia on the outcome of pregnancy in insulin-dependent diabetic women as compared with normal control subjects. *Am J Med* 1980; 68:105–112.

36. Roversi GD, Gugiulo M, Nicolini U, et al; A new approach to the treatment of diabetic pregnant women. *Am J Obstet Gynecol* 1979; 135:567–576.

37. Neave C: Congenital malformation in offspring of diabetics. *Perspect Pediatr Pathol* 1984; 8:213–222.

38. Fuhrmann K, Reiher H, Semmler K, et al: Prevention of congenital malformations in infants of insulin dependent diabetic mothers. *Diabetes Care* 1983; 6:219–223.

39. Dicker D, Feldberg D, Yeshaya A, et al: Pregnancy outcome in gestational diabetes with preconceptional diabetes counselling. *Aust NZ J Obstet Gynaecol* 1987; 27:184–187.

40. Miller E, Hare JW, Cloherty JP, et al: Elevated maternal hemoglobin A$_{1c}$ in early pregnancy and major congenital anomalies in infants of diabetic mothers. *N Engl J Med* 1981; 304:1331–1334.

41. Goldman JA, Dicker D, Feldberg D, et al: Pregnancy outcome in patients with insulin dependent diabetes mellitus with preconceptual diabetes control: A comparative study. *Am J Obstet Gynecol* 1986; 155:293–297.

42. Ballard JL, Holroyde J, Tsang RC, et al: High malformation rates and decreased mortality in infants of diabetic mothers managed after the first trimester (1956–1978). *Am J Obstet Gynecol* 1984; 148:111–118.

43. Mills JL, Knopp RH, Simpson JL, et al: Lack of relation of increase malformation rates in infants of diabetic mothers to glycemic control during organgenerics. *N Engl J Med* 1988; 318:671–676.

44. Bergman M, Newman SA, Seaton JB, et al: Diabetic control and fetal malformations. *N Engl J Med* 1988; 319:647 (Letter to Editor).

45. Landauer W: Rumplessness in chicken embryos produced by the injection of insulin and other chemicals. *J Exp Zool* 1945; 98:65–77.

46. Adam PAJ, Teramo K, Raiha N, et al: Human fetal insulin metabolism early in gestation. *Diabetes* 1969; 18:409–416.

47. Widness JA, Goldman AS, Susa JB, et al: Impermeability of the rat placenta to insulin during organogenesis. *Teratology* 1983; 28:327–332.

48. Perrot LJ, Williamson S, Jimenex JF: The caudal regression syndrome in infants of diabetic mothers. *Ann Clin Lab Sci* 1987; 17:211–220.

49. Davis WS, Allen RP, Favara BE, et al: Neonatal small left colon syndrome. *AJR* 1974; 120:327–329.

50. Way GL, Wolfe RR, Eshughpour E, et al: The natural history of hypertrophic cardiomyopathy in infants of diabetic mothers. *J Pediatr* 1979; 95:1020–1025.

51. Mace S, Hirschfeld SS, Riggs T, et al: Echocardiographic abnormalities in infants of diabetic mothers. *J Pediatr* 1979; 95:1013–1019.

52. Breitweser JA, Mayer RA, Sperling MA, et al: Cardiac septal hypertrophy in hyperinsulinemic infants. *J Pediatr* 1980; 96:535–539.

53. Halliday HL: Hypertrophic cardiomyopathy in infants or poorly controlled diabetic mothers. *Arch Dis Child* 1981; 56:258–263.

54. Molsted-Pedersen L, Pedersen JF: Congenital malformations in diabetic pregnancies. *Acta Paediatr Scand [Suppl]* 1985; 32:79–84.

55. Stern L, Ramos A, Leduc J: Urinary catecholamine excretion in infants of diabetic mothers. *Pediatrics* 1968; 42:598–605.

56. Keenan WJ, Light IJ, Sutherland JM: Effects of exogenous epinephrine on glucose and insulin levels in infants of diabetic mothers. *Biol Neonate* 1972; 21:44–53.

57. Young BJ, Cohen WR, Rappaport EB, et al: High plasma norepinephrine concentrations at birth in infants of diabetic mothers. *Diabetes* 1979; 28:697–699.

58. Artel R, Platt LD, Kammula RK, et al: Sympatho-adrenal activity in infants of diabetic mothers. *Am J Obstet Gynecol* 1982; 42:436–439.

59. Broberger U, Hansson U, Lagercrantz H, et al: Sympatho-adrenal activity and metabolic adjustment during the first 12 hours after birth in infants of diabetic mothers. *Acta Paediatr Scand* 1984; 73:620–625.

60. Cowett RM: Decreased response to catecholamines in the newborn: Effect on glucose kinetics in the lamb. *Metabolism* 1988; 37:736–740.

61. Cowett RM: Alpha adrenergic agonists stimulate neonatal glucose production less than beta adrenergic agonists in the lamb. *Metabolism* 1988; 37:831–836.

62. Lin HC, Maguire CA, Oh W, et al: Accuracy and reliability of glucose reflectance meters in the neonatal intensive care unit (NICU). *J Pediatr* 1989; 115:988–1000.

63. Lilien LD, Pidles RS, Sainivasan G, et al: Treatment of neonatal hypoglycemia with mini-bolus and intravenous glucose infusion. *J Pediatr* 1980; 97:295–298.

64. Persson B, Gentz J, Lunell NO: Diabetes in pregnancy, in Scarpelli EM, Cosmi EV (eds): *Reviews in Perinatal Medicine,* vol 2. New York, Raven Press, 1978, pp 1–53.

65. Kliegman RM, Sparks JW: Perinatal galactose metabolism. *J Pediatr* 1985; 107:831–841.

66. Kliegman RM, Morton S: Galactose assimilation in pups of diabetic canine mothers. *Diabetes* 1987; 36:1280–1285.

67. Pribylova J, Kozlova J: Glucose and galactose infusions in newborns of diabetic and healthy mothers. *Biol Neonate* 1979; 36:193–197.

Chapter 19

Infants With Short Bowel Syndrome*

Sharon F. Taylor, M.D.

Ronald J. Sokol, M.D.

In the first half of this century, infants who underwent resection of large portions of small intestine as a result of a variety of intra-abdominal catastrophes were given little hope of survival. Within the past 2 decades, advances in our knowledge of infant nutrition, coupled with improved diagnostic, surgical, and nutritional support delivery techniques, have greatly improved the outcome of infants with short bowel syndrome (SBS). Currently, the term SBS is used to describe a condition of malabsorption and malnutrition resulting from the loss of significant portions of small bowel. Frequently a shortened or resected colon also is involved in the pathogenesis of the diarrhea; however, essential to the SBS is the loss of surface area in the small intestine, which diminishes the capacity to digest and absorb dietary nutrients.

Short bowel syndrome has been defined by several investigators as loss of a specific length or percentage of small bowel. Rickham[1] defined an extensive resection as that leaving 75 cm of remaining small bowel, and others[2-4] have stated that 50% or more of expected small bowel length must be resected to produce SBS. The problem with these definitions is that SBS is not strictly an anatomic entity; absorption of nutrients may not correlate with length of remaining small intestine if this bowel is damaged. Functionally, an infant may behave as having SBS despite only a moderate foreshortening of bowel.

The cause of small intestine loss can be either prenatal or postnatal, congenital or acquired. Although there are many clinical conditions that may produce the SBS (Table 19–1), the most common causes are necrotizing enterocolitis, intestinal atresias, or volvulus.[2] Necrotizing enterocolitis, which may complicate up to 1% to 2% of admissions to newborn intensive care units, most commonly involves the distal ileum and right colon, and can necessitate resection of long intestinal segments. Atresias and volvulus may result in congenital absence of or necrosis and need for resection of large portions of jejunum and ileum. The management of infants with SBS depends on a basic under-

*Supported in part by USPHS Grant (RR00069) from the General Clinical Resources Centers Branch, Division of Research Resources, NIH.

TABLE 19–1.

Causes of Short Bowel Syndrome in Infants

Necrotizing enterocolitis
Congenital small bowel atresias
   Multiple jejunal and/or ileal
   Christmas tree/apple peel deformities
Midgut volvulus
   Congenital, secondary to malrotation
   Secondary to adhesive bands, congenital or
   acquired
Gastroschisis
Vascular thrombosis of superior mesenteric vein or
   artery
Trauma
Abdominal radiation
Inflammatory bowel disease
Total bowel aganglionosis

standing of normal neonatal gastrointestinal physiology and the phenomena of intestinal adaptation to the early loss of a significant portion of small bowel.

PATHOPHYSIOLOGY

The length of the small intestine in the full-term newborn is approximately 248 ± 40 cm (mean ± SD).[5] During fetal development, 115 ± 21 cm of small bowel is present between 19 and 27 weeks of gestation; the small bowel doubles in length during the 3d trimester. The normal neonatal small bowel has a diameter of 1.5 cm, compared with 3 to 4 cm in the adult. Urban and Weser[3] have demonstrated that there is a relationship between mucosal surface area, body surface area, and body weight. Villi and microvilli present at birth increase the mucosal absorptive surface area approximately 600-fold. However, mucosal surface area is not uniform throughout the length of small bowel; one-half of the total mucosal surface area is contained within the proximal one fourth of the small intestine. In addition, the activity of brush-border enzymes varies along the length of small bowel.

In healthy infants, absorption of fluids and nutrients occurs throughout the length of small bowel, although to a greater degree in the proximal small bowel, influenced by both concentration and osmotic gradients (Table 19–2). The duodenum and jejunum are the main sites for digestion and absorption of carbohydrates, fats, and protein. Most minerals—including iron, calcium, and copper—as well as water-soluble and fat-soluble vitamins are absorbed primarily in the proximal small bowel. The distal small bowel (ileum) has a primary role in the absorption of intrinsic factor-bound vitamin B_{12} and the active transport of conjugated bile salts. In addition, the ileum acts as a functional reserve for substances not absorbed more proximally. The ileocecal valve plays an important role as a physiologic barrier to the emptying of small bowel into colon, thus prolonging transit time, and in preventing colonic bacteria from migrating into and contaminating the small bowel. Colonic absorption reduces fluid and electrolyte losses. The potential nutrient absorptive function of the colon following small bowel resection has not yet been fully evaluated.[6] However, the colon does have the capacity to "salvage" malabsorbed carbohydrate by absorbing the short-chain fatty acids resulting from colonic

TABLE 19–2.

Principal Sites (X) of Intestinal Absorption in Normal
Small Bowel

Nutrient	Proximal (Duodenojejunum)	Distal (Ileum)
Carbohydrate	X	
Protein	X	
Fat	X	
Vitamins (except B_{12})	X	
Minerals (iron, calcium, copper)	X	
Vitamin B_{12}		X
Bile salts		X
Fluids	X	X

fermentation.[7] In this regard, it has been demonstrated that the severity of diarrhea following ileal resection depends in part on the length of contiguous colon removed.[8]

The pathophysiology seen in SBS stems from a loss of surface area for absorption of nutrients. The likelihood of metabolic consequences depends on five factors: (1) the extent of small bowel loss; (2) the location of the bowel loss; (3) the transit time of fluids and nutrients through the remaining small intestine; (4) the presence of the ileocecal valve; and (5) the length of the remaining colon. These factors also affect the resultant intestinal adaptation.

Most investigators report that loss of 50% of the expected small bowel length can be tolerated fairly well by infants if the remaining bowel is normal. The degree of malabsorption is dependent on the amount of lost surface area balanced by the size of the functional reserve. An infant has approximately 2 cm^2 of small intestine to absorb 1 kilocalorie, whereas an adult has 3.5 cm^2.[4] This "intestinal reserve capacity" allows adults to initially tolerate small bowel resection better than infants; however, the intestine in an infant has a far greater potential to increase in length following resection. In fact, premature infants may fare better than full-term infants with identical lengths of remaining small bowel.[5, 9]

The location of small bowel loss is also of importance in assessing the infant with SBS. In general, the more distal the bowel loss, the more severe the morbidity. Proximal small bowel resection is initially associated with malabsorption of most nutrients, particularly carbohydrates and fats. This may be due in part to the decreased secretion of secretin and cholecystokinin by the shortened proximal small bowel, resulting in diminished stimulation of pancreatic secretion.

Hypergastrinemia with acid hypersecretion, detected in 50% of adult patients with intestinal resections,[10] seems more common after proximal small bowel resection,[11] possibly because of loss of a locally produced or humoral inhibitor or reduced catabolism of gastrin.[12] Because gastric acid production is normally reduced in preterm infants, gastric acid hypersecretion is not common after small bowel resection in small infants,[13] unless the resection is massive.[14] It is usually self-limited, decreasing after several months,[15] and often occurs during initial enteral feeding. Hypergastrinemia may have multiple deleterious effects (Table 19–3). Hypergastrinemia may stimulate acid secretion and lead to peptic ulcer disease and breakdown of anastomotic sites. Diarrhea and malabsorption can be exacerbated due to inactivation of pancreatic enzymes by an

TABLE 19–3.

Possible Consequences of Hypergastrinemia

Peptic ulcer disease
Anastomotic site breakdown
Impaired digestion of fats, starches, proteins
Inactivation of pancreatic enzymes
Increased diarrhea

acidic intraluminal milieu. The resulting steatorrhea and impaired digestion of starches and proteins lead to larger intraluminal volumes and osmotic loads, stimulate peristalsis, and increase fluid losses and diarrhea.

Resection of the proximal bowel removes the site of maximal transport of several essential minerals, including iron and calcium. The fat malabsorption associated with proximal bowel resection further aggravates the loss of calcium through formation of insoluble calcium soaps, which preclude absorption of calcium. Hypocalcemia and tetany may result.

Loss of the ileum leads to three major malabsorptive sequelae. The first is vitamin B_{12} deficiency. The ileum is the only portion of the bowel able to selectively transport intrinsic factor–bound vitamin B_{12}; the jejunum has little adaptive potential to assume this function following resection of the distal ileum. If a neonate has less than 15 cm of residual terminal ileum, vitamin B_{12} absorption may be impaired, although there may be a latent period as long as 10 years before B_{12} levels fall.[16]

Bile salt malabsorption has a more immediate effect on the nutritional status of the SBS patient. Unabsorbed conjugated bile salts reaching the colon undergo bacterial deconjugation and dehydroxylation, forming dihydroxy bile acids, which are known to inhibit colonic fluid absorption. In addition, excess fecal excretion of bile salts depletes the bile acid pool, impairing fat absorption and increasing steatorrhea, and increasing the potential for cholelithiasis by producing lithogenic bile. Hydroxylation of unabsorbed fatty acids by bacteria in the contaminated small bowel or in the colon also induces fluid secretion.

Ileal resection can also lead to hyperoxaluria and nephrolithiasis. Normally, dietary oxalates are complexed to calcium intraluminally, forming insoluble calcium oxalate, which is excreted in the feces. After terminal ileal resection, the reduced bile acid pool size impairs micellar solubilization and absorption of fatty acids that are released from hydrolysis of dietary triglycerides. These fatty acids may then complex with intraluminal calcium, leaving the oxalate free to be absorbed and excreted in excessive amounts by the kidneys. In 1974, Valman et al.[17] reported oxaluria in four out of ten children with ileal resections.

The third factor when considering metabolic consequences in SBS is the transit time, or the time nutrients remain in contact with the small bowel absorptive surface. This is determined by the length of remaining bowel, presence or absence of the ileocecal valve, health of remaining small bowel and its innervation, and the amount of malabsorbed luminal contents. Obviously, the more rapid the passage through the small bowel, the more limited is the chance for digestion and absorption of intestinal contents. The roles of the ileocecal valve and of the remaining colon in determining metabolic consequences in SBS have been discussed.

ADAPTATION

In 1955, a well-known pediatric surgeon, Willis Potts,[18] doubted that infants who lost more than 15% of their small bowel could survive. Only 2 years later, Pilling and Cresson[19] described the first successful extensive intestinal resection in two infants, with only 26 and 28 cm of remaining jejunoileum. Subsequently, many anecdotal reports and increasingly larger series of patients have documented survival in infants with even shorter small bowel remnants.[18-26] Early observations stressed compensatory bowel lengthening as the major adaptation response following resection of part of the small bowel,[15, 19, 24] allowing patients to eventually be supported exclusively by enteral nutrition.

Much has been learned since about the morphologic and functional changes of the residual bowel. (For more extensive review of intestinal adaptation, see references 3 and 27 to 29.) The key to survival after massive small bowel resection is the ability of the residual bowel to adapt. Intestinal adaptation begins within 48 hours of resection and probably continues for at least 18 months, although some investigators believe that most adaptation is limited to the 1st year postoperatively. Anatomic changes include lengthening of the remaining small bowel, as well as increased bowel diameter and wall thickness (Table 19–4). Mucosal hyperplasia occurs as the number of cells per villus increases, leading to expansion of villus height and crypt depth. Normally, intestinal epithelial cells divide only at the base of the crypts of Lieberkühn, and then migrate onto villi and differentiate into mature columnar cells capable of nutrient absorption. As villus height diminishes progressively from the jejunum to the distal ileum, cell migration is completed faster.[4] Thus, the distal bowel maintains a greater potential for increasing villus height above normal after a proximal intestinal resection than does the proximal bowel after distal resection. These increases in rate of cell migration and of mucosal mass have been documented by greater mucosal dry weight, deoxyribonucleic acid (DNA), ribonucleic acid, and protein contents.[27] Functional parameters such as glucose and water absorption also correlate with the degree of villous hypertrophy.[27] Studies in humans show that fecal losses of glucose, water, and electrolytes diminish in the postoperative recovery period as segmental absorption increases.[30] Intestinal epithelial cells may exhibit reduced activity of enzymes, such as dipeptidase, suggesting a relative im-

TABLE 19–4.

Adaptive Small Bowel Changes Following Resection

Anatomic
  Increased epithelial cell number/villus
  Increased rate of enterocyte proliferation
  Increased depth of crypts
  Increased villus height
  Increased bowel diameter, wall thickness, and
    length
Functional
  Increased glucose absorption per segment of bowel
  Increased disaccharidase activity segmentally
  Increased enterokinase and peptide hydrolase
    activity
  Increased water, electrolyte, and mineral absorption
    per centimeter of remnant small bowel
  Increased colonic absorption of short-chain fatty
    acids

maturity of the epithelium. Although individual cells during adaptation may have reduced absorptive capacity, the net result is improved nutrient absorption per unit length
of small bowel due to the villus enlargement. The degree of the hyperplasia response is
proportional to the length of small bowel removed,[31] is seen maximally near the anastomosis, and is greatest following proximal rather than distal resections.

Adaptive processes following intestinal resection are stimulated by the enteral intake of nutrients. Although the patient is generally maintained on parenteral nutrition
after massive intestinal resections, the lack of enteral nutrients induces intestinal hypoplasia[32, 33] manifested by delayed migration of intestinal crypt epithelia. Within 3
days of the introduction of total parenteral nutrition (TPN) in the absence of enteral
feeds, hypoplasia and depressed absorptive function can be demonstrated despite maintaining positive nitrogen balance. Clinical studies have shown that this functional impairment can be reversed by instituting enteral feedings. The impaired absorption (as
shown by *d*-xylose absorption) in TPN-fed compared with enterally fed infants has been
improved after introduction of enteral feeds to the TPN group.[28] Animal experiments
have also documented that intraluminal nutrients can prevent or reverse the mucosal hypoplasia seen in isolated loops of bowel or self-emptying blind loops.

As important as it may be, intraluminal nutrition is not the only major factor influencing small bowel adaptation. Postresection adaptive hyperplasia has been documented
even before oral feedings are initiated. Pancreatic and biliary secretions appear to be
important trophic factors. Diversion of pancreatic and biliary secretions directly into the
ileum causes villous hypertrophy.[34] Cholecystokinin and secretin given parenterally can
prevent the mucosal hypoplasia associated with TPN administration in dogs,[35] although
the issue of direct trophic effects of these substances on mucosa vs. stimulation of pan-
creatico-biliary secretions is not completely resolved.

Evidence for the influence of hormones and regulatory peptides has been obtained
from parabiotic animal studies. Intestinal resection in one of the parabionts caused increased cell turnover and mucosal DNA synthesis in the cross-circulated partner.[36] This
humoral stimulation of hyperplasia may be mediated through enteroglucagon, the most
important growth-promoting hormone identified.[29] Circulating levels increase in proportion to the degree of adaptation seen following intestinal resection.[37, 38] The increased
concentration of enteroglucagon normally found in the ileum and colon may explain
why loss of distal small bowel results in less adaptation than loss of proximal bowel.[28]
Epidermal growth factor also appears to play an important role in intestinal and pancreatic adaptive hyperplasia. In mice, epidermal growth factor stimulates gastrointestinal
ornithine decarboxylase activity,[39] which controls the rate-limiting step for polyamine
synthesis in enterocytes. Polyamine synthesis appears to be the most essential step for
the development of postresectional hyperplasia,[29] as polyamines "turn on" rapid cell
growth. Blockage of ornithine decarboxylase inhibits the hyperplastic response. Other
substances that may play a mediating role in intestinal adaptation include prostaglandin
E_2 and human growth hormone analogues. Gastrin induces some stimulation of hyperplasia of the proximal small bowel, but probably does not play a major role in regulation
of adaptation.

SURGICAL MANAGEMENT OF SHORT BOWEL SYNDROME

The routine use of TPN is probably the most significant factor in reduced mortality
of SBS, but advances in diagnostic and surgical techniques also account for decreases in

morbidity and mortality. The surgeon's task is to assess viability of the entire bowel intraoperatively and to preserve bowel length whenever possible. Determination of small intestinal viability can at times be difficult. The use of intraoperative Doppler probe may aid in assessing viability.[40] If massive resection appears to be necessary, consideration should be given to closing the abdomen, providing vigorous fluid and antibiotic support for 24 to 48 hours, and then performing a "second-look" laparotomy. Temporary enterostomies offer an alternative when bowel viability is in question and anastomosis too risky. When severely compromised areas of bowel are scattered and multiple (as may be the case in necrotizing enterocolitis with skip lesions) and preservation of intestinal length is critical, the number of enterostomies can be reduced by a modification of Hartmann's procedure.[41] The proximal end of each remnant of small bowel is oversewn, with exteriorization of the distal end only as a cutaneous enterostomy. Reanastomosis of these segments can be accomplished at a later date. Importantly, the surgeon must measure the unstretched remaining length of bowel along the antimesenteric border and record as accurately as possible its condition to aid in prognostication. The operative report should also reflect whether the ileocecal valve remained intact or required resection. Every effort must be made to preserve this important physiologic barrier as well as every centimeter of viable small bowel.

Other decisions that are part of the initial operative care include placement of a central venous catheter and/or gastrostomy tube. If the infant undergoing extensive bowel resection does not present with or develop signs of sepsis, placement of a semipermanent Silastic catheter for administration of TPN should be considered at the earliest stable postoperative period. Placement of a gastrostomy tube is frequently deferred until wound healing is optimal, often several days to weeks following resection. Some surgeons prefer to fashion the gastrostomy at the time of bowel reanastomosis, between 2 and 6 weeks after the initial small bowel resection. At that time more information is generally available regarding the amount of viable bowel and the success of enteral feeds, and a more reliable estimate given as to the time necessary for bowel adaptation to occur.

With the goal of reducing morbidity and improving the quality of life for the child with SBS, several innovative surgical approaches have been attempted—including intestinal transplantation, increasing the small bowel surface area, and slowing intestinal transit time (Table 19–5).

Intestinal transplantation was attempted as early as 1901; however, a resurgence of interest in bowel transplant was ushered in by R.C. Lillehei and associates in 1959.[42] Although many of the problems of bowel preservation and implant technique have been largely overcome, rejection of the implant by the recipient and graft-vs.-host reactions presented greater barriers to graft survival.[43] Cyclosporine therapy prevented rejection and provided improved outcome of small bowel transplants in rats.[44] Further control of rejection has been achieved with combination therapy using cyclosporine, azathioprine, prednisone, antithymocyte globulin, and monoclonal antibodies. Grafts are currently pretreated with 1,000 rads of x-irradiation to prevent graft-vs.-host disease.[45] Monitoring for rejection may be accomplished through a combination of a functional absorption test (e.g., maltose or glucose absorption) and repeated graft biopsies.[45] Orthotopic small bowel transplantation in rats with SBS has been shown to allow adequate nutritional support to sustain growth and development,[46] but to date there have been no long-term animal or human survivors of small intestine transplantation. Therefore, this therapy should be considered highly experimental and not advocated.

"Splanchnic" transplantation, in which the liver, stomach, entire small bowel, and

TABLE 19–5.

Long-Term Surgical Options in Short Bowel
Syndrome

Intestinal transplantation
    Orthotopic small bowel transplant
    Splanchnic transplant
    Fetal intestinal transplant
Increase small bowel absorptive surface
    Serosal patching
    Intestinal tapering and lengthening
    Strictureplasty
Increase intestinal transit time
    "Valve" operations
    Reversed small bowel segments
    Interposition of colonic segments
    Electrical pacing of small bowel
    Vagotomy/pyloroplasty
    Recirculating intestinal loops

pancreas are transplanted en bloc, was performed in two infants with SBS and liver failure.[47] Although the surgery was initially successful and rejection controlled, the second infant died from a monoclonal B-cell lymphoma. Transplantation of fetal intestine that is initially grown as an implant has been attempted in experimental animals with only limited success.[48] The implanted fetal rat intestine does differentiate and absorb certain substrates, encouraging further work in this area.

Surgical techniques to increase absorptive area include serosal surface patching, intestinal tapering and lengthening, and strictureplasty. Serosal surface patching, if successful, provides for growth of small amounts of new small bowel mucosa in an area of perforation or enterotomy. Colon, abdominal wall muscle, or prosthetic materials may be used to fit over a longitudinal small bowel enterotomy, providing a surface for ingrowth of adjacent mucosa.[43] There has been some interest in evaluating this procedure to substantially increase absorptive surface area, although serosal surface patches to date have been employed mainly in closure of perforations and fistulas. Currently, this may be a useful technique in sealing bowel perforations or anastomotic leaks which otherwise would have required further bowel loss through resection.[49]

Intestinal tapering with lengthening is a procedure described by Bianchi[50] in which dilated small bowel is stapled down the middle longitudinally after division of the mesenteric blood supply. The two hemiloops are anastomosed isoperistaltically, creating two equal-sized loops of bowel and doubling the length of the previously dilated loop. Tapering dilated small bowel can improve transit through that portion of small bowel and help ameliorate the blind loop-stasis syndrome. The lengthening part of the procedure has had more variable success, as the blood supply for the dilated bowel may not be easily divisible.[51] Strictureplasty, in which the strictured bowel is opened longitudinally and closed transversely, has been employed in humans with tubercular strictures, Crohn's disease, and SBS. It appears to be well-tolerated and can prevent resection of the strictured area with further small bowel loss.[49] However, if the strictured area is limited in size and is not functional, little may be gained by deferring resection.

Procedures to slow intestinal transit time originally included vagotomy with pyloroplasty and creation of recirculating intestinal loops, both of which are currently not used. Vagotomy and pyloroplasty to delay gastric emptying and reduce gastric acid hypersecretion had little clinical benefit and may diminish the intestinal adaptation response.[10] Recirculating intestinal loops, formed to increase transit time and provide for re-exposure of luminal nutrients to a limited mucosal absorptive surface, were of unclear benefit in humans. Studies in animals showed a high incidence of bacterial overgrowth and frequent intestinal obstruction.

Small bowel transit time is 3 times faster in patients without ileocecal valves compared with transit time through equivalent bowel lengths with the ileocecal valve present.[52] Therefore, a number of surgical procedures have been aimed at re-creating this valve effect. These "valve" operations include jejunocolic intussusception, anastomosis of the small bowel to the colon by way of a submucosal tunnel,[53] and longitudinal muscle excision, which allows the circular muscle of the intestinal wall to constrict and simulate sphincter action.[54]

Reversal of 2 to 3 cm of distal small bowel in order to produce an antiperistaltic motion and slow small bowel transit time has been accomplished, but partial small bowel obstruction requiring a second surgery makes this approach unsatisfactory.[55] Colonic interposition has been investigated as a solution to ultra-rapid small bowel transit.[53, 55] Isoperistaltic colon segments from 8 to 24 cm have been interposed between the duodenum and jejunum or jejunum and ileum. Limited experience suggests that the longer segments may contribute to *d*-lactic acidemia and obstruction secondary to stasis. Shorter antiperistaltic colon segments have been successfully interposed within the small bowel in experimental animals. Few pediatric surgeons currently employ reversed segments or colonic interposition for this purpose.

Electrical pacing of the intestines is an experimental technique without application as yet to humans.[56] Retrograde electrical pacing of canine jejunum in vivo has led to increased absorption of water, glucose, and sodium.[57] Dogs with SBS were paced postprandially and demonstrated weight gain with reduced fecal fat and nitrogen losses.[58]

The surgical techniques described here are still largely experimental and cannot be recommended routinely.[49] Patient series are generally small, and complication rates are thus unknown. Prevention of resection, with conservation of small intestinal length and the ileocecal valve, are currently the best surgical approach.

MEDICAL MANAGEMENT

Initial medical care in the postoperative period following bowel resection centers on careful assessment and replacement of major fluids and electrolytes, including sodium, potassium, calcium, phosphorus, magnesium, and zinc. Losses can be massive and life-threatening. Initiation of TPN must be accomplished as soon as clinical stability allows, with the nutrients preferably given centrally through an indwelling venous catheter. Peripheral TPN will not achieve adequate caloric and nutrient intake in most neonates, but is preferable to the use of dextrose and saline solutions alone. Infants with enterostomies will often require additional minerals beyond the recommended daily intake for newborns to replace those lost in small bowel effluent. For example, sodium and zinc requirements may double. The TPN should provide adequate total caloric intake, usually 100 to 120 kcal/kg of ideal body weight initially, given as a combination of carbohydrate and fat. After several months, the infant will generally require only 75 to 90 kcal/kg/day. Caloric intake should be adjusted so as to keep the weight-for-height percentile from exceeding the 50th percentile. Recommended protein intake initially is 2 to 2.5 gm/kg/day, based again on ideal body weight. Administration of TPN to neonates with

SBS is the single most important factor in improved survival during the past few decades and must, therefore, be instituted as soon as possible. Not only does TPN provide for growth, it also "buys time" for gradual tolerance of enteral feedings and successful adaptation of the intestine. On the other hand, TPN may be associated with life-threatening complications (e.g., bacterial or fungal sepsis) and contributes to the development of hepatic fibrosis or cirrhosis. However, these risks must be tolerated—as near-normal or normal somatic growth and a high quality of life[23] with near-normal cognitive function are possible on long-term TPN.[59]

Introduction of nutrients into the gut is an important stimulus of intestinal adaptation. Enteral feedings can be initiated as soon as the post-operative ileus resolves in clinically stable patients. Choice of delivery route (oral, nasogastric, or gastrostomy) and frequency (continuous slow drip vs. bolus) depends on the length of the remaining small bowel. Continuous enteral nutrition appears to be the most effective mode of delivery for patients with massive resections (>75% of small bowel),[60] whereas infants with less extensive bowel loss may do well beginning with small amounts of oral bolus feedings. If oral feeds must be deferred, non-nutritive sucking or sham feeds of sterile water should be initiated to prevent later aversion to oral feedings. As progressively larger volumes of continuous drip feeds are tolerated, the infant can often be allowed small oral boluses of formula.

The judicious choice of formula for infants with SBS relies on an understanding of the pathophysiology and adaptive changes accompanying small bowel loss. Routinely, there is a loss of absorptive surface and reduced mucosal enzyme reserve. In terms of carbohydrates, lactose is poorly absorbed in SBS, secondary to lactase deficiency. Sucrose also is a poor choice for initial formulas. For every unit of lactase activity there are 2 units of sucrase activity but 6 to 8 units of maltase activity,[61] providing better absorption of starches and glucose polymers[62] (e.g., the 6-unit straight-chain glucose polymers in corn-syrup solids). Glucose itself may be absorbed without hydrolysis, but its small molecular weight increases the osmolality of formulas. In the normal gastrointestinal tract hypertonic fluids are diluted in the proximal small bowel and absorbed over the length of the bowel. Since absorptive capacity is compromised in SBS patients, the expected carbohydrate malabsorption presents a large carbohydrate load (up to 65% of dietary intake[63]) to the colon, causing large, frequent, acidic water-loss stools that test positive for reducing substances. Malabsorption of glucose polymers may be substantially underestimated by measuring fecal reducing substances, as each polymer molecule behaves as only one reducing equivalent[63]; however, clinically, glucose polymers appear to be fairly well tolerated.

Fat intake routinely needs to be limited in infants with SBS. In addition to loss of absorptive surface and quicker transit times, depletion of bile acids for micelle formation, reduced pancreatic enzyme release, and bacterial contamination contribute to fat malabsorption. Water-insoluble long-chain fats are the least efficiently absorbed nutrient in the normal intestine. Medium-chain triglycerides (MCT) are better absorbed since micellar solubilization by bile acids is not required intraluminally prior to absorption. However, long-chain triglycerides (LCT) may be a more powerful stimulant for small bowel adaptation[64] compared to enteral protein, polysaccharides or MCT.[65] Free fatty acids may be even more potent than LCT. Therefore, a formula using either a combination of LCT plus MCT or small amounts of LCT in addition to a low-fat formula appears to be the best tolerated and most beneficial fat blend.

Protein is better tolerated than other nutrients, because fermentation of malabsorbed protein does not occur in the colon, as it does with carbohydrates. Hydrolyzed proteins are possibly better absorbed than whole proteins, in the face of less absorptive surface area and probable reduction of pancreatic enzyme output. Oligopeptides (two to five amino acids) mimic the protein fragments generally encountered by the small bowel in healthy intestinal tracts and appear to be handled better by brush-border peptidases. Individual amino acids, such as those present in elemental formulas, need no hydrolysis but require specific carriers for absorption. Free amino acids increase the osmolality of a formula dramatically and may require use of more dilute formula. If an elemental formula is chosen for use in infants with SBS, attention must be given to the composition of amino acids. For example, glutamine appears to be the preferred fuel for enterocytes and may be necessary for repair of damaged intestinal mucosa.[66] Glutamine is not stable in TPN solutions, so it must be administered enterally in the formula chosen.

The best formula for feeding infants with SBS has not yet been identified. Elemental formulas induce adaptation, predominantly in the proximal intestine, where they are almost completely absorbed[28]; however, less malabsorbed nutrient reaches the colon to stimulate colonic water and electrolyte secretion. These formulas are usually deficient in essential fatty acid content. In one clinical study, SBS patients with 30 to 150 cm of small bowel remaining were fed a diet of polysaccharides, MCT oil, protein hydrolysates, and high-viscosity tapioca suspension by continuous slow drip, commencing an average of 14 days postoperatively. Because this diet was well-tolerated, the authors[67] concluded that, in their experience, elemental diets were no better than polymeric diets. A formula containing protein hydrolysates, MCTs, and glucose polymers is generally the most logical first choice for enteral feeds in infants with SBS. One-quarter to one-half strength formula at a constant drip rate of 2 to 5 mL/hr (depending on the size of the infant) is started, with advancement of volume and then strength of formula made gradually based on patient tolerance. If feeding intolerance ensues (vomiting, distention, diarrhea), a trial of a more elemental formula containing crystalline amino acids, glucose, and limited fat is warranted. Attention must be paid to the osmolality of these formulas; osmolality under approximately 400 mosm/L is less likely to exacerbate diarrhea in infants with SBS. At times, a modular formula consisting of a protein base with varying concentrations of added carbohydrates and fats proves useful if standard commercially prepared formulas are not tolerated. Causes of persistent diarrhea in patients with SBS are outlined in Table 19–6.

Infants with SBS routinely need both fat-soluble and water-soluble vitamin supplements when TPN has been discontinued and the patient receives full enteral feeds. Following ileal resection, vitamin B_{12} deficiency may develop after a child is 1 or more years on enteral feeds alone. Serum vitamin B_{12} levels, and perhaps serum concentration of methylmalonate and homocysteine, should be periodically checked if vitamin B_{12} is

TABLE 19–6.

Causes of Persistent Diarrhea in Short Bowel Syndrome

Ileal malabsorption of conjugated bile acids
Hydroxylation of malabsorbed fatty acids
Bacterial overgrowth of the small bowel
Hypergastrinemia/gastric acid hypersecretion
Disaccharidase deficiency or acquired monosaccharide
   intolerance
Hyperosmolarity of ingested nutrients
Slow recovery from viral gastroenteritis or other
   exogenous insults

---

not administered prophylactically. A Schilling test can be helpful in determining the necessary duration of B_{12} therapy. A monthly parenteral dose of 100 mcg is recommended. Klish and Putnam[4] advocate parenteral vitamin B_{12} for 4 to 5 years before discontinuation. Patients with a fair degree of adaptation but who still exhibit fat malabsorption require prolonged supplementation of fat-soluble vitamin (vitamins A, D, E, and K). Similarly, mineral deficiencies may be gradual in onset. Insoluble calcium and magnesium soaps form when there is malabsorbed dietary fat and can cause symptomatic deficiency if mineral supplements are not given. Enterostomy or diarrheal losses of zinc, copper, and sodium can also be severe and should be monitored, particularly when the infant develops an acute gastroenteritis. Zinc losses occur as a result of decreased small bowel absorptive surface, rapid transit time, and interruption of the enteropancreatic circulation of the zinc-rich pancreatic juices. Latimer et al.[68] reported two patients with SBS who developed severe zinc deficiency while on parenteral zinc doses of 40 mg/kg/day. Replacement of the large losses of zinc in the stool corrected the clinical manifestations of acrodermatitis, poor weight gain, and abnormal protein metabolism.

Normally, iron is absorbed primarily in the proximal small bowel. Infants who have undergone major proximal small bowel loss are at risk for iron-deficiency anemia, particularly as most pharmacies do not include iron in their TPN mixtures. Two pediatric series[69, 70] including children with SBS on prolonged parenteral nutrition, reported normal iron balance without supplemental iron in the TPN solution. However, some patients had previously been treated with parenteral iron supplements for anemia. Generally, iron requirements can be met by enteral supplements after enteral feeds are successful. If given too early, iron can be irritating to the gastrointestinal mucosa and result in feeding intolerance. Slow parenteral infusions of iron dextran can be given each 1 to 3 months in infants intolerant to oral iron supplements.

Other trace element deficiencies have been detected during TPN administration. Reported levels of selenium and chromium were low in children with SBS on TPN not containing these minerals.[69] Clinical manifestations have been documented with trace element deficiencies; therefore, levels of selenium, chromium, copper, zinc, manganese, and iron must be monitored periodically.

As intestinal adaptation progresses and greater percentages of caloric and fluid requirements are tolerated enterally, TPN can be gradually consolidated to provide a portion of the day free from parenteral infusions. This can usually be accomplished by 6 to 9 months of age. TPN and lipid emulsions are cycled, with an "on" period of 12 to 14 hours each night if an energy source is provided enterally during the daytime "off" period. In addition to allowing greater mobility of the infant for normal exploratory behavior, cycling may decrease the risk of liver disease associated with long-term TPN use. Likewise, lightweight, small, portable pumps for continuous enteral infusion of formula afford more flexibility for those infants otherwise unrestricted during enteral infusions, both in the hospital and at home.

Criteria for discharge from the hospital of infants with SBS vary considerably among institutions. Factors that must be assessed prior to discharge include (1) the infant's overall clinical status and stability; (2) demonstration of consistent growth on a given nutritional intake, whether parenteral, enteral, or likely a combination; (3) parental motivation, compliance, and reliability; (4) adequate home facilities and personnel to allow parenteral or enteral infusions to be accomplished safely; (5) insurance or financial resources; and (6) availability of adequate follow-up medical care. Adaptation may be a lengthy process, particularly if the bowel loss was massive, and as experience with home TPN increases, initial hospital stays for these infants may be markedly reduced.

Other medications may be useful in the management of infants with SBS. Cholestyramine (Questran) and cholestipol (Colestid) are anion-exchange resins that can bind excessive bile acids, ameliorating bile acid–induced diarrhea. When used in a dose of 250 mg/kg/day in three to four divided doses, these medications are useful in patients with limited ileal resections; in extensive resections, they can cause further depletion of the bile acid pool and exacerbate steatorrhea. The exact length of ileal resection in the infant that correlates with response to anion-exchange resins has not been determined. Hyperchloremic acidosis may result from excessive doses; therefore, serum electrolytes must be carefully monitored during initial therapy and periodically thereafter. In addition to binding bile acids, these resins can bind other medications and, therefore, must not be coadministered at the same time of day. Sodium bicarbonate or antacids, given enterally to maintain a stool pH above 6, neutralizes the acidic luminal contents and thus can slow transit time through the bowel. Loperamide hydrochloride (Imodium), a non-narcotic agonist, prolongs transit time, allowing for improved fluid and nutrient absorption with minimal central nervous system side effects. A dose of 0.1 mg/kg given 2 or 3 times daily appears to be well-tolerated. The use of H_2-antagonists such as cimetidine or ranitidine may help combat the problem of gastric acid hypersecretion. Therapy is desirable for only a limited number of months postoperatively, as gastric hypersecretion is a transient phenomenon, and long-term use of H_2-blockers may further compromise vitamin B_{12} absorption by decreasing gastric acid and intrinsic factor secretion, as well as predispose to bacterial contamination of the small bowel. In a rat model of short bowel, Goldman et al.[71] reported earlier and more consistent weight gain during treatment with cimetidine than in identical, untreated rats. Nonabsorbable oral antibiotics such as colistin, gentamicin, neomycin, and metronidazole have been used in SBS patients to eradicate proved or suspected bacterial overgrowth of the remaining small bowel. Pancreatic enzyme supplements theoretically could improve digestion of fats, starches, and proteins if pancreozymin/cholecystokinin secretion is blunted because of loss of bowel, but they are generally not necessary.

Several other medications have received interest, although only anecdotal reports of their use are available. Cisapride, a promotility agent, improved motility in one infant with idiopathic intestinal pseudo-obstruction and SBS.[72] Ohlbaum et al.[73] reported the efficacy of a long-acting somatostatin analogue in reducing profuse ileal output in a 5-year-old child with SBS by prolonging transit time. Other drugs under consideration include ursodeoxycholic acid to treat cholelithiasis and sulfasalazine to treat "short gut colitis," a clinical syndrome characterized by bloody diarrhea and mucosal eosinophilia occurring in some patients with SBS during advancement of enteral feedings.[74] We have found that most SBS infants develop colitis when continuous feedings are aggressively advanced, that 25 to 50 mg/kg/day of sulfasalazine is generally well tolerated (in sequentially increased increments), and that the colitis responds promptly, allowing further advancing of enteral feedings.[74] Neutropenia is the chief toxicity and requires close monitoring.

Absorption of medications prescribed for other indications may be impaired. Antibiotic absorption is proportional to the length of remaining bowel, and independent of the site of resection.[75] Robert et al.[76] reported difficulty in attaining therapeutic cyclosporine levels when given enterally in two children with SBS. This reduced absorption must be taken into account when medications are prescribed and consideration given to parenteral administration if necessary.

OUTCOME

In 1972, Wilmore published a review of 50 infants with small bowel remnants of 75 cm or less.[15] In the pre-TPN era infants less than 2 months' old required at least 15 cm of remaining jejunum or ileum for successful outcome when the ileocecal valve was left intact and greater than 40 cm of jejunoileum if the ileocecal valve was absent. In 1984, Cooper et al.[23] reported an 81% survival rate for 16 neonates with greater than 50% bowel loss who received TPN. Survivors with a mean bowel length of 44 cm required 8 to 26 months of adaptation to sustain themselves on enteral feeds, with near-normal growth. The principal cause of morbidity in their series was liver disease associated with prolonged TPN, with end stage liver disease replacing protein-calorie malnutrition as the most common cause of death.

The series of Rickham et al.[20] in 1977 demonstrated excellent survival in children with 26 to 75 cm of small bowel and suggested 20 cm as the critical length of remaining bowel for survival. In the same year Dorney et al.[59] reported 69% survival in 13 children with very short bowel (<38 cm of jejunoileum). All survivors grew normally, and 8 of 9 had normal development. These authors suggested that infants who have over 10 cm of jejunoileum with an intact ileocecal valve or over 25 cm of jejunoileum without the valve are potential survivors and should be given the benefit of long-term parenteral nutrition to allow adaptation time and weaning off TPN ultimately. However, liver disease was a major complication in their series, and two of their reported patients required TPN for longer than 5 years. Thus, most infants with massive small bowel resections can be given hope of initial survival presuming optimal surgery and no associated anomalies. Currently, the minimum length of remaining small bowel capable of sustaining life via enteral nutrition is undetermined, raising difficult ethical choices.[77] Infants should not be sustained by TPN if there is no hope for intestinal adaptation or for candidacy for intestinal transplantation, as this procedure has not yet been successful long-term in humans.

The key to survival after massive small bowel is the ability of residual bowel to adapt. Morbidity and mortality of infants with SBS depend on (1) the extent and site of bowel resection; (2) adaptive changes in the remaining intestine and colon; (3) persistence of disease in the remaining intestinal mucosa, pancreas, and liver; (4) presence or absence of the ileocecal valve; and (5) associated anomalies. The length of time required for adaptation to full enteral feeds varies but may correlate with the time when a growing infant's caloric requirements decrease proportional to his or her body mass, generally around 1 year of age. Several reports describe children with SBS who are partially dependent on TPN for 4 years or more but who maintain normal growth and nutritional status.[78, 79] Absorption studies indicate that infants with less than 50 cm of small bowel may have prolonged fat and bile acid malabsorption, with low serum levels of 25-hydroxy vitamin D and cholesterol but normal absorptive capacity for sugars and amino acids.[80] Woolf et al.[81] studied 8 patients with SBS who were clinically stable for at least 1 year and determined the percentage absorption of fat (54%), carbohydrate (61%), protein (81%), and total calories (62%). Absorption of divalent cations was 32% for calcium, 34% for magnesium, and 15% for zinc. They concluded that dietary fat and fluid restrictions are not generally necessary once patients have achieved clinical stability. Restriction of high-oxalate foods—including spinach, rhubarb, parsley, citrus fruits, cocoa, tea, chocolate, and cola—appears prudent, however, to prevent hyperoxaluria.

As the mortality of SBS is less commonly due to malnutrition than to TPN-related complications, steps must be taken to insure optimal central venous catheter care to re-

TABLE 19–7.

Steps That May Minimize Liver Disease Associated
With Total Parenteral Nutrition (TPN)

Initiate enteral feeds early
Limit protein intake to ≤ 2.5 g/kg/day
Shield TPN solutions from light
Treat infections promptly and aggressively
Cycle TPN for on/off periods daily
Limit potential hepatotoxins
Monitor hepatic function frequently

duce the incidence of sepsis, mechanical breakage, and thrombosis. End stage liver disease is the most common cause of death in SBS in several series; therefore, minimizing the incidence of TPN-associated cholestasis becomes imperative (Table 19–7). The theoretical factors most often implicated in TPN-associated cholestasis are (1) lack of enteral feeds, (2) high parenteral amino acid loads, (3) toxins formed from photo-oxidation of TPN constituents, (4) infections, and (5) development of a fatty liver from continuous, large infusions of calories. Weaning from TPN while aggressively advancing enteral feeds as rapidly as tolerated appears to minimize the hepatic complications.

Infants with SBS require labor-intensive care during the operative and early adaptive phases; however, most are capable of eventually sustaining themselves by enteral feeds. Long-term morbidity and mortality depend on recognition of and prevention of complications associated with SBS (Table 19–8). Nutritional status must be closely monitored for many years after discharge from the hospital, inasmuch as deficiencies may occur insidiously. Parameters include routine height and weight growth velocity, anthropometrics, scrutinizing physical examinations looking for vitamin or trace element deficiencies, and periodic laboratory evaluation, including assessment of protein adequacy, anemia, and vitamin B_{12} status. The possible development of *D*-lactic acidosis must be kept in mind as the child's diet begins to include more complex starches.[82] Lethargy, ataxia, dysconjugate gaze, metabolic acidosis, and diarrhea should lead the clinician to consider this complication.

The future for treatment of SBS will involve trials of intestinal growth and adaptation-promoting factors along with refinement of surgical bowel lengthening or intestinal transplant techniques. Understanding and preventing metabolic derangements associated with SBS and the use of TPN are major challenges for future investigators.

TABLE 19–8.

Complications of Short Bowel Syndrome

Central venous catheter–related sepsis, thrombosis, mechanical obstruction
Mineral deficiencies (sodium, calcium, phosphorus, zinc, copper)
Vitamin deficiencies
Hypergastrinemia
Metabolic bone disease
Nephrolithiasis/oxaluria
Severe cholestasis, fibrosis, and cirrhosis
D-lactic acidosis
Short gut colitis
Growth failure/malnutrition

REFERENCES

1. Rickham PP: Massive small intestinal resection in newborn infants. *Ann R Coll Surg Engl* 1967; 41:480.
2. Clark JH: Management of short bowel syndrome in the high-risk infant, in Symposium on Continuing Care of the High-Risk Infant. *Clin Perinatol* 1984; 11:189–97.
3. Urban E, Weser E: Intestinal adaptation to bowel resection, in Stollerman GH (ed): *Advances in Internal Medicine,* vol 26. Chicago, Year Book Medical Publishers, Inc, 1980, pp 265–291.
4. Klish WJ, Putnam TC: The short gut. *Am J Dis Child* 1981; 135:1056–1061.
5. Touloukian RJ, Smith GJW: Normal intestinal length in preterm infants. *J Pediatr Surg* 1983; 18:720–723.
6. Masesa PC, Forrester JM: Consequences of partial and subtotal colectomy in the rat. *Gut* 1977; 18:37–44.
7. Ruppin H, Bar-Meir S, Soergel KH, et al: Absorption of short-chain fatty acids by the colon. *Gastroenterology* 1980; 78:1500–1507.
8. Mitchell JE, Breuer KI, Zuckerman L, et al: The colon influences ileal resection diarrhea. *Dig Dis Sci* 1980; 25:33–41.
9. Schwartz MZ, Maeda K: Short bowel syndrome in infants and children. *Pediatr Clin North Am* 1985; 32:1265–1279.
10. Krejs GJ: The small bowel: I. Intestinal resection. Baillieres *Clin Gastroenterol* 1979; 8:373–386.
11. Bohane TD, Haka-Ikse K, Biggar WD, et al: A clinical study of young infants after small intestinal resection. *J Pediatr* 1979; 94:552–558.
12. Meyers WC, Jones RS: Hyperacidity and hypergastrinemia following extensive intestinal resection. *World J Surg* 1979; 3:539–544.
13. Hyman PE, Feldman EJ, Ament ME, et al: Effect of enteral feeding on the maintenance of gastric acid secretory function. *Gastroenterology* 1983; 84:341–345.
14. Hyman PE, Everett SL, Harada T: Gastric acid hypersecretion in short bowel syndrome in infants: Association with extent of resection and enteral feeding. *J Pediatr Gastroenterol Nutr* 1986; 5:191–197.
15. Wilmore DW: Factors correlating with a successful outcome following extensive intestinal resection in newborn infants. *J Pediatr* 1972; 80:88–95.
16. Valman HB, Roberts PD: Vitamin B_{12} absorption after resection of ileum in childhood. *Arch Dis Child* 1974; 49:932–935.
17. Valman HB, Oberholzer VG, Palmer T: Hyperoxaluria after resection of ileum in childhood. *Arch Dis Child* 1974; 49:171–173.
18. Potts WJ: Pediatric surgery. *JAMA* 1955; 157:627–630.
19. Pilling GP, Cresson SL: Massive resection of the small intestine in the neonatal period. Report of two successful cases and review of the literature. *Pediatrics* 1957; 19:940–948.
20. Rickham PP, Irving I, Shmerling DH: Long-term results following extensive small intestinal resection in the neonatal period. *Prog Pediatr Surg* 1977; 10:65–75.
21. Jackson RH: Extensive resection of the small intestine in an infant. *Surg Gynecol Obstet* 1925; 40:55–61.
22. Valman HB: Growth and absorption after resection of ileum in childhood. *Pediatrics* 1976; 88:41–45.
23. Cooper A, Floyd TF, Ross AJ III, et al: Morbidity and mortality of short-bowel syndrome acquired in infancy: An update. *J Pediatr Surg* 1984; 19:711–718.
24. Bell MJ, Martin LW, Schubert WK, et al: Massive small-bowel resection in an infant: Long-term management and intestinal adaptation. *J Pediatr Surg* 1973; 8:197–204.
25. Postuma R, Moroz S, Friesen F: Extreme short-bowel syndrome in an infant. *J Pediatr Surg* 1983; 18:264–268.
26. Holt D, Easa D, Shim W, et al: Survival after massive small intestinal resection in a neonate. *Am J Dis Child* 1982; 136:79–80.

27. Williamson RCN: Intestinal adaptation: Part I. Structural function and cytokinetic changes. Part 2: Mechanisms of control. *N Engl J Med* 1978; 298:1393–1402, 1444–1450.

28. Hughes CA: Intestinal adaptation, in Tanner MS, Stocks RJ: *Neonatal Gastroenterology— Contemporary Issues*. Newcastle Upon Tyne, England, Intercept, 1984.

29. Lentze MJ: Intestinal adaptation in short-bowel syndrome. *Eur J Pediatr* 1989; 148:294–299.

30. Weinstein LD, Shoemaker CP, Hersh T, et al: Enhanced intestinal absorption after small bowel resection in man. *Arch Surg* 1969; 99:560–562.

31. Hanson WR, Osborne JW, Sharp JG: Compensation by the residual intestine after intestinal resection in the rat: I. Influence of amount of tissue removed. *Gastroenterology* 1977; 72:692–700.

32. Johnson LR, Copeland EM, Dudrick SJ, et al: Structural and hormonal alterations in the gastrointestinal tract of parenterally fed rats. *Gastroenterology* 1975; 68:1177–1183.

33. Hughes CA, Dowling RH: Speed of onset of adaptive mucosal hypoplasia and hypofunction in the intestine of parentually fed rats. *Clin Sci* 1980; 59:317–327.

34. Altmann GG: Influence of bile acid and pancreatic secretion on the size of the intestinal villi in the rat. *Am J Anat* 1971; 132:167–168.

35. Hughes CA, Bates T, Dowling RH: Cholecystokinin and secretin prevent the intestinal mucosal hypoplasia of total parenteral nutrition in the dog. *Gastroenterology* 1978; 75:34–41.

36. Williamson RCN, Bucholtz TW, Malt RA: Humoral stimulation of cell proliferation in small bowel after transection and resection in rats. *Gastroenterology* 1978; 75:249–254.

37. Bloom SR, Polak JM: The hormonal pattern of intestinal adaptation. A major role for enteroglucagon. *Scand J Gastroenterol* 1982; 17:91–103.

38. Sagor GR, Almukhtar MYT, Ghatei MA, et al: The effect of altered luminal nutrition on cellular proliferation and plasma concentrations of enteroglucagon and gastrin after small bowel resection in the rat. *Br J Surg* 1982; 69:14–18.

39. Feldman EJ, Aures D, Grossman MI: Epidermal growth factor stimulates ornithine decarboxylase activity in the digestive tract of the mouse. *Proc Soc Exp Biol Med* 1978; 159:400–402.

40. Grosfeld JL, Rescoria FJ, West KW: Short bowel syndrome in infancy and childhood. Analysis of survival of 60 patients. *World J Surg* 1986; 151:41–46.

41. Martinez-Frontanilla LA: Hartmann's procedure for multiple intestinal resections in infants. *Surg Gynecol Obstet* 1987; 164:81.

42. Kirkman RL: Small bowel transplantation. *Transplantation* 1984; 37:429–433.

43. Ziegler MM: Short bowel syndrome in infancy: Etiology and management. *Clin Perinatol* 1986; 13:163–173.

44. Harmel RP Jr, Stanley M: Improved survival after allogeneic small intestinal transplantation in the rat using cyclosporine immunosuppression. *J Pediatr Surg* 1986; 21:214–217.

45. Schraut WH: Current status of small-bowel transplantation. *Gastroenterology* 1988; 94:525–538.

46. Maeda K, Oki K, Nakamura K, et al: Small intestine transplantation: A logical solution for short bowel syndrome? *J Pediatr Surg* 1988; 23:10–15.

47. Williams JW, Sankary HN, Foster PF, et al: Splanchnic transplantation. An approach to the infant dependent on parenteral nutrition who develops irreversible liver disease. *JAMA* 1989; 261:1458–1462.

48. Schwartz MZ, Flye MW, Storozuk RB: Growth and function of transplanted fetal rat intestine: Effect of cyclosporin A. *Surgery* 1985; 97:481–486.

49. Thompson JS: Strategies for preserving intestinal length in the short-bowel syndrome. *Dis Colon Rectum* 1987; 30:208–213.

50. Bianchi A: Intestinal loop lengthening—a technique for increasing small intestinal length. *J Pediatr Surg* 1980; 15:145–151.

51. Thompson JS, Vanderhoof JA, Antonson DL: Intestinal tapering and lengthening for short bowel syndrome. *J Pediatr Gastroenterol Nutr* 1985; 4:495–497.

52. Reid IS: The significance of the ileocecal valve in massive resection of the gut in puppies. *J Pediatr Surg* 1975; 10:507–510.

53. Ricotta J, Zuidema GD, Gadacz TR, et al: Construction of an ileocecal valve and its role in massive resection of the small intestine. *Surg Gynecol Obstet* 1981; 152:310–314.

54. Schiller WR, Didio LJA, Anderson MC: Production of artificial sphincters: Ablation of longitudinal layer of the intestine. *Arch Surg* 1967; 95:436–441.

55. Glick PL, de Lorimier AA, Adzick NS, et al: Colon interposition: An adjuvant operation for short-gut syndrome. *J Pediatr Surg* 1984; 19:719–725.

56. Mitchell A, Watkins RM, Collin J: Surgical treatment of the short bowel syndrome. *Br J Surg* 1984; 71:329–333.

57. Collin J, Kelly KA, Phillips SF: Enhancement of absorption from the intact and transected canine small intestine by electrical pacing. *Gastroenterology* 1979; 76:1422–1428.

58. Layzell T, Collin J: Retrograde electrical pacing of the small intestine—a new treatment for the short bowel syndrome? *Br J Surg* 1981; 68:711–713.

59. Dorney SFA, Ament ME, Berquist WE, et al: Improved survival in very short small bowel of infancy with use of long-term parenteral nutrition. *J Pediatr* 1985; 107:521–525.

60. Parker P, Stroop S, Greene H: A controlled comparison of continuous versus intermittent feeding in the treatment of infants with intestinal disease. *J Pediatr* 1981; 99:360–364.

61. Newcomer AD: Surface digestion of carbohydrates. *Mayo Clin Proc* 1973; 48:620–623.

62. Weser E: Nutritional aspects of malabsorption: Short gut adaptation. *Am J Med* 1979; 67:1014–1020.

63. Ameen V, Powell GK, Jones LA: Quantitation of fecal carbohydrate excretion in patients with short bowel syndrome. *Gastroenterology* 1987; 92:493–500.

64. Simko V, McCarroll AM, Goodman S, et al: High fat diet in short bowel syndrome. Intestinal absorption and gastroenteropancreatic hormone responses. *Dig Dis Sci* 1980; 25:333–339.

65. Grey VL, Garofalo C, Greenberg GR, et al: The adaptation of the small intestine after resection in response to free fatty acids. *Am J Clin Nutr* 1984; 40:1235–1242.

66. Souba WW, Smith RJ, Wilmore DW: Glutamine metabolism by the intestinal tract. *J Parenter Enterol Nutr* 1985; 9:608–617.

67. Levy E, Frileux P, Sandrucci S, et al: Continuous enteral nutrition during the early adaptive stage of the short bowel syndrome. *Br J Surg* 1988; 75:549–553.

68. Latimer JS, McClain CJ, Sharp HL: Clinical zinc deficiency during zinc-supplemented parenteral nutrition. *J Pediatr* 1980; 97:434–437.

69. Dahlstrom KA, Ament ME, Medhin MG, et al: Serum trace elements in children receiving long-term parenteral nutrition. *J Pediatr* 1986; 109:625–630.

70. Engels LGJ, van den Hamer CJA, van Tongeren JHM: Iron, zinc, and copper balance in short bowel patients on oral nutrition. *Am J Clin Nutr* 1984; 40:1038–1041.

71. Goldman CD, Rudloff MA, Ternberg JL: Cimetidine and neonatal small bowel adaptation: An experimental study. *J Pediatr Surg* 1987; 22:484–487.

72. Puntis JW, Booth IW, Buick R: Cisapride in neonatal short gut. *Lancet* 1986; 2:108–109.

73. Ohlbaum P, Galperine RI, Demarquez JL, et al: Use of a long-acting somatostatin analogue (SMS 201-995) in controlling a significant ileal output in a 5-year-old child. *J Pediatr Gastroenterol Nutr* 1987; 6:466–470.

74. Felber SA, Sondheimer JM, Sokol RJ, et al: "Short gut colitis": Characterization and response to treatment. *Clin Res* 1989; 37:181A.

75. Menardi G, Guggenbichler JP: Bioavailability of oral antibiotics in children with short-bowel syndrome. *J Pediatr Surg* 1984; 19:84–86.

76. Robert R, Sketris IS, Abraham I, et al: Cyclosporine absorption in two patients with short-bowel syndrome. *Drug Intell Clin Pharm* 1988; 22:570–572.

77. Caniano DA, Kanoti GA: Newborns with massive intestinal loss: Difficult choices. *N Engl J Med* 1988; 318:703–707.

78. Lin CH, Rossi TM, Heitlinger LA, et al: Nutritional assessment of children with short-

bowel syndrome receiving home parenteral nutrition. *Am J Dis Child* 1987; 141:1093–1098.

79. Vargas JH, Ament ME, Berquist WE: Long-term home parenteral nutrition in pediatrics: Ten years of experience in 102 patients. *J Pediatr Gastroenterol Nutr* 1987; 6:24–32.

80. Ohkohchi N, Igarashi Y, Tazawa Y, et al: Evaluation of the nutritional condition and absorptive capacity of nine infants with short bowel syndrome. *J Pediatr Gastroenterol Nutr* 1986; 5:198–206.

81. Woolf GM, Miller C, Kurian R, et al: Nutritional absorption in short bowel syndrome. Evaluation of fluid, calorie and divalent cation requirements. *Dig Dis Sci* 1987; 32:8–15.

82. Perlmutter DH, Boyle JT, Campos JM, et al: d-lactic acidosis in children: An unusual metabolic complication of small bowel resection. *J Pediatr* 1983; 102:234–238.

Chapter 20

Bile Acid Secretion and Cholestasis

C. Jeffrey Sippel, M.D., Ph.D.

William F. Balistreri, M.D.

NEONATAL HEPATOBILIARY FUNCTION AND NEONATAL CHOLESTASIS

The excretion of bile, which is dependent on an intact and patent hepatobiliary system, involves multiple interrelated processes, including hepatocellular uptake of plasma constituents, transhepatocytic transport, metabolic processing, and an active bile secretory mechanism. An abberation in any of these processes could be manifest as *cholestasis*[1] which, by definition, is a reduction in bile flow. Cholestasis is characterized by the presence of conjugated hyperbilirubinemia and the retention of all substances normally excreted in bile.[2, 3]

For one to define defects in hepatobiliary excretory function clearly, the normal processes generating bile flow—namely bile acid secretion—must first be outlined. Bile acids are catabolic metabolites of cholesterol whose synthesis occurs in hepatic microsomes (Fig 20–1). The resultant amphiphilic compounds—cholanoic acid derivatives referred to as *primary* bile acids—are responsible for the generation of bile flow.[3–5] The two major primary bile acids are cholic acid ($3\alpha,7\alpha,12\alpha$-trihydroxy-5β-cholanic acid) and chenodeoxycholic acid ($3\alpha,7\alpha$-dihydroxy-5β-cholanic acid). These compounds are conjugated with glycine or taurine prior to excretion in bile (Fig 20–2). In healthy adults the glycine conjugates predominate in a ratio of 3.5:1.[3–5]

Intestinal flora dehydroxylate the primary bile acids at the 7α position to form secondary bile acids (Fig 20–3). Cholic acid is deconjugated to deoxycholic acid, and chenodeoxycholic acid is deconjugated to lithocholic acid. Lithocholic acid has a potential to cause cholestasis and may have pathologic implications in conditions such as short gut syndrome, in which bacterial overgrowth of the small intestine can occur. All secondary bile acids can also be conjugated with taurine, glycine, and/or sulfate, which will enhance their detergent properties.[4–7]

The neonate demonstrates a postnatal development of the processes involved in bile acid metabolism and transport. Immature bile acid biosynthetic pathways and transport mechanism in the newborn may have clinical consequences as discussed later.

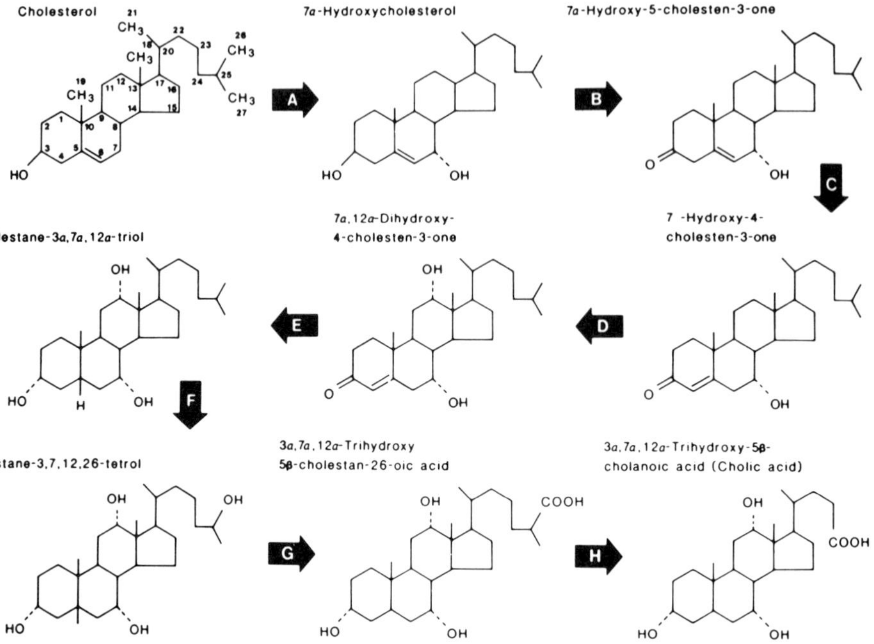

FIG 20–1.
Schematic indicating the important intermediates in the biosynthetic pathways of cholesterol conversion to cholic acid. The individual steps are summarized as follows. **A,** 7α-hydroxylation of cholesterol (addition of -OH group at position 7α configuration). This is the rate-limiting step in the biosynthetic pathway. **B,** oxidation of the 3β-hydroxyl group (to 3-oxo compound). **C,** isomerization of the 5-ene structure. **D,** 12α-hydroxylation. **E,** saturation of the double bond and reduction of the 3-one group. **F,** hydroxylation in the side chain at C26 position. **G,** oxidation to cholestanoic acid. **H,** hydroxylation at C24 and β-oxidation to reduce the length of side chain. (From Balistreri WF, Setchell KDR: Clinical implications of bile acid metabolism, in Silverberg M, Dunn F (eds): *Textbook of Pediatric Gastroenterology*, ed 2. 1987, pp 72–89. Used by permission.)

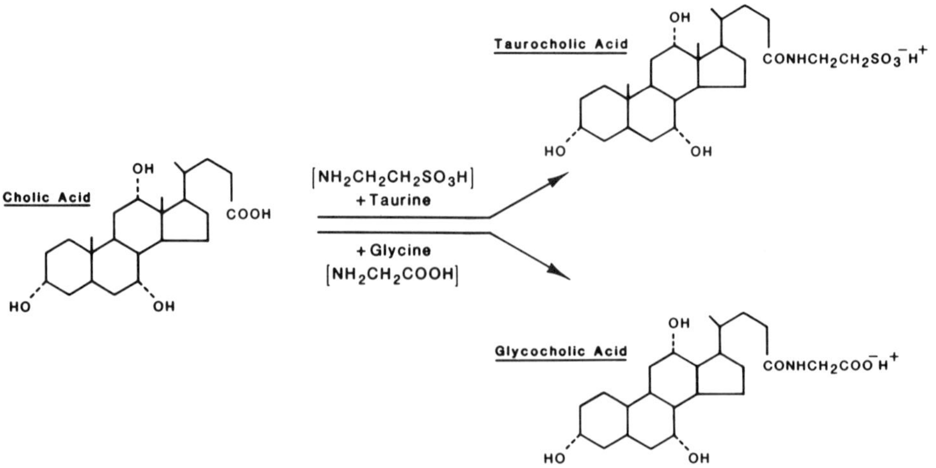

FIG 20–2.
Conjugation of cholic acid with either taurine or glycine. (From Balistreri WF, Setchell KDR: Clinical implications of bile acid metabolism, in Silverberg M, Dunn F (eds): *Textbook of Pediatric Gastroenterology*, ed 2. 1987, pp 72–89. Used by permission.)

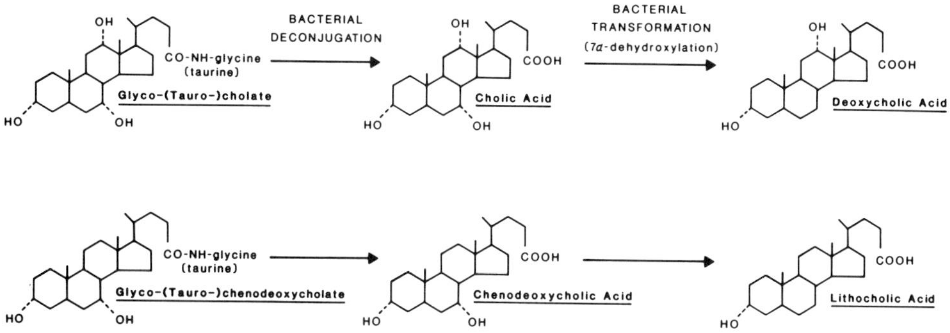

BACTERIAL
DECONJUGATION

BACTERIAL
TRANSFORMATION
(7α-dehydroxylation)

OH
CO-NH-glycine
(taurine)
Glyco-(Tauro-)cholate
HO   OH

OH
COOH
Cholic Acid
HO   OH

OH
COOH
Deoxycholic Acid
HO

CO-NH-glycine
(taurine)
Glyco-(Tauro-)chenodeoxycholate
HO   OH

COOH
Chenodeoxycholic Acid
HO   OH

COOH
Lithocholic Acid
HO

FIG 20–3.
Metabolic steps in the *bacterial* conversion of the primary bile acids (glyco-(tauro-)cholate and glyco-(tauro chenodeoxycholate) to the major secondary bile acids. (From Balistreri WF, Setchell KDR: Clinical implications of bile acid metabolism, in Silverberg M, Dunn F (eds): *Textbook of Pediatric Gastroenterology*, ed 2. 1987, pp 72–89. Used by permission.)

Qualitative and quantitative differences in bile acid synthesis exist between the developing and mature liver, as evidenced by the appearance of atypical bile acids in meconium[6] and tetrahydroxy cholanic acids in infant urine.[7] Human fetal bile contains bile acids with hydroxyl groups at positions C1, C2, and C6, which suggests a different biosynthetic pathway in early life.[8] The ratio of cholic acid to chenodeoxycholic acid is 0.85 for the fetus, 2.5 for the neonate, and 1.6 in the adult, reflecting the immaturity of 12α-hydroxylation during development. The excretion of atypical polyhydroxylated bile acids in the infant may be a response by the neonatal liver to immature bile acid biosynthetic pathways or may result from the "cholestatic" state of the neonate.

ENTEROHEPATIC CIRCULATION OF BILE ACIDS AND ITS ONTOGENIC EXPRESSION

Bile flow is directly dependent on the adequate synthesis, conjugation, secretion, and recirculation of bile acids, as diagramatically depicted in Figure 20–4. The efficient conservation of bile acids is made possible by both intestinal reabsorption and hepatic uptake, referred to as the enterohepatic circulation.

The intestinal reabsorptive phase of bile acid recirculation has been extensively studied.[9, 10] In the developing intestinal tract jejunal absorption predominates early on, with the development of ileal active transport of bile acids occurring later in life.[9, 10] Therefore, the fetal and perinatal enterohepatic circulation appears to be functionally "short circuited" with intraluminal bile acids returning to the liver by way of passive transport from the jejunum, the site where fat solubilization and absorption should occur. The net effect is an exaggeration of the intraluminal bile acid deficiency in the neonate, in the face of excessive fecal loss due to decreased distal active transport. There is also untimely absorption of the bile acids from the proximal intestinal lumen.[9, 10] Bile acid uptake by the liver is also inefficient in the neonate. The postprandial serum bile acid concentration is elevated in healthy newborns and "normalizes" to adult levels near the end of the first 6 months of life, suggesting an increasing capacity for hepatic uptake with maturation.[10] Bile acid pool size, bile acid biosynthesis, and intraluminal (duodenal) bile acid concentrations all quantitatively increase with age (Fig 20–5).[10]

These studies collectively suggest that the ability to synthesize and recover (recircu-

Enterohepatic circulation of bile acids

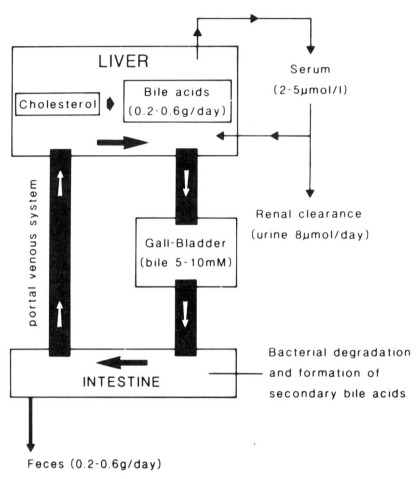

FIG 20-4.
Schematic diagram indicating main compartments and distribution of bile acids in the enterohepatic circulation during health and during impairment of their circulation. (From Balistreri WF, Setchell KDR: Clinical implications of bile acid metabolism, in Silverberg M, Dunn F (eds): *Textbook of Pediatric Gastroenterology*, ed 2. 1987, pp 72-89. Used by permission.)

late) bile acids is a function of age, and that the enterohepatic circulation of bile acids undergoes postnatal maturation.[11] As the newborn can no longer depend on placental excretory function, progressive maturation of both hepatic and intestinal function (the enterohepatic circulation) must occur so that the transition from the fetal to the extrauterine environment can be achieved without the risks of undernutrition and an increased susceptibility to cholestasis.

PHYSIOLOGICAL IMPLICATIONS OF BILE ACID HOMEOSTASIS

Bile acid homeostasis is not only required for efficient hepatic excretory function but also for dietary fat digestion and absorption. The importance of these processes is

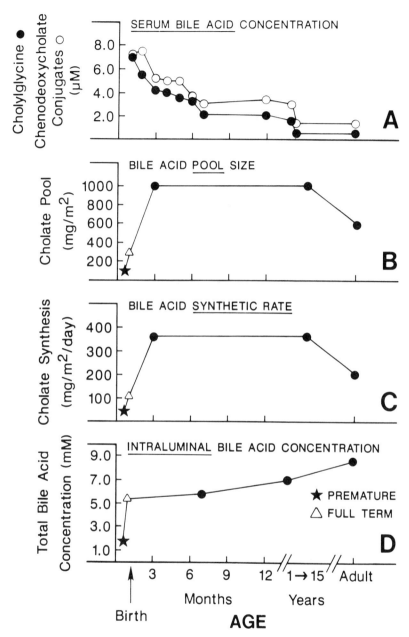

FIG 20–5.
Graphic depictions of compiled data regarding developmental changes in various aspects of bile acid metabolism in *humans*. **A,** progressive decline in the serum concentrations of cholylglycine and conjugated chenodeoxycholate (the primary bile acids) with age. **B,** rapid expansion in bile acid pool size. **C,** rapid increase in bile acid synthetic rate, with age; bile acid kinetics studied by isotopic dilution. **D,** total bile acid concentration measured in duodenal samples. (From Balistreri WF: The enterohepatic circulation of bile acids in early life, in *Neonatal Cholestasis: Causes, Symptoms, Therapies.* Report of the Eighty-seventh Ross Conference on Pediatric Research. Columbus, Ohio, Ross Laboratories, 1984, pp 38–47.)

best demonstrated by the effect of cholestasis (impaired bile acid excretion) on these processes. We will therefore discuss the effect of cholestasis on growth and development, fat-soluble vitamin metabolism, and calcium and phosphorous metabolism.

Effects on Growth and Development

Malnutrition and growth failure in chronic liver disease result from the interaction of multiple factors. There is often decreased nutrient intake due to anorexia, which is often a result of the prescription of unpalatable diets, infection, fat malabsorption, or specific deficiencies such as zinc. Malabsorption is the result of decreased intraluminal bile acids, often with further impairment of absorption because of chronic portal hypertension, mesenteric lymphatic congestion, and altered mucosal nutrient metabolism and transport.[12-14]

Growth failure in chronic liver disease may also be a consequence of decreased secretion of somatomedins (and possibly other growth factors), leading to inefficient glucose oxidation, lipid biosynthesis, and protein biosynthesis.[15]

Delayed sexual development has also been noted in cholestatic liver disease. Postulated mechanisms include an increased prolactin secretion and failure of acquisition of a critical body mass, which may suppress the secretion of gonadotropins.[16, 17] In the presence of cirrhosis and portal hypertension, there may be the shunting of steroid metabolites (such as adrenal and gonadal androgens) to peripheral sites; conversion to estrogen may occur in adipose tissues with resultant further androgenic suppression.[16]

Cholestasis can therefore impair both growth and development through inaccessibility of essential nutrients and the production of altered metabolites.

Altered Fat-Soluble Vitamin Absorption

Fat-soluble vitamins are poorly absorbed in the presence of fat malabsorption, as occurs in cholestasis. The sequelae of vitamin A, D, K, and E malabsorption and subsequent deficiencies are shown in Table 20–1.[12]

Vitamin A is required for optimal opthalmologic function; deficiency can lead to xerophthalmia and a decreased production of *cis*-retinal and *trans*-retinal, which are important components of retinal rod function; therefore, these deficiencies can lead to decreased night vision. Vitamin A also acts as an epidermal lubricant, and its deficiency can lead to excessively dry skin. The diagnosis of vitamin A deficiency can be suggested by measuring serum retinol concentrations which should normally be ≥ 20 μg/dL.[12, 13] Other more accurate means of documenting vitamin A status are needed.

Vitamin K is a cofactor that is essential in the gamma carboxylation of the blood coagulation factors II, VII, IX, and X. Its deficiency in patients with cholestasis therefore can lead to a generalized coagulopathy which can be manifest by petechiae, ecchymosis, purpura, epistaxis, or gastrointestinal and intracranial bleeding. The latter can be devastating, with serious central nervous system (CNS) sequelae or death. Vitamin K levels are not directly assessible; however, vitamin K can be indirectly assessed by measurements of the prothrombin time, which is prolonged in vitamin K deficiency.[12, 13]

Vitamin E is an antioxidant; its presence in cell membranes prevents the oxidation of unsaturated lipids, which are integral components of blood cells and neurons. Vitamin E deficiency leads to a degenerative neuropathy which usually presents with hyporeflexia or areflexia. These lesions are progressive if the vitamin E deficiency is untreated; after age 6 to 8, irreversible neurologic sequelae such as truncal and limb ataxia

TABLE 20–1.

Nutritional Deficiencies in Chronic Cholestasis*

Nutrient Deficiency	Clinical Presentation	Laboratory Diagnosis	Treatment Options
Vitamin A	Xerophthalmia, decreased night vision, thickened skin	Serum retinol concentration < 20 μg/dL	a. 10,000 to 25,000 IU of Aquasol A† b. 100,000 IU IM q 2 mo
Vitamin D	Rickets, osteomalacia	Hypocalemia, hypophosphatemia, low vitamin D levels	a. Vitamin D_2, 5000 to 8000 IU po qd b. 3 to 5 μg/kg/day of 25-hydroxy-cholecalciferol
Vitamin K	Coagulopathy, bleeding, ecchymosis, intracranial bleeding	Hypoprothrombinemia	a. Vitamin K, 2.5 to 5.0 mg IM for infant or adult, respectively b. 2.5 to 5.0 mg po qod thereafter
Vitamin E	Progressive neuropathy (see Fig 21–4)	E/lipid ratio < 0.6 mg/g for infants or < 0.8 mg/g for children > 12 and adults	Oral α-tocopherol, 50 to 400 IU/day
Calcium	Rickets, osteomalacia	Serum calcium level < 8 mg/dL	25 to 100 mg/kg/day of calcium
Phosphorous	Rickets, osteomalacia	Serum phosphorous < 4 mg/dL	25 to 50 mg/kg/day of phosphate

*Modified from Balistreri WF: Neonatal Cholestasis. *J Pediatr* 1985; 106:171–184.
†Armour, Tarrytown, NY.

and peripheral neuropathy may develop. Therefore, vitamin E deficiency should be aggressively treated before these complications occur. The neurologic progression that occurs in patients with vitamin E deficiency is shown in Figure 20–6. Serum vitamin E levels have a linear relationship with serum lipid concentrations, presumably because of partitioning of the vitamin into the serum lipid compartment; consequently, a normal serum vitamin E level does not rule out vitamin E deficiency. Therefore, the ratio of serum vitamin E to total serum lipids has been advocated as a mathematical correction for serum lipid concentration. A serum vitamin E/serum lipid ratio of $\geq$ 0.6 mg/g for infants or young children and $\geq$ 0.8 mg/g for children older than 12 or adults, is considered normal.[13]

Vitamin D facilitates the absorption of Ca^+ from the intestine and kidney, and it also can mobilize Ca^+ from bone; the net effect is to positively assimilate Ca^+ for metabolic purposes. Vitamin D deficiency leads to rickets and osteomalacia. Vitamin D status in cholestatic children should be assessed by measuring calcium, phosphorous, 25-hydroxyvitamin D, and 1,25-dihydroxyvitamin D concentrations and by evaluation with skeletal survey.[12, 13]

The calcium and phosphorous requirements in the presence of cholestasis is not precisely known. In addition, the pathophysiology of bone disease in cholestasis is poorly defined, however. It was once believed that vitamin D deficiency led to calcium malabsorption. Calcium absorption seems unchanged in the cholestatic patient, even those with decreased bone density; thus other mechanisms are probably involved in the development of bone disease in children with chronic cholestasis. Calcium supplements of 25 to 100 mg/kg/day and phosphorous supplements of 25 to 50 mg/kg/day are currently recommended.[12–14]

Water-soluble vitamin and mineral metabolism may be affected by cholestasis. Low

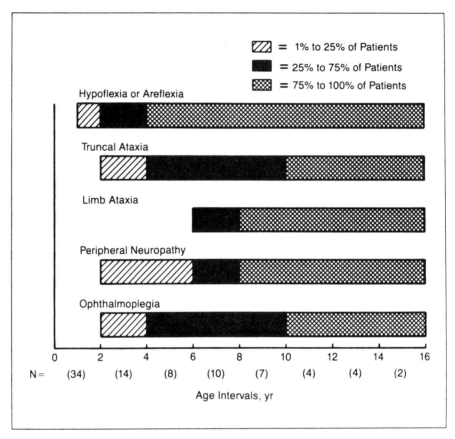

FIG 20–6.
Frequency and clinical progression of neurologic findings in children with vitamin E deficiency. Each bar represents the percent of patients with a specific neurologic finding at each 2-year interval. N = the number of patients studied at each age interval. (From Sokol RJ: Medical management of the infant with cirrhotic liver disease. *Semin Liver Dis* 1987; 7:155–167.)

serum and tissue levels of the water-soluble B complex vitamins have been described in adults with end stage liver disease secondary to alcoholism. Iron deficiency may be a result of chronic blood loss due to bleeding esophageal varices associated with cirrhosis. Hepatic copper accumulation occurs in cholestasis because copper excretion is primarily biliary.[18] Limiting copper intake seems reasonable but has not been shown to alter natural history of the disease.[13]

DIFFERENTIAL DIAGNOSIS OF NEONATAL CHOLESTASIS

The many causes of neonatal cholestasis are outlined in Table 20–2. Despite the diversity of these disease processes, affected patients have a similar clinical presentation of jaundice, dark urine, pale or acholic stools, and hepatomegaly. The diseases that cause cholestasis need to be characterized into those that can be *medically* treated, such as metabolic/endocrine diseases (galactosemia, hypothyroidism, or hypopituitarism) or infectious causes, and *surgically* treatable causes such as extrahepatic biliary atresia or choledocal cysts. Also, the diseases with an unfavorable prognosis such as cystic fibrosis or α-1-antitrypsin deficiency need to be defined such that genetic counseling can be carried out. The relative incidence of the various forms of neonatal cholestasis are presented in Table 20–3.[19]

Disorders of Tyrosine Metabolism

Transient neonatal tyrosinemia, a disorder noted in premature infants, presumably results from decreased activity of tyrosine aminotransferase or a dietary deficiency of vitamin C. This entity is not associated with liver disease, and elevated serum tyrosine levels will abate with age.[20]

Hereditary tyrosinemia is associated with progressive liver failure or cirrhosis and

TABLE 20–2.

Neonatal Cholestasis: Classification of Recognized Disease Entities*

I. Extrahepatic disorders
  A. Biliary atresia
  B. Biliary hypoplasia
  C. Bile duct stenosis
  D. Sclerosing cholangitis
  E. Anomalies of choledochal-pancreatico-ductal junction
  F. Spontaneous perforation of bile duct
  G. Mass (neoplasia, stone)
  H. Bile/mucous plug
II. Intrahepatic disorders
  A. "Idiopathic"
    1. "Idiopathic" neonatal hepatitis
    2. Intrahepatic cholestasis, persistent
      a. Arteriohepatic dysplasia (Alagille syndrome)
      b. Byler disease (severe intrahepatic cholestasis with progressive hepatocellular disease)
      c. Defective bile acid metabolism and cholestasis
        1. Δ 4-3-oxosteroid 5β reductase deficiency
        2. 3β-hydroxy-Δ 5 steroid dehydrogenase-isomerase deficiency
      d. Zellweger syndrome (cerebrohepatorenal syndrome)
      e. Nonsyndromic paucity of intrahepatic ducts (apparent absence of bile ductules)
      f. Microfilament dysfunction
    3. Intrahepatic cholestasis, recurrent (syndromic?)
      a. Familial benign recurrent cholestasis
      b. Hereditary cholestasis with lymphedema (Aagenaes)
  B. "Anatomic"
    1. Congenital hepatic fibrosis/infantile polycystic disease
    2. Caroli disease (cystic dilatation of intrahepatic ducts)
  C. Metabolic disorders
    1. Disorders of amino acid metabolism
      a. Tyrosinemia
      b. Hypermethioninemia (?)
    2. Disorders of lipid metabolism
      a. Wolman disease
      b. Niemann-Pick disease
      c. Gaucher's disease
    3. Disorders of carbohydrate metabolism
      a. Galactosemia
      b. Fructosemia
      c. Glycogenosis III/IV

(Continued.)

TABLE 20–2   (cont.).

4. Metabolic disease (uncharacterized defect)
   a. α-1-antitrypsin deficiency
   b. Cystic fibrosis
   c. Idiopathic hypopituitarism
   d. Hypothyroidism
   e. Neonatal iron storage disease (perinatal hemochromatosis)
   f. Infantile copper overload
   g. Familial erythrophagocytic lymphohistiocytosis
D. Hepatitis
   1. Infectious
      a. Cytomegalovirus
      b. Hepatitis B virus
      c. Rubella virus
      d. Reovirus type 3
      e. Herpes virus
      f. Varicella virus
      g. Coxsackie virus
      h. ECHO virus
      i. Toxoplasmosis
      j. Syphilis
      k. Tuberculosis
      l. Listeriosis
   2. "Toxic"
      a. Cholestasis associated with parenteral nutrition
      b. Sepsis with possible endotoxemia (urinary tract infection, gastroenteritis)
E. Genetic/chromosomal
   1. Trisomy E
   2. Down's syndrome
   3. Donahue syndrome (leprechaunism)
F. Miscellaneous
   1. Histiocytosis X
   2. Shock or hypoperfusion
   3. Intestinal obstruction
   4. Polysplenia syndrome
   5. Hemolysis (?)

*Modified from Balistreri WF: Neonatal cholestasis: Lessons from the past, issues for the future (foreword), in Balistreri WF (ed): *Neonatal Cholestasis.* Seminars in Liver Disease, vol 7. New York, Thieme, 1987.

TABLE 20–3.

Relative Frequency of the Various Clinical Forms of Neonatal Cholestasis (Based on a Composite of Several Published Series Encompassing Over 500 Cases)*

Clinical Form	Cumulative %	Estimated Frequency†
"Idiopathic" neonatal hepatitis	35–40	1.25
Extrahepatic biliary atresia	25–30	0.70
α-1-Antitrypsin deficiency	7–10	0.25
Intrahepatic cholestasis syndromes (e.g., Alagille, Byler)	5–6	0.14
Bacterial sepsis	2	<0.1
Hepatitis		
Cytomegalovirus	1	<0.1
Rubella, herpes	1	<0.1
Endocrine (hypothyroidism, panhypopituitarism)	1	<0.1
Galactosemia	1	<0.1

*Modified from Balistreri WF: Neonatal cholestasis: Lessons from the past, issues for the future (foreword), in Balistreri WF (ed): *Neonatal Cholestasis.* Seminars in Liver Disease, vol 7. New York, Thieme, 1987.
†Per 10,000 live births.

Fanconi's syndrome. The acute form may present in infancy with hepatic failure, failure to thrive, ascites, and hypoprothrombinemia. Chronic tyrosinemia presents later in childhood with cirrhosis, hepatoma, and/or rickets. Both forms may occur within the same family.[20, 21] The enzymatic defect, which has been localized to fumaryl acetoacetase, results in the accumulation of succinyl acetoacetone, succinyl acetone,[20, 21] fumaryl acetoacetate, and maleyl acetoacetate metabolites, which are highly toxic. Treatment consists of dietary restriction of phenylalanine and tyrosine; this may improve the renal tubular dysfunction and but rarely the progression of liver disease. Liver transplantation is necessary in the presence of liver failure, hepatoma, and/or cirrhosis.[21]

Lysosomal Storage Diseases

Wolman disease, an autosomal recessive disease associated with lysosomal acid lipase deficiency, is characterized by diarrhea, failure to thrive, hepatomegaly, and jaundice. The disease is usually fatal during the 1st year of life. There is a generalized accumulation of cholesterol esters and triglycerides in lymphatic tissue, bone marrow, liver, spleen, and adrenal glands. The liver biopsy is highly suggestive with accumulation of lipid droplets in the liver parenchyma. Plasma lipids are usually normal, and all cases are uniformly fatal.[22]

Cholesterol ester storage disease, due to a decrease in acid lipase activity, results in increased cholesterol ester and triglyceride accumulation in the liver and in intestinal mucosa. These patients have hyperbetalipoproteinemia, diagnostic findings on liver biopsy, and a normal life expectancy.[23]

Gaucher's disease (glucosylceramide lipidosis) results from lack of gluco-cerebrosidase. This enzymatic deficiency results in the accumulation of glucosylceramide (glucocerebroside) in lysosomes of reticuloendothelial cells. The clinical spectrum includes cholestasis, hepatosplenomegaly, thrombocytopenia, or neurologic involvement in three varying forms of the disease.[24] Type I, the most common type which is the adult or chronic non-neuronopathic type, results in hepatosplenomegaly, thrombocytopenia, bone pain, and yellow skin pigmentation, and can occur at any age. Type II, also known as infantile or acute neuronopathic, is manifest initially in infants who present with hepatosplenomegaly and progressive neurologic deterioration manifested by strabismus, spasticity, and a characteristic retroflexion of the head with a relentless downhill clinical course. Type III, the juvenile or subacute neuronopathic form, includes children with multiple neurologic abnormalities but prolonged survival. The diagnosis is most commonly made by the combination of clinical features and the demonstration of the characteristic "wrinkled tissue paper" Gaucher cells.

The classic *Niemann-Pick disease* (sphingomyelin lipidoses) is characterized by the accumulation of sphingomyelin in various organs because of absence of sphingomyelinase. At least three distinct deficiency states are recognized; however, five clinical variants of the disease exist.[25] Type A is the acute infantile (neuronopathic) form, and type B is a chronic condition with early visceral involvement but no CNS dysfunction. Type C is a chronic neuronopathic form with neurologic sequelae that occurs after 2 years of age, with associated hepatosplenomegaly. Type D, the Nova Scotia variant, can typically present with cholestasis, perhaps due to obstruction by enlarged lymph nodes. Type E occurs in adults who have visceromegaly but no neurologic involvement.[25] The disease should be suspected in patients with asymptomic hepatomegaly, vomiting, and failure to thrive during the 1st year of life or neurologic deterioration, with motor and intellectual degeneration beginning in the 1st year of life. Approximately 50% of the patients present with the cherry red spot of macular degeneration of the retina. Niemann-Pick foam cells are evident on bone marrow or liver biopsy.[25] The diagnosis can be confirmed by measuring sphinagomyelinase activity in tissue samples.

Disorders of Carbohydrate Metabolism

Galactosemia, an autosomal recessive disorder resulting from the deficiency of galactose-1-phosphate uridyl transferase, results in the toxic accumulation of galactose-1-phosphate, galactitol, and galactosamine.[12, 26] Galactitol is believed to accumulate in the lenses of the eyes and cause cataracts. The liver, renal, ovarian, and neuronal degenerative changes are presumably related to the accumulation of these metabolites in tissues. Due to the inhibition of phosphoglucomutase by galactose-1-phosphate, hypoglycemia may occur especially in a fasting or "galactose challenged" state. A screening test for galactosemia is performed by testing the urine for total reducing (nonglucose) substances. Red blood cells can then be assayed for galactose 1-phosphate uridyl transferase activity. A simple lactose- and galactose-free diet can prevent the serious sequelae of cataracts and progressive liver disease.[12, 26]

Hereditary fructose intolerance can occur in association with three known enzymatic defects in fructose metabolism; only fructose-1-phosphate aldolase deficiency leads to significant hepatic injury.[27] This form of the disease resembles galactosemia in that affected patients present with vomiting, diarrhea, hypoglycemia, hepatomegaly, failure to thrive, and jaundice. The enzymatic defect is manifest in liver, kidney, and jejunal mucosa. Ingestion of fructose leads to hypoglycemia, hypophosphatemia and hyperuricemia, and progressive liver dysfunction. Aversion to sugar (sucrose, fructose, and sorbitol) is evident in older children and adults. Treatment consists of complete elimination of sucrose, fructose, and sorbitol from the diet, which can prevent the symptoms and progressive liver disease.

Glycogen storage disease type III is caused by deficiency of α-1,6-glucosidase (debrancher enzyme).[28] The clinical features of this disorder may range from minimal hepatic dysfunction and little muscle involvement to progressive myopathy and cirrhosis. The diagnosis can be recognized by liver biopsy, which reveals a lack of the enzyme; histologically, hepatocytes will be shown to demonstrate irregular enlargement and nuclear and cytoplasmic accumulation of glycogen. The patient's course can be stabilized by maintaining normoglycemia—either by continuous enteral feedings or by oral feeding of complex carbohydrates such as corn starch to prevent episodes of hypoglycemia.[28]

Glycogen storage disease type IV is characterized by the absence of α-1,4-glycan-6-glucosyl transferase (brancher enzyme).[28, 29] In most cases the disease presents with hepatosplenomegaly and failure to thrive; progressive cirrhosis with portal hypertension, ascites, and esophageal varices will usually result in death in early life. Liver biopsy will demonstrate cirrhotic changes, hepatocytes with eccentric nuclei, and cytoplasmic deposits of the abnormal polysaccharide and a deficiency of the brancher enzyme. Preventing episodes of hypoglycemia through continuous enteral feedings has been observed to improve growth, muscle strength, and liver size; however, this treatment is supportive at best. In most cases, the only hope for survival resides in liver transplantation.[28, 29]

Alpha-1-antitrypsin (A1AT) deficiency is an autosomal recessive disease characterized by the deficiency of the protease inhibitor α-1-antitrypsin. The deficiency of this protease inhibitor results in progressive liver failure in a significant proportion of patients early in life and pulmonary involvement with emphysematous changes usually occurring later in adulthood. The diagnosis is made by immunoelectrophoresis; the normal Pi (protease inhibitor) phenotype is M; the phenotype for the deficiency state is Z. Patients who are homozygous for the deficiency state (Pi ZZ) have serum concentrations 10% to 15% of normal. The liver biopsy obtained from homozygous deficient patients can also be diagnostic, revealing periodic acid-Schiff (PAS)–positive, diastase-resistant globules visualized within the periportal region of the hepatocyte. The prognosis of α-1-antitrypsin deficiency is variable, with 25% of patients progressing to end stage liver disease[30]; a history of severe neonatal cholestasis is a reliable indicator of a poor prognosis.[30, 31] The treatment of A1AT deficiency is supportive at this time. Liver transplantation has been successfully performed in many patients, with the recipient assuming the A1AT phenotype of the donor.[30, 31]

Cystic fibrosis can present as neonatal cholestasis; liver biopsy in these patients reveals inspissated bile plugs and mucous in the bile ducts.[32] Aside from steatosis, focal biliary cirrhosis is the most common hepatic lesion. The incidence of this lesion is 18% in infants under 3 months of age and 27% in children over 1 year of age.[32] The hepatobiliary disease can progress rarely to end stage liver disease with portal hypertension.

Neonatal hypothyroidism may present with prolonged cholestasis in 20% of affected patients. The mechanism of cholestasis is presumed to be secondary to decreased bile flow in the absence of the trophic hormones. The other manifestations of developmental delay, bradycardia, myxedema, or auditory deficiency are unrelated to the frequency of cholestasis.[33]

Hypopituitarism can similarly present as neonatal cholestasis. A history of hypoglycemia, hypernatremia, seizures, or wandering nystagmus will suggest the diagnosis.[34] Endocrine studies reveal suppression of all the major pituitary hormones. The hepatic dysfunction improves with or without treatment of the endocrine abnormalities.[35]

Infectious Causes of Neonatal Cholestasis

Hepatitis A, a common cause of acute hepatitis in children, is a rare cause of hepatitis and cholestasis in neonates.[35, 36] Perinatal transmission has not been reported, and the presence of serologic markers is most likely a consequence of passive placental transfer or transfusion. Even though no reports have documented perinatal transmission, it is recommended that 0.02 mL/kg of serum immune globulin be given intramuscularly to neonates born to icteric mothers with hepatitis A.[35, 36]

Hepatitis B is also an uncommon cause of cholestasis during the neonatal period. In contrast to hepatitis A, hepatitis B is perinatally transmitted to the fetus from mothers who are carriers of hepatitis B surface antigen (HBsAg), and the risk greatly increases if the mothers are also positive for the core protein antigen (HBeAg). Over 90% of infants who acquire hepatitis B virus will become HBsAg-positive chronic carriers. However, only 5% develop acute icteric hepatitis, and most have an uncomplicated course; fulminant hepatic failure may occur rarely.[35, 36] Infants born to HBsAg- and HBeAg-positive mothers should receive hepatitis B immune globulin, 0.5 mL intramuscularly within 12 hours of delivery followed by hepatitis B vaccine during the 1st week of life, and again at 1 and 6 months of age. Their HBsAg levels should be tested at 9 months of age to assess vaccine efficacy and to identify chronic carriers.[35–37]

The absence of viral markers makes the diagnosis of *non A, non B hepatitis* (now called *hepatitis C*) difficult. These patients usually develop anicteric hepatitis between 1 and 2 months after exposure and have the absence of hepatitis A or hepatitis B serologic markers and a liver biopsy revealing hepatocellular involvement. If a mother is presumed to have perinatal non A, non B hepatitis, it is prudent to give serum immune globulin at 0.02 mL/kg even though the literature does not verify the efficacy of this prophylactic measure.[36, 37]

Neonatal cytomegalovirus (CMV) infection may result from perinatal transmission or contact with infected secretions; 5% to 10% of infants with CMV have symptoms ranging from cerebral periventricular calcifications, chorioretinitis, thrombocytopenia, and microcephaly to deafness and psychomotor retardation. Liver biopsies are diagnostic, with evidence of neonatal hepatitis and cytoplasmic and nuclear inclusion bodies. There is no currently approved therapy for recurrent CMV neonatal hepatitis; however, the course is generally benign. The diagnosis is established by urine culture for CMV, with viral titers obtained from the baby and the mother.[38]

Patients with *congenital rubella* may present with patent ductus arteriosus, peripheral pulmonary stenosis, microcephaly, intrauterine growth retardation, deafness, hepatosplenomegaly, purpura, and cataracts. Cholestasis occurs in 15% of cases. Liver biopsies reveal giant cell transformation and extramedullary hematopoiesis. The diagnosis is established by nasopharyngeal viral swabs and by obtaining viral titers from the baby and the mother. The hepatic involvement is usually minimal and reversible, and the involvement of other organ systems more directly relate to the prognosis of the disease.[39]

Herpes simplex virus can attack a multitude of organs including the skin, lungs, spleen, liver, CNS, and retina. The prognosis is usually related to CNS involvement; however, cholestatic liver disease shows characteristic features on liver biopsy. The diagnosis is made by viral cultures of various body fluids and by herpesvirus titers from the baby and the mother. Acyclovir is generally utilized for herpes simplex encephalitis.[40]

Toxoplasmosis infection may be associated with disseminated intracranial calcification, meningoencephalitis, intrauterine growth retardation, and chorioretinitis. Forty percent of patients present with cholestasis. The diagnosis may be made by culture of cerebrospinal fluid or throat cultures. Toxoplasmosis titers from the baby and mother are again helpful. The treatment involves concomitant administrate sulfasalazine, pyrimethemine, and folinic acid.[38]

Syphilis infection in the perinatal period is usually manifest as anemia, rash, periostosis, mucosal lesions, hepatomegaly, and cholestasis. The liver biopsy can be suggestive; however, the diagnosis is usually made by positive serology. Dark field examination of mucosal or skin lesions will also reveal spirochetes. Treatment with penicillin usually completely reverses the hepatic involvement of the disease.

Listerosis presents with the clinical signs of sepsis and cholestasis. Liver biopsy reveals granulomatous and hepatic changes. The hepatic involvement usually reverses with adequate antibiotic therapy.[35]

Coxsackie B virus usually involves the heart, liver, kidney, and CNS. The diagnosis is established by liver biopsy, which reveals focal hepatitis and viral isolation from the liver or cerebrospinal fluid.

ECHO virus presents with a "sepsis-like" picture. ECHO and coxsackie viruses can progress to fulminant hepatic failure. Therapy is supportive.

Tuberculosis rarely causes cholestatic jaundice; infected patients usually present with failure to thrive, pulmonary, or CNS involvement. Cerebrospinal fluid and gastric aspirates cultured for mycobacterium and acid-fast stain can confirm the diagnosis as can skin testing at 1 to 3 months of age. Treatment involves the utilization of at least isoniazid and rifampin. The liver disease usually improves with time.[41]

Infantile Cholangiopathies

There appears to be a clinical and histologic continuum from idiopathic neonatal hepatitis to extra-hepatic biliary atresia that are collectively termed "the idiopathic obstructive cholangiopathies." It has been suggested that extrahepatic biliary atresia and sporadic idiopathic neonatal hepatitis are a result of viral-induced biliary ductal obliteration and hepatocellular injury, respectively. Familial forms of neonatal cholestasis are suggested to be genetic diseases resulting from defects in hepatocellular excretion or bile acid synthesis. There are vast areas of overlap among the idiopathic cholangiopathies (Fig 20–7).[19]

The cause or causes of these infantile cholangiopathies remain unsolved, and definitive efforts at treatment are therefore not available. Further investigations will be necessary to understand the pathophysiology of these diseases and their treatment.

Extrahepatic biliary atresia patients have been found to have a 15% to 20% incidence of congenital anomalies such as polysplenia, cardiovascular anomalies, and malrotation which *might* suggest a congenital insult. In contrast, biliary atresia has also been found at autopsy in infants previously shown to have patent extrahepatic ducts, which might indicate a late perinatal or postnatal progressive obliteration. In an attempt to reconcile this paradox, a fetal and perinatal form have been delineated.[42] In the postulated *fetal form* (comprising approximately 33% of the cases) infants were found to be jaundiced from birth with progressive cholestasis. These children also had high incidence of malrotation and other congenital anomalies. In these infants no bile duct rem-

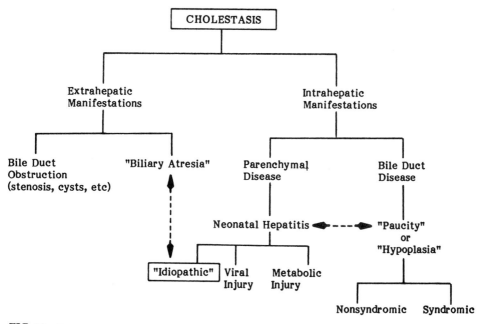

FIG 20–7.
Conceptualization of neonatal cholestasis based on the presumed nature of the hepatobiliary injury. Potential areas of overlap or suggested routes of evolution are indicated by *broken arrows;* for example, progressive duct disappearance in a patient with idiopathic neonatal hepatitis may be manifested in later life as bile duct paucity. Similarly, cholestatic patients with documented extrahepatic bile duct patency in early life have been found to have biliary atresia on reevaluation. (From Balistreri WF: Neonatal cholestasis: Lessons from the past, issues for the future (foreword), in Balistreri WF (ed): *Neonatal Cholestasis.* Seminars in Liver Disease, vol 7. New York, Thieme, 1987.)

nants were visualized at the porta hepatis. The postulated *perinatal* form presented later in life (6 to 8 weeks) with liver disease, and bile duct remnants were often found at the porta hepatis, suggesting that bile ducts are formed but are obliterated by a cholangiolytic process; there were no associated congenital anomalies. The fetal form generally had a greater propensity to a progressive course with liver failure and cirrhosis than did the perinatal form.[42]

Infants with biliary atresia generally look well at birth and are of appropriate size for gestational age. Cholestasis is usually noted at 3 to 6 weeks of age, with an enlarged, firm liver and conjugated hyperbilirubinemia. Liver biopsy reveals periportal inflammation, proliferating bile ducts, and bile plugs. The diagnosis is confirmed with an intraoperative cholangiogram, which also defines the anatomy for the hepatic portoenterostomy to follow. It is critical that the diagnosis be made as soon as possible. Authors have suggested that bile flow can be established in up to 90% of patients who undergo surgery at less than 2 months of age; however, the success rate drops to 20% in infants older than 3 months of age.[43] Infants with uncorrectable forms of extrahepatic biliary atresia should undergo portal dissection with apposition of the resected surface of the porta hepatis to the bowel mucosa of a limb of jejunum.[43] A proportion of patients with biliary atresia will benefit from the portoenterostomy; however, the majority will continue to show evidence of hepatic dysfunction. In the latter cases, the goal is to allow adequate growth in hopes of an ultimate successful liver transplantation.[43]

Choledochal cysts present with clinical symptoms that are very similar to extrahepatic biliary atresia; the incidence ranges from 1 in 1,000 to 1 in 10,000 births. These structures are dilatations and diverticula off of the extrahepatic biliary tree and there are multiple anatomical variations.[43]

Abdominal ultrasound, hepatobiliary scintigraphy, and intraoperative cholangiograms are utilized in the diagnosis of this anomaly. The treatment is surgical and involves either the anastomosis of the cyst to the duodenum or a Roux-en-Y jejunal loop or excision of the cyst with primary biliary reconstruction.[43]

Intrahepatic Bile Duct Paucity

Syndromic Paucity of Intrahepatic Bile Ducts (Alagille's Syndrome)

This autosomal dominant syndrome is characterized by a decreased number of interlobular bile ducts (which by definition is < 0.5 interlobular bile ducts per portal triad).[44, 45] The combination of extrahepatic features vary but include prominent forehead, hypertelorism, deep-set eyes, a saddle or straight nasal bridge, hemivertebrae or butterfly vertebrae, decreased interpeduncular distance on radiographic examination, posterior embryotoxon on opthalmologic slit-lamp examination, and peripheral pulmonic stenosis, along with the cholestasis. Less frequently mental retardation, mesangiolipidosis, and growth retardation related to the cholestasis may occur. Hepatic histology in affected patient over 6 months of age classically reveals intrahepatic bile duct paucity with occasional evidence of hepatocellular unrest. The early biopsy picture is indistinct, with inflammation predominating. Serum bile acid, alkaline phosphatase, cholesterol, phospholipid, and triglyceride levels are all increased. The clinical course is marked by recurrent episodes of cholestasis which are most severe during the first 4 years of life and decrease thereafter. Xanthomas occur during the 1st decade but diminish thereafter in parallel with decreasing serum cholesterol. Pruritus is the most troublesome feature. The prognosis in infancy is usually related to the severity of cardiovascular disease, and the long-term prognosis is usually excellent—with progressive liver disease occurring only in 5% of cases.

Nonsyndromic Paucity of the Intrahepatic Bile Ducts

The clinical course and prognosis in nonsyndromic paucity are generally worse than in Alagille's syndrome, but are variable, reflecting the heterogenous nature of this group of diseases, which are often familial.[45]

Idiopathic neonatal hepatitis is the most common cause of neonatal cholestasis and is a diagnosis made by liver biopsy and by exclusion after all other forms of neonatal hepatocellular disease have been ruled out.[12, 19] On liver biopsy there is hepatocellular swelling, necrosis, multinucleated giant cell formation, and extramedullary hematopoeisis. This is in contrast to extrahepatic biliary atresia, in which periportal inflammation, bile duct proliferation, and bile plug predominate. This syndrome of idiopathic neonatal hepatitis has presumed multiple causes, and thus the clinical course may be variable; however, certain features characterize the illness. Over 50% of neonatal hepatitis present with jaundice during the 1st week of life, and many of these children are clinically stable and thrive; approximately 33% have a fulminant downhill course. The presence of associated symptoms (thrombocytopenia, hydrocephaly, chorioretinitis, microcephaly) are unusual and suggest alternative causes such as congenital infections.

It is difficult to estimate a prognosis for individual cases of neonatal hepatitis as there are no laboratory or clinical parameters that can quantitatively gauge the disease. It also seems that sporadic cases seem to have a more favorable prognosis than familial cases. Treatment is supportive, as discussed below.[12, 13, 18, 19]

Hematological causes of cholestasis are usually related to hemolytic anemias or increased loading of blood products (as in exchange transfusions), with a subsequent increased load of bilirubin to be metabolized and secreted by the hepatobiliary tract. When the hepatobiliary load is excessive, sludging occurs with subsequent obstructive jaundice. This phenomenon, referred to as the "inspissated bile syndrome," should be suspected in the face of a hemolytic anemia and cholestasis. The diagnosis is established by ultrasound, which will often reveal biliary sludge and extrahepatic duct dilatation proximal to the point of maximal sludging.

Evaluation of the cause of the hemolytic anemia should include Coombs testing of the baby and the mother, reticulocyte count, osmotic fragility tests for hereditary spherocytosis, or glucose-6-phosphate dehydrogenase assays for infants who have family members with this deficiency. The therapy of the associated cholestasis includes treating the underlying cause of the hemolytic anemia, reducing the amount of blood cells transfused, and increasing enteral feedings when possible to stimulate choleresis.

Cholestasis Associated With Total Parenteral Nutrition

Total parenteral nutrition (TPN) may be complicated by the development of cholestasis in very low birth weight infants.[46] This entity is a diagnosis of exclusion after all other causes of neonatal cholestasis have been ruled out. Jaundice and hepatomegaly are the presenting clinical features in an infant who generally has received TPN for a period exceeding 2 weeks. The liver biopsy will reveal several histologic features; giant cell transformation, hepatocellular damage, extramedullary hematopoeisis, and portal fibrosis may be seen. Cholestasis associated with TPN has a good prognosis, provided enteral feedings can be rapidly instituted. Fewer than 10% of patients progress to end stage liver disease with cirrhosis. The cause is unknown.[46] The key to reversing the progression of this disease is the institution of enteral feeding. Fat-soluble vitamins and medium-chain triglycerides should be supplemented during severe cholestasis, as fat-soluble vitamins and long-chain triglycerides are usually malabsorbed during the active stage of the disease.[46]

EVALUATION OF INFANTS WITH PRESUMED CHOLESTASIS

Our recommendations for the evaluation for neonatal cholestasis are listed in Table 20–4. The goals of evaluation of the infant with prolonged conjugated hyperbilirubinemia are to rule out specific treatable entities and to identify the infant who may require surgical intervention. The laboratory tests listed in Table 20–4 will yield information as to the treatable causes of diseases such as hypothyroidism, galactosemia and sepsis. The patient who requires surgery can be assessed by ultrasound scanning of the abdomen, liver biopsy, or intraoperative cholangiogram. Hepatobiliary scintigraphy deserves mention: a radionuclide scanner traces technetium-labeled iminodiacetic acid as it is taken

TABLE 20–4.

Evaluation of the Infant Presenting With Protracted Conjugated Hyperbilirubinemia*

Complete blood count, reticulocyte count, platelet
  count
Coagulation profile (before and after parenteral
  vitamin K)
Radiologic studies (skull, long bones, upper
  gastrointestinal series)
Abdominal ultrasound
Cultures (bacterial and viral)
TORCH complex and serology, VDRL, HBsAg
  (infant and maternal)†
Total protein, immunoglobulin levels
Bilirubin (fractionated), SGOT, SGPT‡
Alkaline phosphatase, 5′-nucleotidase
Cholesterol, triglycerides
α-1-Antitrypsin phenotype
Serum bile acids (qualitative and quantitative analysis)
α-Fetoprotein, ferritin
Urinalysis (reducing substances, amino acid screen,
  urobilinogen)
Serum amino acid profile
Stool examination (color, urobilinogen), ? steatorrhea
Sweat electrolytes, T_4, (levothyroxine),
  thyroid-stimulating hormone
Hepatobiliary scintigraphy
Liver biopsy (culture, hemotoxylin-eosin staining,
  electron microscopy)

*From references 12 and 19. Each test or procedure has been used in conjunction with historical data and clinical examination in an attempt to provide discriminatory value in the differential diagnosis of neonatal cholestasis.
†TORCH = toxoplasmosis, other (syphillis, hepatitis, Zoster), rubella, cytomegalovirus, and herpes simplex. VDRL = syphilis test. HBsAg = hepatitis B surface antigen.
‡SGOT = serum glutamic oxaloocetic transaminase. SGPT = serum glutamic pyruvic transaminose.

TABLE 20–5.

Frequency of Clinical Features Associated With Intrahepatic and Extrahepatic Cholestasis*

Feature	Intrahepatic Cholestasis	Extrahepatic Cholestasis
Mean birth weight, g	2,680	3,230
Male gender, %	66	45
Congenital anomalies, %	32	17
Mean age of onset of jaundice, days	23	11
Mean age of onset of acholic stools, days	30	16
Acholic stool > 10 days of admission, %	26	79
Firm or hard liver consistency, %	53	87
Portal fibrosis, %	47	94
Bile duct proliferation, %	30	86
Intraportal bile thrombi, %	1	63

*Modified from Alagille D: Cholestasis in the first three months of life, in Popper H, Schaffner R (eds): *Progress in Liver Disease*, vol 6. New York, Corrine and Sharon, 1979, pp 471–485.

up by the liver and excreted into the biliary tree and out into the intestinal lumen. In biliary atresia, uptake of the agent is nonimpaired, but its excretion into the intestine is absent. In neonatal hepatitis, the uptake of the agent by the liver parenchyma is delayed, but its excretion into the intestine eventually occurs if the degree of cholestasis is not too severe. The oral administration of phenobarbitol, 5 mg/kg/day, for 5 days prior to scintigraphy may enhance biliary excretion of the isotope and therefore increase the discriminatory value.[12, 19, 47]

The most useful procedure in the evaluation of the cholestatic infant is liver biopsy, which can be performed by the Menghini technique with local anesthesia. Liver biopsy interpreted by an experienced pathologist will correctly distinguish biliary atresia from other forms of neonatal cholestasis in 90% to 95% of cases, thus avoiding unnecessary surgery in patients with intrahepatic disease.[12, 18, 47]

Because of the importance of distinguishing between biliary atresia and neonatal hepatitis, many clinicians have attempted to identify clinical and histologic findings that correlate with each condition. Alagille has found that the following features occurred more frequently in infants with neonatal hepatitis than in those with biliary atresia: low birth weight, male gender, the presence of other congenital anomalies, later onset of jaundice, and later onset of acholic stools (Table 20–5).[45] On the other hand, acholic stools within 10 days after admission and hepatic enlargement with a firm or hard consistency are more likely to occur in infants with biliary atresia.[45] Discriminant analysis using the variables shown in Table 20–5 permitted accurate distinction between intrahepatic and extrahepatic cholestasis in 85% of the patients tested.[45]

In those patients thought to have biliary atresia on the basis of clinical, biochemical, and histologic features, exploratory laparotomy and intraoperative cholangiography are indicated to determine the presence and location of the extrahepatic biliary obstruction. If the diagnosis of extrahepatic biliary atresia is confirmed, then surgical treatment can be performed.

GENERAL MEDICAL MANAGEMENT OF NEONATAL CHOLESTASIS

In most cases treatment with a specific modality is not possible; therefore, management usually consists of addressing the sequalae of cholestasis. These patients have steatorrhea secondary to the deficiency of intraluminal bile acids in the small intestine. Therefore, malabsorption of lipids and fat-soluble vitamins occur. Medium-chain triglycerides do not require bile salt solubilization and are absorbed directly into portal blood. Therefore formulas containing medium-chain triglycerides, such as Pregestimil (Mead Johnson Nutritionals), are indicated. The patient should also receive fat-soluble vitamins A, D, K, and E as supplements (see Table 20–1).

Vitamin A can be given in supplemental doses from 10,000 to 25,000 IU/day as a water-miscible vitamin (Aquasol A; Armour, Tarrytown, NY) orally or 100,000 IU of vitamin A (30 mg retinyl palmitate) intramuscularly every 2 months.[12, 13, 19, 47]

Vitamin D supplements in the form of vitamin D_2 (5,000 to 8,000 IU/day or 3 to 5 μg/kg/day of 25-hydroxycholecalciferol) should be given orally. In children with deficient absorption, alternative forms of supplementation such as parental vitamin D should be administered.[12, 13, 19, 47]

Initially vitamin E should be supplemented as oral α-tocopherol at 50 to 400 IU/day. The ratio of serum vitamin E to lipid should be assessed every 2 to 3 months and a neurologic examination conducted. Children may fail to respond to massive doses of oral vitamin E. In this situation, tocopherol polyethylene glycol succinate at 15 to 25 IU/kg/day has been shown to be effective in clinical trials.[13]

Vitamin K therapy is indicated for all patients with significant cholestasis. The infant dose is 2.5 mg orally every other day (qod) or every 3 days (q3d). In cholestatic infants with a prolonged prothrombin time, vitamin K can be given and after 24 hours and follow-up prothrombin time values can be obtained to determine the relative importance of vitamin K deficiency and hepatic synthesis of coagulation factors. If there is good response to intramuscular vitamin K then menadiol, a water-soluble vitamin K derivative, can be given orally in dosages ranging from 2.5 mg to 5.0 mg qod or q3d.[12, 13]

Hypercholesterolemia, xanthomas, and pruritus are also common complications of chronic cholestasis. The treatment for hypercholesterolemia includes increasing catabolism of cholesterol to bile acids with phenobarbitol therapy or removal of feedback inhibition of cholesterol metabolism by removal of the bile acid end products with bile acid binding resins such as cholesytramine and colestipol.[12, 13, 18, 47] Pruritus may be relieved by increasing choleresis with the above agents or by the utilization of antihistamines.[12, 13, 19, 47]

MANAGEMENT OF PROGRESSIVE FIBROSIS AND CIRRHOSIS

The prognosis of any child with chronic liver disease depends not only on the degree of fibrosis and cirrhosis that develops, but also on the nature and refractoriness of the resultant complications. The most difficult complications of cirrhosis to manage are ascites, variceal hemorrhage, and end stage liver disease (decompensation).

Ascites

Impairment in sodium and water excretion results in ascites and edema often with hyponatremia. These complications are progressive in nature and often become refractory to therapy.[48] The development of ascites is a poor prognostic sign in a patient with chronic liver disease. The treatment of ascites does not alter the natural history of the underlying disease process. Therefore, the decision to treat ascites should be dictated by the risk of respiratory compromise, risk of bacterial infection of the ascitic fluid, and the patient's comfort. It is important to avoid rapid correction of the ascites, especially in patients without peripheral edema. Excessive diuresis can result in hypokalemia, alkalosis, hypotension, or hepatic encephalopathy. Dietary sodium should be restricted in patients with ascites to 1 to 2 mEq/kg/day. Fluid intake should be closely monitored as well; if signs of free water retention occur, then fluid intake may need to be restricted to 1,000 mL/m^2/day. Patients who continue to have ascites despite sodium and water restriction may need diuretic therapy. Spironolactone, an aldosterone antagonist, can be given at an initial dose of 3 to 5 mg/kg/day in three or four divided doses and increased at 72-hour intervals up to a maximum dose of 10 to 12 mg/kg/day if no response is noted. Monitoring urinary sodium and potassium excretion may be helpful in assessing the adequacy of diuretic therapy; the urinary sodium concentration should increase and urinary potassium decrease in response to adequate therapy. In addition, serum electrolytes and fluid balance should be serially assessed. Patients whose ascites is unresponsive to spironolactone may require the addition of furosemide, 1 to 2 mg/kg/day. Alternatively, diuresis may be achieved by the intravenous infusion of albumin 1 g/kg/dose, followed by intravenous furosemide. Large-volume paracentesis followed by intravenous albumin infusion has been shown to be a safe and effective method of treatment in adults. Head-out-of-water immersion is a form of therapy that has been used to manage adults with resistant ascites.[12, 47, 48] Water immersion compresses the peripheral vasculature, which produces central volume expansion and a natriuresis and diuresis. There are no data on the efficacy of head-out-of-water immersion in children.

Esophageal Varices

Esophageal varices are present to some degree in virtually all patients with severe portal hypertension. Patients with esophageal varices should be instructed to avoid salicylates, alcohol, and sharp-surfaced foods. Patients who do present with an acute variceal hemorrhage should be aggressively managed; initially venous access should be established and blood volume maintained. Cold saline gastric lavage should be used to control gastrointestinal bleeding. Some patients may require intravenous vasopressin or emergent variceal sclerosis for control of variceal bleeding. Balloon tamponade, which is frequently used in adults, is rarely utilized in children. Endoscopic sclerotherapy may be useful for both the management of acute variceal bleeding and for prophylaxis against recurrent episodes of variceal bleeding.[12, 47]

Hepatic Encephalopathy

Hepatic failure and encephalopathy will eventually develop in patient with end stage liver disease. Children whose liver disease has progressed to this stage should be considered for liver transplantation unless other contraindications exist. Hepatic encephalopathy may be precipitated by gastrointestinal bleeding, sedatives, tranquilizers, hypovolemia, electrolyte abnormalities, or infections. Clinical findings depend on the stage of encephalopathy. In the infant the early stages may develop insidiously. Stage I encephalopathy is characterized by periods of lethargy and hypotonia alternating with periods of normal alertness. Stage II encephalopathy is present when reversal of day-night sleep pattern, disorientation, agitation, and confusion occur. A stage III encephalopathic patient presents with stupor and coma, but maintains his response to pain with decerebrate posturing, spasticity, and hyperreflexia. Stage IV hepatic coma includes those patients who are unresponsive and areflexic. The pathophysiology of hepatic coma is probably multifactorial, and several mechanisms have been implicated. Accumulations of toxins such as ammonia, mercaptans, and short-chain and medium-chain fatty acids may be contributory. In addition, plasma amino acid abnormalities and the synthesis of false neurotransmitters may play a role in the development of encephalopathy. Treatment of hepatic encephalopathy is supportive, and no therapy other than orthotopic liver transplantation has been shown to alter the underlying disease process. Fluid, sodium, and protein restriction should be instituted. The administration of an amino acid preparation high in branched chain amino acids in an attempt to normalize serum amino acid concentrations has not been shown to alter survival. Biochemical abnormalities, especially hypoglycemia and hypophosphatemia, should be monitored for and aggressively corrected. Oral lactulose and neomycin can be helpful in reducing serum ammonia concentrations. Plasmapheresis, exchange transfusions, or charcoal hemoperfusion, have not been proved to improve survival in patients with end stage liver disease and hepatic encephalopathy, but have assumed an important role in the stabilization of the patient in anticipation of liver transplantation.[12, 47]

MONITORING THE PATIENT WITH CHRONIC LIVER DISEASE

The emergence of orthotopic liver transplantation as a viable option for treatment of irreversible liver disease has increased the importance of careful monitoring of the infant or child with liver disease.[12, 47] Prognostic scores have been developed for guidance in choosing a pediatric recipient for orthotopic liver transplantation. These prognostic indicators were assessed in potential liver transplant patients in Pittsburgh, and the risk of mortality was then assessed based on these parameters (Table 20–6).[49] Future investigations may determine if other tests are useful in children with liver disease to help determine the optimum time for liver transplantation and to assess the function of potential donor organs.

TABLE 20–6.

Prognostic Score for Orthotopic Liver Transplantation. Relative Importance of Each Prognostic Variable*

Weighting Factor	Variable
+15	If cholesterol < 100 mg/dL
+15	If positive history of ascites
+13	If bilirubin (indirect) > 6 mg/dL
+11	If bilirubin (indirect) 3 to 6 mg/dL
+10	If partial thromboplastin time is prolonged > 20 sec

Total Score	Patient Group	Risk of Dying Within 6 mo of Evaluation
0–27	Low risk	< 25%
28–39	Moderate risk	25% to 75%
≥ 40	High risk	> 75%

*Modified from Malatack JJ, Schnaid JP, Urbach AH, et al: Choosing a pediatric recipient for orthotopic liver transplantation. *J Pediatr* 1987; 111:479–489.

FUTURE GOALS

It will be necessary to further define the nature of unknown causes of neonatal cholestasis by defining groups of patients with metabolic and enzymatic defects that were previously unknown.[12, 19, 47]

Alpha-1-antitrypsin deficiency was previously classified in the group of idiopathic neonatal hepatitis, but now has been separated as a specific disease. This disease could serve as a prototype for other undefined causes of neonatal cholestasis.

If an inborn error of bile acid metabolism can be identified, it may be possible to supplement with bile acids distal to the metabolic block. In transport protein defects, cloning of the gene and parenteral administration or incorporation of that defective gene into the host genome may be necessary to reverse that form of neonatal cholestasis. Advances in antifibrotic therapy for cirrhosis, such as colchicine therapy,[50] choleretic agents for cholestasis, and supportive care for progressive liver disease may reverse the progressive nature of previously untreatable diseases or prolong the stabilization of a patient who is awaiting liver transplantation.

REFERENCES

1. Phillips JM, Poucell S, Oda M: Biology of disease, mechanisms of cholestasis. *Lab Invest* 1986; 54:593–608.
2. Popper H, Schaffner F: The pathophysiology of cholestasis. *Hum Pathol* 1970; 1:1–24.
3. Hofmann AF, Roda A: Physiocochemical properties of bile acids and their relationship to biological properties: An overview of the problem. *J Lipid Res* 1984; 25:1477–1489.
4. Setchell KDR, Street JM: Inborn errors of bile acid synthesis. *Semin Liver Dis* 1987; 7:85.
5. Balistreri WF, Setchell KDR: Clinical implications of bile acid metabolism, in Silverberg M, Dunn F (eds): *Textbook of Pediatric Gastroenterology,* 2 ed. 1987, pp 72–89.
6. Back P, Walter K: Developmental pattern of bile acid metabolism as revealed by bile acid analysis of meconium. *Gastroenterology* 1970; 78:671–678.
7. Strandvik B, Wikstrom SA: Tetrahydroxylated Bile Acids in Healthy Human Newborns. *Eur J Clin Invest* 1982; 12:301–305.
8. Columbo C, Zulani G, Rochi M, et al: Biliary acid composition of the human fetus in early gestation. *Pediatr Res* 1987; 21:197–200.
9. de Belle RC, Bauphas V, Vitullo BB, et al: Intestinal absorption of bile salts: Immature development in the neonate. *J Pediatr* 1979; 94:472–476.
10. Balistreri WF: The enterohepatic circulation of bile acids in early life, in *Neonatal Cholestasis: Causes, Syndromes, Therapies.* Report of the Eighty-seventh Ross Conference on Pediatric Research. Columbus, Ohio, Ross Laboratories, 1984, pp 38–47.
11. Suchy FJ, Bucuvalas JC, Novak DA: Determinants of bile formation during development: Ontogeny of hepatic bile acid metabolism and transport. *Semin Liver Dis* 1987; 7:77–84.
12. Balistreri WF: Neonatal cholestasis. *J Pediatr* 1985; 106:171–184.
13. Sokol RJ: Medical management of the infant with chronic liver disease. *Semin Liver Dis* 1987; 7:155–167.
14. Weber A, Roy CC: The malabsorption associated with chronic liver disease in children. *Pediatrics* 1982; 50:73–83.
15. Takano K, Hizuka N, Shizume K, et al: Serum somatomedin peptides measured by somatomedin: A radio receptor assay in chronic liver diseases. *J Clin Endocrinol Metab* 1977; 45:828–832.
16. Van Thiel DH, Gavaler JS, Cobb CF, et al: An evaluation of the respective roles of portosystemic shunting and portal hypertension in rats upon the production of gonadal dysfunction in cirrhosis. *Gastroenterology* 1983; 85:154–159.

17. Frisch RE, Revelle R: Height and weight at menarch and a hypothesis of critical body weights and adolescent events. *Science* 1970; 169:397–399.
18. Evans J, Newman S, Sherlock S: Liver copper levels in intrahepatic cholestasis of childhood. *Gastroenterology* 1978; 75:875–878.
19. Balistreri WF: Neonatal cholestasis: Lessons from the past, issues for the future (foreword), in Balistreri WF (ed): *Neonatal Cholestasis.* Seminars in Liver Disease, vol 7. New York, Thieme, 1987.
20. Avery ME, et al: Transient tyrosinemia of the newborn. *Pediatrics* 1967; 39:378–384.
21. Starzl TE, Zitelli BJ, Shaw et al: Changing concepts: Liver replacement for hereditary tyrosinemia and hepatoma. *J Pediatr* 1985; 106:604–606.
22. Patrick AD, Lake BD: Deficiency of an acid lipase in Wolman's disease. *Nature* 1969; 222:1067–1068.
23. Schiff L, et al: Hepatic cholesterol ester storage disease: A familial disorder. I: Clinic aspects. *Am J Med* 1968; 44:538–546.
24. Brady RO, Bavanger JS: Glucosyl ceramide lipidosis (Gaucher's disease), in Stanbury JB, et al (eds): *The Metabolic Basis of Inherited Disease.* New York, McGraw-Hill Book Co, 1983, pp 842.
25. Brady RO, et al: The metabolism of sphingomyelin: Evidence of an enzymatic block in Niemann-Pick disease. *Proc Natl Acad Sci USA* 1966; 55:366–369.
26. Kliegman PM, Sparks: Perinatal galactose metabolism. *J Pediatr* 1985; 107:837–841.
27. Baerlocher K, et al: Hereditary fructose intolerance in early childhood: A major diagnostic challenge. *Helv Pediatr Acta* 1978; 33:465–487.
28. Hug G: Glycogen storage disease, in Kelley UC (ed): *Practice of Pediatrics.* Philadelphia, Harper & Row, 1985.
29. Greene HL, Brown BA, McClenathan, et al: A new variant of type IV glycogenosis: Deficiency of branch enzyme activity without apparent progressive liver disease. *Hepatology* 1988; 8:302–306.
30. Odievre M, et al: Alpha-1-antitrypsin deficiency and liver disease in children: Phenotypes, manifestations and prognosis. *Pediatrics* 1976; 57:226–231.
31. Ghishan FL, Greene HL: Liver disease in children with PIZZ alpha-antitrypsin deficiency. *Hepatology* 1988; 8:307–310.
32. Borowitz SM, Ghishan FK: Advances in cystic fibrosis. *Compr Ther* 1986; 12:20–27.
33. Weldon AP, Danks DM: Congenital hypothyroidism and neonatal jaundice. *Arch Dis Child* 1972; 47:469–471.
34. Kaufman F, Costin G, Thurias D: Neonatal cholestasis and hypopituitarism. *Arch Dis Child* 1984; 59:787–789.
35. Committee on Infectious Diseases: *Report of the Committee on Infectious Disease,* ed 20. Elk Grove Village, Ill, American Academy of Pediatrics, 1986.
36. Balistreri WF: Viral hepatitis. *Pediatr Clin North Am* 1988; 35:637–669.
37. Tong MJ, Thursby M, Rahela J, et al: Studies on the maternal infant transmission of the viruses which cause acute hepatitis. *Gastroenterology* 1981; 80:999–1004.
38. Marks MI, Marks MI (eds): *Pediatric Infectious Disease for the Practitioner.* New York, Springer Verlag, 1985, p 141.
39. Esterly JR, Slusser RJ, Riebner BH: Hepatic lesions in the congenital rubella syndrome. *J Pediatr* 1967; 71:676–685.
40. Stagno S, Whitley RJ: Herpesvirus infections of pregnancy: Part I. Cytomegalovirus and Epstein-Barr virus infections: Part II. Herpes simples virus and Varicella-Zoster virus infections. *N Engl J Med* 1985; 313:1270, 1327.
41. Congenital tuberculosis: Critical reappraisal of clinical findings and diagnostic procedures. *Pediatrics* 1980; 66:980–984.
42. Schweizer P, Muller G (eds): *Gallengangsatresie, Cholestase-Syndrome in Neugeborenen und Sauglingsatter.* Bibliothek fur Kinderchirurgie. Stuggart, Hippokrates, 1984.
43. Ryckman FC, Noseworthy J: Neonatal cholestastic conditions requiring surgical reconstruction. *Semin Liver Dis* 1987; 7:134–154.

44. Alagille D, et al: Syndromic paucity of interlobular bile ducts (Alagille syndrome of arterio-hepatic dysplasia). *J Pediatr* 1987; 10:195–200.

45. Alagille D: Cholestasis in the first three months of life, in Popper H, Schaffner R (eds): *Progress in Liver Disease,* vol 6. New York, Grune & Stratton, 1979, pp 471–485.

46. Balistreri WF, Novak DA, Farrell MK: Bile acid metabolism, total parenteral nutrition and cholestasis, in Lebenthal E (ed): *Total Parenteral Nutrition—Indications, Complications, and Pathophysiological Considerations in Total Parenteral Nutrition and Home Total Parenteral Nutrition.* New York, Raven Press, 1986, pp 319–334.

47. Gremse DA, Balistreri WF: Neonatal cholestasis, in Lebenthal E (ed): *Textbook of Gastroenterology and Nutrition in Early Childhood,* 2 ed. New York, Raven Press.

48. Cosby R, Yec B, Shapiro M, et al: Prognostic factors in cirrhosis. *Kidney Int* 1986; 29:184.

49. Malatack JJ, Schnaid JP, Urbach AH, et al: Choosing a pediatric recipient for orthotopic liver transplantation. *J Pediatr* 1987; 111:479–489.

50. Kershenobich D, et al: Colchicine in the treatment of cirrhosis of the liver. *N Engl J Med* 1988; 318:1709–1713.

Chapter 21

Acute Respiratory Failure and Bronchopulmonary Dysplasia

John E. E. Van Aerde, M.D.

Feeding the critically ill patient with acute or chronic respiratory failure is a challenge for the intensivist. In the adult intensive care unit, the main goal is to maintain an acceptable energy balance without imposing extra metabolic and respiratory stress on the organism. In newborn infants, the caloric cost for growth has to be added to the energy balance; this means that the energy intake has to exceed the infant's maintenance energy requirements to allow growth. It also means that additional respiratory demands will be imposed on the neonate to cover the energy cost for growth: that is, the growth process itself produces carbon dioxide and consumes oxygen. Consequently, feeding a patient with respiratory failure is more complicated in a neonatal than in an adult intensive care setting.

Several recent reviews have focused on interactions between nutrition and different aspects of the respiratory system.[14, 46, 51, 58] Nutritional status affects the respiratory system directly by providing energy for the respiratory muscles and development of lung structure and function; indirectly, the level of energy intake and the dietary macronutrient composition modify the metabolic demands and affect the respiratory system by modifying central ventilatory drive and the respiratory gaseous exchange (Fig 21–1). In this chapter the effect of energy intake and dietary macronutrients on the development and function of the respiratory system in newborns with respiratory problems is emphasized. The effect of micronutrients, minerals, and vitamins is addressed, but is not the primary topic of discussion. The first portion describes the interactions between nutrition and structural, biochemical, and functional changes in the lung of the neonate and the adult. The second part addresses growth and energy efficiency of infants with lung disease in general and chronic lung disease in particular. The third and fourth sections describe the effects of energy intake and/or diet composition on respiratory gas exchange and energy metabolism in the intravenously fed infant with acute respiratory distress and in the orally fed neonate with chronic lung disease respectively. Finally, areas for future research are noted and some suggestions for feeding newborn infants with acute and chronic lung disease are made.

Studies investigating interactions between nutrition and the respiratory system are very limited. Throughout this chapter, many extrapolations from animal studies have been made. Some of the links suggested might not be entirely applicable to the human

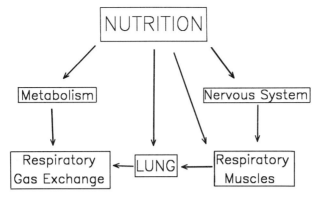

FIG 21–1.
Nutritional interactions with the respiratory system. Dietary composition and energy intake affect ventilation and respiratory gas exchange indirectly by modifying the metabolic demand. The central ventilatory drive, respiratory muscle function, and lung function/structure are directly affected by the nutritional status.

infant; nevertheless, it is reasonable to make these assumptions, first because they might really exist, and second because they will highlight which areas need to be researched.

NUTRITION, METABOLISM, AND THE RESPIRATORY SYSTEM

Lung Development and Morphology

The preterm infant with a birth weight of 1,000 g has an expendable nonprotein energy reserve of less than 200 kcal, with 1% to 2% of the body weight as fat and less than 1% as glycogen. Because accretion of expendable energy stores are late gestational processes, energy depletion in the very low birth weight (VLBW) newborn infant is rapid after short periods of insufficient nutritional intake. This depletion will be accelerated and protein catabolism induced when serious respiratory distress increases the infant's energy demands.

Interference with somatic growth may affect lung structure, as lung size, alveolar number, and alveolar surface area are stature-dependent. In two studies of newborn rats with reduced food intake during the first 21 days of life (i.e., 50% to 65% of the energy rations of control animals), the lung weight was lower than in the control group. There seems to be a permanent reduction in the number of lung cells, as assessed by measuring deoxyribonucleic acid (DNA) in lung during subsequent developmental stages, as well as a permanent reduction in ribonucleic acid.[69, 191] When food restriction of equal duration is imposed later in the course of lung development, there is less of an effect on lung growth. Whereas early malnutrition impedes cell division with no recovery when feeding is reinstituted, malnutrition at a later stage of growth results in a reduction of cell size rather than absolute cell number allowing recovery when refeeding occurs.[191] In adult rats receiving 20% to 33% of the control energy intake for periods of 1 to 6 weeks, the alveolar diameter increases, with a decrease in alveolar surface area and dissolution of connective tissue elements from within alveolar septa,[153, 154] resulting in morphological lung changes similar to those seen in emphysema. The reduced alveolar surface area is further accompanied by reduced in vivo pulmonary diffusing capacity.[85] In the starved human, emphysematous lesions have also been found in all age groups from childhood to senility.[168]

In the newborn guinea pig, a 50% reduction in energy intake in the prenatal and weanling period results in reduced lung tissue volumes, reduced alveolar and capillary surface areas, and diminished pulmonary diffusion capacity. As guinea pigs have more mature lungs than other rodents at birth, the postnatal lung is more resistant to alveolar hypoplasia than the prenatal lung; this is confirmed by complete recovery when the starved weanlings are refed, whereas animals starved prenatally show residual starvation effects as adult animals, demonstrating reduced tissue volumes, reduced alveolar and capillary surface areas, and diminished pulmonary diffusing capacity.[113] The development of lungs of prenatally starved guinea pigs is retarded to the saccular phase. Further, the newborn guinea pig is born with considerable adipose tissue reserves, and pulmonary growth retardation seems minimized during starvation; lung growth might be protected by these energy reserves. In VLBW infants, alveolarization has not developed and energy reserves are minimal; alveolar development might therefore be delayed in preterm infants when fed inappropriately, as suggested by one report of an infant with bronchopulmonary dysplasia.[165]

Even short-term starvation or malnutrition (50% of energy of control group given as glucose for 60 hours) leads to failure of lung growth in terms of weight, protein content, and cell size in 21-day-old rats.[72]

Changes in connective tissue composition of the lung are also known to occur during malnutrition. In adult rats, receiving only one fifth of the energy compared to a controlled group, body and lung weight as well as lung content of crude connective tissue, elastin, hydroxyproline, and protein in the lung drop significantly.[152] After refeeding, elastin and protein content do not return to control values, indicating that the emphysema-like changes in the lungs of malnourished rats are at least partly related to loss of connective tissue elements. The diet-induced loss of elastic recoil forces persists and resembles mechanical and morphological changes of experimental, elastase-induced emphysema.[153, 154] Apart from energy deprivation, protein deficiency also seems to be a major dietary factor contributing to nutrition-induced emphysema in rats.[105, 128]

In summary, apart from gross reduction in the content of various connective tissue components, the major impact of food restriction on the lung during early life is interference with normal lung growth and alveolar development. All data in animal studies support the fact that lung growth is certainly affected by the state of nutrition during the postnatal period. In rats, the severity and reversibility of the changes appear to depend on the stage of the lung growth during which food deprivation occurs. These are interesting findings in view of the fact that undernutrition early on in life has been mentioned to be a major contributing factor in the pathogenesis of bronchopulmonary dysplasia (BPD).[58]

Nutrition and Surfactant Synthesis

Phosphatidylcholine (PC), particularly disaturated phosphatidylcholine (DSPC) and phosphatidylglycerol (PG), are the main phospholipids of lung surfactant.[181] Food deprivation in adult rats for 2 to 3 days results in a decrease of total phospholipids and PC in total lung tissue expressed per DNA content,[50] but the ratio of saturated over unsaturated fatty acids in PC is maintained.[63] There is a reduced rate of phosphate incorporation with slower rate of secretion of phospholipid into the airway lavage material of 48-hour starved vs. fed adult rats, suggesting reduced surfactant synthesis and diminished release into the alveoli as a result of short-term food deprivation.[151] In 21-day-old rats who fasted for 60 hours, phospholipid and PC content of lavage fluid and lung tissue per cell but not per unit cell mass is also reduced.[72] Brown et al. confirmed that fasting or calorie deprivation for 24-72 hours in adult rats results in diminished pools of total phospholipids, PC, DSPC, and PG in the intracellular fractions of the lung when expressed on a DNA basis; nevertheless, after 96 hours of complete fasting or 192 hours of calorie deprivation, the pool sizes return to control levels.[27] The percentage of total phospholipids found as phosphatidylcholine is decreased in the intracellular as well as in the extracellular surfactant fraction, but the ratio of saturated to unsaturated phosphatidylcholine only changes in the intracellular and not in the extracellular fraction.[27] After 96 hours, compensation for the absolute reduced quantity of DSPC appears to take place as a greater percentage of PC is made available as the disaturated species in the extracellular surfactant fraction. The activity of the enzyme choline-phosphate cytidylyl transferase, which is considered to be the main regulatory enzyme in the synthesis of PC, increases markedly with the duration of fasting with maximum activity after 72 hours.[27, 28] Sahebjami and Macgee[152] studied effects of more prolonged partial food deprivation on lung surfactant. Adult rats receiving one fifth of their normal, measured daily food consumption for 3 weeks show a significant reduction in DSPC content both in lung tissue and lavage fluid compared with the age-matched control-fed group. The content of DSPC per total lung DNA is also significantly lower in starved than in the control-fed group. After a period of refeeding for 7 to 10 days, the DSPC content of both tissue and lavage fluid returns to normal.[152]

Gail et al. have shown that alveolar stability is maintained despite decreased surfactant phospholipids, probably by maintaining the ratio of saturated to unsaturated phosphatidylcholine in the extracellular surfactant fraction.[63] Whereas the reserve of pulmonary surfactant appears to be sufficient in the energy-deprived animal, it remains speculative whether the same is true for the infant with respiratory distress syndrome, particularly because the preterm infant starts off with a biochemically deficient lung.

It is interesting to speculate whether diet composition, without energy deprivation, can also alter the quality of surfactant. Feeding a diet deficient in essential fatty acids to weanling rats for 12 to 14 weeks does not change the content of total PC in lung tissue and lavage material, but the content of DSPC is reduced significantly.[111] Within 24 hours of refeeding with essential fatty acids, the return towards control fatty acid composition is evident and gradually completed in 7 to 14 days. As in energy deprivation, the relationship between surfactant phospholipids is maintained in the extracellular but not in the intracellular surfactant fraction.[51] As in animals,[111] alteration in the fatty acid composition of lung PC might also occur in infants with essential fatty acid deficiency.[61] There is preliminary evidence that dietary fatty acid composition with normal provision of energy and without essential fatty acid deficiency can affect fatty acid composition of lung surfactant phospholipids[166] and the resistance against oxygen toxicity. In the next section we discuss the effect of dietary fatty acids as defense mechanism against oxygen toxicity.

Finally, two substrates that have been considered to have potential nutritional value for surfactant synthesis are choline and inositol. After birth, neither glycogen nor exogenous choline seems to have a regulatory influence on lung lipid synthesis, but glucose continues to be an important precursor. As in energy deprivation, the surfactant PC poolsize in lungs shows very little change with established choline deficiency, and the maximal choline incorporation into PC is unchanged by dietary choline deficiency.[51] Whereas there doesn't seem to be a need for feeding choline, there might be a place for inositol. Inositol administered by the intragastric or intravenous route tends to decrease the severity of respiratory distress syndrome (RDS),[81] probably secondary to an increased ratio of saturated phosphatidylcholine to sphingomyelin.[80]

In summary, even for short periods, food and calorie deprivation alters surfactant metabolism, leading to inadequate tissue stores and intra-alveolar levels; the quality of the surfactant on the alveolar surface is not altered considerably. It appears that the lung is capable of shifting its metabolic activity during short-term food deprivation toward maintaining essential lipid components in order to preserve the stability of lung mechanics.[145] Although the surfactant phosphoplipid production by the type II cells of the lungs eventually returns to normal, the initial marked reduction in surfactant production during experimental malnutrition might be important during the first few days of life in the VLBW infant who is in a catabolic state. There is no knowledge on the relative contribution of exogenous and endogenous fatty acids to the formation of surfactant lipids in humans. It is also unknown whether specific dietary substrates can promote reduced surfactant production.

Lung Defense Mechanisms

Nutritional interventions affect lung defense mechanisms and hence possibly prevent oxygen toxicity, barotrauma, and lung infection. Because of the limited energy stores of the VLBW infant, the lung structure and biochemistry, its repair capability, adaptive capacity, and defense mechanisms might be compromised unless early nutritional support is instituted. The degree of damage depends on the magnitude of the imbalance between lung injury and repair capabilities.

Oxygen

The molecular mechanism of lung injury in oxygen toxicity is still not understood, although much of the recent literature supports the oxygen free radical theory. Highly reactive oxygen products are generated which cause peroxidation of unsaturated membrane lipids, alteration of DNA, and depolymerization of cellular polysaccharides. There are several defense mechanisms against oxygen-free radicals (Table 21–1). These

TABLE 21–1.

Antioxidant Protective Systems in the Developing Lung

Enzymatic
  Glutathione peroxidase* (selenium, cysteine, methionine)
  Superoxide dismutase* (copper, zinc, manganese)
  Catalase
  Indoleamine 2, 3-dioxygenase
  Glutathione S-transferases
  Ferroxidases(*) (transferrin, ceruloplasmin)
Nonenzymatic
  Vitamin E*
  Vitamin C*
  Vitamin A*
  Glutathione* (sulphur-containing amino acids)
  Uric acid
  Polyunsaturated fatty acids*

*Indicates factor that can be nutritionally affected.

are divided into two large categories: (1) enzymatic and (2) nonenzymatic protective systems.[146] Only those defense mechanisms that can be affected nutritionally are discussed here.

Exposure to high levels of oxygen is poorly tolerated in undernourished newborn rats.[54] The inhibitory effects of oxygen and undernutrition on body growth, lung growth, and lung DNA are additive with an especially marked depression of lung DNA content. The survival rate of undernourished rats in a high oxygen environment is only half that of well-nourished pups despite the presence of comparable levels of antioxidant enzymes. The normal repair function of the lung in the undernourished organism is also compromised.[76]

The normal rise in lung antioxidant enzyme activities in late gestation is absent or delayed in prematurely born animals of several species.[56, 57] Intrauterine nutritional deprivation can exert a detrimental effect on the oxygen tolerance of the newborn. Rat pups born at 75% normal birth weight show accelerated oxygen-induced lung lesions.[55] In contrast, newborn lambs fed a high-calorie formula survive high oxygen exposure twice as long as lambs fed a normocaloric diet.[123] Similarly, VLBW infants might have an increased susceptibility to oxygen-induced lung damage if the catabolic state is not prevented or reversed in the acute stage of the illness during the first days of life.

Not only total energy supply, but also provision of an adequate amount of specific nutrients, may be important to improve the protective antioxygen defense mechanisms of the lung.

Glutathione peroxidase is a selenoprotein, and selenium-deficient rats have decreased enzyme activity in the lungs.[40] The effects of sulphur-containing amino acids and selenium have been tested on the survival rate of young rats in a high-oxygen environment.[53] Whereas the mortality is 35% to 40% for both the selenium-deficient and cysteine/methionine-deficient groups, all rats fed a diet containing selenium, cysteine, and methionine survive. The potentiation of oxygen toxicity in rats with protein deficiency can be reversed only by administering sulphur-containing feeds and not by feeding any other amino acids.[41]

Superoxide dismutase exists in two forms: one is a copper- and zinc-containing cytosolic enzyme, the other is a manganese-containing mitochrondrial enzyme. Copper deficiency in the rat decreases lung activity of the copper/zinc dependent superoxide dismutase, whereas glutathione peroxidase and catalase activities do not change.[97, 140] The copper-deficient rats exhibit increased mortality and enhanced pulmonary oxygen toxicity during exposure to 85% oxygen.

Sulphur-containing amino acids and trace elements might be of particular importance for infants on total parenteral nutrition. On the other hand, there is no evidence that administration of pharmacologic amounts to nondeficient organisms will provide more efficient protective systems.

Iron is thought to facilitate formation of highly reactive hydroxyl radicals, whereas nutritional iron deficiency is protective in oxygen radical–mediated injury.[171] Early supplements of iron are therefore not advisable, particularly in view of the developmentally low levels of ceruloplasmin and transferrin in preterm infants. Plasma transfusions early in life might increase the levels of those ferroxidases.[171]

Nonenzymatic systems against oxygen toxicity that can be manipulated nutritionally are vitamins E and C as well as dietary fatty acids; vitamin A is discussed later in the section on barotrauma.

Vitamin E is the major natural antioxidant in the body. It protects cell membranes against oxidative injury and is thought to play a role in preventing neonatal oxygen toxicity.[18] However, the early reported success in reducing the incidence and severity of BPD in premature infants requiring oxygen[47] has not been substantiated by more extensive randomized double-blind controlled clinical trials.[48, 155] Neonatal animals are born with low levels of vitamin E and depend on their mother's milk to raise tissue levels to adult norms; premature infants with pulmonary disease are generally denied oral intake for some time. Vitamin E deficiency enhances susceptibility to oxygen-induced injury,[183, 187] while supplementation restores these defences. Supplementing animals that have adequate stores of vitamin E does not offer enhanced protection beyond the normal state.[30, 84] Similar results have been replicated in human newborns who are fed human milk or one of today's commercial formulas for preterm infants: supplementation offered no protection against the development of BPD compared to control infants with adequate vitamin E stores.[48, 155, 142] This seems logical, as the amount of vitamin E that can enter cellular lipid membranes is limited by biophysical considerations and cannot be increased by supplementation over and above amounts dictated by the composition of the membrane lipids.[124, 194] Infants who cannot be fed and who will not receive oral feedings within the first days of life should probably receive some form of tocopherol supplement.[141] The limited vitamin E stores in VLBW infants and the high ratio of polyunsaturated fatty acids to vitamin E in intravenous lipid emulsions indicates that there is a potential risk for developing real or functional vitamin E deficiency during the acute stage of the respiratory disease.

Vitamin C may be synergistic with vitamin E through its ability to support the reductive regeneration of oxidized vitamin E.[131] Tissue ascorbic acid content in humans depends on nutritional intake. Ascorbic acid levels during fetal rat development are largely unchanged during the late stages of gestation.[107] Exposure of adult animals to elevated oxygen concentrations causes a decrease in the ascorbic acid content of the lungs.[193] There is no information available on the influence of oxygen exposure on newborn lung ascorbic acid levels.

Beta-carotene is an efficient quencher of singlet oxygen and oxygen-centered radicals.[108] Apart from being a possible protective agent against processes that can lead to cellular damage by oxygen free radical mechanisms, it is also involved in repair mechanisms. (See the following section.)

There is evidence that dietary fatty acid composition can affect the phospholipid composition of surfactant in rats. Greater saturation of lung fatty acids leads to 100% mortality after 3 days in oxygen-exposed rats on a coconut oil diet. Only half of the rats die after 4 days when being fed either a standard rat diet or a cod liver oil-enriched diet for 33 days prior to entering the experiment.[102] Developmental changes in surfactant-associated lung lipid can be induced in rat pups of dams fed diets of differing fat composition for at least 3 weeks before and during pregnancy.[129] Although transplacental accretion of fatty acid is more extensive in rats than in humans, maternal nutrition might play a role in the lung lipid fatty acid accretion of the developing fetus. More recently it has been reported that postnatal dietary manipulation over the first 7 days of life induces fatty acid changes in the lung triglycerides and phospholipids.[2, 166] There is no difference in antioxidant enzyme levels between rat pups receiving a diet high in polyunsaturated fatty acid (PUFA) vs. a low-PUFA-level diet,[166] but with the changes in fatty acid composition of the lung lipids, a significantly superior hyperoxic survival is noted in the group receiving the high-PUFA diet.

Barotrauma

General underfeeding or malnutrition will impair the repair capabilities of airway epithelial cell damage secondary to pressure during artificial ventilation. Recently, emphasis has been focused on the importance of vitamin A in restorative processes. Retinol is essential for maintenance of epithelial cell integrity and differentiation[5]; its deficiency in animals and humans is associated with altered cell type and composition in the tracheobronchial tree with loss of cilia and squamous metaplasia[5, 19] (i.e., the histology is similar to that found in patients with bronchopulmonary dysplasia).[135] Glutathione content and glutathione-S-transferase activity in lungs of rats exposed to oxygen are reduced in vitamin A deficiency[43]; recent animal[167] and early human studies[163] suggest there is a role for vitamin A supplementation in premature infants. Cord blood retinol-binding protein is decreased in patients with RDS compared with its levels in premature infants without RDS; infants who develop BPD have lower cord and day 21 plasma retinol levels than those without BPD.[95] Plasma retinol in infants with BPD is lower than in infants without BPD at days 4, 14, 21, and 28.[162] Vitamin A administration results in significantly higher mean plasma concentrations of vitamin A and retinol-binding protein. Early achievement and maintenance of normal vitamin A concentration is associated with decreased morbidity related to BPD in susceptible VLBW infants who require supplemental oxygen and mechanical ventilation. In infants given vitamin A supplements, the overall incidence of BPD is reduced by almost 50% and there is a progressive decrease of ventilatory requirements during the 1st month of postnatal life.[163] Before an increase in the current recommendations of vitamin A requirements can be justified, more clinical investigations have to confirm the findings of this one report.

It has been suggested that high fluid intake, pulmonary edema, and development of BPD are interrelated.[26] Infants with pulmonary overperfusion and interstitial pulmonary edema secondary to a large ventricular septal defect have increased peripheral airway resistance and impaired gas exchange, necessitating higher ventilatory settings.[91] Hypocaloric dextrose infusion during short-term mechanical ventilation after oleic acid–induced lung injury decreases serum albumin and protein in previously healthy baboons; this is probably the result of capillary protein leak and albumin pooling in the lung.[144]

Excessive fluid intake,[22] surfactant deficiency/dysfunction,[137] and low colloid osmotic pressure in plasma as a result of low protein concentration[22, 138] are factors involved in development of pulmonary edema and can all be affected by the nutritional status of the neonate. It can be speculated that by manipulating the diet accordingly, pulmonary interstitial edema could be kept to a minimum, reducing the ventilatory requirements and thus limiting barotrauma.

Infection

Pulmonary defense mechanisms against infection depend on the integrity of the respiratory epithelium and the immune system, as described in several review papers.[33, 118, 147] In all species studied, including humans, the main aspects of immunity that are affected in protein-calorie malnutrition include impaired macrophage and lymphocyte functions, circulatory IgA antibody response, the complement system, and bactericidal capacity of neutrophils.[33, 46] In the premature newborn infant with marginal nutritional status, depressed defenses against infectious complications will be additional to the suppressive actions of hyperoxia on the lung's antibacterial defense mechanisms.[92] Pulmonary clearance mechanisms are altered by prolonged oxygen exposure and barotrauma; there is toxic loss of ciliated airway cells and ciliary action, injury to alveolar macrophages, and depletion of anti-proteolytic/anti-elastase protection.[92, 126] Some patients with nutritional impairment have more tracheal bacterial adherence and are more frequently colonized by *Pseudomonas* species.[130] In malnourished rat pups, pulmonary clearance of *Listeria monocytogenes* is markedly impaired because the T lymphocytes in the lung fail to activate alveolar macrophages[117] and the death rate is higher than in well-nourished rats. Malnourished children have marked reductions of secretory IgA in respiratory fluids.[169] The inhibition of normal defenses against infection by a combination of nutritional, hyperoxic, and mechanical insults explains at least part of the high incidence of infectious lung complications in the VLBW infant. Adequate nutritional support very early on could prevent some of these infectious complications.

Nutrition and Respiratory Muscles

Nutritional studies in animals and adult humans suggest that energy utilization and protein synthesis in viscera during undernutrition are maintained by degradation of skeletal muscle protein.[66] Despite their continuous use, the respiratory muscles are not spared from atrophy during nutritional deprivation. Two to 3 days of starvation cause the rate of protein synthesis in isolated rat diaphragm strips to fall by half and to more than double the rate of protein degradation.[62, 67] In adults, undernutrition is associated with diaphragmatic muscle atrophy and a decrease in muscle force output.[6, 7, 103] The minority of the preterm diaphragmatic muscle fibers are of the fast-oxidative fatigue-resistant type,[101] indicating that the ventilatory muscles of the newborn infant are very susceptible to fatigue, particularly if there is superimposed lung disease.[127] And yet, in food-restricted hamsters, there is a greater reduction in those fast-glycolytic and fast-oxidative fibers than in slow oxidative fatigue-sensitive fibers.[104] There is controversy in this area, particularly as other investigators have found a high oxidative capacity and, in contrast to the findings of Keens et al.,[101] they found fatigue resistance in neonates[119, 120] and piglets.[121] Because of the highly compliant rib cage, a substantial fraction of the force of the diaphragm is dissipated in distorting the rib cage rather than affecting gas volume exchange. Tachypnea is characteristic of lung disease in infancy, and the faster the repetition rate of muscle contraction, the shorter the time of its endurance. As in other skeletal muscles,[59] when the available chemical energy becomes limited, force generation will fail. The ability to sustain contractions has been found to depend on intramuscular glycogen stores.[38, 68] Diaphragmatic glycogen depletion resulting in loss of force has been demonstrated.[15] It is interesting to note that the diaphragm at birth is rich in glycogen,[77] but it is unknown for how long these reserves are sufficient to cover the respiratory needs of the newborn infant. Apnea of prematurity has at least in part been attributed to respiratory muscle fatigue. Apart from the increased work of breathing due to the high chest wall compliance and paucity of high oxidative type fibers in the diaphragm of the preterm infant,[127] relative substrate deficiency has also been hypothesized to play a role.[172, 173] Budin, the grandfather of today's neonatology, already recognized that apnea was more common in underfed infants.[31] More recently a reduction in frequency of apneas was observed in a group of preterm infants receiving amino acids and glucose intravenously compared with a group receiving only glucose.[29] This might have resulted from either the higher energy intake or an increase in ventilatory drive caused by amino acids, as is discussed in the next section.

Muscle fatigue can be hastened by insufficient energy supply/stores and/or elevated energy demands. Energy availability is a problem not only for the acutely ill infant with limited energy reserves but also for the infant with chronic lung disease who fails to grow. In the BPD patient, energy demands are increased because of higher energy expenditure from increased work of breathing, which in turn is secondary to increased resistive load, reduced respiratory muscle efficiency, and flattened diaphragm due to hyperinflation (see the following section). In the ventilated infant, energy demands may be increased after removal of mechanical ventilation, and if a particular infant is in a precarious nutritional state, the question arises as to whether maintenance of mechanical ventilation should be used to allow return to a state of higher energy reserve; malnourished adults, for example, have a higher need for mechanical ventilatory support.[17, 44]

Nutrition, Metabolism, and Ventilatory Drive

Apart from the nutritional interactions with the respiratory system already discussed, there are two more ways in which nutrition can affect the respiratory system: (1) directly by stimulating the central nervous ventilatory drive, and (2) indirectly by modifying metabolism, and consequently the metabolic rate and respiratory gaseous exchange. In adults and infants, cardiac output and heart rate closely parallel changes in oxygen consumption,[35, 89] whereas carbon dioxide production affects minute ventilation.[89] When adults are weaning from mandatory ventilation, the ability to breathe spontaneously is dependent on an appropriate level of energy intake[112]; in contrast, overfeeding might result in hypercapnea in the patient with borderline lung function.[89] In the latter situation, the ventilatory response to carbon dioxide may be diminished, either secondary to decreased chemosensitivity or because changes in ventilatory mechanics limit the response.[89] It can be speculated that the same rules apply to the preterm infant. On the one hand, the intensivist has the difficult task of minimizing oxygen demands and carbon dioxide burden in patients with borderline lung function; on the other hand, enough energy has to be provided to allow weaning from the ventilator. In newborn infants, there is the additional necessity of giving sufficient energy to allow structural lung maturation and growth of the body. This brittle balance might be particularly difficult to achieve in the very small premature infant and, as Frank and Sosenko indicate[58]: "This may help to explain why weaning the VLBW infant to room air often is fraught with difficulty."

Doekel et al.[42] have demonstrated in adults that one interaction between nutrition and ventilation is a marked depression of hypoxic ventilatory drive during semistarvation. The ventilatory responses to hypoxia and hypercapnea decrease in parallel with the fall in metabolic rate, which occurs during a 10-day period of semistarvation in the healthy human, and they return to normal after refeeding.[42] It is not known whether similar mechanisms exist in the critically ill infant who is not nourished appropriately during the first days of life. Zwillich et al. have suggested that the interaction between nutrition and ventilation is a direct effect of nutritional intake on metabolic rate.[199] Studies in healthy subjects receiving 5% dextrose for a 7-day period reveal a diminished respiratory response to carbon dioxide which returns to normal with an infusion of isotonic amino acids for a 4-hour period.[186] High levels of protein intake lead to pronounced increases in the ventilatory response to carbon dioxide.[13] These effects may be due to the increased metabolic rate and oxygen consumption that follow protein feeding or might result from changes in the plasma amino acid profile. Some studies indicate that the augmented respiratory effects are due to the branched chain amino acids.[175] The sympathetic nervous system is probably also involved, as indicated by elevated levels of circulating catecholamines.[175] In contrast, L-tryptophan decreases the chemosensitivity to carbon dioxide and acts as a respiratory depressant.[12]

Whereas increasing the amino acid content of total parenteral nutrition increases the ventilatory demand by increasing both oxygen consumption and ventilatory drive, the high carbohydrate component seems to increase minute ventilation by way of an increased carbon dioxide production in adults.[9, 39, 199] A similar correlation between glucose intake and carbon dioxide production has been reported in newborn infants receiving fat-free intravenous nutrition.[34, 177, 179] It remains to be proved whether minute ventilation increases as well.

The rise in carbon dioxide production can cause an increase in the level of ventilation required. Without the ability of the chest wall and lung system to adequately respond, increasing the ventilatory drive in infants with limited lung function might cause problems. In those infants who cannot respond adequately, this may precipitate respiratory failure; in the infants that do respond, the increase in workload may lead to an excessively high level of work of breathing and induce respiratory muscle fatigue. Clearly, one is dealing with a difficult dilemma: on one hand energy intake has to be sufficient to maintain bodily functions and support adequate growth; on the other hand, too much energy intake and unbalanced dietary composition might induce or accelerate respiratory failure in the infant with borderline lung function.

GROWTH, ENERGY BALANCE, AND CHRONIC LUNG DISEASE

Growth and Bronchopulmonary Dysplasia

The degree of growth delay in infants who have BPD is directly related to the severity and duration of the disease. Acceleration of growth in length, accompanied by a small increase in rate of weight gain, is usually seen within a few months of improvement in lung function.[115] Adequate oxygenation, decreased work of breathing, and/or reduction in oxygen consumption have been postulated as mechanisms for the improvement in growth.[106, 115] Although growth rates increase with age, infants with BPD remain relatively small, such that by 2 years of corrected age, weight is between the 3d and the 10th percentile, length between the 10th and the 25th, and head circumference on the 50th percentile.[115, 196] Head growth is least affected, but 2 out of 3 infants are under the 10th percentile for weight, and 1 out of 4 is below the 3d percentile for length and weight.[115, 196] By 3 years of age, 1 out of 3 BPD survivors have length and/or weight below the 3d percentile.[134]

Although some studies did not find a difference in growth between infants suffering from BPD vs. matched controls,[182] most studies find a persistent delay in growth in BPD infants with weight, length, head circumference, and arm muscle mass frequently below the 10th percentile.[125, 160] More recently, Sell and Vaucher[161] also demonstrated persistent growth delay throughout early childhood. It takes 4 to 5 years before the BPD patients have caught up with the control group in length, weight, and head circumference. Variables most predictive of growth are early growth parameters; the data of Sell and Vaucher indicate that even infants with less severe BPD remain significantly smaller on a long-term basis primarily because of their size at birth.[161] Differences in growth outcome may at least in part relate to the severity and chronicity of BPD in the different studies.[109, 110] Further growth in BPD patients is possible only when oxygen saturation is kept at 90% to 95% or arterial oxygen pressure (tension) (Pa_{O_2}) above 60 torr.[138]

Besides delay in total body growth and lung development, it should be mentioned that there is a major nutritional impact on developmental outcome by modifying brain growth. Indeed, although the head circumference is least affected, many studies report the head growth to be below normal when compared with that of control infants. Differences in energy intake and severity of the disease are probably the major reasons why head growth is less preserved in some studies than in others. This might be the most significant aspect of growth retardation, as head circumference directly reflects brain mass.[191, 192] Interference with brain growth during the critical period of dendritic multiplication may significantly influence long-term brain function.[75] Indeed chronic, severe malnutrition during infancy can restrict brain growth and is associated with developmental delay even after reinstitution of adequate nutrition.[149] Retarded head growth has been reported in VLBW infants with energy intakes of less than 85 kcal/kg/day for 4 weeks,[64] resulting in adverse effects on long-term neurodevelopmental outcome at 2 years of age.[73] This situation often exists in BPD patients with a limited energy intake due to fluid restriction and with low energy storage due to high energy expenditure.

Bronchopulmonary Dysplasia and Energy Balance

Several explanations have been offered to understand growth failure in infants with BPD: restricted fluid intake and reduced energy supply, poor gastrointestinal absorption, increased energy expenditure related to higher mechanical work of breathing, and/or other mechanisms possibly related to chronic hypoxia.

Fluid restriction with caloric deprivation is often a major factor in growth delay.[184, 195] Nevertheless, most infants receiving an appropriate amount of energy also demonstrate growth retardation.[100, 109] Previously it has been suggested that higher energy losses in the stool contribute to poor weight gain,[82] but this has clearly been dis-

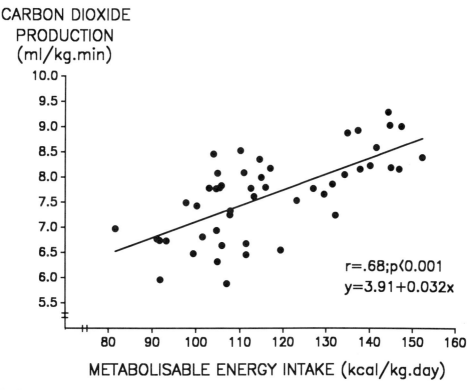

FIG 21–2.
Effect of increasing metabolizable energy intake on carbon dioxide production in orally fed, growing, preterm infants. In a group of 49 orally fed, growing, preterm infants receiving a milk formula with 12% of the energy as protein, 40% as carbohydrate, and 48% as lipid, the carbon dioxide production rises 0.032 mL/kg/min for each additional kilocalorie of energy absorbed. (See also Figs 21–6 and 21–7.)

proved recently.[109, 195] There are at least three contributing factors as to why energy expenditure is elevated. First, in infants receiving calorie-dense formula, the higher energy intake will induce a rise in energy expenditure and carbon dioxide production.[178] For every 10 additional kilocalories administered, 460 mL/kg/day of extra carbon dioxide is produced (Fig 21–2; see also section on BPD and enteral feedings), which can induce either an increase in minute ventilation or respiratory acidosis.

Second, increased work of breathing is another factor contributing to the elevated energy expenditure.[184] Interestingly, treatment of BPD patients with theophylline and furosemide improves pulmonary mechanics and mechanical work of breathing, but does not decrease oxygen consumption[100]; this suggests that the elevated metabolic rate and oxygen consumption in infants with BPD is not primarily, or not exclusively, induced by increased work of breathing and that a third, unknown factor contributes to the elevated energy expenditure. Similarly, Kurzner et al.[110] could only partially account for the elevated oxygen consumption by abnormalities of pulmonary mechanics. Although they speculate that compromised systemic oxygen transport and impaired intermediary metabolism are contributing causes to the growth failure, this is unlikely as the energy efficiency (energy storage divided by intake) is similar in BPD patients either with or without growth failure. Third, for those studies that compare infants in a high oxygen environment to infants studied in room air, part of the elevated oxygen consumption could be attributed to an error in measurement of oxygen consumption which increases with rising forced inspiratory oxygen (F_{IO_2}).[45]

Not only is weight gain lower, but the energy content per gram of weight gain is also less in BPD patients, indicating low fat deposition with high fluid content.[195] This leaves the BPD patient with low energy reserves.

It is difficult to identify all factors that may contribute to poor growth because the BPD population is very heterogenous. Summarizing the few studies on energy balance in infants with BPD, we can conclude as follows:

1. The energy intake is often low because of fluid restriction.
2. Energy losses in stool are not higher than in neonatal control infants.
3. Energy expenditure and oxygen consumption are elevated compared with controls. Only part of the increase can be explained by increased work of breathing.
4. The composition of tissue gain might have a higher water content than that of healthy infants.

ACUTE RESPIRATORY DISTRESS AND TOTAL PARENTERAL NUTRITION

Undernutrition has been suggested to be a contributing factor in the pathogenesis of BPD.[58] Many VLBW infants whose birth weight is under 1,000 g are in a catabolic state during the most acute phase of their respiratory illness.[58, 64] Although their energy stores are limited, providing too much energy might overload the already compromised lung function.

It has been reported that total parenteral nutrition is the only source of nutrition during the 1st week of life in 80% of the infants weighing less than 1,000 g. The other 20% receive combined parenteral and enteral feedings.[36] In infants with a birth weight under 1,250 g, appropriate nutrition should be introduced after 36 to 48 hours.[173] The initial goal is not to attain weight gain but to provide adequate calories and nitrogen to prevent catabolism and promote positive nitrogen balance. The provision of 60 kcal/kg/day and 2 to 2.5 g/kg/day of amino acids results in a positive nitrogen balance.[4] Whether that amount of energy is given as glucose or as lipid does not make a difference in nitrogen retention, emphasizing the importance of energy provision per se for achieving nitrogen retention.[150] When 50 kcal/kg/day are given as glucose only, without amino acids, infants excrete nitrogen at a rate of approximately 130 mg/kg/day.[4]

For those infants requiring parenteral nutrition for longer periods of time, the second goal, weight gain, must be achieved. Energy intakes above 70 kcal/kg/day (including 2.7 to 3.5 g of protein per kilogram per day) result in nitrogen accretion rates similar to in utero values,[197] indicating that basal and muscular activity caloric needs have been met. The combined effect of energy and nitrogen intake seems to be such that, at any level of energy intake, increasing nitrogen intake increases nitrogen retention; similarly, at any level of nitrogen intake, increasing energy intake up to 120 kcal/kg/day increases nitrogen retention.[198] Unfortunately, in infants with birth weights less than 1,000 g, metabolic acidosis can develop even with low intake of protein (1 to 1.5 g/kg/day).[1] Whereas reasonable estimations of nitrogen requirements are available for preterm infants, the ideal amino acid composition of the intravenous solutions is still being investigated.[1]

Improving Energy Intake by Increasing Glucose Supply

Glucose is the main energy source of total parenteral nutrition. When feeding human milk, the glucose intake of the newborn infant is around 1.75 g/kg/day during the first 2 days, increasing to 2.75 g/kg/day on days 3 and 4, and to 6.3 g/kg/day 1 week after birth.[16] It has been demonstrated that low energy intake provided by glucose (38 kcal/kg/day) results in diminished activity of the sympathetic nervous system.[185] Increasing glucose intake from 38 to 64 kcal/kg/day induces a rise in energy expenditure, which is related to a surge in catecholamines; this indicates that the sympathetic nervous system in the preterm infant responds to varying levels of energy intake in a manner similar to that in the human adult. We have investigated energy metabolism and respiratory gaseous exchange in full-term infants receiving fat-free intravenous nutrition.[177] Twelve infants (group 1) received glucose between 3.5 and 10 g/kg/day (2.4 to 7.0 mg/kg/min), equivalent to an energy intake ranging from 13.1 to 37.5 kcal/kg/day. Twenty-six infants (group 2) received increasing amounts of a glucose/amino acid solution totaling between 10.9 and 24.1 g/kg/day for glucose, 2.06 to 3.90 g/kg/day for amino acids, and 51 to 105 kcal/kg/day for energy intake. There was no increase in energy expenditure with increasing glucose intake in group 1. For group 2, diet-induced-thermogenesis caused by the glucose-amino acid infusion resulted in an increment in resting energy expenditure of 0.31 kcal per extra kilocalorie supplied (Fig 21–3). The major portion of this rise is due to increasing lipogenesis from glucose with increasing glucose intake[159] (Fig 21–4). There is some controversy to what extent the increasing amount of amino acids intake contributes to the rise in energy expenditure. In the preterm neonate, Weinstein et al.[185] have demonstrated that a moderate amount of intravenous amino acids (2 g/kg/day) does not affect energy expenditure compared to when glucose is given alone. In contrast, in adults, intravenous amino acids cause a rise in oxygen consumption and in energy expenditure, which is related to an increase in respiratory drive and circulating norepinephrine.[175] In preterm infants, there is also evidence of increasing energy expenditure with rising protein gain.[32, 157]

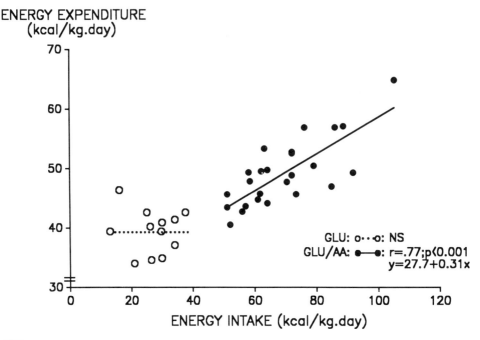

ENERGY EXPENDITURE (kcal/kg.day)

ENERGY INTAKE (kcal/kg.day)

GLU: o··o: NS
GLU/AA: ●—●: r=.77;p<0.001
y=27.7+0.31x

FIG 21–3.
Effect of energy intake on energy expenditure in full-term infants receiving fat-free intravenous nutrition. Energy expenditure increases with increasing energy intake for the glucose/amino acid group; the diet-induced thermogenesis costs 0.31 kcal per kilocalorie administered. Diet-induced thermogenesis can not be demonstrated in the glucose group with energy intakes below maintenance energy requirements.

In adults, high glucose loads increase resting energy expenditure[9, 11, 133] and can induce temperature instability.[10] High glucose loads have also been demonstrated to increase carbon dioxide production,[8, 9, 49, 93, 148] resulting in a higher minute ventilation.[9, 10, 65, 148, 156] This can exacerbate respiratory failure in the patient on ventilatory support and with borderline lung function.[9, 39, 88]

We did not demonstrate a rise in carbon dioxide production or oxygen consumption below glucose intakes equivalent to 40 kcal/kg/day in full-term infants on fat-free parenteral nutrition. Nonprotein carbon dioxide production almost doubles from 4.7 to 7.9 mL/kg/min when the glucose intake increases from 10 to 24 g/kg/day (Fig 21–5). Nonprotein oxygen consumption rises slower and equals non-protein carbon dioxide production at a glucose intake of approximately 18 g/kg/day.[177] This is similar to findings in preterm infants on fat-free parenteral nutrition.[34]

The difference between the slopes of nonprotein carbon dioxide production and nonprotein oxygen consumption in Figure 21–5 is the result of increasing lipogenesis with increasing glucose intake, as confirmed by Sauer et al.[159] Lipogenesis from glucose produces more carbon dioxide than it consumes oxygen[60] and will cause an increase in energy expenditure, because up to 24% of the glucose energy is required to cover the energy requirements for fatty acid synthesis from glucose.[52] This accounts at least partially for the rise in metabolic rate from 43 to 60 kcal/kg/day (group 2; glu/aa) observed in Figure 21–3.

A large carbohydrate load given to healthy adults increases carbon dioxide production by 43% and oxygen consumption by 13%, which results in a 47% increase in alveolar ventilation.[156] In adults with airway disease without carbon dioxide retention, a

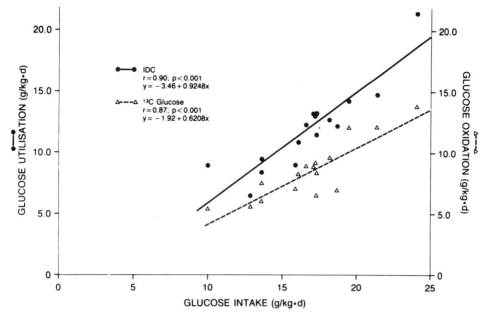

FIG 21-4.

Glucose utilization measured with indirect calorimetry *(solid line)* vs. glucose oxidation measured with U-^{13}C-glucose *(broken line)* in infants on fat-free parenteral nutrition. The increment in glucose oxidation is only two thirds of the increment in glucose utilization; the difference between the two techniques gives an estimate of glucose carbon stored as fat. Energy expenditure rises by approximately 1 kcal for each additional gram of glucose administered and can in part be attributed to increasing lipogenesis from glucose. (From Sauer P, Van Aerde J, Pencharz P, et al: *Clin Sci* 1986; 70:587-593. Used by permission.)

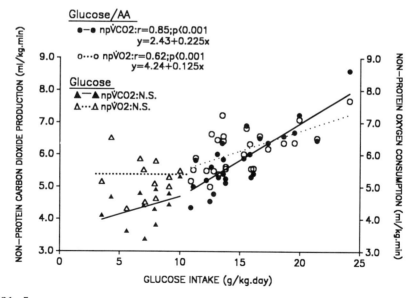

FIG 21-5.

Effect of glucose intake on nonprotein respiratory gas exchange in full-term infants receiving fat-free intravenous nutrition. Nonprotein carbon dioxide production (np$\dot{V}CO_2$, *closed circles*), rose 0.225 ml/kg/min for each additional gram of glucose administered and nonprotein oxygen consumption (np$\dot{V}O_2$, *open circles*) rose 0.125 ml/kg/min in 26 full-term infants receiving a fat-free diet of glucose and amino acids (glucose/AA). Nonprotein respiratory quotient = 1.0 at a glucose intake of approximately 18 g/kg/day. Below an energy intake sufficient to cover maintenance energy requirements *(triangles)*, there was no effect of glucose intake on respiratory gas exchange.

large oral carbohydrate load causes an increase in minute ventilation from 10.3 to 12.8 L/min.[65] Assuming that the basic caloric requirement for a full-term 3-kg neonate is equal to the average hepatic endogenous glucose production of 6 mg/kg/min[20, 99] and assuming that the respiratory frequency averages 40 breaths/min, the nonprotein carbon dioxide production will total 13.1 mL/min (see Fig 21–5) or 0.33 mL per breath. Raising the glucose intake to 15 mg/kg/min will increase the nonprotein carbon dioxide production to 21.9 mL/min, an increase of 8.8 mL/min or approximately 67%. To eliminate this extra carbon dioxide, the minute ventilation will increase either by augmenting respiratory rate or volume. Assuming constant tidal volume, the respiratory rate would rise to approximately 65 breaths per minute. The workload of additional ventilation imposed by the increased carbon dioxide production occasioned by a high load of intravenous glucose could precipitate respiratory failure when respiratory function is compromised, and weaning from ventilatory support could be impeded. In summary, the practice of increasing the energy supply progressively by only increasing glucose and amino acid intake imposes an additional workload on the respiratory system.

Improving Energy Supply by Administering Intravenous Lipid Emulsions

In adults, a combination of intravenous glucose and lipid as the nonprotein energy source appears to be more physiologic than infusion of glucose alone.[90, 132, 176] Nose et al. found a substantial increase in basal metabolic rate in infants and children on total parenteral nutrition with glucose and amino acids alone compared with lipid-supplemented patients.[136] On the other hand, when intravenous fat alone is given as the nonprotein energy source, an increase in oxygen consumption has been reported.[86]

We compared two groups of full-term infants on total parenteral nutrition with similar energy and protein intakes, but with a nonprotein energy supply of either only glucose or a combination of glucose and lipid with a caloric ratio of 3:1. At a caloric intake of approximately 85 kcal/kg/day, energy expenditure decreases significantly when isocaloric amounts of fats are substituted for glucose, leaving more energy for storage and growth. Nonprotein carbon dioxide production decreases by 15% from 6.5 to 5.5 mL/kg/min, and nonprotein oxygen consumption decreases as well.[179] The significant differences in carbon dioxide production, oxygen consumption, and metabolic rate between the two groups are due to suppression of lipogenesis from glucose in the lipid-supplemented group. This has been confirmed by studies combining indirect calorimetry and U-^{13}C-glucose.[180]

These data and the earlier work of Heim et al.[86] indicate that administering either glucose or fat as the only nonprotein energy source results in "metabolic stress," with an increase in oxygen consumption, carbon dioxide production, and energy expenditure. From the point of view of energy balance and respiratory gaseous exchange, intravenous nonprotein calories should be given as a combination of glucose and lipid, but the ideal ratio still has to be determined.

Effect of Intravenous Lipid Emulsions On Lung Function

In spite of the theoretical and clinical benefits for routine use of intravenous lipid emulsions as a calorie source, lipid emulsions have been suspected of causing potential pulmonary dysfunction. There is a lot of controversy on this subject—which probably reflects differences in dose, infusion rate, duration of lipid infusion, type of animal models, and type of patients. The lung dysfunction observed has initially been attributed to the associated hyperlipidemia[70]; this might in fact only be correct with fat overload syndrome. More recent studies, however, have indicated that the decrease in PaO_2 is a result of ventilation/perfusion inequalities caused by changes in prostanoid metabolism causing alterations in the pulmonary vascular tone.[78, 79, 96, 122, 164] Whereas a bolus of prostaglandin precursors has resulted in higher pulmonary pressure responses, continuous infusion has yielded net vasodilator responses in some studies[78, 94, 98] or no effect in other studies.[24] There is a much larger volume of studies in animals[37, 74, 122, 174] demonstrating a vasoconstrictor response in the pulmonary circulation after either a bolus or low-dose continuous infusion. In human neonates, after 90 minutes of intravenous lipid infusion, the ratio of right ventricular pre-ejection period to ejection time rises significantly, suggesting pulmonary hypertension due to an increase in pulmonary vascular tone.[114] Infusion of soybean oil–based intravenous lipid emulsions might increase the incidence of BPD, and it is postulated that this effect is related to thromboxane A_2[82, 83] and leukotrienes.[25] In contrast, high levels of dietary linoleic acid have been related to a decrease in oxygen toxicity.[166] The reason for the contradictory results might be related to differences in duration and in rate of infusion of the lipid emulsions in the respective studies and the resulting differences in the ratio of vasodilating over vasoconstricting eicosanoids. During a bolus or a rapid infusion, however, the excessive amount of substrate may overwhelm the enzymatic pathways for PGI_2 (prostacyclin) and PGE_2 (dinoprostone) metabolism, resulting in an increased production of potent vasoconstrictive thromboxanes.[164] Although some data from animal studies are available, there is presently insufficient clinical evidence to withhold intravenous lipid emulsions for pulmonary reasons. The fact that early undernutrition adversely affects lung development, plus the fact that there is improved hyperoxic tolerance with diet high in polyunsaturated fatty acids, should form the basis for contemplating clinical trials in which polyunsatured fat emulsions are provided very early in life. Selective blockers for prostanoid or leukotriene synthesis and addition of different prostaglandin precursors to the intravenous lipid emulsions are currently under investigation (J. Van Aerde and Y. Coe, unpublished data).

Insufficient data are available to define the "normal" triglyceride level in VLBW infants. Brans et al. claim that triglyceride levels as high as 9.58 mmol/L have no undesirable effects on the alveolar-arteriolar oxygen gradient.[23] Certainly these data are only preliminary, and more clinical studies are absolutely mandatory to confirm the safety of these high triglyceride levels before they can be accepted as a general recommendation.

In summary, during the acute stage of respiratory disease, catabolism should be avoided and a positive nitrogen balance achieved, to support lung repair and development, and to safeguard that appropriate amounts of nutrients are given during the "critical epochs" of growth and development.[189] After 36 to 48 hours of the infant's life, the nutritional management should provide approximately 60 kcal/kg/day—10 to 12 g/kg/day as glucose, 0.5 to 1.0 g/kg/day of intravenous lipid (which is enough to prevent essential fatty acid deficiency),[1] and amino acid intake rising to 2 g/kg/day. Whereas fluid overload and the risk for lung edema[26] can be limited with this regimen, hyperglycemia is often a serious problem in the smallest preterm infants. Continuous infusion of low-dose insulin improves glucose tolerance in extremely low-birth-weight infants,[21, 139] but there are no data regarding the effect on metabolic rate, respiratory gaseous exchange, or metabolic rate of glucose.

After a few days, one should aim for a more positive energy balance by progressively increasing the intravenous lipid intake to 3 to 4 g/kg/day, while monitoring the triglyceride levels.[24] A glucose:lipid ratio of 3:1 to 2:1 on a caloric basis minimizes the carbon dioxide stress on the neonate, which is particularly important during the acute stage of impaired lung function. A progressive increase of protein intake should also be aimed for. Clearly, in the absence of absolute contraindications, it is advisable to start oral-enteral feedings as soon as possible.[173]

BRONCHOPULMONARY DYSPLASIA AND ENTERAL FEEDING

Energy Intake and Respiratory Function

Whereas energy and macronutrient intake are mainly provided parenterally during the early, acute phase of the respiratory disease, oral feeding is the main energy source for infants with chronic lung disease during the later stages.

In adults, the change in metabolic rate, carbon dioxide production, and oxygen consumption is determined by the infusion rate of the oral dietary formula, the fuel composition, and the subject's health status.[89, 90] From baseline fasting measurements to a maintenance energy infusion rate, no change is observed in oxygen consumption, carbon dioxide production, energy expenditure, and minute ventilation. We made similar observations in intravenously fed infants receiving fewer calories than the maintenance energy requirements (see Fig 21–3). Heymsfield et al.[89, 90] further reported that as the energy infusion rate is advanced into the repletion range, oxygen consumption, carbon dioxide production, minute ventilation, and metabolic rate rise linearly, and a rise in cardiac output, heart rate, and myocardial oxygen consumption is observed. We have made similar observations in a group of 49 formula-fed, growing, preterm infants with birth weights under 1,300 gm. Their energy intake ranged between 102 and 171 kcal/kg/day by modifying fluid intake or formula concentration. The diet composition was kept constant—with 40% of the energy provided as carbohydrate, 48% as fat, and 12% as protein. Metabolizable energy intake increased with total energy intake, and the energy losses increased proportionally as well, resulting in a constant digestibility of 86%. As indicated in Figure 21–6, about one fourth of each additional kilocalorie absorbed is expended; this indicates increasing substrate oxidation and/or conversion into new tissue—disposable material for growth. In this group of stable, growing, preterm infants, the growth component is probably predominant, whereas in BPD patients the oxidation component might be more important to cover the higher energy expenditure demands. In any case, fast growth might decompensate an organism with borderline lung function by imposing more metabolic and respiratory demands. Indeed, the increase in metabolizable energy intake also induces a drastic rise in carbon dioxide production (see Fig 21–2) and oxygen consumption (Fig 21–7). It is interesting to note that the intercept of Figure 21–6 equals 32 kcal/kg/day; that is, when no energy is administered at all, the energy expenditure is similar to the fetal energy expenditure, which ranges between 30 and 35 kcal/kg/day.

Diet Composition, Energy Expenditure, and Respiratory Gaseous Exchange

The second determinant of the energetic response to enteral feeding in adults is dietary formula composition.[89] The nature of the fuel supplied directly influences metabolic rate, respiratory gas exchange, and minute ventilation.[90] When dietary protein is held constant, progressively increasing the proportion of formula carbohydrate is associated with an increase in carbon dioxide production compared to a high-fat formula.

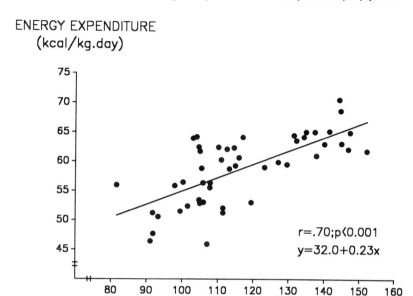

FIG 21–6.

Effect of energy intake on energy expenditure in a group of 49 orally fed, preterm, growing infants receiving a metabolizable energy intake between 80 and 150 kcal/kg/day. Approximately one fourth of each additional kilocalorie absorbed is expended. Milk formula composition: 12% of the energy as protein, 40% as carbohydrate, and 48% as lipid.

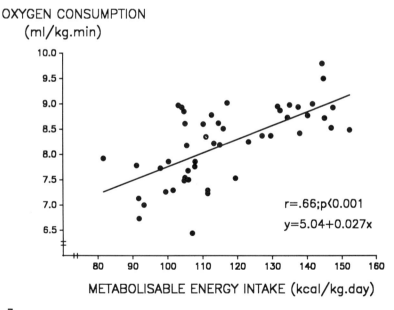

FIG 21–7.

Effect of energy intake on oxygen consumption. Oxygen consumption increases when metabolizable energy intake is increased from 80 to 150 kcal/kg/day in orally fed, preterm infants. (See also Fig 21–6.)

Since minute ventilation is primarily determined by carbon dioxide production and $PaCO_2$, high-carbohydrate solutions also tend to increase minute ventilation. As there is only a small difference in oxygen consumption between high-carbohydrate and high-fat solutions, measurable differences in cardiac output and heart rate could not be detected.[90] This experiment confirms the generally accepted relation between carbon dioxide production and ventilatory drive. The differences in carbon dioxide production between low-fat and high-fat formulas noted by Heymsfield et al.[89] are attributed to the different pathways involved in triglyceride biosynthesis. Lipogenesis from glucose is more energy costly, carbon dioxide producing, and oxygen consuming than when synthesized from fat.

Although no similar data are available for orally fed neonates, we have demonstrated a reduction in energy expenditure, carbon dioxide production, and oxygen consumption in intravenously fed infants when some of the glucose calories are isocalorically replaced by intravenous fat, while keeping protein and energy intake constant (see previous section).[158, 180] We have also demonstrated that this reduction is due to a decrease in lipogenesis from glucose.[180]

Whyte and Sinclair[188] have speculated about what might happen if the diet of the BPD infant were supplemented with medium-chain triglycerides or with glucose polymers in order to simulate acceptable growth rates and energy storage. If this energy were supplied as fat, there would only be a minor effect on carbon dioxide production, but if provided as carbohydrate, carbon dioxide production would be substantially increased. It is questionable whether an infant with restricted alveolar ventilation could actually excrete the additional carbon dioxide generated so that respiratory acidosis could be made worse.

The exact caloric needs of infants with BPD are presently not known, in part because of the heterogenicity of the disease, in part because there are very limited data on energy balance in these patients. The energy intake has to be at least equal to and probably more than in normal growing preterm infants. For those infants with the worst lung disease, too high intakes might be disadvantageous, as every additional 10 kcal/kg/day fed produces approximately 0.5 L of extra carbon dioxide and consumes an additional 0.33 L of oxygen. As the energy intake is very often too low because of fluid restriction, 24, 27, or 30 kcal/oz formulas can be administered. Although fluid restriction is generally recommended as part of the treatment of BPD, its value has never been investigated.

Some caution is necessary with gavage tube feeding. There is evidence that small, intermittent feeds over a longer duration might decrease the bolus effect of feeding on lung volume. Indeed, the functional residual capacity decreases and respiratory rate and minute ventilation increase following nasogastric bolus feeds in infants recovering from respiratory disease.[143] Stocks found a significant increase in nasal resistance and total airway resistance when a nasogastric tube is in situ.[170] This was reconfirmed by Martin et al., who also reported on the effect of the head position.[116] Additionally, with a nasogastric tube in place, there seems to be an increased diaphragmatic workload,[87] a reduction in PaO_2, and an increased incidence of apnea.[190] It is therefore advisable to feed infants with BPD frequent small amounts of formula, with intermittent insertion of an orogastric tube. If nasogastric tubes are used, then they should never be left in place.

Finally, a word on oxygen therapy. It has been suggested that compromised systemic oxygen transport and impaired intermediate metabolism contribute to growth failure. Keeping the oxygen tension over 55 to 60 mm Hg and/or oxygen saturation over 92% seems to promote weight gain in BPD patients.[71, 138] There is no decisive proof on the need for booster blood transfusions, and more prospective studies are to be done.[3] In summary, optimizing the energy balance is much more difficult in the patient with chronic lung disease than in the healthy, growing, preterm infant. Too little energy intake results in growth failure and inability to promote lung growth; too much energy intake can result in respiratory decompensation. With current knowledge and technology, it is difficult, if not impossible, to find the brittle equilibrium for each individual patient.

SUMMARY

The survival of smaller and smaller infants over the past decade stresses the unique nutritional requirements of prematurely born infants who inherently have high caloric requirements that are difficult to meet during the first weeks of life.

Many premature infants with RDS show evidence of malnutrition during the acute illness; the tendency to restrict fluids and treat BPD patients with potent diuretics that cause mineral losses might aggravate the condition of these infants.

Whereas data are available on energy requirements for the stable, growing infant, nourished either orally or intravenously, very limited data are available on the critically ill, ventilated, preterm infant. The estimation of maintenance energy requirements derived from data on the stable newborn infant underestimate the true requirements of the very small, sick infant. New standards have to be set and, ideally, the requirements should be determined for each infant individually. On a long-term basis, limited intake of energy and nutrients affects the development of the fast-growing nervous system, but it also affects lung growth and might contribute to the development of bronchopulmonary dysplasia. It seems clear that in addition to the commonly held notion that lung immaturity, hyperoxia, and barotrauma are causative factors of bronchopulmonary dysplasia, the frequent state of malnutrition seen in most distressed premature infants contributes to the development or worsening of the lung disease. On one hand, a negative energy balance in infants with limited energy stores affects mortality and morbidity of the smallest preterm infants. On the other hand, feeding "too much" or "an inappropriate mix" results in high carbon dioxide production, with a potential for respiratory acidosis and an increase in energy expenditure. Finding the brittle equilibrium is a key part in the nutritional management of these infants.

Although animal and human adult data are available, more research is needed in the human neonatal area investigating interactions between nutrition and lung development, surfactant synthesis, and respiratory muscles. The question of why infants with bronchopulmonary dysplasia have a high energy expenditure has only been answered in part. How much of this is due to increased work of breathing? Does the metabolism of sick and hypoxic neonates intrinsically change? The issue of chronic hypoxia and alterations in metabolism is still unanswered, and appropriate animal models for chronic hypoxia should provide some answers. Even the most essential, most clinically oriented question has not been answered: how can we improve the energy balance and growth in babies with BPD, and what type of nonprotein substrate should be given? Clearly, this area in nutritional metabolism is just at the beginning of its development. Is there a place for prevention by providing adequate nutrition in the immediate period after birth in an attempt to decrease the incidence of BPD? Is the capacity for repair of ongoing lung injury or normal lung growth limited? Alterations in composition of lung surfactant occurring in essential fatty acid and energy deficiency may explain in part why some infants are slow in recovering from RDS. The data discussed on substrate availability and enzyme regulation of surfactant synthesis also have potential clinical importance. In vitro models are necessary for an investigation of how nutrients influence surfactant synthesis on a cellular level.

Data are available on the effect of severe malnutrition and starvation on the mechanics of the respiratory system in adults. Studies investigating less extreme nutritional conditions in newborn animals are currently lacking. There is clear evidence that certain amino acids and the nonprotein substrates influence the ventilatory drive in adults, but no data concern newborn animals or infants. In adults and neonates, providing more energy by increasing the fat-free intravenous nutrition results in an increase in energy expenditure, carbon dioxide production, and oxygen consumption. Increasing the energy intake by offering a more balanced intravenous diet containing a moderate amount of lipid does not impose this extra metabolic and respiratory strain.

Based on the studies reviewed in this chapter, early appropriate nutrition should be part of the total management of the prematurely born infant: this is important not only on a short-term basis for the acutely ill infant with limited energy reserves, but also in the long term, as it might limit lung damage leading to BPD. Minimizing "metabolic and respiratory stress" are primary goals when providing the necessary energy for infants with acute or chronic lung disease.

In managing the preterm infant, failing organs and body systems cannot be treated separately but have to be seen as part of a complex interaction in which energy balance and metabolism take a central position from the very beginning. The energy efficiency of any type of burning furnace or engine depends mainly on the fuel administered.

REFERENCES

1. Adamkin D: Nutrition in very low birth weight infants. *Clin Perinatol* 1986; 13:419–443.
2. Alam S, Alam B: Lung surfactant and fatty acid composition of lung tissue and lavage of rats fed diets containing different lipids. *Lipids* 1984; 19:39–43.
3. Alverson D, Isken V, Cotren R: Effect of booster blood transfusions on oxygen utilization in infants with bronchopulmonary dysplasia. *J Pediatr* 1988; 113:722–726.
4. Anderson T, Muttart C, Bieber M, et al: A controlled trial of glucose versus glucose and amino acids in preterm infants. *J Pediatr* 1979; 94:947–951.
5. Anzano M, Olson J, Lamb A: Morphologic alterations in the trachea and the salivary gland following the induction of rapid synchronous vitamin A deficiency in rats. *Am J Pathol* 1982; 98:717–732.
6. Arora N, Rochester D: Respiratory muscle strength and maximal voluntary ventilation in undernourished patients. *Am Rev Respir Dis* 1982; 126:6–8.
7. Arora N, Rochester D: Effect of body weight and muscularity on human diaphragm muscle mass, thickness and area. *J Appl Physiol* 1982; 52:64–70.
8. Askanazi J, Carpentier Y, Elwyn D, et al: Influence of total parenteral nutrition on fuel utilization in injury and sepsis. *Am Surg* 1979; 191:40–46.
9. Askanazi J, Elwyn D, Silverberg P, et al: Respiratory distress secondary to a high carbohydrate load. *Surgery* 1980; 87:596–598.
10. Askanazi J, Rosenbaum S, Michelsen C, et al: Increased body temperature secondary to total parenteral nutrition. *Crit Care Med* 1980; 8:736–737.
11. Askanazi J, Rosenbaum S, Hyman A, et al: Respiratory changes induced by the large glucose loads of total parenteral nutrition. *JAMA* 1980; 14:1444–1447.
12. Askanazi J, Weissman C, Lasala P, et al: Nutrients and ventilation. *Adv Shock Res* 1983; 9:69–70.

13. Askanazi J, Weissman C, Lasala P, et al: Effect of protein intake on ventilatory drive. *Anesthesiology* 1984; 60:106–110.
14. Askanazi J, Weissman C, Rosenbaum S, et al: Nutrition and the respiratory system. *Crit Care Med* 1982; 10:163–172.
15. Aubier M, Trippenbach T, Roussos C: Respiratory muscle fatigue during cardiogenic shock. *J Appl Physiol* 1981; 51:499–508.
16. Aynsley-Green A, Soltesz G: The regulation of carbohydrate metabolism, in Aynsley-Green A, Soltesz G (eds): *Hypoglycemia in Infancy and Childhood.* Edinburgh, Churchill Livingstone, 1985, pp 1–27.
17. Bassili H, Dietel M: Effect of nutritional support on weaning patients off mechanical ventilators. *J Parenter Enteral Nutr* 1981; 5:161–163.
18. Bell E, Filer L: The role of vitamin E in the nutrition of premature infants. *Am J Clin Nutr* 1981; 34:414–422.
19. Berman W, Katz R, Yabek S: Long-term follow-up of bronchopulmonary dysplasia. *J Pediatr* 1986; 109:45–50.
20. Bier D, Leake R, Haymond M, et al: Measurement of "true" glucose production rates in infancy and childhood with 6,6-dideutero-glucose. *Diabetes* 1977; 26:1016–1023.
21. Binder N, Raschko P, Benda G, et al: Insulin infusion with parenteral nutrition in extremely low birth weight infants with hyperglycemia. *J Pediatr* 1989; 114:273–280.
22. Bland R: Edema formation in the newborn lung. *Clin Perinatol* 1982; 9:593–612.
23. Brans Y, Andrew D, Carrillo D, et al: Tolerance of fat emulsions in very-low-birthweight neonates. *Am J Perinatol* 1988; 5:8–12.
24. Brans Y, Dutton E, Andrew D, et al: Fat emulsion tolerance in very low birth weight neonates. Effect on diffusion of oxygen in the lungs and on blood pH. *Pediatrics* 1986; 78:79–84.
25. Broderick K, Tyrala E: Leukotrienes and their role in the development of bronchopulmonary dysplasia in the newborn. *Pediatr Res* 1987; 21:445A.
26. Brown E, Stark A, Sosenko I, et al: Bronchopulmonary dysplasia. Possible relationship to pulmonary edema. *J Pediatr* 1978; 92:982–984.
27. Brown L, Bliss A, Longshore W: Effect of nutritional status on the lung surfactant system. Food deprivation and caloric restriction. *Exp Lung Res* 1984; 6:133–147.
28. Bruno J, McMahon K, Farrell P: Lung surfactant phospholipids as related to hydration and choline status of fasted rats. *J Nutr* 1985; 115:85–89.
29. Bryan M, Wei P, Hamilton J, et al: Supplemental intravenous alimentation in low-birth-weight infants. *J Pediatr* 1973; 82:940–944.
30. Bucher J, Roberts R: Effects of alpha-tocopherol treatment on newborn rat lung development and injury in hyperoxia. *Pediatr Pharmacol* 1982; 3:1–9.
31. Budin P: The feeding and hygiene of premature and full term infants, in *The Nursling.* Authorized translation by WJ Maloney of "Le Nourisson" (1900). London, Caxton Publishing Co, 1907.
32. Catzeflis C, Schutz Y, Micheli J, et al: Whole body protein synthesis and energy expenditure. *Pediatr Res* 1985; 19:679–687.
33. Chandra RK: Nutrition, immunity and infection: Present knowledge and future directions. *Lancet* 1983; 1:688–691.
34. Chessex P, Putet G, Verellen G, et al: Influence of glucose load on the energy metabolism of preterm infants on fat-free parenteral nutrition. *Pediatr Res* 1984; 18:192A.
35. Chessex P, Reichman B, Verellen G, et al: Relation between heart rate and energy expenditure in the newborn. *Pediatr Res* 1981; 15:1077–1082.
36. Churella H, Bachuber B, MacLean W: Survey: Methods of feeding low-birth-weight infants. *Pediatrics* 1985; 76:243–249.
37. Coe J, Van Aerde J, Kolatat T, et al: Intralipid induced pulmonary vasoconstrictions in newborn piglets. *Clin Invest Med* 1988; 11:D34.
38. Costill D, Gollnick P, Jansson E, et al: Glycogen depletion pattern in human muscle fibers during distance running. *Acta Physiol Scand* 1973; 9:374–389.

39. Covelli H, Black J, Olsen M, et al: Respiratory failure precipitated by high carbohydrate loads. *Ann Intern Med* 1981; 95:579–581.

40. Cross C, Hasegawa G, Reddy K, et al: Enhanced lung toxicity of oxygen in selenium-deficient rats. *Res Commun Chem Pathol Pharmacol* 1977; 16:695–700.

41. Deneke S, Gershoff S, Fanburg B: Potentiation of oxygen toxicity in rats by dietary protein or amino acid deficiency. *J Appl Physiol* 1983; 54:147–151.

42. Doekel R, Zwillich C, Scoggin C: Clinical semistarvation: Depression of hypoxic ventilatory response. *N Engl J Med* 1976; 895:358–365.

43. Dogra S, Khanduja K, Sharma R: Effect of vitamin A on the levels of glutathione and glutathione-S-transferase activity in rat lung and liver. *Experientia* 1981; 38:903–904.

44. Driver A, Lebrun M: Iatrogenic malnutrition in patients receiving ventilation support. *JAMA* 1980; 244:2195–2196.

45. Eccles R, Swinamer D, Jones R: Validation of a compact system for measuring gas exchange. *Crit Care Med* 1986; 64:807–811.

46. Edelman N, Rucker R, Peavy H: Nutrition and the respiratory system: Chronic obstructive pulmonary disease. *Am Rev Respir Dis* 1986; 134:347–352.

47. Ehrenkranz R, Bonta B, Ablow R, et al: Amelioration of bronchopulmonary dysplasia after vitamin E administration. *N Engl J Med* 1978; 299:564–569.

48. Ehrenkranz R, Bonta B, Ablow R, et al: Effect of vitamin E on the development of oxygen-induced lung injury in neonates. *Ann NY Acad Sci* 1982; 93:452–466.

49. Elwyn D, Kinney J, Gump F, et al: Some metabolic effects of fat infusions in depleted patients. *Metabolism* 1980; 29:125–132.

50. Faridy E: Effect of food and water deprivation on surface elasticity of lungs of rats. *J Appl Physiol* 1970; 29:493–498.

51. Farrell P: Nutrition and infant lung functions. *Pediatr Pulmonol* 1986; 2:44–59.

52. Flatt J: The biochemistry of energy expenditure: in Bray G (ed): *Recent Advances in Obesity Research II*. Washington DC, Newman Publishers, 1977, pp 211–228.

53. Forman M, Rotman E, Fisher A: Roles of selenium and sulfur-containing amino acids in protection against oxygen toxicity. *Lab Invest* 1983; 49:148–153.

54. Frank L, Groseclose E: Oxygen toxicity in newborn rats: The adverse effects of undernutrition. *J Appl Physiol* 1982; 53:1248–1255.

55. Frank L, Lewis PL, Garcia-Pons T: Intrauterine growth-retarded rat pups show increased susceptibility to pulmonary oxygen toxicity. *Pediatr Res* 1985; 19:281–286.

56. Frank L, Sosenko I: Development of lung antioxidant enzyme system in late gestation: Possible implications for the prematurely-born infant. *J Pediatr* 1987; 110:9–14.

57. Frank L, Sosenko I: Prenatal development of lung antioxidant enzymes in four species. *J Pediatr* 1987; 110:106–110.

58. Frank L, Sosenko I: Undernutrition as a major contributing factor in the pathogenesis of bronchopulmonary dysplasia. *Am Rev Respir Dis* 1988; 138:725–729.

59. Fraser I, Jeejeebhoy K, Atwood H: Hypocaloric diet impairs force-length adaptation in the rat soleus. *Fed Proc* 1984; 43:533.

60. Frayn K: Calculation of substrate oxidation rate in vivo from gaseous exchange. *J Appl Physiol* 1983; 55:628–634.

61. Friedman Z, Rosenberg A: Abnormal lung surfactant related to essential fatty acid deficiency in a neonate. *Pediatrics* 1979; 63:855–859.

62. Fulks R, Li J, Goldberg A: Effects of insulin, glucose and amino acids on protein turnover in rat diaphragm. *J Biol Chem* 1975; 250:290–298.

63. Gail D, Hassaro G, Hassaro D: Influence of fasting on the lung. *J Appl Physiol* 1977; 42:88–92.

64. Georgieff M, Hoffman J, Pereira G, et al: Effect of neonatal caloric deprivation on head growth and 1-year developmental status in preterm infants. *J Pediatr* 1985; 107:581–587.

65. Gieseke T, Gurushanthaiah G, Glauser F: Effects of carbohydrate on carbon dioxide excretion in patients with airway disease. *Chest* 1977; 71:55–58.

66. Goldberg A, Chane T: Regulation and significance of amino acid metabolism in skeletal muscle. *Fed Proc* 1978; 37:2301–2307.
67. Goldberg A, Odessey R: Oxidation of amino acids by diaphragm from fed and fasted rats. *Am J Physiol* 1972; 223:1384–1391.
68. Gollnick P, Pieml K, Saubert C, et al: Diet, exercise and glycogen changes in human muscle fibers. *J Appl Physiol* 1972; 33:421–425.
69. Goswami T, Vu M, Srivastava U: Quantitative changes in the DNA, RNA and protein content of various organs of the young of undernourished female rats. *J Nutr* 1974; 104:1257–1264.
70. Greene H, Hazlett D, Demaree R: Relationship between Intralipid-induced hyperlipemia and pulmonary function. *Am J Clin Nutr* 1976; 29:127–135.
71. Groothuis J, Rosenberg A: Home oxygen promotes weight gain in infants with bronchopulmonary dysplasia. *Am J Dis Child* 1987; 141:992–995.
72. Gross I, Ilic I, Wilson C, et al: The influence of postnatal nutritional deprivation on the phospholipid content of developing rat lung. *Biochim Biophys Acta* 1976; 441:412–422.
73. Gross S, Eckerman C: Normative early head growth in very-low-birth-weight infants. *J Pediatr* 1983; 103:946–949.
74. Gurtner G, Knoblauch A, Smith P, et al: Oxidant- and lipid-induced pulmonary vasoconstriction mediated by arachidonic acid metabolites. *J Appl Physiol* 1983; 55:949–954.
75. Hack M, Breslau N: Very low birth weight infants. Effect of brain growth during infancy on intelligence quotient at 3 years of age. *Pediatrics* 1986; 77:196–202.
76. Hackney J, Evans M, Bils R, et al: Effects of oxygen at high concentration and food deprivation on cell division in lung alveoli of mice. *Exp Mol Pathol* 1977; 26:350–358.
77. Haddad G, Akabas S: Adaptation of respiratory muscles to acute and chronic stress. Considerations on energy and fuels. *Clin Chest Med* 1986; 7:79–89.
78. Hageman J, McCulloch K, Gora P, et al: Intralipid alterations in pulmonary prostaglandin metabolism and gas exchange. *Crit Care Med* 1983; 10:794–798.
79. Hageman J, Hunt C: Fat emulsions and lung function. *Clin Chest Med* 1986; 7:69–77.
80. Hallman M, Arjomaa P, Hoppu K: Inositol supplementation in respiratory distress syndrome. Relationship between serum concentration, renal excretion, and lung effluent phospholipids. *J Pediatr* 1987; 110:604–610.
81. Hallman M, Jarvenpaa AI, Pohjavuori M: Respiratory distress syndrome and inositol supplementation in preterm infants. *Arch Dis Child* 1986; 61:1076–1083.
82. Hammerman C, Aramburo M: Decreased lipid intake reduces morbidity in sick premature neonates. *J Pediatr* 1988; 113:1083–1088.
83. Hammerman C, Valaitis S, Aramburo M: Thromboxanes: The link between Intralipid and pulmonary vasoconstriction in the newborn. *Pediatr Res* 1987; 21:236A.
84. Hansen T, Hazinsi T, Bland R: Vitamin E does not prevent oxygen-induced lung injury in newborn lambs. *Pediatr Res* 1982; 16:583–587.
85. Harkema J, Mauderly J, Gregory R, et al: A comparison of starvation and elastase models of emphysema in the rat. *Am Rev Respir Dis* 1984; 129:584–591.
86. Heim T, Putet G, Verellen G, et al: Energy cost of intravenous alimentation in the newborn infant, in Stern L, Salle B, Friis-Hansen B (eds): *Intensive Care in the Newborn III.* New York, Masson Publishing, 1981, pp 219–238.
87. Heldt S: The effect of gavage feeding on the mechanics of the lung, chest wall, and diaphragm of preterm infants. *Pediatr Res* 1988; 24:55–58.
88. Herve P, Simonneau G, Girard P, et al: Hypercapnic acidosis induced by nutrition in mechanically ventilated patients: Glucose versus fat. *Crit Care Med* 1985; 13:537–543.
89. Heymsfield S, Erbland M, Casper K, et al: Enteral nutritional support: Metabolic, cardiovascular, and pulmonary interrelations. *Clin Chest Med* 1986; 7:41–67.
90. Heymsfield S, Head A, McManus C, et al: Respiratory, cardiovascular and metabolic effects of enteral hyperalimentation: Influence of formula dose and composition. *Am J Clin Nutr* 1984; 40:116–130.

91. Hordof A, Mellins R, Gersony W, et al: Reversibility of chronic obstructive lung disease in infants following repair of ventricular septal defect. *J Pediatr* 1977; 90:187–191.

92. Huber G, Laforce P: Comparative effects of ozone and oxygen on pulmonary antibacterial defense mechanisms. *Antimicrob Agents Chemother* 1970; 10:129–136.

93. Hunker F, Bruton C, Hunker E, et al: Metabolic and nutritional evaluation of patients supported with mechanical ventilation. *Crit Care Med* 1980; 8:628–632.

94. Hunt C, Pachman L, Hageman J et al: Liposyn infusion increases plasma prostaglandin concentrations. *Pediatr Pulmonol* 1986; 2:154–158.

95. Hustead V, Gutcher G, Anderson S: Relationship of vitamin A status to lung disease in the preterm infant. *J Pediatr* 1984; 105:610–615.

96. Inwood R, Gora P, Hunt C: Indomethacin inhibition of intralipid induced lung dysfunction. *Prostaglandins Med* 1981; 6:503–514.

97. Jenkinson S, Lawrence R, Grafton W, et al: Enhanced pulmonary toxicity in copper-deficient rats exposed to hyperoxia. *Fundam Appl Toxicol* 1984; 4:170–177.

98. Kadowitz P, Spannhake E, Levin J: Differential actions of the prostaglandins on the pulmonary vascular bed. *Adv Prostaglandin Thromboxane Res* 1980; 7:731–743.

99. Kalhan S, Savin S, Adam P, et al: Estimation of glucose turnover with stable tracer glucose-1-^{13}C. *J Lab Clin Med* 1977; 80:285–294.

100. Kao L, Durand D, Nickerson B: Improving pulmonary function does not decrease oxygen consumption in infants with bronchopulmonary dysplasia. *J Pediatr* 1988; 112:612–621.

101. Keens T, Bryan A, Levison H, et al: Developmental pattern of muscle fiber types in human ventilatory muscles. *J Appl Physiol* 1978; 44:909–913.

102. Kehrer J, Autor A: The effect of dietary fatty acids on the composition of adult rat lung lipids: Relationship to oxygen toxicity. *Toxicol Appl Pharmacol* 1978; 44:423–430.

103. Kelly S, Rosa A, Field S: Inspiratory muscle strength and body composition in patients receiving total parenteral nutrition therapy. *Am Rev Respir Dis* 1984; 130:33–37.

104. Kelsen S, Ference M, Kapoor S: Effects of prolonged undernutrition on structure and function of the diaphragm. *J Appl Physiol* 1985; 58:1354–1359.

105. Kerr J, Riley D, Lanza-Jacoby S, et al: Nutritional emphysema in the rat. *Am Rev Respir Dis* 1985; 131:644–650.

106. Koops B, Abhan S, Accurso F: Outpatient management and follow-up of bronchopulmonary dysplasia. *Clin Perinatol* 1984; 11:101–122.

107. Kratzing C, Kell J: Tissue levels of ascorbic acid during rat gestation. *Int J Vitam Nutr Res* 1982; 52:326–332.

108. Krinsky N, Deneke S: Interaction of oxygen and oxy-radicals with carotenoids. *J Natl Cancer Inst* 1982; 69:205–210.

109. Kurzner S, Garg M, Bautista D, et al: Growth failure in infants with bronchopulmonary dysplasia: Nutrition and elevated resting metabolic expenditure. *Pediatrics* 1988; 81:379–384.

110. Kurzner S, Garg M, Bautista D, et al: Growth failure in bronchopulmonary dysplasia: Elevated metabolic rates and pulmonary mechanics. *J Pediatr* 1988; 112:73–80.

111. Kyriakides E, Beeler D, Edmonds R, et al: Alterations in phosphatidylcholine species and their reversal in pulmonary surfactant during essential fatty acid deficiency. *Biochim Biophys Acta* 1976; 431:399–407.

112. Laaban J, Lemaire F, Baron J, et al: Influence of caloric intake on the respiratory mode during mandatory minute volume ventilation. *Chest* 1985; 87:67–78.

113. Lechner A: Perinatal age determines the severity of retarded lung development induced by starvation. *Am Rev Resp Dis* 1985; 131:638–643.

114. Lloyd T, Boucek M: Effect of Intralipid on the neonatal pulmonary bed: An echographic study. *J Pediatr* 1986; 108:130–133.

115. Markestad T, Fitzhardinge P: Growth and development in children recovering from bronchopulmonary dysplasia. *J Pediatr* 1981; 98:597–608.

116. Martin R, Sinner B, Carlo W, et al: Effect of head position on distribution of nasal airflow in preterm infants. *J Pediatr* 1988; 112:99–103.

117. Martin T, Altman Z, Alvares O: The effects of severe protein-calorie malnutrition on antibacterial defense mechanisms in the rat lung. *Am Rev Respir Dis* 1983; 128:1013–1019.
118. Mata L: The malnutrition-infection complex and its environmental factors. *Proc Nutr Soc* 1979; 38:29–40.
119. Maxwell L, Kuehl Y, Robotham J, et al: Temporal changes after death in primate diaphragm muscle oxidative enzyme activity. *Am Rev Respir Dis* 1984; 130:1147–1151.
120. Maxwell L, McCarter R, Kuehl T, et al: Development of histochemical and functional properties of baboon respiratory muscles. *J Appl Physiol* 1983; 54:551–561.
121. Maycock D, Hall J, Watchko J, et al: Diaphragmatic muscle fiber type development in swine. *Pediatr Res* 1987; 22:449–454.
122. McKeen C, Brigham K, Bowers R: Pulmonary vascular effects of fat emulsion infusion in unanesthetized sheep. *J Clin Invest* 1978; 61:1291–1297.
123. McMillan D, Gordon N: The role of antioxidants and diet in the prevention or treatment of oxygen-induced microvascular injury. *Ann NY Acad Sci* 1982; 384:535–543.
124. Mead J, Wu C, Stein R: Mechanisms of protection against membrane peroxidation, in Yagi K (ed): *Lipid Peroxides in Biology and Medicine.* New York, Academic Press, 1982, pp 161–178.
125. Meisels S, Plunkett J, Roloff D, et al: Growth and development of preterm infants with respiratory distress syndrome and bronchopulmonary dysplasia. *Pediatrics* 1986; 77:345–352.
126. Merritt T: Oxygen exposure in the newborn guinea pig. Lung lavage cell populations, chemotactic and elastase response: A possible relationship to neonatal bronchopulmonary dysplasia. *Pediatr Res* 1982; 16:798–805.
127. Muller N, Gulston G, Cade D, et al: Diaphragmatic muscle fatigue in the newborn. *J Appl Physiol* 1979; 46:688–695.
128. Myers B, Dubick M, Gerreits J, et al: Protein deficiency: Effects on lung mechanics and the accumulation of collagen and elastin in rat lung. *J Nutr* 1983; 113:2308–2315.
129. Nelson G, McPherson J, Perling L, et al: The effect of maternal dietary fat on fetal pulmonary maturation in rats. *Am J Obstet Gynecol* 1980; 138:466–470.
130. Niederman M, Merrill W, Farranti R: Nutritional status and bacterial binding in the lower respiratory tract in patients with chronic tracheostomies. *Ann Intern Med* 1984; 100:795–800.
131. Niki E, Saito T, Kawakami A: Inhibition of oxidation of methyllinoleate in solution by vitamin E and vitamin C. *J Biol Chem* 1984; 259:4177–4182.
132. Nordenstrom J, Carpentier Y, Askanazi J, et al: Metabolic utilization of intravenous fat emulsion during total parenteral nutrition. *Ann Surg* 1982; 196:221–231.
133. Nordenstrom J, Jeevanandam M, Elwyn D, et al: Increasing glucose intake during total parenteral nutrition increases norepinephrine excretion in trauma and sepsis. *Clin Physiol* 1981; 1:525–534.
134. Northway W: Observations on bronchopulmonary dysplasia. *J Pediatr* 1979; 95:815–818.
135. Northway W, Rosan R, Porter D: Pulmonary disease following respiratory therapy of hyaline membrane disease: Bronchopulmonary dysplasia. *N Engl J Med* 1967; 276:357–368.
136. Nose O, Tipton J, Ament M, et al: Effect of the energy source on changes in energy expenditure, respiratory quotient and nitrogen balance during total parenteral nutrition in children. *Pediatr Res* 1987; 21:538–541.
137. O'Brodovich H, Coates A: Pulmonary edema in respiratory distress syndrome and bronchopulmonary dysplasia, in Merritt T, Northway W, Boynton B (eds): *Bronchopulmonary Dysplasia.* Boston, Blackwell Scientific Publications, 1988, pp 143–160.
138. O'Brodovich H, Mellins R: Bronchopulmonary dysplasia. *Am Rev Respir Dis* 1985; 132:694–709.
139. Ostertag G, Jovanovic L, Lewis B, et al: Insulin pump therapy in the very low birth weight infant. *Pediatrics* 1986; 78:625–630.
140. Paynter D, Moir R, Underwood E: Changes in activity of the Cu-Zn superoxide dismutase enzyme in tissues of the rat with changes in dietary copper. *J Nutr* 1979; 109:1570–1576.

141. Phelps D: The role of vitamin E therapy in high risk neonates. *Clin Perinatol* 1988; 15:955–963.

142. Phelps D, Rosenbaum A, Isenberg S, et al: Tocopherol efficiency and safety for preventing retinopathy of prematurity: A randomized, controlled, double-masked trial. *Pediatrics* 1987; 79:489–500.

143. Pitcher-Wilmot R, Shutack J, Fox W: Decreased lung volume after nasogastric feeding of neonates recovering from respiratory disease. *J Pediatr* 1979; 95:119–121.

144. Polk G, Jenkinson S, Johanson W: Nutritional changes in nonhuman animals during mechanical ventilation. *Am J Clin Nutr* 1987; 46:900–904.

145. Rhoades R: Influence of starvation on the lung: Effect of glucose and palmitate utilization. *J Appl Physiol* 1975; 38:513–516.

146. Roberts R: Antioxidant systems of the developing lung, *Bronchopulmonary Dysplasia and Related Chronic Respiratory Disorders,* in Report of the 90th Ross Conference on Pediatric Research. Columbus, Ohio, Ross Laboratories, 1986, pp 24–32.

147. Rochester D, Esau S: Malnutrition and the respiratory system. *Chest* 1984; 85:411–415.

148. Rodriguez J, Weissman C, Askanazi J, et al: Metabolic and respiratory effects of glucose infusion. *Anesthesiology* 1982; 57:A199.

149. Rosso P. Winick M: Relation of nutrition to physical and mental development. *Pediatr Ann* 1973; 2:33–43.

150. Rubecz I, Mestyan J, Varga P, et al: Energy metabolism, substrate utilization, and nitrogen balance in parenterally fed postoperative neonates and infants. *J Pediatr* 1981; 98:42–46.

151. Rubin J, Clowes G, Macnicol M: Impaired pulmonary surfactant synthesis in starvation and severe nonthoracic sepsis. *Am J Surg* 1972; 123:461–467.

152. Sahebjami H, Macgee J: Changes in connective tissue composition of the lung in starvation and refeeding. *Am Rev Respir Dis* 1983; 128:644–647.

153. Sahebjami H, Vassalo C: Effects of starvation and refeeding on lung mechanics and morphometry. *Am Rev Respir Dis* 1979; 119:443–451.

154. Sahebjami H, Wirman J: Emphysema-like changes in the lungs of starved rats. *Am Rev Respir Dis* 1981; 124:619–624.

155. Saldanha R, Cepeda E, Poland R: The effect of vitamin E prophylaxis on the incidence and severity of bronchopulmonary dysplasia. *J Pediatr* 1982; 101:89–93.

156. Saltzman H, Salzano J: Effects of carbohydrate metabolism upon respiratory gas exchange in normal men. *J Appl Physiol* 1971; 30:228–231.

157. Sauer P, Van Aerde J, Beesley J, et al: Energy partition of protein synthesis in resting energy expenditure of neonates on TPN. *Pediatr Res* 1984; 18:339A.

158. Sauer P, Van Aerde J, Pencharz P, et al: Beneficial effect of the lipid system on energy metabolism in the intravenously alimented newborn. *Pediatr Res* 1986; 20:248A.

159. Sauer P, Van Aerde J, Pencharz P, et al: Glucose oxidation rates in newborn infants measured with indirect calorimetry and U-^{13}C-glucose. *Clin Sci* 1986; 70:587–593.

160. Sauve R, Singhal N: Long-term morbidity of infants with bronchopulmonary dysplasia. *Pediatrics* 1985; 76:725–733.

161. Sell E, Vaucher Y: Growth and neurodevelopmental outcome of infants who had bronchopulmonary dysplasia, in Merritt T, Northway W, Boynton B (eds): *Bronchopulmonary Dysplasia.* Boston, Blackwell Scientific Publications, 1988; pp 403–420.

162. Shenai J, Chytil F, Stahlman M: Vitamin A status of neonates with bronchopulmonary dysplasia. *Pediatr Res* 1985; 19:185–189.

163. Shenai J, Kennedy K, Chytil F, et al: Clinical trial of vitamin A supplementation in infants susceptible to bronchopulmonary dysplasia. *J Pediatr* 1987; 111:269–277.

164. Skeie B, Askanazi J, Rothkopf M, et al: Intravenous fat emulsions and lung emulsions: A review. *Crit Care Med* 1988; 16:183–194.

165. Sobonya R, Logvinoff M, Taussig L, et al: Morphometric analysis of the lung in prolonged bronchopulmonary dysplasia. *Pediatr Res* 1983; 16:969–972.

166. Sosenko I, Innis S, Frank L: Polyunsaturated fatty acids and protection of newborn rats from oxygen toxicity. *J Pediatr* 1988; 112:630–637.

167. Stahlman M, Gray M, Chytil F, et al: Effects of retinol on fetal lamb tracheal epithelium, with and without epidermal growth factor: A model for the effect of retinol on the healing lung of human premature infants. *Lab Invest* 1988; 59:25–35.

168. Stein J, Fenigstein H: Anatomie pathologigue de la maladie de famine, in Apfelbaum E (ed): *Maladie de Famine*. American Joint Distribution Committee, 1946, pp 21–27.

169. Stiehm E: Humoral immunity in malnutrition. *Fed Proc* 1980; 39:3093–3097.

170. Stocks J: Effect of nasogastric tubes on nasal resistance during infancy. *Arch Dis Child* 1980; 55:17–21.

171. Sullivan J: Iron, plasma antioxidants, and the oxygen radical disease of prematurity. *Am J Dis Child* 1988; 142:1341–1344.

172. Swyer P: Nutrition, growth and metabolism in the newborn, in Prakash O (ed): *Critical Care of the Child*. Boston, Martinus Nijhoff, 1984, pp 1–27.

173. Swyer P, Heim T: Nutrition in the high-risk newborn, in Fanaroff A, Martin R (eds): *Neonatal-Perinatal Medicine*. St Louis, CV Mosby Co, 1987, pp 445–459.

174. Tague W, Ray U, Braun D, et al: Lung vascular effects of lipid infusion in awake lambs. *Pediatr Res* 1987; 22:714–719.

175. Takala J, Askanazi J, Weissman C, et al: Changes in respiratory control induced by amino acids infusions. *Crit Care Med* 1988; 16:465–469.

176. Thiebaud D, Acheson K, Schutz Y, et al: Stimulation of thermogenesis in man after combined glucose–long-chain-triglyceride infusion. *Am J Clin Nutr* 1983; 37:603–611.

177. Van Aerde J, Sauer P, Heim T, et al: Effect of increasing glucose loads on respiratory gaseous exchange in the newborn infant. *Pediatr Res* 1986; 20:420A.

178. Van Aerde J, Sauer P, Heim T, et al: Is bountiful nutrient intake beneficial for the orally fed very low birth weight infant? *Pediatr Res* 1988; 23:427A.

179. Van Aerde J, Sauer P, Pencharz P, et al: Glucose and fat requirements in the intravenously fed newborn infant, in Stern L, Friis-Hansen B, Orzalesi M (eds): *Physiologic Foundations of Perinatal Care*, vol 3. New York, Elsevier Scientific Publishing Co., 1989, pp 60–74.

180. Van Aerde J, Sauer P, Pencharz P, et al: The effect of replacing glucose with lipid on the energy metabolism of newborn infants. *Clin Sci* 1989; 76:581–588.

181. Van Golde L, Batenburg J, Robertson B: The pulmonary surfactant system: Biochemical aspects and functional significance. *Physiol Rev* 1988; 68:374–455.

182. Vohr B, Bell E, Oh W: Infants with bronchopulmonary dysplasia. Growth pattern and neurologic and developmental outcome. *Am J Dis Child* 1982; 136:443–447.

183. Ward J, Roberts R: Vitamin E inhibition of the effects of hyperoxia on the pulmonary surfactant system of the newborn rabbit. *Pediatr Res* 1984; 18:329–334.

184. Weinstein M, Oh W: Oxygen consumption in infants with bronchopulmonary dysplasia. *J Pediatr* 1981; 99:958–961.

185. Weinstein M, Haugen K, Bauer J, et al: Intravenous energy and amino acids in the preterm newborn infant: Effects on metabolic rate and potential mechanisms of action. *J Pediatr* 1987; 111:119–123.

186. Weissman C, Askanazi J, Rosenbaum S, et al: Amino acids and respiration. *Ann Intern Med* 1983; 98:41–44.

187. Wender D, Thulin G, Walker Smith G, et al: Vitamin E affects lung biochemical and morphologic response to hyperoxia in the newborn rabbit. *Pediatr Res* 1981; 15:262–268.

188. Whyte R, Sinclair J: Discussion on nutritional management of infants with bronchopulmonary dysplasia (Oh W), in *Bronchopulmonary Dysplasia and Related Chronic Respiratory Disorders*. Report of the 90th Ross Conference on Pediatric Research. Columbus, Ohio, Ross Laboratories, 1986, pp 96–104.

189. Widdowson E, McCance R: A review: New thoughts on growth. *Pediatr Res* 1975; 9:154–156.

190. Wilkinson A, Yu V: Intermediate effects of feeding on blood gases and some cardiorespiratory functions in ill newborn infants. *Lancet* 1974; 6:1083–1085.

191. Winick M, Noble A: Cellular response in rats during malnutrition at various ages. *J Nutr* 1966; 89:300–306.

192. Winick M, Rosso P: Head circumference and cellular growth of the brain in normal and marasmic children. *J Pediatr* 1969; 74:774–778.

193. Wispe J, Roberts R: Development of antioxidant systems, in Merritt TA, Northway WH, Boynton BR (eds): *Bronchopulmonary Dysplasia*. Boston, Blackwell Scientific Publications, 1988, pp 103–116.

194. Witting L: Vitamin E and lipid antioxidants in free-radical-initiated reactions, in Pryor WA (ed): *Free Radicals in Biology,* vol 4. New York, Academic Press, 1980, pp 295–319.

195. Yeh T, McClenan D, Ajayi O, et al:. Metabolic rate and energy balance in infants with bronchopulmonary dysplasia. *J Pediatr* 1989; 114:448–451.

196. Yu V, Orgill A, Lim S, et al: Growth and development of very low birth weight infants recovering from bronchopulmonary dysplasia. *Arch Dis Child* 1983; 58:791–794.

197. Zlotkin S, Bryan M, Anderson G: Intravenous nitrogen and energy intakes required to duplicate in utero nitrogen accretion in prematurely born human infants. *J Pediatr* 1981; 99:115–120.

198. Zlotkin S: Protein-energy interactions in humans, in Fomon S, Heird W (eds): *Energy and Protein Needs During Infancy*. Orlando, Fla, Academic Press, 1986, pp 157–174.

199. Zwillich C, Sahn S, Weil J: Effects of hypermetabolism on ventilation and chemosensitivity. *J Clin Invest* 1977; 60:900–906.

Chapter 22

Nutrition Therapies for Inborn Errors of Metabolism

Steven Yannicelli, M.M.Sc., R.D.

Carol L. Greene, M.D.

Inborn errors of metabolism are individually rare but collectively important in the neonate. They cause significant morbidity and mortality that can in some cases be ameliorated or prevented by nutritional treatment. In addition, inborn errors are "experiments of nature" that provide clues to human biochemistry and nutritional requirements. An increasingly large number of inborn errors of metabolism are being described, many of which present or can be identified in the newborn period.

Premature infants have no less risk of inborn errors of metabolism than full-term neonates. However, inborn errors may be less frequently suspected in the premature infant because symptoms may resemble more common problems expected in those patients. In addition, diagnostic tests in the premature infant may be altered by common treatments. For example, whole blood transfusions can give false negative results on newborn screening for galactosemia. Premature infants are actually at higher risk for transient forms of some inborn errors for which a critical enzyme shows maturation in the perinatal period.

Garrod's discovery of alcaptonuria in 1908[1] was the first description of an inborn error of metabolism. Discovery of phenylketonuria (PKU) by Fölling in 1934[2] identified a significant population in whom risk of mental retardation could be predicted by neonatal biochemical tests. Development in technology has lead to the description of numerous inborn errors of metabolism. For each disorder, identification of specific abnormal metabolites leads to understanding the unique biochemistry of the disorder and is the key to developing approaches to management.

Nutrition has played an important role in the development of strategies for management of the inborn errors of metabolism. The benefit of a phenylalanine-restricted diet for PKU was described by Bickel and associates in 1953,[3] after it was shown that modification of dietary intake could alter the biochemical imbalances of the patient. Studies have since revealed that diet therapy can result in normal intellectual development in patients with classic PKU.

The nutrition management of inborn errors has contributed to our knowledge of the requirements for various essential amino acids, fats, carbohydrates, vitamins, and minerals in healthy infants as well as infants with metabolic disorders. The first special dietary formulations for inborn errors of metabolism (e.g., PKU) were made from casein hydrolysates or free amino acids. It was not until several years later that commercially prepared special metabolic formulas were available for widespread use. Currently, a wide variety of commercial metabolic formulas are available for treatment of various inborn errors, and are used in combination with other nutritional and medical therapies to treat patients with these disorders.

The focus of this chapter is limited solely to inborn errors of metabolism that can be diagnosed in the newborn period, and for which efficacy of nutritional management in that period has been demonstrated. A variety of inherited enzymatic defects that may respond to specific nutritional therapies are shown in Table 22–1. It is not in the scope of this chapter to discuss diagnostic approaches or criteria for these disorders. It should be pointed out that treatment of these disorders (which may present with nonspecific symptoms) can be successful only if an inborn error of metabolism is suspected and identified by appropriate biochemical studies. With identification and appropriate treatment, neonates with the inborn errors of metabolism considered in this chapter can be expected to show improved, and sometimes normal, mental and physical development.

TABLE 22–1.

Nutrition Therapies in Selected Metabolic Disorders

Disorder	Nutrition Therapy†
Aminoacidopathies	
Phenylketonuria (classic)	Phenylalanine restriction
	Tyrosine supplementation
Hyperphenylalaninemia	Usually not indicated but may be same as phenylketonuria
Biopterin deficiency	Phenylalanine restriction
	Tetrahydrobiopterin and dopaminergic drugs
Tyrosinemia type I	Phenylalanine/tyrosine restriction
	Cysteine supplementation (?)
Neonatal tyrosinemia	Low-protein
	Ascorbic acid*
Tyrosinemia type II (Richner-Hanhart)	Phenylalanine/tyrosine restriction
Maple syrup urine disease (branched-chain ketoacidosis)	Branched-chain amino acid restriction
	Thiamine*
Valinemia	Valine restriction
Homocystinuria	Methionine restriction
	Cystine supplementation
	Betaine (?), folate (?)
	Pyridoxine*
Cystathioninuria	Pyridoxine
Methylmalonic acidemia/homocystinuria complex	None; a low protein diet with methionine supplementation may be indicated; hydroxycobalamin,* betaine
Organic acidemias	
Isovaleric acidemia	Leucine restriction and/or low protein diet
	Carnitine and glycine supplementation
Methylmalonic acidemia	Propiogenic amino acid restriction
	Hydroxycobalamin,* L-alanine supplementation (?), carnitine
Propionic acidemia	Propiogenic amino acid restriction
	Biotin,* L-alanine supplementation (?), carnitine
Pyruvate carboxylase deficiency	High fat, low carbohydrate
	Modified ketogenic diet, biotin*
Pyruvate dehydrogenase deficiency	Same as above, thiamine,* biotin,* lipoic acid*
Glutaric acidemia type 1	Lysine and tryptophan restriction

	Riboflavin,* carnitine
Glutaric acidemia type 2	Dietary restriction not indicated
	Riboflavin*
Alcaptonuria	Phenylalanine/tyrosine restricted diet (?), ascorbic acid (?)
Histidemia	Histidine restriction (?), low protein
Urea cycle disorders	
	Low protein diet with essential amino acids
	Arginine supplementation EXCEPT in Argininemia
Carbohydrate disorders	
Galactosemia (classic)	Galactose-free
Galactosemia (Duarte)	Galactose-free diet indicated for first year of life
Galactokinase deficiency	Galactose-free
Hereditary fructose intolerance	Fructose-free, sorbitol-free
Glycogen storage diseases	
Type I (glucose-6-phosphatase deficiency)	Galactose/fructose-free, low fat, moderate protein
	Frequent feedings, noctural drip
Type III (amylo-1,6-glucosidase deficiency)	Same as Type I except high protein included
Type IV (phosphorylase deficiency)	Frequent feedings
Type VIII (phosphorylase kinase deficiency)	Frequent feedings, high protein
Lipid disorders	
Medium-chain acyl-CoA Dehydrogenase deficiency	Frequent feedings, low fat, carnitine supplementation
Abetalipoproteinemia	Restriction of long-chain fatty acids, Fat-soluble vitamins A, E, and K, folate and iron Supplementation
Peroxisomal disorders	
Adrenoleukodystrophy	Low fat diet Supplementation with monosaturated fatty acids (erucic and oleic)

*These products are prescribed in pharmacologic doses to patients who are considered clinically responsive to cofactor therapy. Those patients that are clinically responsive may not require other nutritional therapies.
†Diet therapies denoted by a (?) indicate therapies that are investigative and/or questionable in regards to their effectiveness.

PHYSIOLOGY, PATHOPHYSIOLOGY, DEVELOPMENT, AND DISEASE

General principles of metabolism are illustrated in Figure 22–1. All metabolism is mediated by enzymes coded for by genes. Some enzymes function independently, while some require a cofactor or a coenzyme, which may itself be synthesized or recycled by enzyme-mediated steps. Some biochemical pathways are necessary for every cell and are therefore present in all tissues, while some reactions are organ- or tissue-specific. These variations of enzyme activity in tissues of the healthy individual must be the result of timed tissue-specific development. Only a few maturational defects of metabolic paths have been suspected or demonstrated to cause human disease (e.g. transient hyperammonemia of the neonate, neonatal tyrosinemia). Most inborn errors of metabolism are single gene defects, usually autosomal recessive but occasionally X-linked, dominant, or mitochondrially inherited.

There is a wide range of expression of each inborn error of metabolism. Phenotypic variation is most marked between families, but there may be significant variation between siblings and within a single patient over time. Variation of the defective enzyme activity between families and variation within families in the activity of other relevant pathways of metabolism alter the tolerance of and requirements for nutrients. Clinical

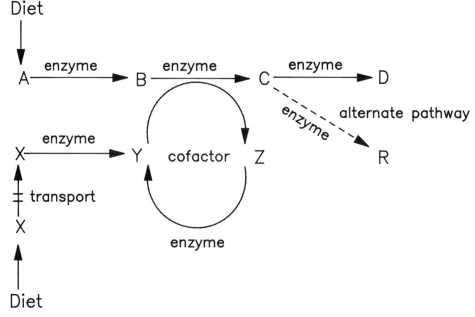

FIG 22–1.
General principles of metabolism. Virtually all reactions are controlled by enzymes coded for by genes. Any compound can have more than one metabolic fate or origin, and some reactions may proceed in either direction depending on biochemical conditions. A transport system, enzyme, or cofactor may serve a single metabolic pathway or may be important for several. Any step that requires mediation of an enzyme is at risk for genetic error. A metabolic block may cause a decrease in levels of compounds after the block unless there is an alternative mechanism by which to produce the compound. Similarly, there is accumulation of compounds before a block depending on availability of other pathways of disposal or alternative metabolism of the compound.

variation is also due to different requirements for energy and for cell growth between individuals and over time. These variations, along with differences in feeding practices govern timing and severity of presentation of each disorder. There is little information for each disorder about the special issues in the premature infant.

The clinical symptoms of each inborn error of metabolism must result from the abnormal metabolism. Usually, clinical expression can be related to elevated or depressed concentrations of some measurable metabolite, but in many cases the exact pathophysiology remains a mystery. For most disorders there are short-term reversible effects and long-term irreversible damage in the untreated patient. Either deficiency or excess of a specific metabolite may directly or indirectly have an effect on the infant. "Direct effects" are usually well understood but may be only a part of the pathophysiology of a disorder. An example of direct action is the formation of cataracts by galactitol accumulation in the lens of patients with galactosemia. In galactokinase deficiency, one form of galactosemia, the accumulation of galactitol explains all the clinical manifestations of the disorder. In classic galactosemia, which is due to galactose-1-phosphate uridyl transferase deficiency, the accumulation of galactitol also causes cataracts. However, these patients also have liver, kidney, and brain injury related to blood levels of galactose-1-phosphate levels. The manner in which galactose-1-phosphate causes this multiorgan injury is unclear.

In some diseases, secondary biochemical alterations occur. An example of this is in methylmalonic acidemia, in which some patients have hyperammonemia presumably due to interference with the urea cycle resulting from metabolites of methylmalonic acid. Secondary deficiencies can also be found in some inborn errors. For example, secondary carnitine deficiencies have been identified in patients with organic acidemias, possibly resulting from the increased excretion of acylcarnitine esters.

Finally, many nutrients require enzyme-mediated transport across membranes to reach target organs, or for absorption and excretion. In many cases transport systems are shared and alterations in ratios of metabolites may be muted or magnified by transport competition between metabolites. An example of this is the shared transport of phenylalanine and branched-chain amino acids into nerve cells, which has led to the suggestion that high levels of phenylalanine may cause a clinically important intracellular defect of branched-chain amino acids. Transport systems or other enzymes may be further modified by other physiologic systems, such as the induction of specific amino acid transport by insulin. The interdependence and interconnectedness of the biochemical pathways makes it unlikely that simple explanations such as the effect of one biochemical pathway on one physiologic or developmental system will account for the expression of an inborn error of metabolism.

PRINCIPLES OF NUTRITION SUPPORT

The basic principle in the management of inborn errors of metabolism is to manipulate the biochemistry so that the metabolite(s) is as normal as possible in the tissue where the defect has its pathophysiologic effect(s). The goals for nutrition support are:

1. To provide all essential nutrients in quantities adequate to promote optimal physical and mental development.
2. To supply the optimal amount of any nutrient that is restricted or supplemented, in order to promote growth while preventing or correcting metabolic imbalances.

For each disease, management depends on the specific biochemistry and pathophysiology of the disease. The main strategies of nutrition support are:

1. Dietary restriction of any compound or precursors of metabolites that accumulate as a result of the enzyme block.
2. Replenishing any deficient end product distal to the enzyme block.
3. Supplementing compounds that may combine with a toxic metabolite to promote its excretion or its safe metabolism.
4. Providing cofactor in therapeutic dose, if cofactor is deficient or if the enzyme can be activated by cofactor excess.

The use of nutrition support to treat inborn errors of metabolism has helped to clarify specific nutrient requirements in the healthy infant. When a specific nutrient (e.g., phenylalanine in PKU) has been overrestricted, failure to thrive and protein malnutrition has resulted.

Substrate restriction in the treatment of inborn errors of metabolism can be very specific (a single amino acid, sugar, or fatty acid) or general (total protein, total carbohydrate, or total fat). When one specific nutrient is being restricted, it may be difficult to insure adequate intake of other related nutrients. It is the challenge to the clinician to insure optimal nutrition despite the restrictions of one or many nutrients.

Nutritional management of amino acid disorders requires the use of synthetic formulas that have been created based on a knowledge of nutrition requirements in the healthy infant. Some of the variety of special metabolic formulas now available in the United States can be seen in the Appendix. Special diets for amino acid disorders are designed individually using combinations of special metabolic formulas and natural protein sources from standard infant formulas, evaporated milk, human milk, or foods.

Each diet prescription is calculated to provide specific amounts of protein, energy, fluid, and the specific nutrients that must be restricted and or supplemented. Depending on the disorder, a prescription may require a restriction in the amount or type of carbohydrates, proteins, fat or of specific amino acids. In some instances, the diet regimen may also specify avoidance of fasting, as many metabolic disorders worsen acutely in catabolism. Guidelines for calculating specific nutrient needs for amino acid disorders are found in Table 22–2. Computer software programs are currently available for calculating nutrient needs for a variety of amino acid disorders. These programs are useful because of the individuality of each diet prescription.[4, 5]

Diet prescriptions should be evaluated for vitamin and mineral adequacy. Research has shown that trace mineral status of children treated with special metabolic formulas may be compromised.[6] The reliance on chemically defined metabolic formulas used in

TABLE 22–2.

Recommended Nutrient Intakes for Inborn Errors of Amino Acid Metabolism Which Require Specific Amino Acid Restrictions

Nutrient	Unit	Age			
		0 < 3 mo	3 < 6 mo	6 < 9 mo	9 < 12 mo
Energy	kcal/kg	145–100	130–95	130–90	120–85
Fluid	ml/kg	150–125	140–115	125–110	120–100
Protein (total)	g/kg	2.5	2.5	2.2	2.0
Carbohydrate	% total energy	← - - - - - - - - - - - - - - - - - 50–35 - - - - - - - - - - - - - - - - - →			
Fat	% total energy	← - - - - - - - - - - - - - - - - - 50–40 - - - - - - - - - - - - - - - - - →			
Isoleucine[1, 2]	mg/kg	120–30	100–30	80–30	80–30
Leucine[1, 3]	mg/kg	110–60	100–40	80–40	70–40
Valine[1, 2]	mg/kg	105–40	80–40	80–35	75–30
Phenylalanine[4]	mg/kg	70–40	50–25	40–25	35–20
Methionine[2, 5, 8]	mg/kg	60–20	50–20	40–15	40–15
Lysine[6]	mg/kg	150–90	120–85	120–85	115–80
Tryptophan[6]	mg/kg	40–15	30–11	30–11	30–11
Histidine[7]	mg/kg	35–20	35–10	35–10	30–10
Threonine[2]	mg/kg	90–45	90–40	75–40	55–45
Tyrosine[8]	mg/kg	95–55	85–45	75–35	70–30

*Protein amounts are total amounts and do not reflect amounts of natural or whole protein as a percentage of the total protein. In addition, the values for protein do not apply to disorders where total protein must be restricted, i.e., urea cycle disorders. Further information on protein restrictions are mentioned in the text for each disorder.
[1]Maple syrup urine disease.
[2]Methylmalonic and propionic acidemia.
[3]Isovaleric acidemia.
[6]Glutaric acidemia Type 1.
[7]Histidinemia.
[8]Tyrosinemia.

amino acid disorders can affect the bioavailability of several trace elements, including copper, zinc, and iron. A number of the special metabolic formulas are without certain recognized essential nutrients, such as selenium, molybdenum, chromium, taurine, and carnitine. Periodic assessment of trace mineral status needs to be considered.

The special metabolic formulas are specific for each disorder and provide essential and nonessential amino acids, vitamins, minerals, and energy. Some formulas provide no fat or linoleic acid, and therefore less energy than others (see the Appendix Tables 22A–1 to 22A–6). Metabolic formulas are usually necessary to meet long-term protein requirements whenever specific amino acid(s) must be restricted. A "low-protein" diet alone using only standard infant formula to adequately restrict one or more specific amino acids will usually overrestrict other essential amino acids. The total protein recommendations for many amino acid disorders are higher than the Recommended Dietary Allowances (RDA) when the majority of protein is supplied by synthetic amino acids.

If the special metabolic formula chosen has a low energy:protein ratio, supplementation with a protein-free energy module is indicated. Protein-Free Diet Powder, Product 80056 (Mead Johnson Nutritionals), which contains needed vitamins and minerals in addition to fat and carbohydrates, is preferable to using separate fat and carbohydrate sources for energy.

Many of the special metabolic formulas used to treat amino acid disorders are potentially hyperosmolar. Presence or absence of a fat source and the nature of the carbohydrates in the formula will affect osmolality. Hyperosmolar feedings may result in vomiting, diarrhea, and dehydration, which can trigger a catabolic crisis. If additional energy modules are indicated in the formulation it may be preferable to use a fat source and or glucose polymers as carbohydrate to keep osmolality within acceptable limits. Osmolality of formula should be analyzed when calculations suggest hyperosmolality.

Because of the heterogeneity found in most inborn errors of metabolism, the nutrition support must be individualized and constantly reevaluated according to the patient's clinical assessment and biochemical parameters. The dietary prescription must allow for age-related biochemical parameters, growth acceleration, and level of stress in acute situations. The metabolic status of the infant will also determine the energy, protein, and fluid requirements. Frequent dietary changes in infancy are usually necessary to meet the demands of the rapidly developing infant. Management for all disorders includes anthropometrics and visceral protein status. Other biochemical parameters measured are specific to each disorder. For a number of disorders, assessment of plasma concentrations of carnitine should be performed, and levels of any cofactor that is supplemented should be monitored.

It is now recognized that infants diagnosed with inborn errors of metabolism require lifelong nutrition therapy. Providing optimal nutrients during infancy may set precedents for future potential in regard to both mental and physical development and growth.

Counseling and education of the family are a part of the dietary management of inborn errors. The success of the diet regimen requires cooperation between the clinicians and family. The clinicians must provide accurate instructions on all aspects of the diet including formula preparation and diet record keeping. Continued support, education, and encouragement increases the compliance with the diet.

In this chapter, discussion of management for each disorder is generally restricted to the newborn period, but principles of chronic management are described, as these are important issues for the counseling of the family. Also, we restrict discussion to nutritional management generally, assuming that basic principles of medical management of vascular access, fluids, resuscitation, and so forth are applied. These issues are addressed only for disorders in which special problems related to the nutritional management of the disorder are expected.

AMINOACIDOPATHIES

Phenylketonuria

Classic PKU, an autosomal recessive disease, was first described by Fölling in 1934.[2] It occurs in 1 of every 12,000 Caucasians and if untreated causes severe retardation and seizures in most affected individuals. The defect in PKU (Fig 22–2) causes failure to metabolize phenylalanine, an essential amino acid, to tyrosine. This enzymatic pathway is the major fate of phenylalanine, and defects cause significant elevation of phenylalanine and of metabolites of phenylalanine. Tyrosine becomes an essential amino acid in infants with PKU. The cause of mental retardation in PKU is not completely understood but clearly correlates with the blood level of phenylalanine and is characterized by abnormal myelination. Alteration of levels of biogenic amines, for which tyrosine is a precursor, are demonstrable in patients with hyperphenylalaninemia.

The percentage of dietary phenylalanine that is hydroxylated to tyrosine is dependent on person's age and rate of growth. In the rapidly growing infant approximately 50% to 60% of the phenylalanine is used for protein synthesis, compared to 10% in the normal adult.

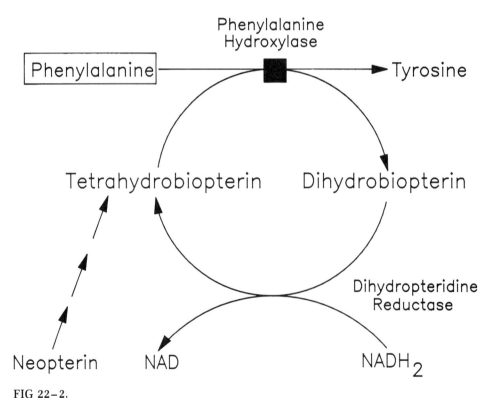

FIG 22–2.
Phenylalanine metabolism. Tetrahydrobiopterin, synthesized from neopterin by a series of reactions, is the cofactor for phenylalanine hydroxylase. The tetrahydrobiopterin is oxidized to dihydrobiopterin in the reaction and is recycled by dihydropteridine reductase.

Classic PKU is generally diagnosed by newborn screening programs. Milder forms of phenylalanine hydroxylase deficiency are also detected with frequency similar to classic PKU, and there is apparently a transient form of enzyme deficiency probably due to a maturational defect. Hyperphenylalaninemia may also be due to defects in the synthesis of tetrahydrobiopterin, a coenzyme in the phenylalanine hydroxylase enzyme system. These disorders must be rapidly distinguished from classic PKU in the newborn period, as their management and outcome are quite different. Mild and transient hyperphenylalaninemia usually do not require treatment, and dietary restriction of phenylalanine in these individuals may be harmful to growth and development. Patients with cofactor defects will show a response of blood phenylalanine levels to dietary phenylalanine restriction, but retardation will not be prevented. Finally, offspring of mothers with PKU may present with a high phenylalanine on newborn screening if the screen is done earlier than recommended. These babies do not require dietary treatment. Overall, the most common error in nutritional management of PKU is probably the inappropriate institution of diet in a baby who does not require restriction.

Therapy

Nutritional therapy begun in the 1st month of life, with blood phenylalanine levels maintained between 125 and 480 μmol/L, has resulted in normal mental and physical development for a majority of patients. It was previously believed that the phenylalanine-restricted diet could be discontinued in childhood, but results from the National PKU Collaborative Study[7] and the problems associated with maternal PKU syndrome[8] now support lifelong continuation of diet.

The components of a phenylalanine-restricted diet prescription include phenylalanine, tyrosine, protein, and energy (see Table 22–2). The phenylalanine requirement must be individualized and is determined by age, growth acceleration, and the presence of any residual enzyme activity. Tyrosine supplementation may be necessary if blood tyrosine concentrations remain less than 44 μmol/L.

The basis for nutrition support of PKU is the use of low-phenylalanine or phenylalanine-free special metabolic formulas (see Appendix, Table 22A–1). Lofenalac was one of the first commercially available special formulas used for the treatment of PKU. Throughout infancy these special formulas supply approximately 80% of the total protein requirement and are used in conjunction with standard cow's milk infant formulas, human milk, or evaporated milk to meet the infant's requirements for phenylalanine and tyrosine. As the infant grows, natural foods are introduced into the dietary regimen. With time, the entire phenylalanine requirement will be supplied by natural foods. The PKU diet has been falsely labeled as a low-protein diet. Because the majority of the protein consumed by the infant with PKU comes from either a casein hydrolysate or free amino acid source, the diet prescription is calculated to supply a total protein intake greater than the recommended intakes for healthy infants.

Alternative methods for treating PKU have been attempted with limited success. Supplementation of branched-chain amino acids in patients with PKU resulted in decreased concentrations of phenylalanine in cerebrospinal fluid. The branched-chain amino acids may compete with phenylalanine at the blood-brain barrier since they follow similar transport systems. This approach has had limited success and should not replace the phenylalanine-restricted diet.

Blood phenylalanine concentrations should be obtained at least weekly in infancy, and tyrosine concentrations are required periodically. Trace mineral status, including iron indices, should be monitored.

Causes of hyperphenylalaninemia in the treated infant with PKU include illness leading to catabolism, improper dietary prescription, inaccurate measurement of formula/food components, or decreased formula/food consumption. The clinician must be aware of hidden sources of phenylalanine, such as Nutrasweet, which may be found in cough medicines.

Hereditary Tyrosinemias

Type I

Type I tyrosinemia, an autosomal recessive disorder, is a defect in the metabolism of tyrosine, due to a defect in the enzyme fumarylacetoacetic acid hydrolase or in some patients of maleylacetoacetic acid isomerase (Fig 22–3). Tyrosine and methionine are elevated in blood, and the elevated tyrosine correlates with the symptoms. The acute form of the disease expresses itself in the neonatal period with findings of failure to thrive, vomiting, renal tubular dysfunction, jaundice, and hepatosplenomegaly. Death usually occurs in the neonatal period, but the course may be more chronic.

Therapy.—The goal of therapy is to prevent, delay, or ameliorate the liver and kidney damage, growth failure, mental retardation, and death. A restricted phenylalanine, tyrosine, and methionine diet may decrease the formation of toxic metabolites, but the actual benefit of the diet is not well established. Dietary therapy may better prepare the infant for liver transplantation. Nutrition therapy definitely decreases plasma concentra-

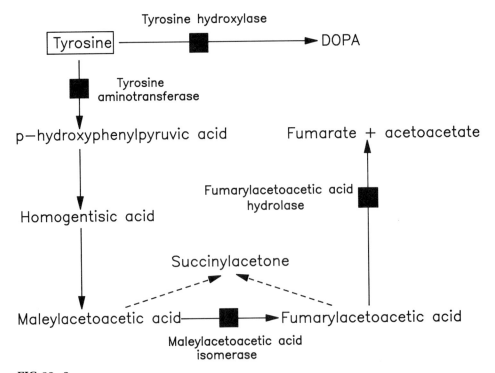

FIG 22–3.
Tyrosine metabolism. The enzymes illustrated lead to primary disorders of tyrosine metabolism. Succinylacetone *(broken line)* is a result of an alternate pathway of metabolism in the neonatal form of tyrosinemia with liver disease.

tions of tyrosine, but this alone may not affect renal dysfunction.[9] Since elevations of plasma methionine apparently reflect the extent of liver insult rather than dietary intake of methionine, plasma methionine should not be aggressively regulated by dietary restriction. Little data are available from which to develop specific recommendations, but a safe guideline may be to use the upper limit of recommendations for methionine found in Table 22–2. Plasma phenylalanine and tyrosine concentrations are well correlated with dietary intake. Overrestriction of phenylalanine and tyrosine will lead to a phenylalanine-tyrosine deficiency syndrome, which has been found in the management of this disease.[10] Requirements for phenylalanine may be higher than that in patients with PKU, most likely because that the enzyme defect is further down the metabolic pathway of phenylalanine. The amounts of nutrients required are determined by the patient's tolerance of these amino acids as monitored by plasma amino acid profiles.

Energy intakes should be high to prevent failure to thrive. Where growth delay has already occurred, catch-up growth can be achieved only by provision of the maximum calories tolerated by the infant. A standard rule of thumb is to provide up to 150% of calories based on ideal body weight for height, when height is calculated as being at the 50th percentile for chronological age.

Special metabolic formulas free of phenylalanine, tyrosine, and in some formulas methionine, are an essential component to nutrition support (see Appendix, Table 22A–2). Evaporated milk or standard infant formulas supply the prescribed amounts of amino acids and additional nutrients necessary for growth. Additional protein-free energy supplements may be needed. Some researchers have recommended that high-carbohydrate feedings—up to 75% of total energy—should be given.[11] In at least one patient with hereditary tyrosinemia, L-cysteine supplementation was found beneficial.[12] L-cysteine may be essential if methionine is restricted.

Neonatal Tyrosinemia

Neonatal tyrosinemia is a transient disorder caused by immaturity of *p*-hydroxyphenylpyruvate oxidase and is more frequent in premature infants. The patients are asymptomatic and are usually identified through state newborn screening programs. The outcome of neonatal tyrosinemia is variable. Although it is considered a benign disorder, mental retardation has been associated with persistent hypertyrosinemia in some patients.

Incidence of transient tyrosinemia varies in neonates of various population groups, apparently according to infant feeding practices. The decreased incidence of this disease in infants weighing over 2,500 grams in Scandinavian countries has been attributed to the increase in breast-feeding and use of lower protein cow's-milk infant formula.[12a]

Protein restriction to 1.5 to 2.0 g/kg/day can reduce plasma tyrosine levels. This can be achieved in part by changing from higher protein infant formulas such as soy-protein–based infant formulas to standard cow's-milk formula or human milk. Therapeutic dosages of ascorbic acid, 400 mg daily, has had some limited success in treating this disorder. Ascorbic acid supplementation may help accelerate maturation of the enzyme *p*-hydroxyphenylpyruvate oxidase.

Tyrosinemia Type II

Unlike other tyrosinemias, type II tyrosinemia (Richner-Hanhart syndrome) is a chronic disorder. It results from a defect in hepatic cystosol tyrosine aminotransferase, the rate-limiting enzyme in tyrosine metabolism (see Fig 22–3). The clinical findings are highly correlated with plasma tyrosine levels and include hyperkeratotic skin lesions

on the palms and soles, and ocular lesions. While more than 50% of patients are severely retarded, mental status varies from normal to severe retardation and is not
strongly correlated with age of diagnosis. The age of presentation may vary from infancy up to adulthood. This disease is particularly frequent in persons of Italian origin.

Therapy.—The goal of nutrition therapy is the amelioration of hyperkeratotic skin
lesions through reduction of dietary tyrosine and phenylalanine. Information on early
treatment in infants is limited, but patients treated early with a tyrosine/phenylalanine
restricted diet have shown normal psychomotor development.[13, 14]

The degree of tyrosine/phenylalanine restriction (see Table 22–2) will vary depending on individual tolerance as demonstrated by monitoring of plasma levels. In the infant it is beneficial to monitor tyrosine/phenylalanine concentrations at least weekly
throughout the 1st year of life. Plasma tyrosine concentrations ranging from 607 to 994
μmol/L can reduce the clinical signs and symptoms associated with this disorder. Untreated levels may be greater than 3,313 μmol/L; a normal level is less than
221 μmol/L.

Maple Syrup Urine Disease (Branched-Chain Ketoaciduria)

Maple syrup urine disease (MSUD) is an autosomal recessive disorder of the metabolism of the branched-chain amino acids leucine, isoleucine, and valine (Fig 22–4). Elevations in plasma and branched-chain ketoacids, and the presence of alloisoleucine,
correlate with clinical symptoms.

Classic MSUD presents in neonates who at first appear normal but within several
days develop lethargy, failure to thrive, poor suck and feeding, vomiting, and ketoacidosis. The urine may smell like maple syrup. Variant forms of the disease exist, with
milder clinical features. Some mild variants have symptoms only after febrile illness,
infections, or a protein load. Early diagnosis and treatment can prevent death, severe
mental retardation, and neurologic deficits. Despite early treatment and diagnosis, some
patients still present with compromised mental status.[15]

Another variant of MSUD is the thiamine-responsive type, first described by Scriver
et al. in 1971[16] in an infant with MSUD who responded to therapeutic dosages of thiamine (10 mg/day). Other researchers have since identified similar patients who have improved biochemical parameters with varying dosages of thiamine, up to 1,000 mg/day.
The effects of pharmacologic dosages of thiamine may not be expressed for several
weeks.[17]

Therapy

The neonate with classic MSUD must be treated aggressively. The acutely ill infant
frequently requires withdrawal from formula and may require dialysis if the acidosis is
severe. Prevention or inhibition of catabolism is essential. If the oral route is not possible, then parenteral nutrition utilizing glucose and lipids is indicated. Only recently have
amino acid solutions free of branched-chain amino acids been available for use in total
parenteral nutrition.

Once formula is tolerated, a total restriction of branched-chain amino acids may still
be necessary for a rapid reduction of their levels in plasma. This can be accomplished
by the use of branched-chain amino acid–free special metabolic formulas (see Appendix, Table 22A–3) alone to provide the recommended amounts of protein (see Table
22–2). Higher total protein intakes may be required because of the source of protein

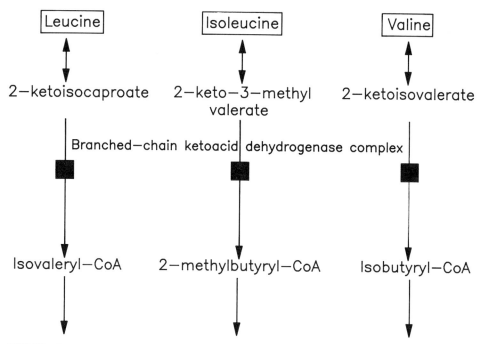

FIG 22−4.
Branched-chain amino acid metabolism. The branched-chain amino acids share a common enzyme for decarboxylation, and defects of that dehydrogenase complex cause maple syrup urine disease. Other steps not discussed here are specific to the pathways of one or two branched chain amino acids or their metabolites.

from these special formulas. Intakes of 2.5 to 3.0 g/kg/day of protein supplied by special metabolic formulas may be needed to inhibit catabolism in the infant recovering from an acute episode. Extra energy is also needed during recovery, and protein-free energy modules may be used to provide these calories.

The total restriction of branched-chain amino acids will require daily monitoring of plasma amino acid concentrations to prevent a prolonged overrestriction of these essential amino acids. After several days of treatment, blood concentrations of valine and isoleucine may be reduced to therapeutic range while leucine is still elevated. Supplemental L-isoleucine (Ile) and L-valine (val) may be required. It has been suggested that supplementation of L-Ile and L-val at 40 to 45 mg/kg without the addition of leucine will help normalize all three branched-chain amino acids within a few days.[18] Once the patient has been stabilized and the plasma concentrations of branched-chain amino acids are within the therapeutic range, natural protein sources such as human milk, evaporated milk, or standard infant formulas can be incorporated into the nutrition therapy.

Requirements for the branched-chain amino acids depends on age, growth velocity, state of health, and residual enzyme activity. Because most infants with classic MSUD have 0% to 2% of the enzyme activity, the restriction of branched-chain amino acids is usually significant (see Table 22−2). MSUD Diet Powder (see Appendix, Table 22A−3), a standard formulation used in infants with MSUD, has a high energy-to-protein ratio of 47:1, so that supplying the required amount of protein may result in a formula that is hyperosmolar. Therefore, MSUD Diet Powder is often combined with MSUD 1, a low energy:protein ratio formula. Analog MSUD has a more balanced energy to protein ratio (36:1) and may be used alone. (Components of these formulas are shown in the Appendix, Table 22A−3.)

In nature, leucine makes up a larger portion of all natural protein (8.5%) than valine and isoleucine. Tolerance to dietary leucine may significantly drop within the first 6 months of life. The dietary restriction of leucine necessary to obtain a therapeutic range may overrestrict valine and isoleucine. Supplementation of these two amino acids as a solution (10 mg/ml) may be necessary. An excess or deficiency of any of these amino acids will have clinical consequences.

Analysis of plasma branched-chain amino acids should be performed at least weekly for the 1st year of life. Families are instructed on home monitoring of urine for presence of keto acids using either 2,4-dinitrophenylhydrazine or ketone test strips to assess impending illness.

Nutrition therapy in thiamine nonresponsive classic MSUD is lifelong. During episodes of illness, additional nutrients and energy to inhibit or prevent catabolism and acidosis may be needed. With time, these patients may develop increased tolerance to episodes of illness, but any ketosis or illness that causes decreased nutrient and fluid intake must be treated aggressively.

Homocystinuria

Homocystinuria (HCU) may result from a variety of enzyme defects. The most common cause is a deficiency of cystathionine β-synthase (Fig 22–5) that results in the accumulation of methionine and homocystine with a concurrent depletion of cystine. Homocystine is also found in the urine of these patients. Because animals with high methionine levels are healthy, it is believed that homocystine and not methionine is the

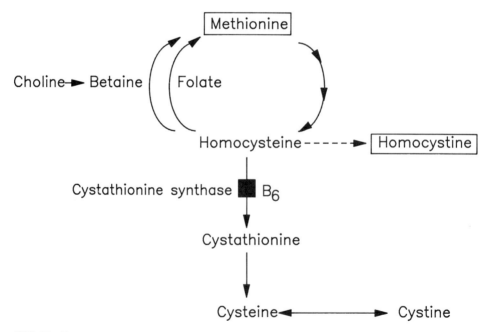

FIG 22–5.
Sulphur amino acid metabolism. Simple diagram of metabolic origin and fate of methionine from exogenous and endogenous protein. Formation of homocystine is represented by a *broken line* since it is not a normal pathway for homocysteine metabolism. Folate is required for metabolism of homocysteine to methionine, and pyridoxine is a required cofactor for action of cystathionine synthase. Betaine and choline favor conversion of homocysteine to methionine through remethylation.

major toxic compound in the pathophysiology of homocystinuria.[19] The presence of homocystine and low blood levels of methionine is also found in the disorder of methylmalonic acidemia/homocystinuria complex.[20, 21]

Screening tests which measure methionine in the blood of newborns lead to diagnosis of homocystinuria in 1 in 200,000 live births. The mode of inheritance is autosomal recessive. Untreated patients may clinically present with dislocated optic lenses, osteoporosis and thromboembolic events, and a limited life expectancy. Mentation is variable, with treated patients having less severe manifestations of the disorder.

Pyridoxine responsiveness is found in 12.7% to 36.7% of patients with homocystinuria.[22] Those responsive to pyridoxine are clinically healthier and tolerate more methionine than nonresponders.[23] Some completely responsive patients require no special diet. The majority of patients diagnosed by newborn screening are pyridoxine nonresponders.[22, 23]

Therapy

On diagnosis of homocystinuria the patient should be tried on therapeutic dosages of pyridoxine. Oral doses of pyridoxine ranging from 250 to 750 mg/day have resulted in decreases in plasma methionine concentrations and a significant reduction in plasma and urine homocystine. It may take from days to several weeks of pharmacologic doses before a biochemical response is noted. If the patient does not respond to a trial of pyridoxine, the pyridoxine should be discontinued because prolonged periods of high doses of pyridoxine may be harmful.[24] Total elimination of homocystine from plasma and urine should be attempted. Exogenous sources of methionine are restricted to maintain plasma methionine concentrations in the normal range of about 50 μmol/L.

In patients not responsive to pyridoxine, supplementation of L-cysteine is necessary because cysteine becomes an essential amino acid. The amount of supplementation is variable. Total cysteine intake should range from 200 to 300 mg/kg/day in infants up to 12 months of age. Actual cysteine supplementation will need to be adjusted to maintain normal plasma concentrations.

The dietary prescription for the infant with homocystinuria includes a methionine-free special metabolic formula and a prescribed amount of natural protein from either evaporated milk, standard infant formulas, or human milk to supply the requirements for methionine (see Table 22–2). Although breast-feeding of an infant being treated for homocystinuria has not been reported, it seems physiologically appropriate because human milk is low in methionine and has a unique 1:1 ratio of methionine to cystine. In contrast to human milk, some soy and hypoallergenic infant formulas contain more methionine than found even in standard cow's milk infant formulas. A change from soy formulas to other natural protein sources may assist in reducing plasma methionine.

Some special metabolic formulas used in the treatment of homocystinuria have a low ratio of energy to protein (see Appendix, Table 22A–4). Therefore, a protein-free energy module such as Protein-Free Diet Powder, Product 80056, is indicated. Methionine requirements in nature are small in comparison to other essential amino acids. This limits the amounts of foods available for consumption.

Weekly analysis of plasma concentrations are recommended for the infant up to 6 months of age. Biweekly assessment is recommended from 6 months to 1 year of age. Assessment of nutrition support should include protein, iron, and folate status. Because a large percentage of the protein is from synthetic amino acids, protein needs may be greater than the RDA. Folic acid is utilized in the remethylation of homocysteine to methionine, and has been used with limited success in the treatment of this disorder. Therefore, supplementation of folic acid may be helpful to some patients. Bougle et al.[25] stated that the low levels of molybdenum in preterm human milk may contribute to hypermethioninemia in the premature infant. As with other special formulas, trace minerals may be suboptimal, and periodic assessment of intake is warranted.

Betaine, and its precursor choline, have been used to reduce homocystine in patients with homocystinuria. These two methyl donors likely increase the remethylation of homocysteine to methionine and result in elevation of plasma methionine and a subsequent reduction of plasma homocystine. These drugs are still considered experimental in the treatment of cystathionine β-synthase deficiency.

ORGANIC ACIDEMIAS

Isovaleric Acidemia

Isovaleric acidemia, an autosomal recessive disorder, was the first organic acidemia to be described in humans, in 1966.[26] A defect in the metabolism of leucine (Fig 22–6) results in the accumulation of isovaleric acid (IVA) and isovalerylglycine. The presence of excess IVA is responsible for the distinctive "sweaty-feet odor" associated with this disease.

Isovaleric acidemia may be acute or chronic. Patients with acute isovaleric acidemia appear normal at birth but within several days develop vomiting, lethargy, and coma. If not aggressively treated, death occurs, either from severe infection, ketoacidosis, or hyperammonemia. If the patient survives this severe neonatal episode, the subsequent course is similar to that of patients with chronic intermittent isovaleric acidemia and is characterized by recurrent episodes of vomiting, acidosis, lethargy, and coma. Symptoms are usually triggered by infections or protein loads. Metabolic acidosis may occur frequently in early infancy and childhood but subsides with maturity. Mental development is variable.

Therapy

Limiting the production of isovaleric acid and enhancing its excretion can reduce the frequency and severity of acute ketotic episodes. During acute episodes of metabolic acidosis it is advisable to provide a leucine-free or drastically reduced leucine dietary regimen. In acute crisis, adequate protein and energy can be supplied by leucine-free special metabolic formulas alone or in conjunction with protein-free energy modules. Parenteral nutrition using glucose and lipids have been used in treating acute episodes.

Glycine and isovaleryl-coenzyme A (CoA) form isovalerylglycine, which is easily excreted, reducing accumulation of isovaleric acid.[27] During acute crisis, glycine supplementation ranging from 150 to 600 mg/kg has been used.[28] The amount of glycine needed for chronic therapy varies but 150 mg glycine/kg body weight may be optimal.[29]

Secondary carnitine deficiency has been identified in this disorder.[30] This may be due to the increased excretion of isovalerylcarnitine, found in the urine of these patients. L-Carnitine can conjugate with isovaleryl-CoA, the toxic acyl-CoA compound of this disorder. The use of L-carnitine supplementation has been suggested to both replenish depleted tissue stores and as a prophylactic treatment for removal of isovaleryl-CoA. Recommended intake of carnitine in this disorder ranges from 100 to 300 mg/kg/day.

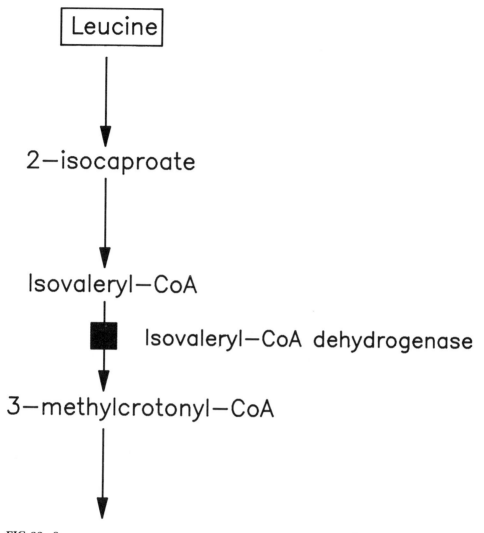

FIG 22–6.
Leucine metabolism. Part of leucine metabolism, shared with other branched-chain amino acids, is shown in Figure 22–4. Isovaleric acidemia is a defect of an enzyme specific to leucine metabolism.

Carnitine is generally tolerated orally, but intravenous preparations of L-carnitine are now available as an investigative drug.

Dietary prescription is based on a leucine-free special metabolic formula and standard cow's milk formula or evaporated milk to provide leucine requirements. Previously, dietary prescriptions for treatment were calculated using MSUD Diet Powder (Mead Johnson Nutritional) and supplementation with L-valine and L-isoleucine. Analog XLEU (Ross Laboratories) is also leucine-free but contains L-valine and L-isoleucine, so supplementation is usually not necessary. This special formulation is currently undergoing clinical studies and is currently available for widespread use.

Low-protein diets alone (1.2 to 1.5 g/kg/day in infants), without the use of special metabolic formulas, have been successful in reducing clinical symptoms. Infants may tolerate up to 120 mg leucine/kg body weight because of the efficiency of the glycine conjugating system. In 3- to 5-year old children, as much as 1,300 mg/day of leucine could be handled by this system.[31] However, for infants the use of protein restriction alone is not recommended, as without supplemental leucine-free protein from special metabolic formulas, their protein intake may not be sufficient for optimal growth.

Methylmalonic/Propionic Acidemia

Propionic Acidemia (Ketotic Hyperglycinemia)

Propionic acidemia is an autosomal recessive disorder of propionate metabolism (Fig 22–7). Propionic acid is normally metabolized to methylmalonic acid, and metabolic blocks result in accumulation of propionic acid. The defect can result from deficiency of the holoenzyme propionyl-CoA carboxylase or deficiency of the biotin cofactor. The propiogenic amino acids isoleucine, valine, threonine, and methionine are the major precursors of propionyl-CoA. Only a few patients with the carboxylase defect are clinically responsive to biotin therapy, although their cells often show a response to biotin, with increased enzyme activity.[32] A trial period of therapeutic dosages of 5 to 10 mg biotin per day should be attempted.

Methylmalonic Acidemia

Methylmalonic acidemia results from decreased activity of the enzyme methylmalonyl-CoA mutase, which converts L-methylmalonyl-CoA to succinyl-CoA. High levels

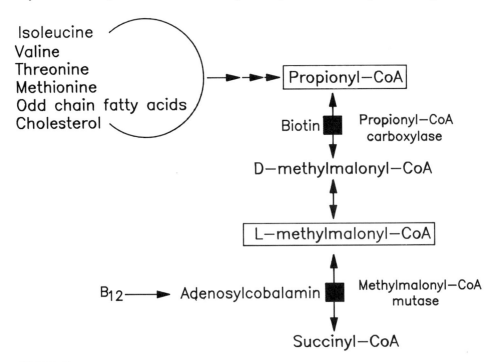

FIG 22–7.
Propionic and methylmalonic acid metabolism. Propionic acid is formed from propiogenic amino acids, fatty acids, and cholesterol. Defects in priopionyl-CoA carboxylase may be primary or may result from deficiency of the biotin cofactor. Similarly, defects in methylmalonyl-CoA mutase may be primary or result from abnormal B_{12} metabolism or deficiency of B_{12}. No inborn errors of the conversion of D- to L-methylmalonyl-CoA have been described.

of methylmalonic acid appear to correlate with clinical symptoms in these disorders. Several autosomal recessive mutations of this enzyme system have been identified. Defects in the mutase enzyme are most common. When the defect is in biosynthesis of adenosylcobalamin, a cofactor in the mutase enzyme system, the patient may be responsive to pharmacologic doses of cobalamin (vitamin B_{12}). Since cobalamin is also needed in metabolism of homocystine, these patients excrete homocystine as well. Patients responsive to pharmacologic doses of vitamin B_{12} may not require nutritional therapy. Prenatal vitamin B_{12} therapy in diagnosed fetus has been utilized.[33]

There have been cases of methylmalonic aciduria due to B_{12} deficiency in infants who were breast-fed from vegan B_{12} deficient mothers.[34, 35]

Diagnosis/Clinical Presentation

Both methylmalonic and propionic acidemias usually present in the neonatal period with vomiting, poor feeding, failure to thrive, profound metabolic acidosis, ketonuria, and lethargy. Hyperammonemia may be present and contribute to clinical symptoms. These patients may also present with clinically significant neutropenia or thrombocytopenia. The infant who presents later in infancy, at 1 to 3 months of age, may have a history of breast-feeding with failure to thrive.[36] Failure to thrive is more a prominent feature of methylmalonic acidemia than propionic acidemia. In the classic form of both disorders, seizures, coma, and death are common in the neonate, and severe neurologic damage is expected unless the condition is successfully treated.

Therapy

During acute presentation, correction of acidosis and provision of calories to reverse catabolism are essential. As management progresses to oral or nasogastric feedings, electrolyte solutions with a mixture of glucose polymers to make a 20 kcal per fluid ounce solution can assist in providing fluids and energy.

Once formula is tolerated, the diet prescription should include the following: (1) Ile, Met, Thr, Val; (2) protein (natural and synthetic); (3) energy (carbohydrate, fat); and (4) fluid (see Table 22–2 and Appendix, Table 22A–5). Propiogenic amino acids are restricted, but total protein is not restricted unless hyperammonemia is present. Natural protein sources, from either standard infant formulas, evaporated milk, or foods, supply the requirements for the essential propiogenic acids, while the additional protein requirements are supplied by synthetic amino acids from special metabolic formulas. Special metabolic formulas, free of propiogenic amino acids, can provide additional nitrogen for protein synthesis and assist in promoting anabolism.[37] The exact nutrients provided are determined by the child's age, biochemical data, growth parameters, and tolerance of propiogenic amino acids. An example of a diet prescription for a 5-month-old infant with methylmalonic acidemia is shown in Table 22–3.

The protein requirements of children with methylmalonic and propionic acidemia are not well established. Reports of protein intake in an infant with methylmalonic acidemia show an intake of 1.25 g/kg of natural protein was necessary for maximal nitrogen retention, with slight retention at 0.75 g/kg in the same infant.[38] Our experience has shown that the provision of 1.25 g natural protein/kg/day in addition to synthetic amino acids equal to 0.5 to 0.9 g protein/kg/day achieved adequate growth and biochemical indices up to 12 months of age. Total protein intakes equaling 70% to 85% of the RDA for protein for infants can provide adequate visceral and somatic protein stores and help reduce acidotic episodes. Optimal energy from carbohydrate and fat must be supplied to protect the infant's protein stores. Although researchers have shown that biotin- and vi-

TABLE 22–3.

Sample Diet Prescription for a Five-Month-Old Infant With Methylmalonic Acidemia*

Weight = 6.0 kg	Amount	Isoleucine (mg)	Methionine (mg)	Threonine (mg)	Valine (mg)	Protein (gm)	Energy (Kcal)
Enfamil powder	65 gm	453	142	392	463	7.8	345
OS 1	13 gm	0	0	0	0	5.5	36
Protein-free diet							
Powder (80056)	69 gm	0	0	0	0	0.0	338
Safflower oil	15 ml	0	0	0	0	0.0	120
Total per day		453	142	392	463	13.3	839
Total/kg		76	24	65	77	2.2	140

*Water to equal a total volume of 900 ml (150 ml/kg).
Osmolality = 392 mOsm/kg water.
Above prescription provides 1.3 gm natural protein/kg/day.

tamin B_{12}-deficient animals process linoleic acid into the propionate pathway, a restriction of lipids in patients with methylmalonic acidemia has not been warranted.[39]

The restriction of the propiogenic amino acids sufficient to maintain normal plasma concentrations of methionine and threonine may overrestrict isoleucine and valine, and supplementation is recommended to balance the plasma profiles.

Many infants with methylmalonic acidemia or propionic acidemia develop anorexia and a poor suck early in infancy, and may require nasogastric feedings. Gastrostomy tubes are recommended if long-term tube feedings are expected. Some children also experience dysphagia and hyperactive gag reflex, both of which interfere with the provision of nutrients. The anorexia and food refusal may be both physiologic and behavioral. The physiologic component may be the result of an altered serotonin metabolism.[40]

Frequent infections and vomiting make it difficult to provide optimal nutrients for any extended period of time. Children are prone to recurrent infections and illness.[41, 42] During times of illness, the special formula mixture may need to be temporarily stopped. Parenteral nutrition calculated to provide the prescribed amounts of amino acids in conjunction with carbohydrate and fat can limit catabolism.

Adjunct therapies to the treatment of these disorders include supplementations of L-alanine and carnitine. Secondary carnitine deficiency has been identified in organic acidemias.[43, 44] Prophylactic treatment of 100 mg/kg/day of oral carnitine must be considered. During acute crisis, intravenous carnitine up to 300 mg/kg/day has been utilized in patients with these disorders. The supplementation of exogenous L-alanine into the dietary regimen may spare the catabolism of branched-chain amino acids. Supplementation of 250 mg alanine/kg/day enhanced nitrogen balance and may promote growth at lower intakes of protein.[45]

UREA CYCLE DISORDERS

Urea cycle disorders (Fig 22–8) compromise a variety of enzymatic defects in the production of urea, the end product of nitrogen metabolism. The enzyme defects include:

1. Carbamoyl-phosphate synthetase deficiency.
2. Ornithine transcarbamoylase (OTC) deficiency.

3. Argininosuccinic acid synthetase deficiency (citrullinemia).
4. Argininosuccinic acid lyase deficiency.
5. Arginase deficiency (arginemia).
6. N-acetylglutamate synthetase deficiency.

In OTC deficiency, inheritance is X-linked. The other defects of the cycle are transmitted as autosomal recessive traits.

The degradation of amino acids releases ammonia, which enters the urea cycle by way of carbamyl phosphate. Hyperammonemia is the major biochemical abnormality of all the urea cycles and the ammonia itself is apparently an important neurotoxin. With the exception of argininemia, the neonatal clinical features usually include vomiting, poor feeding, lethargy, respiratory distress, seizures, and coma. Although mental retardation is common in infants surviving the neonatal course, rapid resolution of hyperammonemia may preserve mental development. Researchers have found a correlation between length of neonatal hyperammonemic coma, intelligence quotient, and abnormal appearance on computed tomographic scans.[46] The survival rate in infancy depends on the location of the enzymatic defect in the cycle, level of enzyme activity, and recognition and treatment of the disorder. In general, defects early in the cycle and patients with lower enzyme activity have the highest mortality. Mortality is highest for CPS deficiency and boys with classic OTC deficiency, and these respond poorly to therapy. Heterozygote girls with OTC deficiency may present neonatally or may be symptomatic only after a protein load or infection in childhood.[47] Family histories from female heterozygotes for OTC may reveal an intolerance and avoidance of high-protein foods.

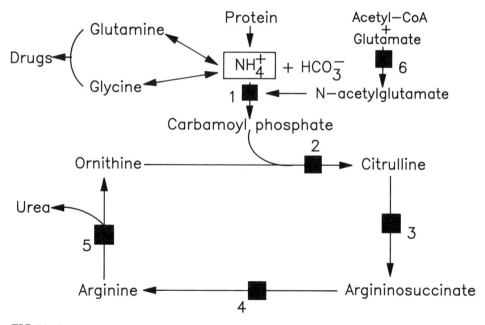

FIG 22–8.
Urea cycle. Amino groups from exogenous and endogenous protein are the source of ammonia. The enzymes are *(1)* carbamoyl phosphate synthetase, *(2)* ornithine carbamoyl transferase, *(3)* argininosuccinate synthetase, *(4)* argininosuccinate lyase, *(5)* arginase, and *(6)* N-acetylglutamate synthetase. The equilibrium of glutamine and glycine with ammonia may be used for disposal of ammonia by use of drugs such as sodium benzoate and sodium phenylacetate, which form complexes with glycine and glutamine that are excreted in the urine.

Therapy

The components of the treatment regimen of urea cycle disorders include: (1) removal of waste nitrogen by promoting urinary excretion using sodium benzoate and/or sodium phenylacetate, (2) limitation of production of waste nitrogen through restriction of intake of amino acids and protein, and (3) removal of waste nitrogen by supplementation of urea cycle intermediates distal to the enzymatic block.

During acute hyperammonemic episodes, the major goal is to reduce plasma ammonia levels immediately. Aggressive measures using peritoneal dialysis, hemodialysis, or exchange transfusion may be necessary. Peritoneal dialysis is the most effective and exchange transfusion the least effective means for reducing ammonia, although peritoneal dialysis may be somewhat slower in initial reduction.[47] Sodium benzoate and sodium phenylacetate are standard drugs for reducing ammonia concentrations. They act by forming compounds with ammonia which are excreted in the urine.[48] Sodium benzoate at doses of 200 to 500 mg/kg/day has not resulted in significant toxicity.[49] Intravenous L-arginine at doses ranging from 250 to 500 mg/kg, with standard dose of 210 mg/kg/day, should be added, except for patients diagnosed with arginase deficiency.

During acute crisis all exogenous protein sources are stopped. However, nonprotein energy sources by intravenous or oragastric feedings are necessary to inhibit or prevent catabolism. A protein-free carbohydrate and fat module is useful if oragastric feeds are tolerated. Reintroduction of protein should be performed slowly, starting at 0.5 g/kg/day and titrating to a tolerated intake approximately 1.0 to 1.5 g/kg/day.

To promote anabolism a dietary prescription providing 145 kcal/kg/day and 1.0 to 1.5 g protein/kg/day is recommended as a baseline once the patient is ready for chronic therapy. Restricting protein intake to a minimum daily requirement may be sufficient to support protein synthesis and growth. It is essential that optimal calories from fat and carbohydrates be provided to inhibit gluconeogenesis. No less than 100 kcal/kg/day should be given to the infant up to 12 months of age.

The use of a mixture of essential L-amino acids prescribed as a percentage of the total protein may improve nitrogen retention and reduce waste nitrogen. However, use of the essential amino acids alone as the total protein intake may be limiting. The Inherited Metabolic Diseases Clinic (IMD) at the University of Colorado Health Sciences Center has used a regimen of high biological value protein (HBV), in the form of standard infant formulas or evaporated milk, and pure essential amino acids in a 50:50 ratio to supply the total protein required. This regimen has been successful in promoting optimal visceral and somatic protein status and growth and has been successfully used by others.[50] Because protein intake is a small percentage of the total caloric intake per day (7% to 10%), carbohydrates and fat must balance out the required energy. The IMD Clinic has had success using 45% of the remaining energy intake as carbohydrate and 45% to 50% as fat. Use of L-keto analogs of essential amino acids has been attempted in treating these disorders with varying success.[51]

UCD 1 (see Appendix, Table 22A–6) is an essential amino acid formulation available for use in infants. In addition to essential amino acids it contains L-tyrosine, L-cystine, vitamins, minerals, and small amounts of carbohydrate. UCD 1 should be used in conjunction with HBV protein and protein-free energy supplements to provide the required nutrients for the infant.

To provide adequate plasma arginine concentrations, oral supplementation of L-arginine is required in the treatment of urea cycle disorders, with the exception of arginase deficiency. Recommended intakes are 175 to 250 mg/kg of L-arginine. Actual supplementation may need to be adjusted to maintain adequate plasma concentrations.

Dietary restriction of protein alone has had limited success.[47] The use of benzoate and phenylacetate therapy in conjunction with nutrition therapy can improve metabolic control. Ucephan (Kendall McGaw Pharmaceuticals), a 10% solution of these compounds, is now available in the United States. However, use of separate formulations of these drugs, available through a research protocol, will allow independent variation of doses as needed. A new compound, sodium phenylbotyrate, to promote urinary nitrogen is currently being tested.

Secondary carnitine deficiency may occur in patients with urea cycle disorders.[52] The deficiency may be more pronounced during hyperammonemic episodes. Prophylactic supplementation of oral L-carnitine (100 mg/kg/day) should be considered.

Infants on low-protein diets should be monitored at least monthly for the first year. Analysis of plasma amino acid profiles, ammonia, visceral protein status, anthropometrics, and growth assessment are recommended.

DISORDERS OF CARBOHYDRATE METABOLISM

Galactosemia

Galactosemia is a biochemical defect in the metabolism of galactose, a monosaccharide milk sugar. The defect in classic galactosemia is deficiency of galactose-1-phosphate uridyl transferase (gal-1-P transferase), an enzyme necessary for the conversion of galactose to glucose (Fig 22–9). Galactosemia can also occur due to enzymatic defects of galactokinase, and UDP-galactose-4-epimerase.

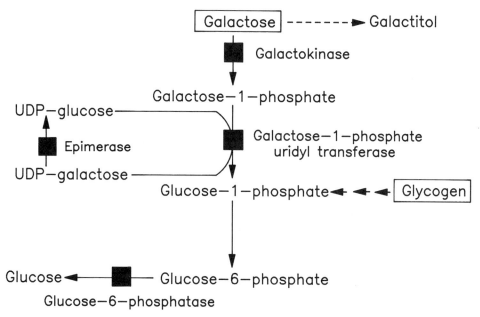

FIG 22–9.

Selected pathways of carbohydrate metabolism. Galactose must be converted to glucose for use in energy metabolism. Any defect in galactose metabolism results in accumulation of galactitol as a result of an alternate pathway *(broken line)*. Glucose-1-phosphate from any source including glycogen must be converted to free glucose for a variety of metabolic functions. Defects in glucose-6-phosphatase cause hypoglycemia and accumulation of glycogen.

Neonatal presentation in patients with classic transferase deficiency can be catastrophic and includes vomiting, failure to thrive, liver disease, and occasionally *Escherichia coli* sepsis and cataracts.[53] Symptoms occur within a few days after birth, once the infant is exposed to lactose-containing formulas or to human milk. If undiagnosed, the infant may die or follow a course of recurring symptoms with failure to thrive and mental retardation. Various genotypes of transferase deficiency have been identified and have implications for the severity of illness.[54] Galactokinase deficiency presents with only cataracts. Many states perform newborn screening for galactosemia by assay of transferase activity and/or galactose level in blood.

Despite newborn screening and early intervention, patients with classic galactosemia may still have significant problems. Longitudinal studies have shown that infants diagnosed early and well managed have improved mental status and intellectual function but are still below the intellectual quotients measured in their unaffected siblings.[55] Other findings in this same population include speech and language deficits,[56] ovarian failure,[57] and neurologic defects.[58] Recent questions whether early diagnosis and treatment significantly alter the neurologic outcome are currently being addressed by a national collaborative study.

Therapy

A galactose-restricted diet regimen is used for patients with both classic transferase and galactokinase deficiency. Patients with some variants of transferase deficiency may also benefit from a galactose-restricted diet.[59]

Infants suspected of having galactosemia should immediately be removed from lactose-containing formulas. Although false positive newborn screening tests are common when the screen tests enzyme activity, treatment should be started while diagnosis is ruled out or confirmed. Acceptable formula alternatives are Nutramigen, a casein hydrolysate (Mead Johnson Nutritionals), or soy protein formulas, such as ProSobee (Mead Johnson Nutritionals) and Isomil (Ross Laboratories). At one time the use of soy-protein formulas were questioned because of raffinose and stachyose, two galactose-containing oligosaccharides found in soybeans. Researchers now have shown that these sugars are not absorbed by human gut mucosa.[60] Soy-based formulas have since been used successfully in patients with galactosemia.

Free galactose sugars are not commonly found in natural foods. Lactose, a common disaccharide, comprising galactose and glucose, yields 50% galactose on hydrolysis. Therefore, all lactose-containing foods, such as milk and milk products, must be totally excluded from the diet. It is difficult to provide a diet regimen that is entirely free of exogenous galactose. Lactose is used in many processed foods including bread, cereals, dry mixes, and candies. Hidden sources of lactose are found in many "pill-form" medications and vitamin supplements, and as extenders in artificial sweeteners. The steady increase in the use of processed foods has challenged many families. Food label reading is an absolute necessity for anyone managing a galactose-restricted diet. Some investigators have suggested that the diet can be relaxed in school-age children,[61] but the consensus is now to continue the dietary regimen indefinitely.

There are major discrepancies in food lists for galactose-restricted diets. Some "questionable" foods that may contain either galactose or sugars that may be metabolized to galactose include green peas and other legumes, molasses, monosodium glutamate, sugar beets, soy sauce, and canned tuna fish. The lack of consensus regarding these foods has caused frustration for both families and practitioners.

The nutritional requirements for the patient with galactosemia are similar to those of healthy infants and children. The need for supplementation of calcium or vitamin D is dependent on the quantity and quality of milk-substitute infant formulas and natural foods supplied. If calcium or other vitamin–mineral supplements are indicated, care must be taken to ascertain whether they contain lactose fillers. Liquid preparations do not contain lactose. A list of medications that are galactose-free is now available.[62] All medications should first be checked by a physician or pharmacist.

Type I Glycogen Storage Disease

Type I glycogen storage disease (GSD; von Gierke's disease) is an inherited disorder of carbohydrate metabolism. It results from an enzymatic deficiency of glucose-6-phosphatase, significantly impairing glycogenolysis and gluconeogensis (see Fig 6–9).

The young infant with type I GSD presents with failure to thrive, severe hypoglycemia, hepatomegaly, and lactic acidosis. Biochemical abnormalities include elevation of blood lactate, pyruvate, triglycerides, cholesterol, and uric acid. Blood ketone concentrations are surprisingly not elevated. These patients are resistant to ketosis possibly through a mechanism whereby high pyruvate supplies sufficient oxaloacetate to inhibit accumulation of acetyl-CoA.[63]

Therapy

The goals of nutrition support for type I GSD include:

1. Steady supply of exogenous glucose to prevent hypoglycemia and reduce the biochemical derangements, while
2. Avoiding excess glucose or energy to inhibit hepatic glycogen storage.

The dietary prescription is a fructose-restricted galactose-restricted diet with limited fat intake and moderate protein. Fructose (sucrose) and galactose (lactose) should be avoided because they cannot metabolize to glucose by the gluconeogenic pathway and may contribute to elevated blood lactate. Carbohydrate should be in the form of glucose and glucose polymers. Total fat ingestion should be restricted to prevent overaccumulation of triglycerides, but hypertriglyceridemia may be a consequence of hypoglycemia rather than exogenous fat. The use of medium-chain triglycerides as a substitute for other fat sources may reduce blood triglycerides. Excess protein in the diet is not useful because amino acids cannot be readily converted to free glucose. An energy distribution of 60% to 75% of calories as carbohydrate, 10% to 15% as protein, and 20% to 30% as fat is recommended.

Daytime formula feedings providing 1.5 to 2.5 g/kg/feed of predominantly complex carbohydrate every 3 hours have been beneficial in maintaining normoglycemia. The actual amount of prescribed carbohydrate per feed will depend on the individual infant and the source and physical nature of the carbohydrate. Adjustments of exogenous glucose may be necessary based on ascertainment of blood glucose levels before, after, and between feedings. Infants less than 6 months of age can use soy-based formulas without sucrose (ProSobee), or carbohydrate-free formulations RCF (Ross) as the major nutrient source. These formulas must be used with either glucose polymers (Polycose, Ross; Moducal, Mead Johnson) or raw cornstarch. Glucose polymers are necessary to allow for a slow absorption of glucose between feedings. Recently, Vital High Nitrogen (Ross), a chemically-defined formula with glucose polymers as a carbohydrate source, has been used for daytime feedings. The high carbohydrate and low fat ratio in Vital

High Nitrogen appears beneficial in preventing childhood obesity and promoting an acceptable blood glucose response. Ultimately, raw cornstarch provides a better blood glucose response than either dextrose or Polycose, but the decreased pancreatic amylase activity of young infants limits its use in neonates. However, pancreatic amylase activity can be stimulated with ingestion of oral starch, and partial digestion by salivary amylase if the oral route is utilized. Because of the variability of each infant's amylase enzyme activity, tolerance to cornstarch ingestion should be attempted in gradual dosages at later infancy.

Nocturnal continuous drip feedings of chemically defined formulas or dextrose have been beneficial in preventing hypoglycemia, reducing biochemical aberrations, and potentiating optimal growth. Tolerex (Norwich Eaton), and Vital High Nitrogen both contain oligosaccharides as their sole carbohydrate source and are indicated for use. Infusion rates providing 7 to 12 mg glucose/kg/min can prevent hypoglycemia. This rate of infusion is higher than glucose production rates of term neonates (6.07 ± 0.46 mg/kg/min).[64] Intragastric feedings using dextrose alone instead of chemically defined formulas in these patients has also been used.[65]

Gastrostomy tube placements are indicated because of the long-term dependence on nocturnal feedings. The gastrostomy tubes also provide an entry for feedings during times of illness or anorexia when the oral route is not sufficient for the provision of nutrients.

The recommended dietary needs for the infant with type I GSD are similar to those of healthy infants. Special attention should be given to insuring adequate intake of calcium, vitamin D, and ascorbic acid, as foods that supply these nutrients are restricted.

The use of frequent daytime high-carbohydrate feedings in conjunction with nocturnal infusion of carbohydrate result in optimal growth in these patients. Careful monitoring of blood glucose concentrations and prevention of hyperglycemia and hypoglycemia can minimize the biochemical abnormalities associated with this disorder. Parents need to be taught to monitor for hypoglycemia at home.

PRIMARY LACTIC ACIDOSIS

Lactic acidosis will not be discussed at length but does deserve mention in a discussion of nutritional therapy of inborn errors of metabolism presenting in the neonate. One of the many causes of primary lactic acidosis, severe pyruvate dehydrogenase deficiency, presenting with overwhelming acidosis in the neonate, has the distinction of being the only inborn error of metabolism to worsen acutely with intravenous glucose. Generally, clinical intervention makes little difference to the outcome in neonates with severe pyruvate dehydrogenase deficiency. Treatment has been attempted in these and in more mildly affected patients with a modified-ketogenic diet and various drugs and vitamins or other cofactor supplements.[66, 67] Response to treatment has been reported in a limited number of patients.

Another group of patients with primary lactic acidosis have gluconeogenic disorders and present with hypoglycemia and acidosis. These patients require treatment with provision of a steady glucose source. One important subset of this group are patients with disorders of fructose metabolism. Although there may be some lactic acidosis in the absence of fructose ingestion, significant symptoms usually occur only after fructose exposure.[68] Some neonates are exposed to fructose by certain feeding practices and medications. A few patients with lactic acidosis due to disorders of the respiratory chain present as neonates. These patients usually do not respond to dietary manipulation.[67] Infrequently, patients with primary lactic acidosis of various or unknown cause will present with hyperammonemia and protein intolerance. Understanding of the various presentations of and strategies for therapy of primary lactic acidosis is rapidly changing, and it is likely that any attempt to discuss more extensively the place of nutrition in the management of neonates with these disorders would be out of date at publication.

Acknowledgment

The authors gratefully acknowledge Dr. Anthony Luder, who graciously assisted in the preparation of the figures in this chapter as well as providing technical assistance.

REFERENCES

1. Garrod AE: Inborn errors of metabolism (Croonian lectures). *Lancet* 1908; 2:1–7, 73–79, 142–148, 214–220.
2. Fölling A: Uber Ausscheidung von Phenylbrenztraub en saure in den Harn als Stoffwechsel anomalie in Verbindemgmit Imbezillitat. *Hoppe-Seylers Z Physiol Chem* 1934; 277:169–176.
3. Bickel H, Gerrard J, Hickmans EM: Influence of phenylalanine intake on phenylketonuria. *Lancet* 1953; 265:812–813.
4. Kennedy B, Anderson K, Acosta PB: Nutrition support of inborn errors of amino acid metabolism. *Int J Biomed Comput* 1985; 17:69–76.
5. Anderson K, Kennedy B, Acosta PB: Computer implemented nutrition support of phenylketonuria. *J Am Diet Assoc* 1985; 85:1623–1624.
6. Acosta PB, Fernhoff PM, Warshaw H, et al: Zinc and copper status of treated children with phenylketonuria. *J Parenter Enteral Nutr* 1981; 5:406–409.
7. Koch R, Friedman EG, Azen CG, et al: Report from the United States Collaborative Study of Children Treated for Phenylketonuria (PKU), in Bickel H, Wachtel U (eds): *Inherited Diseases of Amino Acid Metabolism.* Stuttgart, Federal Republic of Germany, George Thieme, 1985, pp 134–150.
8. Lenke RR, Levy HL: Maternal phenylketonuria and hyperphenylalaninemia: An international survey of the outcome of untreated and treated pregnancies. *N Engl J Med* 1980; 303:1202–1208.
9. Susuki Y, Konda MI, Imai I, et al: Effect of dietary treatment on the renal tubular function in a patient with hereditary tyrosinemia. *Int J Pediatr Nephrol* 1987; 8:171–176.
10. Cohn RM, Yudkoff M, Yost B, et al: Phenylalanine-tyrosine deficiency syndrome as a complication of the management of hereditary tyrosinemia. *Am J Clin Nutr* 1977; 30:209–214.
11. Bonkowsky HL, Magnussen CR, Collins AR, et al: Comparative effects of glycerol and dextrose on porphyrin, precursor excretion in acute intermittent porphyria. *Metabolism* 1976; 25:405–414.
12. Soirdahl S, Lie SO, Jellum E, et al: Increased need for L-cysteine in hereditary tyrosinemia (abstract). *Pediatr Res* 1979; 13:74.
12a. Halvorsen S: Screening for disorders of tyrosine metabolism, in Bickel H, Guthrie R, Hammersen G (eds): *Neonatal Screening for Inborn Errors of Metabolism.* New York, Springer-Verlag, 1980, p 45.
13. Buist NRM, Kennaway NG, Fellman JH: Tyrosinemia Type II: Hepatic cytosol tyrosine aminotransferase deficiency, in Bickel H, Wachtel U (eds): *Inherited Diseases of Amino Acid Metabolism.* Stuttgart, Federal Republic of German, George Thieme, 1985, pp 203–235.
14. Halvorsen S, Skjelkvale L: Tyrosine aminotransferase deficiency (TATD): First case diag-

nosed on newborn screening and successfully treated with Phe-Tyr restricted diet from early age. *Pediatr Res* 1977; 11:1017.

15. Rousson R, Guilbaud P: Long term outcome of organic acidurias: Survey of 105 French cases (1967–1983). *J Inherited Metab Dis* 1984; 7(suppl 1):10–12.

16. Scriver CR, Mackenzie S, Clow CL, et al: Thiamine-responsive maple syrup urine disease. *Lancet* 1971; 1:310–312.

17. Elsas L, Danner D, Lubitz D, et al: Metabolic consequence in inherited defects in branched-chain alpha ketoacid dehydrogenase: Mechanism of thiamine action, in Walser M, Williamsen JR (eds): *Metabolism and Clinical Implications of Branched Chain Amino and Ketoacids*. New York, Elsevier/North-Holland, 1981, p 369.

18. Naglak M, Elsas LJ: Nutrition support of maple syrup urine disease. *Metabolic Currents* 1989; 1(3):15–20. Ross Laboratories, Columbus, Ohio.

19. McCully KS: Vascular pathology of homocysteinemia: Implications for the pathogenesis of arteriosclerosis. *Am J Pathol* 1969; 56:111–128.

20. Carson NAJ, Neill DW: Metabolic abnormalities detected in a survey of mentally backward individuals in Northern Ireland. *Arch Dis Child* 1962; 37:505–513.

21. Mudd SH, Finkelstein JD, Irreverre F, et al: Homocystinuria: An enzymatic defect. *Science* 1964; 143:1443–1445.

22. Mudd SH, Skovby F, Levy HL, et al: The natural history of homocystinuria due to cystathionine beta-synthase deficiency. *Am J Hum Genet* 1985; 37:1–31.

23. Fowler B: Recent advances in the mechanism of pyridoxine-responsive disorders. J Inherited Metab Dis 1985; 8(suppl 1):76–83.

24. Yoshida I, Sakaguchi Y, Nakano M, et al: Pyridoxal phosphate-induced liver injury in a patient with homocystinuria. *J Inherited Metab Dis* 1985; 8:91.

25. Bougle D, Bureau F, Foucault P, et al: Molybdenum content of term and preterm human milk during the first 2 months of lactation. *Am J Clin Nutr* 1988; 48:652–654.

26. Tanaka K, Budd MA, Efron ML, et al: Isovaleric acidemia: A new genetic defect of leucine metabolism. *Proc Natl Acad Sci USA* 1966; 56:236–242.

27. Kreiger I, Tanaka K: Therapeutic effects of glycine in isovaleric acidemia. *Pediatr Res* 1976; 10:25–29.

28. Cohn RM, Yudkoff M, Rothman R, et al: Isovaleric acidemia: Use of glycine therapy in neonates. *N Engl J Med* 1978; 299:996–999.

29. Naglak M, Madsen K, Dembure P, et al: The treatment of isovaleric acidemia with glycine supplements. *Clin Res* 1987; 35:60A.

30. Roe CR, Millington DS, Maltby DA, et al: L-carnitine therapy in isovaleric acidemia. *J Clin Invest* 1984; 74:2290–2295.

31. Tanaka K, Ikeda Y: Isovaleric acidemia: Clinical manifestations in biochemistry and genetics, in Bickel H, Wachtel U (eds): *Inherited Diseases of Amino Acid Metabolism*. Stuttgart, Federal Republic of Germany, George Thieme, 1985, pp 203–235.

32. Wolf B: Reassessment of biotin-responsiveness in "unresponsive" propionyl-CoA carboxylase deficiency. *J Pediatr* 1980; 97:964–966.

33. Ampola MG, Mahoney MJ, Nakamura E, et al: Prenatal therapy of a patient with vitamin-B12-responsive methylmalonic acidemia. *N Engl J Med* 1975; 293:313–317.

34. Specker BL, Miller D, Norman EJ, et al: Increased urinary methylmalonic acid excretion in breast-fed infants of vegetarian mothers and identification of an acceptable dietary source of vitamin B12. *Am J Clin Nutr* 1988; 47:89–92.

35. Higginbottom MC, Sweetman L, Nyhan WL: A syndrome of methylmalonic aciduria, homocystinuria, megaloblastic anemia and neurologic abnormalities in a vitamin B12 deficient breast-fed infant of a strict vegetarian. *N Engl J Med* 1978; 299:317–323.

36. Nyhan WL: Understanding Inherited Metabolic Disease, in Brass A (ed): *Clinical Symposia*, vol 32 (5). Summit, New Jersey, CIBA Pharmaceutical Company, 1980, pp 1–35.

37. Queen PM, Fernhoff PM, Acosta PB: Protein and essential amino acid requirements in a child with propionic acidemia. *J Am Diet Assoc* 1981; 79:562–565.

38. Ney D, Bay C, Sandubray JM, et al: An evaluation of protein requirements in methyl-malonic acidemia. *J Inherited Metab Dis* 1985; 8:132–142.
39. Wolff JA, Sweetman L, Nyhan WL: The role of lipid in the management of methylmalonic acidaemia: Administration of linoleic acid does not increase excretion of methylmalonic acid. *J Inherited Metab Dis* 1985; 8:100.
40. Hyman SL, Porter CA, Page TJ, et al: Behavior management of feeding disturbances in urea cycle and organic acid disorder. *J Pediatr* 1987; 111:558–562.
41. Inoue S, Krieger I, Sarnaik A, et al: Inhibition of bone marrow stem cell growth in vitro by methylmalonic acid: A mechanism for pancytopenia in a patient with methylmalonic acidemia. *Pediatr Res* 1981; 15:95–98.
42. Stork LC, Ambruso DR, Wallner SF, et al: Pancytopenia in propionic acidemia: Hematologic evaluation and studies of hematopoiesis in vitro. *Pediatr Res* 1986; 20:783–788.
43. DiDonato S, Rimoldi M, Garavaglia B, et al: Propionyl-carnitine excretion in propionic and methylmalonic acidurias: A cause of carnitine deficiency. *Clin Chim Acta* 1984; 139:13–21.
44. Chalmers RA, Stacy TE, Tracey BM, et al: L-carnitine insufficiency in disorders of organic acid metabolism: Response to L-carnitine by patients with methylmalonic acidemia and 3-hydroxy-3-methyl-glutaric acidemia. *J Inherited Metab Dis* 1984; 7(suppl 2):108–110.
45. Kelts DG, Ney D, Bay C, et al: Studies on requirements for amino acids in infants with disorders of amino acid metabolism: I. Effect of alanine. *Pediatr Res* 1985; 19:86–91.
46. Msall M, Batshaw ML, Suss R, et al: Neurologic outcome in children with inborn errors of urea synthesis. *N Engl J Med* 1984; 310:1500–1505.
47. Batshaw ML, Thomas GH, Brusilow SW: New approaches to the diagnosis and treatment of inborn errors of urea synthesis. *Pediatrics* 1981; 68:290–297.
48. Brusilow S, Tinker J, Batshaw ML: Amino acid acylation: A mechanism of nitrogen excretion in inborn errors of urea synthesis. *Science* 1980; 207:659–661.
49. Walser M: Urea cycle disorders and other hereditary hyperammonemic syndromes, in Stanbury JB, Wyngaarden JB, Fredrickson DS, et al (eds): *The Metabolic Basis of Inherited Disease,* ed 5. New York, McGraw-Hill Book Co, 1983, pp 402–438.
50. Batshaw ML, Brusilow S, Waber L, et al: Treatment of inborn errors of urea synthesis: Activation of alternate pathways of waste nitrogen synthesis. *N Engl J Med* 1982; 306:1387–1392.
51. Walser M, Stewart PM: Organic acidemia and hyperammonaemia: A review. *J Inherited Metab Dis* 1981; 4:177–182.
52. Matsuda I, Ohtani Y, Ohyanagi K, et al: Hyperammonemia related to carnitine metabolism with particular emphasis on ornithine transcarbamylase deficiency. Recent advances in inborn errors of metabolism. Proc 4th Int Congr, Sendai: *Enzyme* 1987; 38:251–255.
53. Levy HL, Sept SJ, Shih VE, et al: Sepsis due to *Escherichia coli* in neonates with galactosemia. *N Engl J Med* 1977; 297:823–825.
54. Segal S: Disorders of galactose metabolism, in Stanbury JB, Wyngaarden JB, Fredrickson DS, et al (eds): *The Metabolic Basis of Inherited Disease,* ed 5. New York, McGraw-Hill Book Co, 1983, pp 167–191.
55. Fishler K, Donnell GN, Bergren WR, et al: Intellectual and personality development in children with galactosemia. *Pediatrics* 1972; 50:412–419.
56. Waisbren SE, Norman TR, Schnell RR, et al: Speech and language deficits in early-treated children with galactosemia. *J Pediatr* 1983; 102:75–77.
57. Kaufman FR, Donnell GN, Roe TF, et al: Gonadal function in patients with galactosemia. *J Inherited Metab Dis* 1986; 9:140–146.
58. Lo W, Packman S, Nash S, et al: Curious neurologic sequelae in galactosemia. *Pediatrics* 1984; 73:309–312.
59. Schwarz HP, Zuppinger KA, Zimmerman A, et al: Galactose intolerance with double heterozygosity for duarte variant and galactosemia. *J Pediatr* 1982; 100:704–709.
60. Gitzelman R, Aurricchio S: The handling of soya alpha-galactosides by a normal and galactosemia child. *Pediatrics* 1965; 36:231–235.

61. Kowrower GM: Galactosemia: Thirty years on: The experience of a generation. *J Inherited Metab Dis* 1982; 5(suppl 2):96–104.

62. Meyer BA, Wappner RS: Galactose-free and lactose-free medications, supplement to Roberts RS, Meyer BA: *Living With Galactosemia: A Handbook for Families*. Indianapolis, Metabolism Clinic, James Whitcomb Riley Hospital for Children, 1985.

63. Howell RR, Williams JC: The glycogen storage diseases, in Stanbury JB, Wyngaarden JB, Fredrickson DS, et al (eds): *The Metabolic Basis of Inherited Disease,* ed 5. New York, McGraw-Hill Book Co, 1983, pp 141–166.

64. Bier DM, Leake RD, Haymond MW, et al: Measurement of "true" glucose production rates in infancy and childhood with 6,6-dideutero glucose. *Diabetes* 1977; 26:1016–1023.

65. Stanley CA, Mills JL, Baker L: Intragastric feeding in type I glycogen storage disease: Factors affecting the control of lactic acidemia. *Pediatr Res* 1981; 15:1504–1508.

66. Falk RE, Cederbaum SD, Blass JP, et al: Ketogenic diet in the management of pyruvate dehydrogenase deficiency. *Pediatrics* 1976; 58:713–721.

67. Przyrembel H: Therapy of mitochondrial disorders. *J Inherited Metab Dis* 1987; 10:129–146.

68. Gitzelmann R, Steinmann B, Van Den Berghe G: Essential fructosuria, hereditary fructose intolerance, and fructose-1,6-diphosphatase deficiency, in Stanbury JB, Wyngaarden JB, Fredrickson DS, et al (eds): *The Metabolic Basis of Inherited Disease,* ed 5. New York, McGraw-Hill Book Co, 1983, pp 118–140.

APPENDIX

TABLE 22A–1.

Nutrient Composition (per 100 g) of Special Metabolic Formulas for Infants With Phenylketonuria

Nutrient Component	Analog XP Powder*	Lofenalac Powder†	PKU 1 Powder‡
Energy, kcal	475.0	460.0	278.0
Protein, g	13.0	15.0	50.3
Carbohydrate, g	59.0	60.0	19.3
Fat, g	20.9	18.0	0.0
Linoleic acid, g	2.85	9.2	0.0
Essential amino acids			
Arginine, g	1.03	0.56	2.00
Cystine, g	0.38	0.06	1.40
Histidine, g	0.59	0.48	1.40
Isoleucine, g	0.90	0.87	3.40
Leucine, g	1.55	1.66	5.70
Lysine, g	1.06	1.65	4.00
Methionine, g	0.25	0.54	1.40
Phenylalanine, g	Trace	0.08	Trace
Threonine, g	0.76	0.78	2.70
Tryptophan, g	0.30	0.20	1.00
Tyrosine, g	1.37	0.80	3.40
Valine, g	0.99	1.38	4.00
Minerals			
Calcium, mg	325.0	434.0	2,400.0
Chloride, mEq	8.2	9.2	47.0
Chromium, μg	15.0	0.0	0.0
Cooper, mg	0.45	0.43	6.7
Iodine, μg	47.0	32.0	230.0
Iron, mg	7.0	8.6	34.0
Magnesium, mg	34.0	50.0	520.0
Manganese, mg	0.6	0.14	2.4
Molybdenum, μg	35.0	0.0	107.0
Phosphorus, mg	230.0	324.0	1,860.0
Potassium, mEq	10.7	12.0	59.0
Selenium, μg	15.0	10.4	0.0
Sodium, mEq	5.2	9.4	46.5
Zinc, mg	5.0	3.6	26.0
Vitamins			
A, μg RE	530.0	432.0	2,800.0
D, μg	8.5	7.2	25.0
E, mg alpha-TE	4.9	14.4	34.0
K, μg	21.0	72.0	167.0
Ascorbic acid, mg	40.0	37.0	230.0
Biotin, μg	26.0	36.0	100.0
Pyridoxine, mg	0.52	0.29	2.2
B-12, μg	1.25	1.4	7.9
Choline, mg	50.0	61.0	430.0
Folate, μg	38.0	72.0	340.0
Inositol, mg	100.0	22.0	500.0
Niacin equivalent, mg	9.5	9.13	71.0
Pantothenic acid, mg	2.7	2.2	25.0
Riboflavin, mg	0.6	0.43	4.0
Thiamine, mg	0.5	0.36	2.70
Additional nutrients			
Carnitine, mg	9.5	8.6	0.0
Taurine, mg	19.0	27.0	0.0

* Ross Laboratories, Columbus, Ohio; 7.7 g Analog XP = 1.0 g protein.
† Mead Johnson Nutritionals, Evansville, Ind; 6.7 g Lofenalac = 1.0 g protein.
‡ Mead Johnson Nutritionals, Evansville, Ind; 2.0 g PKU 1 = 1.0 g protein.

TABLE 22A–2.

Nutrient Composition (per 100 g) of Special Metabolic Formulas for Infants With Tyrosinemia Type 1

Nutrient Component/100g	Analog XPHEN, TYR Powder*	Low PHE/TYR Diet Powder†	TYR 1 Powder‡
Energy, kcal	475.0	460.0	270.0
Protein, g	13.0	15.0	47.0
Carbohydrate, g	59.0	60.0	21.0
Fat, g	20.9	18.0	0.0
Linoleic acid, g	2.9	9.2	0.0
Essential amino acids			
Arginine, g	1.12	0.56	2.00
Cystine, g	0.42	0.06	1.40
Histidine, g	0.64	0.45	1.40
Isoleucine, g	1.00	0.87	3.40
Leucine, g	1.72	1.66	5.70
Lysine, g	1.17	1.65	4.00
Methionine, g	0.27	0.54	1.40
Phenylalanine, g	Trace	0.08	Trace
Threonine, g	0.84	0.78	2.70
Tryptophan, g	0.34	0.20	1.00
Tyrosine, g	Trace	<0.04	Trace
Valine, g	1.10	1.38	4.00
Minerals			
Calcium, mg	325.0	430.0	2,400.0
Chloride, mEq	8.2	9.1	47.0
Chromium, μg	15.0	0.0	0.0
Copper, mg	0.45	0.43	6.7
Iodine, μg	47.0	32.0	230.0
Iron, mg	7.0	8.6	34.0
Magnesium, mg	34.0	50.0	520.0
Manganese, mg	0.6	0.14	2.4
Molybdenum, μg	35.0	0.0	107.0
Phosphorus, mg	230.0	320.0	1,860.0
Potassium, mEq	10.7	12.0	59.0
Selenium, μg	15.0	14.2	0.0
Sodium, mEq	5.2	9.6	46.5
Zinc, mg	5.0	3.6	26.0
Vitamins			
A, μg RE	530.0	432.0	2,800.0
D, μg	8.5	7.2	25.0
E, mg alpha TE	4.9	14.4	34.0
K, μg	21.0	72.0	167.0
Ascorbic acid, mg	40.0	37.0	230.0
Biotin, μg	26.0	36.0	100.0
Pyridoxine, mg	0.52	0.3	2.2
B-12, μg	1.25	1.4	7.9
Choline, mg	50.0	61.0	430.0
Folate, μg	38.0	72.0	340.0
Inositol, mg	100.0	22.0	500.0
Niacin equivalent, mg	9.5	9.1	70.7
Pantothenic acid, mg	2.65	2.2	25.0
Riboflavin, mg	0.6	0.43	4.0
Thiamine, mg	0.5	0.36	2.7
Additional nutrients			
Carnitine, mg	9.5	8.6	0.0
Taurine, mg	19.0	27.0	0.0

* Ross Laboratories, Columbus, Ohio; 7.7 g Analog XPHEN, TYR = 1.0 g protein. Note: Analog is also available without methionine (Analog XPHEN, TYR, MET) for the treatment of neonatal tyrosinemia.
† Mead Johnson Nutritionals, Evansville, Ind; 6.7 g Low PHE/TYR Diet Powder = 1.0 g protein.
‡ Mead Johnson Nutritionals, Columbus, Ohio; 2.1 g TYR 1 = 1.0 g protein.

TABLE 22A – 3.

Nutrient Composition of Special Metabolic Formulas for Infants With Maple Syrup Urine Disease

Nutrient Component	Analog MSUD Powder*	MSUD Diet Powder†	MSUD 1 Powder‡
Energy, kcal	475.0	466.0	286.0
Protein, g	13.0	9.9	40.9
Carbohydrate, g	59.0	63.3	30.5
Fat, g	20.9	20.0	0.0
Linoleic acid, g	2.9	10.6	0.0
Essential amino acids			
Arginine, g	1.34	0.49	2.00
Cystine, g	0.49	0.30	1.40
Histidine, g	0.76	0.30	1.40
Isoleucine, g	Trace	Trace	Trace
Leucine, g	Trace	Trace	Trace
Lysine, g	1.38	0.61	4.00
Methionine, g	0.32	0.30	1.40
Phenylalanine, g	0.90	0.66	2.40
Threonine, g	1.00	0.66	2.70
Tryptophan, g	0.40	0.24	1.00
Tyrosine, g	0.90	0.78	2.90
Valine, g	Trace	Trace	Trace
Minerals			
Calcium, mg	325.0	490.0	2,400.0
Chloride, mEq	8.2	10.6	47.0
Chromium, μg	15.0	0.0	0.0
Copper, mg	0.45	0.44	6.7
Iodine, μg	47.0	33.0	230.0
Iron, mg	7.0	8.9	34.0
Magnesium, mg	34.0	52.0	520.0
Manganese, mg	0.6	0.15	2.4
Molybdenum, μg	35.0	0.0	107.0
Phosphorus, mg	230.0	270.0	1,860.0
Potassium, mEq	10.7	12.5	59.0
Selenium, μg	15.0	2.8	0.0
Sodium, mEq	5.2	8.0	46.5
Zinc, mg	5.0	3.7	26.0
Vitamins			
A, μg RE	530.0	444.0	2,800.0
D, μg	8.5	7.4	25.0
E, mg alpha TE	4.9	14.8	34.0
K, μg	21.0	74.0	167.0
Ascorbic acid, mg	40.0	38.0	230.0
Biotin, μg	26.0	37.0	100.0
Pyridoxine, mg	0.52	0.3	2.2
B-12, μg	1.25	1.5	7.9
Choline, mg	50.0	63.0	430.0
Folate, μg	38.0	74.0	340.0
Inositol, mg	100.0	22.0	500.0
Niacin equivalent, mg	11.2	9.2	78.0
Pantothenic acid, mg	2.65	2.2	25.0
Riboflavin, mg	0.6	0.44	4.0
Thiamine, mg	0.5	0.37	2.7
Additional nutrients			
Carnitine, mg	9.5	8.9	0.0
Taurine, mg	19.0	28.0	0.0

* Ross Laboratories, Columbus, Ohio; 7.7 g Analog MSUD = 1.0 g protein.
† Mead Johnson Nutritionals, Evansville, Ind; 12.2 g MSUD Diet Powder = 1.0 g protein.
‡ Mead Johnson Nutritionals, Evansville, Ind; 2.4 g MSUD 1 = 1.0 g protein.

TABLE 22A–4.

Nutrient Composition (per 100 g) of Special Metabolic Formulas for Infants With Homocystinuria

Nutrient Component/100g	Analog XMET Powder*	Low Methionine Diet Powder†	HOM 1 Powder‡
Energy, kcal	475.0	515.0	277.0
Protein, g	13.0	15.5	51.6
Carbohydrate, g	59.0	51.0	17.7
Fat, g	20.9	28.0	0.0
Linoleic acid, g	2.85	6.2	0.0
Essential amino acids			
Arginine, g	1.04	0.88	2.00
Cystine, g	0.39	0.14	2.50
Histidine, g	0.59	0.36	1.40
Isoleucine, g	0.93	0.71	3.40
Leucine, g	1.59	1.18	5.70
Lysine, g	1.08	0.93	4.00
Methionine, g	Trace	0.16	Trace
Phenylalanine, g	0.70	0.76	2.40
Threonine, g	0.78	0.50	2.70
Tryptophan, g	0.31	0.19	1.00
Tyrosine, g	0.30	0.53	2.90
Valine, g	1.01	0.71	4.00
Minerals			
Calcium, mg	325.0	480.0	2,400.0
Chloride, mEq	8.2	12.0	47.0
Chromium, μg	15.0	0.0	0.0
Copper, mg	0.45	0.48	6.7
Iodine, μg	47.0	52.0	230.0
Iron, mg	7.0	9.7	34.0
Magnesium, mg	34.0	56.0	520.0
Manganese, mg	0.6	0.13	2.4
Molybdenum, μg	35.0	0.0	107.0
Phosphorus, mg	230.0	380.0	1,860.0
Potassium, mEq	10.7	16.0	59.0
Selenium, μg	15.0	4.3	0.0
Sodium, mEq	5.2	8.0	46.5
Zinc, mg	5.0	4.0	26.0
Vitamins			
A, μg RE	530.0	480.0	2,800.0
D, μg	8.5	8.0	25.0
E, mg alpha TE	4.9	16.0	34.0
K, μg	21.0	81.0	167.0
Ascorbic acid, mg	40.0	42.0	230.0
Biotin, μg	26.0	40.0	100.0
Pyridoxine, mg	0.52	0.32	2.2
B-12, μg	1.25	1.61	7.9
Choline, mg	50.0	40.0	430.0
Folate, μg	38.0	81.0	340.0
Inositol, mg	100.0	24.0	500.0
Niacin equivalent, mg	9.7	9.6	70.7
Pantothenic acid, mg	2.65	2.4	25.0
Riboflavin, mg	0.6	0.48	4.0
Thiamine, mg	0.5	0.4	2.7
Additional nutrients			
Carnitine, mg	9.5	9.7	0.0
Taurine, mg	19.0	31.0	0.0

* Ross Laboratories, Columbus, Ohio; 7.7 g Analog XMET = 1.0 g protein.
† Mead Johnson Nutritionals, Evansville, Ind; 6.5 g Low Methionine Diet Powder = 1.0 g protein.
‡ Mead Johnson Nutritionals, Evansville, Ind; 1.94 g HOM 1 = 1.0 g protein.

TABLE 22A–5.

Nutrient Composition of Special Metabolic Formulas for Infants With Methylmalonic and Propionic Acidemia

Nutrient Component	Analog XMET, THRE, VAL, ISOLEU Powder*	OS 1 Powder†
Energy, kcal	475.0	285.0
Protein, g	13.0	42.3
Carbohydrate, g	59.0	28.9
Fat, g	20.9	0.0
Linoleic acid, g	2.85	0.0
Essential amino acids		
Arginine, g	1.32	2.00
Cystine, g	0.49	1.40
Histidine, g	0.89	1.40
Isoleucine, g	<0.035	0.10
Leucine, g	2.00	5.70
Lysine, g	1.36	4.00
Methionine, g	Trace	Trace
Phenylalanine, g	0.88	2.40
Threonine, g	Trace	Trace
Tryptophan, g	0.39	1.00
Tyrosine, g	0.88	2.90
Valine, g	Trace	Trace
Minerals		
Calcium, mg	325.0	2,400.0
Chloride, mEq	8.2	47.0
Chromium, μg	15.0	0.0
Copper, mg	0.45	6.7
Iodine, μg	47.0	230.0
Iron, mg	7.0	34.0
Magnesium, mg	34.0	520.0
Manganese, mg	0.6	2.4
Molybdenum, μg	35.0	107.0
Phosphorus, mg	230.0	1,860.0
Potassium, mEq	10.7	59.0
Selenium, μg	15.0	0.0
Sodium, mEq	5.2	46.4
Zinc, mg	5.0	26.0
Vitamins		
A, μg RE	530.0	2,800.0
D, μg	8.5	25.0
E, mg alpha TE	4.9	34.0
K, μg	21.0	167.0
Ascorbic acid, mg	40.0	230.0
Biotin, μg	26.0	100.0
Pyridoxine, mg	0.52	2.2
B-12, μg	1.25	7.9
Choline, mg	50.0	430.0
Folate, μg	38.0	340.0
Inositol, mg	100.0	500.0
Niacin equivalent, mg	11.0	78.0
Pantothenic acid, mg	2.65	25.0
Riboflavin, mg	0.6	4.0
Thiamine, mg	0.5	2.7
Additional nutrients		
Carnitine, mg	9.5	0.0
Taurine, mg	19.0	0.0

* Ross Laboratories, Columbus, Ohio 7.7 grams of Analog XMET, THRE, VAL, ISOLEU = 1.0 g protein
† Mead Johnson Nutritionals, Evansville, Indiana 2.4 grams of OS 1 = 1.0 g protein

TABLE 22A–6.

Nutrient Composition of a Special Metabolic Formula for Infants With Urea Cycle Disorders

Nutrient Component	UCD 1 Powder*
Energy, kcal	260.0
Protein, g	56.4
Carbohydrate, g	8.0
Fat, g	0.0
Linoleic acid, g	0.0
Essential amino acids	
Arginine, g	0.0
Cystine, g	3.1
Histidine, g	3.1
Isoleucine, g	7.6
Leucine, g	12.8
Lysine, g	9.0
Methionine, g	3.1
Phenylalanine, g	5.3
Threonine, g	6.0
Tryptophan, g	2.2
Tyrosine, g	6.5
Valine, g	9.0
Minerals	
Calcium, mg	2,400.0
Chloride, mEq	47.0
Chromium, μg	0.0
Copper, mg	6.7
Iodine, μg	230.0
Iron, mg	34.0
Magnesium, mg	520.0
Manganese, mg	2.4
Molybdenum, μg	107.0
Phosphorus, mg	1,860.0
Potassium, mEq	59.0
Selenium, μg	0.0
Sodium, mEq	46.0
Zinc, mg	26.0
Vitamins	
A, μg RE	2,800.0
D, μg	25.0
E, mg alpha TE	34.0
K, μg	167.0
Ascorbic acid, mg	230.0
Biotin, μg	100.0
Pyridoxine, mg	2.2
B-12, μg	7.9
Choline, mg	430.0
Folate, μg	340.0
Inositol, mg	71.0
Niacin equivalent, mg	78.0
Pantothenic acid, mg	25.0
Riboflavin, mg	4.0
Thiamine, mg	2.7
Additional nutrients	
Carnitine, mg	0.0
Taurine, mg	0.0

*Ross Laboratories, Columbus, Ohio; 1.77 g UCD 1 = 1.0 g protein.

Index

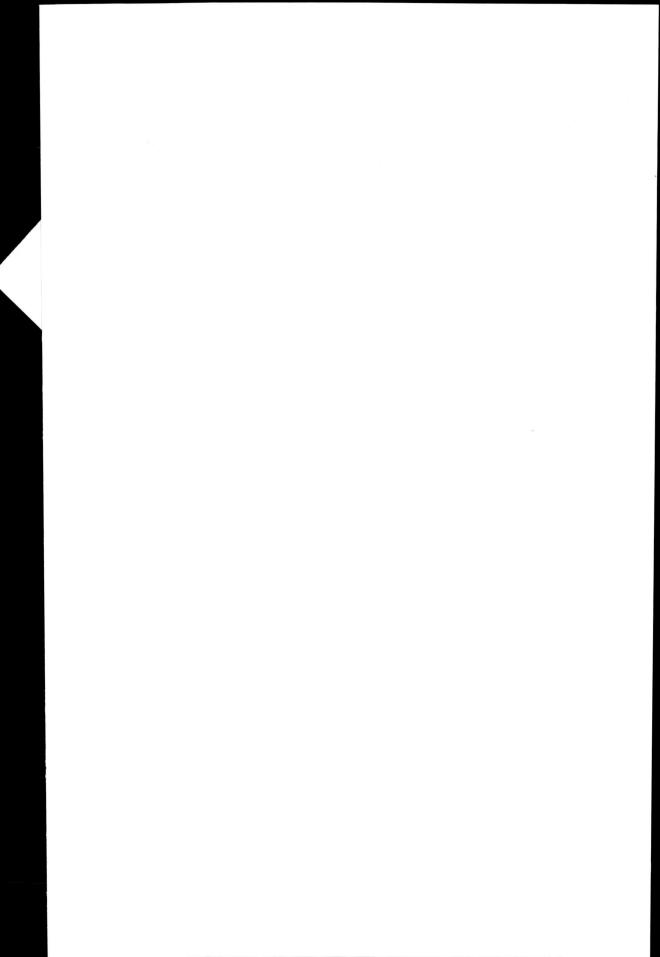

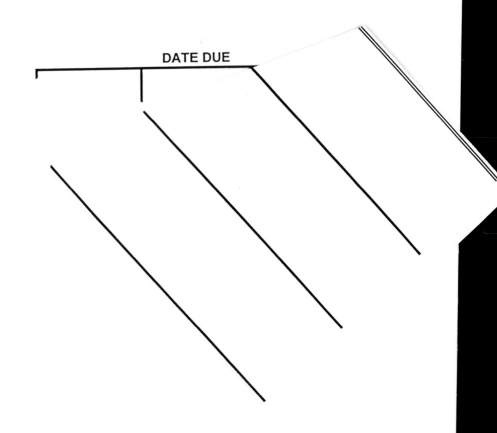

DATE DUE